FROM THE LIBRARY OF

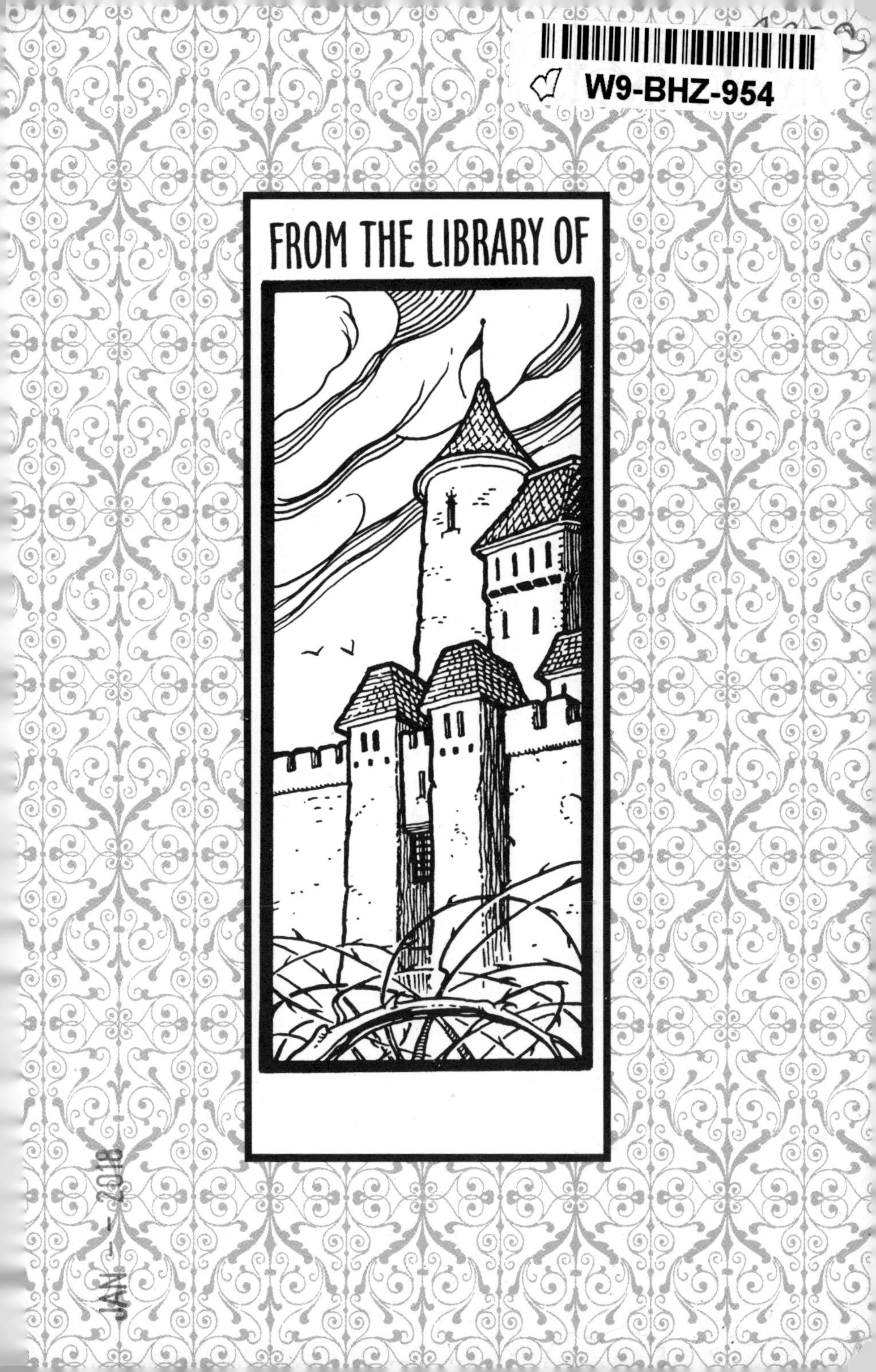

"The black-and-white drawings are precisely crafted, with small, endearing touches that render each character entirely unique. The dialogue is clever and filled with subtle grace notes of drollness and humor. The set will be especially appealing to readers of all ages who enjoy seeing and reading traditional fairy tale tropes teased and played with, all with a sense of good-humored fun."
– Nancy Pearl, *NPR*

"The charming blend of original and well-known fairy tale characters into one slightly dysfunctional castle household only gets better as it progresses." – *School Library Journal*

"*Castle Waiting* creates a vibrant fantasy world not unlike *The Lord of the Rings*' Middle-earth but with a focus on the lives of women. Gorgeously illustrated in black and white, the book combines Christian and mythological imagery, including a bearded female saint, Rumpelstiltskin and various animal-headed characters. Fun to read and look at, *Castle Waiting* will enthrall fantasy readers of both genders." – *Time*

"A set of linked nouveaux fairy tales, this graphic novel extends the story of Sleeping Beauty into a modern, feminist Chaucer. Medley's art is both exquisitely detailed and fantastically lighthearted. Though appropriate for all ages, this one-of-a-kind graphic novel is likely to appeal most to smart women in their 20s and older — much older — and to any man who believes in feminism and knows how to laugh." – *Publishers Weekly* (starred review)

"There's a clear salute to the power of sisterhood in *Castle Waiting*'s stories of battered and exploited women banding together with kindly men to make a new world... The *Castle Waiting* castle draws people looking for a safe place to rest. The *Castle Waiting* book draws readers looking for much the same. Club rating: A-"
– *The Onion A.V. Club*

"Medley's big book ranks with Jeff Smith's *Bone* as a nearly-all-ages graphic-novel triumph." – *Booklist* "Core Collection: Graphic Women"

"Have you ever wondered what happened after 'Happily Ever After'? This graphic novel [*Castle Waiting*] is a modern tale that incorporates fairytale characters and settings. Funny, thoughtful and not at all what you'd expect." – *The Victoria Times Colonist*

"...*Castle Waiting* has been one of the most joyous comics discoveries for me of the last couple years. ...[D]espite this volume clocking in at 375 pages I read the whole thing in one sitting...and enjoyed every freaking second of it. I laughed repeatedly and more often than not was caught just smiling like an idiot as I read about these beautifully crafted characters and their completely boring but somehow also completely fascinating lives. It doesn't hurt that Medley is truly an incredible illustrator." – Kelly Thompson, *Comic Book Resources*

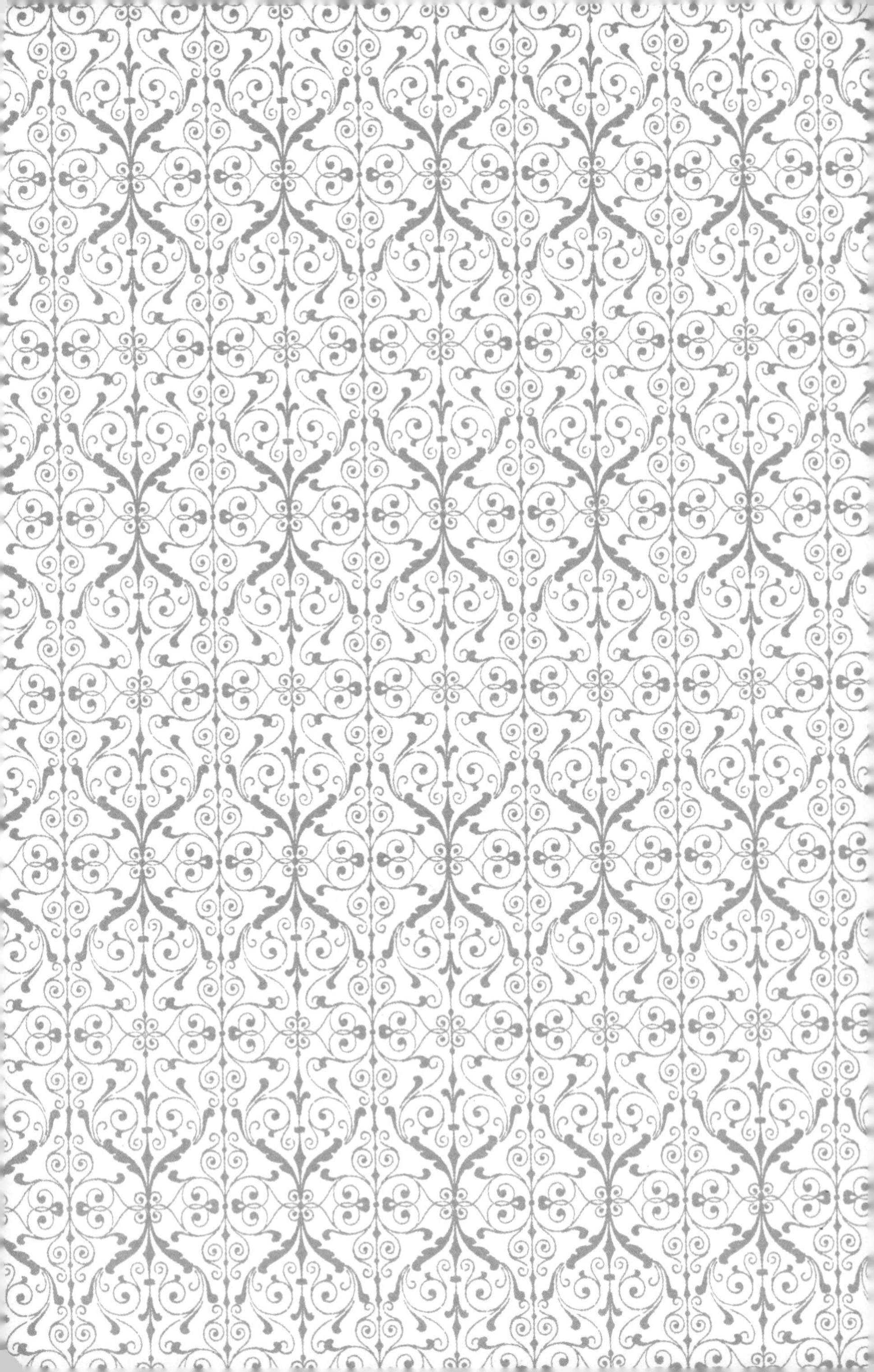

Castle Waiting

VOLUME I · BY LINDA MEDLEY

SANCTUM OMNIUM-GATHERUM

FANTAGRAPHICS BOOKS

EDITOR: GARY GROTH.
DESIGNER: ADAM GRANO.
REPRINT DESIGN: EMORY LIU.
LETTERING: TODD KLEIN.
ASSOCIATE PUBLISHER: ERIC REYNOLDS.
PUBLISHER: GARY GROTH & KIM THOMPSON.

 Fantagraphics Books, Inc. 7563 Lake City Way, Seattle, WA 98115.

To receive a free catalogue of fine comics and books, call 1-800-657-1100 or visit our website at Fantagraphics.com.

ISBN: 978-1-60699-602-7
First Printing, November 2012.
Printed in Hong Kong.

Chapter 1.

· THE CURSE OF BRAMBLY HEDGE PT. I ·

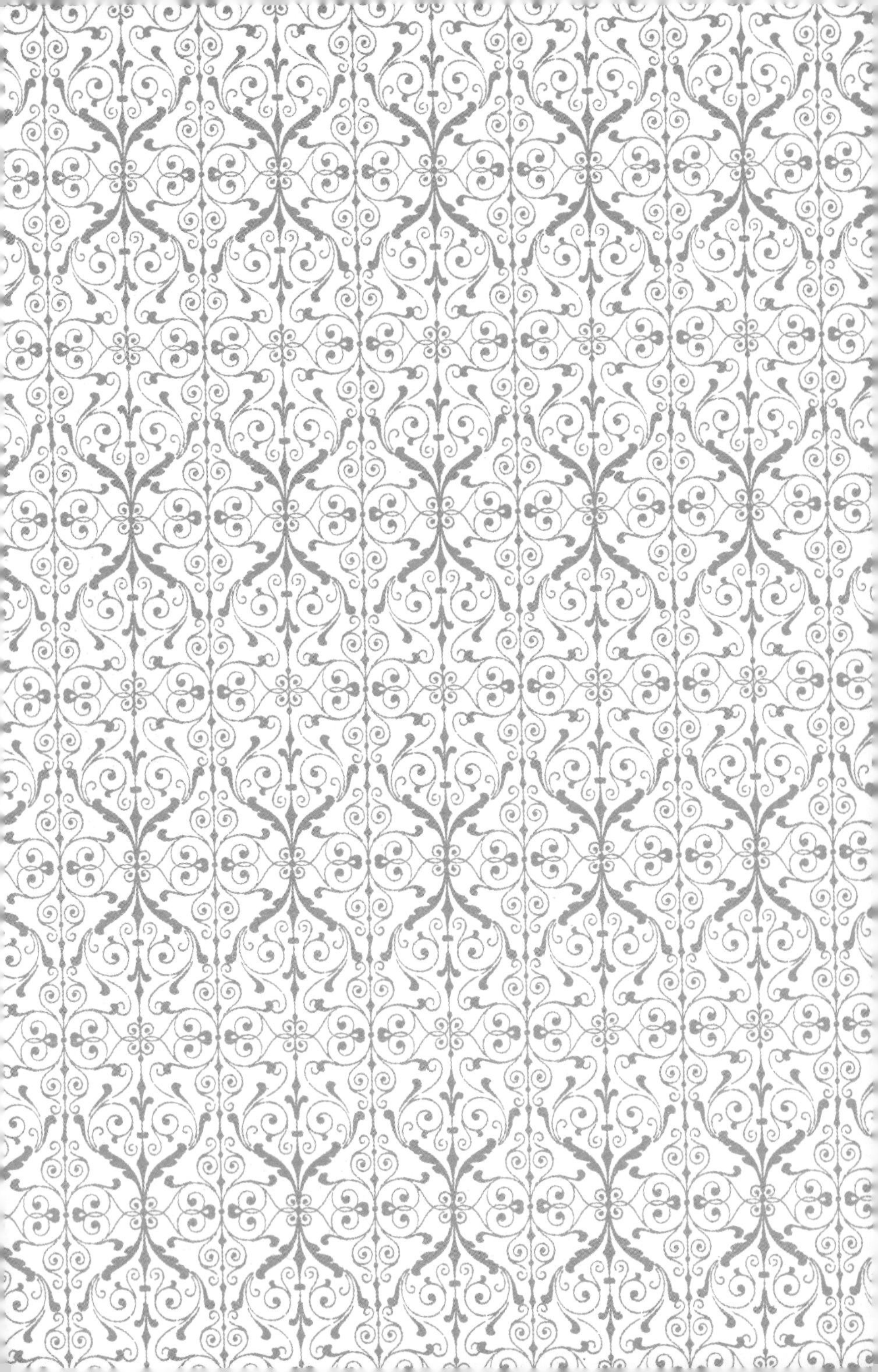

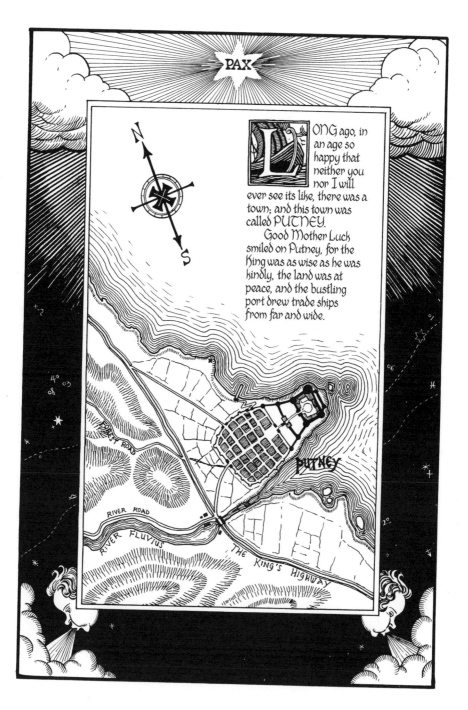

PAX

LONG ago, in an age so happy that neither you nor I will ever see its like, there was a town; and this town was called PUTNEY.

Good Mother Luck smiled on Putney, for the King was as wise as he was kindly, the land was at peace, and the bustling port drew trade ships from far and wide.

FOREST ROAD

PUTNEY

RIVER ROAD

RIVER FLUVIUS

THE KING'S HIGHWAY

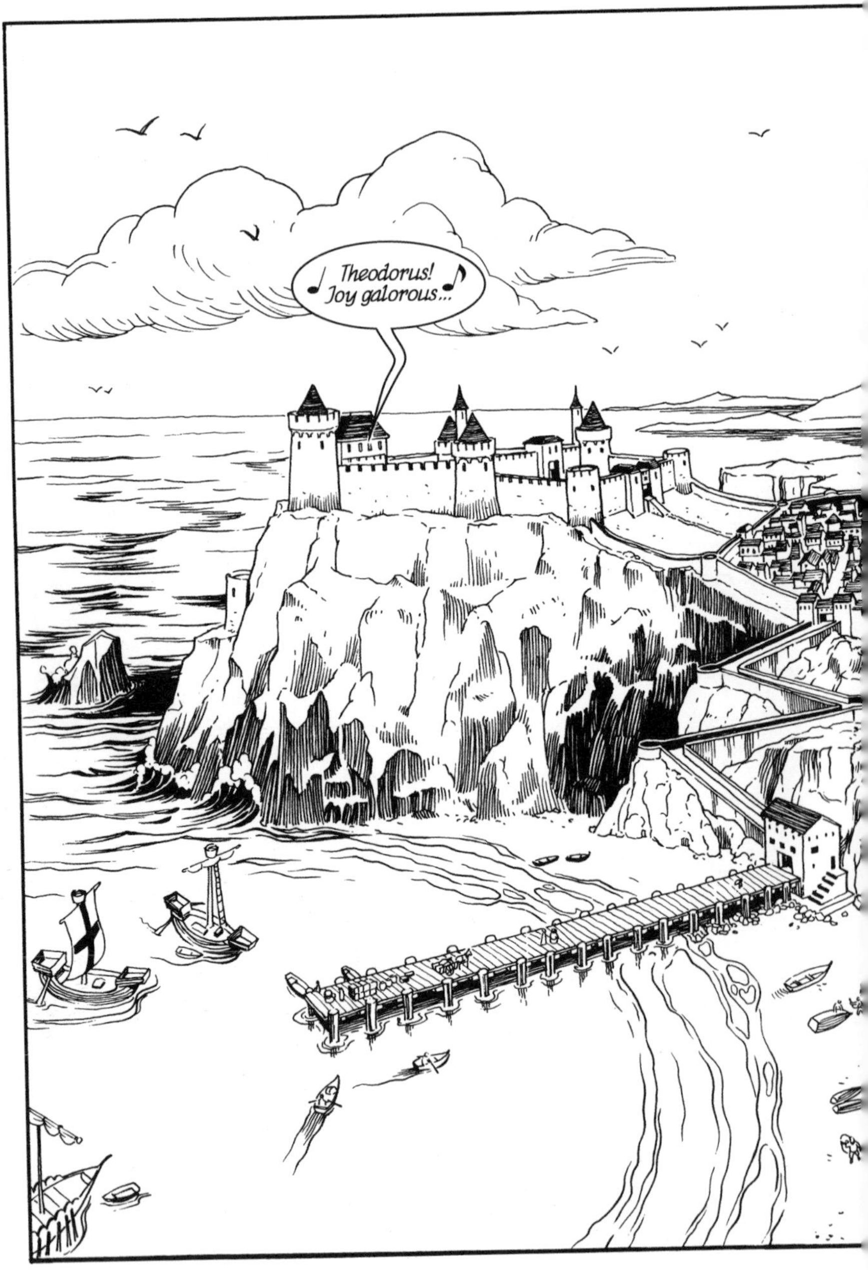
♩ Theodorus! Joy galorous... ♪

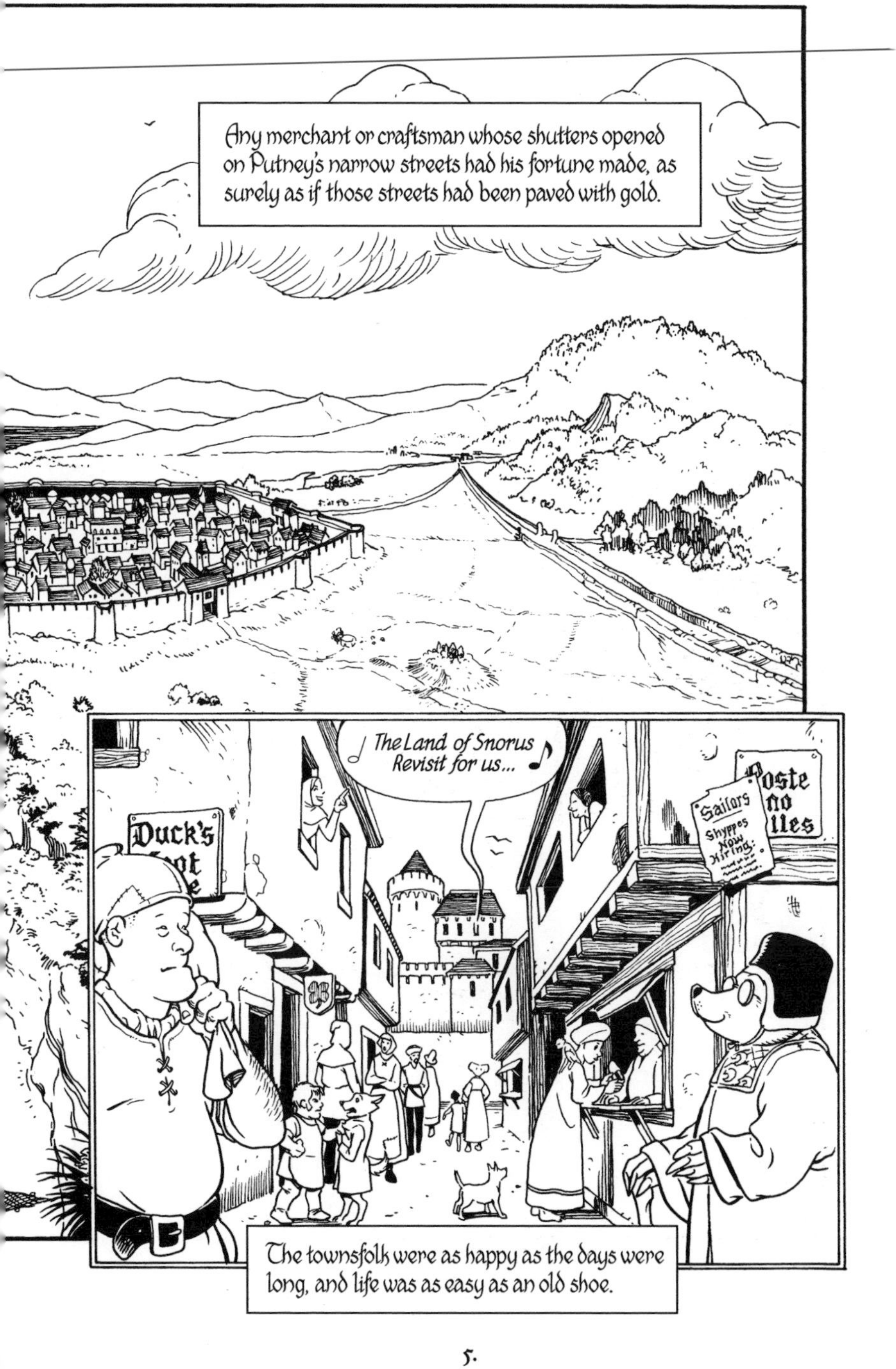
Any merchant or craftsman whose shutters opened on Putney's narrow streets had his fortune made, as surely as if those streets had been paved with gold.
The Land of Snorus Revisit for us...
Sailors
Shyppes Now Hiring:
The townsfolk were as happy as the days were long, and life was as easy as an old shoe.

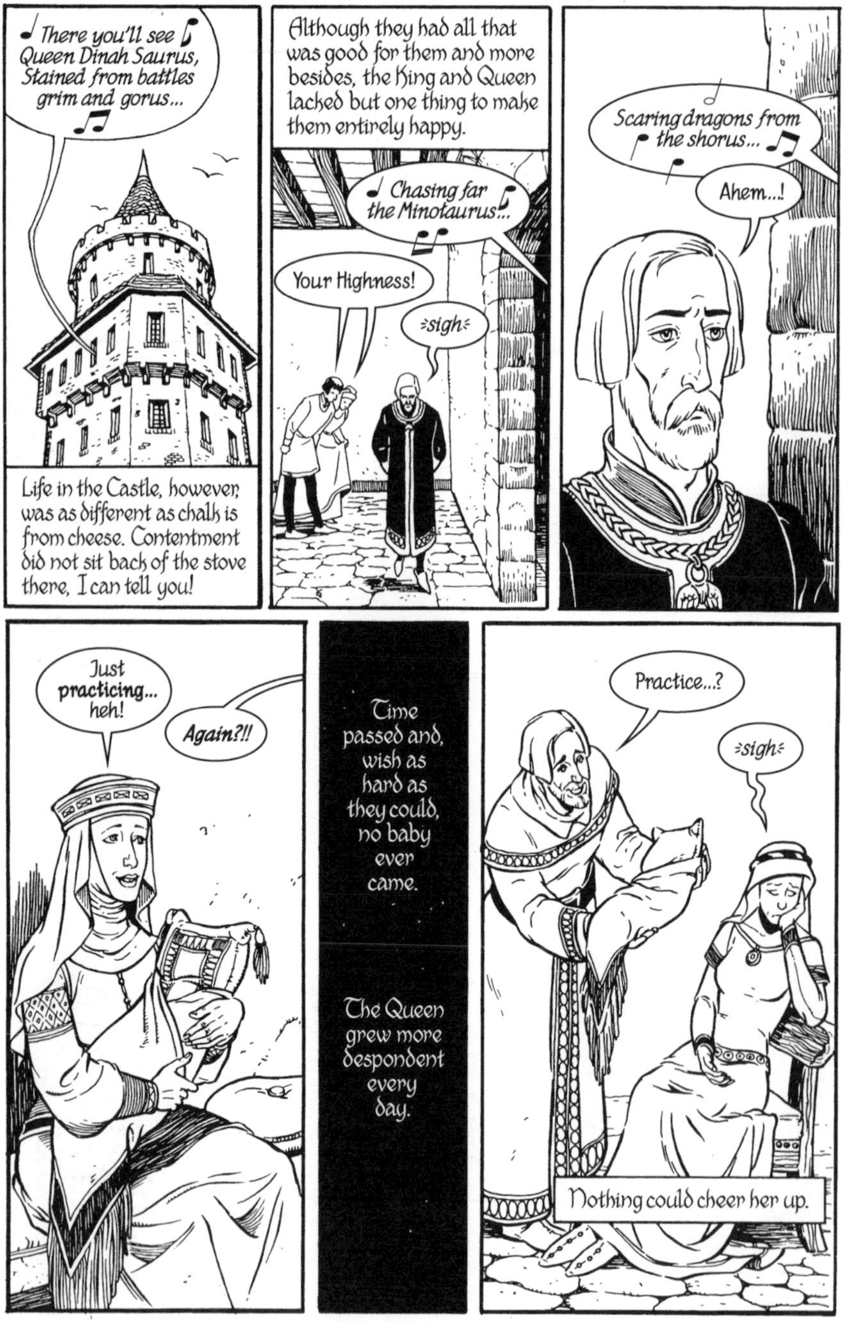
There you'll see Queen Dinah Saurus, Stained from battles grim and gorus...
Life in the Castle, however, was as different as chalk is from cheese. Contentment did not sit back of the stove there, I can tell you!
Although they had all that was good for them and more besides, the King and Queen lacked but one thing to make them entirely happy.
Chasing far the Minotaurus...
Your Highness!
sigh
Scaring dragons from the shorus...
Ahem...!
Just practicing... heh!
Again?!!
Time passed and, wish as hard as they could, no baby ever came.
The Queen grew more despondent every day.
Practice...?
sigh
Nothing could cheer her up.

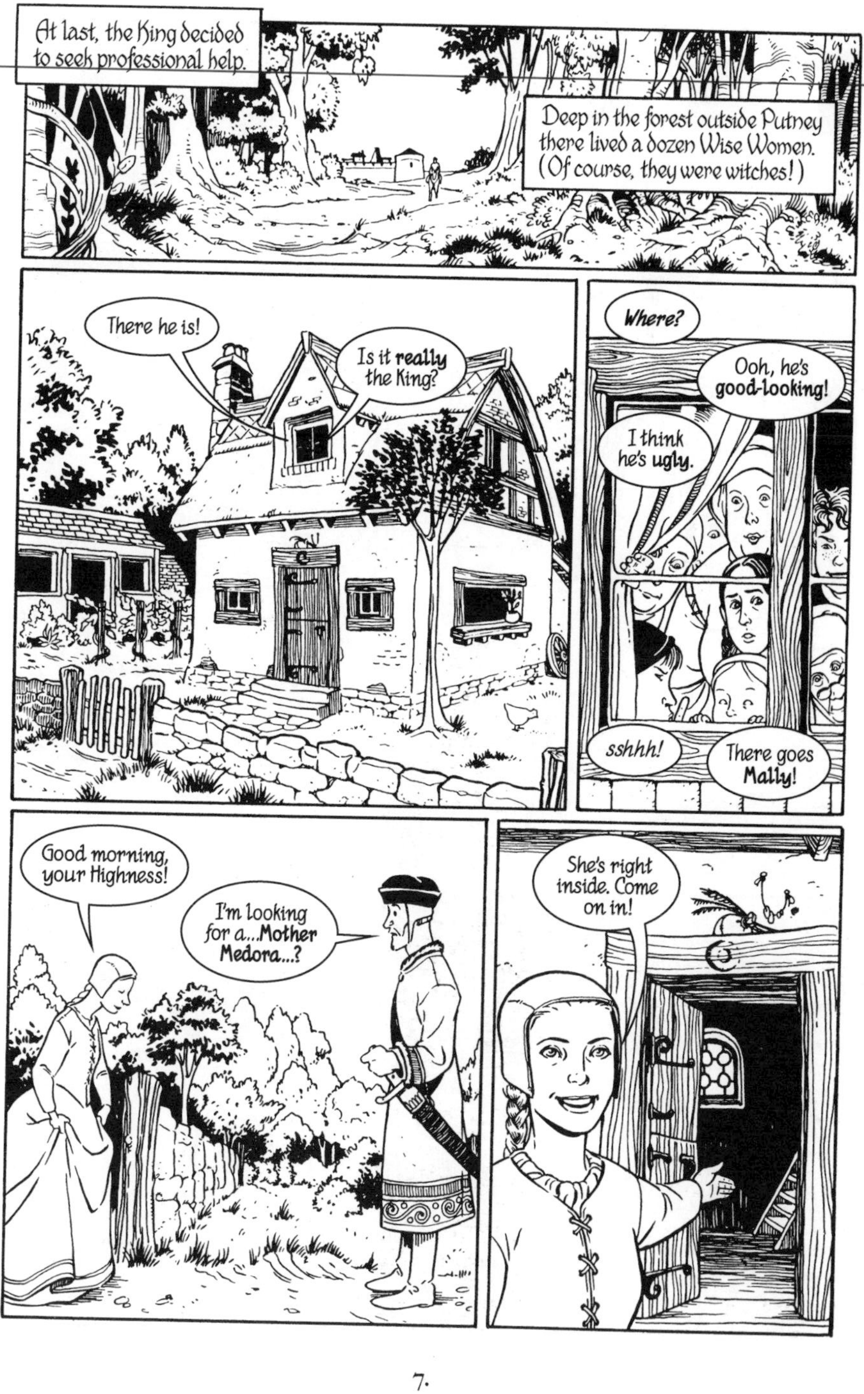
At last, the King decided to seek professional help.
Deep in the forest outside Putney there lived a dozen Wise Women. (Of course, they were witches!)
There he is!
Is it **really** the King?
Where?
Ooh, he's **good-looking!**
I think he's **ugly.**
sshhh!
There goes **Mally!**
Good morning, your Highness!
I'm looking for a...**Mother Medora...?**
She's right inside. Come on in!

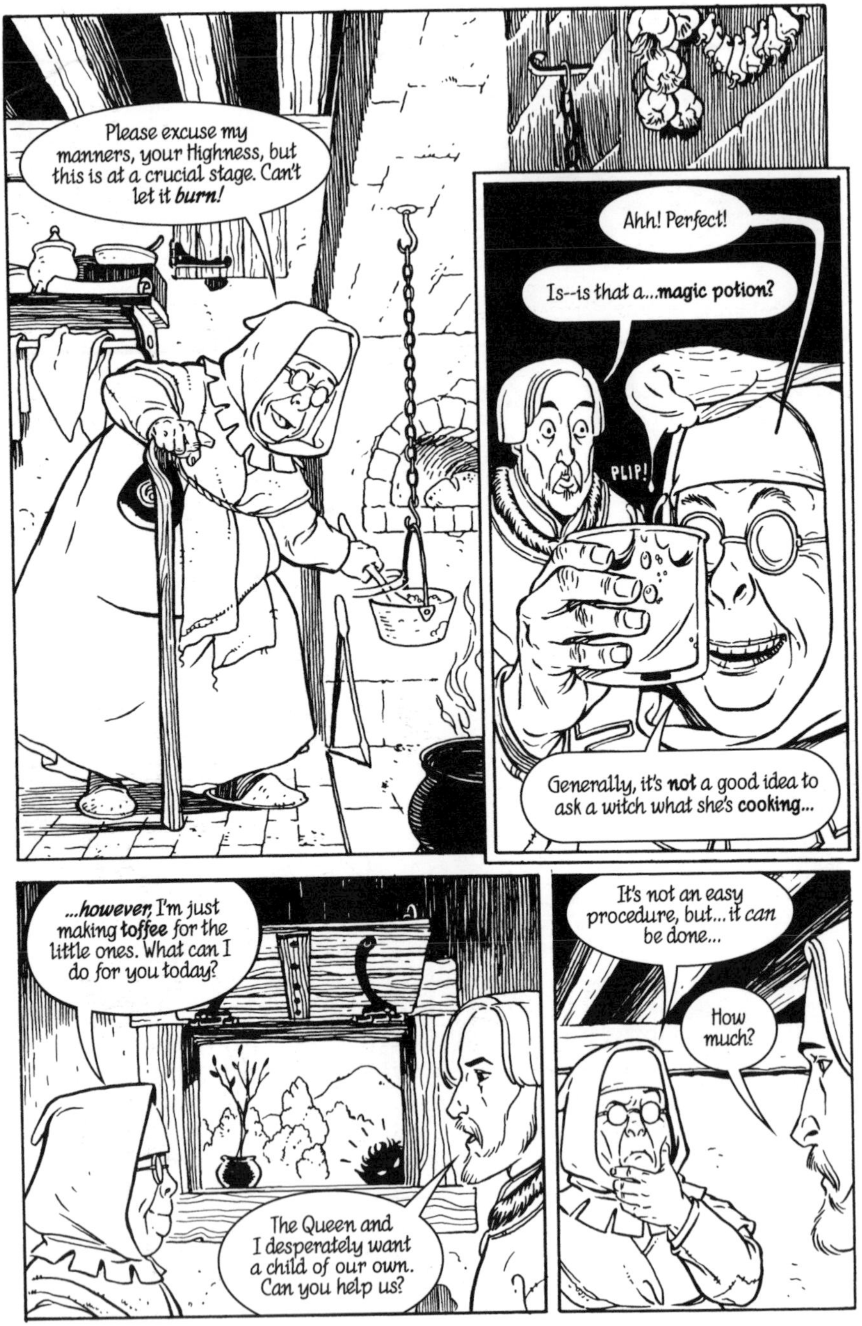
Please excuse my manners, your Highness, but this is at a crucial stage. Can't let it *burn!*
Ahh! Perfect!
Is--is that a...**magic potion?**
PLIP!
Generally, it's **not** a good idea to ask a witch what she's **cooking...**
...however, I'm just making **toffee** for the little ones. What can I do for you today?
The Queen and I desperately want a child of our own. Can you help us?
It's not an easy procedure, but... it *can* be done...
How much?

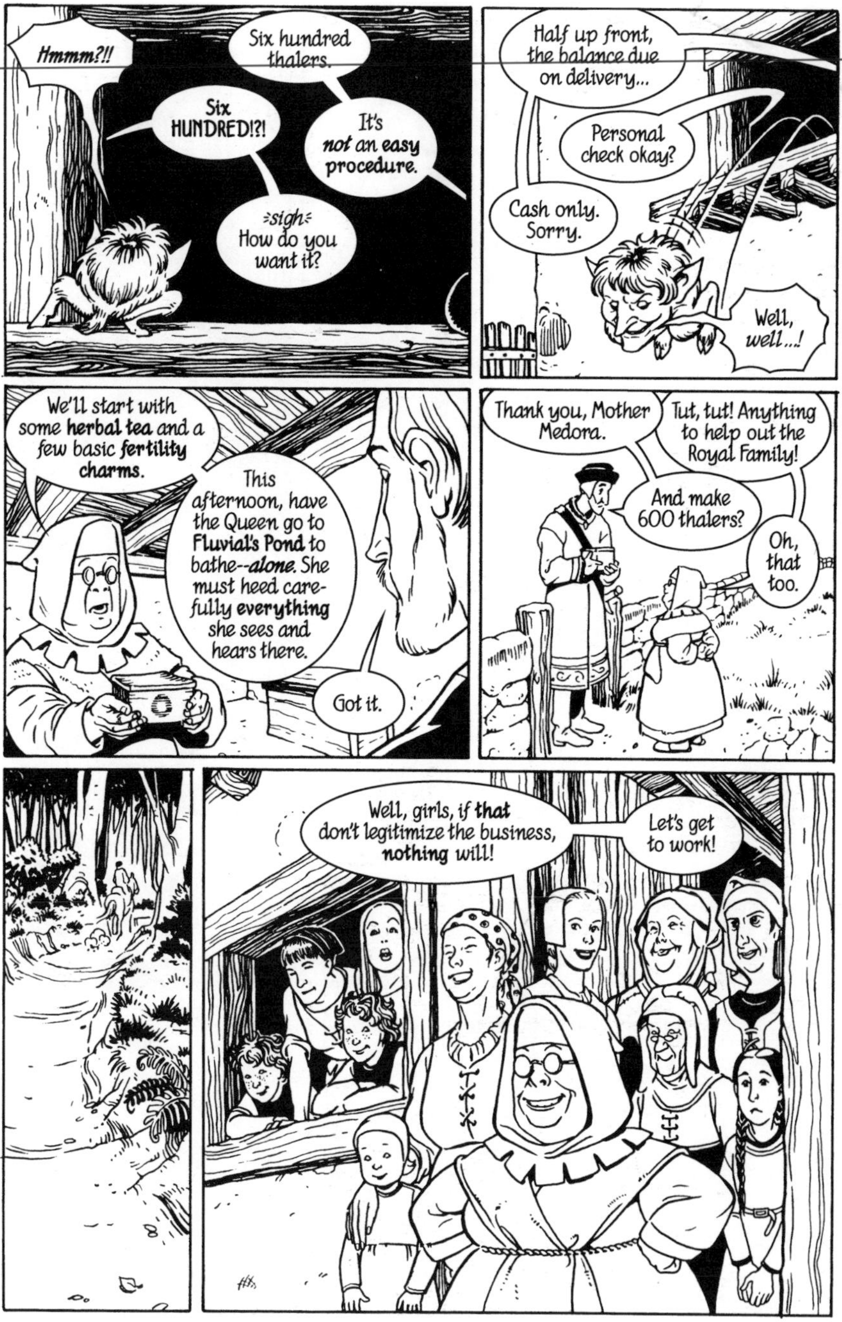
Hmmm?!!
Six hundred thalers.
Six HUNDRED!?!
It's *not* an easy procedure.
sigh
How do you want it?
Half up front, the balance due on delivery...
Personal check okay?
Cash only. Sorry.
Well, well...!
We'll start with some herbal tea and a few basic fertility charms.
This afternoon, have the Queen go to Fluvial's Pond to bathe--*alone*. She must heed carefully everything she sees and hears there.
Got it.
Thank you, Mother Medora.
Tut, tut! Anything to help out the Royal Family!
And make 600 thalers?
Oh, that too.
Well, girls, if that don't legitimize the business, nothing will!
Let's get to work!

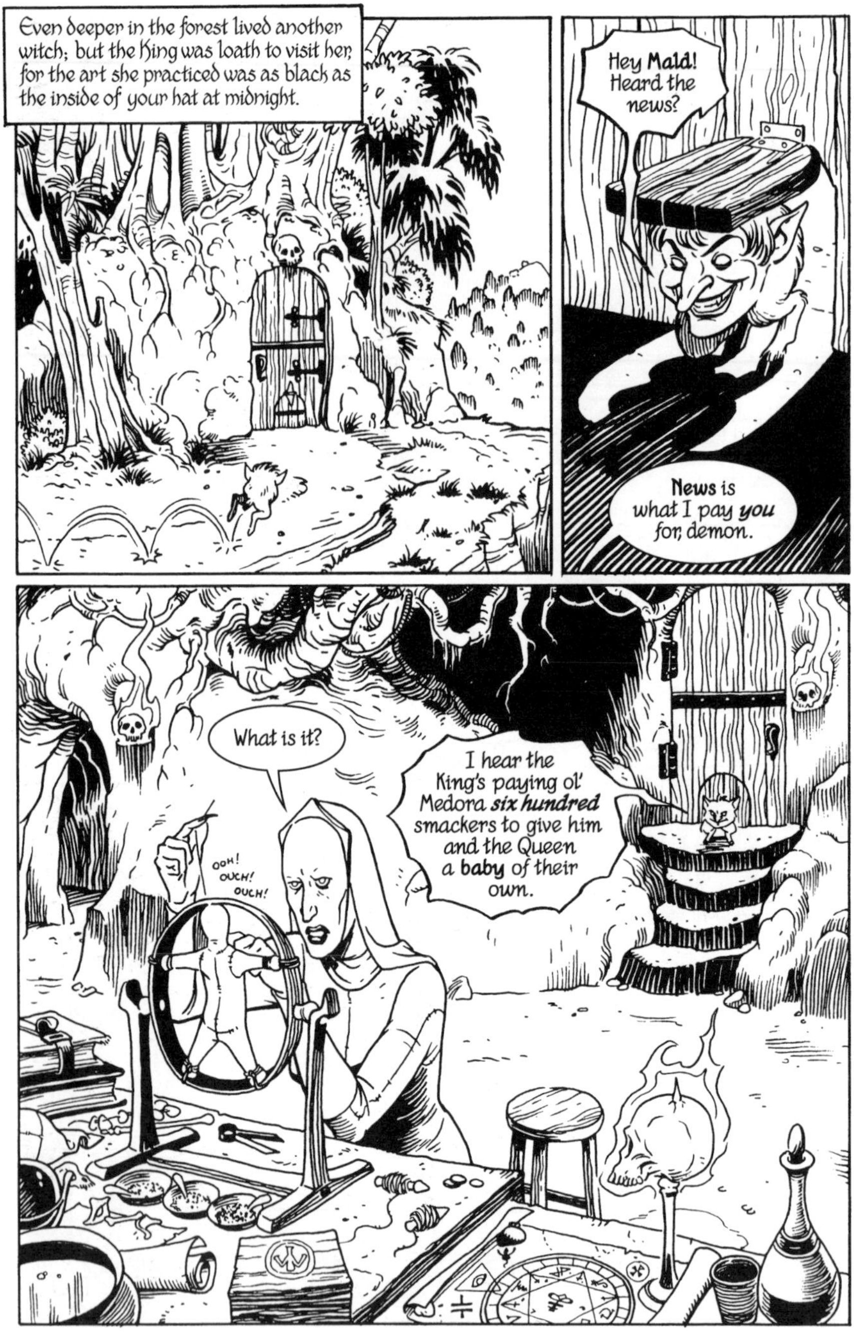
Even deeper in the forest lived another witch; but the King was loath to visit her, for the art she practiced was as black as the inside of your hat at midnight.
Hey Mald! Heard the news?
News is what I pay you for, demon.
What is it?
I hear the King's paying ol' Medora six hundred smackers to give him and the Queen a baby of their own.
OOH! OUCH! OUCH!

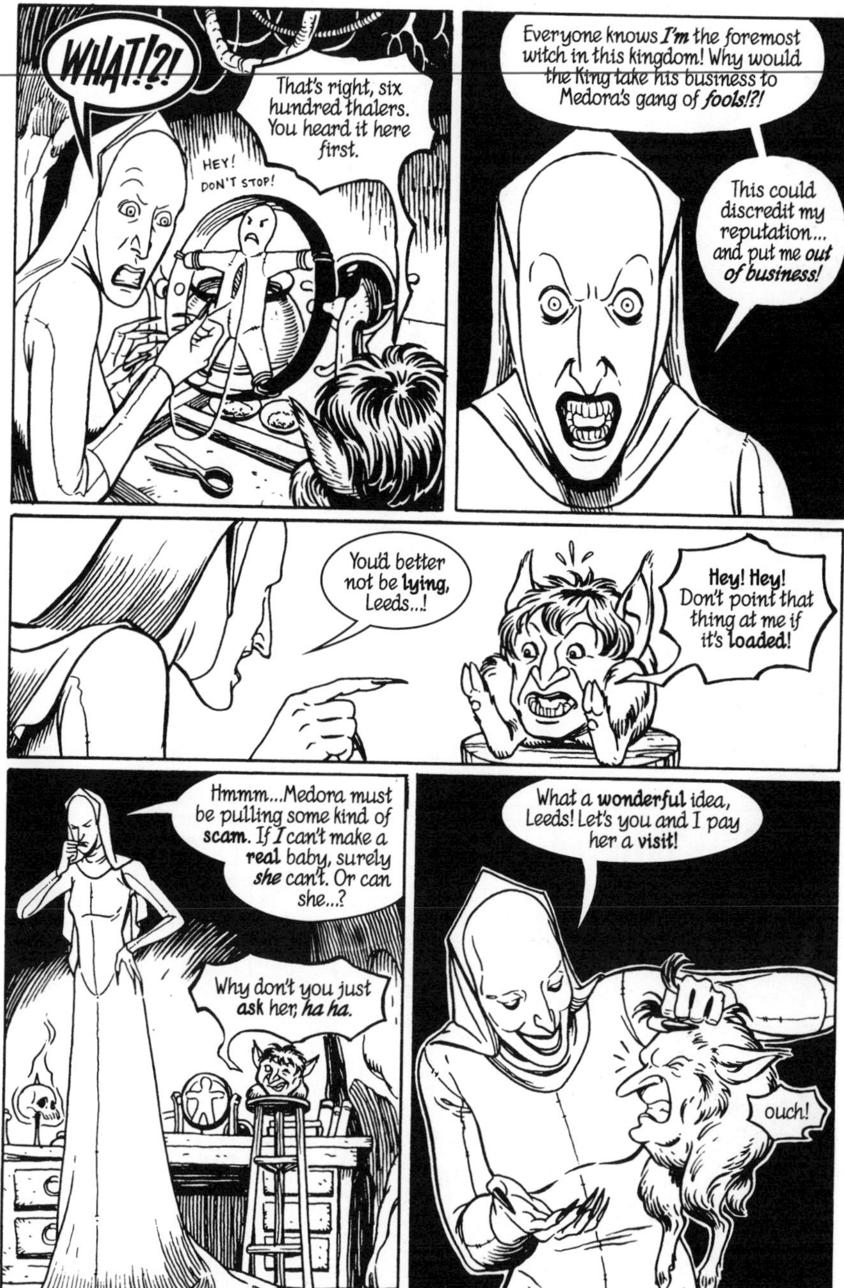
WHAT!?!
That's right, six hundred thalers. You heard it here first.
HEY! DON'T STOP!
Everyone knows I'm the foremost witch in this kingdom! Why would the King take his business to Medora's gang of fools!?!
This could discredit my reputation... and put me out of business!
You'd better not be lying, Leeds...!
Hey! Hey! Don't point that thing at me if it's loaded!
Hmmm...Medora must be pulling some kind of scam. If I can't make a real baby, surely she can't. Or can she...?
Why don't you just ask her, ha ha.
What a wonderful idea, Leeds! Let's you and I pay her a visit!
ouch!

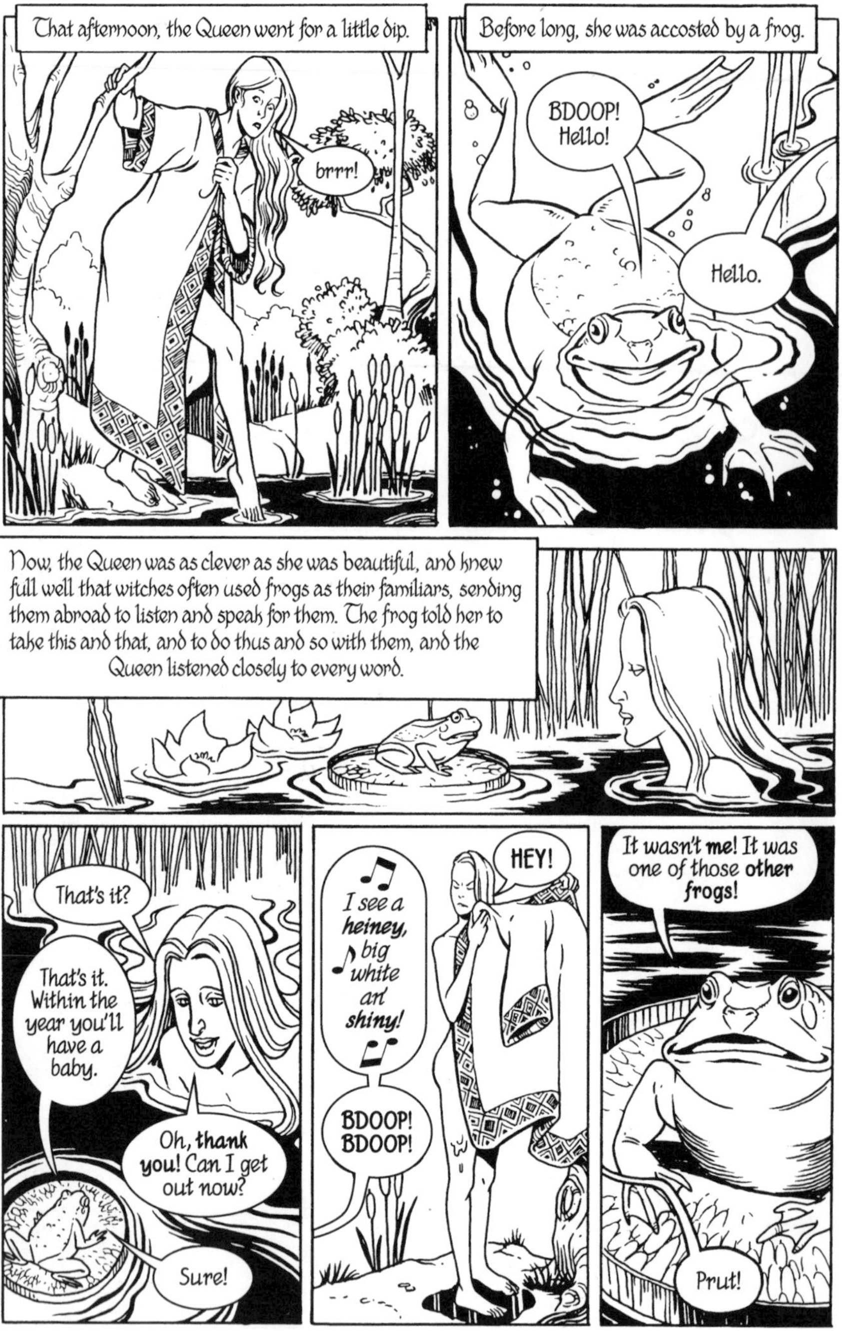
That afternoon, the Queen went for a little dip.
brrr!
Before long, she was accosted by a frog.
BDOOP! Hello!
Hello.
Now, the Queen was as clever as she was beautiful, and knew full well that witches often used frogs as their familiars, sending them abroad to listen and speak for them. The frog told her to take this and that, and to do thus and so with them, and the Queen listened closely to every word.
That's it?
That's it. Within the year you'll have a baby.
Oh, **thank you**! Can I get out now?
Sure!
*I see a **heiney,** big white an' **shiny!***
BDOOP! BDOOP!
HEY!
It wasn't **me**! It was one of those **other frogs**!
Prut!

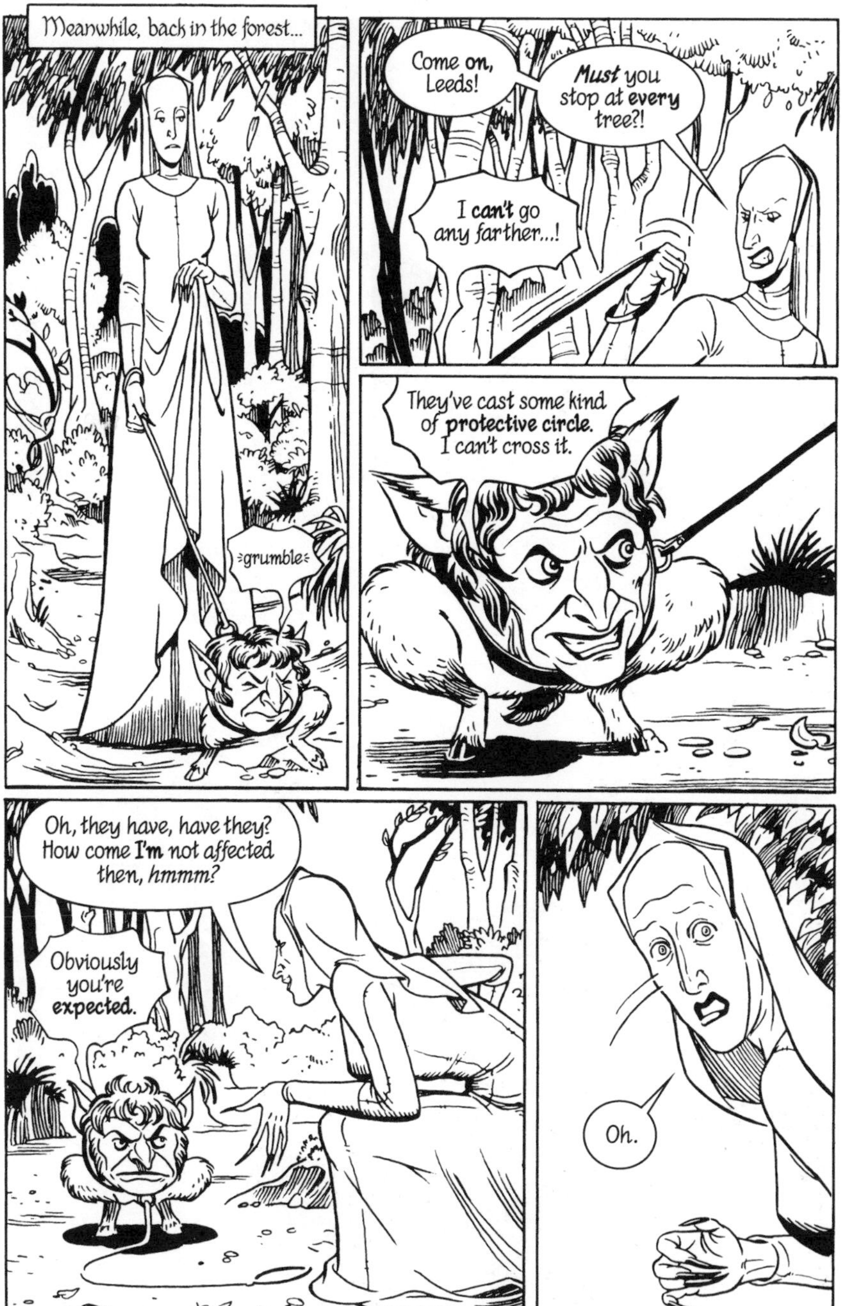
Meanwhile, back in the forest...
grumble
Come on, Leeds!
Must you stop at every tree?!
I can't go any farther...!
They've cast some kind of protective circle. I can't cross it.
Oh, they have, have they? How come I'm not affected then, hmmm?
Obviously you're expected.
Oh.

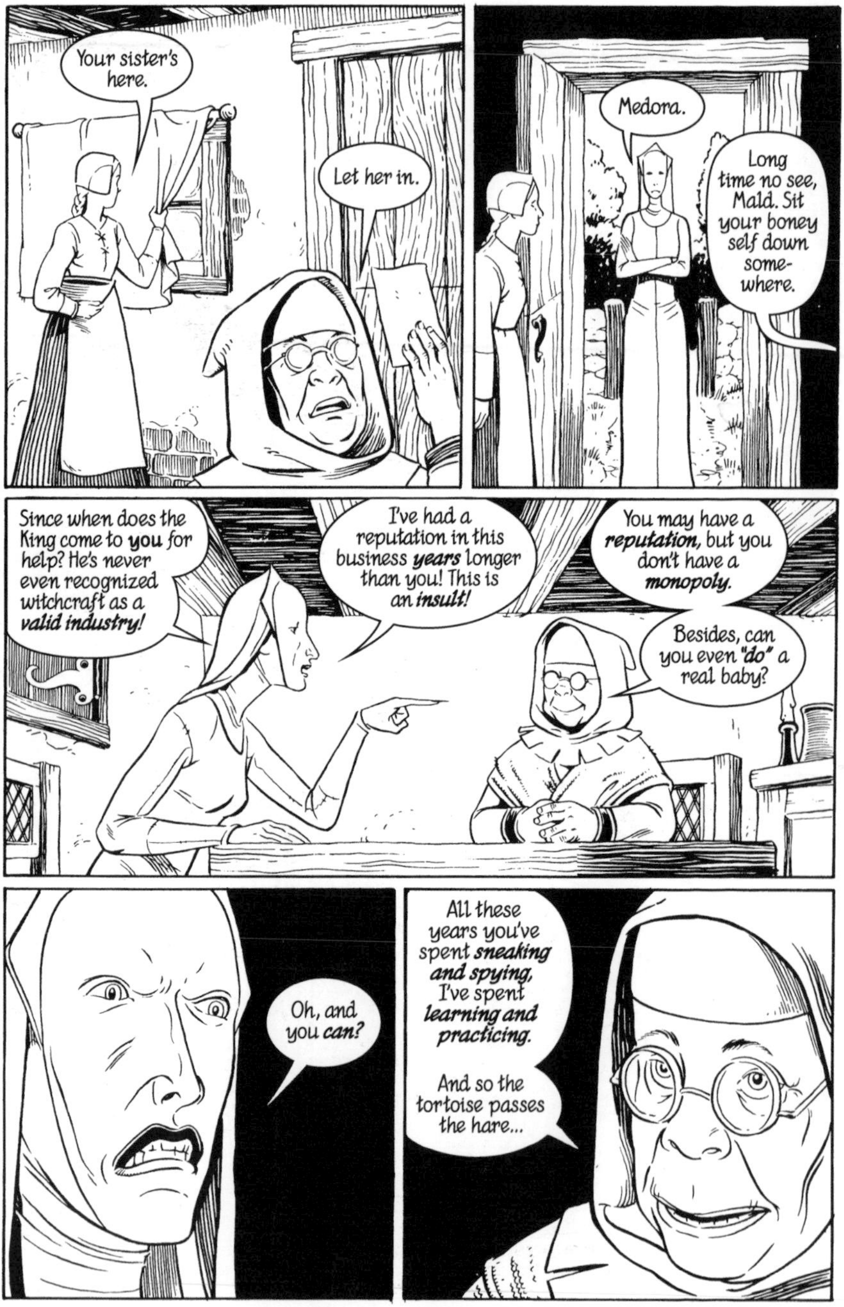
Your sister's here.
Let her in.
Medora.
Long time no see, Mald. Sit your boney self down some-where.
Since when does the King come to **you** for help? He's never even recognized witchcraft as a ***valid industry!***
I've had a reputation in this business ***years*** longer than you! This is an ***insult!***
You may have a ***reputation,*** but you don't have a ***monopoly.***
Besides, can you even ***"do"*** a real baby?
Oh, and you ***can?***
All these years you've spent ***sneaking and spying,*** I've spent ***learning and practicing.***
And so the tortoise passes the hare...

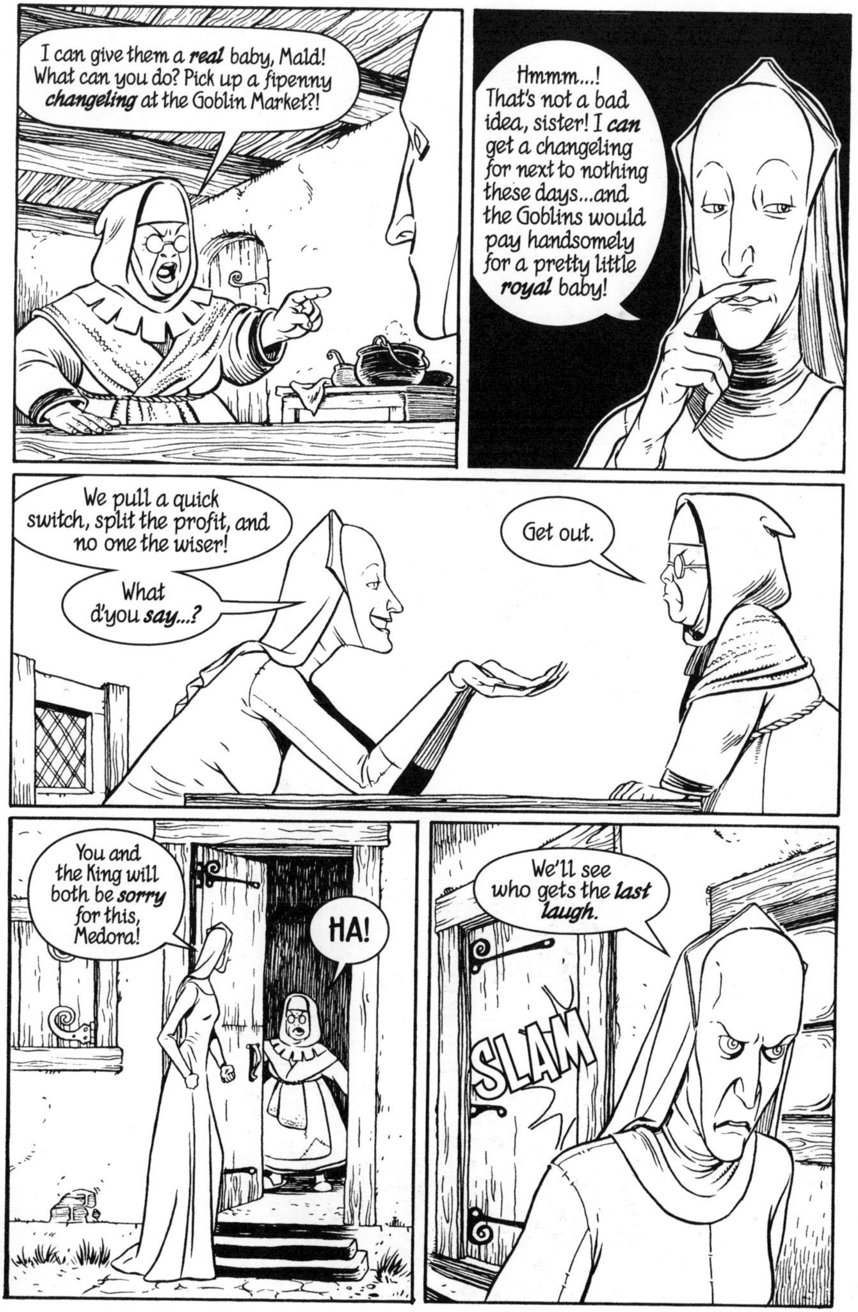
I can give them a real baby, Mald! What can you do? Pick up a fipenny changeling at the Goblin Market?!
Hmmm...! That's not a bad idea, sister! I can get a changeling for next to nothing these days...and the Goblins would pay handsomely for a pretty little royal baby!
We pull a quick switch, split the profit, and no one the wiser!
What d'you say...?
Get out.
You and the King will both be sorry for this, Medora!
HA!
We'll see who gets the last laugh.
SLAM

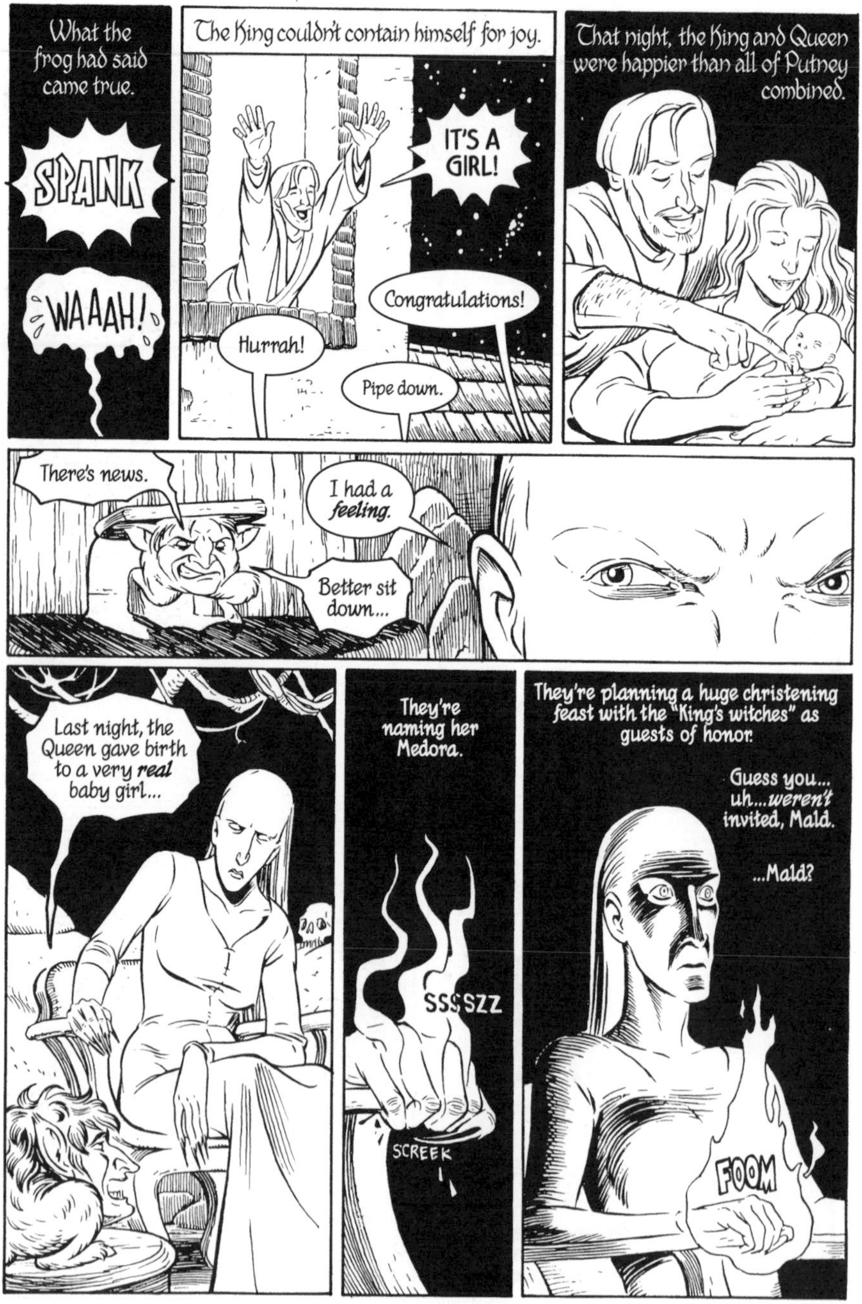
What the frog had said came true.
SPANK
WAAAH!
The King couldn't contain himself for joy.
IT'S A GIRL!
Congratulations!
Hurrah!
Pipe down.
That night, the King and Queen were happier than all of Putney combined.
There's news.
I had a *feeling*.
Better sit down...
Last night, the Queen gave birth to a very *real* baby girl...
They're naming her Medora.
SSSSZZ
SCREEK
They're planning a huge christening feast with the "King's witches" as guests of honor.
Guess you... uh...*weren't* invited, Mald.
...Mald?
FOOM

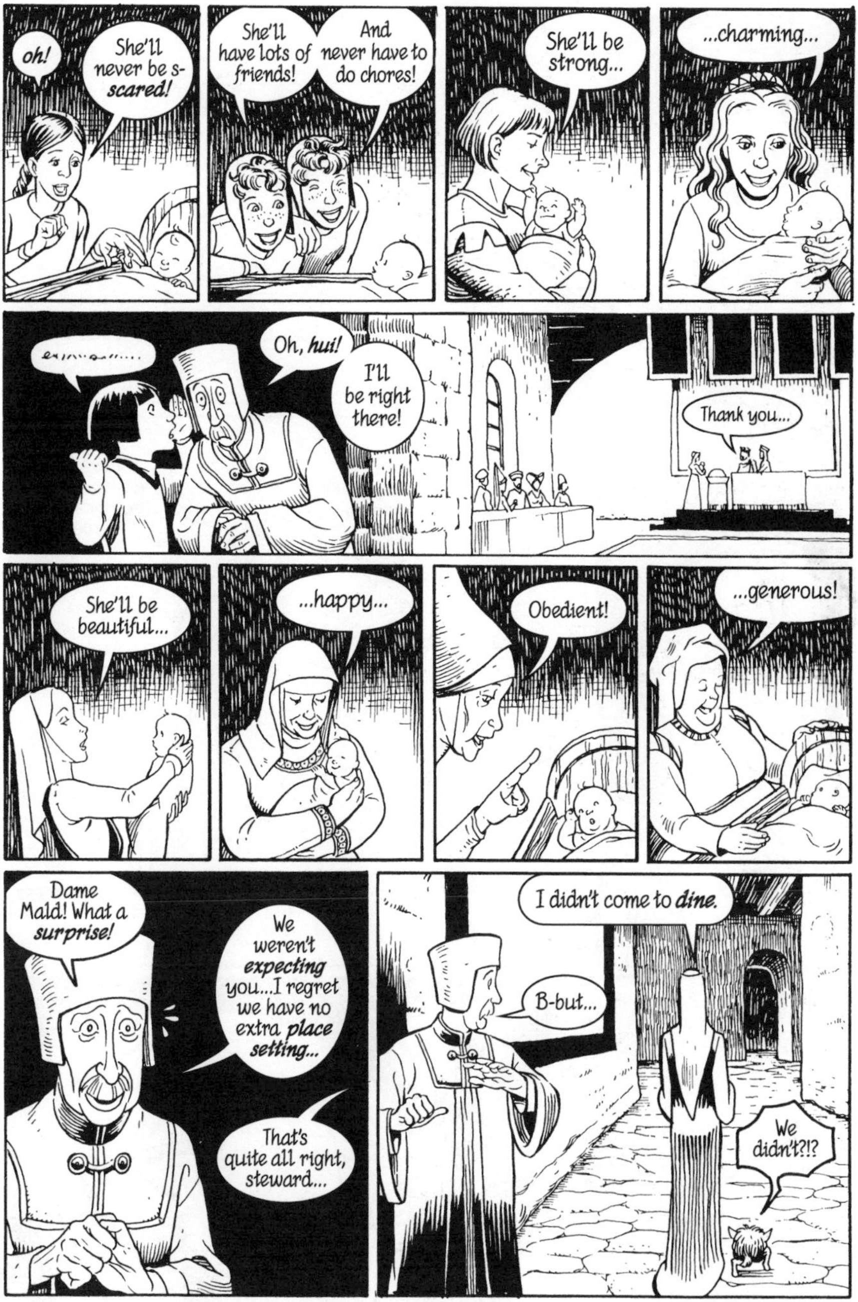
oh!
She'll never be s-scared!
She'll have lots of friends!
And never have to do chores!
She'll be strong...
...charming...
Oh, hui!
I'll be right there!
Thank you...
She'll be beautiful...
...happy...
Obedient!
...generous!
Dame Mald! What a surprise!
We weren't expecting you...I regret we have no extra place setting...
That's quite all right, steward...
I didn't come to dine.
B-but...
We didn't?!?

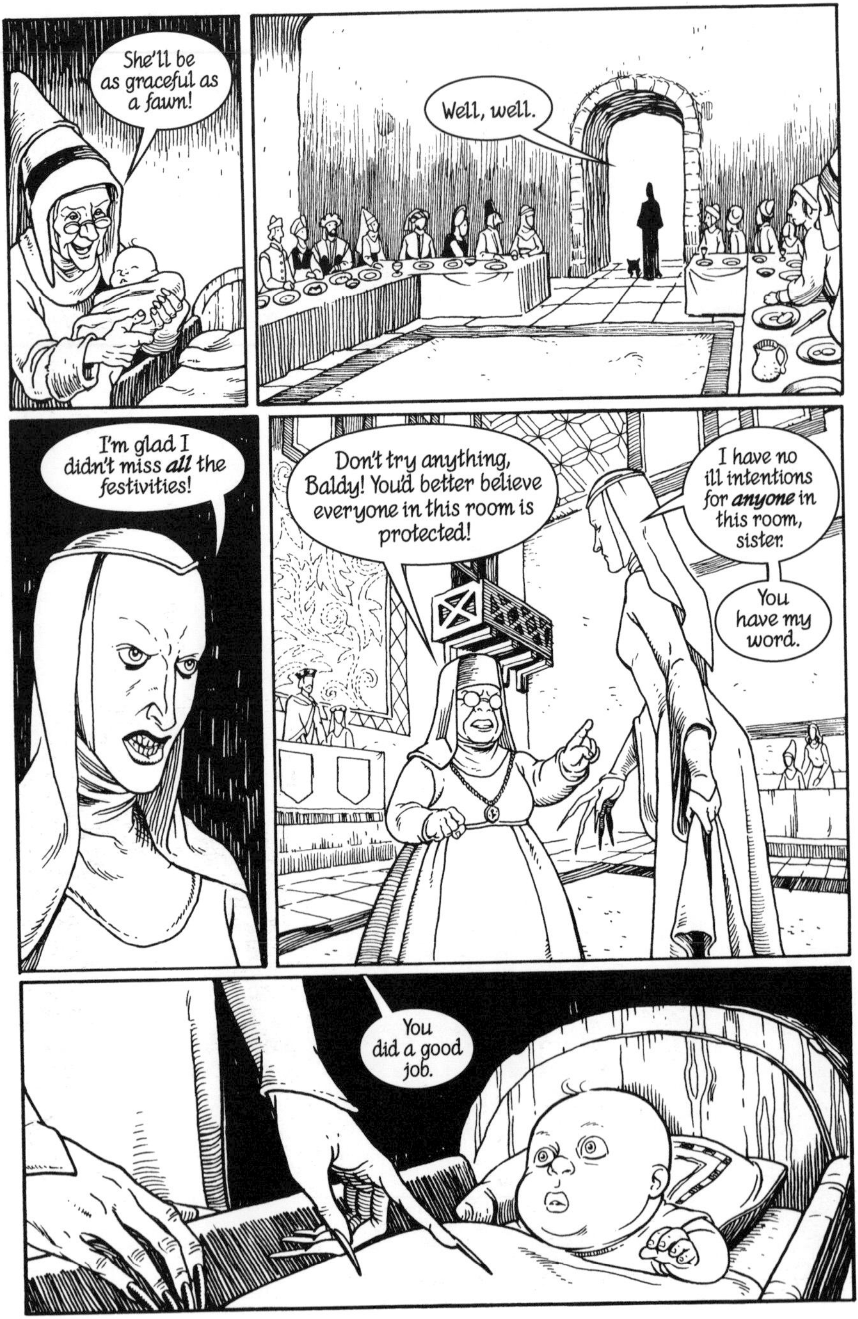
She'll be as graceful as a fawn!
Well, well.
I'm glad I didn't miss *all* the festivities!
Don't try anything, Baldy! You'd better believe everyone in this room is protected!
I have no ill intentions for *anyone* in this room, sister.
You have my word.
You did a good job.

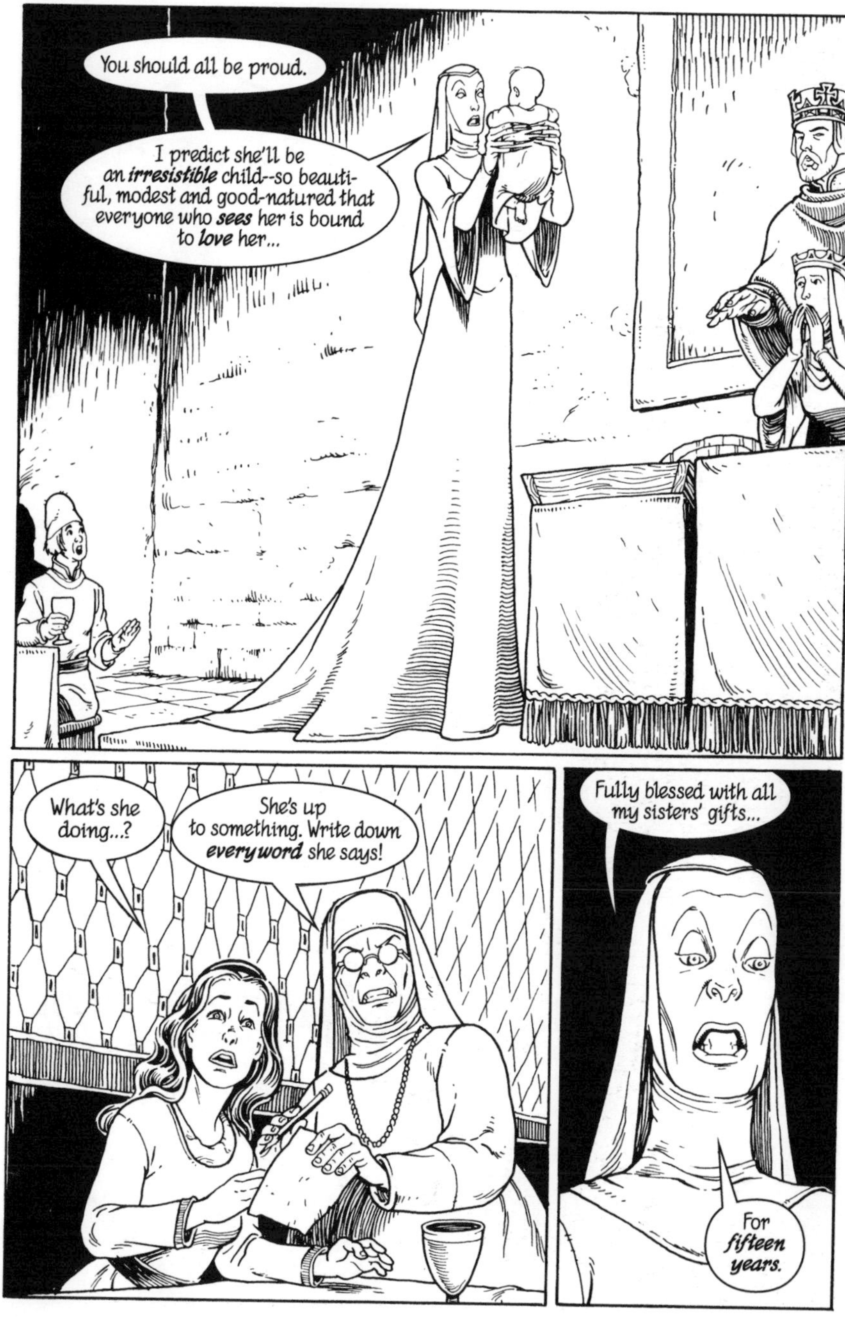

You should all be proud.
I predict she'll be an *irresistible* child--so beautiful, modest and good-natured that everyone who *sees* her is bound to *love* her...
What's she doing...?
She's up to something. Write down *every word* she says!
Fully blessed with all my sisters' gifts...
For *fifteen years.*

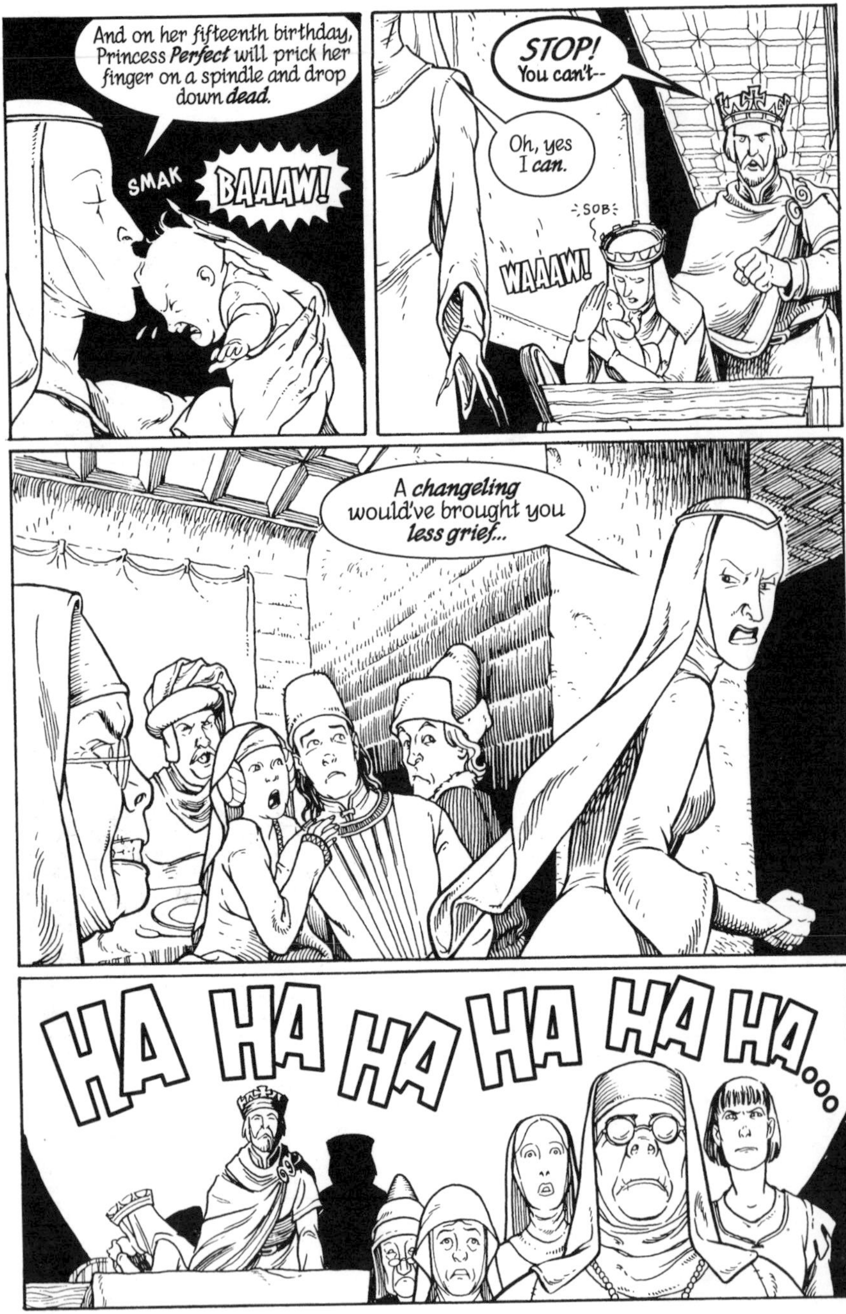
And on her fifteenth birthday, Princess *Perfect* will prick her finger on a spindle and drop down *dead*.
SMAK
BAAAW!
STOP! You can't--
Oh, yes I *can*.
SOB
WAAAW!
A *changeling* would've brought you *less grief*...
HA HA HA HA HA HA...

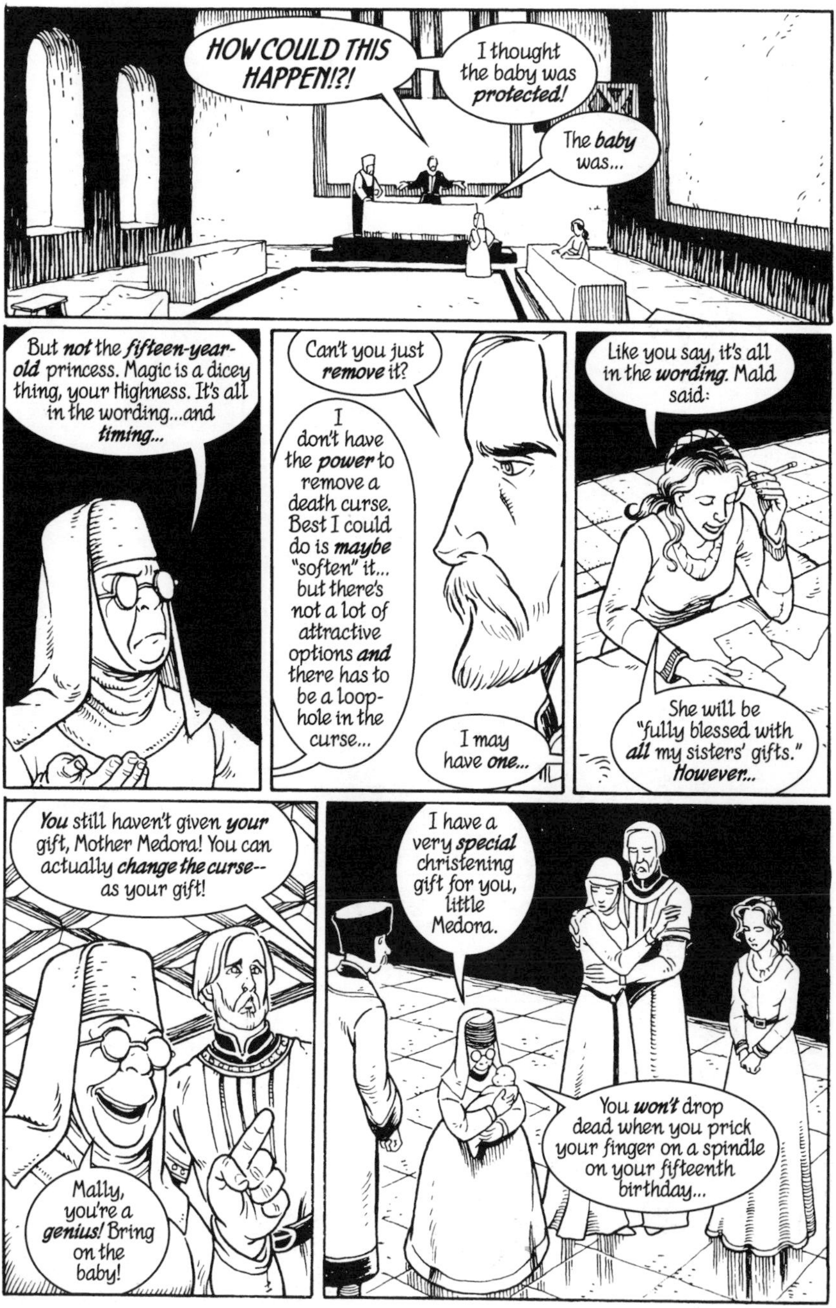
HOW COULD THIS HAPPEN!?!
I thought the baby was *protected!*
The *baby* was...
But *not* the *fifteen-year-old* princess. Magic is a dicey thing, your Highness. It's all in the wording...and *timing...*
Can't you just *remove* it?
I don't have the *power* to remove a death curse. Best I could do is *maybe* "soften" it... but there's not a lot of attractive options *and* there has to be a loop-hole in the curse...
I may have *one...*
Like you say, it's all in the *wording*. Mald said:
She will be "fully blessed with *all* my sisters' gifts." *However...*
You still haven't given *your* gift, Mother Medora! You can actually *change the curse*-- as your gift!
Mally, you're a *genius!* Bring on the baby!
I have a very *special* christening gift for you, little Medora.
You *won't* drop dead when you prick your finger on a spindle on your fifteenth birthday...

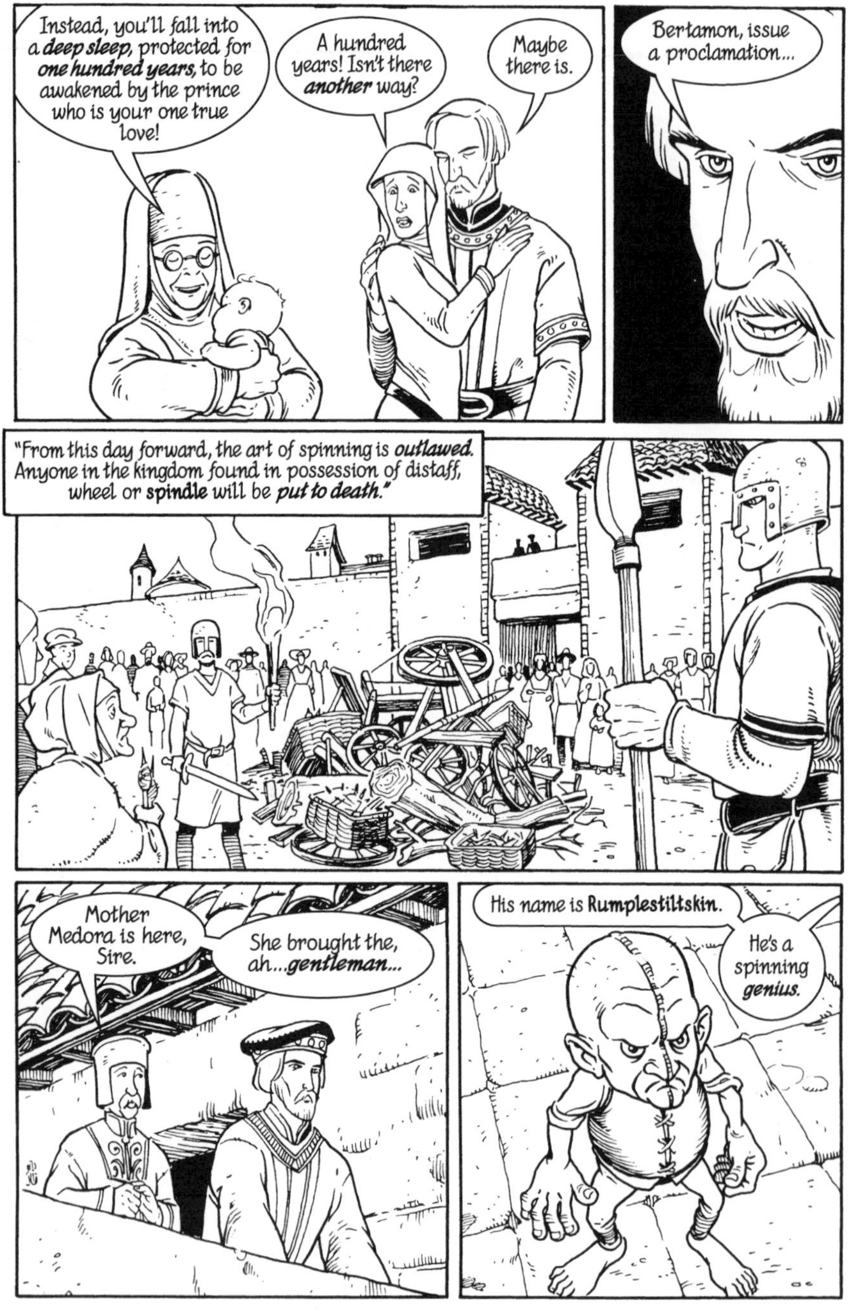
Instead, you'll fall into a *deep sleep*, protected for *one hundred years*, to be awakened by the prince who is your one true love!
A hundred years! Isn't there *another* way?
Maybe there is.
Bertamon, issue a proclamation...
"From this day forward, the art of spinning is *outlawed*. Anyone in the kingdom found in possession of distaff, wheel or **spindle** will be *put to death*."
Mother Medora is here, Sire.
She brought the, ah...*gentleman*...
His name is **Rumplestiltskin**.
He's a spinning *genius*.

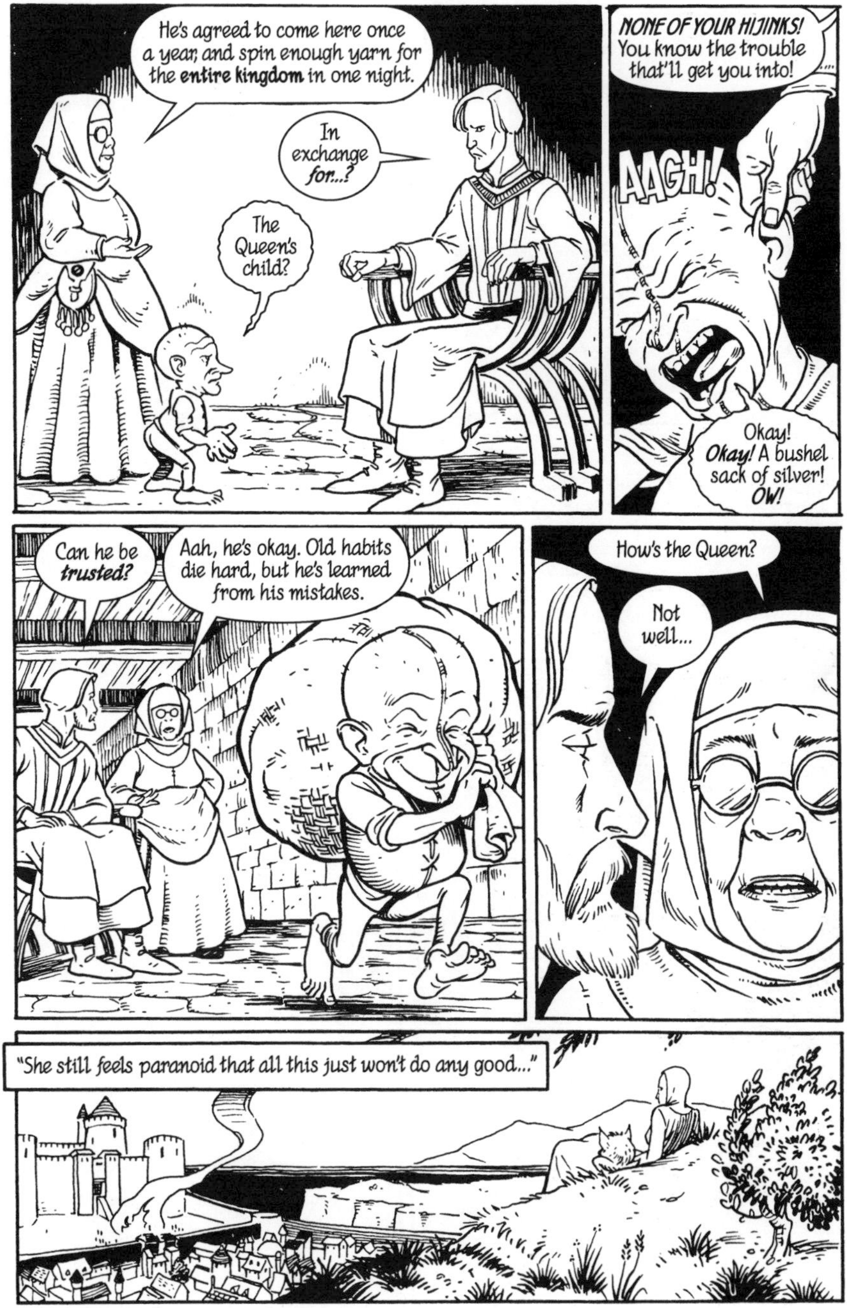
He's agreed to come here once a year, and spin enough yarn for the **entire kingdom** in one night.
In exchange ***for...?***
The Queen's child?
NONE OF YOUR HIJINKS! You know the trouble that'll get you into!
AAGH!
Okay! ***Okay!*** A bushel sack of silver! ***OW!***
Can he be ***trusted?***
Aah, he's okay. Old habits die hard, but he's learned from his mistakes.
How's the Queen?
Not well...
"She still *feels* paranoid that all this just won't do any good..."

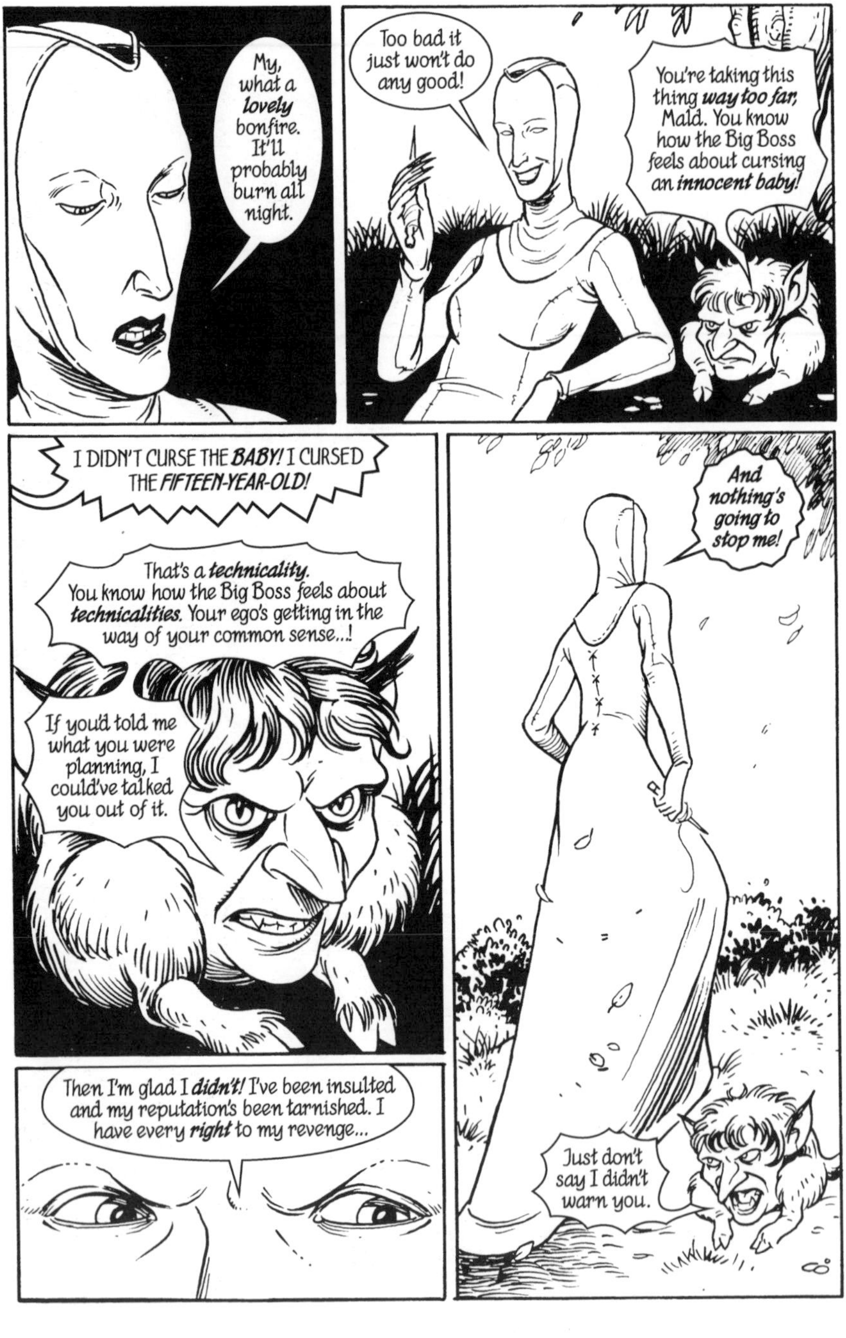
My, what a *lovely* bonfire. It'll probably burn all night.
Too bad it just won't do any good!
You're taking this thing *way too far,* Mald. You know how the Big Boss feels about cursing an *innocent baby!*
I DIDN'T CURSE THE *BABY!* I CURSED THE *FIFTEEN-YEAR-OLD!*
That's a *technicality.* You know how the Big Boss feels about *technicalities.* Your ego's getting in the way of your common sense...!
If you'd told me what you were planning, I could've talked you out of it.
Then I'm glad I *didn't!* I've been insulted and my reputation's been tarnished. I have every *right* to my revenge...
And nothing's going to stop me!
Just don't say I didn't warn you.

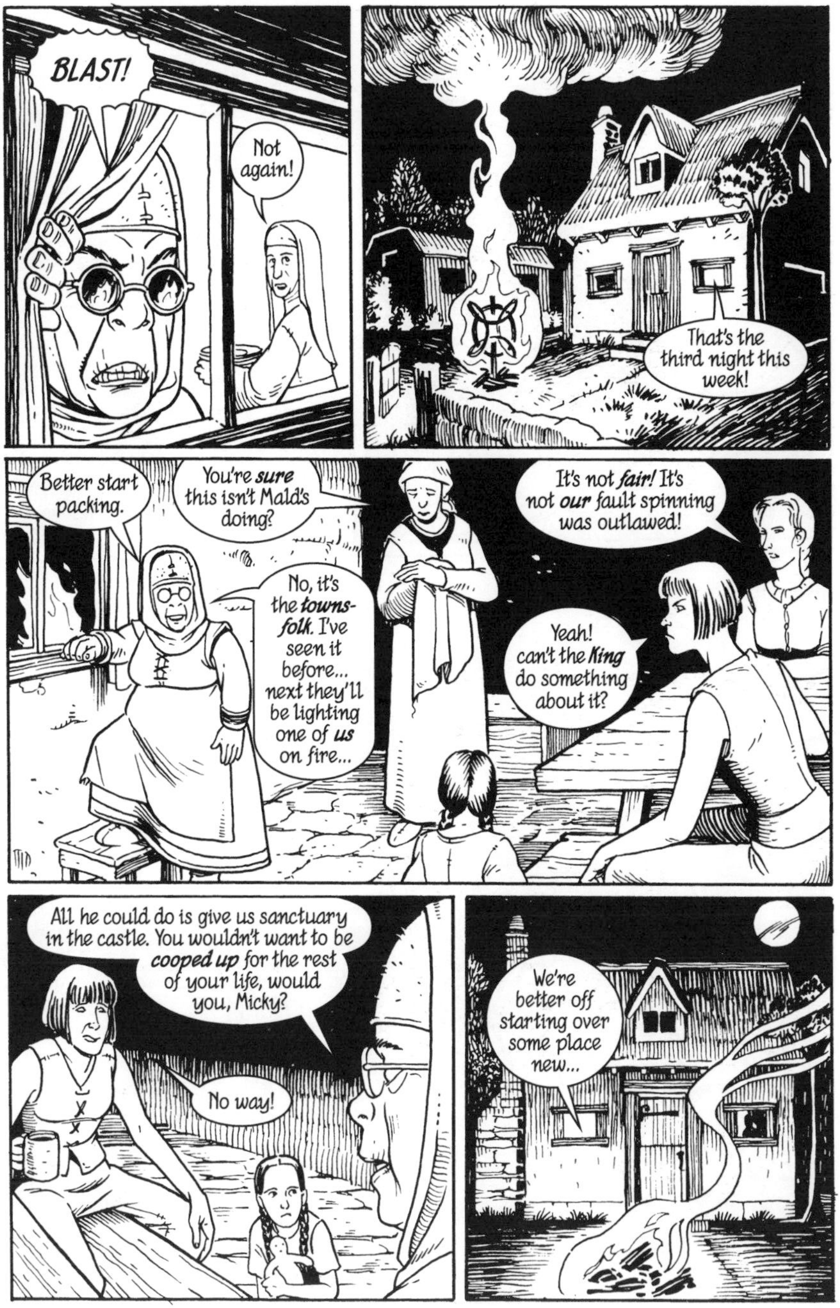
BLAST!
Not again!
That's the third night this week!
Better start packing.
You're sure this isn't Mald's doing?
No, it's the townsfolk. I've seen it before... next they'll be lighting one of us on fire...
It's not fair! It's not our fault spinning was outlawed!
Yeah! can't the King do something about it?
All he could do is give us sanctuary in the castle. You wouldn't want to be cooped up for the rest of your life, would you, Micky?
No way!
We're better off starting over some place new...

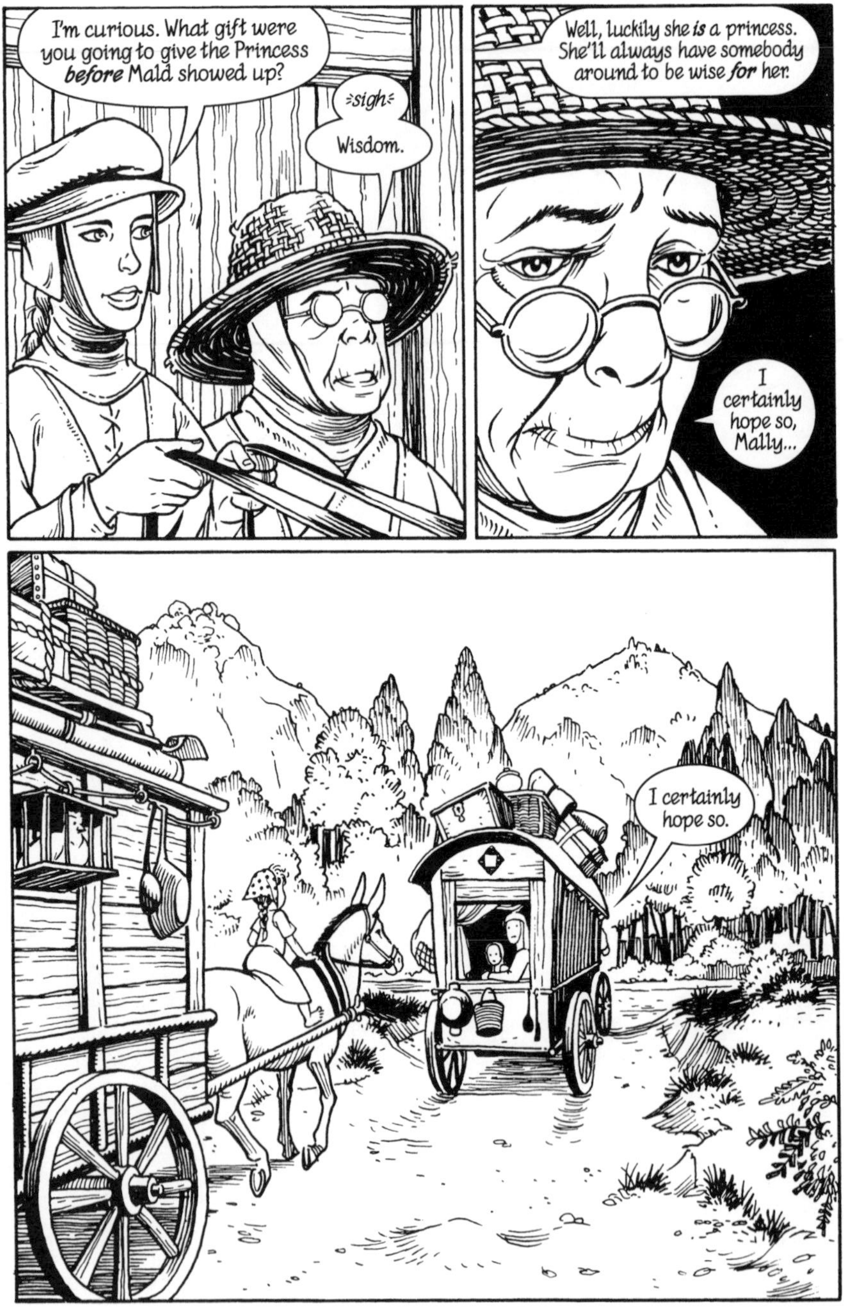
I'm curious. What gift were you going to give the Princess *before* Mald showed up?
sigh
Wisdom.
Well, luckily she *is* a princess. She'll always have somebody around to be wise *for* her.
I certainly hope so, Mally...
I certainly hope so.

Chapter 2.

· THE CURSE OF BRAMBLY HEDGE PT. 2 ·

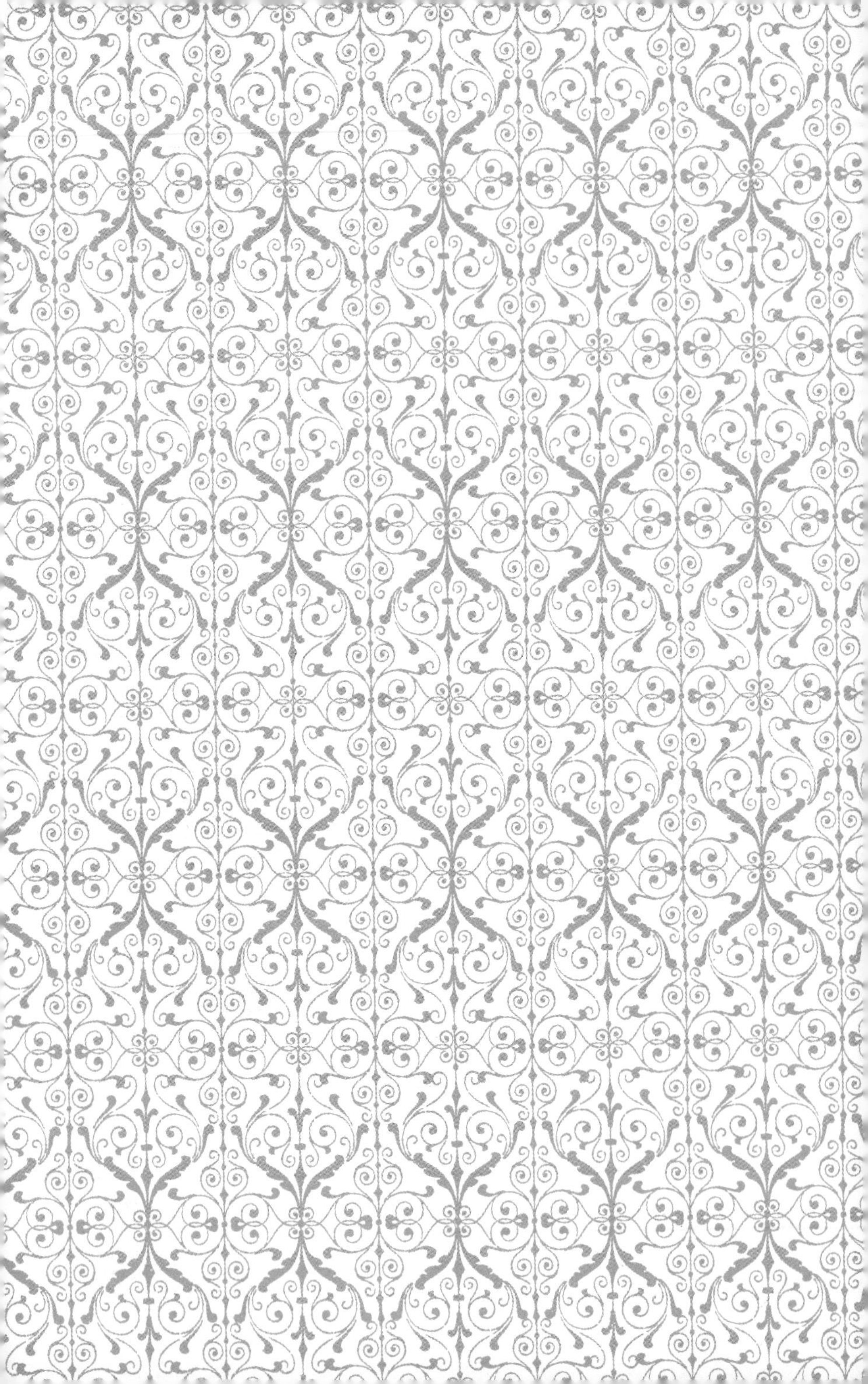

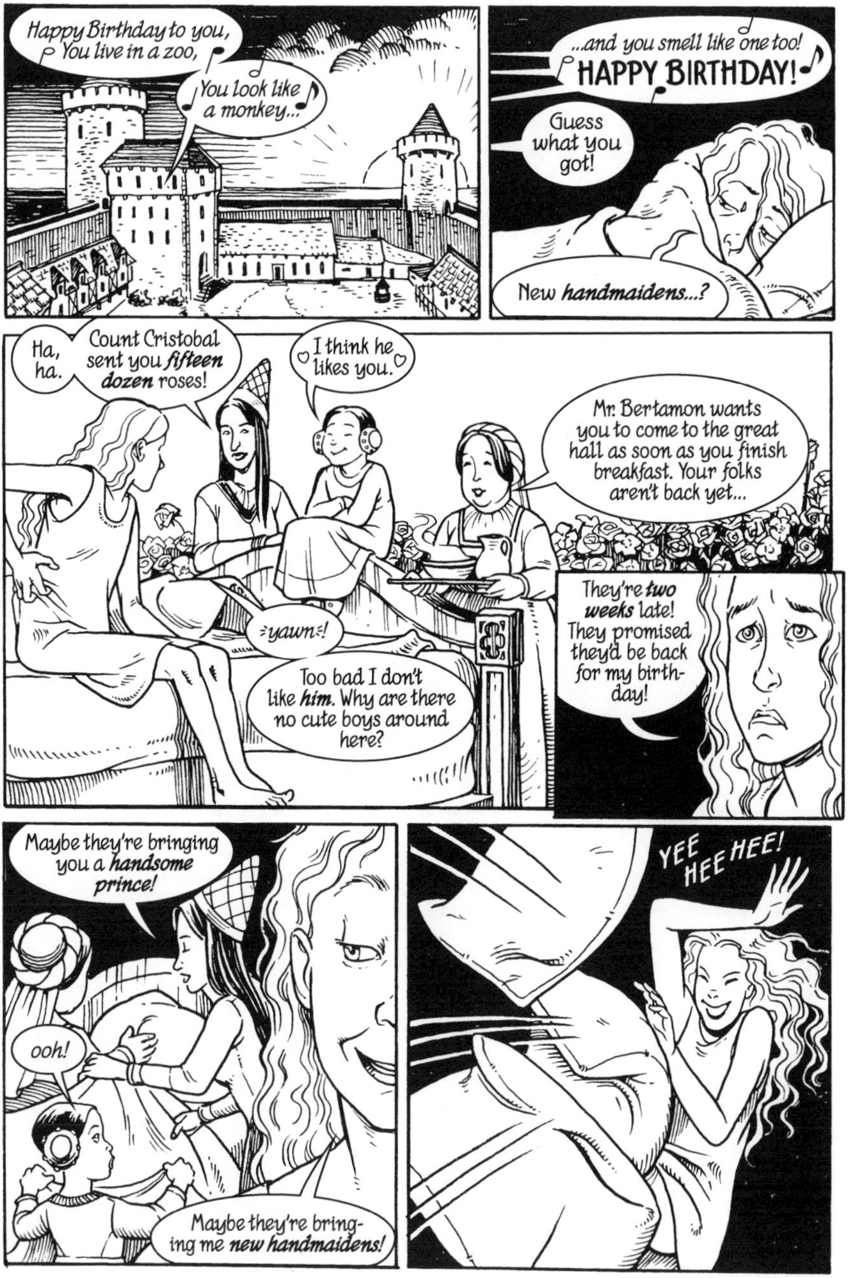

Happy Birthday to you, You live in a zoo,
You look like a monkey...
...and you smell like one too!
HAPPY BIRTHDAY!
Guess what you got!
New handmaidens...?
Ha, ha.
Count Cristobal sent you fifteen dozen roses!
I think he likes you.
Mr. Bertamon wants you to come to the great hall as soon as you finish breakfast. Your folks aren't back yet...
yawn!
Too bad I don't like him. Why are there no cute boys around here?
They're two weeks late! They promised they'd be back for my birthday!
Maybe they're bringing you a handsome prince!
ooh!
Maybe they're bringing me new handmaidens!
YEE HEE HEE!

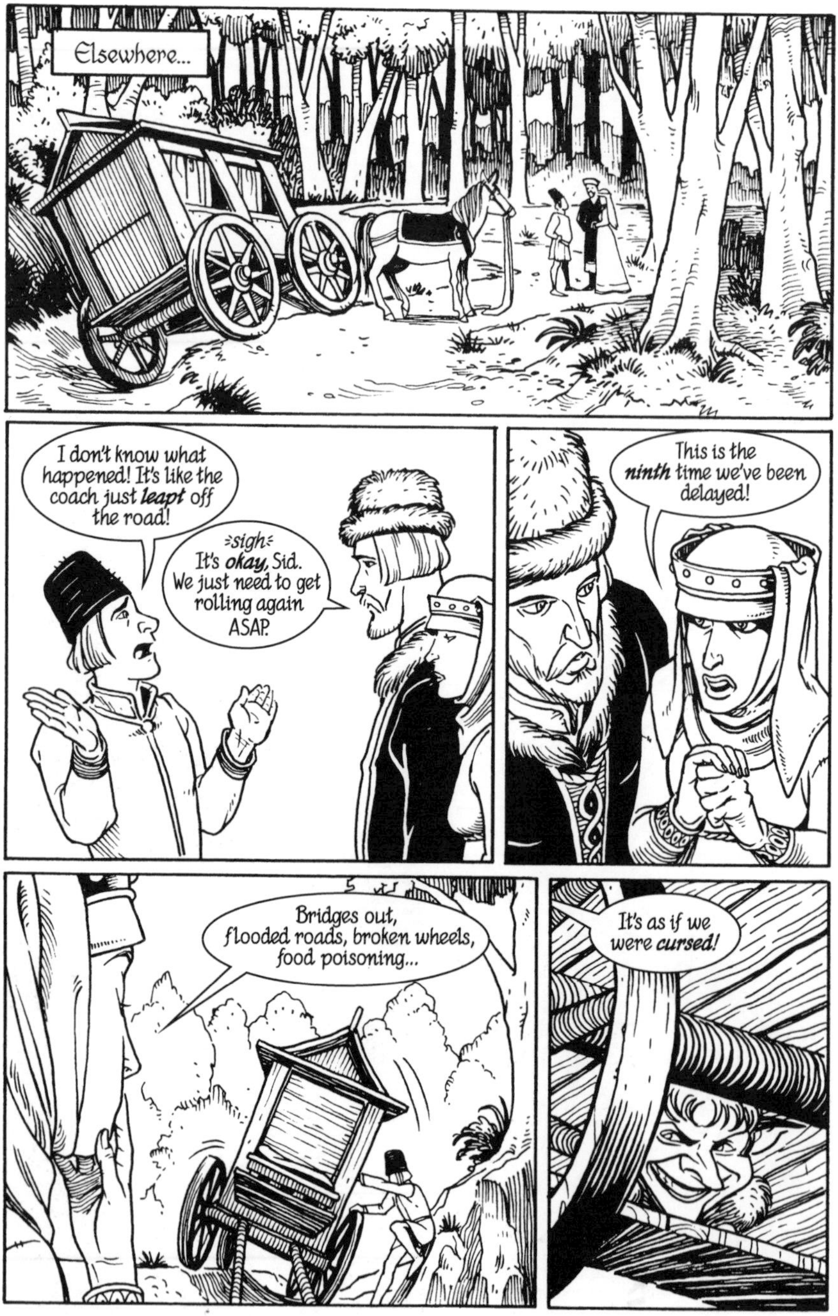
Elsewhere...
I don't know what happened! It's like the coach just *leapt* off the road!
≈sigh≈ It's *okay,* Sid. We just need to get rolling again ASAP.
This is the *ninth* time we've been delayed!
Bridges out, flooded roads, broken wheels, food poisoning...
It's as if we were *cursed!*

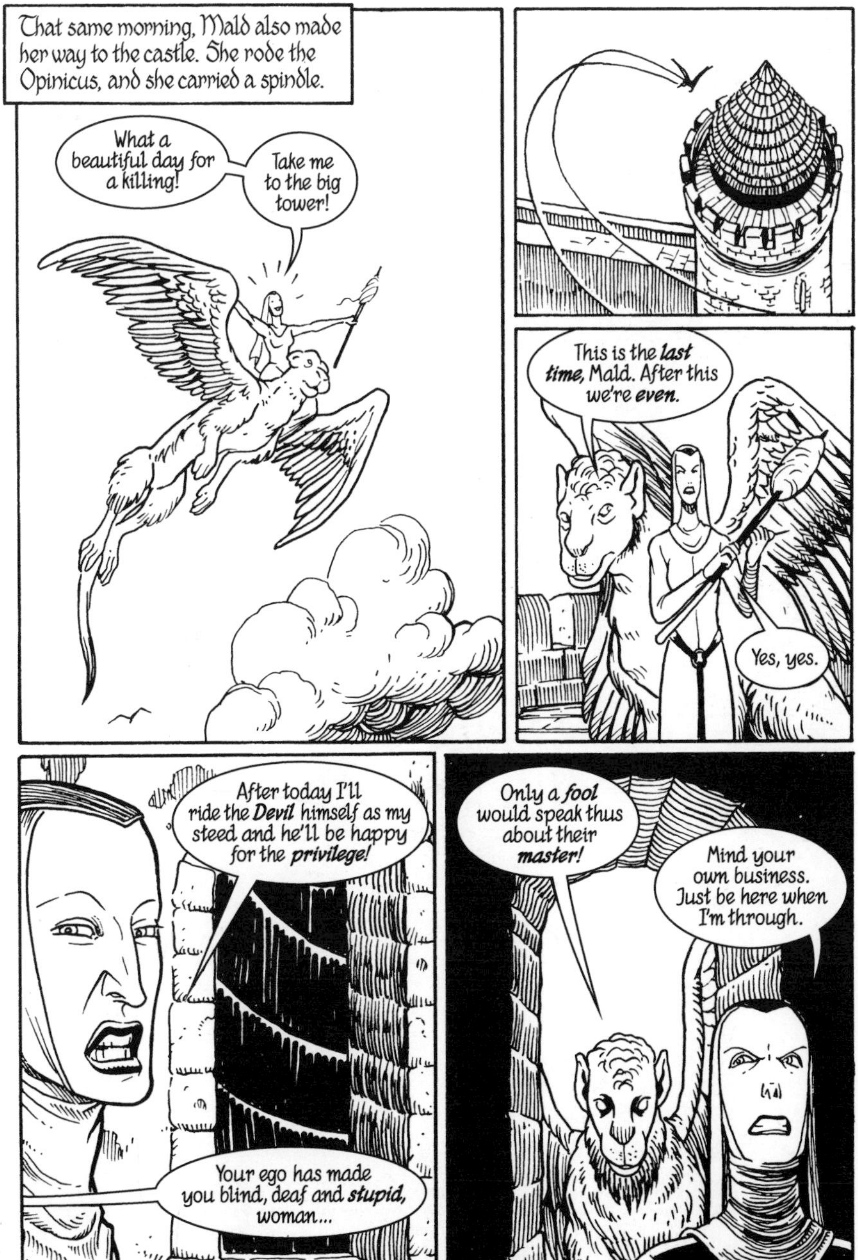
That same morning, Mald also made her way to the castle. She rode the Opinicus, and she carried a spindle.
What a beautiful day for a killing!
Take me to the big tower!
This is the *last time,* Mald. After this we're *even.*
Yes, yes.
After today I'll ride the *Devil* himself as my steed and he'll be happy for the *privilege!*
Your ego has made you blind, deaf and *stupid,* woman...
Only a *fool* would speak thus about their *master!*
Mind your own business. Just be here when I'm through.

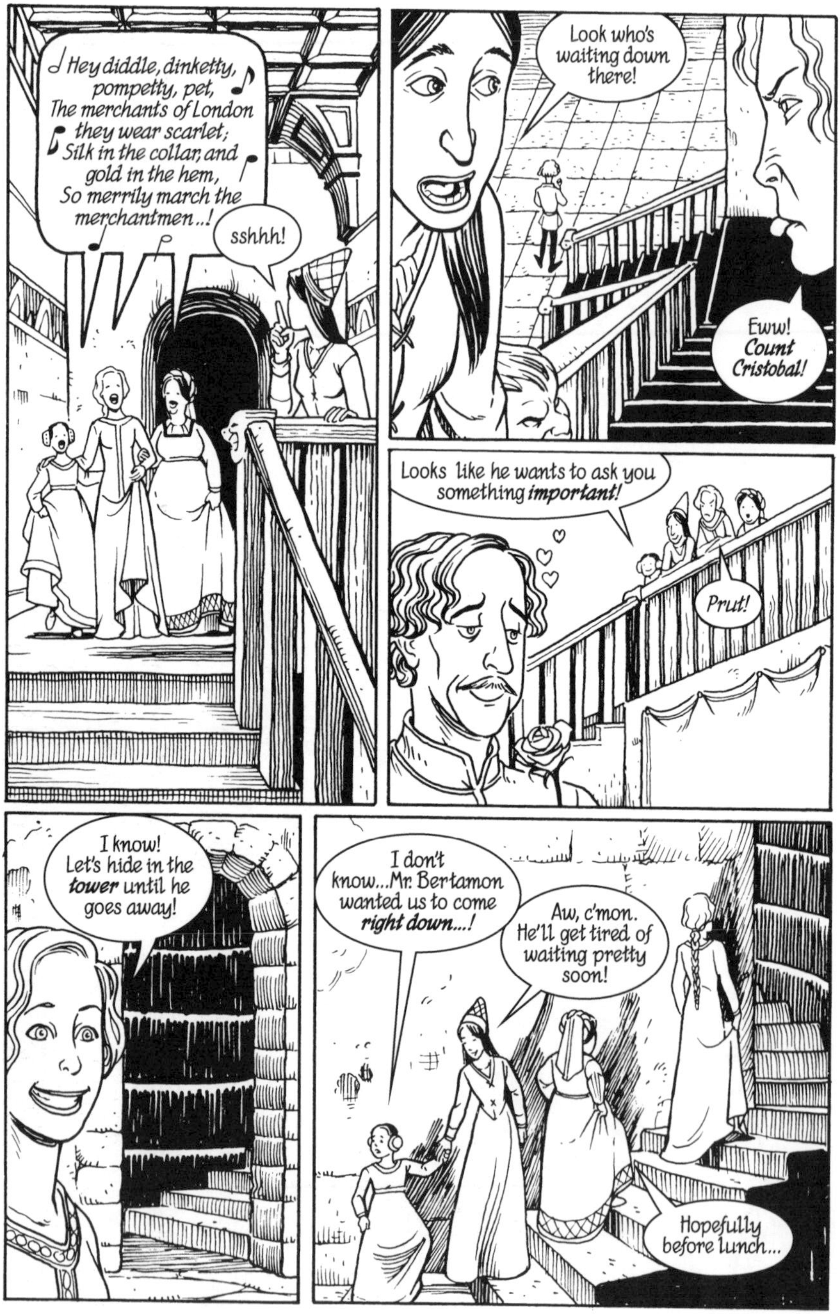
Hey diddle, dinketty, pompetty, pet, The merchants of London they wear scarlet; Silk in the collar, and gold in the hem, So merrily march the merchantmen...!
sshhh!
Look who's waiting down there!
Eww! Count Cristobal!
Looks like he wants to ask you something important!
Prut!
I know! Let's hide in the tower until he goes away!
I don't know...Mr. Bertamon wanted us to come right down...!
Aw, c'mon. He'll get tired of waiting pretty soon!
Hopefully before lunch...

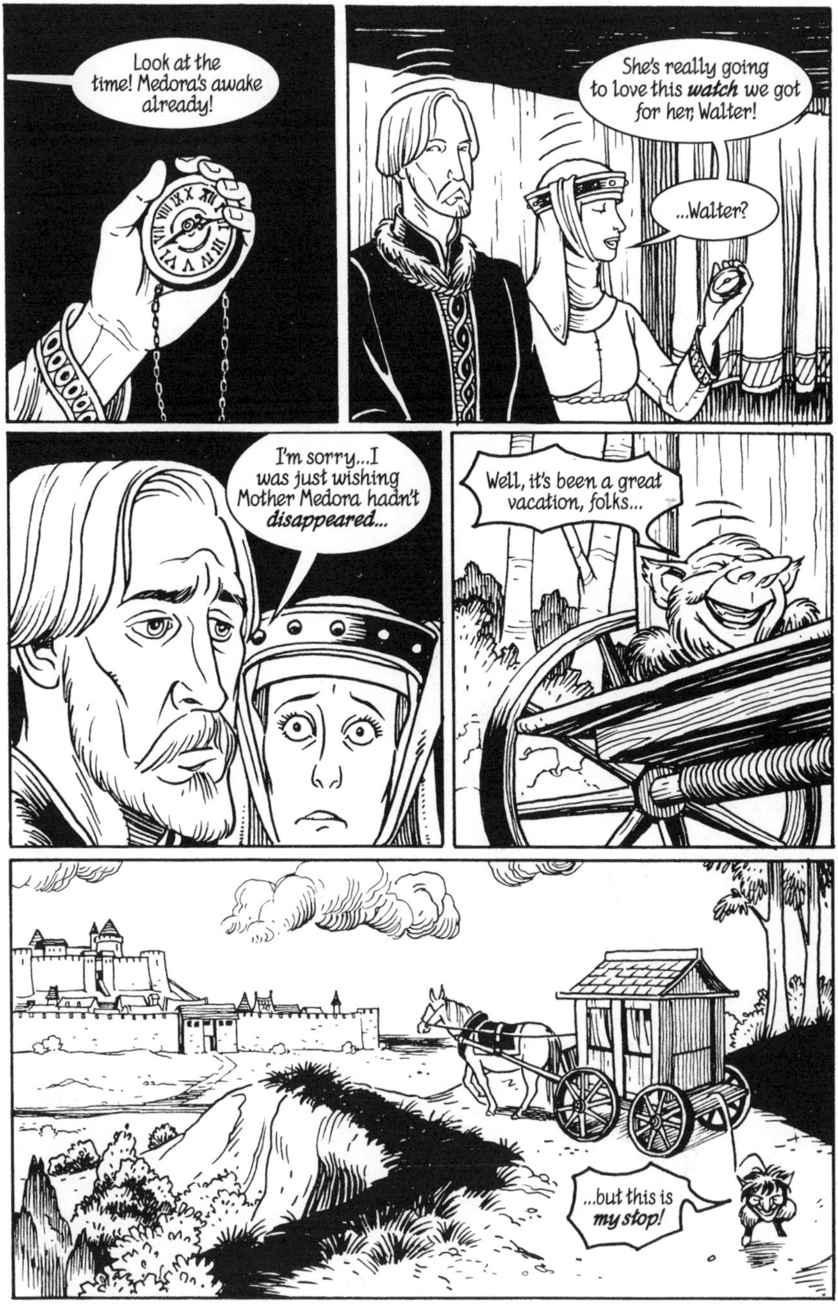

Look at the time! Medora's awake already!
She's really going to love this **watch** we got for her, Walter!
...Walter?
I'm sorry...I was just wishing Mother Medora hadn't **disappeared...**
Well, it's been a great vacation, folks...
...but this is **my stop!**

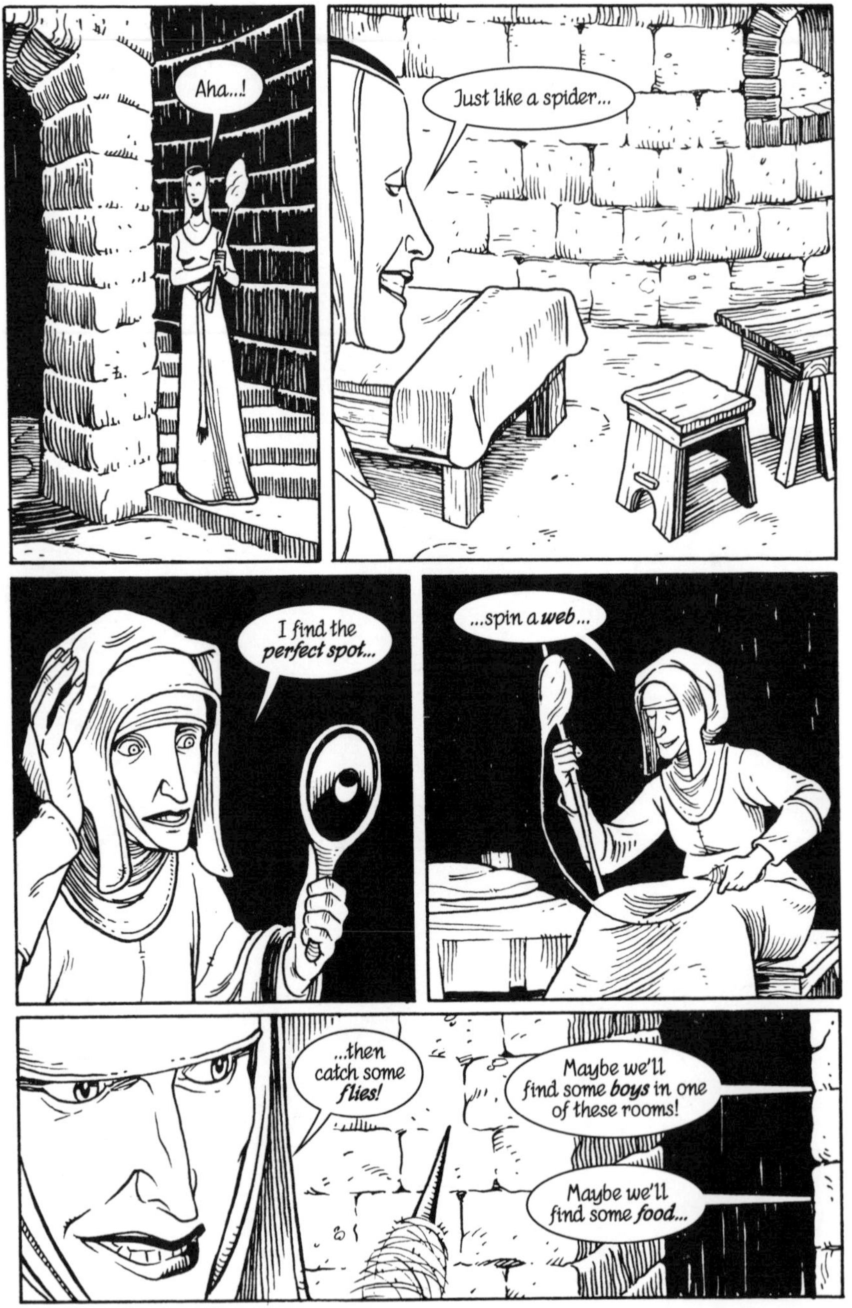
Aha...!
Just like a spider...
I find the *perfect spot...*
...spin a *web...*
...then catch some *flies!*
Maybe we'll find some *boys* in one of these rooms!
Maybe we'll find some *food...*

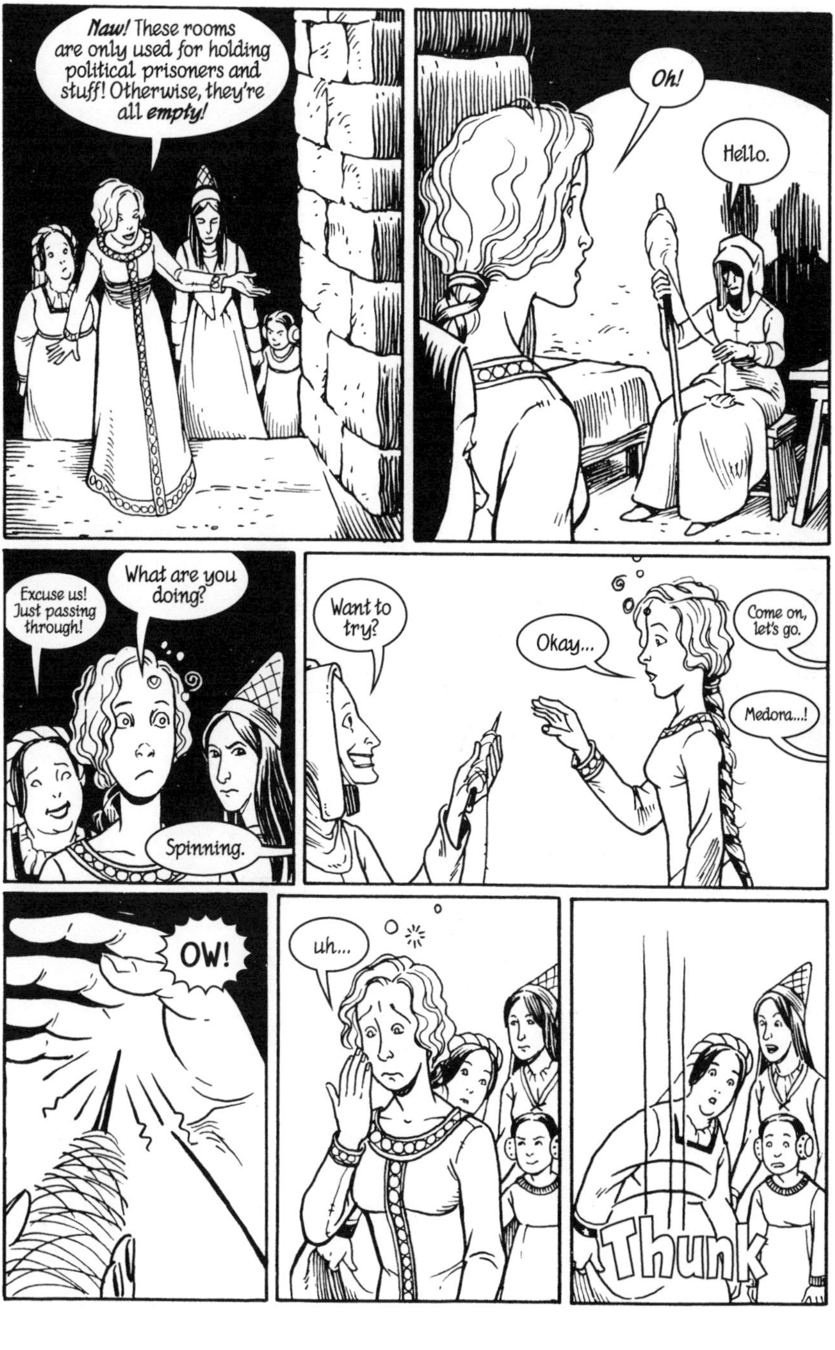
Naw! These rooms are only used for holding political prisoners and stuff! Otherwise, they're all *empty!*
Oh!
Hello.
Excuse us! Just passing through!
What are you doing?
Spinning.
Want to try?
Okay...
Come on, let's go.
Medora...!
OW!
uh...
Thunk

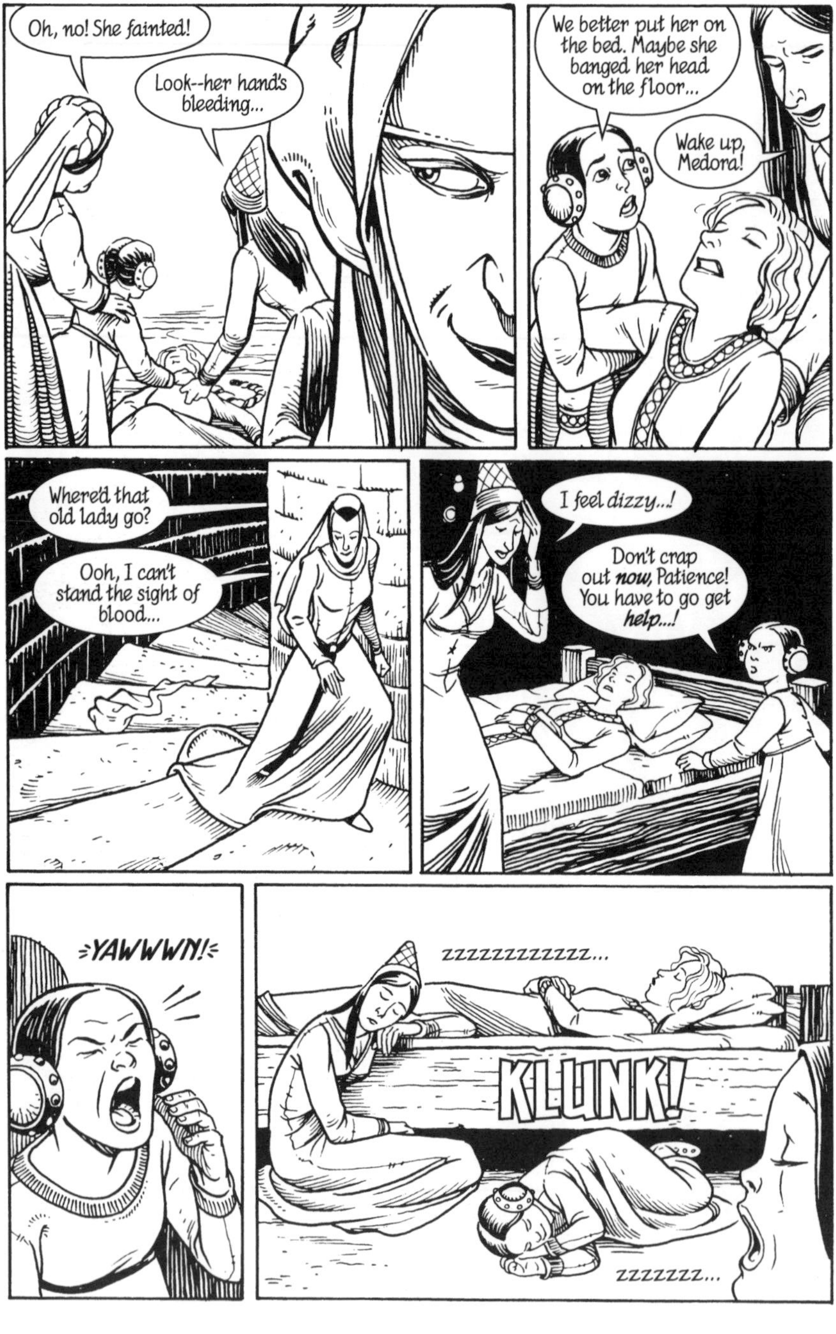
Oh, no! She fainted!
Look--her hand's bleeding...
We better put her on the bed. Maybe she banged her head on the floor...
Wake up, Medora!
Where'd that old lady go?
Ooh, I can't stand the sight of blood...
I feel dizzy...!
Don't crap out **now**, Patience! You have to go get **help**...!
YAWWWN!
ZZZZZZZZZZZZ...
KLUNK!
ZZZZZZZ...

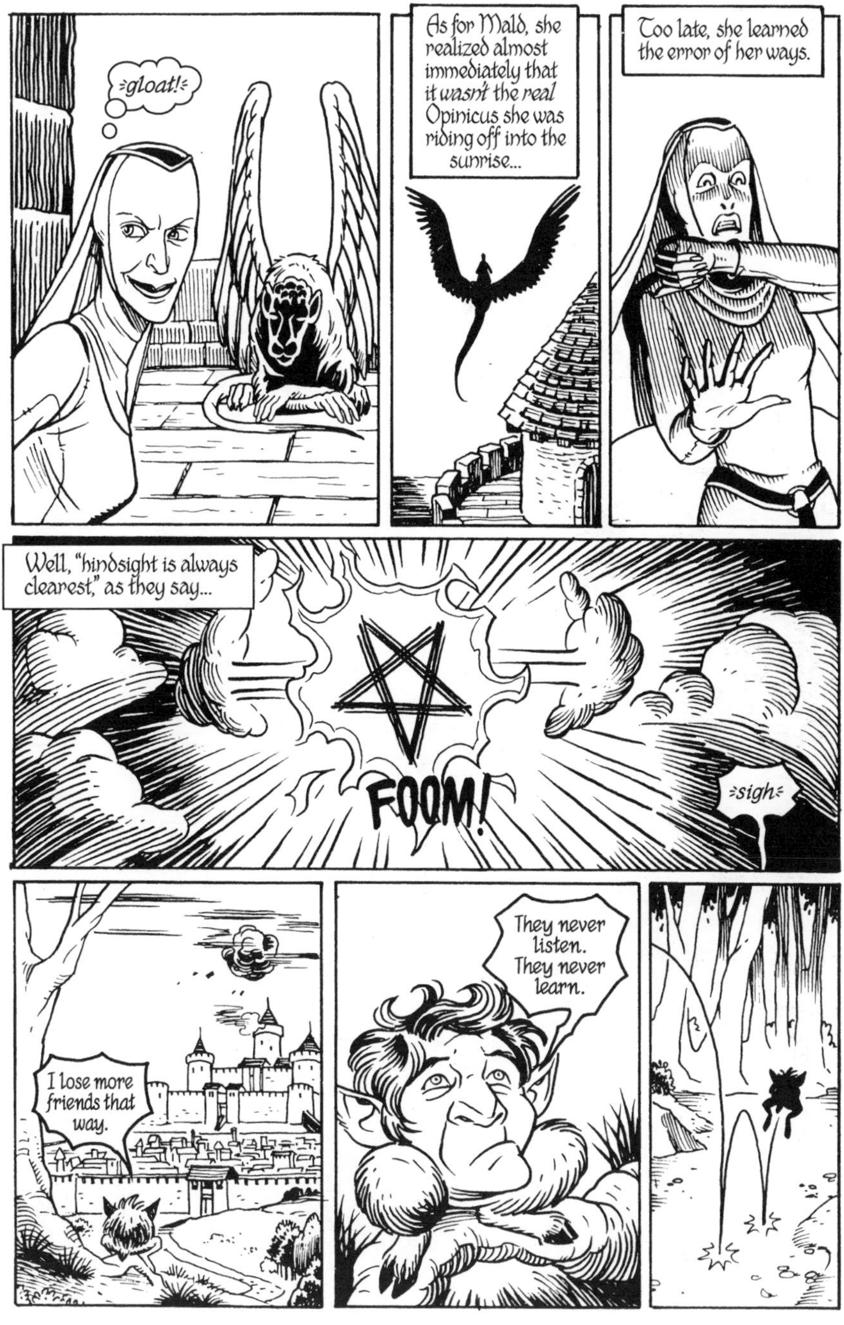
gloat!
As for Mald, she realized almost immediately that it *wasn't* the *real* Opinicus she was riding off into the sunrise...
Too late, she learned the error of her ways.
Well, "hindsight is always clearest," as they say...
FOOM!
sigh
I lose more friends that way.
They never listen. They never learn.

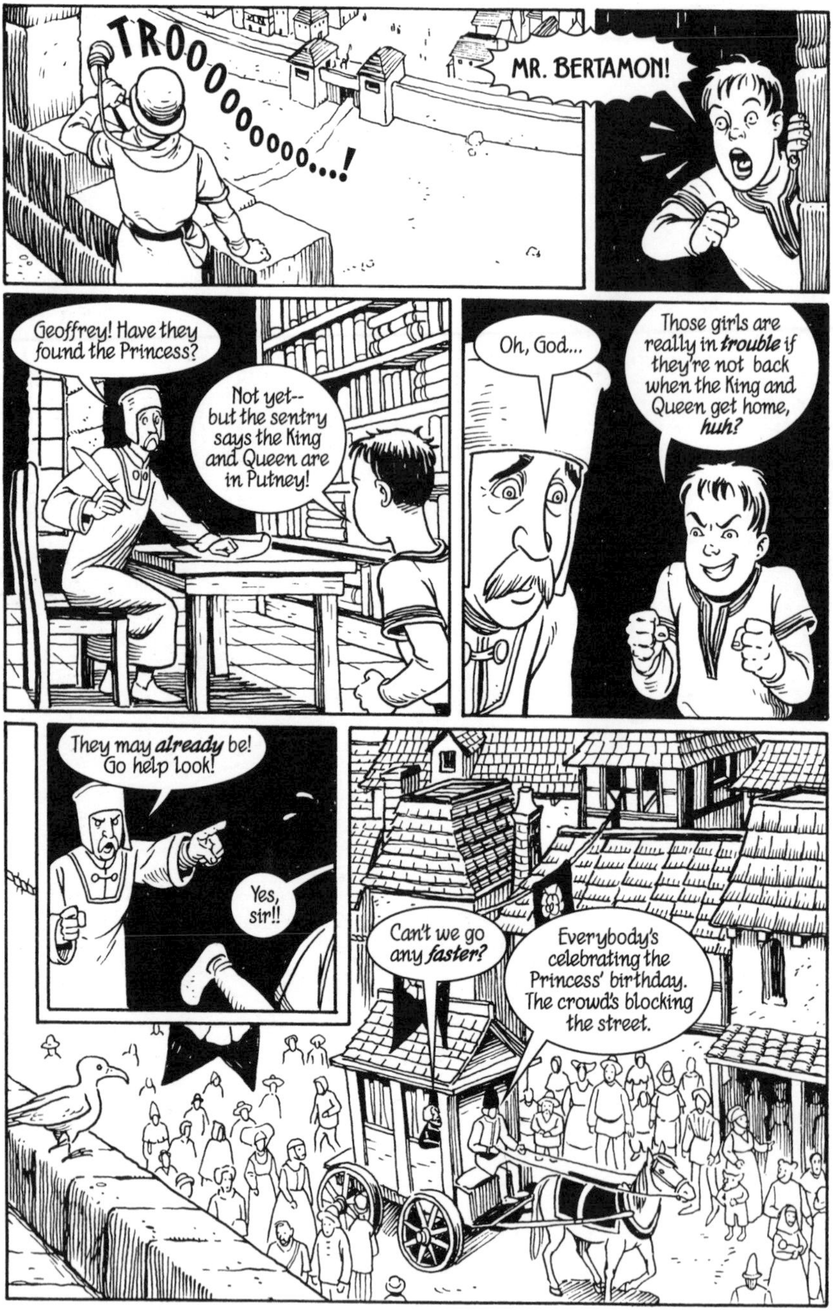
TROOOOOOOOOO...!
MR. BERTAMON!
Geoffrey! Have they found the Princess?
Not yet-- but the sentry says the King and Queen are in Putney!
Oh, God...
Those girls are really in *trouble* if they're not back when the King and Queen get home, *huh?*
They may *already* be! Go help look!
Yes, sir!!
Can't we go any *faster?*
Everybody's celebrating the Princess' birthday. The crowd's blocking the street.

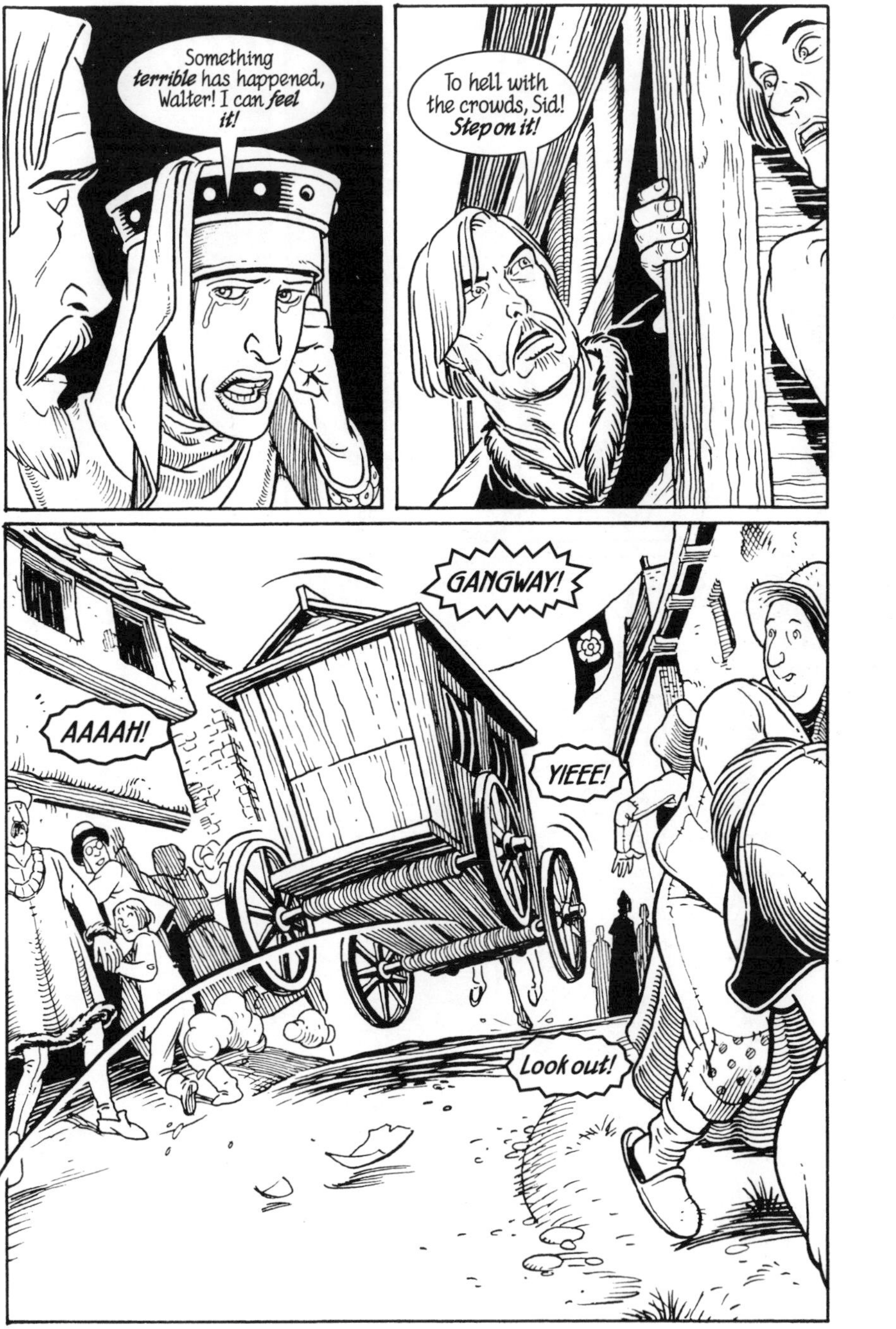
Something *terrible* has happened, Walter! I can *feel* it!
To hell with the crowds, Sid! *Step on it!*
GANGWAY!
AAAAH!
YIEEE!
Look out!

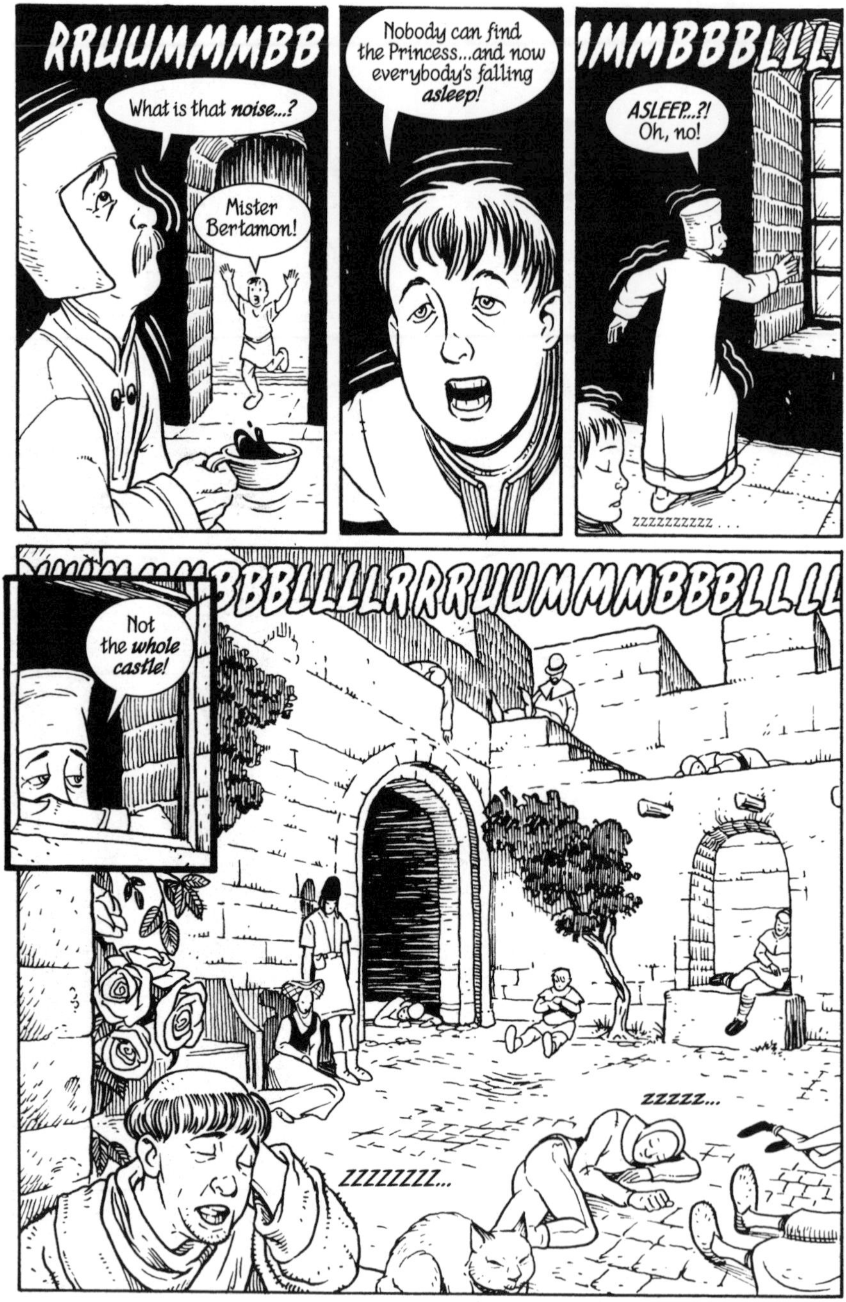
RRUUMMMBB
What is that noise...?
Mister Bertamon!
Nobody can find the Princess...and now everybody's falling asleep!
MMBBBLLL
ASLEEP...?! Oh, no!
ZZZZZZZZZZ . . .
BBBLLLLRRRUUMMMMBBBLLLL
Not the whole castle!
ZZZZZ...
ZZZZZZZ...

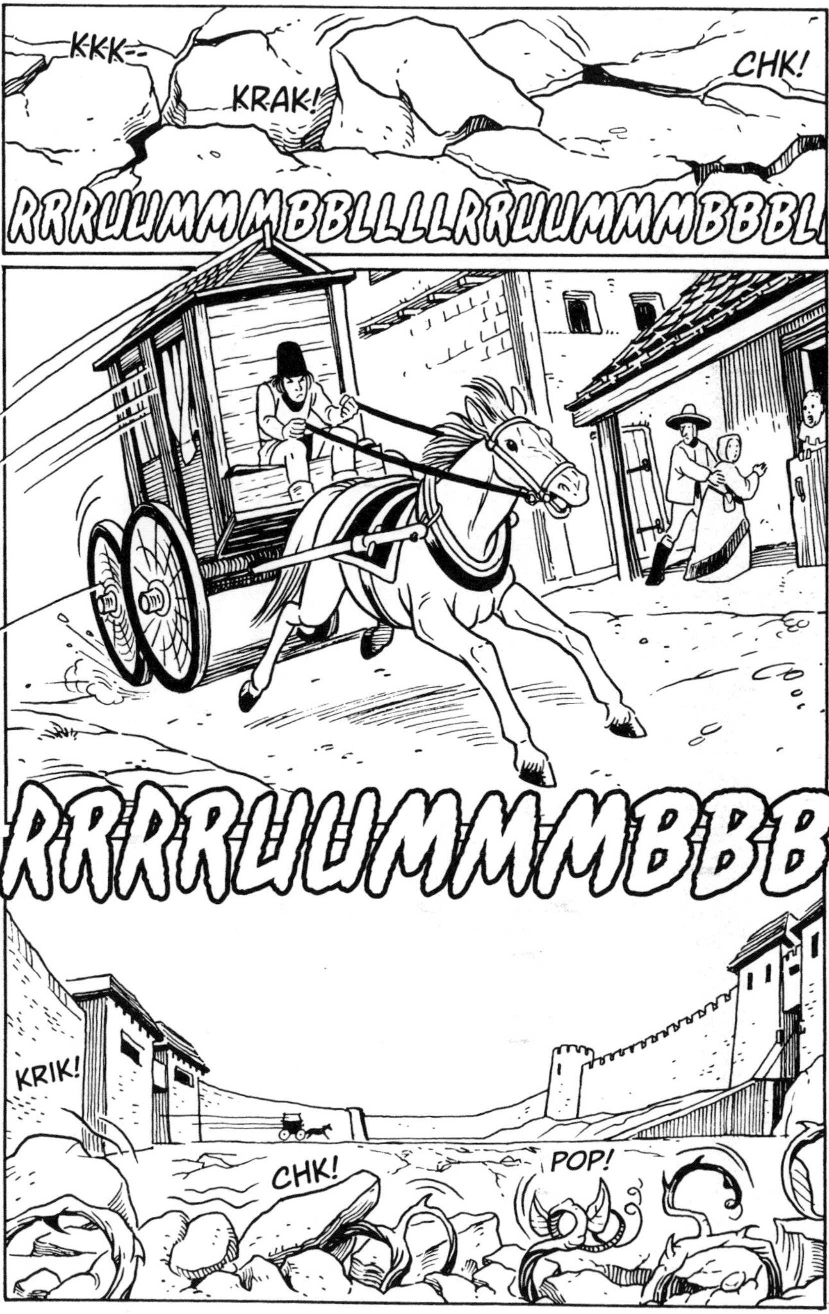
K-K-K-
KRAK!
CHK!
RRRUUMMMBBLLLLRRRUUMMMMBBBL
RRRRUUMMMMBBB
KRIK!
CHK!
POP!

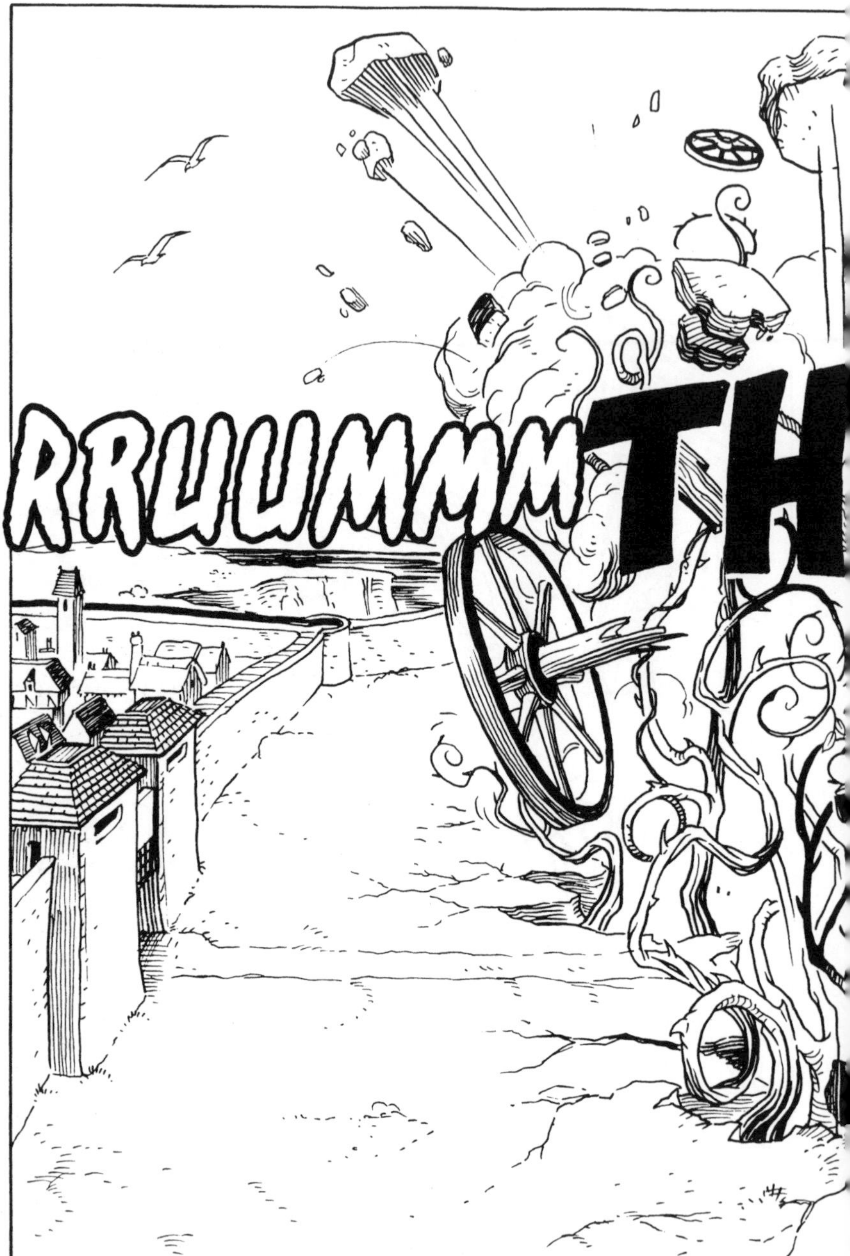
RRUUMMMTH

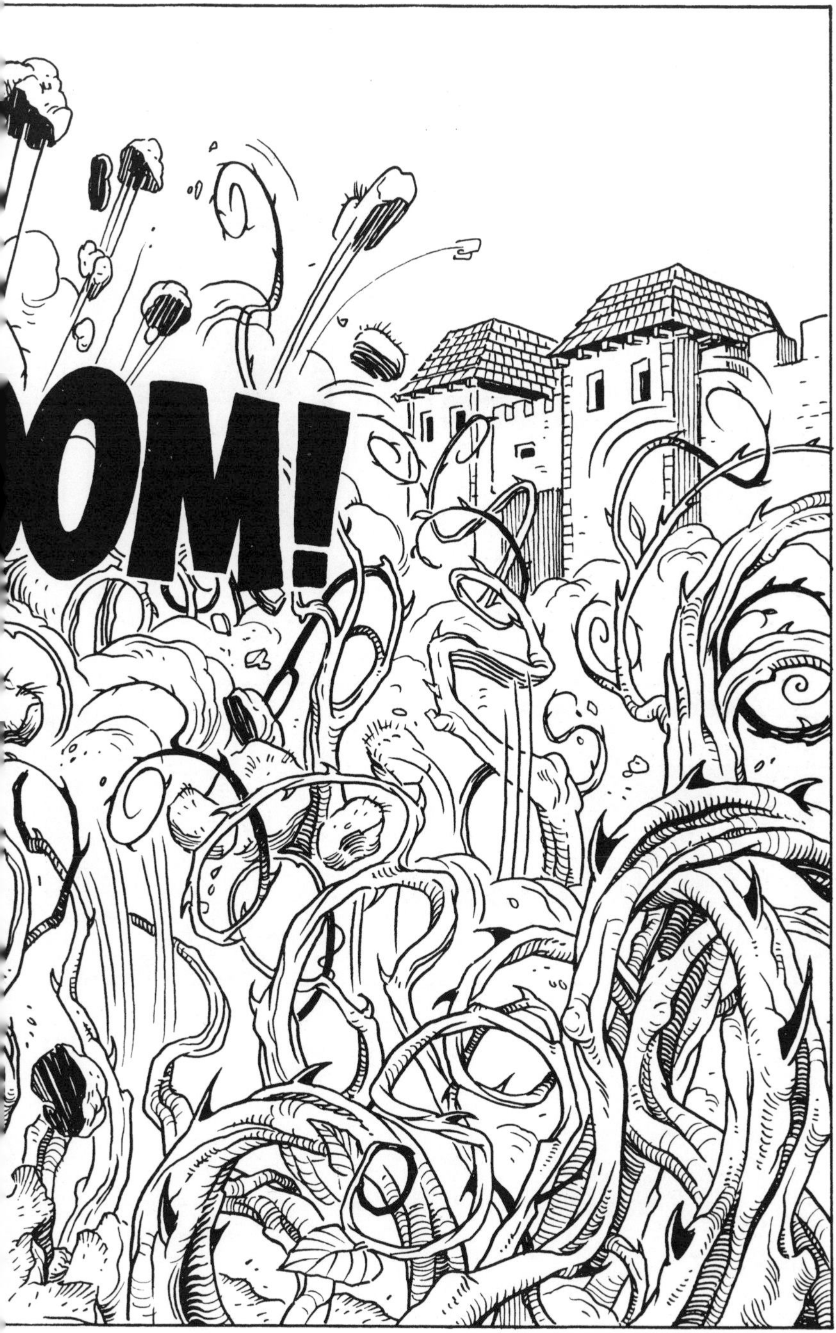
OM!

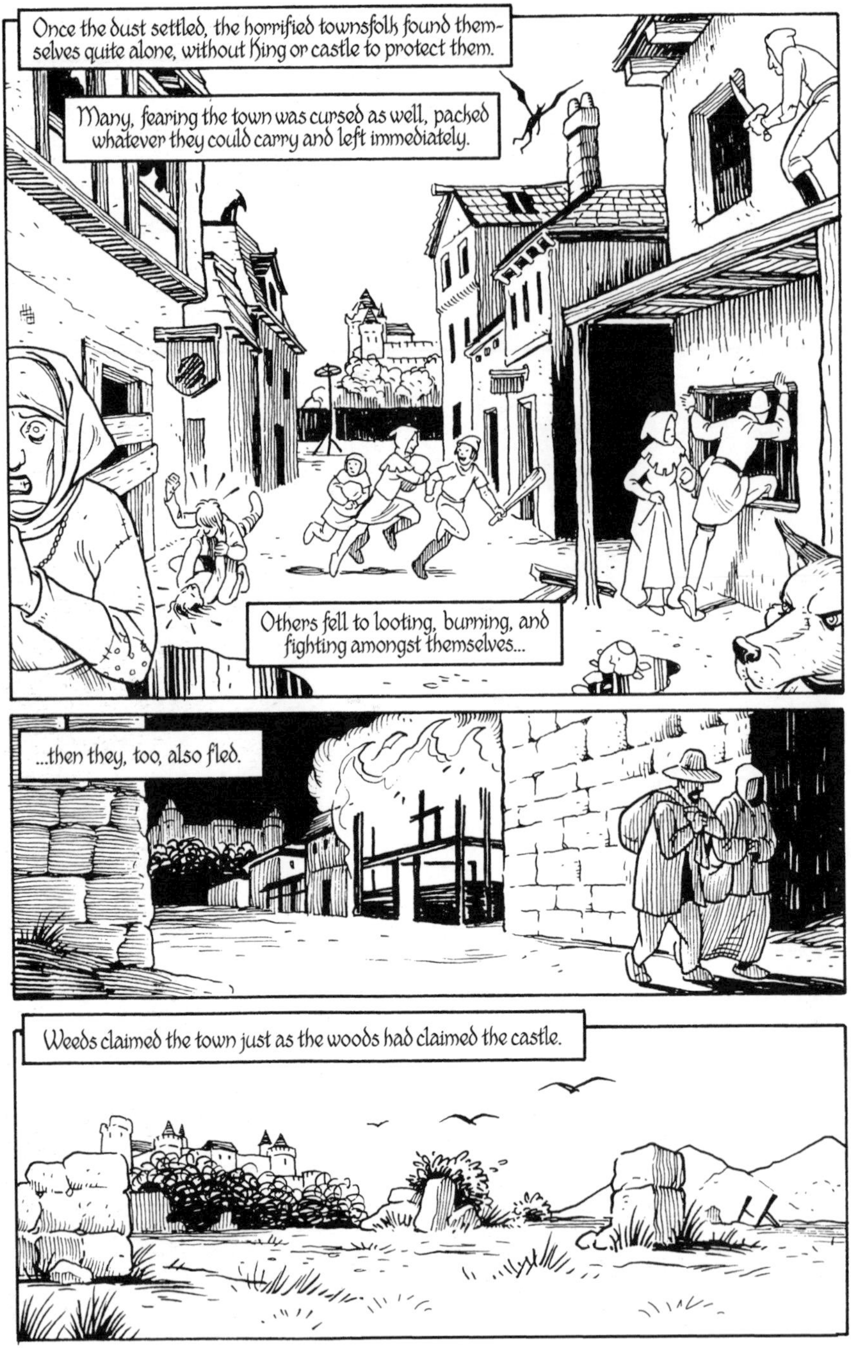
Once the dust settled, the horrified townsfolk found themselves quite alone, without King or castle to protect them.
Many, fearing the town was cursed as well, packed whatever they could carry and left immediately.
Others fell to looting, burning, and fighting amongst themselves...
...then they, too, also fled.
Weeds claimed the town just as the woods had claimed the castle.

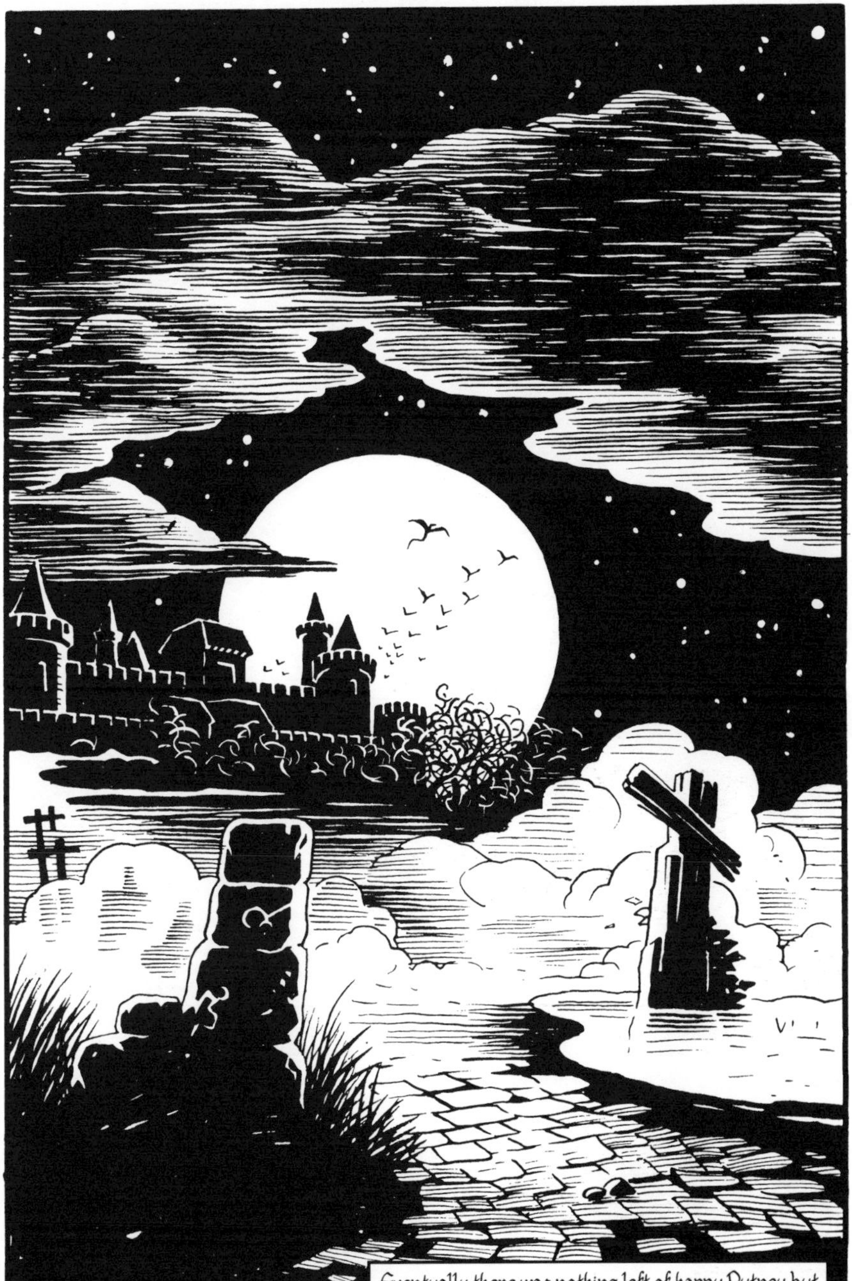
Eventually there was nothing left of happy Putney but silence, and ruins, and the legend of a haunted castle.

Chapter 3.

· THE CURSE OF BRAMBLY HEDGE PT. 3 ·

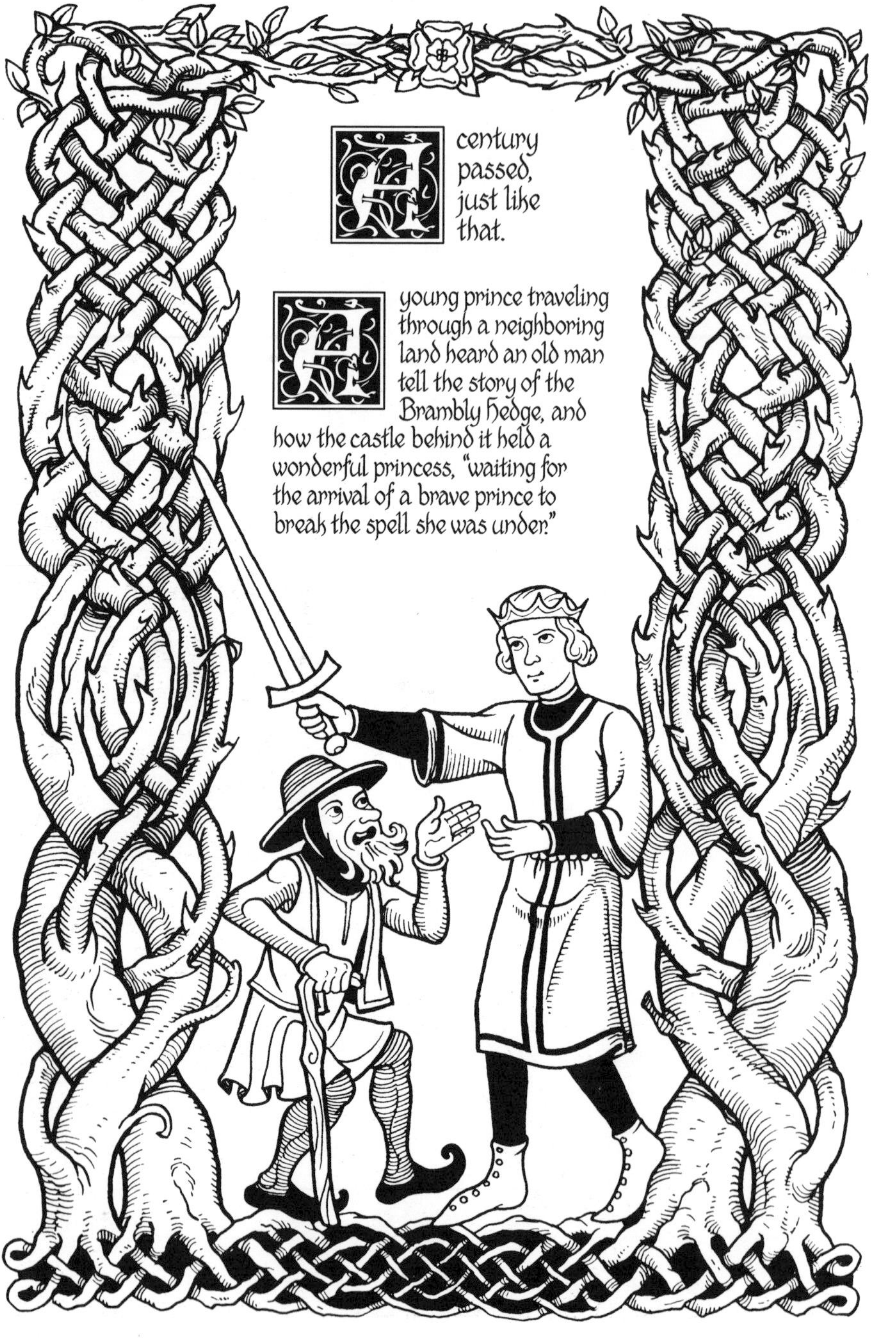

A century passed, just like that.

A young prince traveling through a neighboring land heard an old man tell the story of the Brambly Hedge, and how the castle behind it held a wonderful princess, "waiting for the arrival of a brave prince to break the spell she was under."

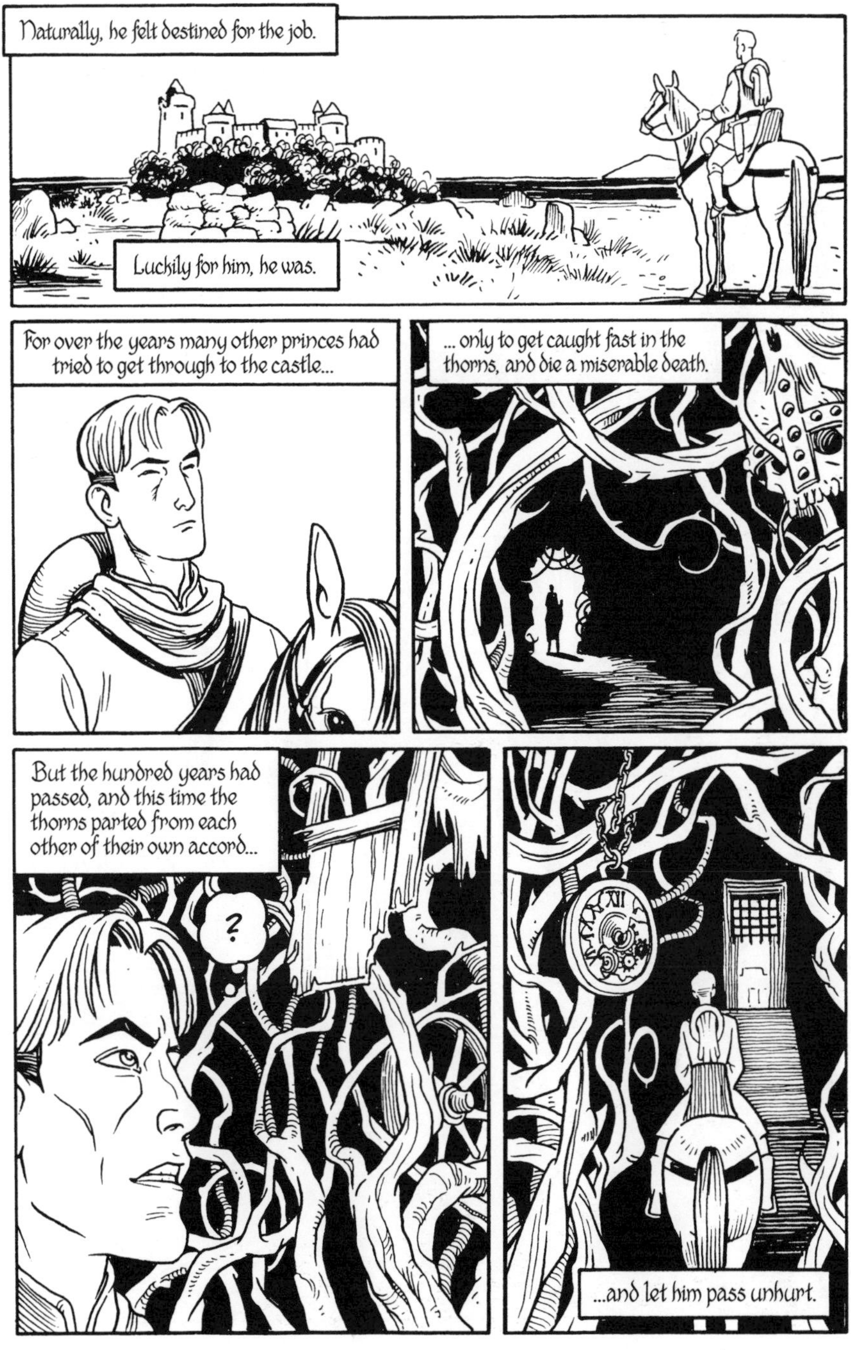
Naturally, he felt destined for the job.
Luckily for him, he was.
For over the years many other princes had tried to get through to the castle...
... only to get caught fast in the thorns, and die a miserable death.
But the hundred years had passed, and this time the thorns parted from each other of their own accord...
?
...and let him pass unhurt.

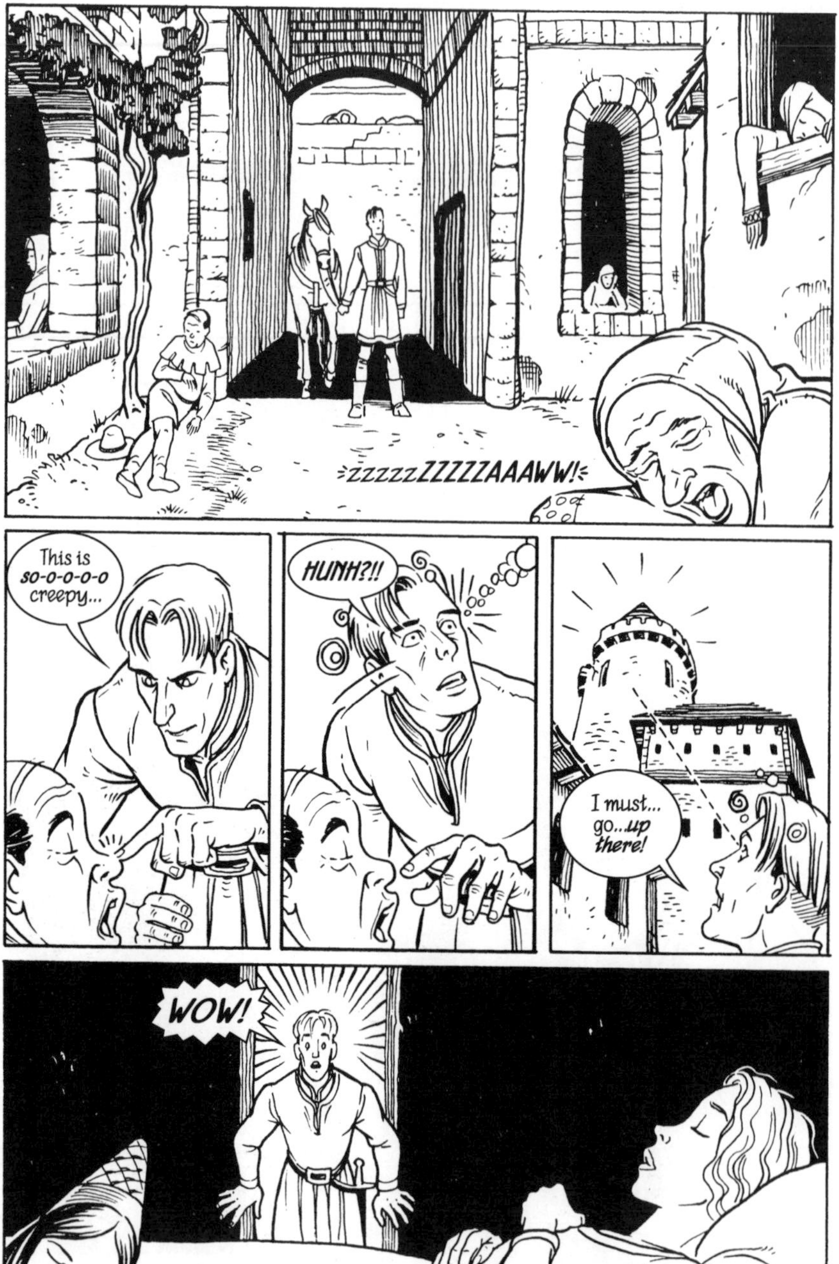
ZZZZZZZZZZAAAWW!
This is so-o-o-o-o creepy...
HUNH?!!
I must... go...up there!
WOW!

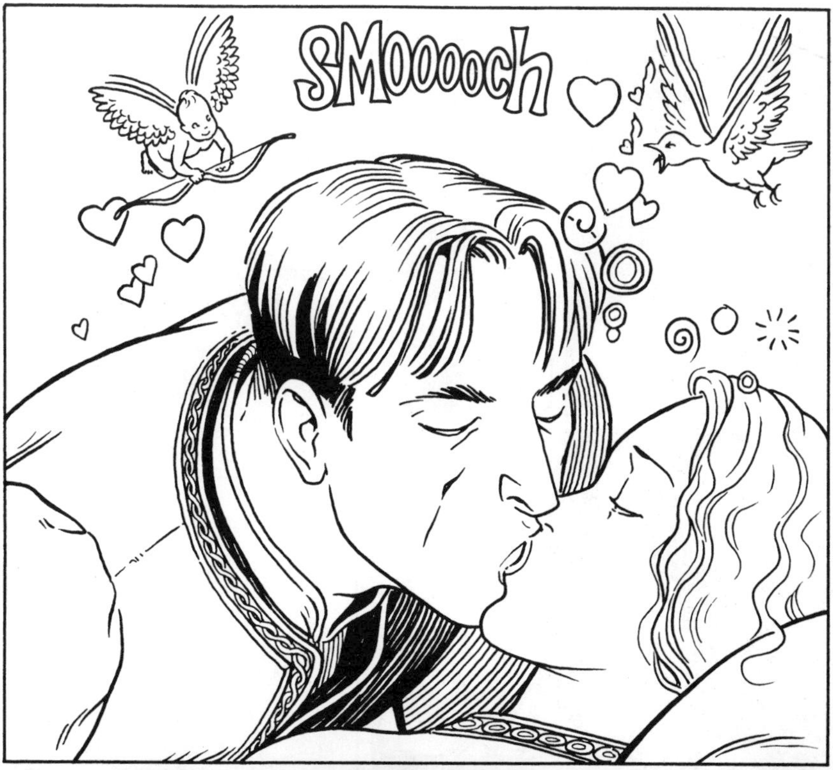
SMOooch

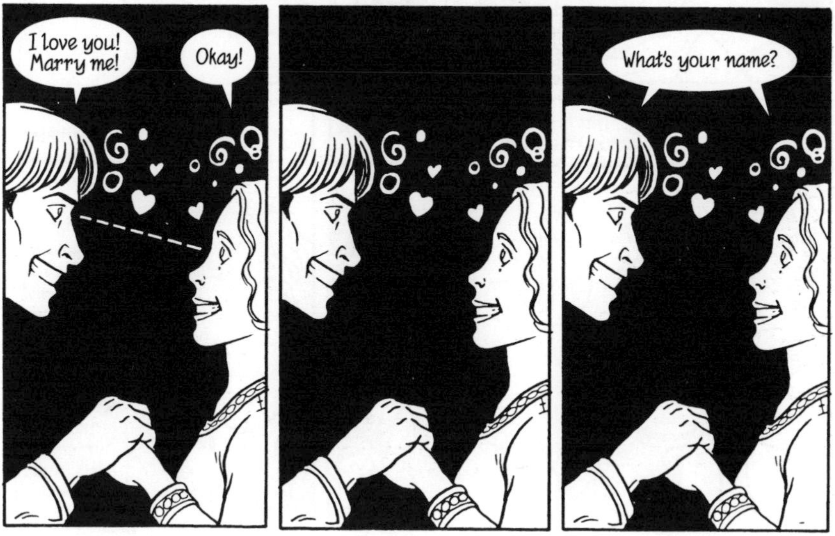
I love you! Marry me!
Okay!
What's your name?

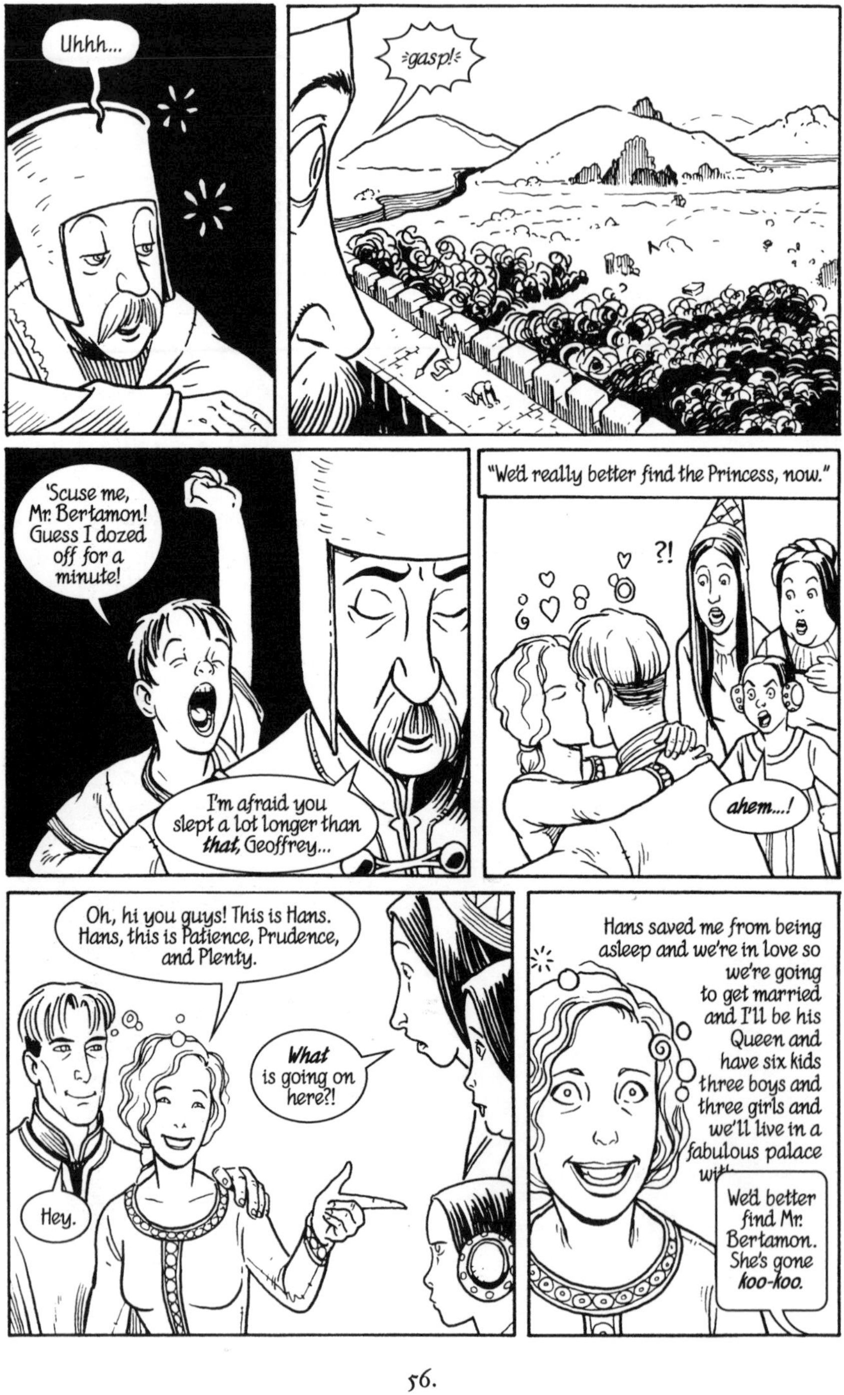
Uhhh...
gasp!
'Scuse me, Mr. Bertamon! Guess I dozed off for a minute!
I'm afraid you slept a lot longer than *that,* Geoffrey...
"We'd really better find the Princess, now."
?!
ahem...!
Oh, hi you guys! This is Hans. Hans, this is Patience, Prudence, and Plenty.
Hey.
What is going on here?!
Hans saved me from being asleep and we're in love so we're going to get married and I'll be his Queen and have six kids three boys and three girls and we'll live in a fabulous palace
We'd better find Mr. Bertamon. She's gone *koo-koo.*

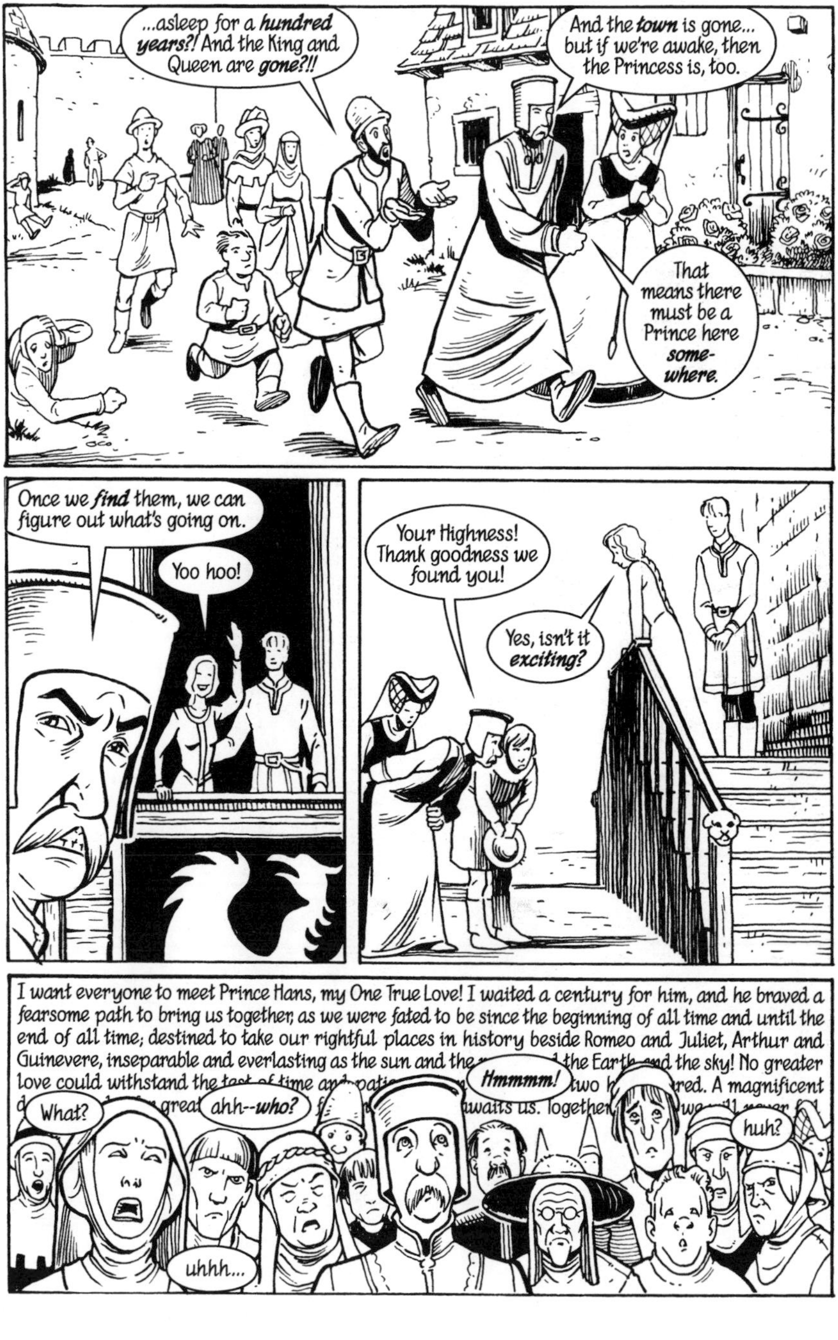
...asleep for a **hundred years?!** And the King and Queen are **gone?!!**
And the **town** is gone... but if we're awake, then the Princess is, too.
That means there must be a Prince here **some-where.**
Once we **find** them, we can figure out what's going on.
Yoo hoo!
Your Highness! Thank goodness we found you!
Yes, isn't it **exciting?**
I want everyone to meet Prince Hans, my One True Love! I waited a century for him, and he braved a fearsome path to bring us together, as we were fated to be since the beginning of all time and until the end of all time; destined to take our rightful places in history beside Romeo and Juliet, Arthur and Guinevere, inseparable and everlasting as the sun and the
the Earth
the sky! No greater love could withstand the
two
red. A magnificent
great
awaits us. Together
What?
ahh--**who?**
Hmmmm!
huh?
uhhh...

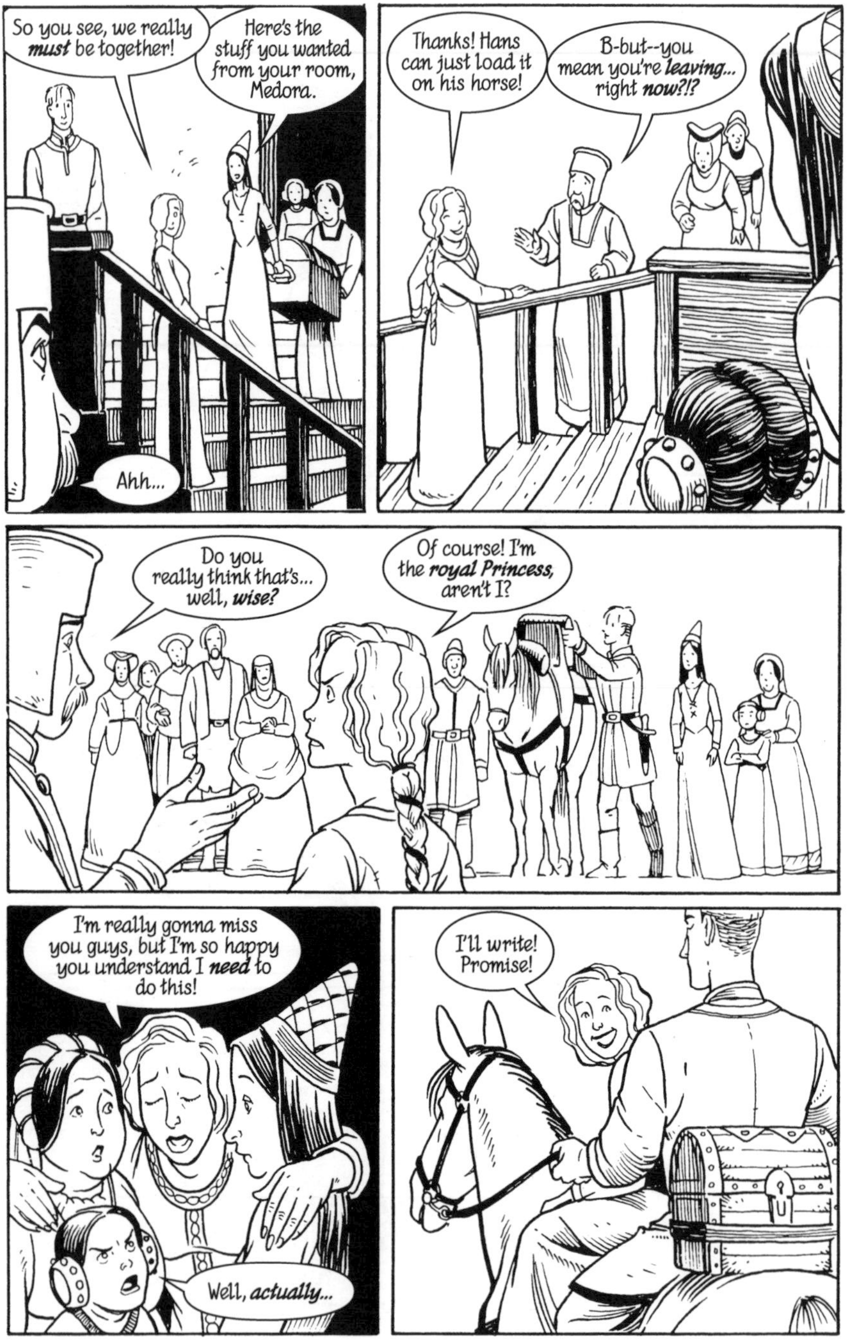
So you see, we really *must* be together!
Here's the stuff you wanted from your room, Medora.
Ahh...
Thanks! Hans can just load it on his horse!
B-but--you mean you're *leaving*... right *now?!?*
Do you really think that's... well, *wise?*
Of course! I'm the *royal Princess,* aren't I?
I'm really gonna miss you guys, but I'm so happy you understand I *need* to do this!
Well, *actually*...
I'll write! Promise!

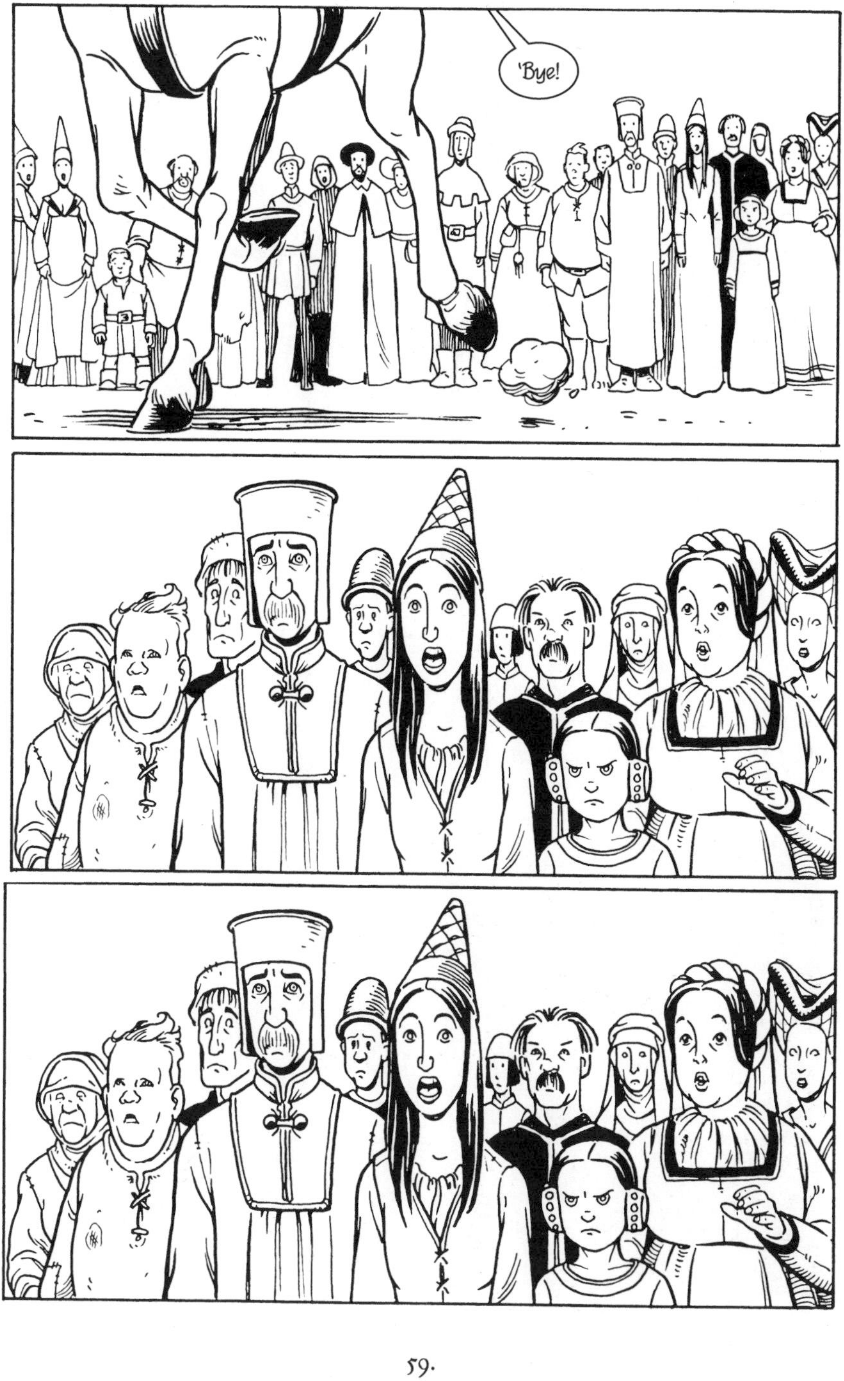
'Bye!

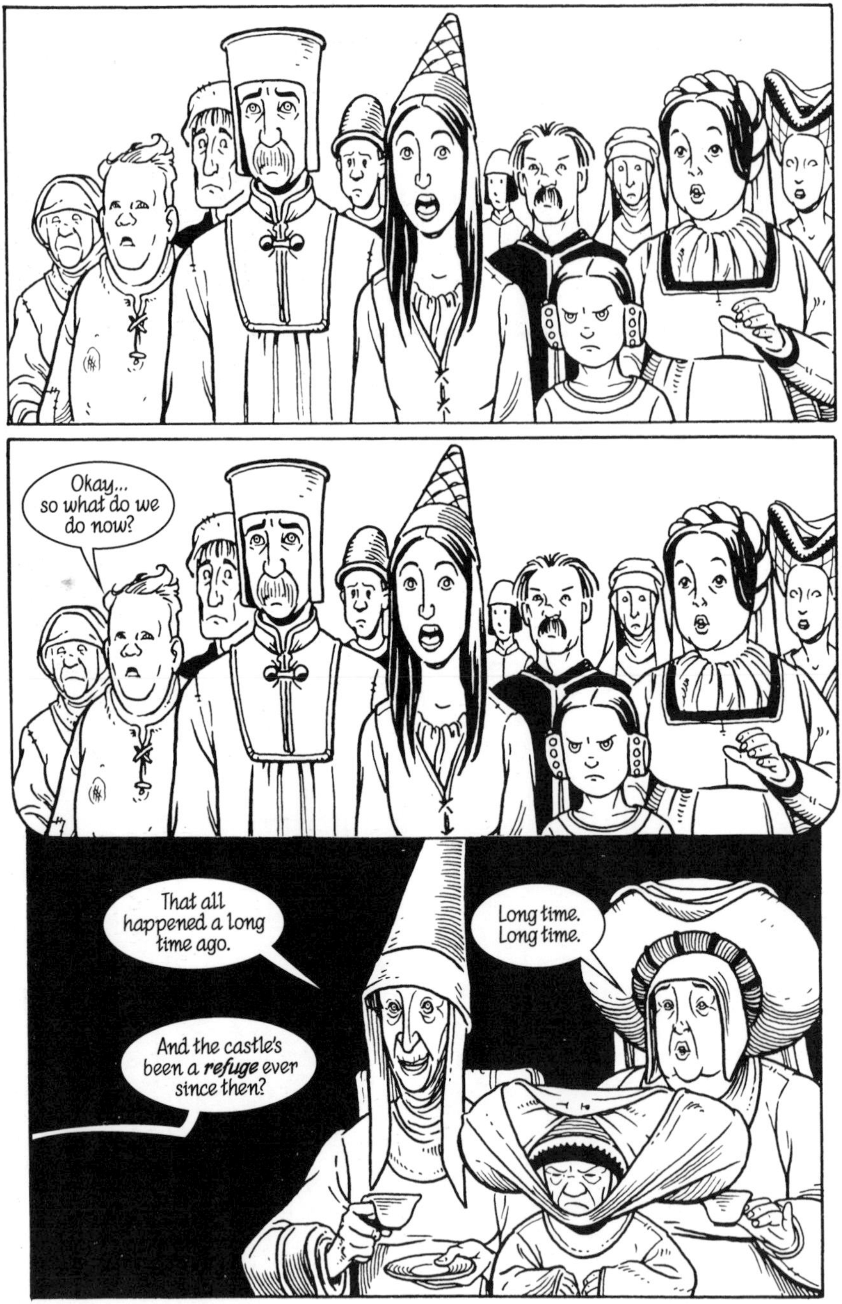
Okay... so what do we do now?
That all happened a long time ago.
Long time. Long time.
And the castle's been a *refuge* ever since then?

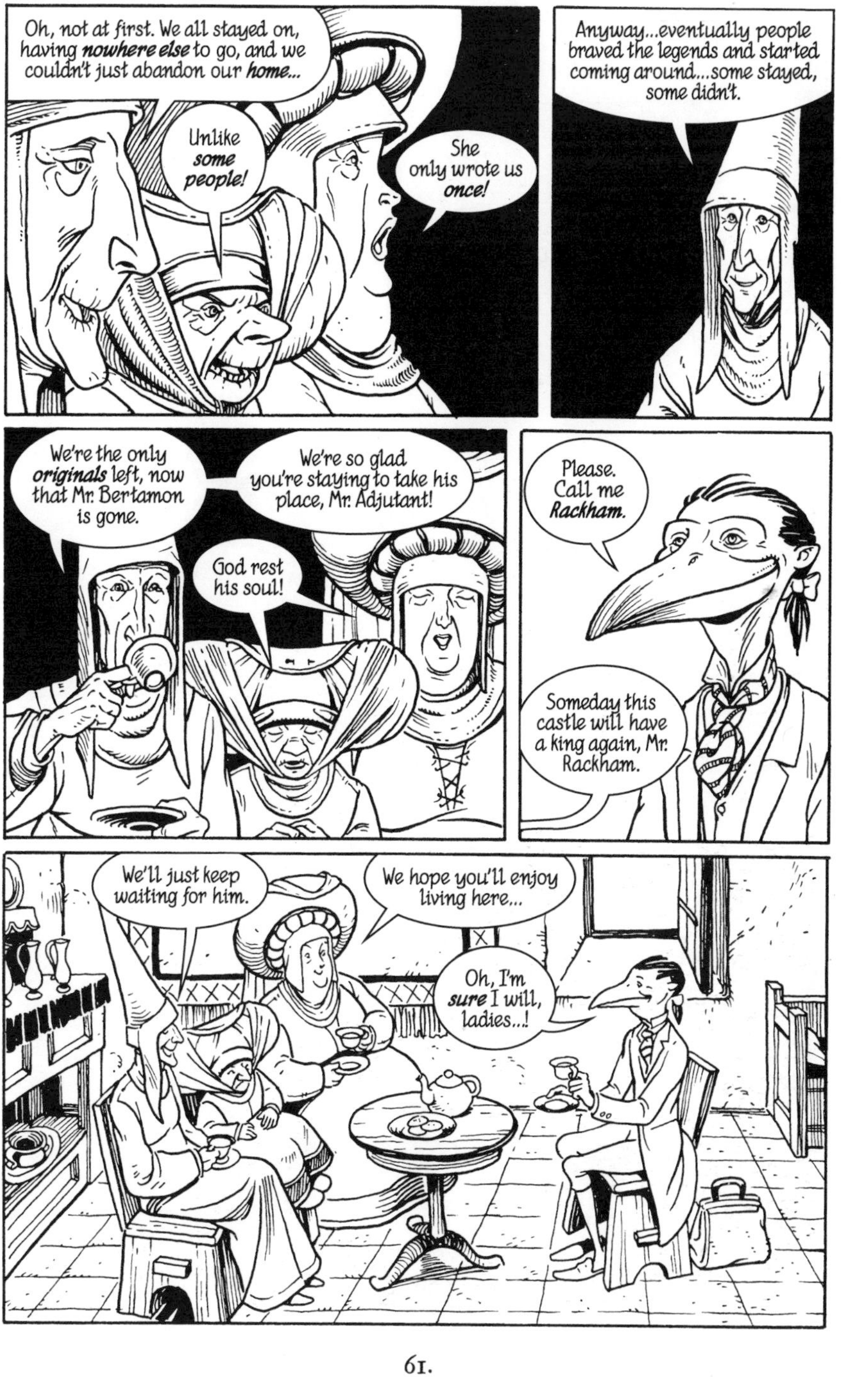
Oh, not at first. We all stayed on, having *nowhere else* to go, and we couldn't just abandon our *home...*
Unlike *some people!*
She only wrote us *once!*
Anyway...eventually people braved the legends and started coming around...some stayed, some didn't.
We're the only *originals* left, now that Mr. Bertamon is gone.
We're so glad you're staying to take his place, Mr. Adjutant!
God rest his soul!
Please. Call me *Rackham.*
Someday this castle will have a king again, Mr. Rackham.
We'll just keep waiting for him.
We hope you'll enjoy living here...
Oh, I'm *sure* I will, ladies...!

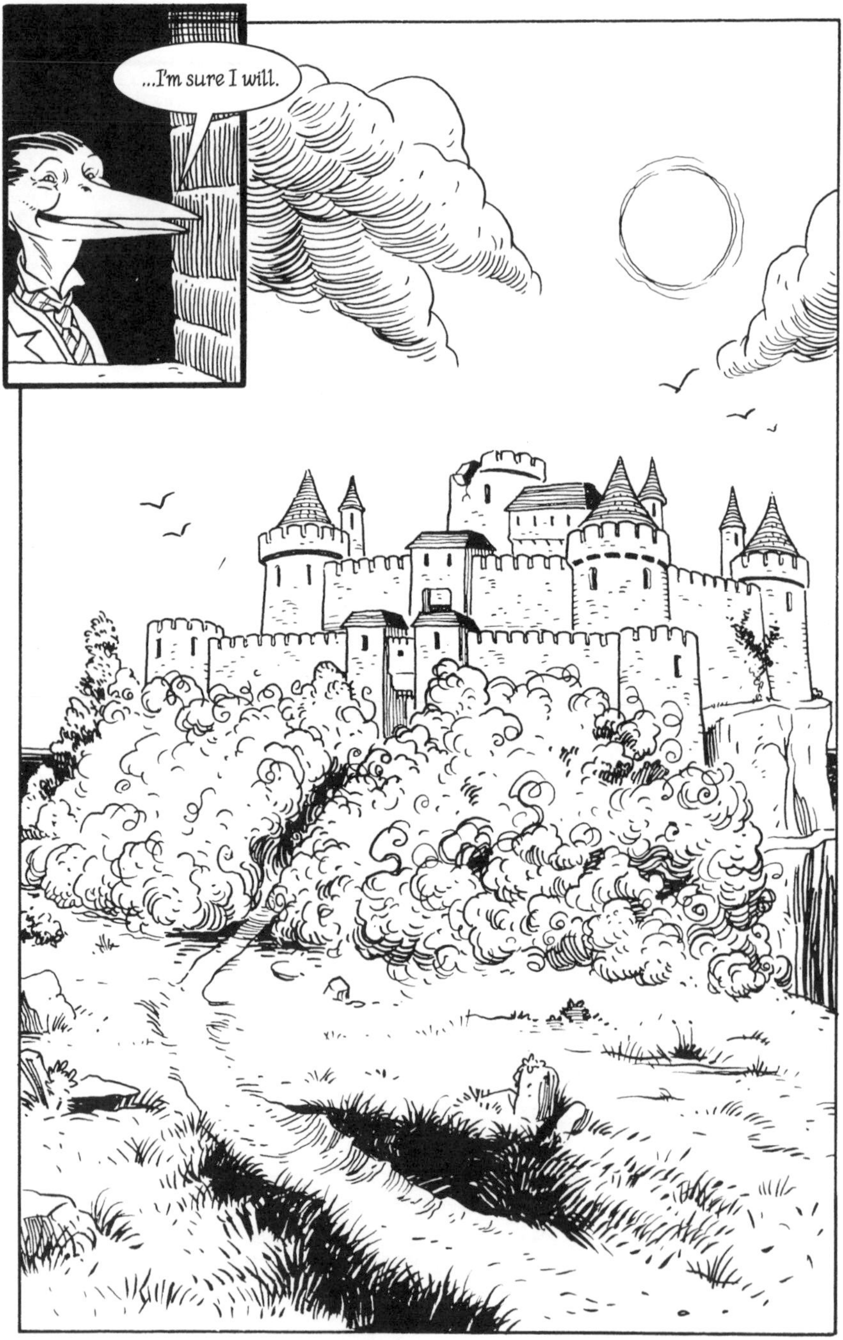
...I'm sure I will.

Chapter 4.

· BAHTALO DROM ·

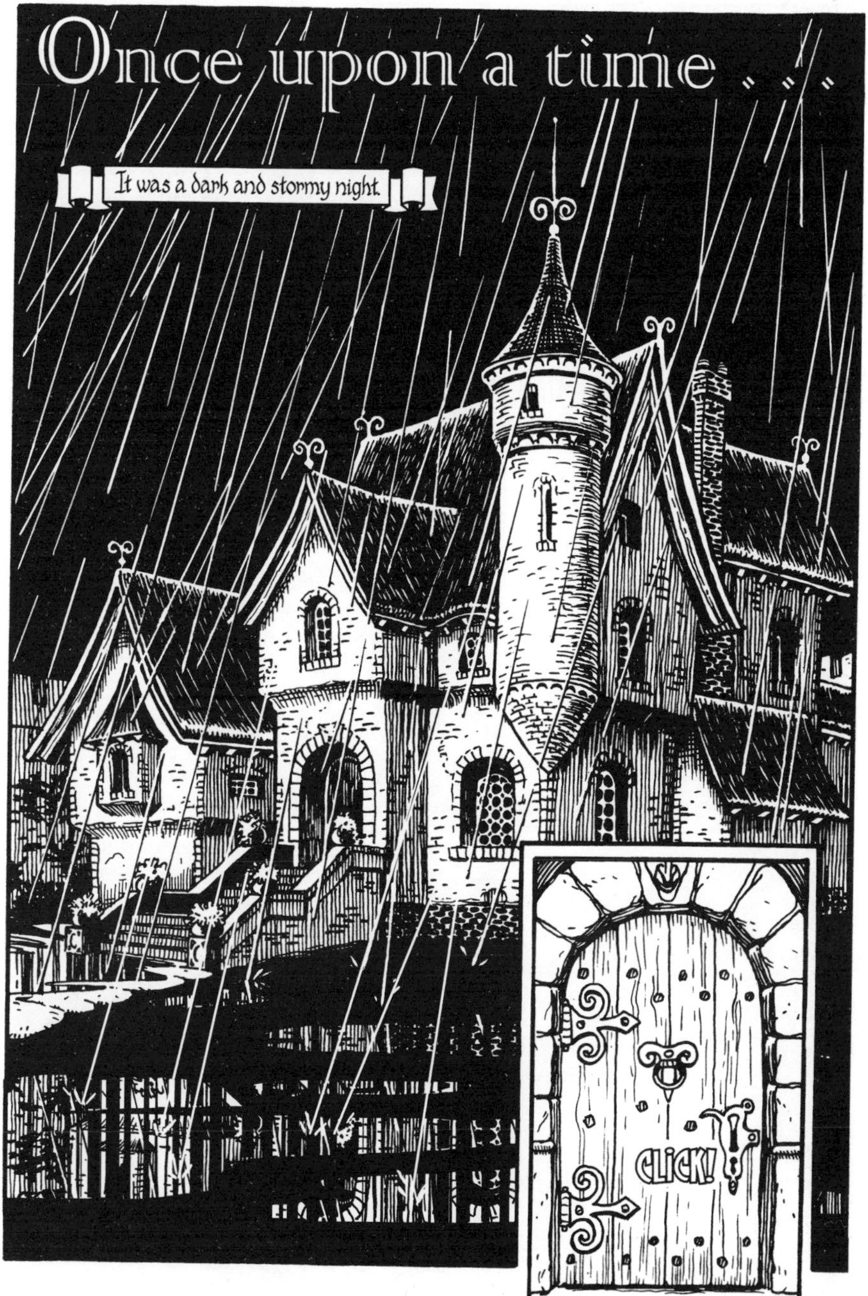
Once upon a time . . .
It was a dark and stormy night.
CLICK!

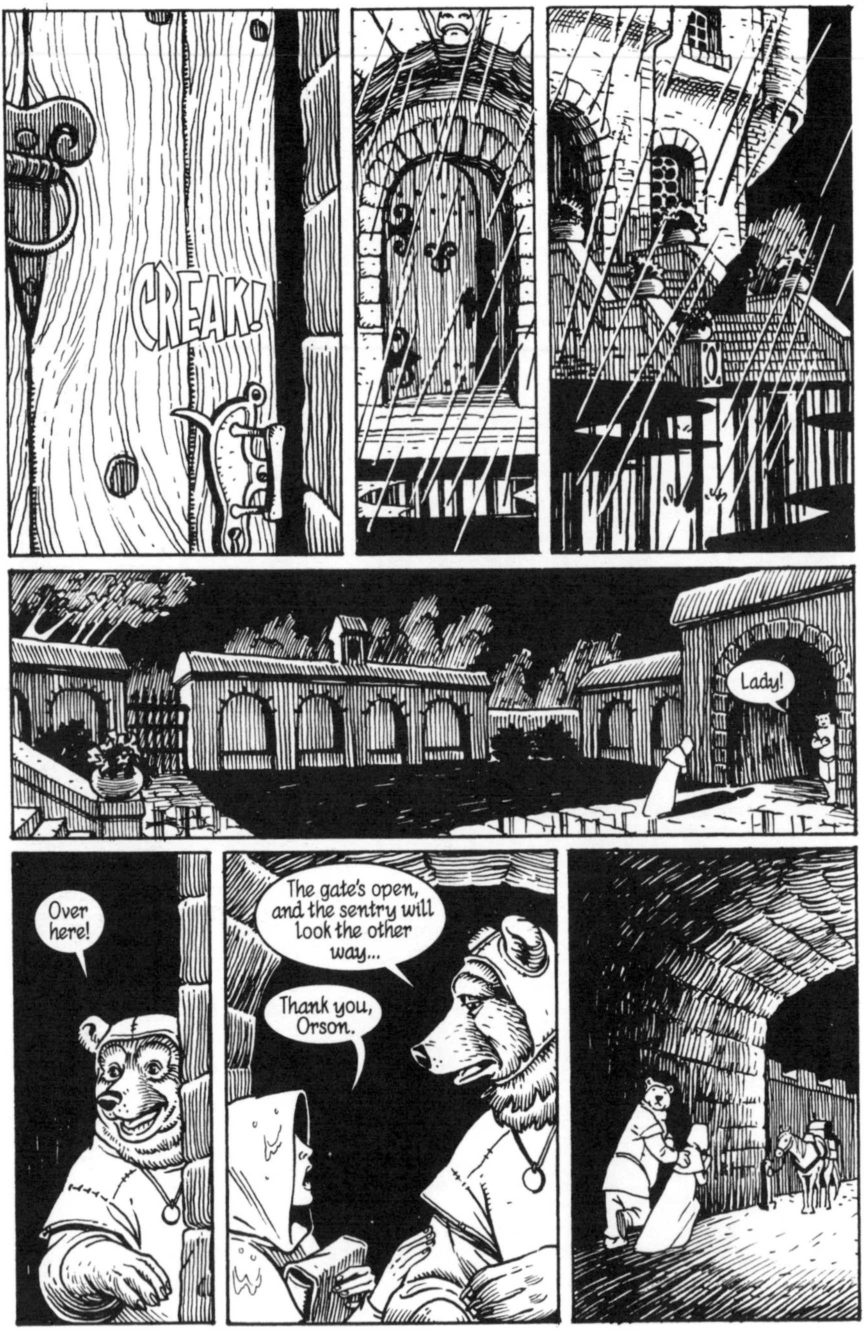
CREAK!
Lady!
Over here!
The gate's open, and the sentry will look the other way...
Thank you, Orson.

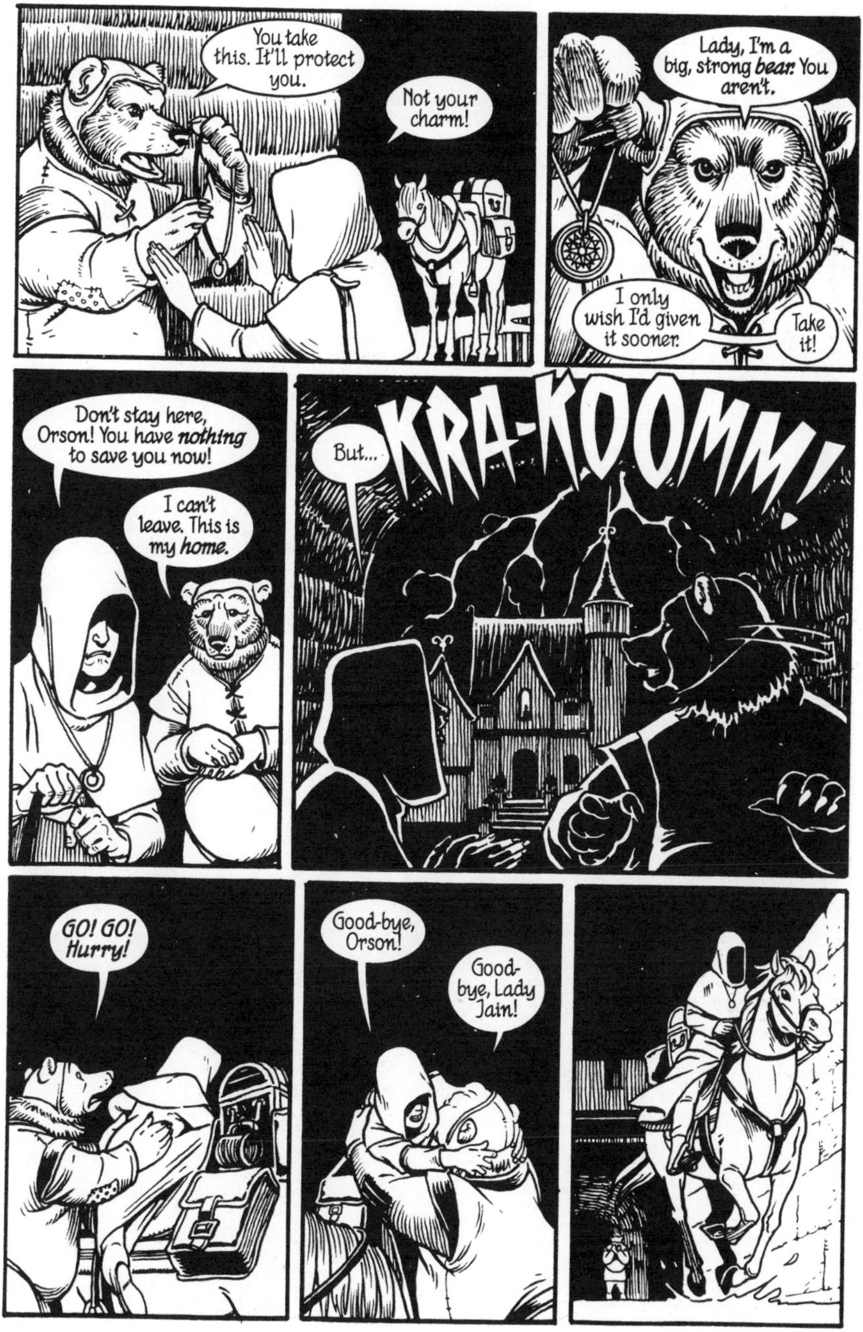

You take this. It'll protect you.
Not your charm!
Lady, I'm a big, strong *bear.* You aren't.
I only wish I'd given it sooner.
Take it!
Don't stay here, Orson! You have *nothing* to save you now!
I can't leave. This is my *home.*
But...
KRA-KOOMM!
GO! GO! Hurry!
Good-bye, Orson!
Good-bye, Lady Jain!

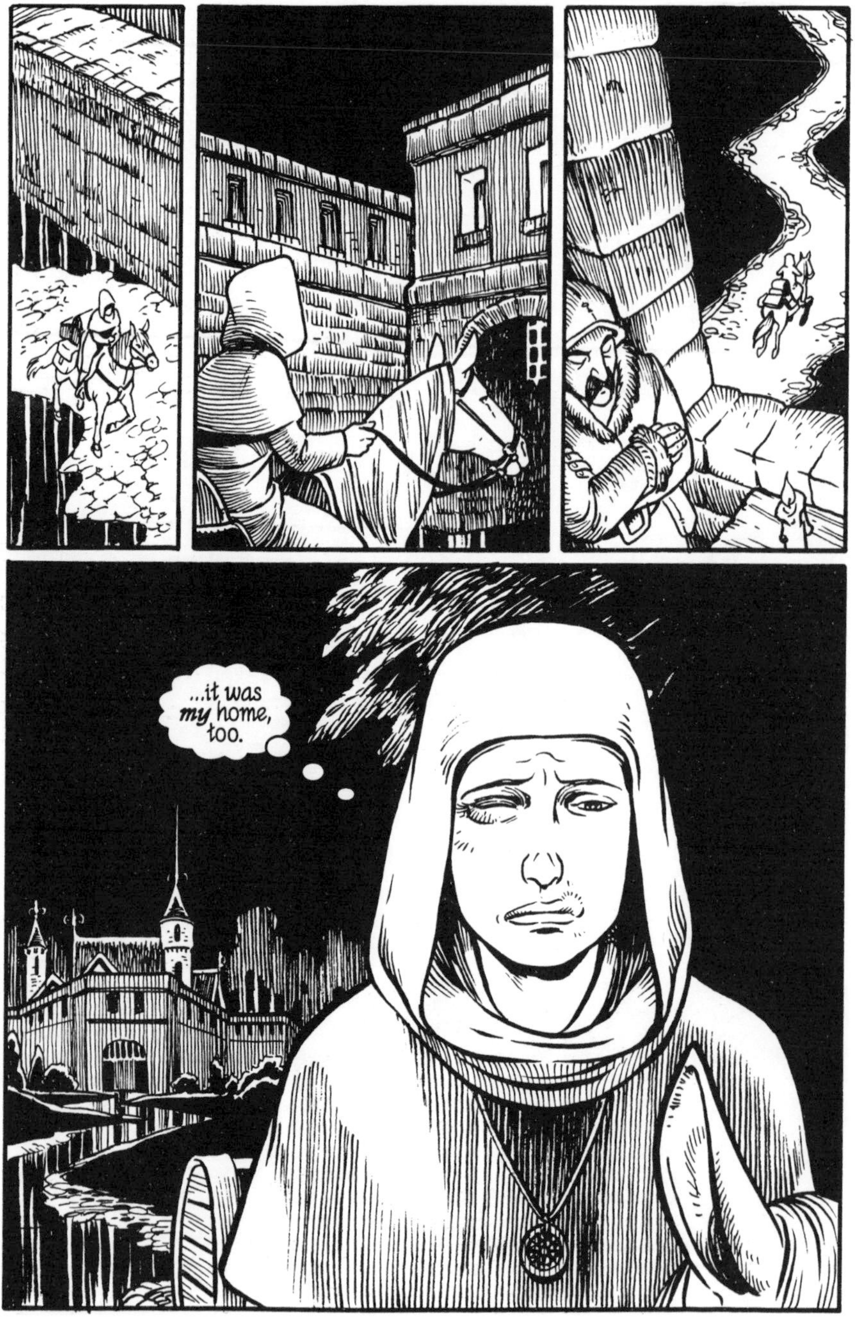
...it was **my** home, too.

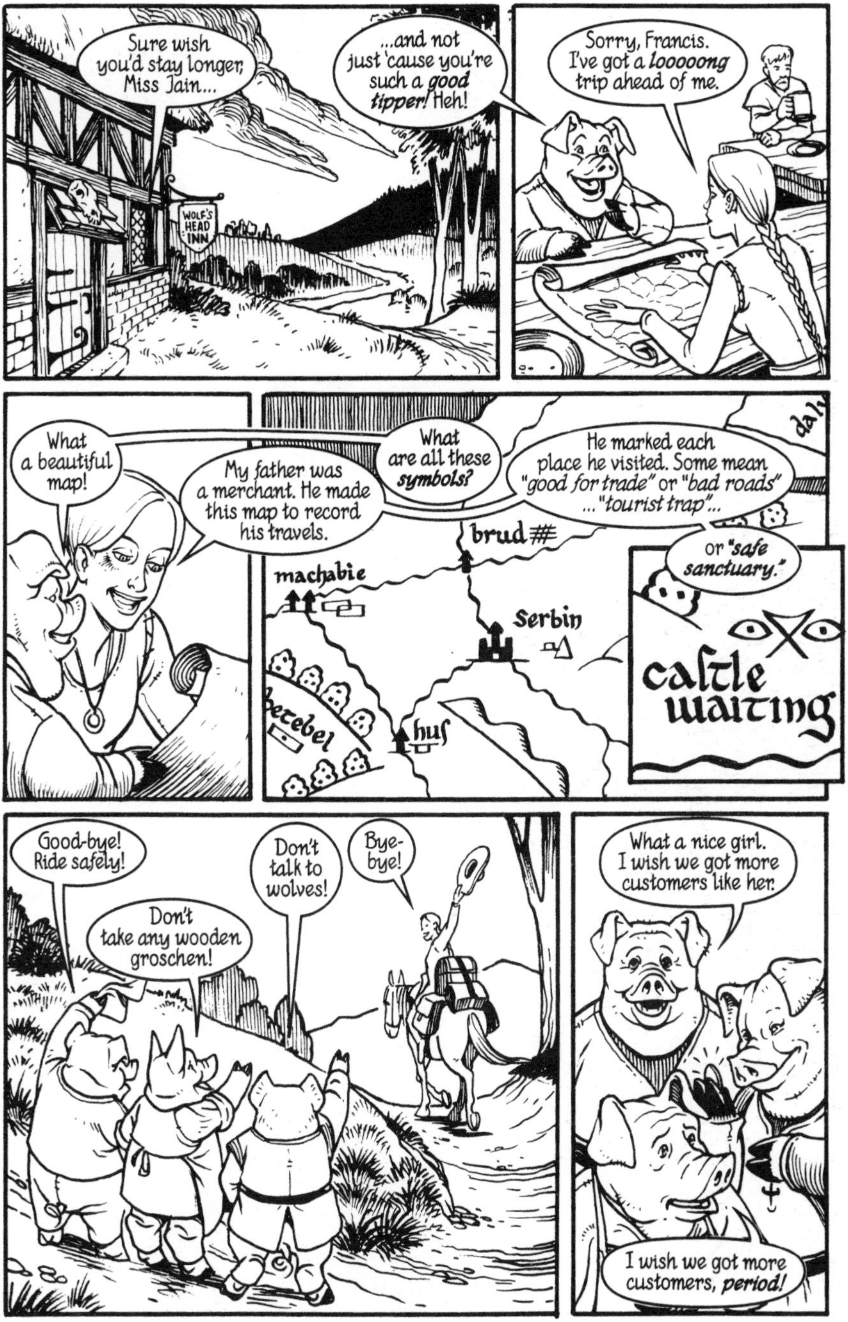

Sure wish you'd stay longer, Miss Jain...
...and not just 'cause you're such a *good tipper!* Heh!
WOLF'S HEAD INN
Sorry, Francis. I've got a *looooong* trip ahead of me.
What a beautiful map!
My father was a merchant. He made this map to record his travels.
What are all these *symbols?*
He marked each place he visited. Some mean *"good for trade"* or *"bad roads"* ...*"tourist trap"*...
or *"safe sanctuary."*
brud
machabie
Serbin
betebel
hus
castle waiting
Good-bye! Ride safely!
Don't take any wooden groschen!
Don't talk to wolves!
Bye-bye!
What a nice girl. I wish we got more customers like her.
I wish we got more customers, *period!*

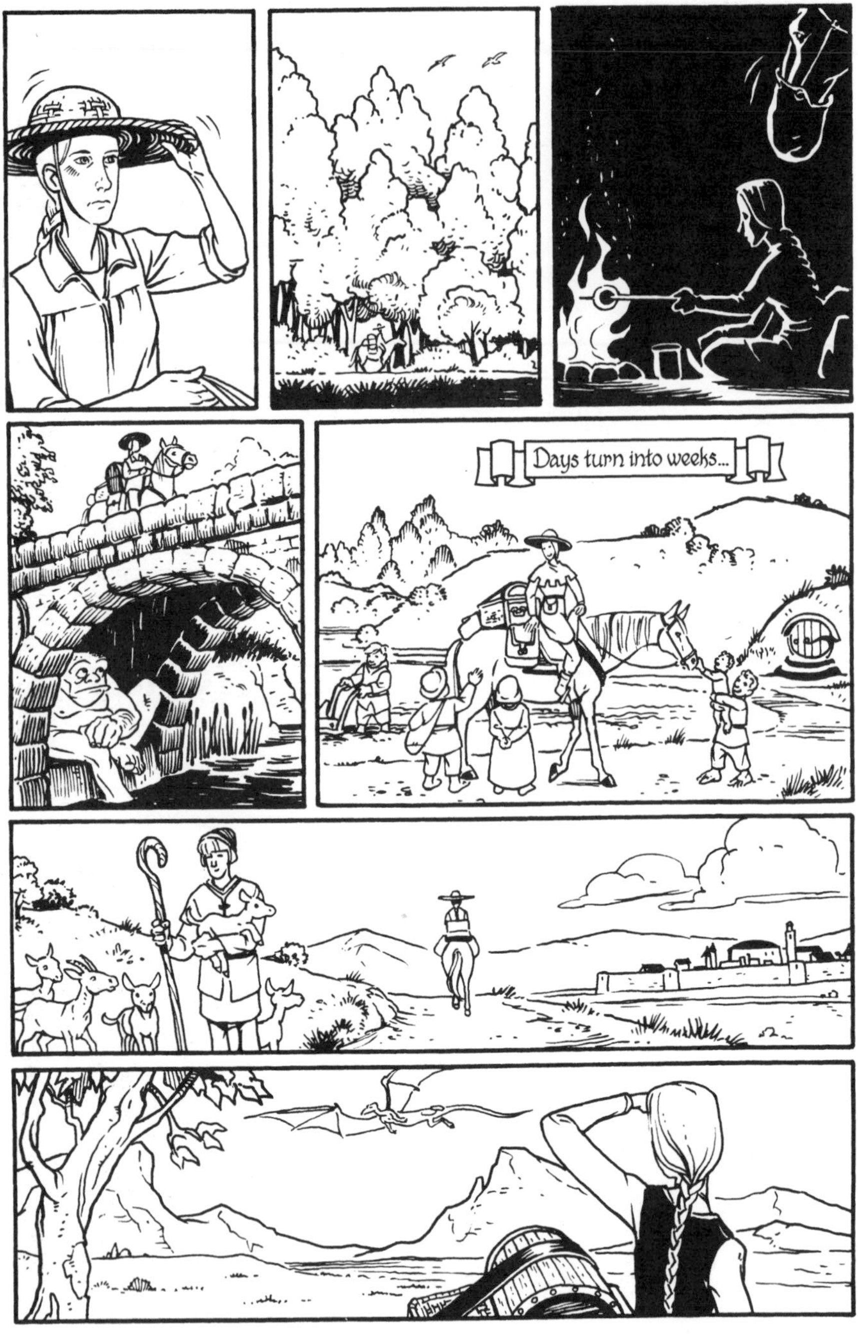
Days turn into weeks...

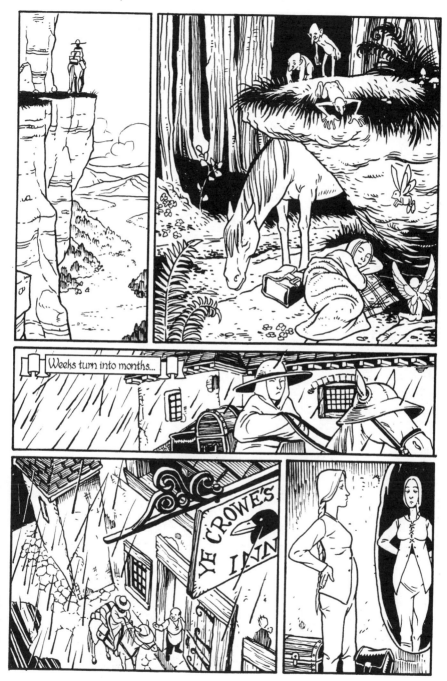

Weeks turn into months...

YE CROWE'S INN

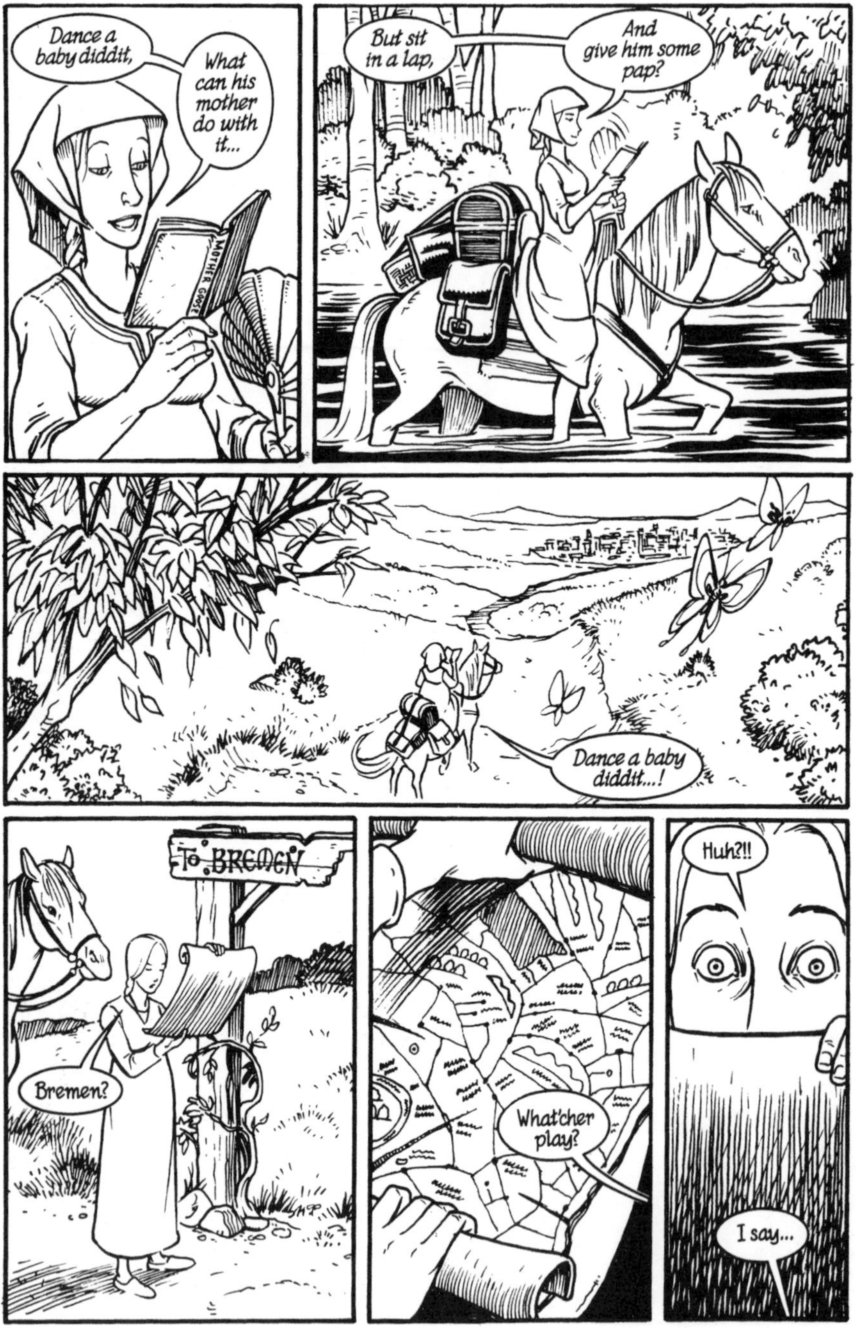
Dance a baby diddit,
What can his mother do with it...
But sit in a lap,
And give him some pap?
MOTHER GOOSE
Dance a baby diddit...!
TO BREMEN
Bremen?
What'cher play?
Huh?!!
I say...

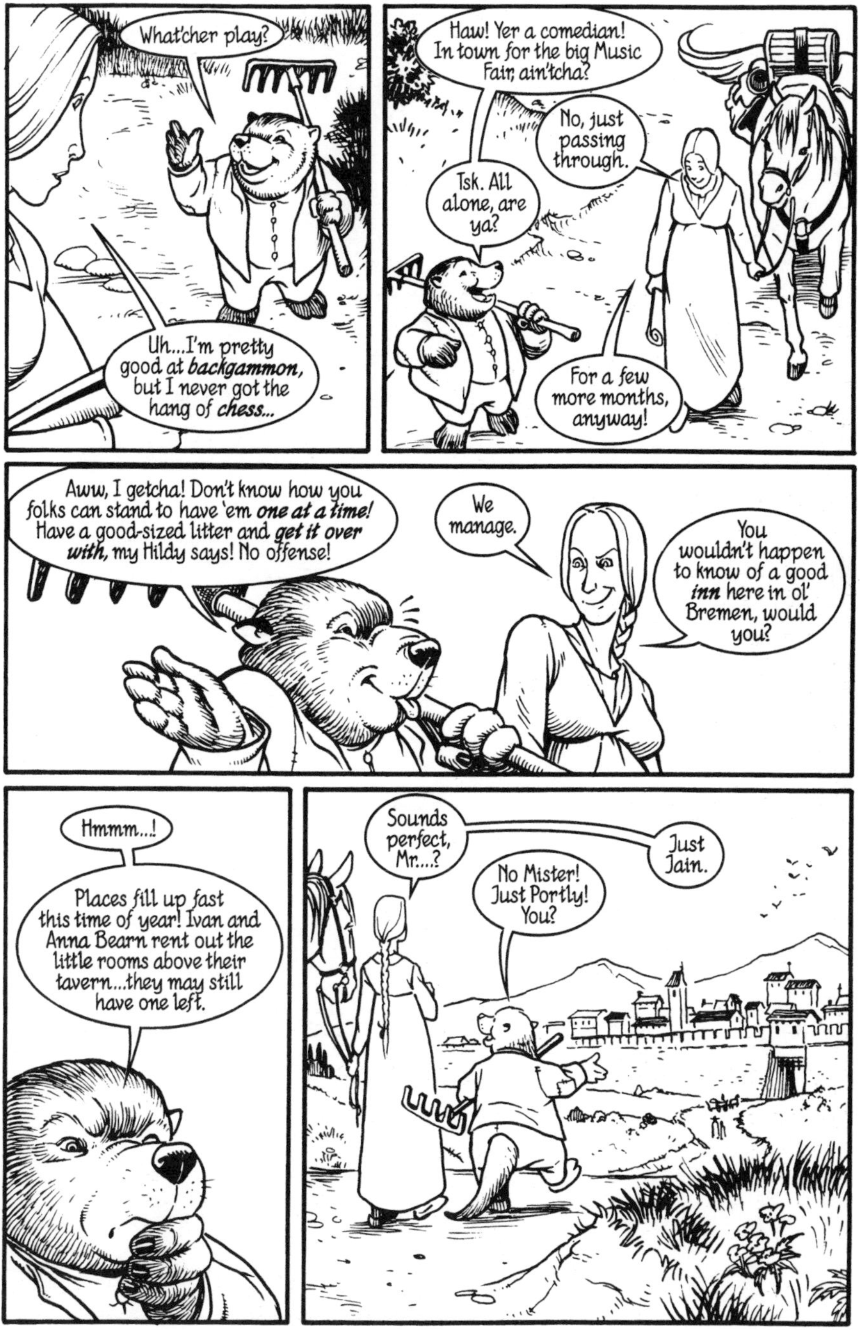
What'cher play?
Uh...I'm pretty good at *backgammon*, but I never got the hang of *chess*...
Haw! Yer a comedian! In town for the big Music Fair, ain'tcha?
No, just passing through.
Tsk. All alone, are ya?
For a few more months, anyway!
Aww, I getcha! Don't know how you folks can stand to have 'em *one at a time*! Have a good-sized litter and *get it over with*, my Hildy says! No offense!
We manage.
You wouldn't happen to know of a good *inn* here in ol' Bremen, would you?
Hmmm...!
Places fill up fast this time of year! Ivan and Anna Bearn rent out the little rooms above their tavern...they may still have one left.
Sounds perfect, Mr....?
No Mister! Just Portly! You?
Just Jain.

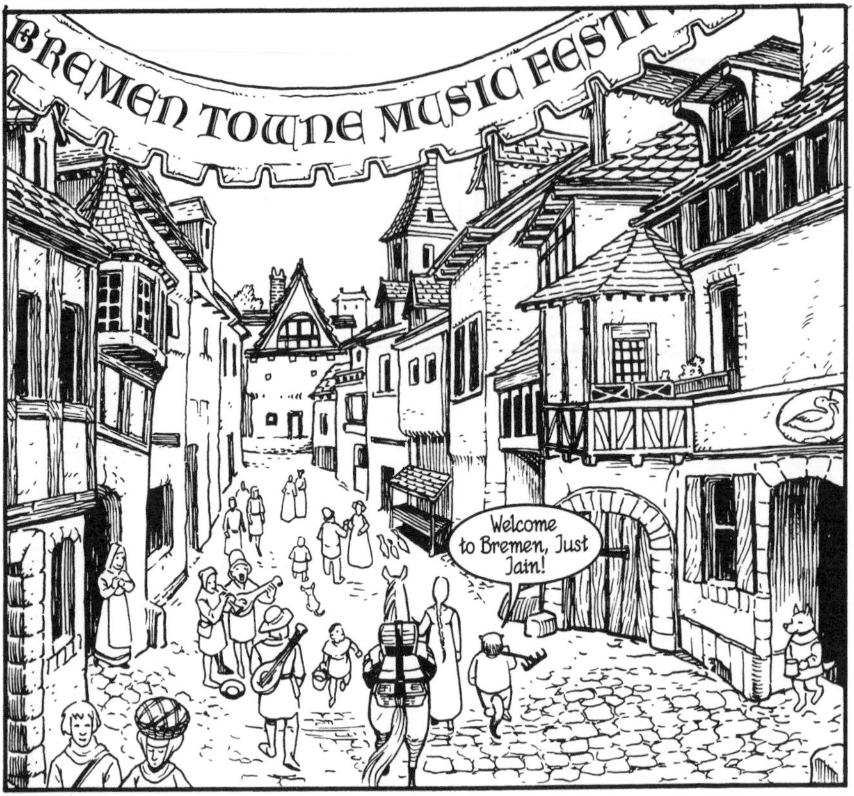
BREMEN TOWNE MUSIC FESTI
Welcome to Bremen, Just Jain!

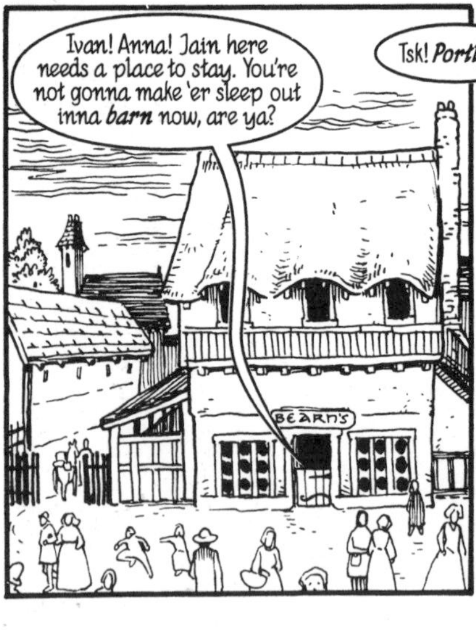
Ivan! Anna! Jain here needs a place to stay. You're not gonna make 'er sleep out inna *barn* now, are ya?
BEARN'S

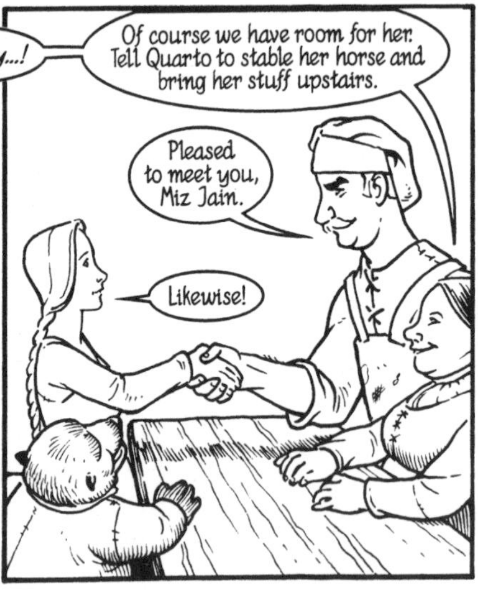
Tsk! *Portly...!*
Of course we have room for her. Tell Quarto to stable her horse and bring her stuff upstairs.
Pleased to meet you, Miz Jain.
Likewise!

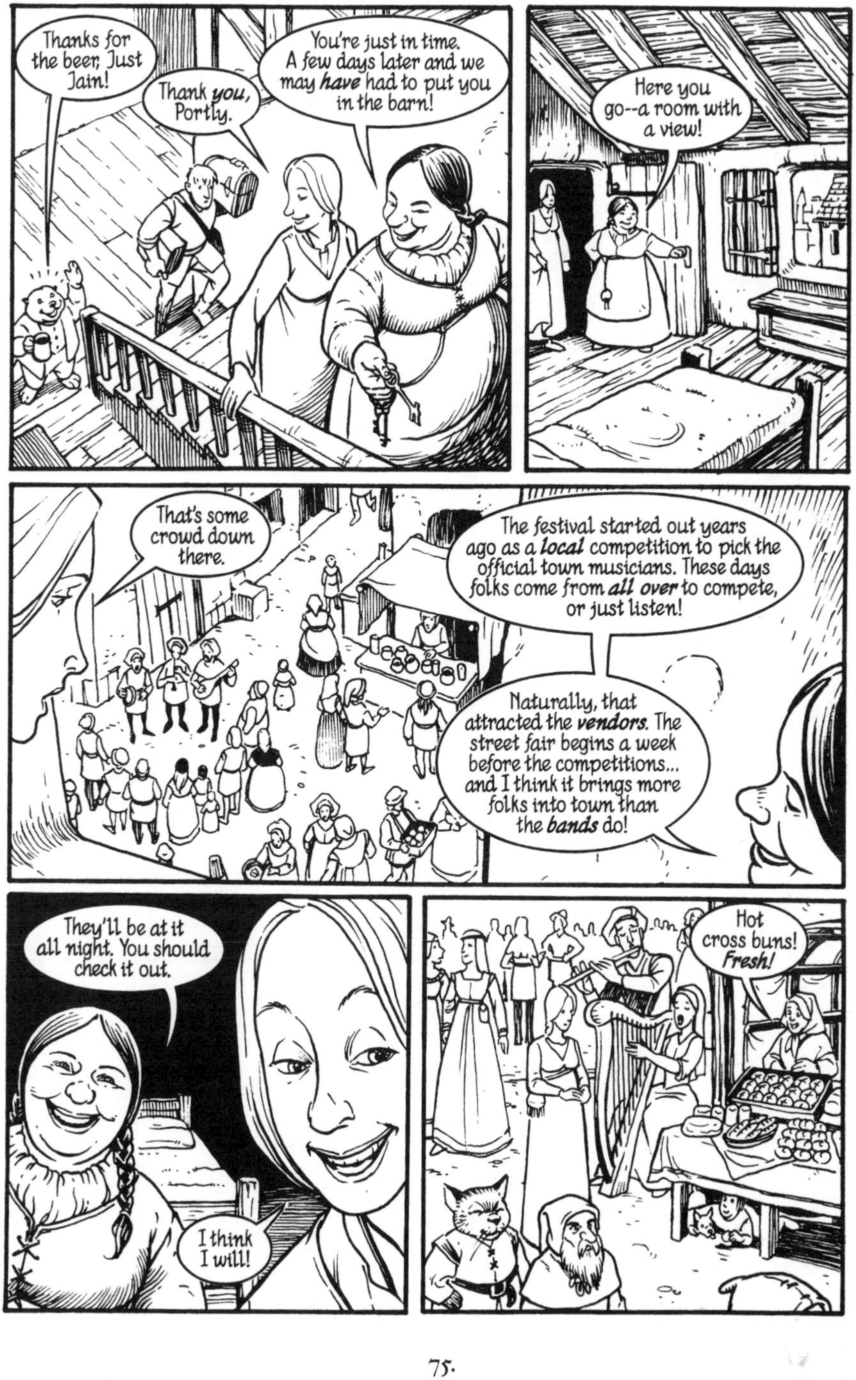
Thanks for the beer, Just Jain!
Thank *you*, Portly.
You're just in time. A few days later and we may *have* had to put you in the barn!
Here you go--a room with a view!
That's some crowd down there.
The festival started out years ago as a *local* competition to pick the official town musicians. These days folks come from *all over* to compete, or just listen!
Naturally, that attracted the *vendors*. The street fair begins a week before the competitions... and I think it brings more folks into town than the *bands* do!
They'll be at it all night. You should check it out.
I think I will!
Hot cross buns! *Fresh!*

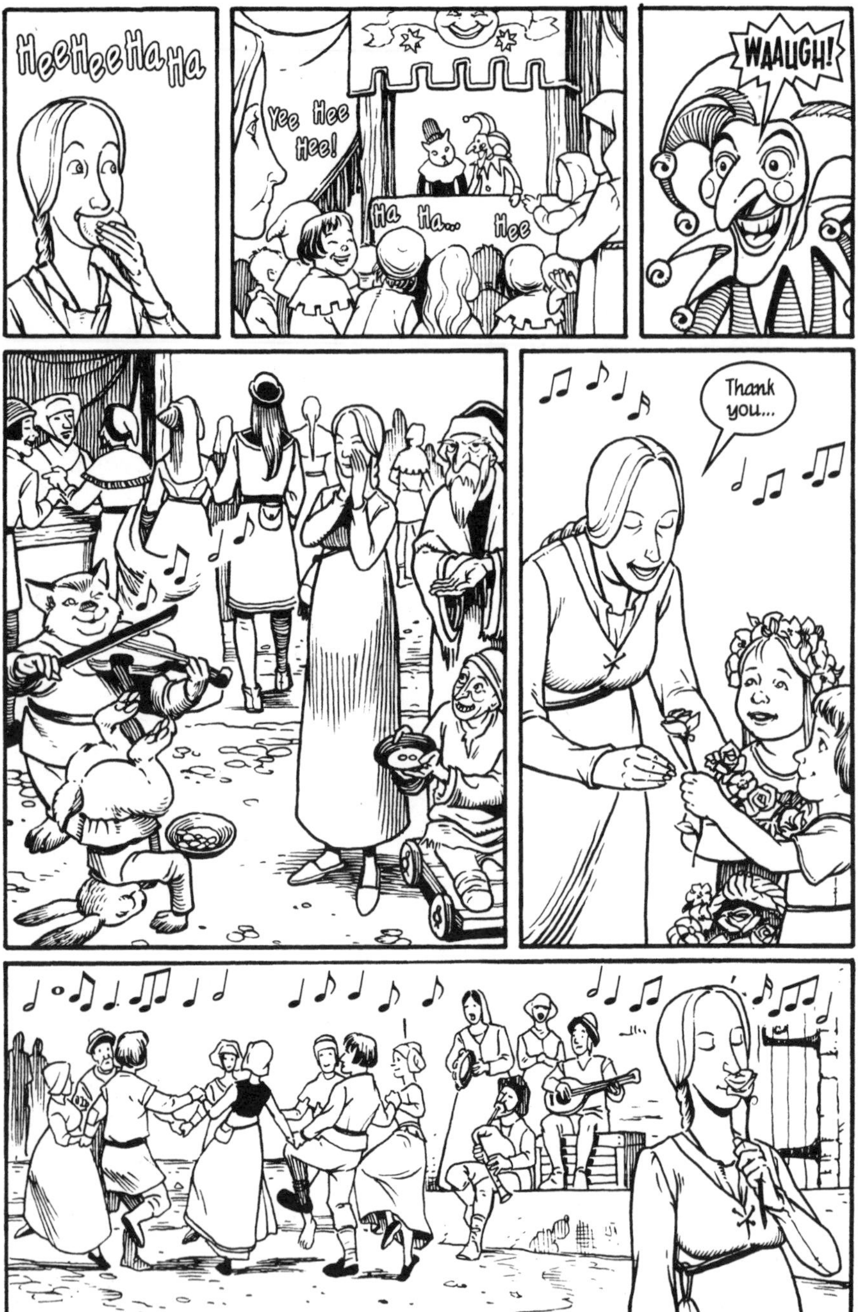
HeeHeeHaHa Ha
Yee Hee Hee!
Ha Ha... Hee
WAAUGH!
Thank you...

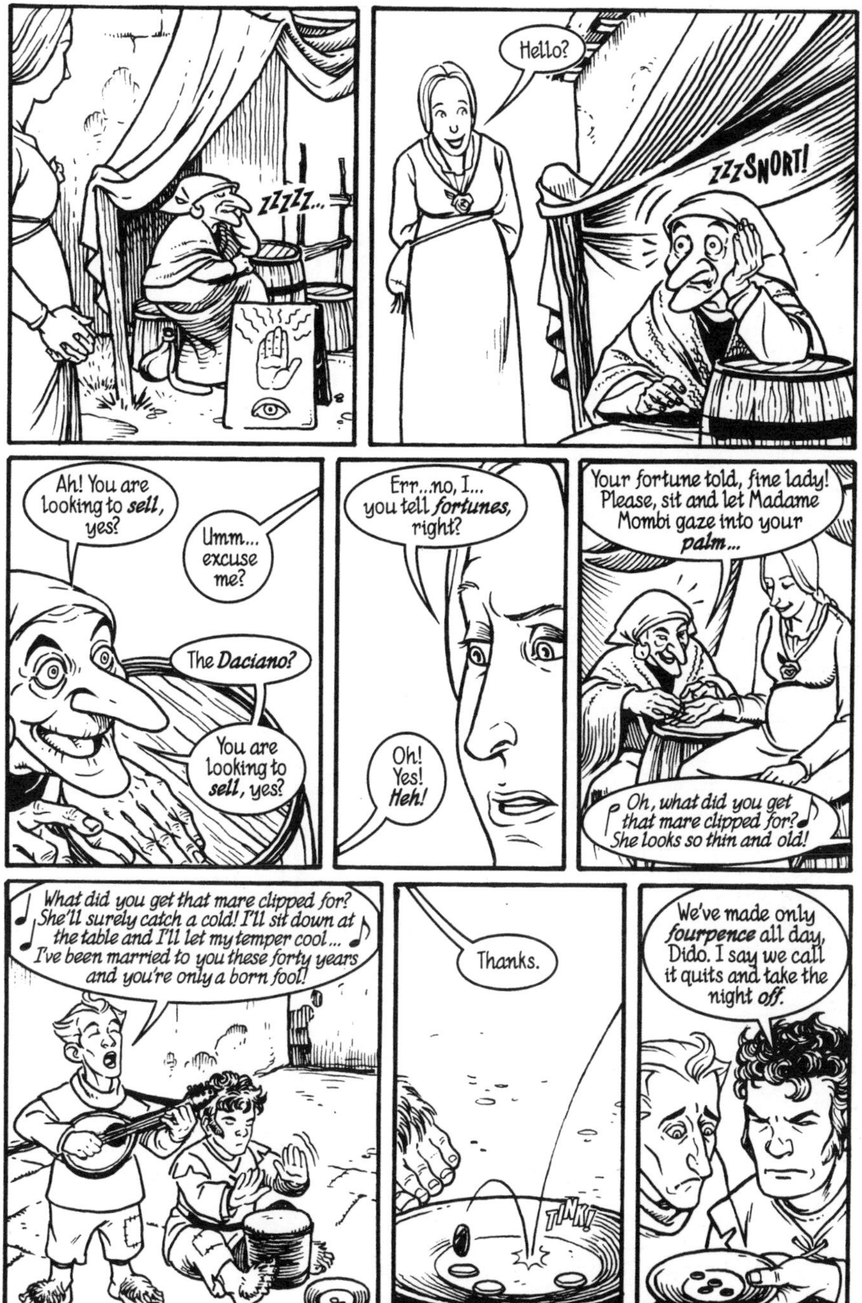

ZZZZZ...
Hello?
ZZZSNORT!
Ah! You are looking to sell, yes?
Umm... excuse me?
The Daciano?
You are looking to sell, yes?
Err...no, I... you tell fortunes, right?
Oh! Yes! Heh!
Your fortune told, fine lady! Please, sit and let Madame Mombi gaze into your palm...
Oh, what did you get that mare clipped for? She looks so thin and old!
What did you get that mare clipped for? She'll surely catch a cold! I'll sit down at the table and I'll let my temper cool... I've been married to you these forty years and you're only a born fool!
Thanks.
TINK!
We've made only fourpence all day, Dido. I say we call it quits and take the night off.

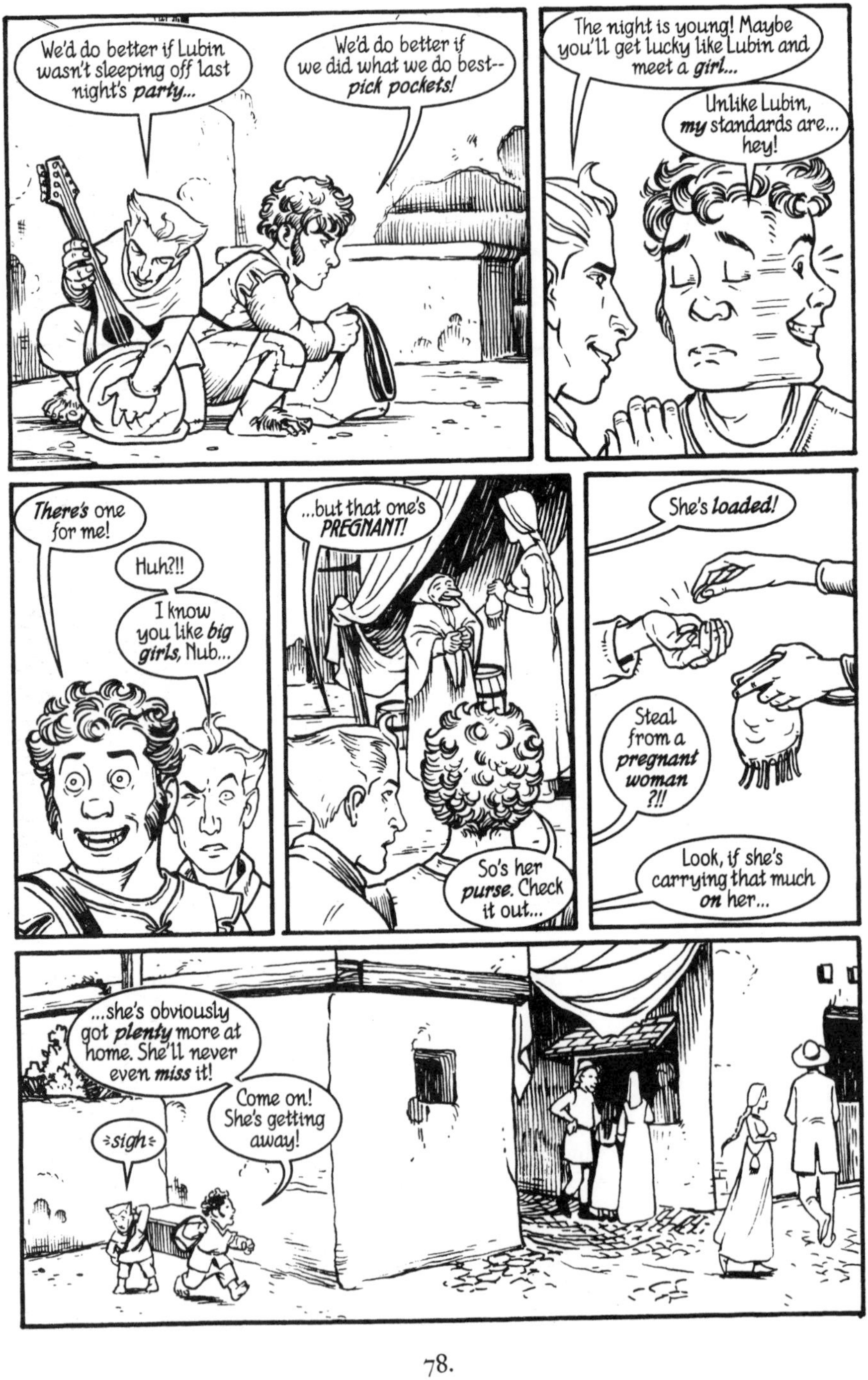
We'd do better if Lubin wasn't sleeping off last night's *party...*
We'd do better if we did what we do best-- *pick pockets!*
The night is young! Maybe you'll get lucky like Lubin and meet a *girl...*
Unlike Lubin, *my* standards are... hey!
There's one for me!
Huh?!!
I know you like *big girls,* Nub...
...but that one's *PREGNANT!*
So's her *purse.* Check it out...
She's *loaded!*
Steal from a *pregnant woman* ?!!
Look, if she's carrying that much *on* her...
...she's obviously got *plenty* more at home. She'll never even *miss* it!
sigh
Come on! She's getting away!

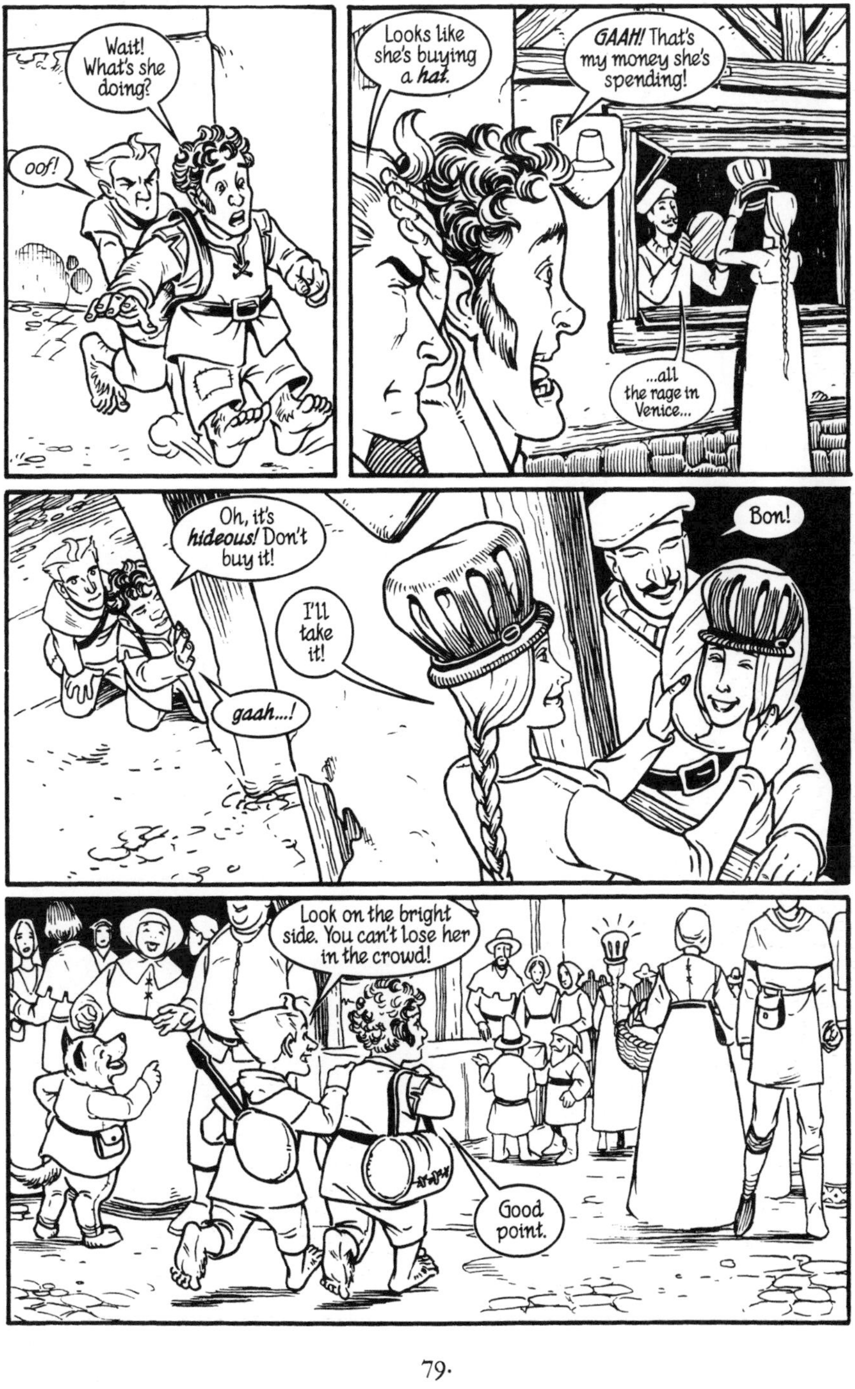
Wait! What's she doing?
oof!
Looks like she's buying a *hat*.
GAAH! That's my money she's spending!
...all the rage in Venice...
Oh, it's *hideous!* Don't buy it!
gaah...!
I'll take it!
Bon!
Look on the bright side. You can't lose her in the crowd!
Good point.

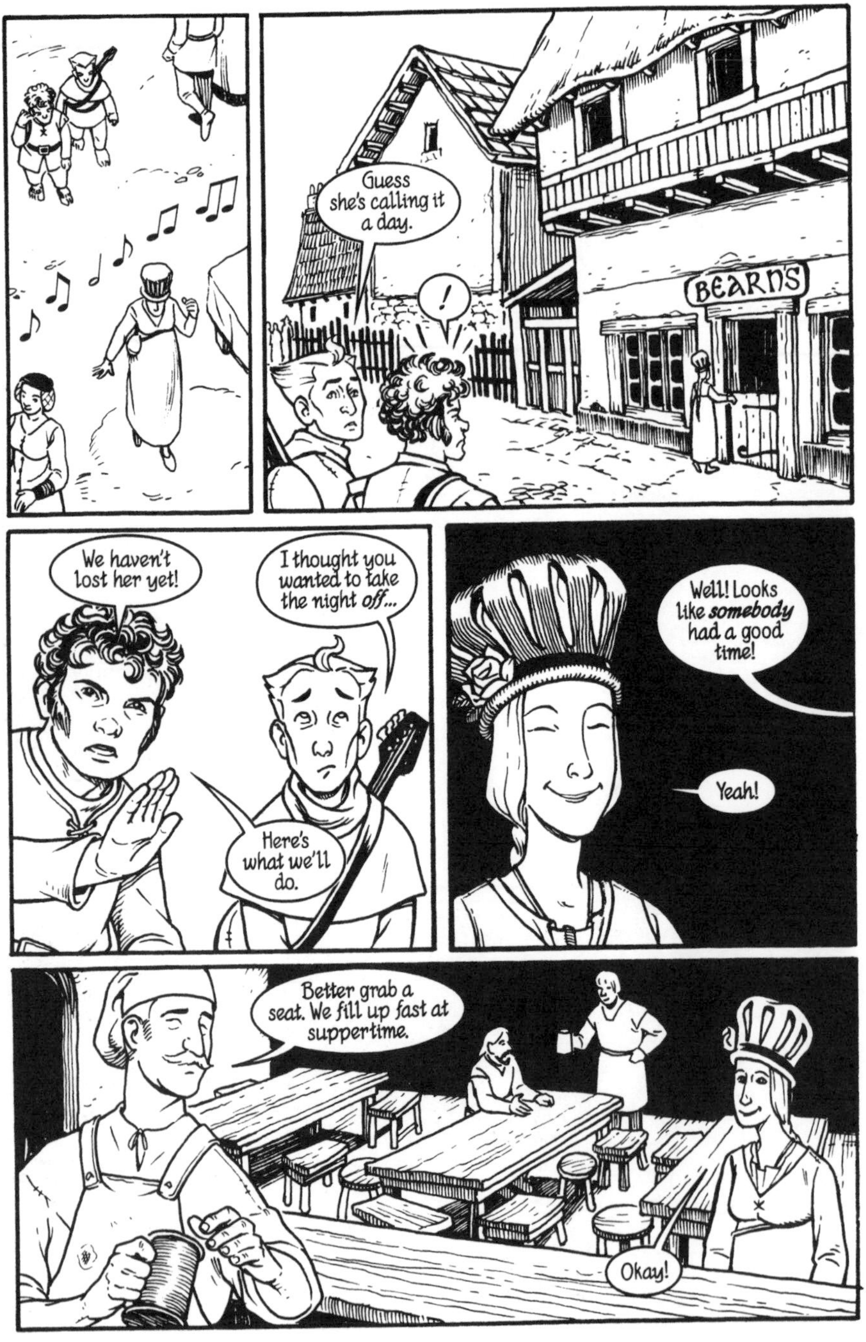
Guess she's calling it a day.
!
BEARN'S
We haven't lost her yet!
I thought you wanted to take the night *off*...
Here's what we'll do.
Well! Looks like ***somebody*** had a good time!
Yeah!
Better grab a seat. We fill up fast at suppertime.
Okay!

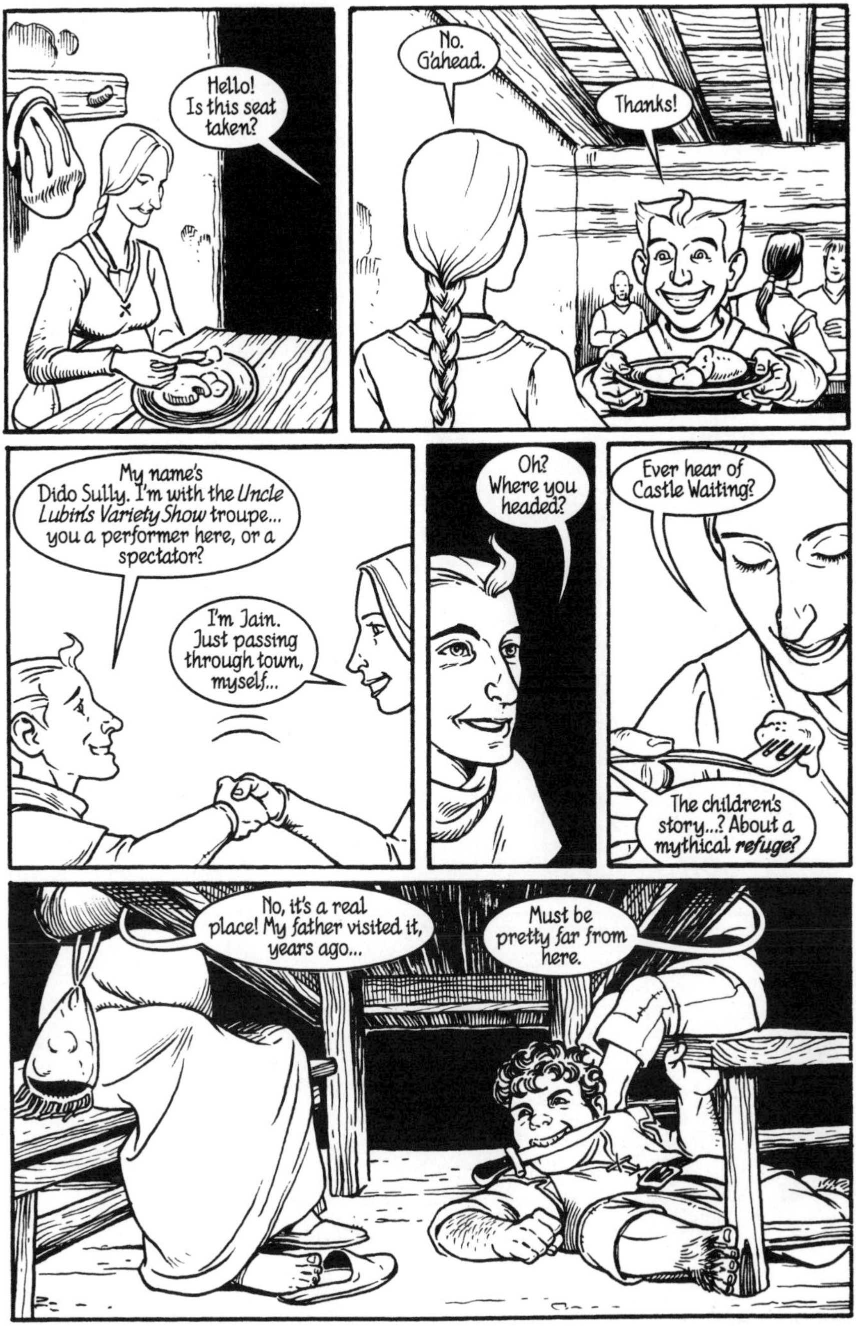
Hello! Is this seat taken?
No. G'ahead.
Thanks!
My name's Dido Sully. I'm with the *Uncle Lubin's Variety Show* troupe... you a performer here, or a spectator?
I'm Jain. Just passing through town, myself...
Oh? Where you headed?
Ever hear of Castle Waiting?
The children's story...? About a mythical *refuge?*
No, it's a real place! My father visited it, years ago...
Must be pretty far from here.

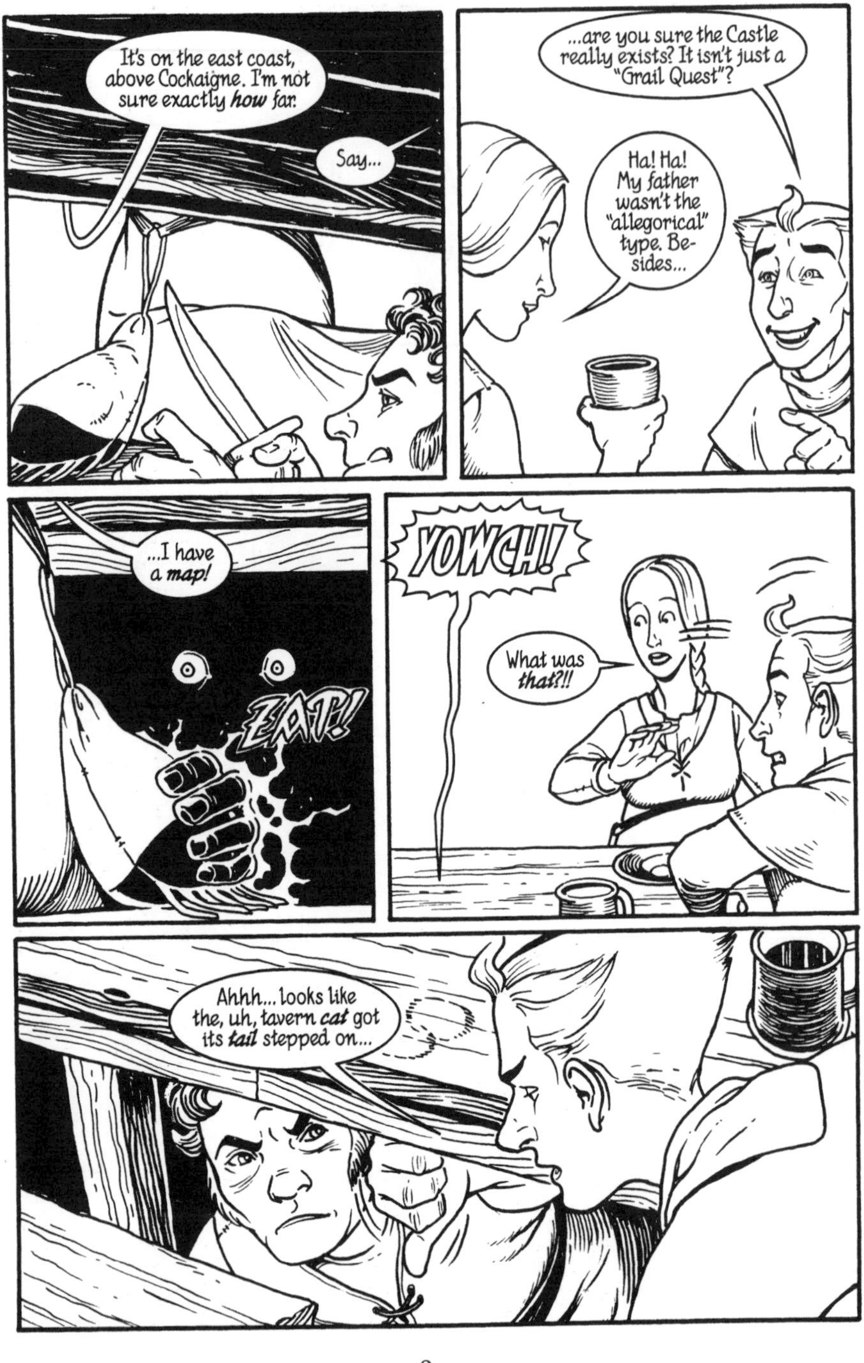
It's on the east coast, above Cockaigne. I'm not sure exactly *how* far.
Say...
...are you sure the Castle really exists? It isn't just a "Grail Quest"?
Ha! Ha! My father wasn't the "allegorical" type. Besides...
...I have a *map!*
ZAT!
YOWCH!
What was *that?!!*
Ahhh... looks like the, uh, tavern *cat* got its *tail* stepped on...

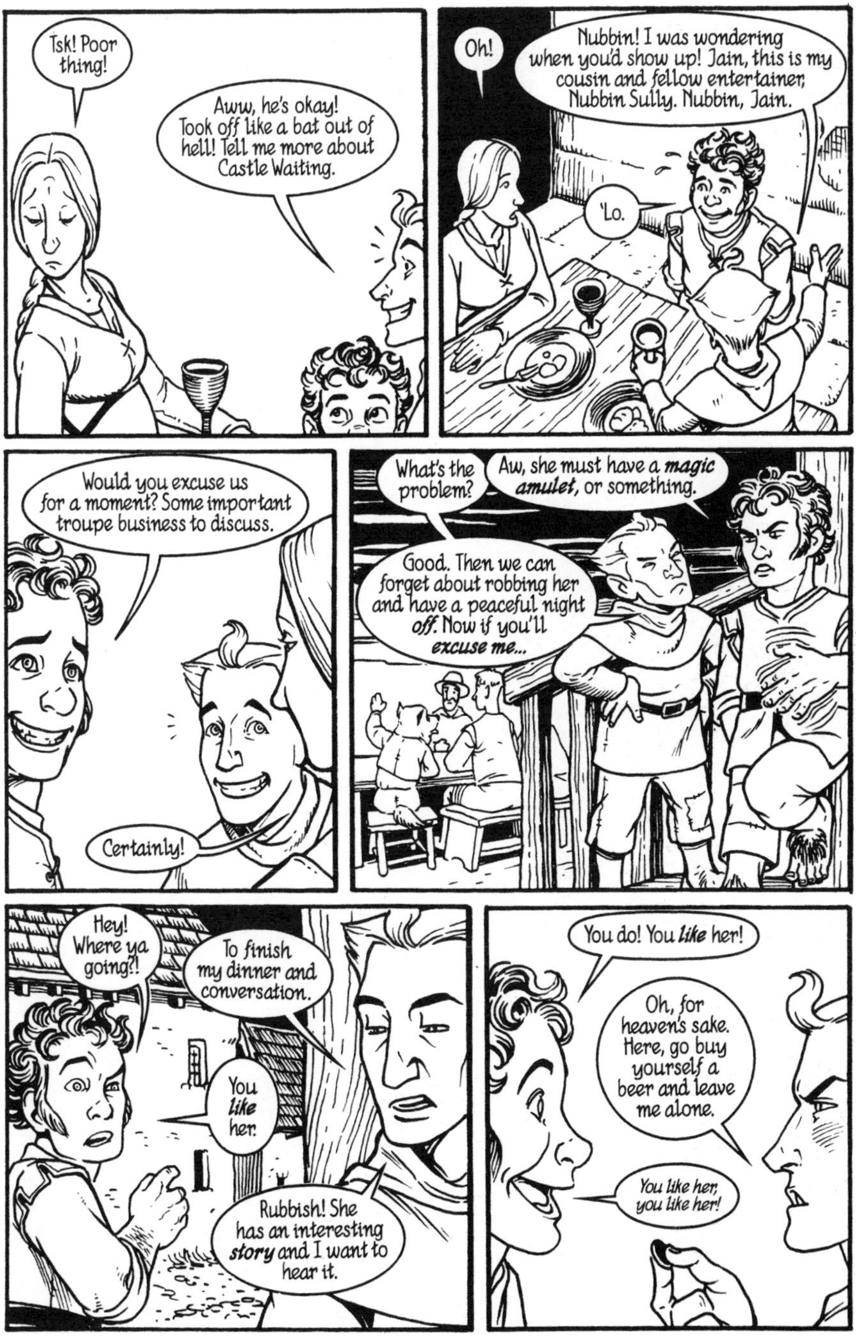
Tsk! Poor thing!
Aww, he's okay! Took off like a bat out of hell! Tell me more about Castle Waiting.
Oh!
Nubbin! I was wondering when you'd show up! Jain, this is my cousin and fellow entertainer, Nubbin Sully. Nubbin, Jain.
'Lo.
Would you excuse us for a moment? Some important troupe business to discuss.
Certainly!
What's the problem?
Aw, she must have a magic amulet, or something.
Good. Then we can forget about robbing her and have a peaceful night off. Now if you'll excuse me...
Hey! Where ya going?!
To finish my dinner and conversation.
You like her.
Rubbish! She has an interesting story and I want to hear it.
You do! You like her!
Oh, for heaven's sake. Here, go buy yourself a beer and leave me alone.
You like her, you like her!

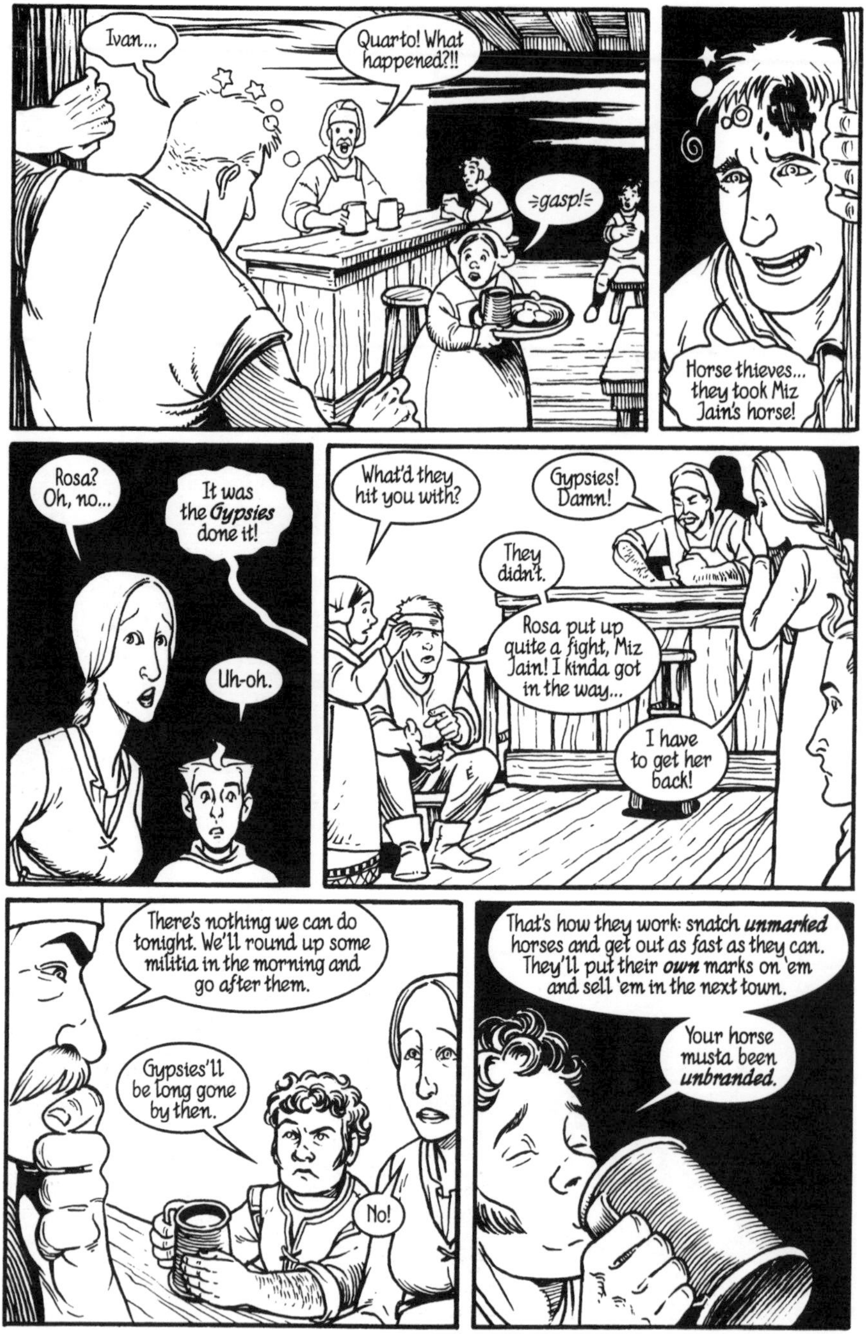
Ivan...
Quarto! What happened?!!
gasp!
Horse thieves... they took Miz Jain's horse!
Rosa? Oh, no...
It was the *Gypsies* done it!
Uh-oh.
What'd they hit you with?
Gypsies! Damn!
They didn't.
Rosa put up quite a fight, Miz Jain! I kinda got in the way...
I have to get her back!
There's nothing we can do tonight. We'll round up some militia in the morning and go *after* them.
Gypsies'll be long gone by then.
No!
That's how they work: snatch ***unmarked*** horses and get out as fast as they can. They'll put their ***own*** marks on 'em and sell 'em in the next town.
Your horse musta been ***unbranded***.

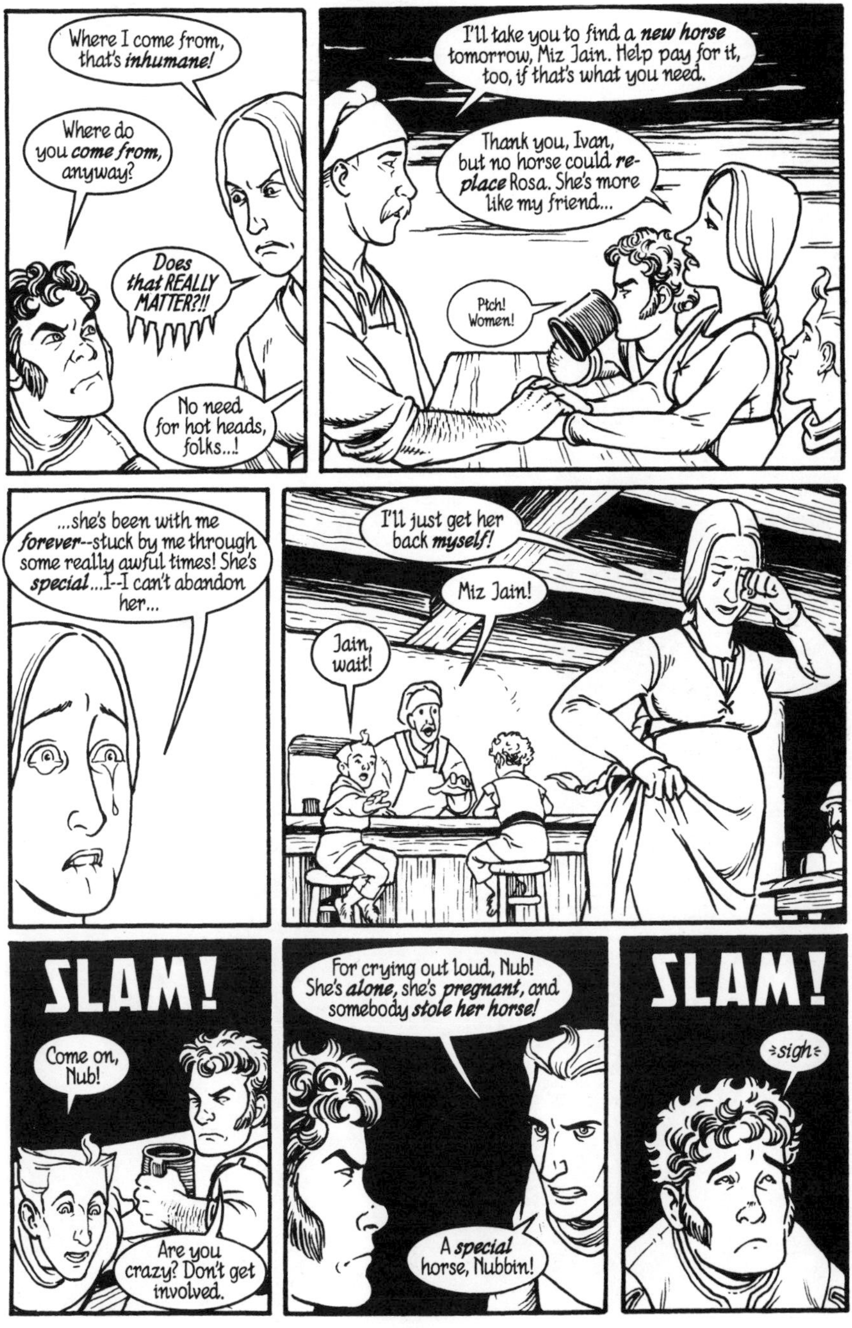
Where I come from, that's *inhumane!*
Where do you *come from,* anyway?
Does that REALLY MATTER?!!
No need for hot heads, folks...!
I'll take you to find a *new horse* tomorrow, Miz Jain. Help pay for it, too, if that's what you need.
Thank you, Ivan, but no horse could *replace* Rosa. She's more like my friend...
Ptch! Women!
...she's been with me *forever*--stuck by me through some really awful times! She's *special*...I--I can't abandon her...
I'll just get her back *myself!*
Miz Jain!
Jain, wait!
SLAM!
Come on, Nub!
Are you crazy? Don't get involved.
For crying out loud, Nub! She's *alone*, she's *pregnant*, and somebody *stole her horse!*
A *special* horse, Nubbin!
SLAM!
sigh

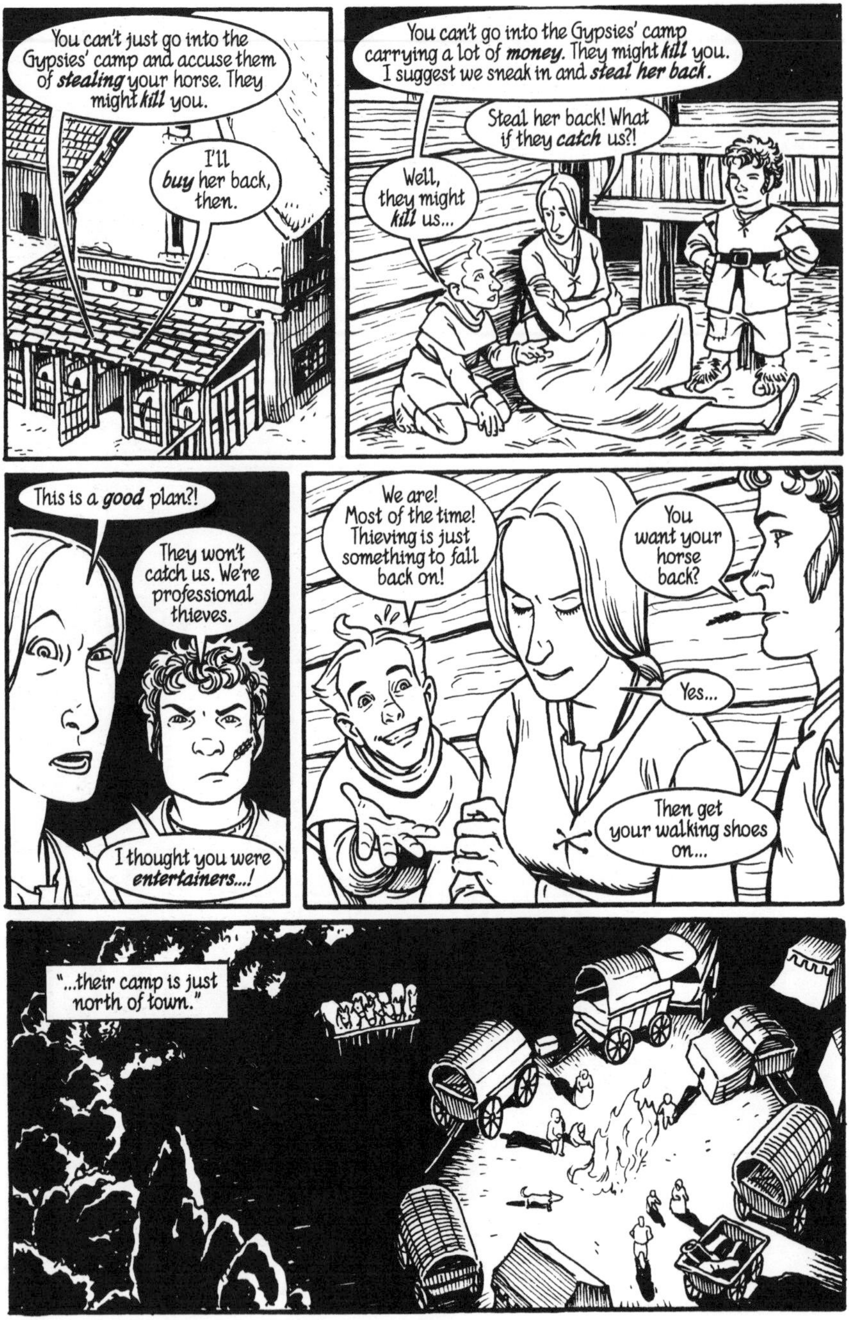
You can't just go into the Gypsies' camp and accuse them of stealing your horse. They might kill you.
I'll buy her back, then.
You can't go into the Gypsies' camp carrying a lot of money. They might kill you. I suggest we sneak in and steal her back.
Steal her back! What if they catch us?!
Well, they might kill us...
This is a good plan?!
They won't catch us. We're professional thieves.
I thought you were entertainers...!
We are! Most of the time! Thieving is just something to fall back on!
You want your horse back?
Yes...
Then get your walking shoes on...
"...their camp is just north of town."

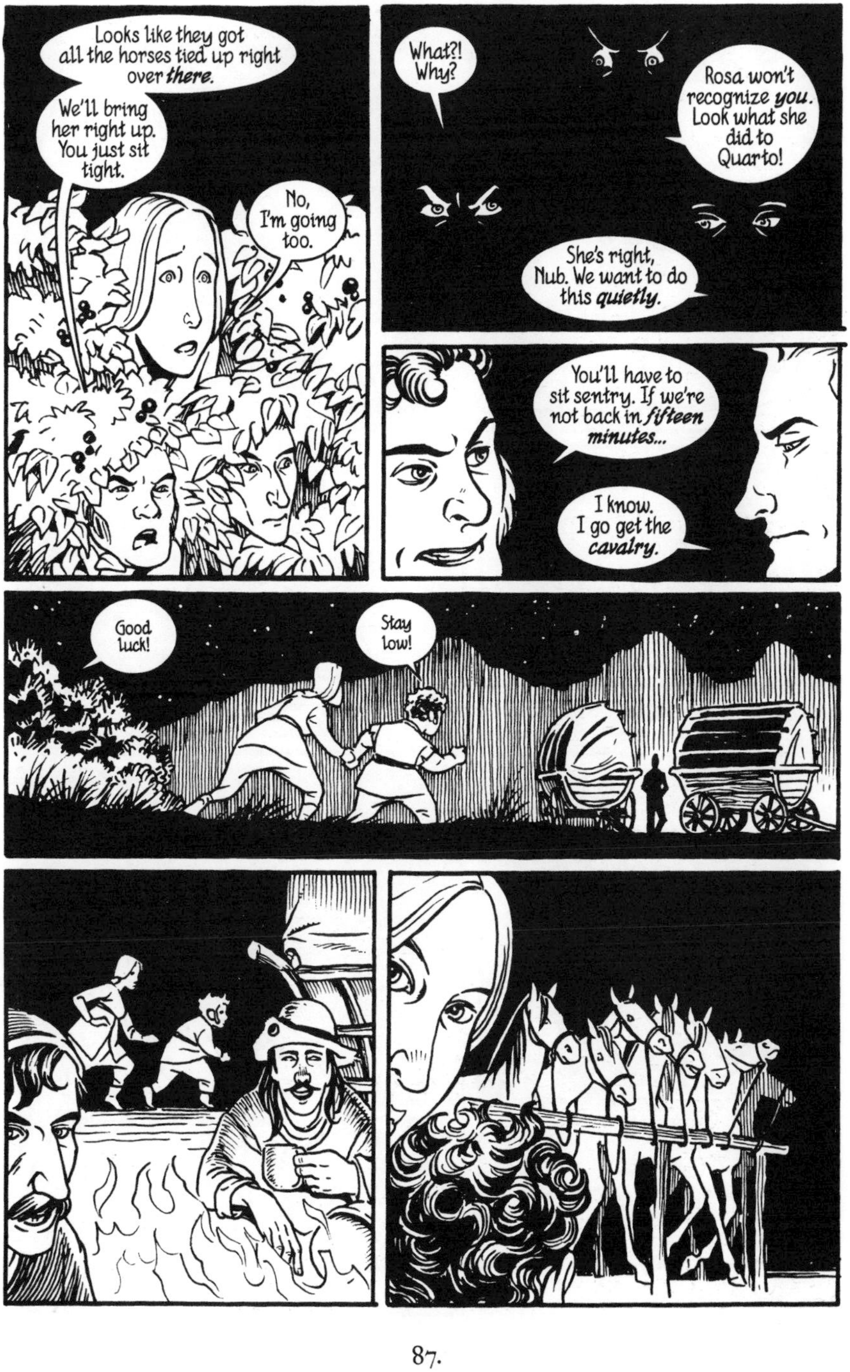
Looks like they got all the horses tied up right over *there*.
We'll bring her right up. You just sit tight.
No, I'm going too.
What?! Why?
Rosa won't recognize *you*. Look what she did to Quarto!
She's right, Nub. We want to do this *quietly*.
You'll have to sit sentry. If we're not back in *fifteen minutes...*
I know. I go get the *cavalry*.
Good luck!
Stay low!

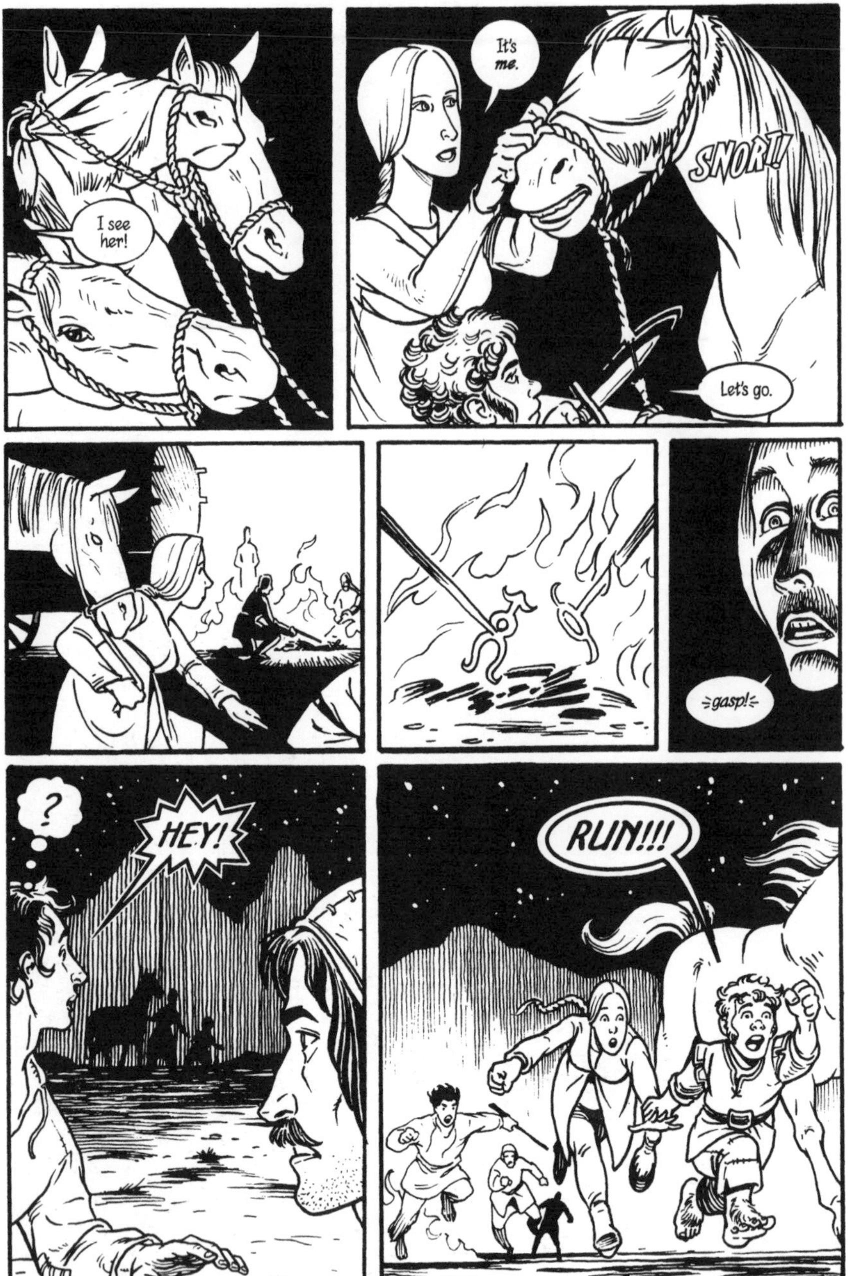
I see her!
It's me.
SNORT!
Let's go.
gasp!
?
HEY!
RUN!!!

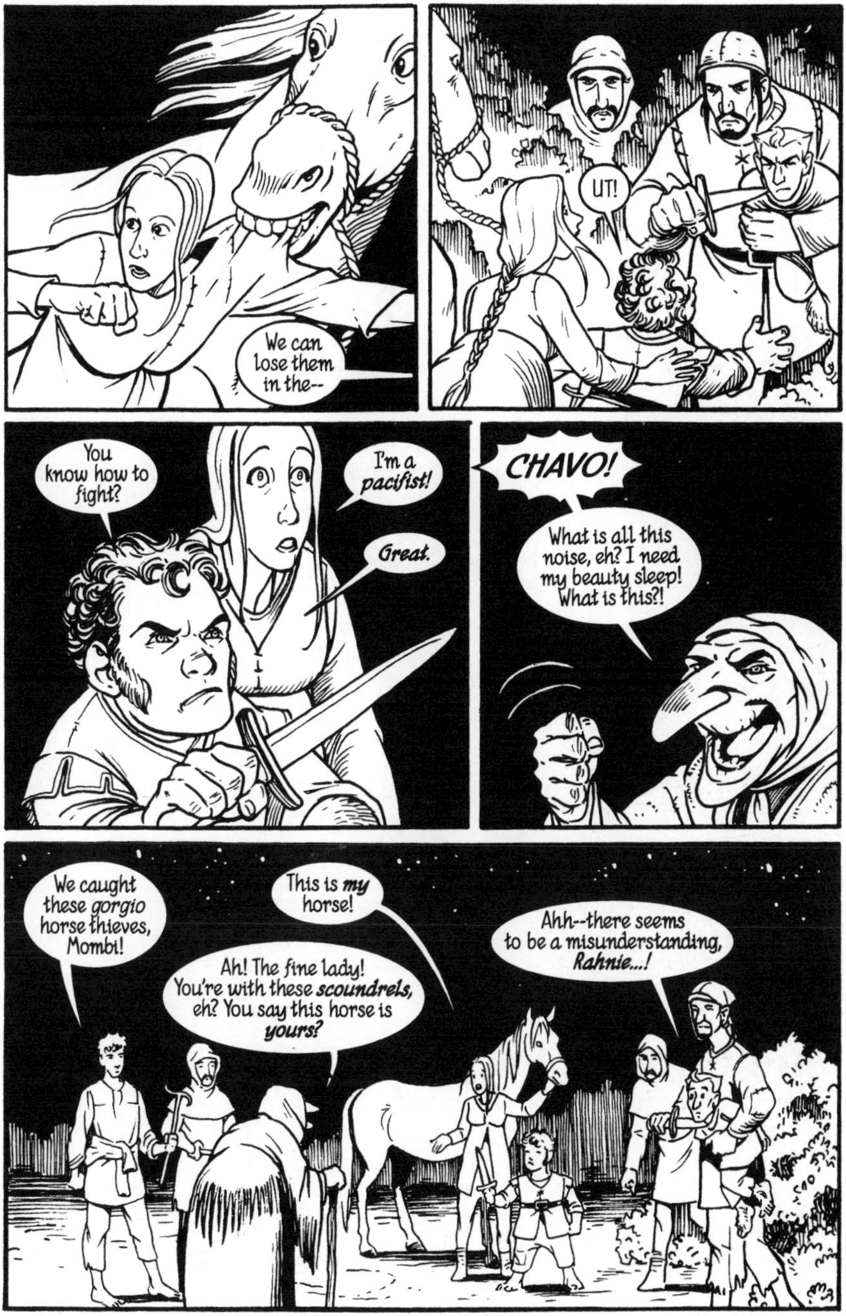
We can lose them in the--
UT!
You know how to fight?
I'm a *pacifist!*
Great.
CHAVO!
What is all this noise, eh? I need my beauty sleep! What is this?!
We caught these *gorgio* horse thieves, Mombi!
This is *my* horse!
Ah! The fine lady! You're with these *scoundrels,* eh? You say this horse is *yours?*
Ahh--there seems to be a misunderstanding, *Rahnie...!*

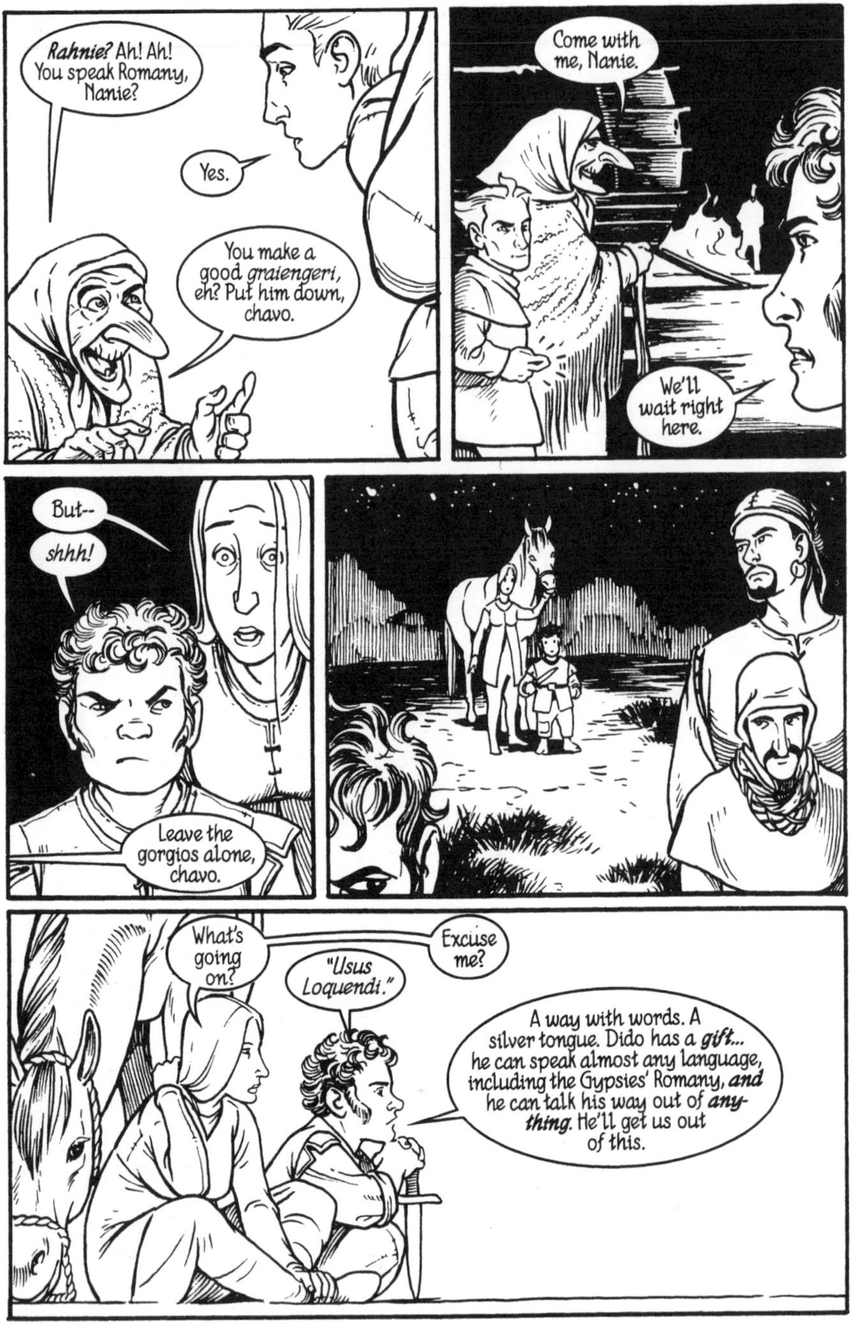
Rahnie? Ah! Ah! You speak Romany, Nanie?
Yes.
You make a good *graiengeri*, eh? Put him down, chavo.
Come with me, Nanie.
We'll wait right here.
But--
shhh!
Leave the gorgios alone, chavo.
What's going on?
Excuse me?
"Usus Loquendi."
A way with words. A silver tongue. Dido has a ***gift...*** he can speak almost any language, including the Gypsies' Romany, ***and*** he can talk his way out of ***any-thing***. He'll get us out of this.

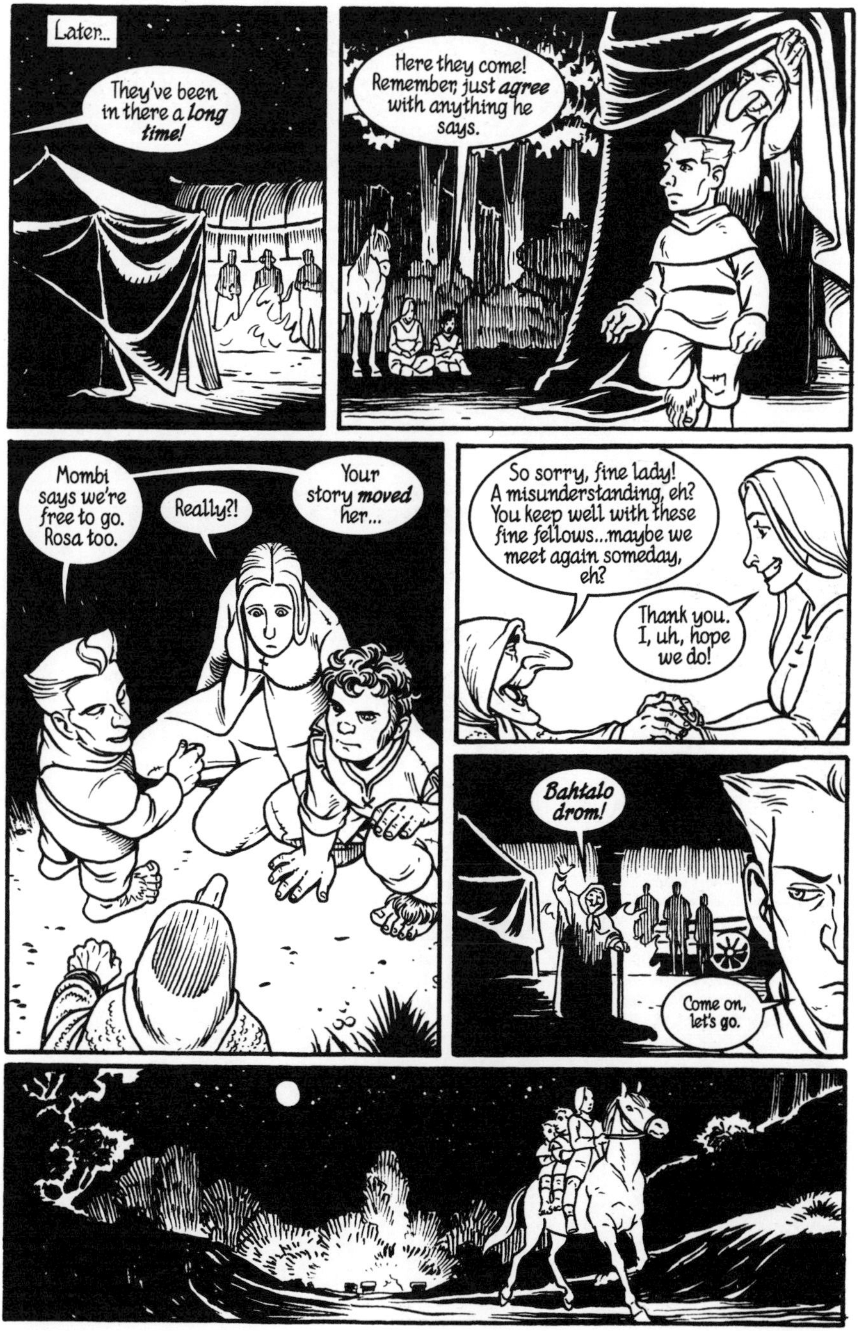
Later...
They've been in there a *long time!*
Here they come! Remember, just *agree* with anything he says.
Mombi says we're free to go. Rosa too.
Really?!
Your story *moved* her...
So sorry, fine lady! A misunderstanding, eh? You keep well with these fine fellows...maybe we meet again someday, eh?
Thank you. I, uh, hope we do!
Bahtalo drom!
Come on, let's go.

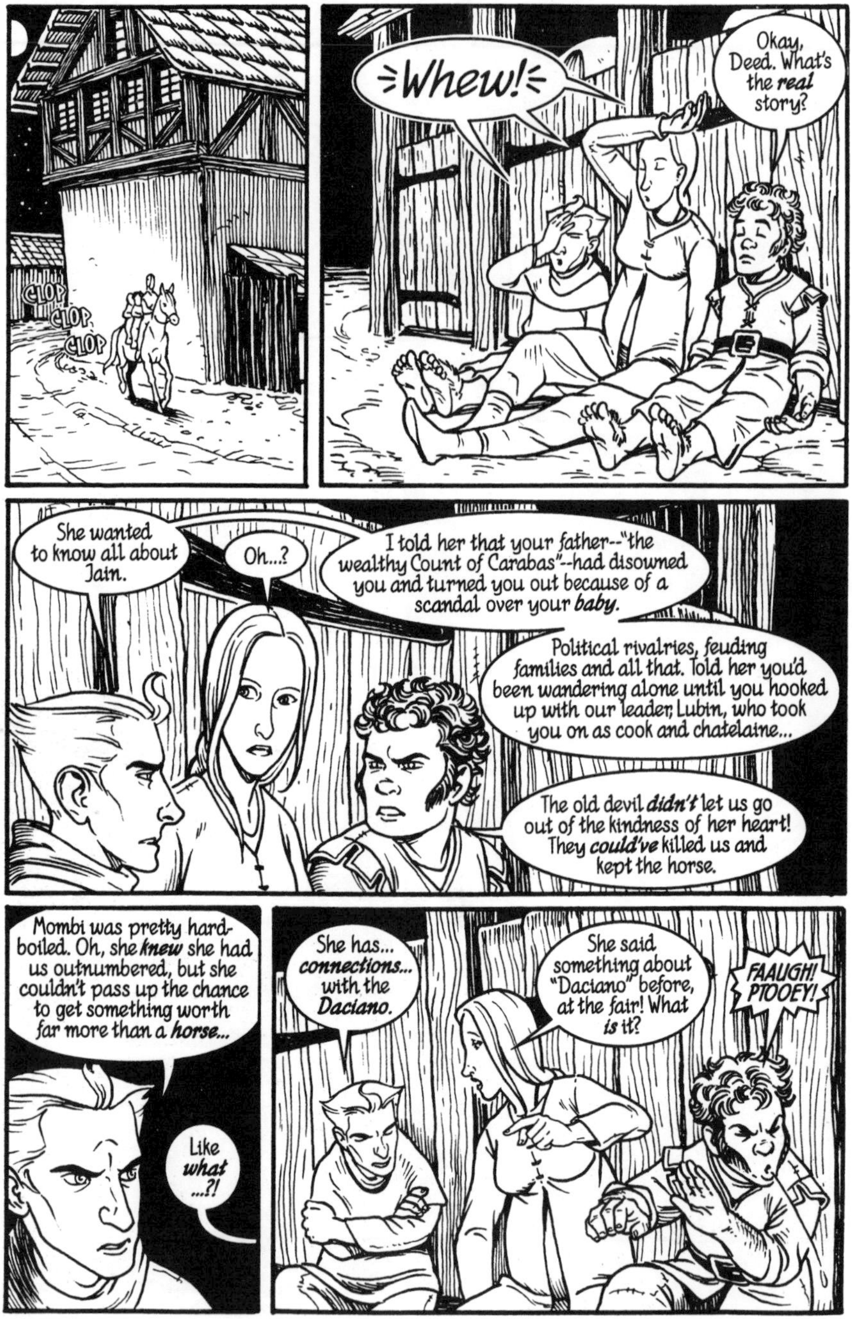
CLOP
CLOP
CLOP
Whew!
Okay, Deed. What's the *real* story?
She wanted to know all about Jain.
Oh...?
I told her that your father--"the wealthy Count of Carabas"--had disowned you and turned you out because of a scandal over your *baby*.
Political rivalries, feuding families and all that. Told her you'd been wandering alone until you hooked up with our leader, Lubin, who took you on as cook and chatelaine...
The old devil *didn't* let us go out of the kindness of her heart! They *could've* killed us and kept the horse.
Mombi was pretty hard-boiled. Oh, she *knew* she had us outnumbered, but she couldn't pass up the chance to get something worth far more than a *horse*...
Like *what* ...?!
She has... *connections*... with the *Daciano*.
She said something about "Daciano" before, at the fair! What *is* it?
FAAUGH! PTOOEY!

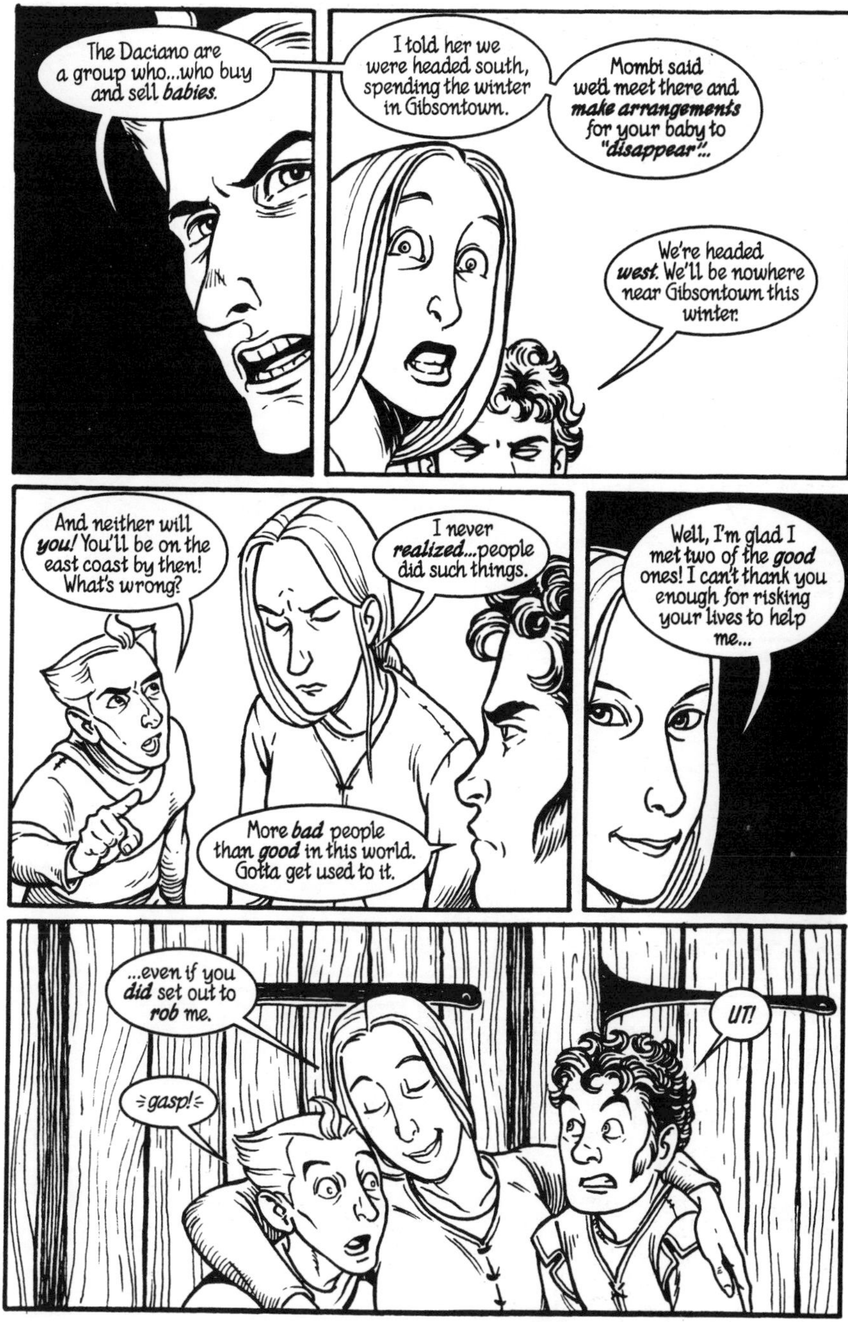
The Daciano are a group who...who buy and sell *babies*.
I told her we were headed south, spending the winter in Gibsontown.
Mombi said we'd meet there and *make arrangements* for your baby to "*disappear*"...
We're headed *west*. We'll be nowhere near Gibsontown this winter.
And neither will *you!* You'll be on the east coast by then! What's wrong?
I never *realized*...people did such things.
More *bad* people than *good* in this world. Gotta get used to it.
Well, I'm glad I met two of the *good* ones! I can't thank you enough for risking your lives to help me...
...even if you *did* set out to *rob* me.
UT!
gasp!

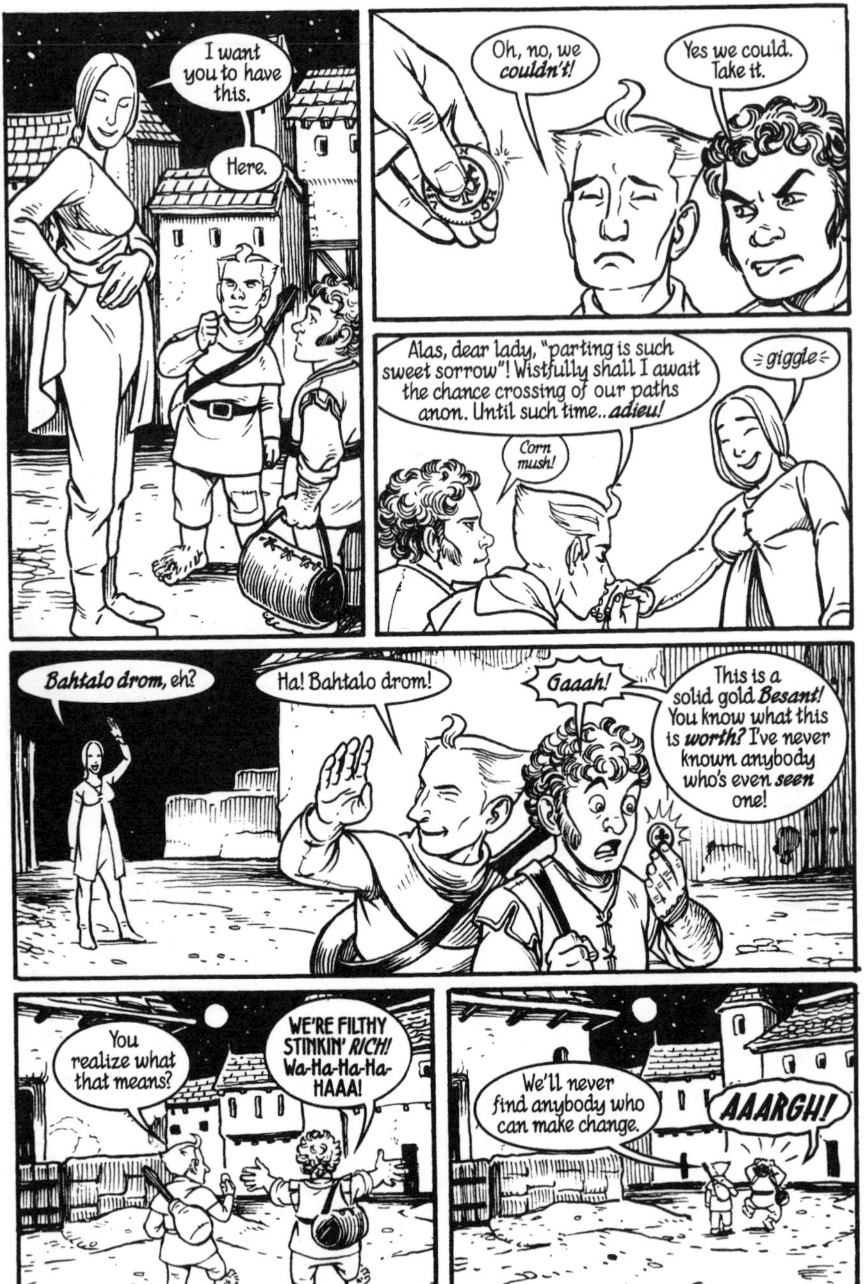
I want you to have this.
Here.
Oh, no, we couldn't!
Yes we could. Take it.
Alas, dear lady, "parting is such sweet sorrow"! Wistfully shall I await the chance crossing of our paths anon. Until such time... adieu!
giggle
Corn mush!
Bahtalo drom, eh?
Ha! Bahtalo drom!
Gaaah!
This is a solid gold Besant! You know what this is worth? I've never known anybody who's even seen one!
You realize what that means?
WE'RE FILTHY STINKIN' RICH! Wa-Ha-Ha-Ha-HAAA!
We'll never find anybody who can make change.
AAARGH!

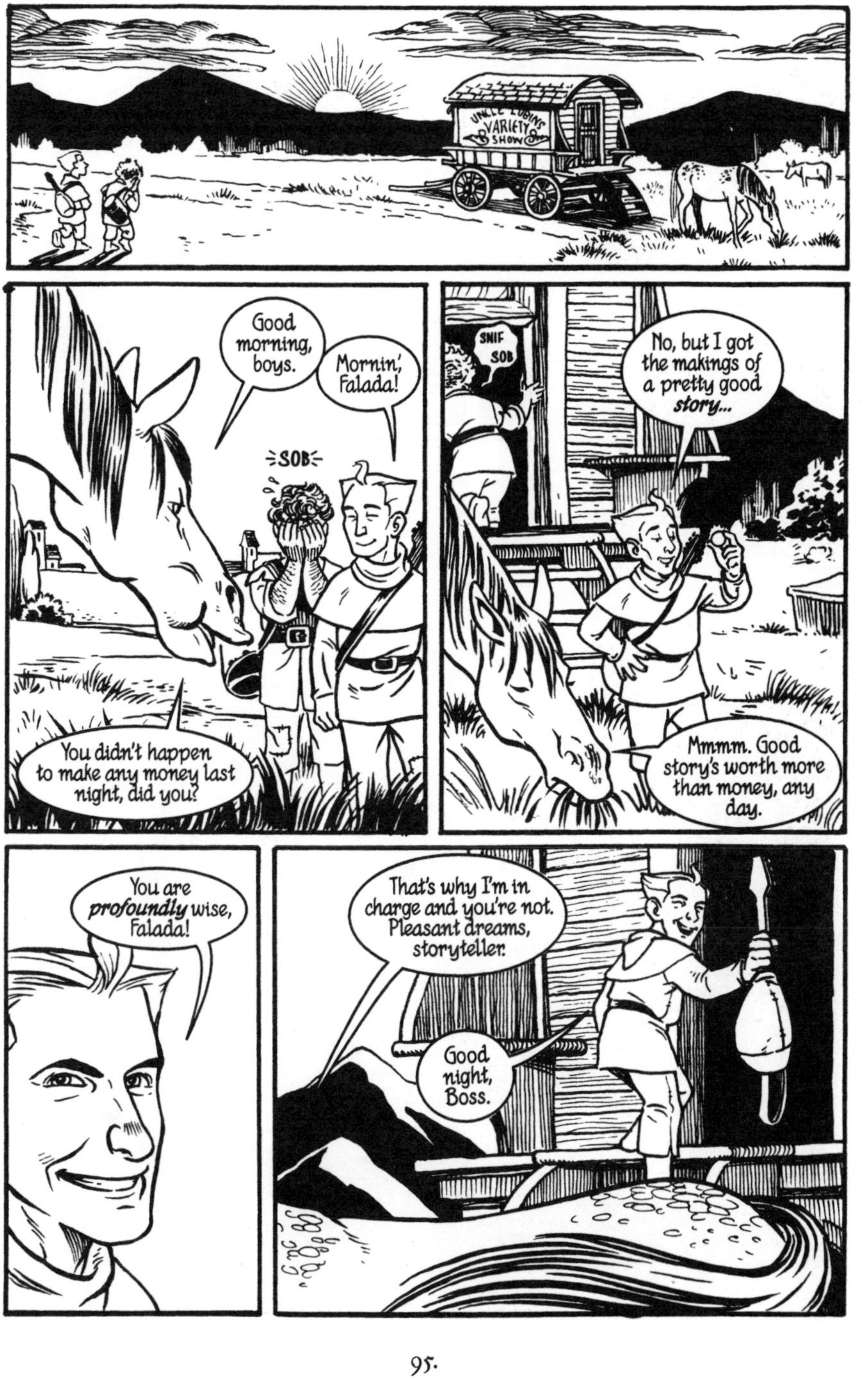
UNCLE LUBIN'S VARIETY SHOW
Good morning, boys.
Mornin', Falada!
SOB
You didn't happen to make any money last night, did you?
SNIF SOB
No, but I got the makings of a pretty good *story...*
Mmmm. Good story's worth more than money, any day.
You are *profoundly* wise, Falada!
That's why I'm in charge and you're not. Pleasant dreams, storyteller.
Good night, Boss.

rom: gypsy	*chavo:* boy
rahnie: great lady	*gorgio:* non-gypsy
graiengeri: horsetrader	*bahtalo drom:* "lucky road"

Chapter 5.

· YOUR CASTLE IS YOUR HOME ·

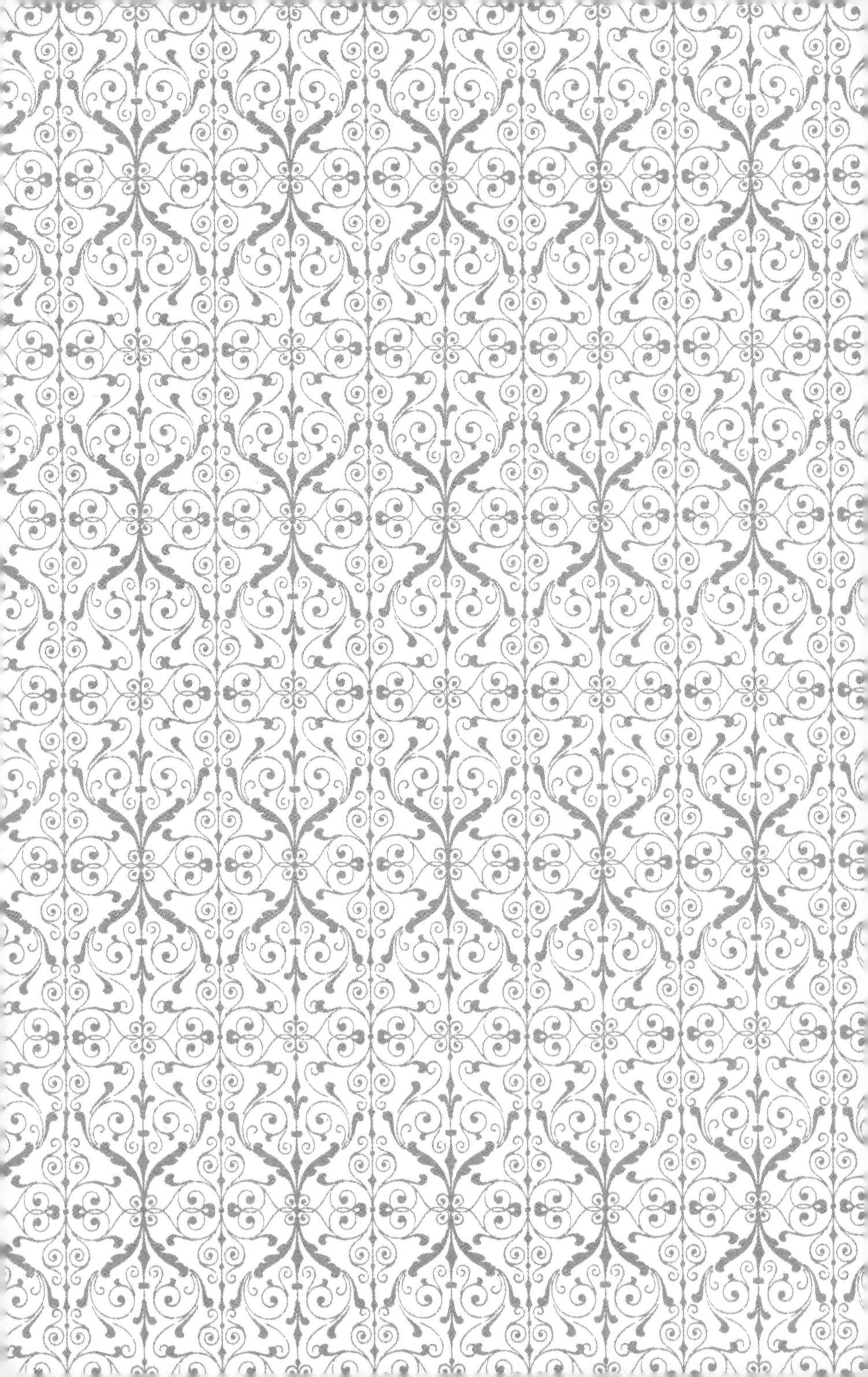

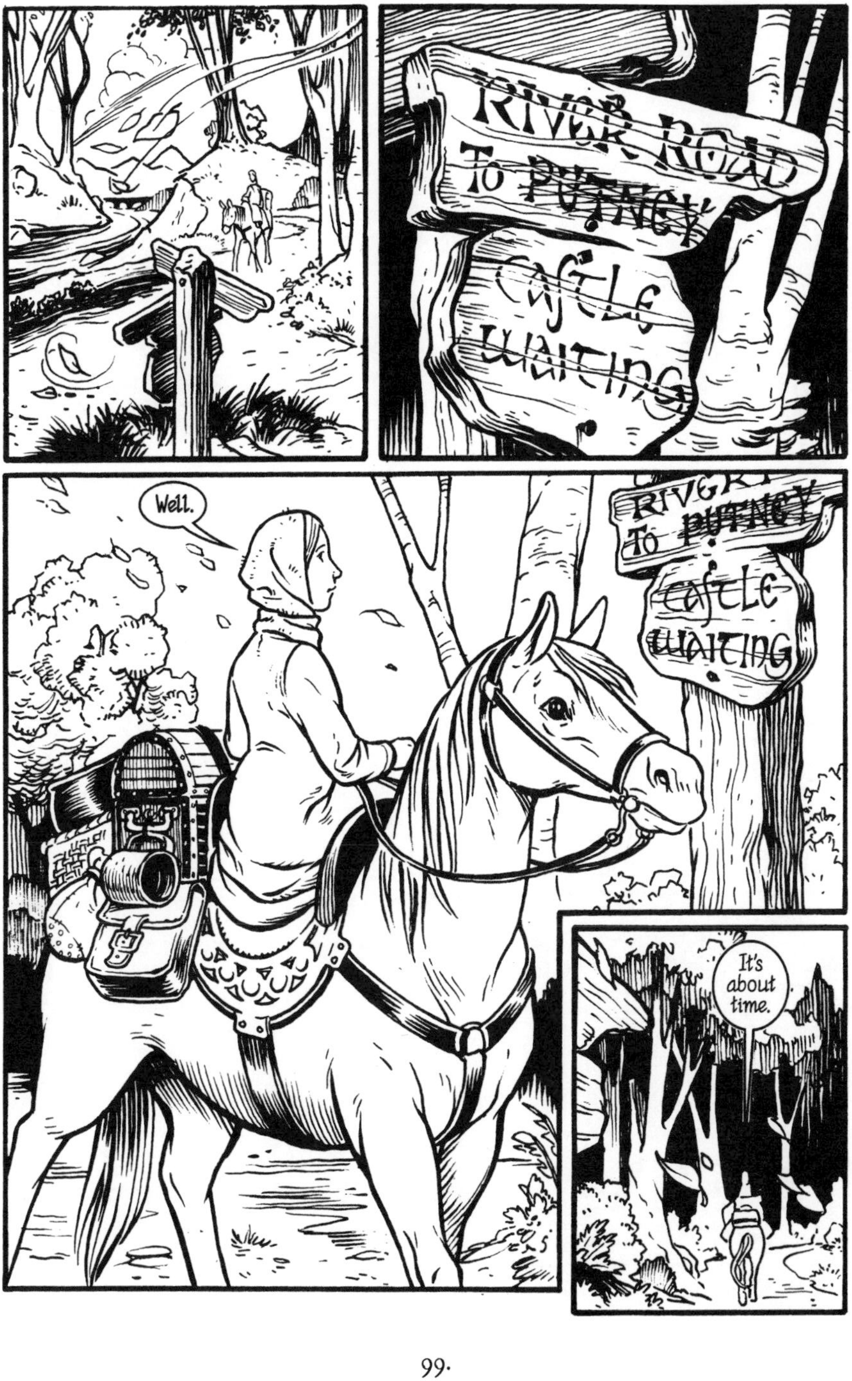
RIVER ROAD
TO PUTNEY
CASTLE
WAITING
Well.
RIVER
TO PUTNEY
CASTLE
WAITING
It's about time.

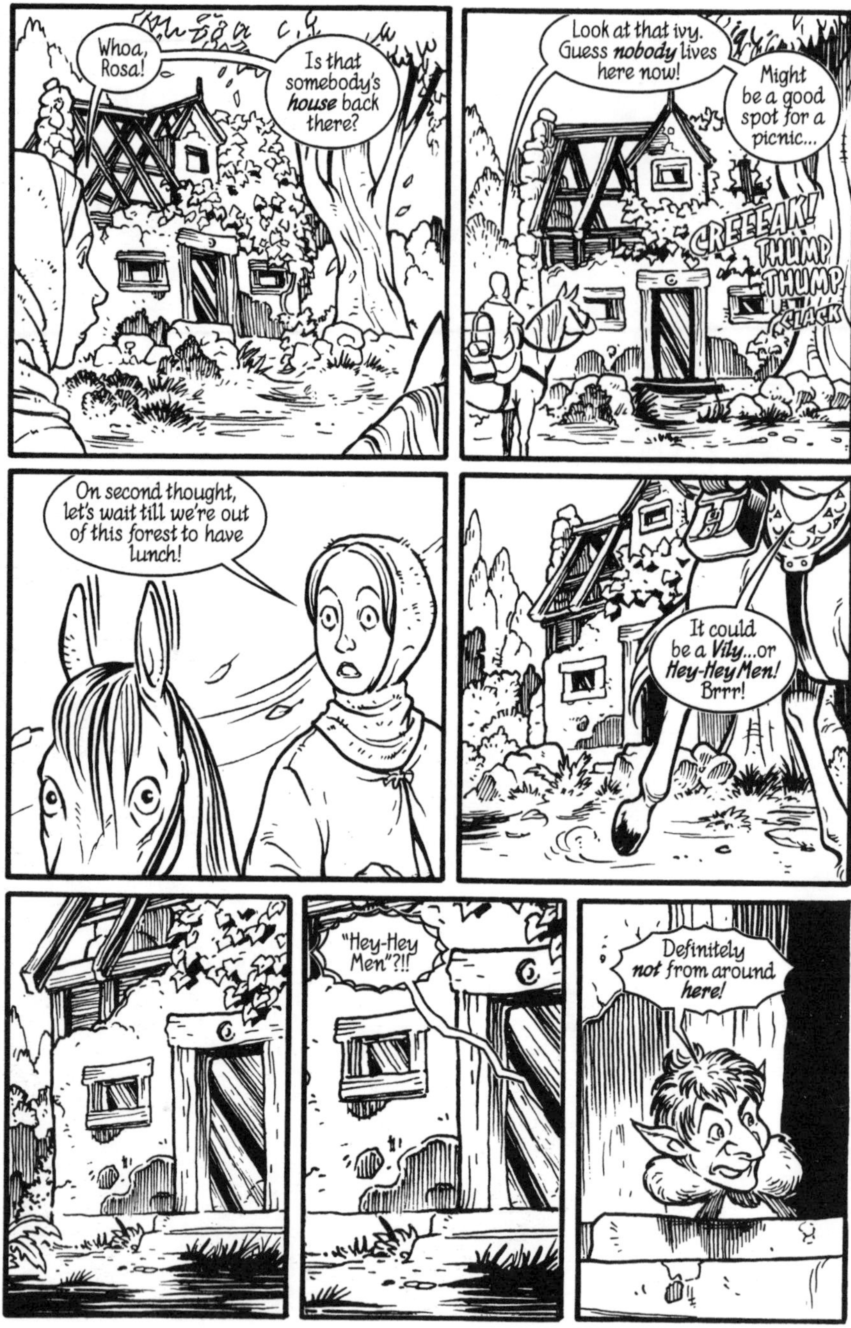
Whoa, Rosa!
Is that somebody's **house** back there?
Look at that ivy. Guess **nobody** lives here now!
Might be a good spot for a picnic...
CREEEAK!
THUMP
THUMP
CLACK
On second thought, let's wait till we're out of this forest to have lunch!
It could be a ***Vily***...or ***Hey-Hey Men!*** Brrr!
"Hey-Hey Men"?!!
Definitely ***not*** from around ***here!***

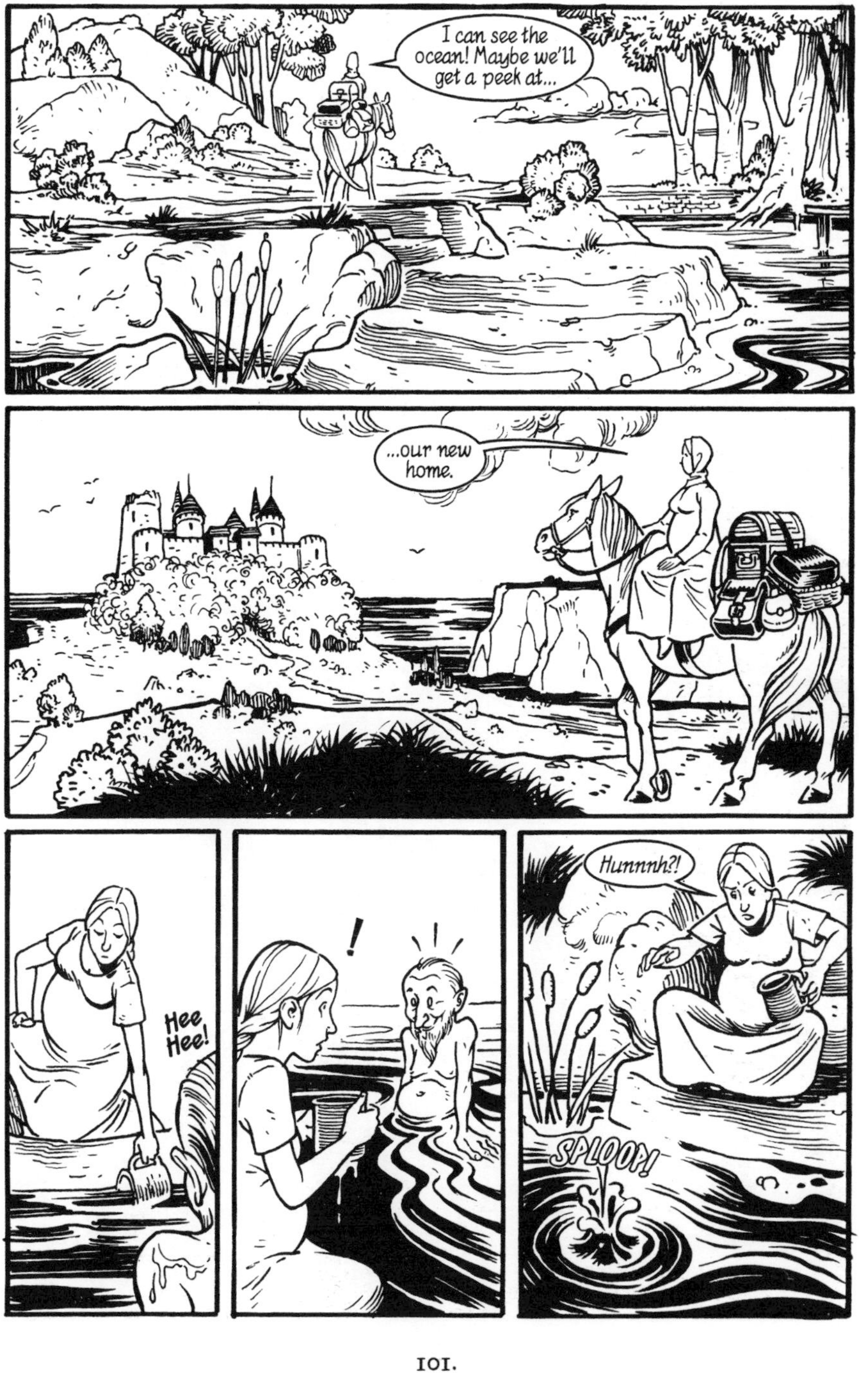
I can see the ocean! Maybe we'll get a peek at...
...our new home.
Hee Hee!
!
Hunnnh?!
SPLOOP!

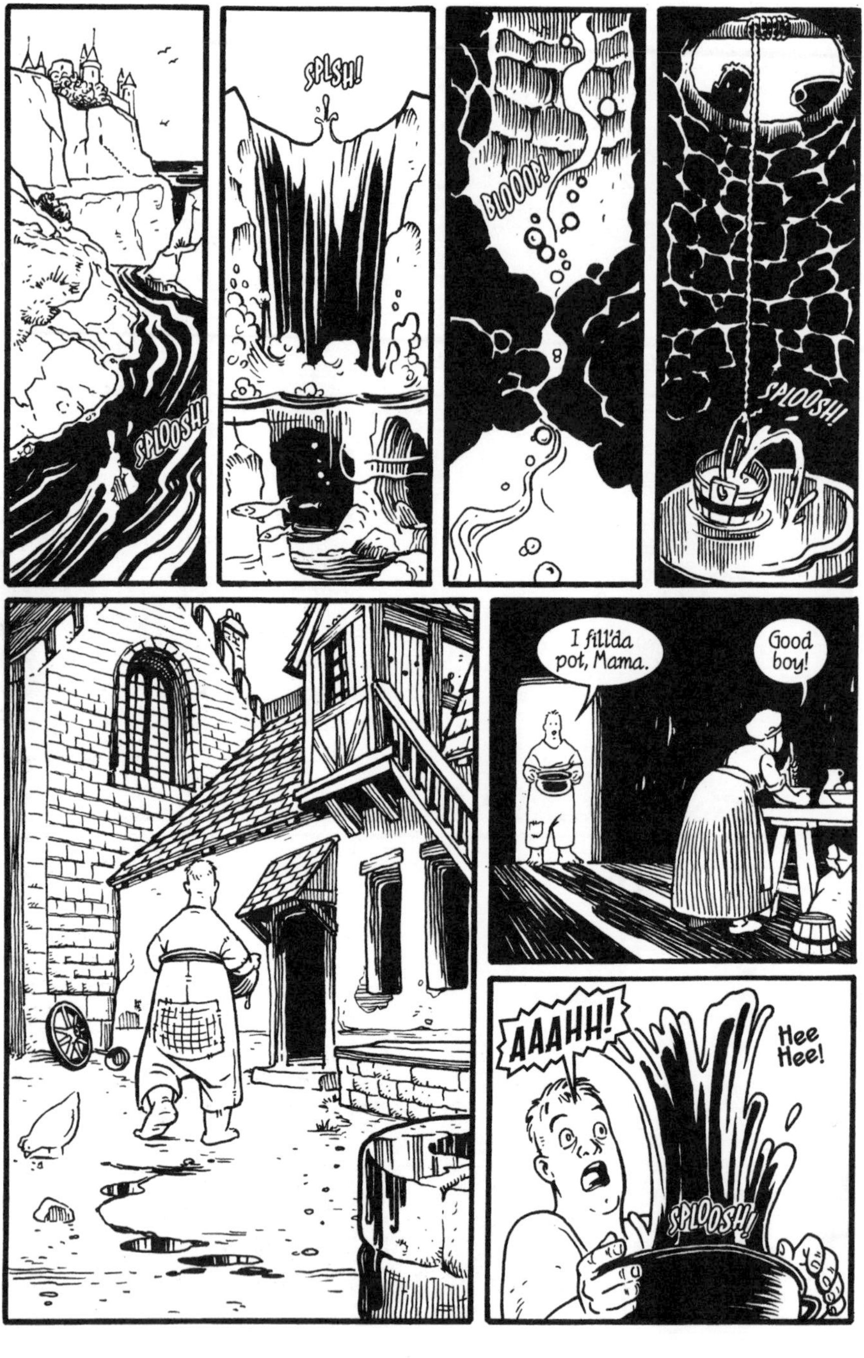
SPLOOSH!
SPLSH!
BLOOOP!
SPLOOSH!
I fill'da pot, Mama.
Good boy!
AAAHH!
Hee Hee!
SPLOOSH!

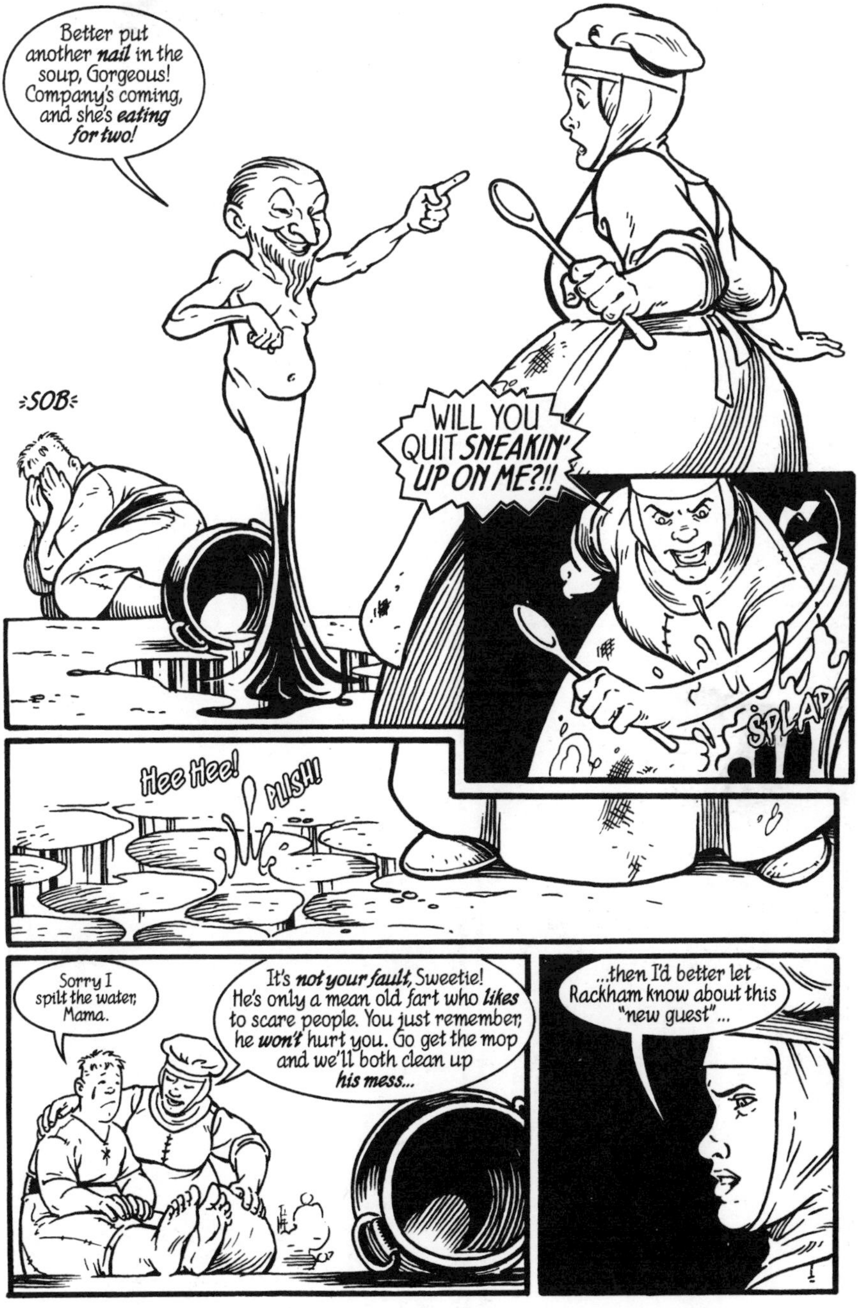
Better put another *nail* in the soup, Gorgeous! Company's coming, and she's *eating for two!*
SOB
WILL YOU QUIT *SNEAKIN'* UP ON ME?!!
SPLAP
Hee Hee!
PLISH!
Sorry I spilt the water, Mama.
It's *not your fault,* Sweetie! He's only a mean old fart who *likes* to scare people. You just remember, he *won't* hurt you. Go get the mop and we'll both clean up *his mess...*
...then I'd better let Rackham know about this "new guest"...

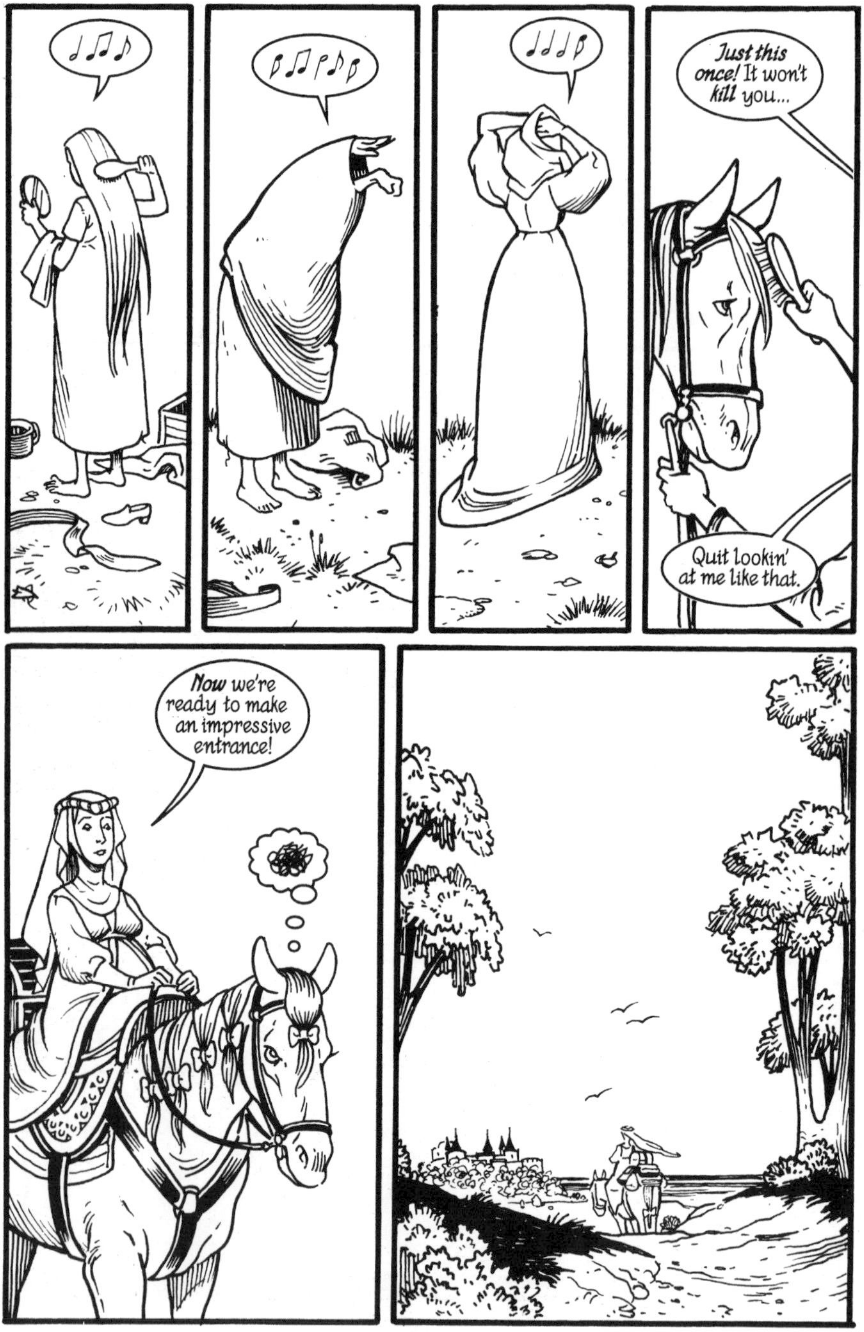
Just this once! It won't kill you...
Quit lookin' at me like that.
Now we're ready to make an impressive entrance!

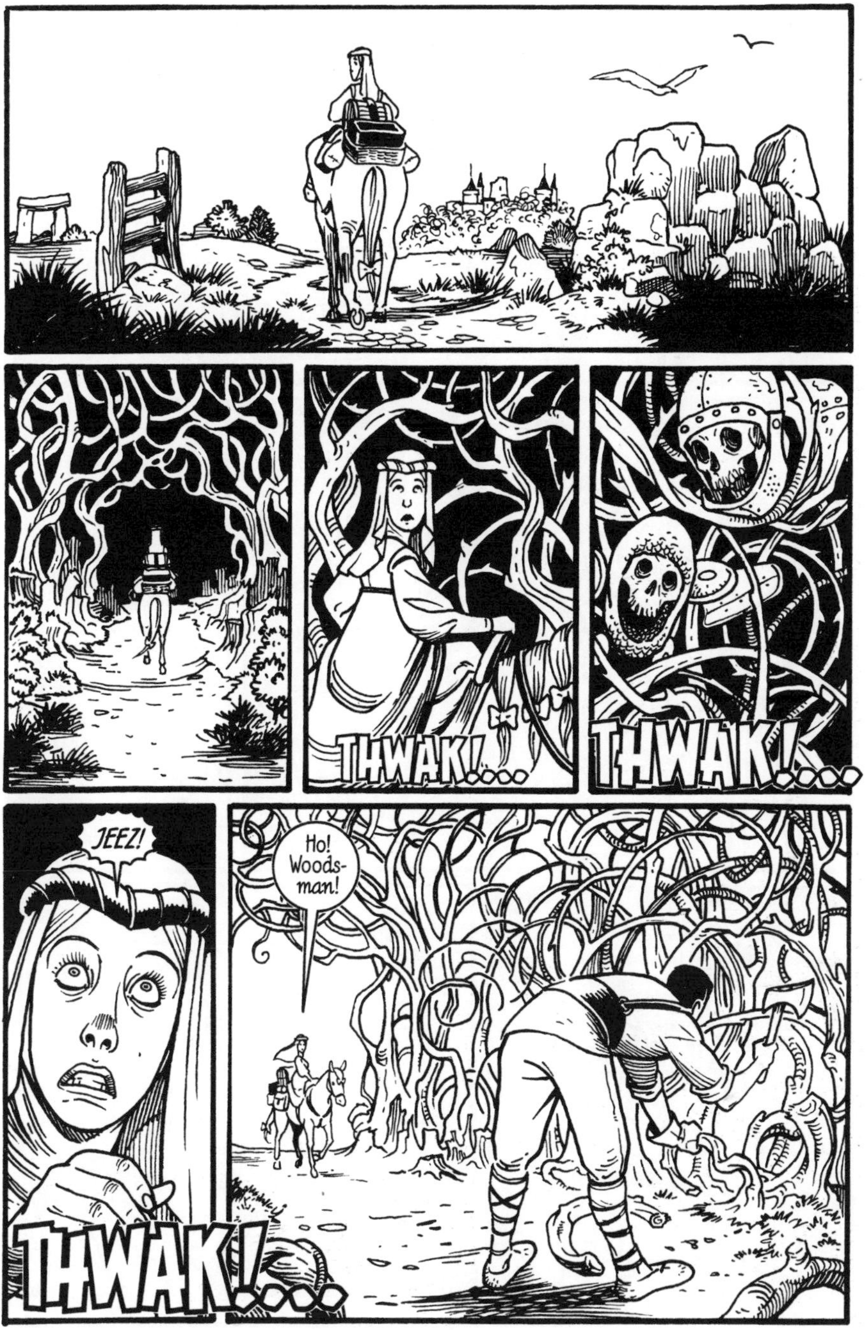
THWAK!....
THWAK!....
JEEZ!
THWAK!....
Ho! Woods-man!

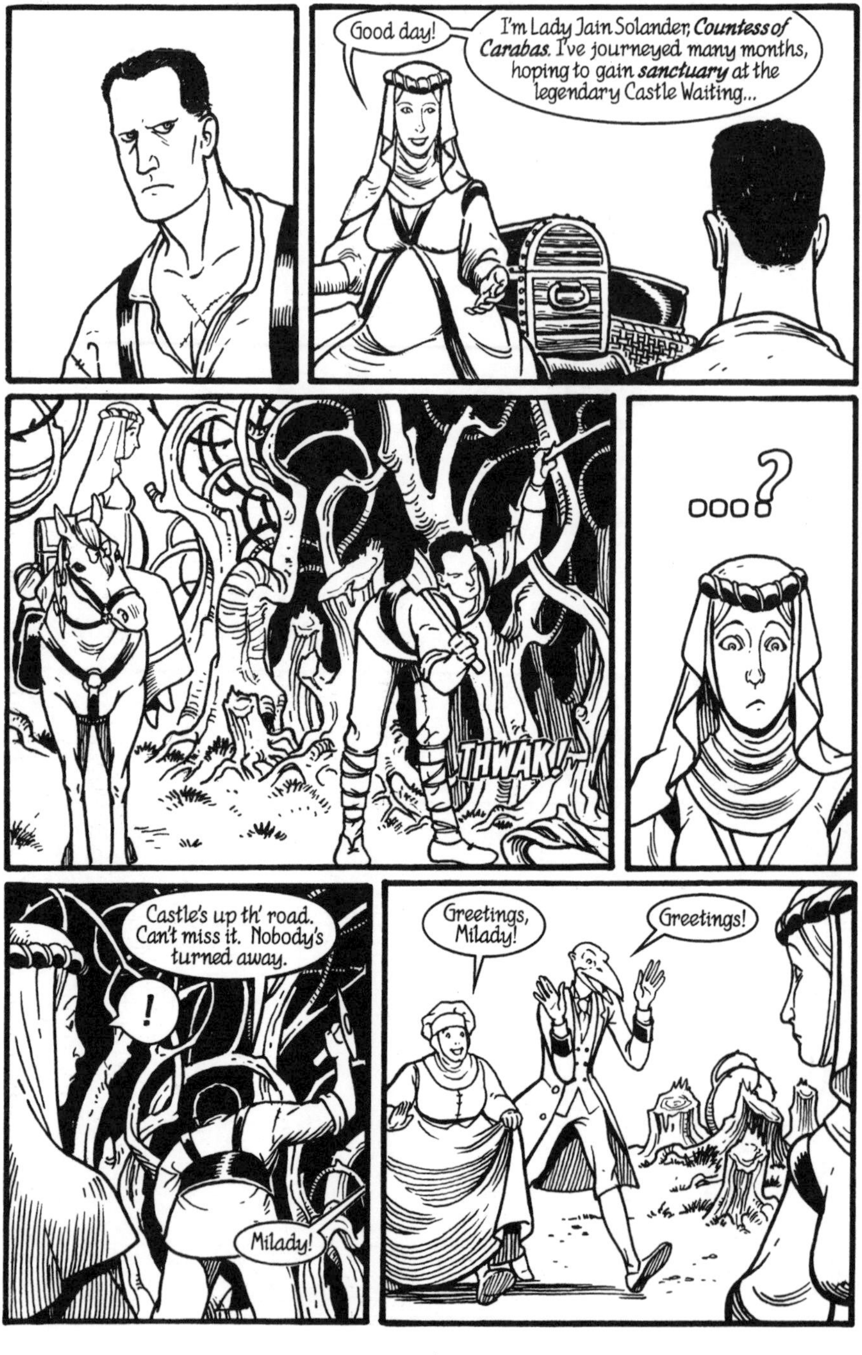
Good day!
I'm Lady Jain Solander, *Countess of Carabas.* I've journeyed many months, hoping to gain *sanctuary* at the legendary Castle Waiting...
THWAK!
...?
Castle's up th' road. Can't miss it. Nobody's turned away.
!
Milady!
Greetings, Milady!
Greetings!

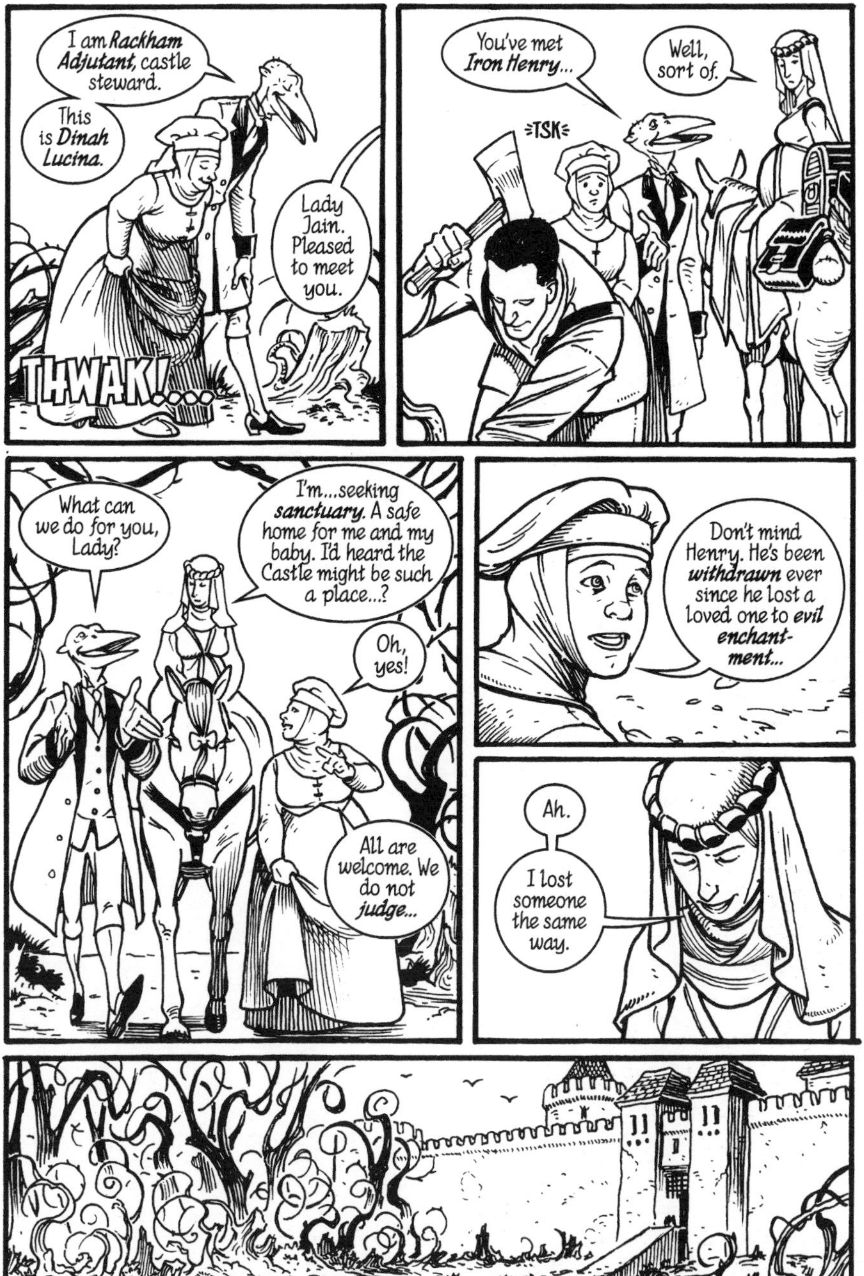
I am *Rackham Adjutant*, castle steward.
This is *Dinah Lucina*.
Lady Jain. Pleased to meet you.
THWAK!...
You've met *Iron Henry*...
Well, sort of.
TSK
What can we do for you, Lady?
I'm...seeking *sanctuary*. A safe home for me and my baby. I'd heard the Castle might be such a place...?
Oh, yes!
All are welcome. We do not *judge*...
Don't mind Henry. He's been *withdrawn* ever since he lost a loved one to *evil enchant-ment*...
Ah.
I lost someone the same way.

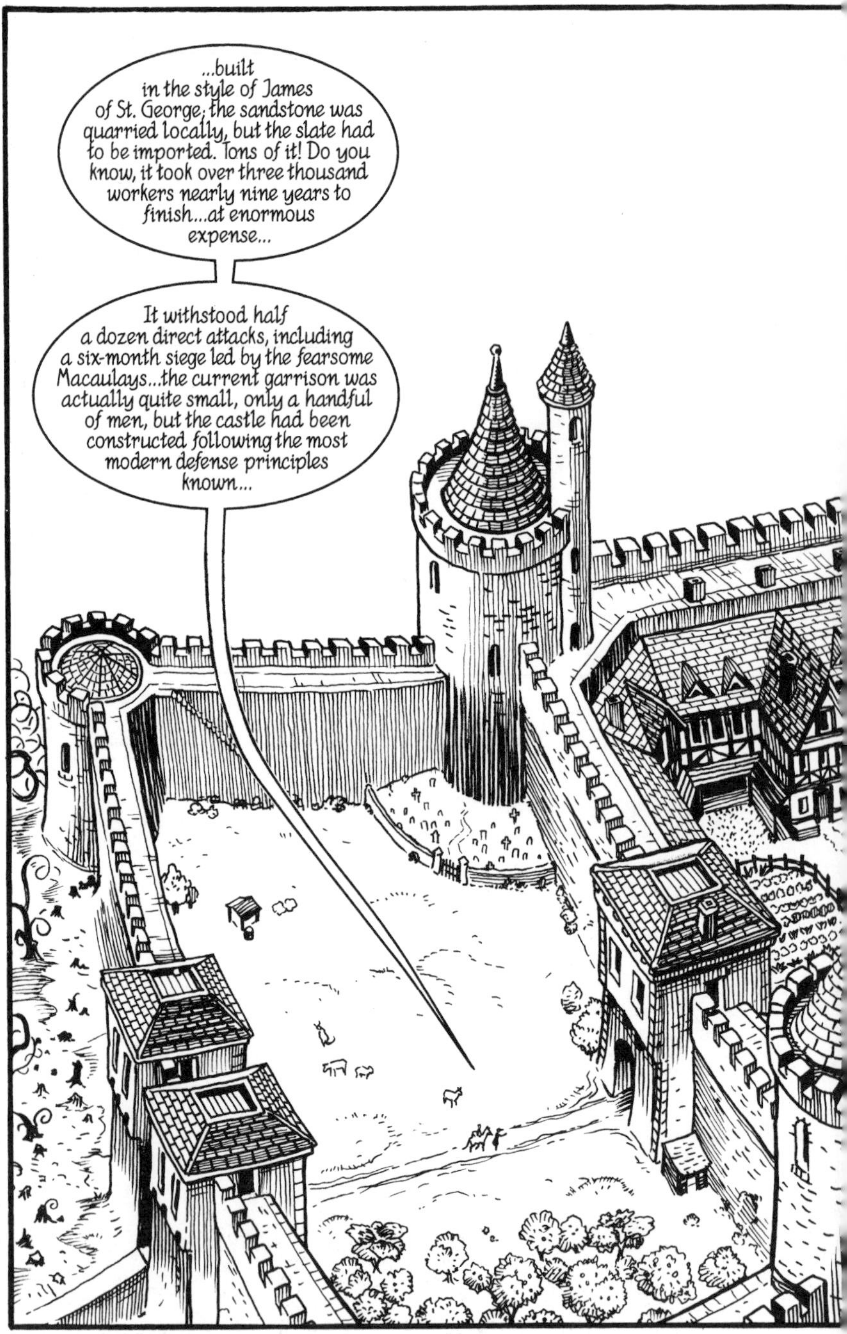
...built in the style of James of St. George; the sandstone was quarried locally, but the slate had to be imported. Tons of it! Do you know, it took over three thousand workers nearly nine years to finish...at enormous expense...
It withstood half a dozen direct attacks, including a six-month siege led by the fearsome Macaulays...the current garrison was actually quite small, only a handful of men, but the castle had been constructed following the most modern defense principles known...

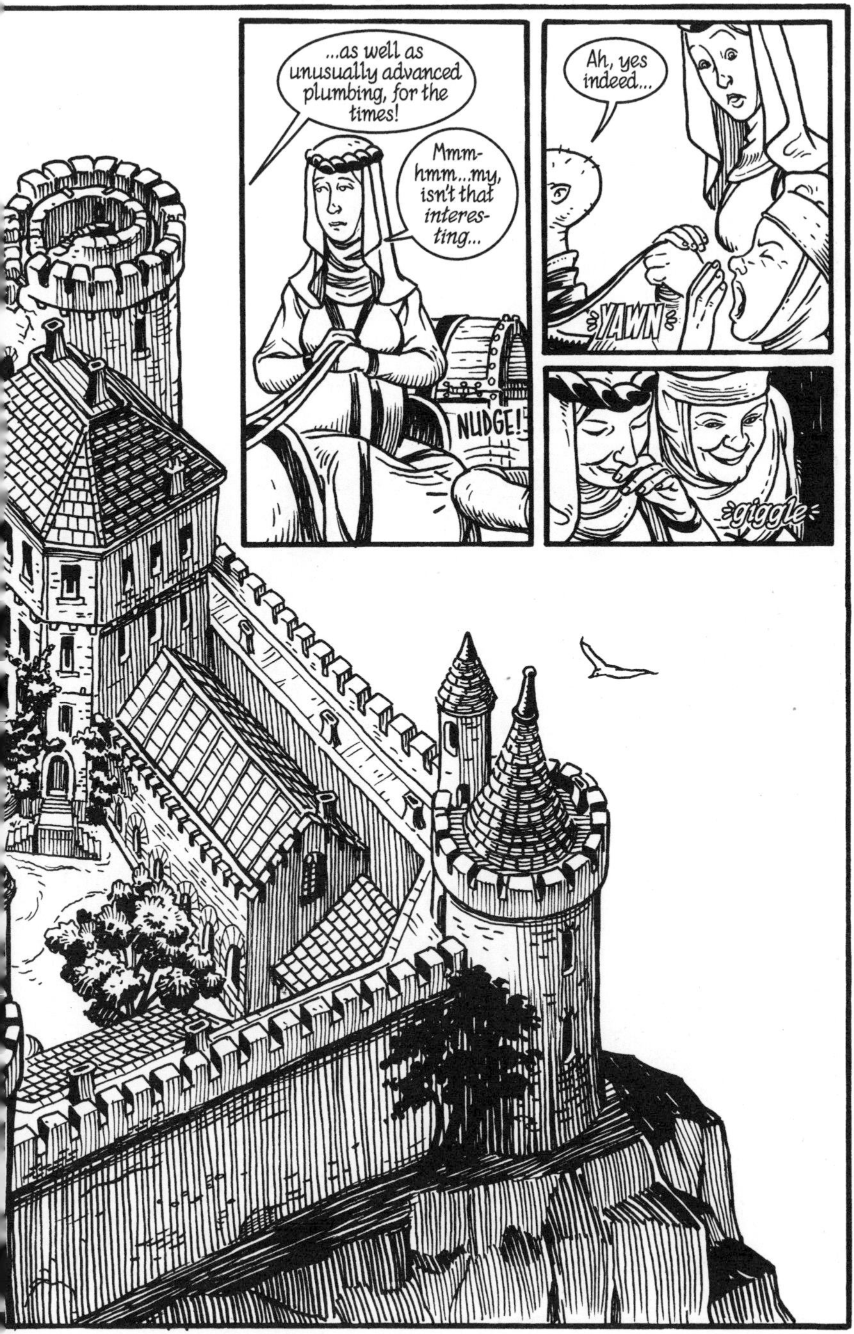

...as well as unusually advanced plumbing, for the times!
Mmm-hmm...my, isn't that interes-ting...
NUDGE!
Ah, yes indeed...
YAWN
giggle

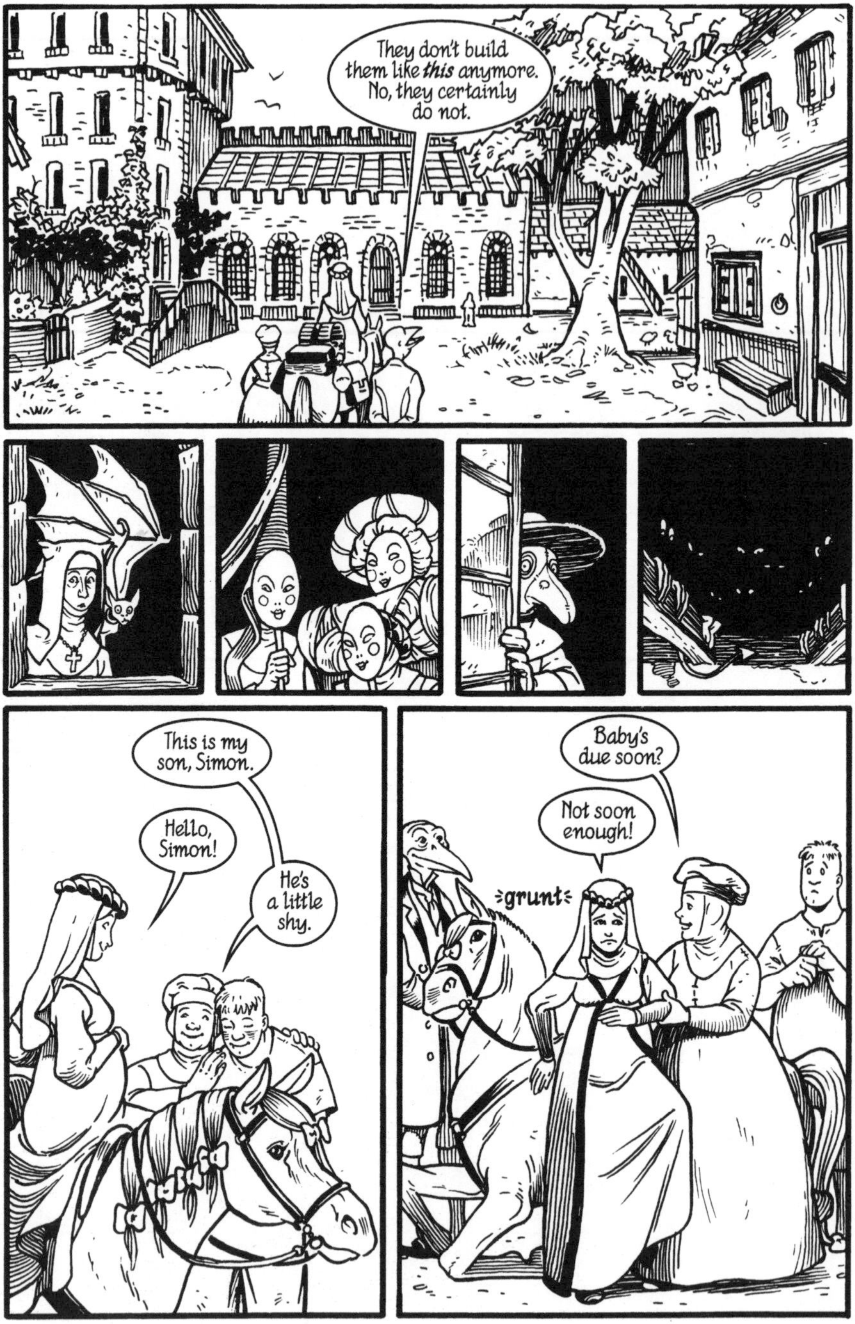
They don't build them like *this* anymore. No, they certainly do not.
This is my son, Simon.
Hello, Simon!
He's a little shy.
Baby's due soon?
Not soon enough!
grunt

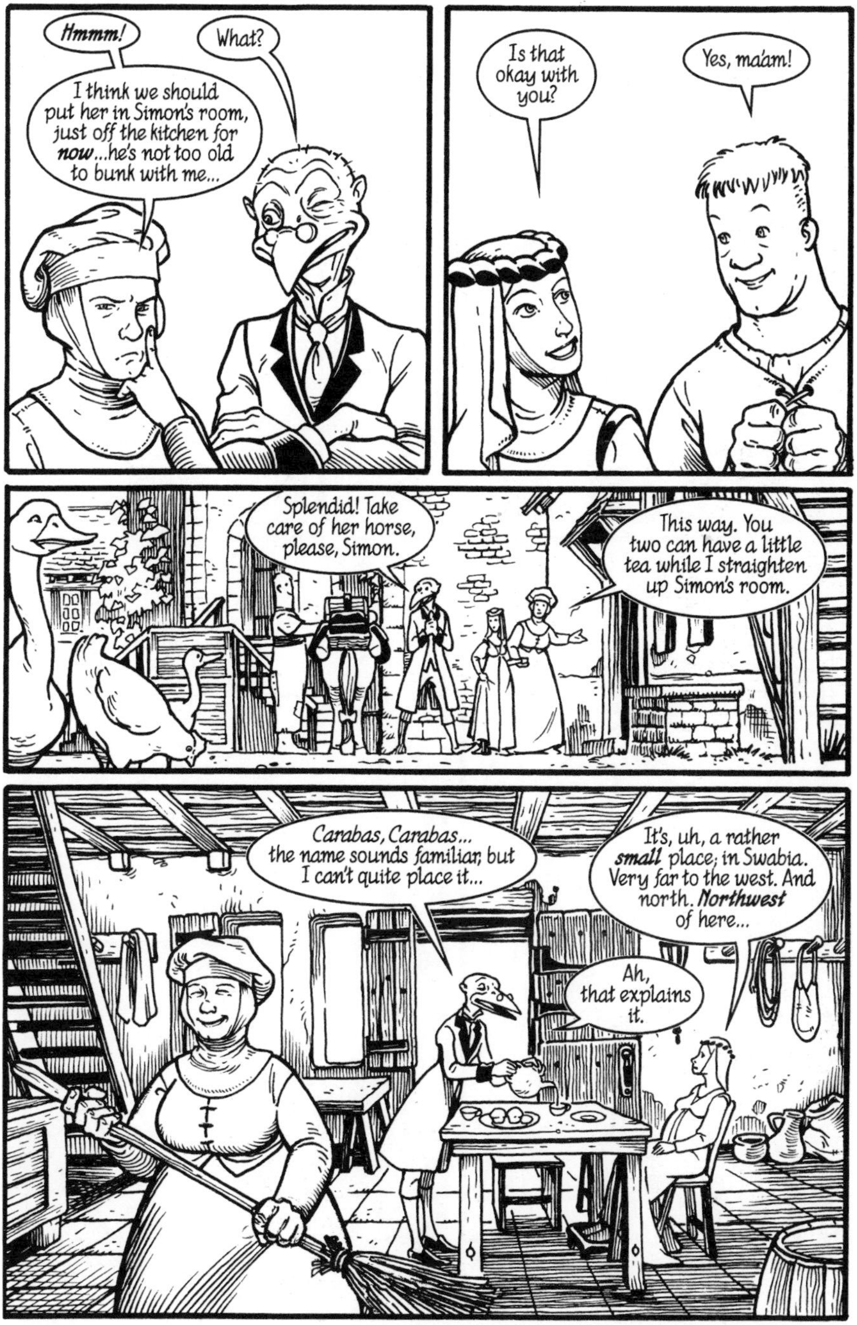
Hmmm!
What?
I think we should put her in Simon's room, just off the kitchen for **now**...he's not too old to bunk with me...
Is that okay with you?
Yes, ma'am!
Splendid! Take care of her horse, please, Simon.
This way. You two can have a little tea while I straighten up Simon's room.
Carabas, Carabas... the name sounds familiar, but I can't quite place it...
It's, uh, a rather **small** place; in Swabia. Very far to the west. And north. ***Northwest*** of here...
Ah, that explains it.

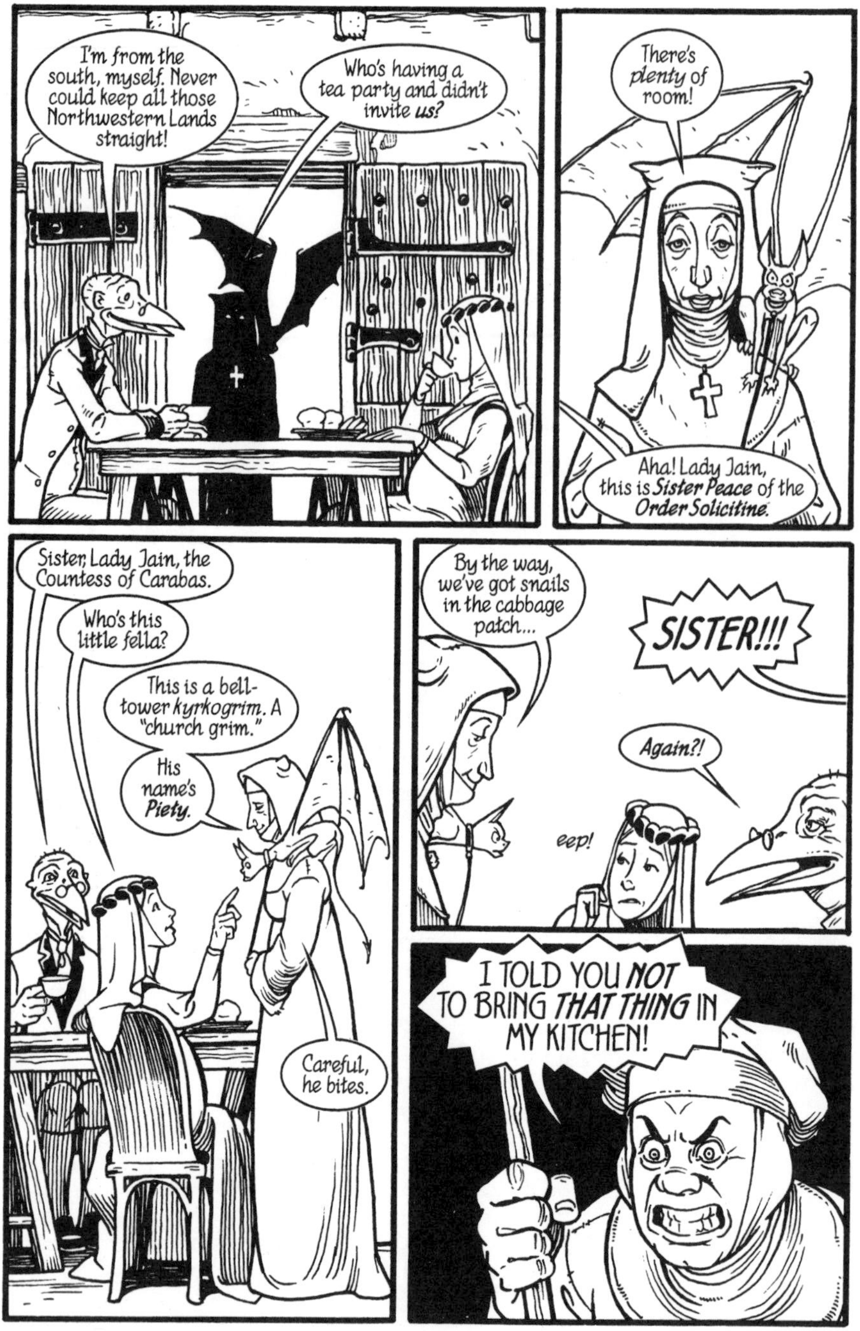
I'm from the south, myself. Never could keep all those Northwestern Lands straight!
Who's having a tea party and didn't invite *us?*
There's *plenty* of room!
Aha! Lady Jain, this is ***Sister Peace*** of the ***Order Solicitine.***
Sister, Lady Jain, the Countess of Carabas.
Who's this little fella?
This is a bell-tower *kyrkogrim*. A "church grim."
His name's ***Piety.***
Careful, he bites.
By the way, we've got snails in the cabbage patch...
SISTER!!!
Again?!
eep!
I TOLD YOU *NOT* TO BRING *THAT THING* IN MY KITCHEN!

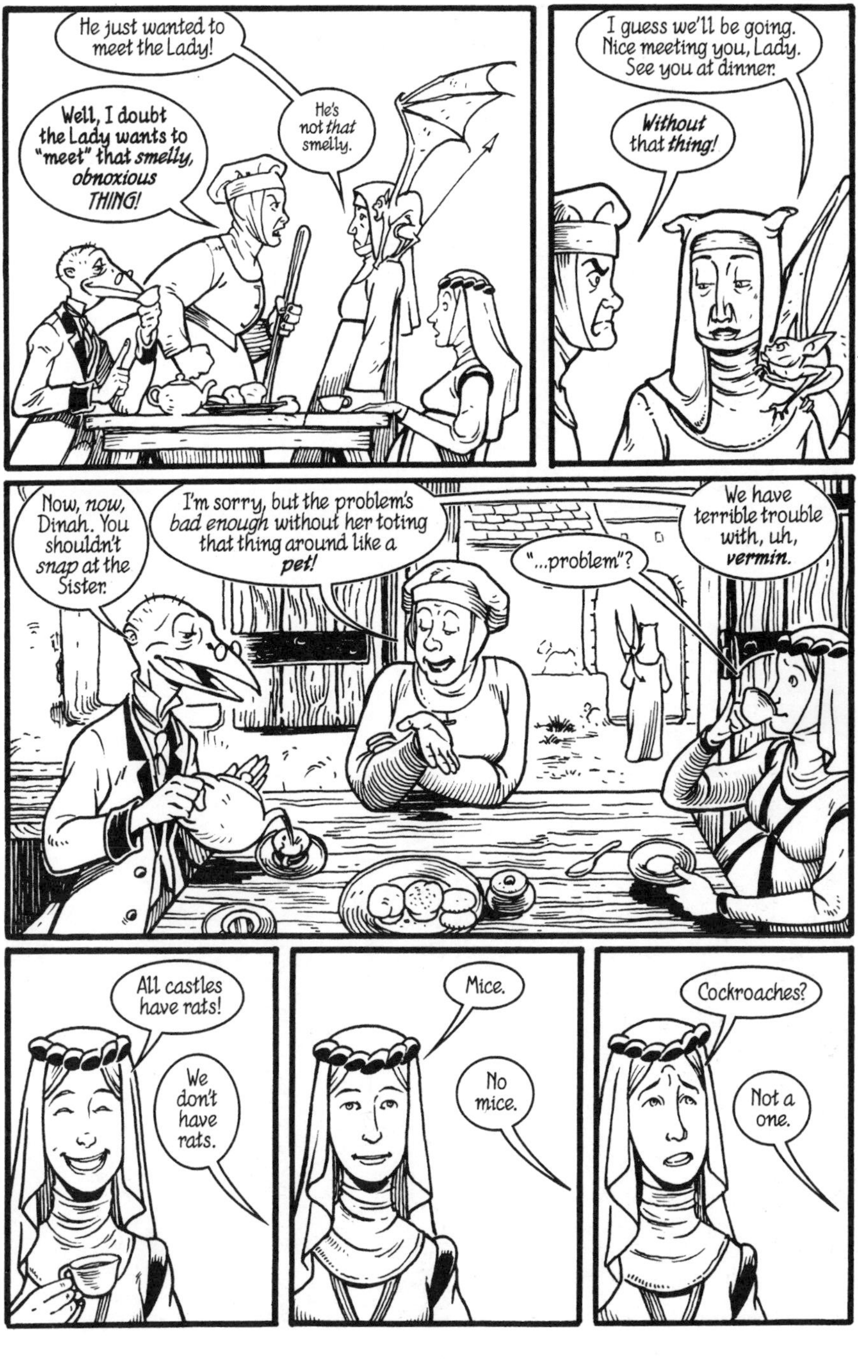
He just wanted to meet the Lady!
Well, I doubt the Lady wants to "meet" that *smelly*, *obnoxious* *THING!*
He's not *that* smelly.
I guess we'll be going. Nice meeting you, Lady. See you at dinner.
Without that ***thing!***
Now, *now*, Dinah. You shouldn't *snap* at the Sister.
I'm sorry, but the problem's *bad enough* without her toting that thing around like a ***pet!***
"...problem"?
We have terrible trouble with, uh, ***vermin.***
All castles have rats!
We don't have rats.
Mice.
No mice.
Cockroaches?
Not a one.

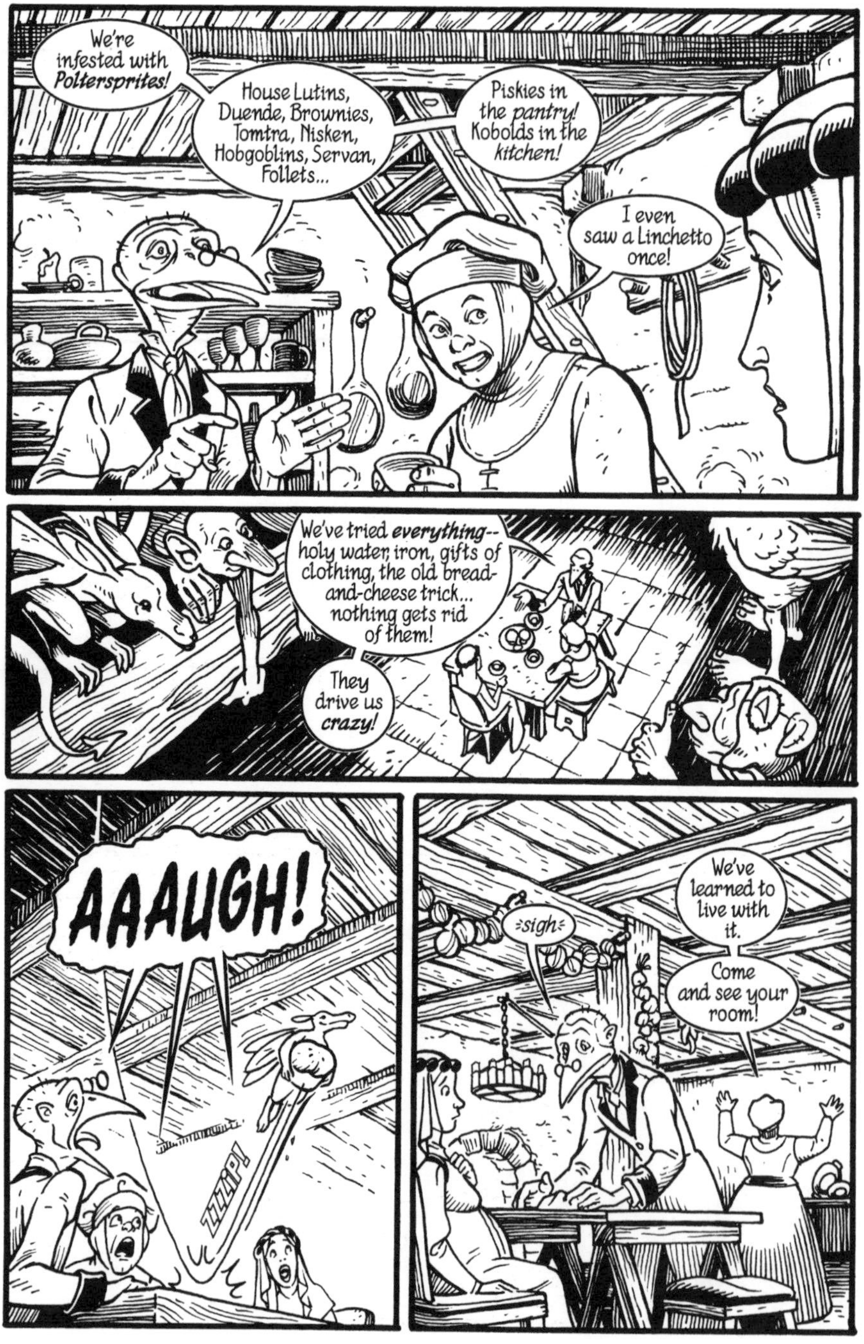
We're infested with *Poltersprites!*
House Lutins, Duende, Brownies, Tomtra, Nisken, Hobgoblins, Servan, Follets...
Piskies in the *pantry!* Kobolds in the *kitchen!*
I even saw a Linchetto once!
We've tried ***everything***-- holy water, iron, gifts of clothing, the old bread-and-cheese trick... nothing gets rid of them!
They drive us ***crazy!***
AAAUGH!
ZZZIP!
sigh
We've learned to live with it.
Come and see your room!

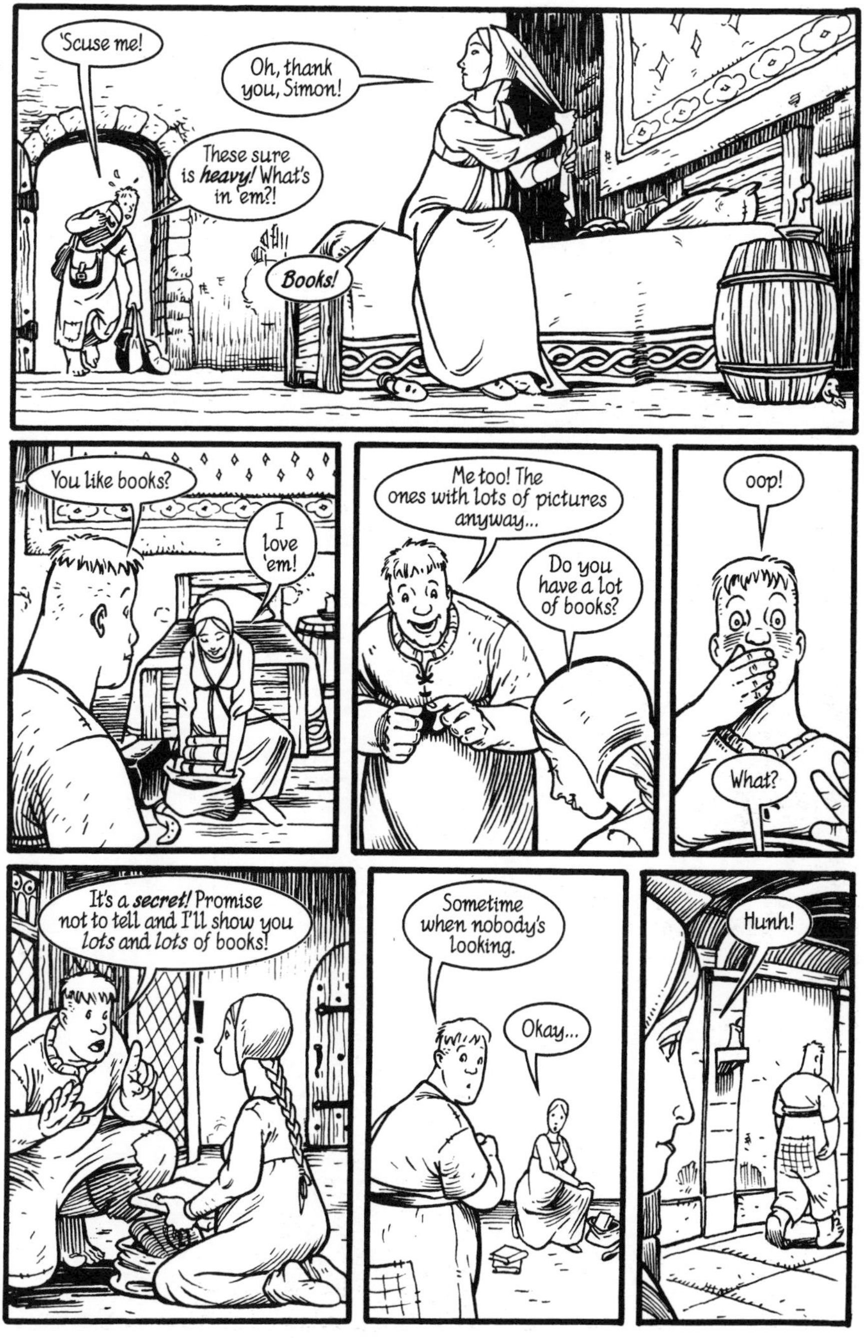
'Scuse me!
Oh, thank you, Simon!
These sure is *heavy!* What's in 'em?!
Books!
You like books?
I love 'em!
Me too! The ones with lots of pictures anyway...
Do you have a lot of books?
oop!
What?
It's a ***secret!*** Promise not to tell and I'll show you *lots and lots* of books!
Sometime when nobody's looking.
Okay...
Hunh!

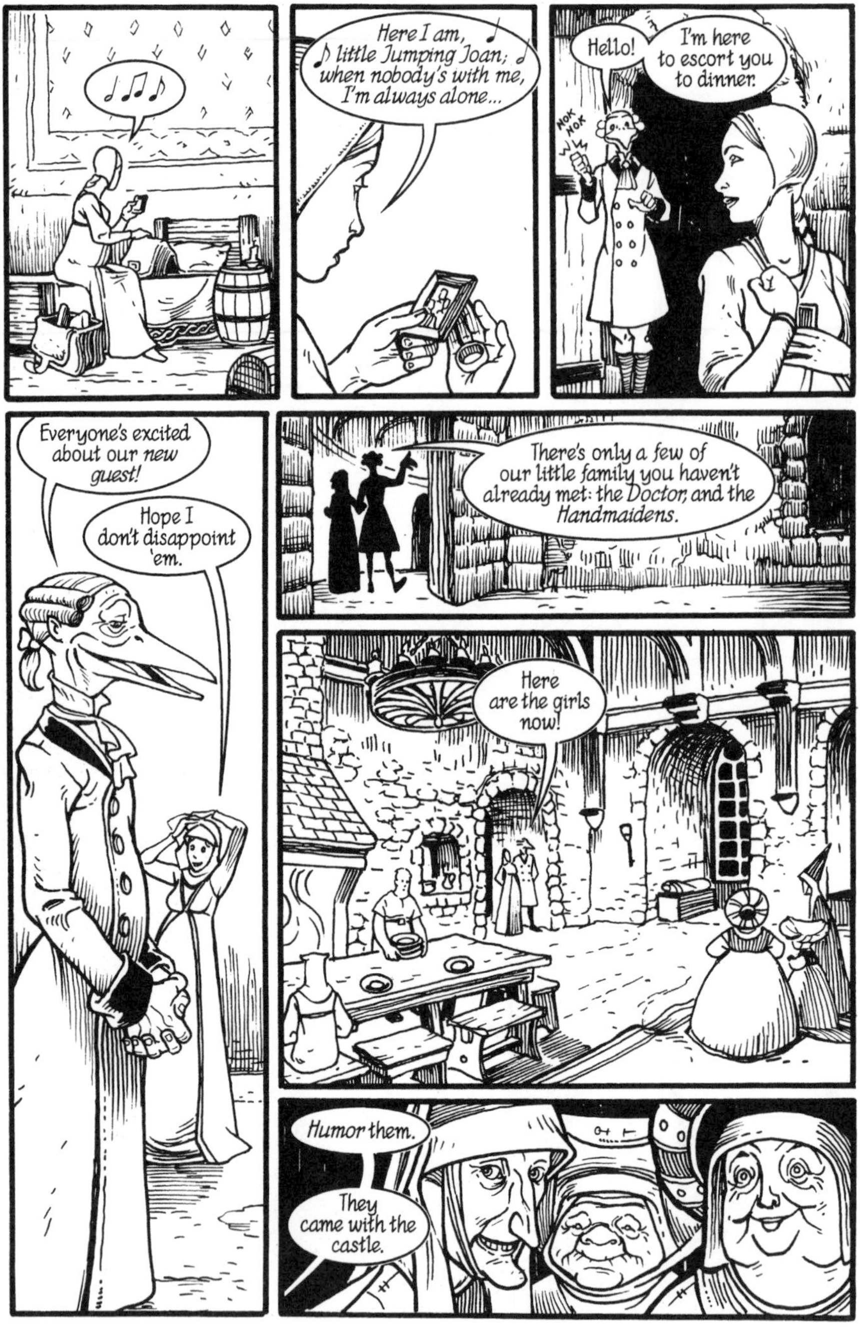
♪♫♪
Here I am, ♩ ♪ little Jumping Joan; ♩ when nobody's with me, I'm always alone...
Hello!
I'm here to escort you to dinner.
NOK NOK
Everyone's excited about our new guest!
Hope I don't disappoint 'em.
There's only a few of our little family you haven't already met: the Doctor, and the Handmaidens.
Here are the girls now!
Humor them.
They came with the castle.

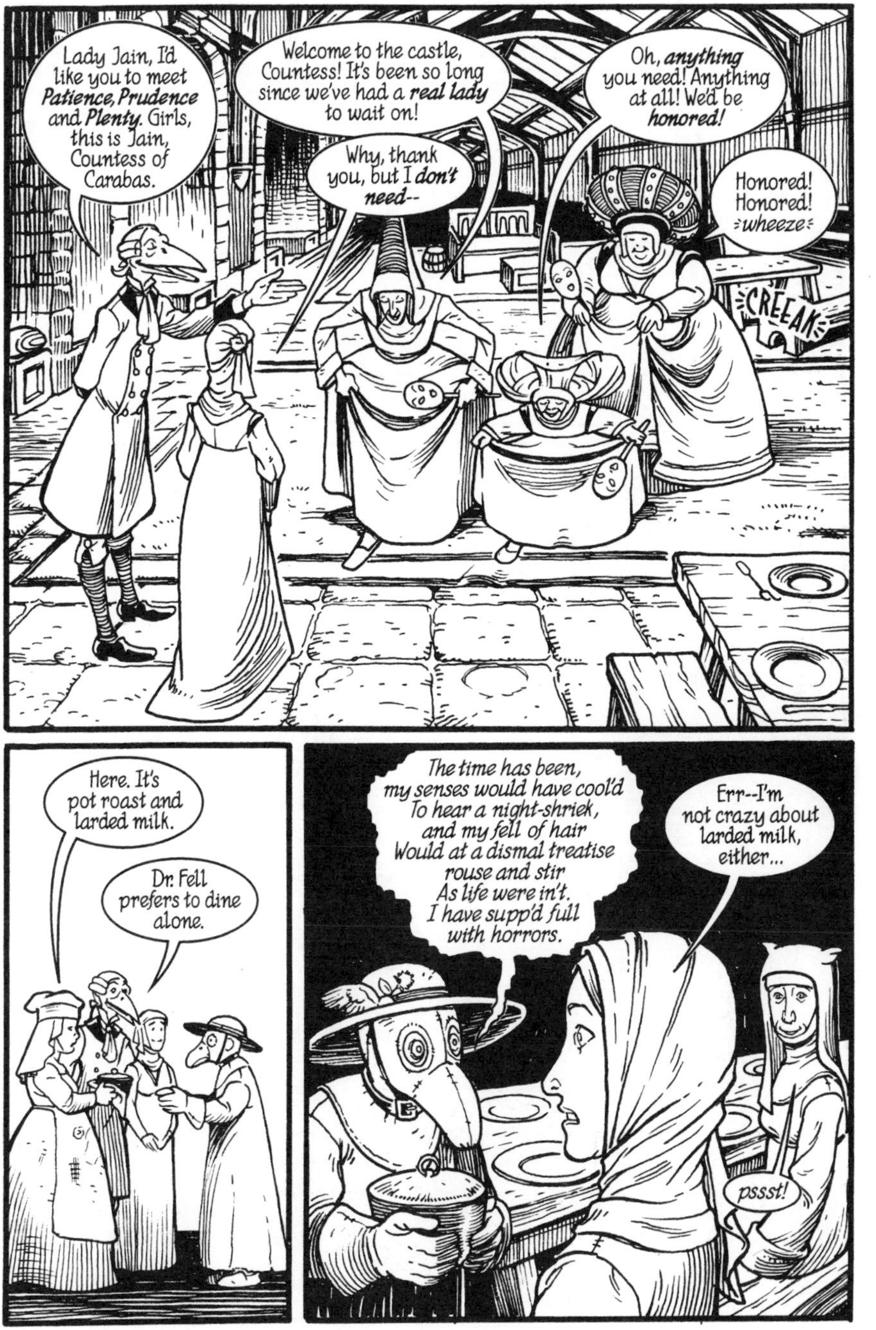
Lady Jain, I'd like you to meet **Patience, Prudence** and **Plenty**. Girls, this is Jain, Countess of Carabas.
Welcome to the castle, Countess! It's been so long since we've had a **real lady** to wait on!
Why, thank you, but I **don't need**--
Oh, **anything** you need! Anything at all! We'd be **honored!**
Honored! Honored! *wheeze*
CREEAK
Here. It's pot roast and larded milk.
Dr. Fell prefers to dine alone.
The time has been, my senses would have cool'd To hear a night-shriek, and my fell of hair Would at a dismal treatise rouse and stir As life were in't. I have supp'd full with horrors.
Err--I'm not crazy about larded milk, either...
pssst!

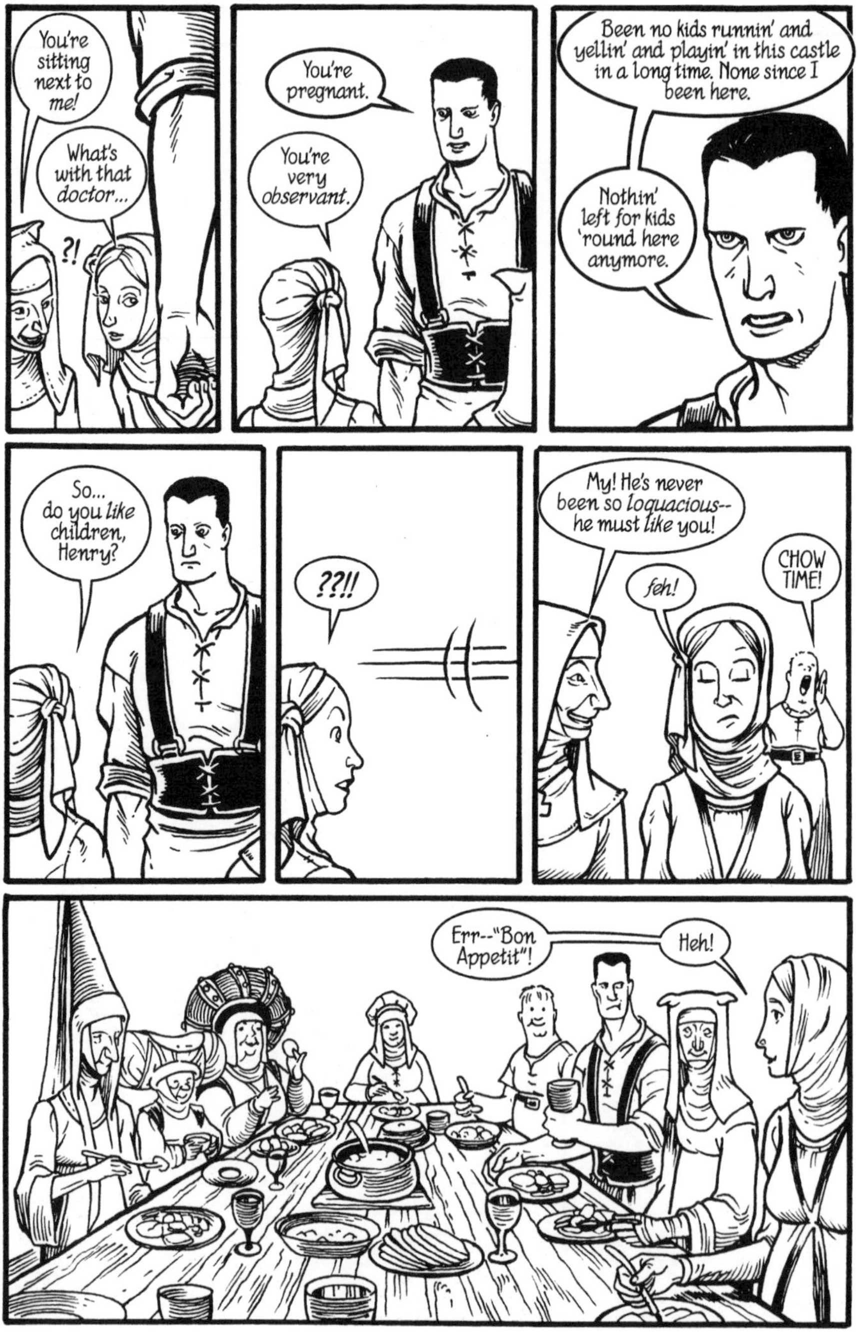
You're sitting next to me!
What's with that doctor...
?!
You're pregnant.
You're very observant.
Been no kids runnin' and yellin' and playin' in this castle in a long time. None since I been here.
Nothin' left for kids 'round here anymore.
So... do you like children, Henry?
??!!
My! He's never been so loquacious-- he must like you!
feh!
CHOW TIME!
Err--"Bon Appetit"!
Heh!

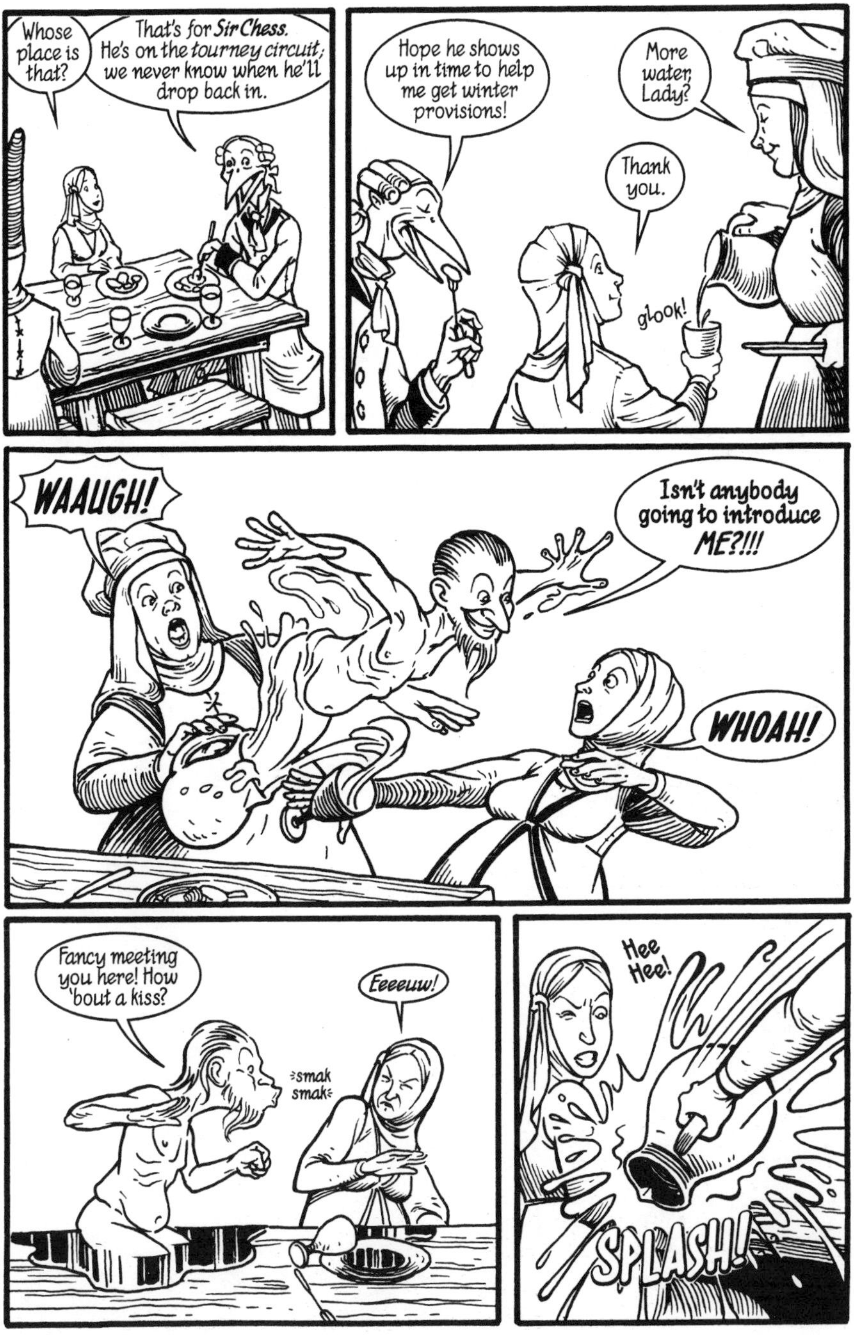
Whose place is that?
That's for Sir Chess. He's on the tourney circuit; we never know when he'll drop back in.
Hope he shows up in time to help me get winter provisions!
More water, Lady?
Thank you.
glook!
WAAUGH!
Isn't anybody going to introduce ME?!!!
WHOAH!
Fancy meeting you here! How 'bout a kiss?
Eeeeuw!
smak smak
Hee Hee!
SPLASH!

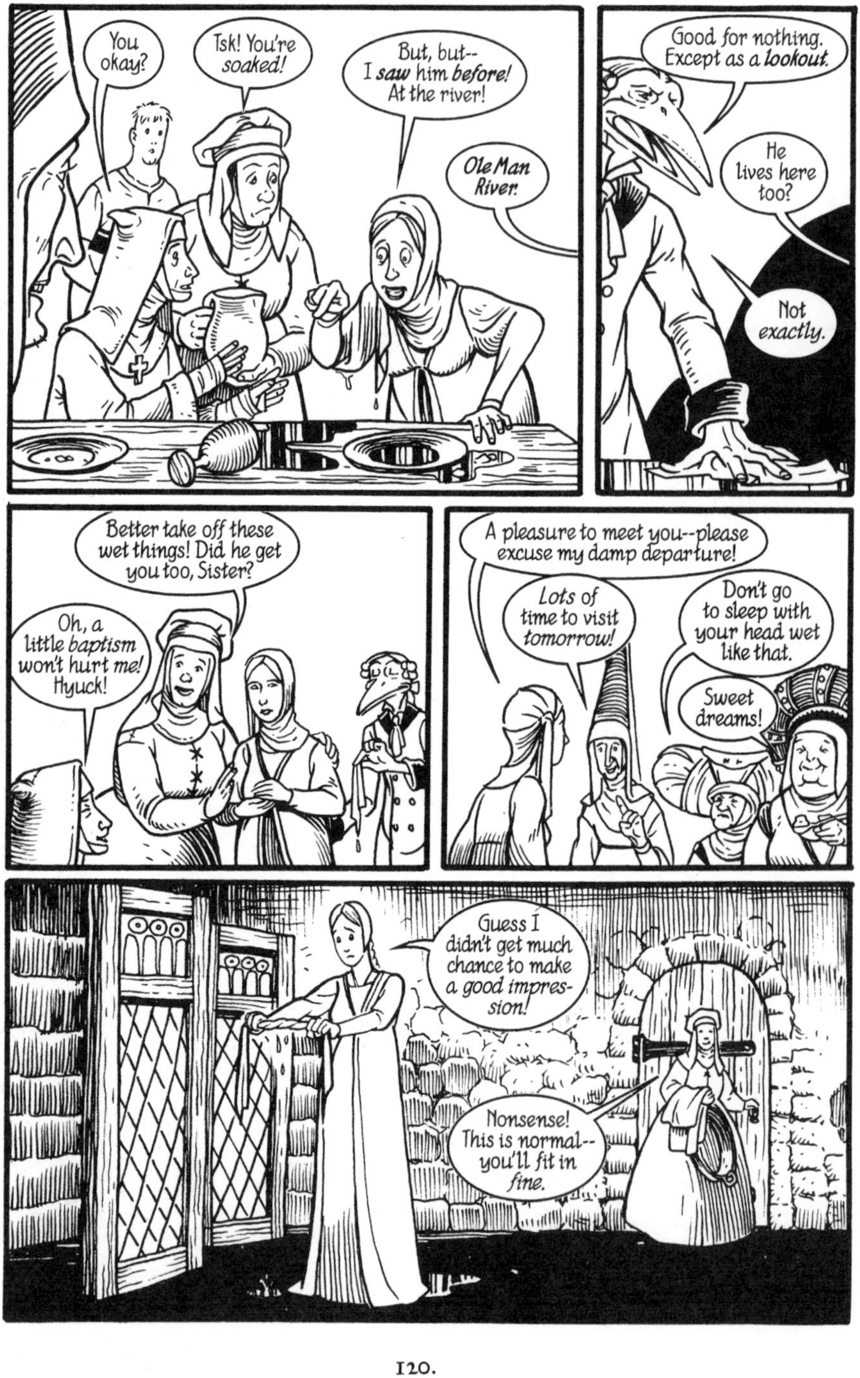
You okay?
Tsk! You're soaked!
But, but-- I saw him before! At the river!
Ole Man River.
Good for nothing. Except as a lookout.
He lives here too?
Not exactly.
Better take off these wet things! Did he get you too, Sister?
Oh, a little baptism won't hurt me! Hyuck!
A pleasure to meet you--please excuse my damp departure!
Lots of time to visit tomorrow!
Don't go to sleep with your head wet like that.
Sweet dreams!
Guess I didn't get much chance to make a good impres-sion!
Nonsense! This is normal--you'll fit in fine.

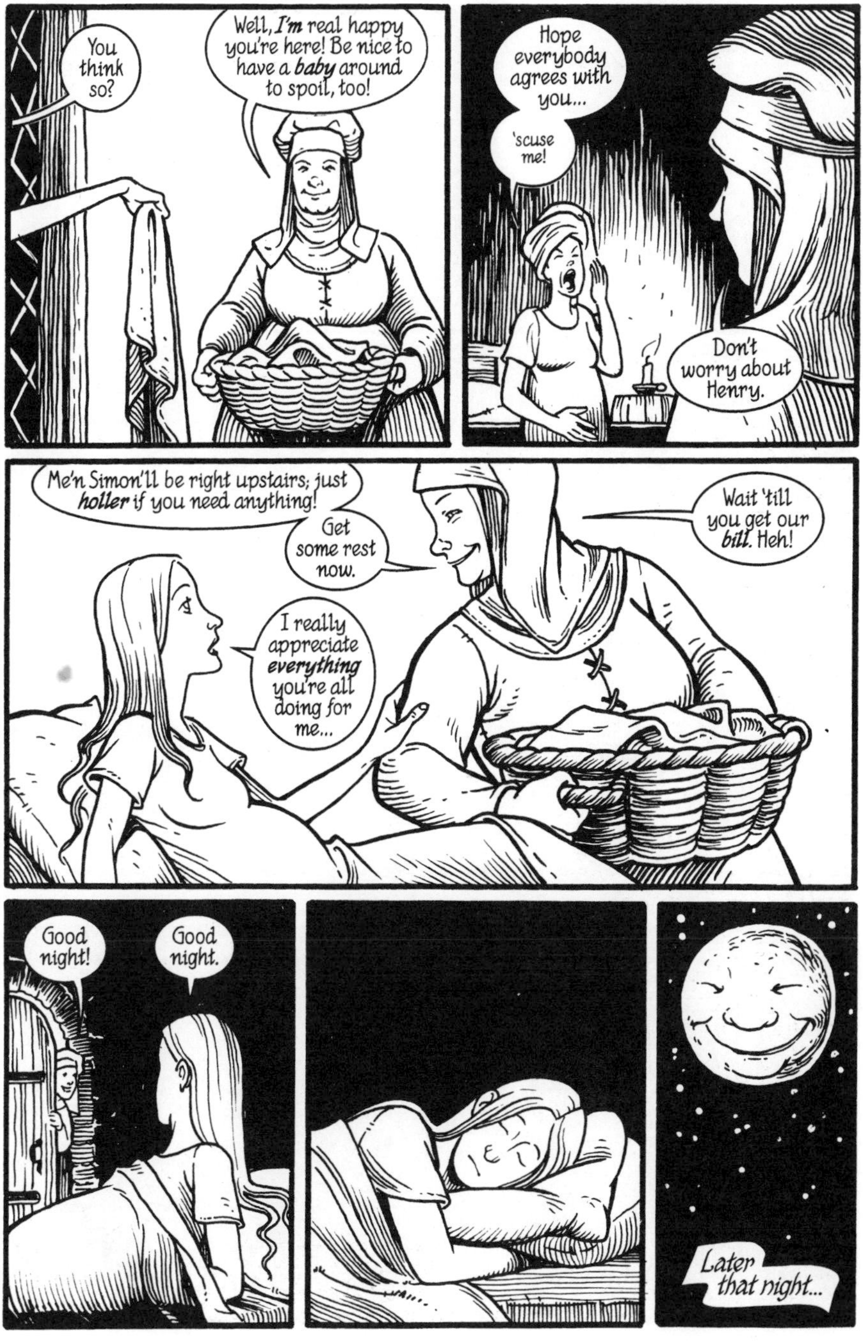
You think so?
Well, *I'm* real happy you're here! Be nice to have a *baby* around to spoil, too!
Hope everybody agrees with you...
'scuse me!
Don't worry about Henry.
Me'n Simon'll be right upstairs; just *holler* if you need anything!
Get some rest now.
Wait 'till you get our *bill*. Heh!
I really appreciate *everything* you're all doing for me...
Good night!
Good night.
Later that night...

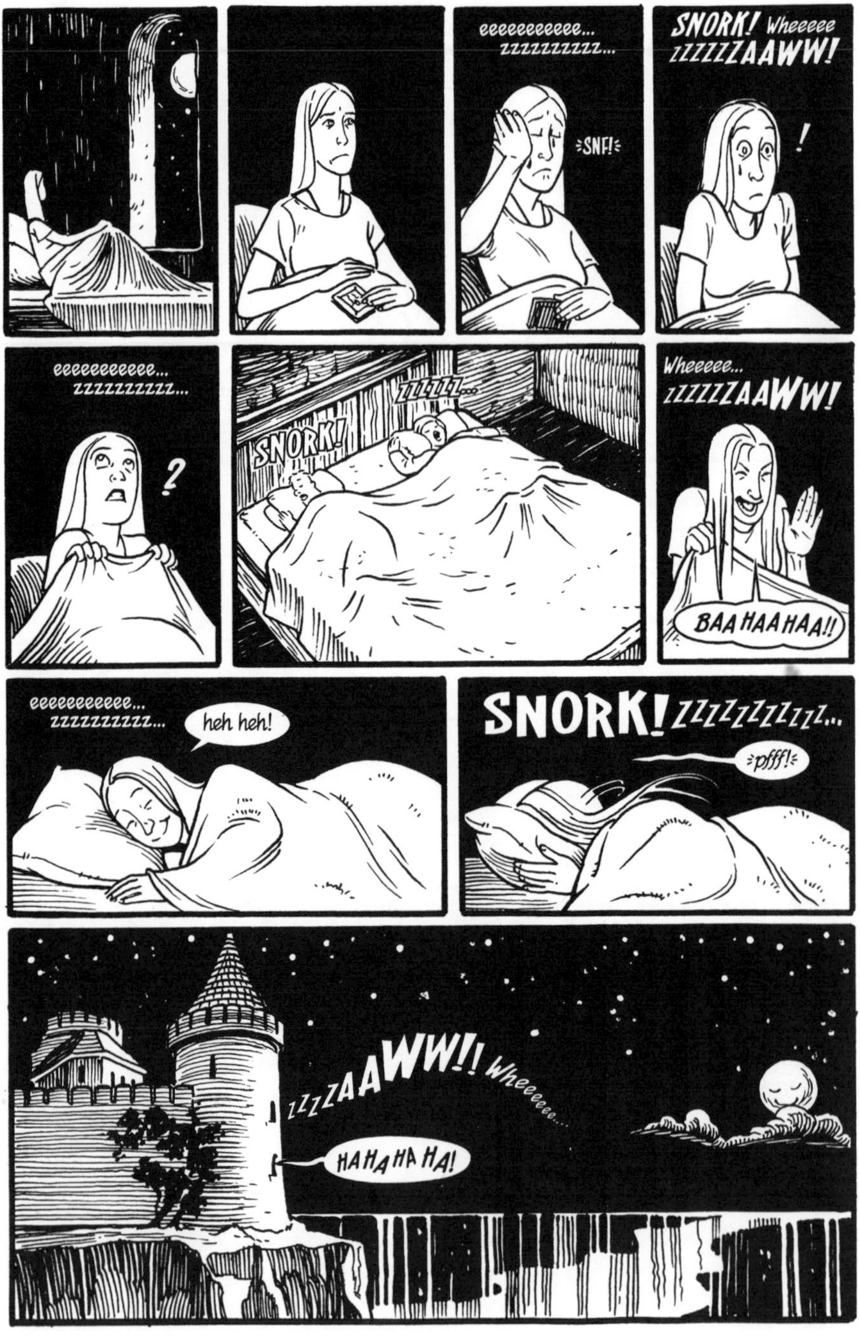
eeeeeeeeeee...
zzzzzzzzzz...
SNF!
SNORK! Wheeeee
zzzzzZAAWW!
!
eeeeeeeeeee...
zzzzzzzzzz...
?
ZZZZZ...
SNORK!
Wheeeee...
zzzzzZAAWW!
BAA HAA HAA!!
eeeeeeeeeee...
zzzzzzzzzz...
heh heh!
SNORK! zzzzzzzzzz...
pfff!
zzzzZAAWW!! Wheeeeee...
HA HA HA HA HA!

Chapter 6.

· LABORS OF LOVE ·

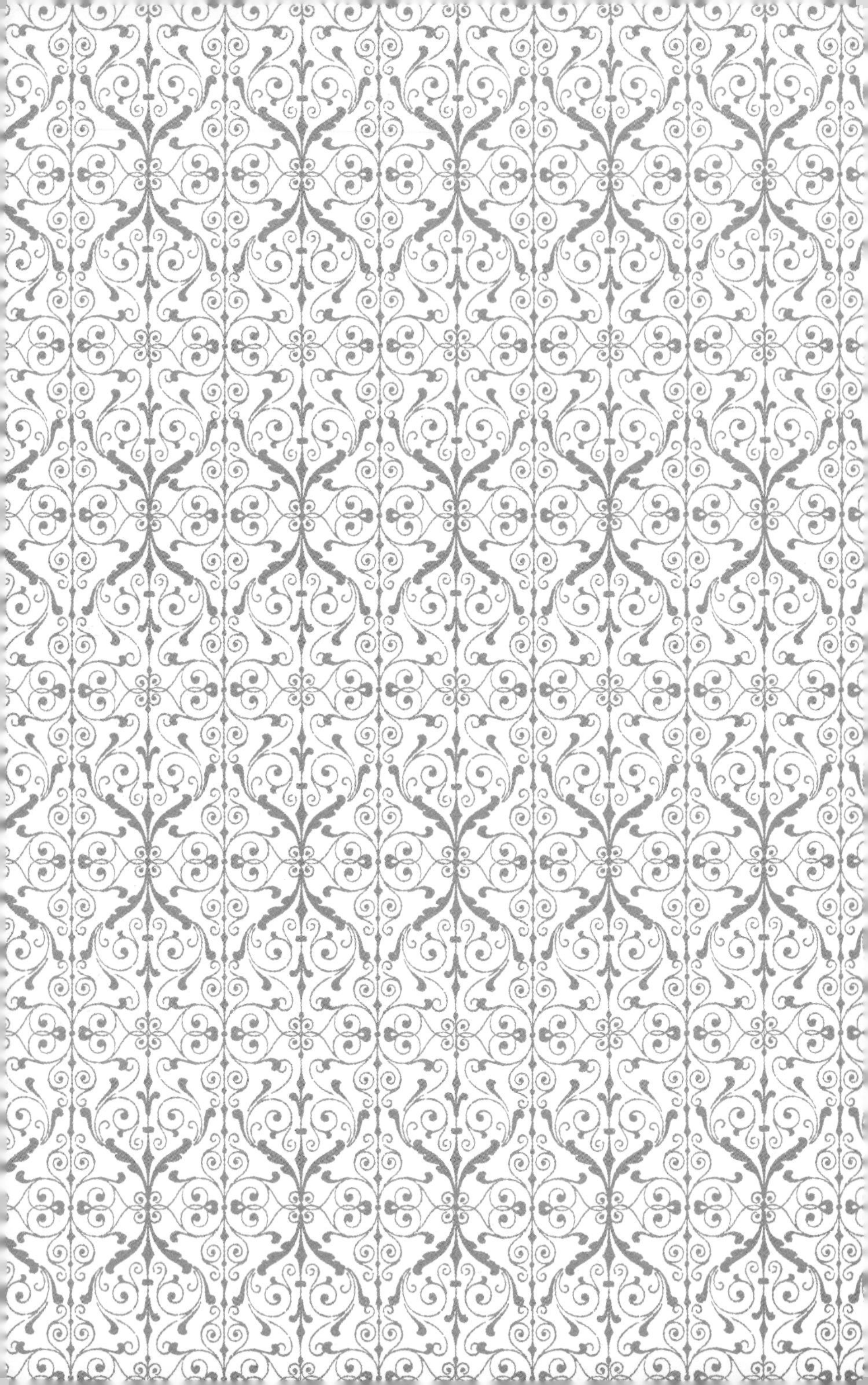

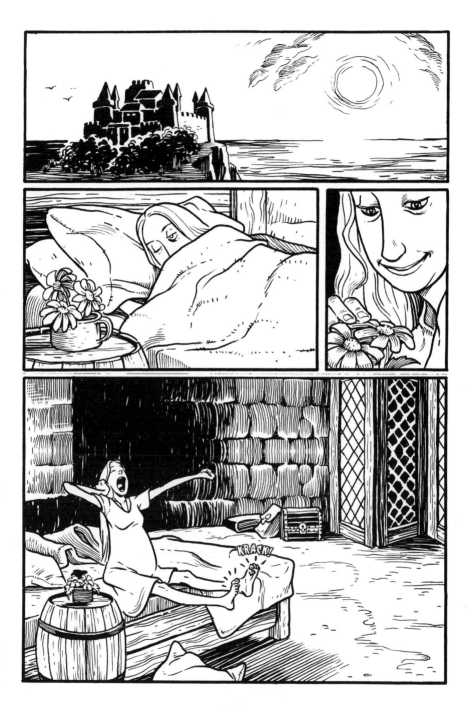

KRACK!

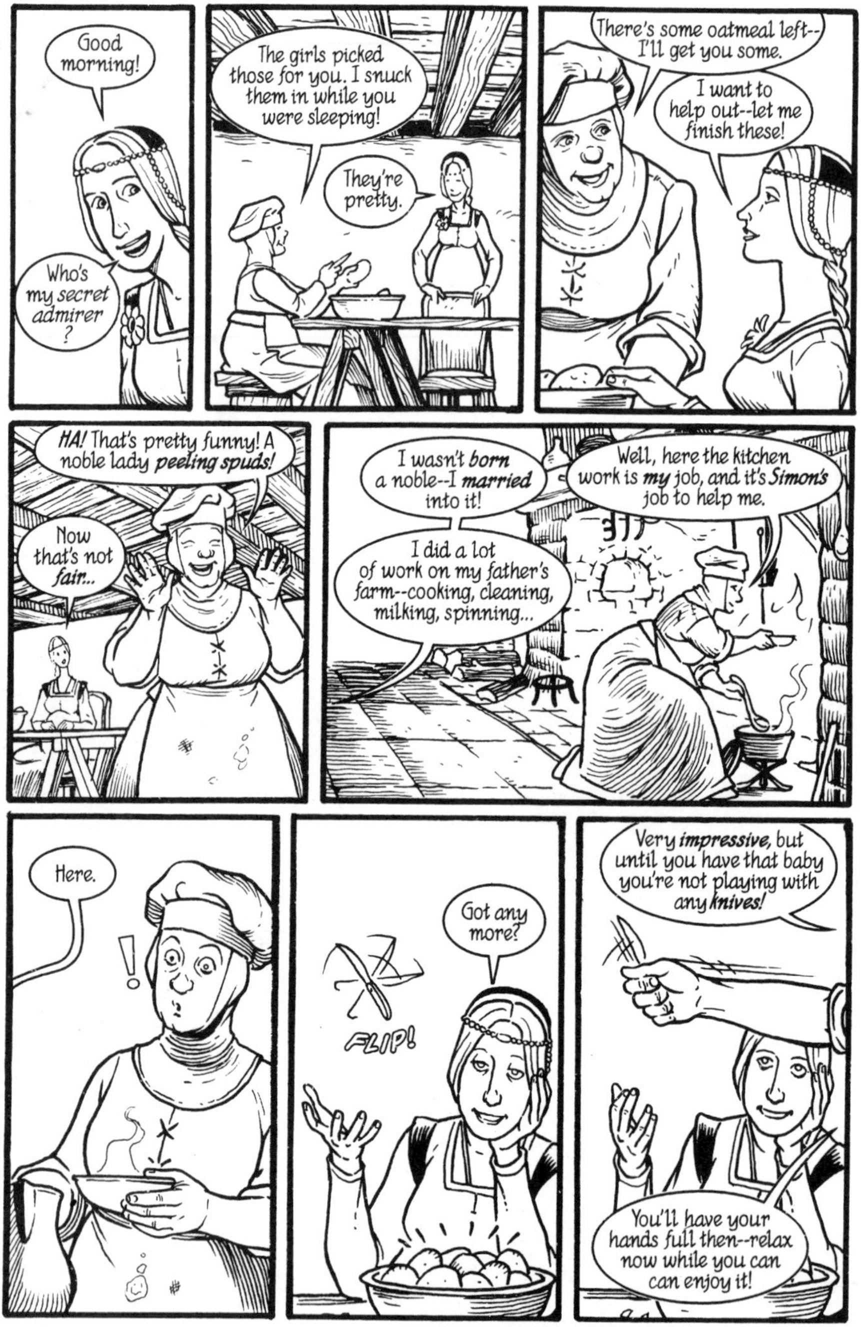
Good morning!
Who's my *secret* admirer?
The girls picked those for you. I snuck them in while you were sleeping!
They're pretty.
There's some oatmeal left-- I'll get you some.
I want to help out--let me finish these!
HA! That's pretty funny! A noble lady ***peeling spuds!***
Now that's not *fair*...
I wasn't ***born*** a noble--I ***married*** into it!
I did a lot of work on my father's farm--cooking, cleaning, milking, spinning...
Well, here the kitchen work is ***my*** job, and it's ***Simon's*** job to help me.
Here.
!
Got any more?
FLIP!
Very ***impressive,*** but until you have that baby you're not playing with any ***knives!***
You'll have your hands full then--relax now while you can can enjoy it!

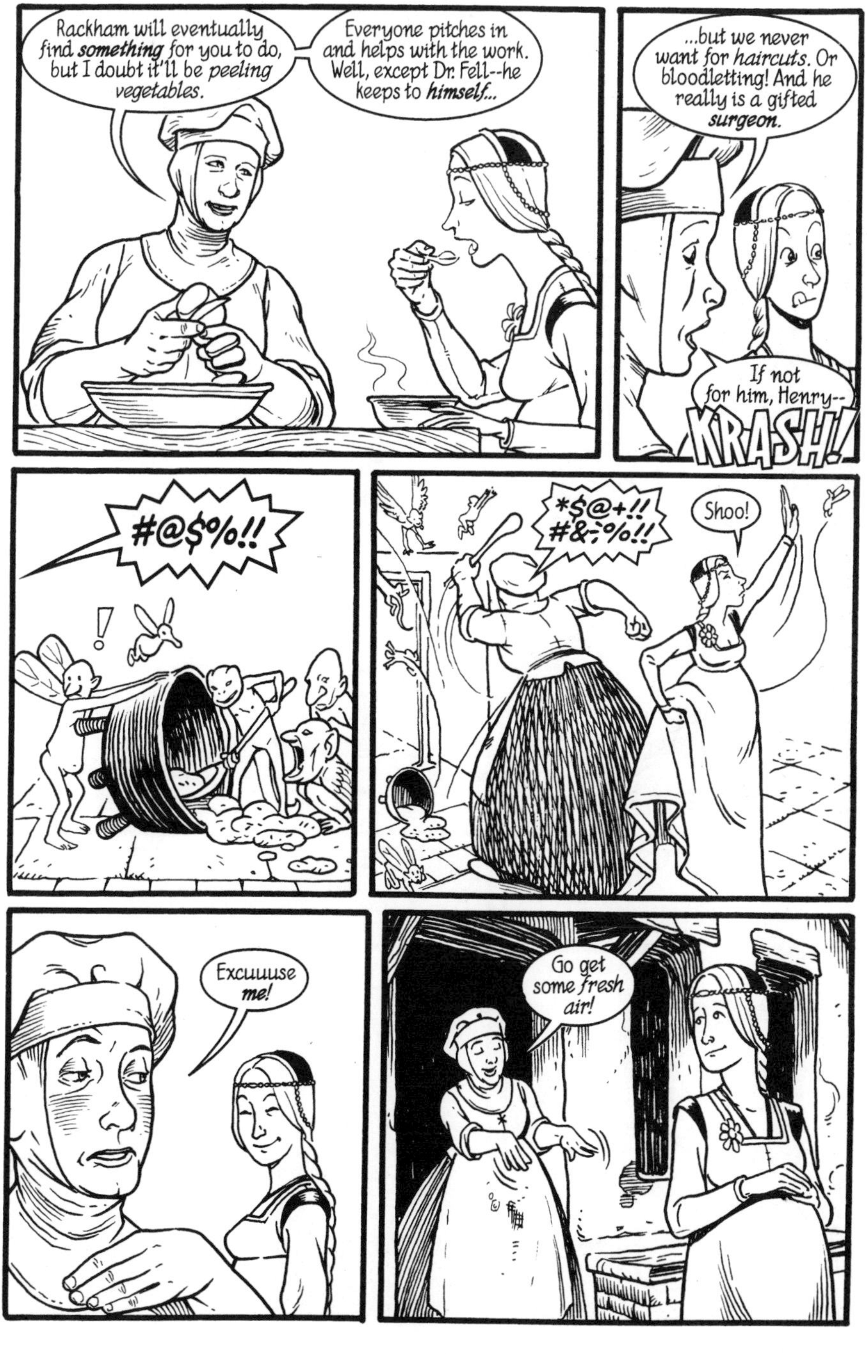
Rackham will eventually find **something** for you to do, but I doubt it'll be *peeling vegetables*.
Everyone pitches in and helps with the work. Well, except Dr. Fell--he keeps to ***himself***...
...but we never want for *haircuts*. Or bloodletting! And he really is a gifted ***surgeon***.
If not for him, Henry--
KRASH!
#@$%!!
!
*$@+!! #&;%!!
Shoo!
Excuuuse ***me!***
Go get some *fresh* air!

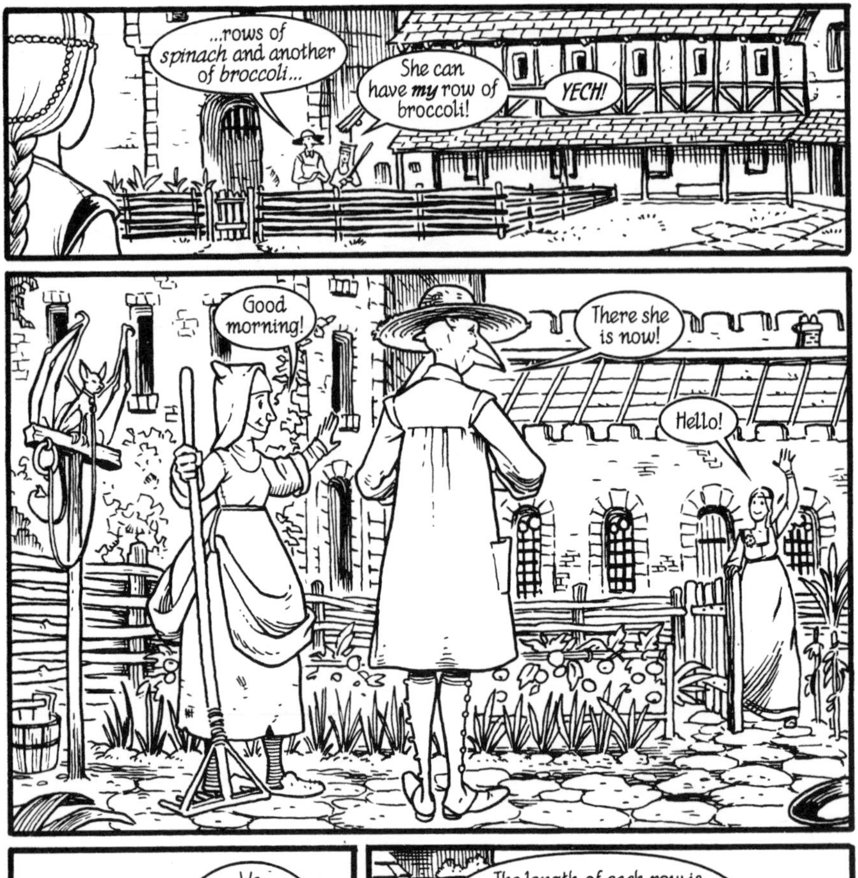
...rows of spinach and another of broccoli...
She can have my row of broccoli!
YECH!
Good morning!
There she is now!
Hello!
We were just planning your space in the garden.
The length of each row is scientifically calculated to feed one person...whenever we get a new person, we just add one row of each!
Everyone helps out!

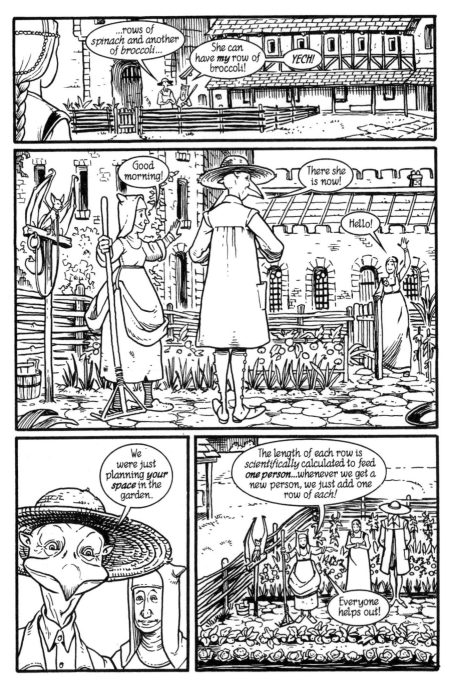

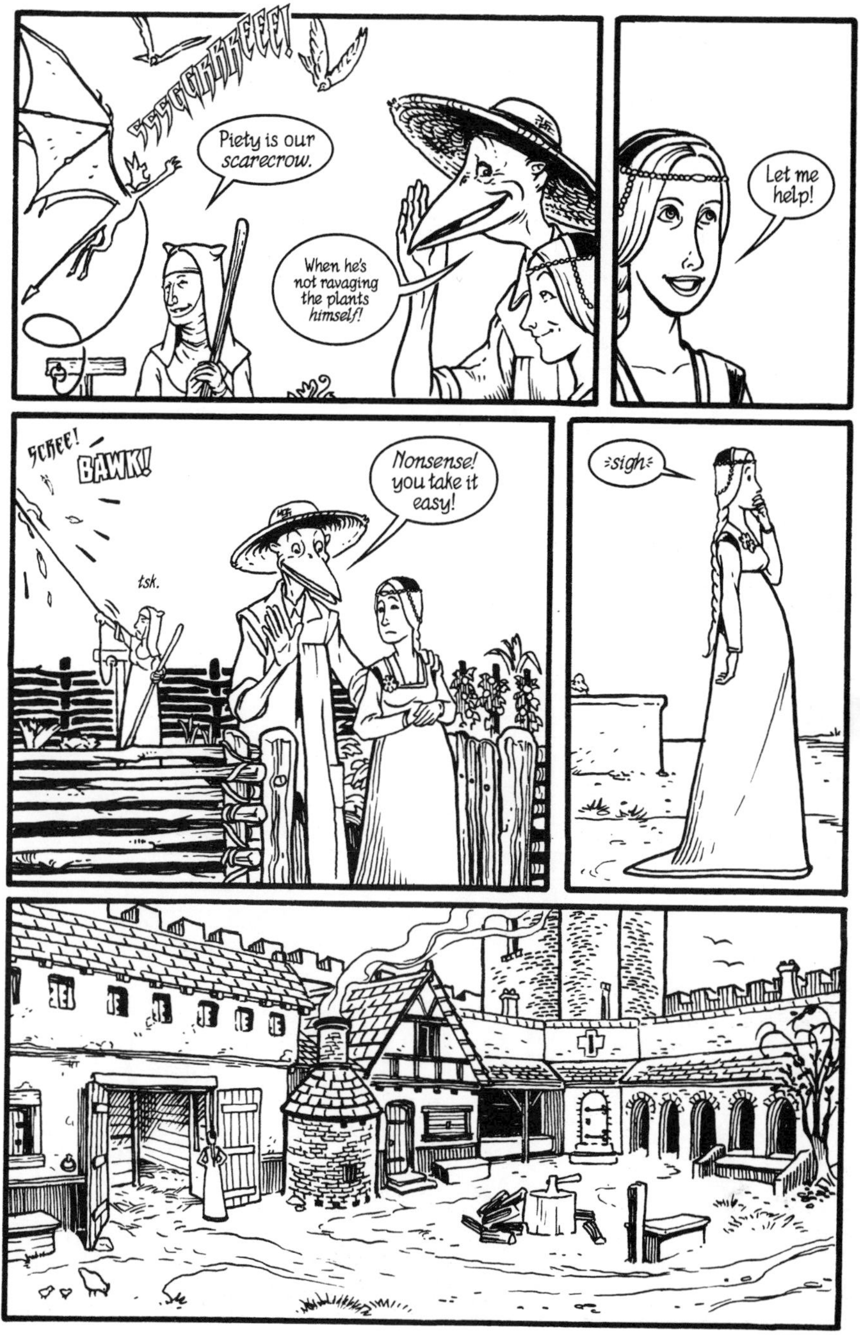
SSSCRRREEE!
Piety is our scarecrow.
When he's not ravaging the plants himself!
Let me help!
SCREE!
BAWK!
Nonsense! you take it easy!
tsk.
sigh

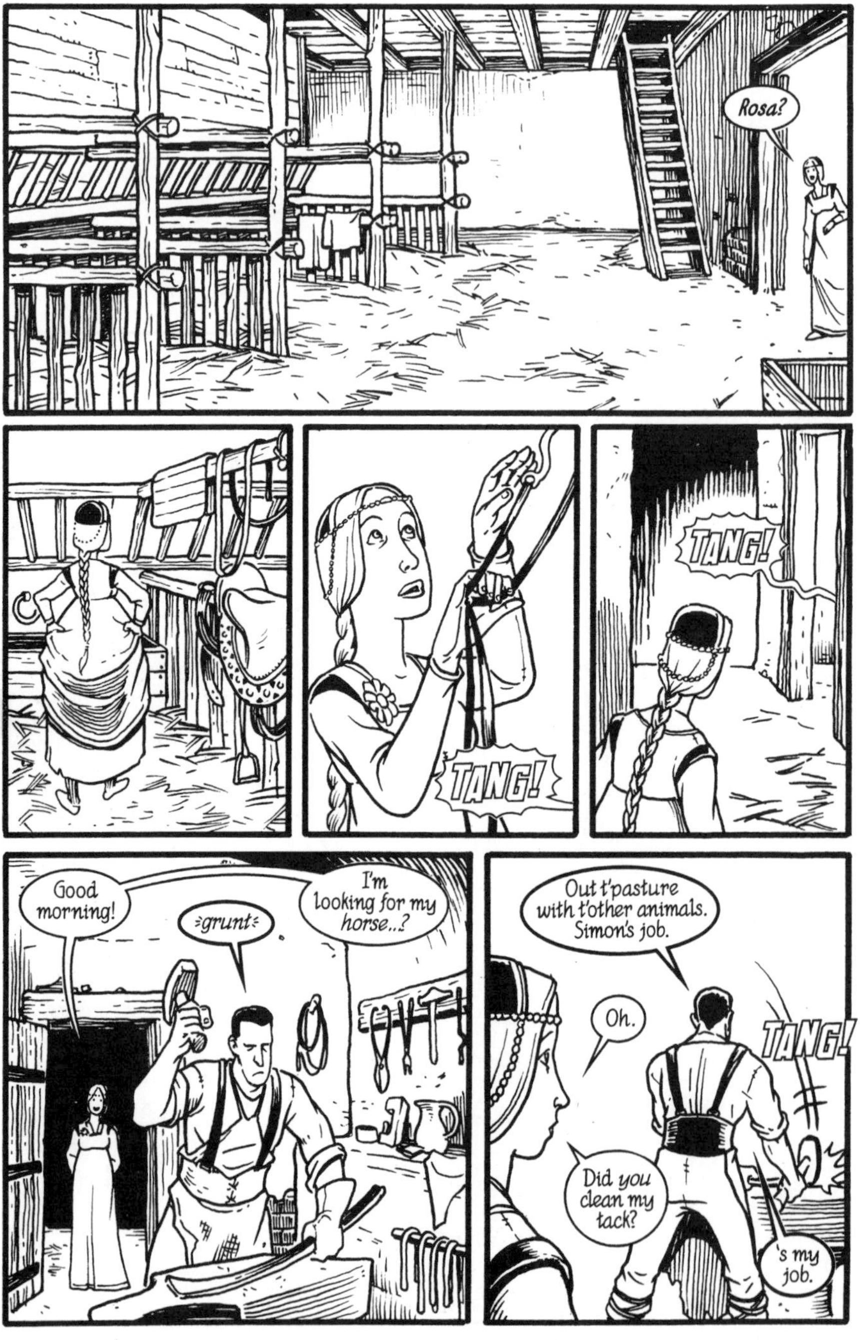
Rosa?
TANG!
TANG!
Good morning!
grunt
I'm looking for my horse...?
Out t'pasture with t'other animals. Simon's job.
Oh.
TANG!
Did you clean my tack?
's my job.

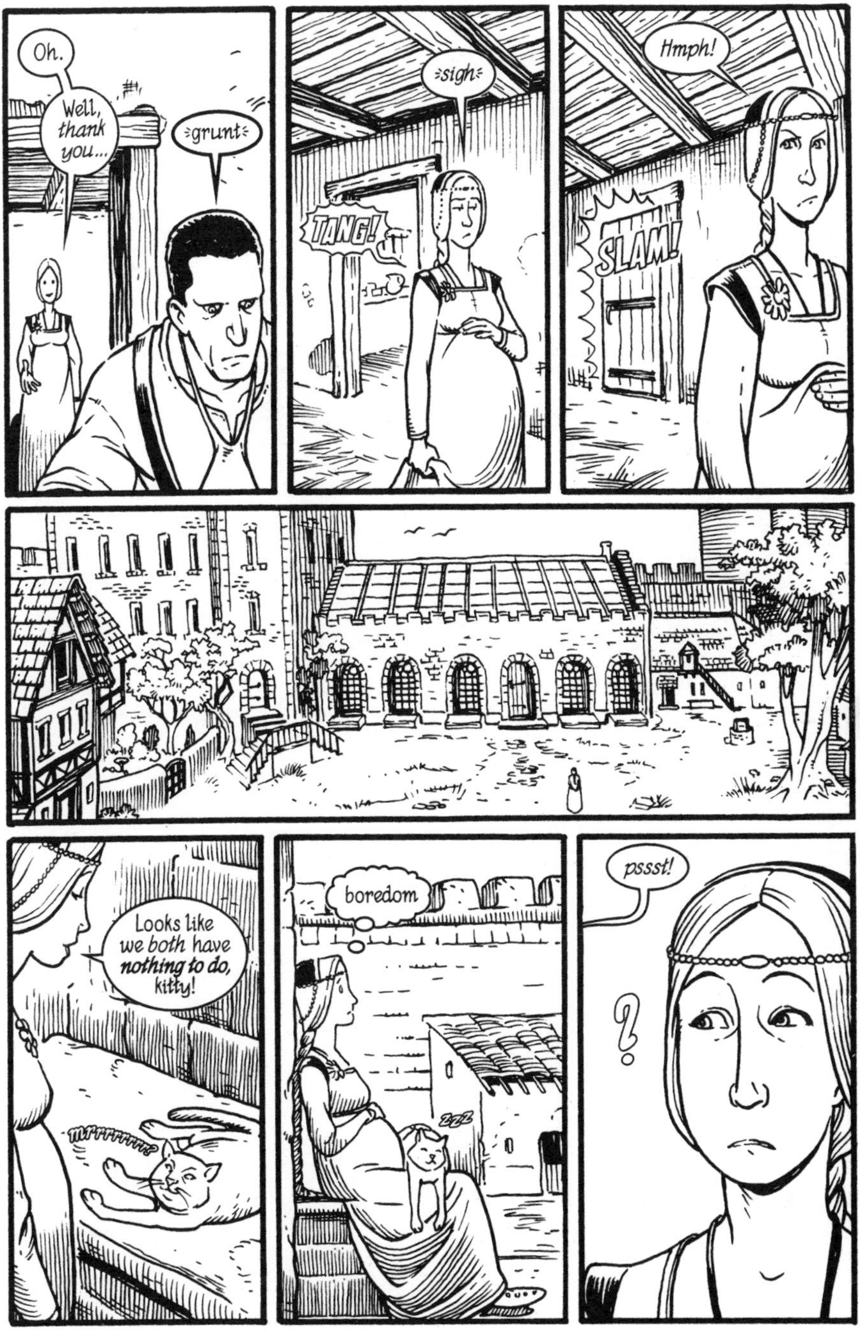
Oh.
Well, thank you...
grunt
sigh
TANG!
Hmph!
SLAM!
Looks like we both have *nothing to do*, kitty!
mrrrrrrrrr?
boredom
zzz
pssst!
?

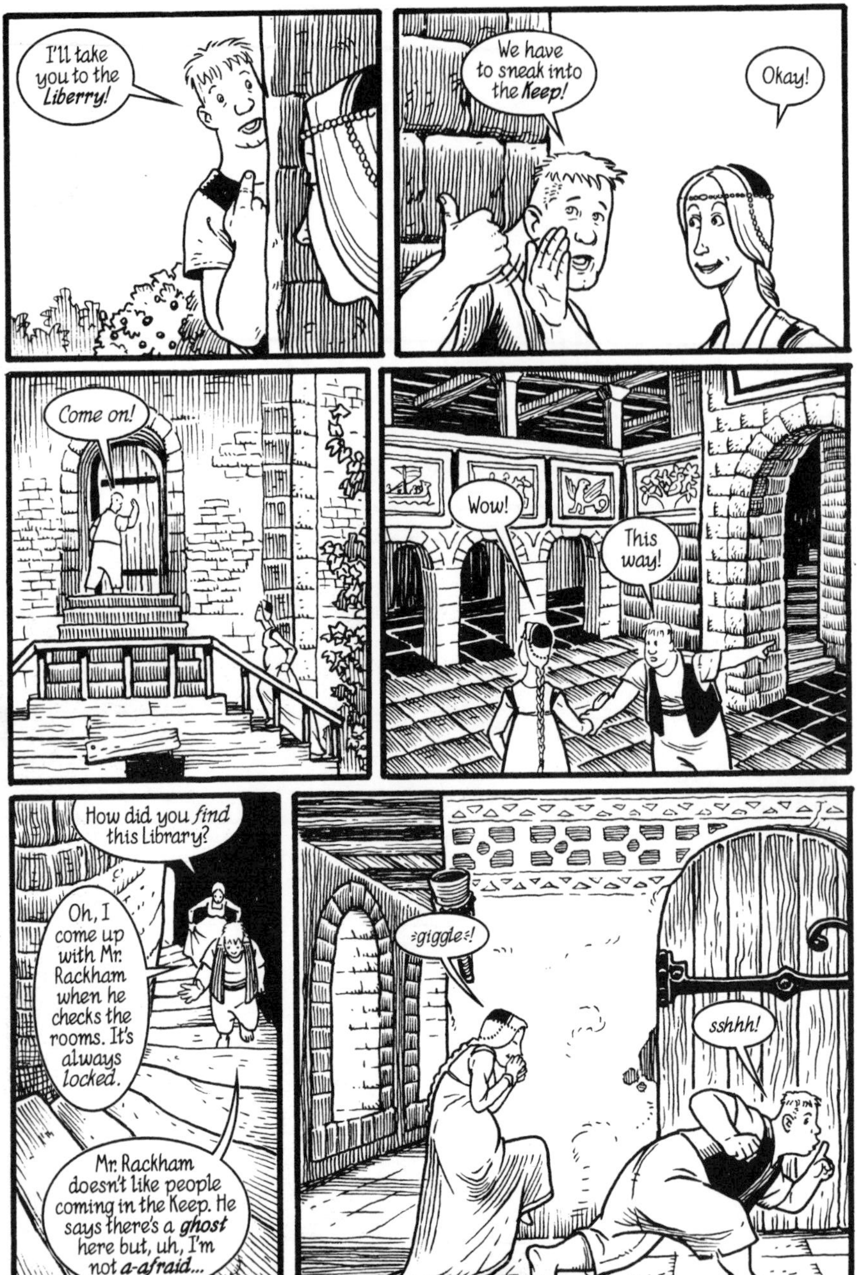
I'll take you to the *Liberry!*
We have to sneak into the *Keep!*
Okay!
Come on!
Wow!
This way!
How did you *find* this Library?
Oh, I come up with Mr. Rackham when he checks the rooms. It's always *locked*.
Mr. Rackham doesn't like people coming in the Keep. He says there's a *ghost* here but, uh, I'm not *a-afraid...*
giggle!
sshhh!

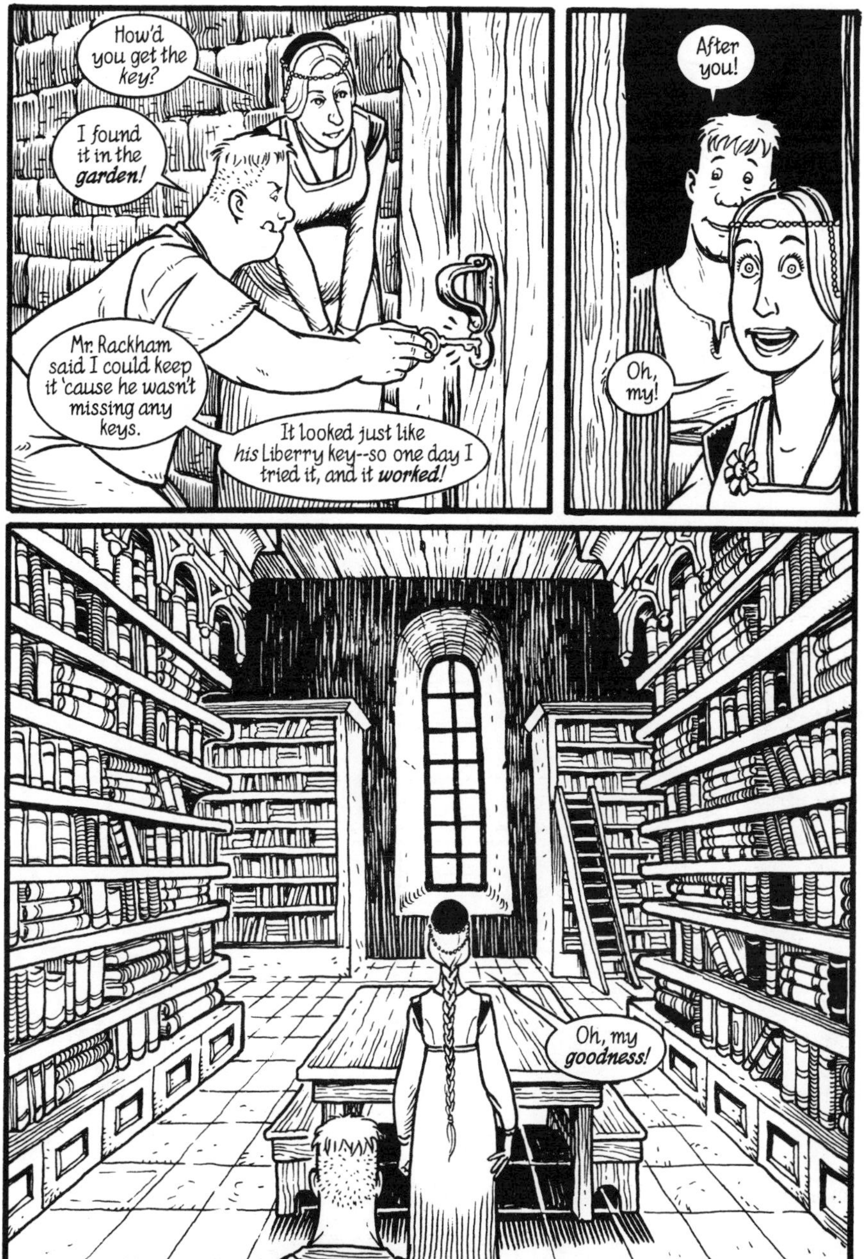
How'd you get the key?
I found it in the ***garden!***
Mr. Rackham said I could keep it 'cause he wasn't missing any keys.
It looked just like *his* Liberry key--so one day I tried it, and it ***worked!***
After you!
Oh, my!
Oh, my ***goodness!***

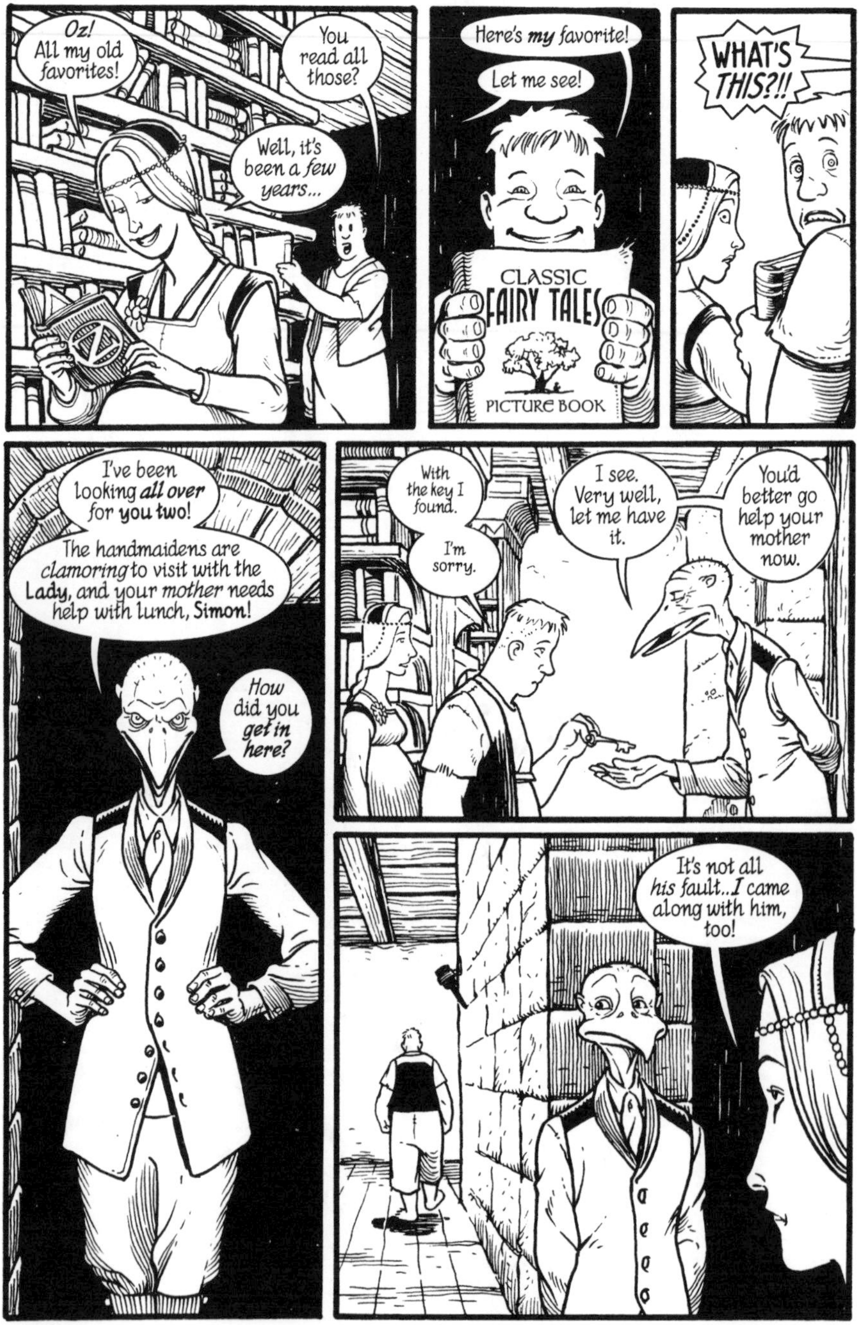
Oz! All my old favorites!
You read all those?
Well, it's been a few years...
Here's my favorite!
Let me see!
CLASSIC FAIRY TALES
PICTURE BOOK
WHAT'S THIS?!!
I've been looking all over for you two!
The handmaidens are clamoring to visit with the Lady, and your mother needs help with lunch, Simon!
How did you get in here?
With the key I found.
I'm sorry.
I see. Very well, let me have it.
You'd better go help your mother now.
It's not all his fault...I came along with him, too!

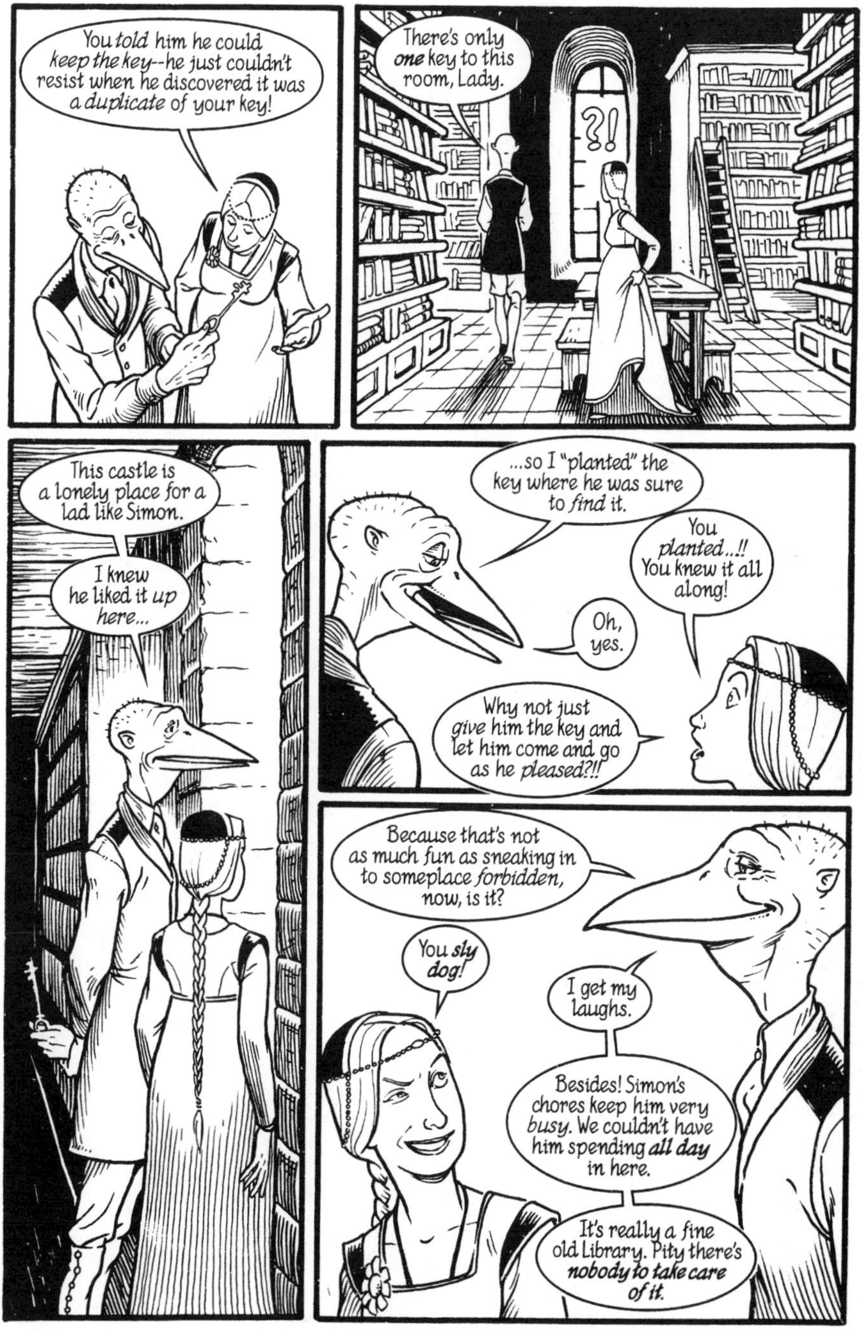
You *told* him he could *keep the key*--he just couldn't resist when he discovered it was a *duplicate* of your key!
There's only ***one*** key to this room, Lady.
?!
This castle is a lonely place for a lad like Simon.
I knew he liked it *up here*...
...so I "planted" the key where he was sure to *find* it.
You *planted*...!! You knew it all along!
Oh, yes.
Why not just *give* him the key and let him come and go as he *pleased?!!*
Because that's not as much fun as sneaking in to someplace *forbidden*, now, is it?
You ***sly dog!***
I get my laughs.
Besides! Simon's chores keep him very *busy*. We couldn't have him spending ***all day*** in here.
It's really a fine old Library. Pity there's ***nobody to take care of it.***

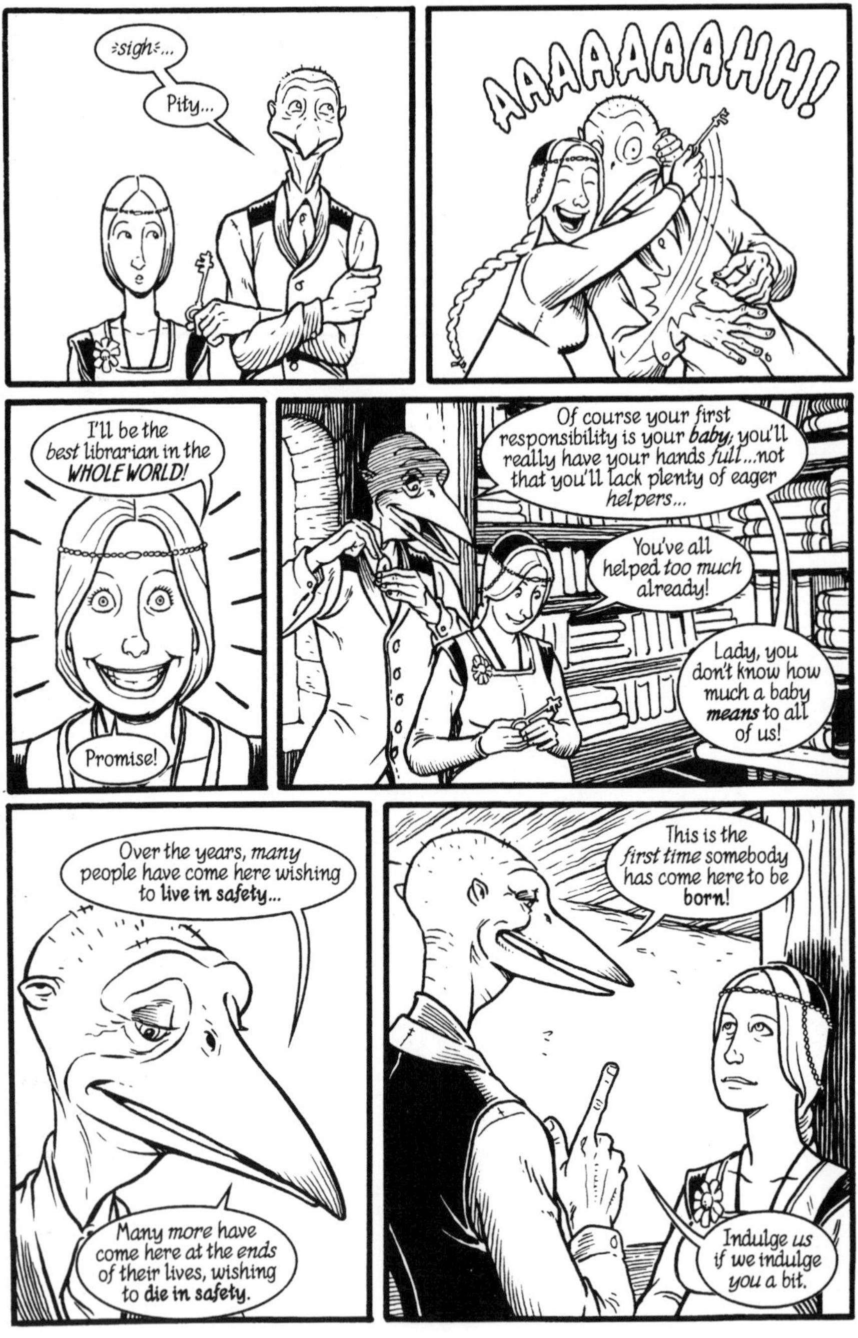

sigh...
Pity...
AAAAAAAAHH!
I'll be the *best* librarian in the **WHOLE WORLD!**
Promise!
Of course your first responsibility is your ***baby***; you'll really have your hands *full*...not that you'll lack plenty of eager *helpers*...
You've all helped *too much* already!
Lady, you don't know how much a baby ***means*** to all of us!
Over the years, *many* people have come here wishing to **live in safety**...
Many *more* have come here at the *ends* of their lives, wishing to **die in safety**.
This is the *first time* somebody has come here to be **born**!
Indulge *us* if we indulge *you* a bit.

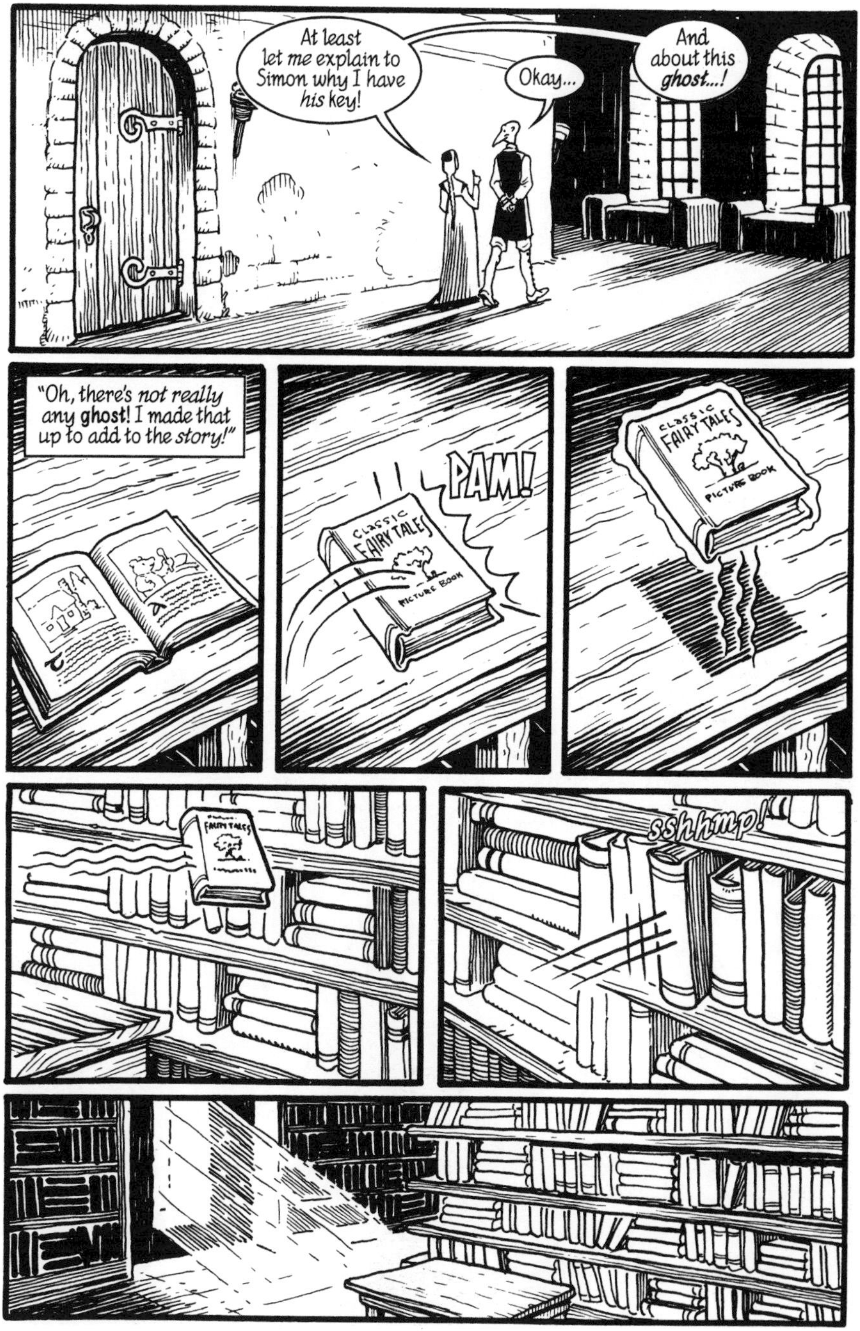
At least let me explain to Simon why I have his key!
Okay...
And about this ghost...!
"Oh, there's not really any ghost! I made that up to add to the story!"
PAM!
CLASSIC FAIRY TALES PICTURE BOOK
sshhmp!

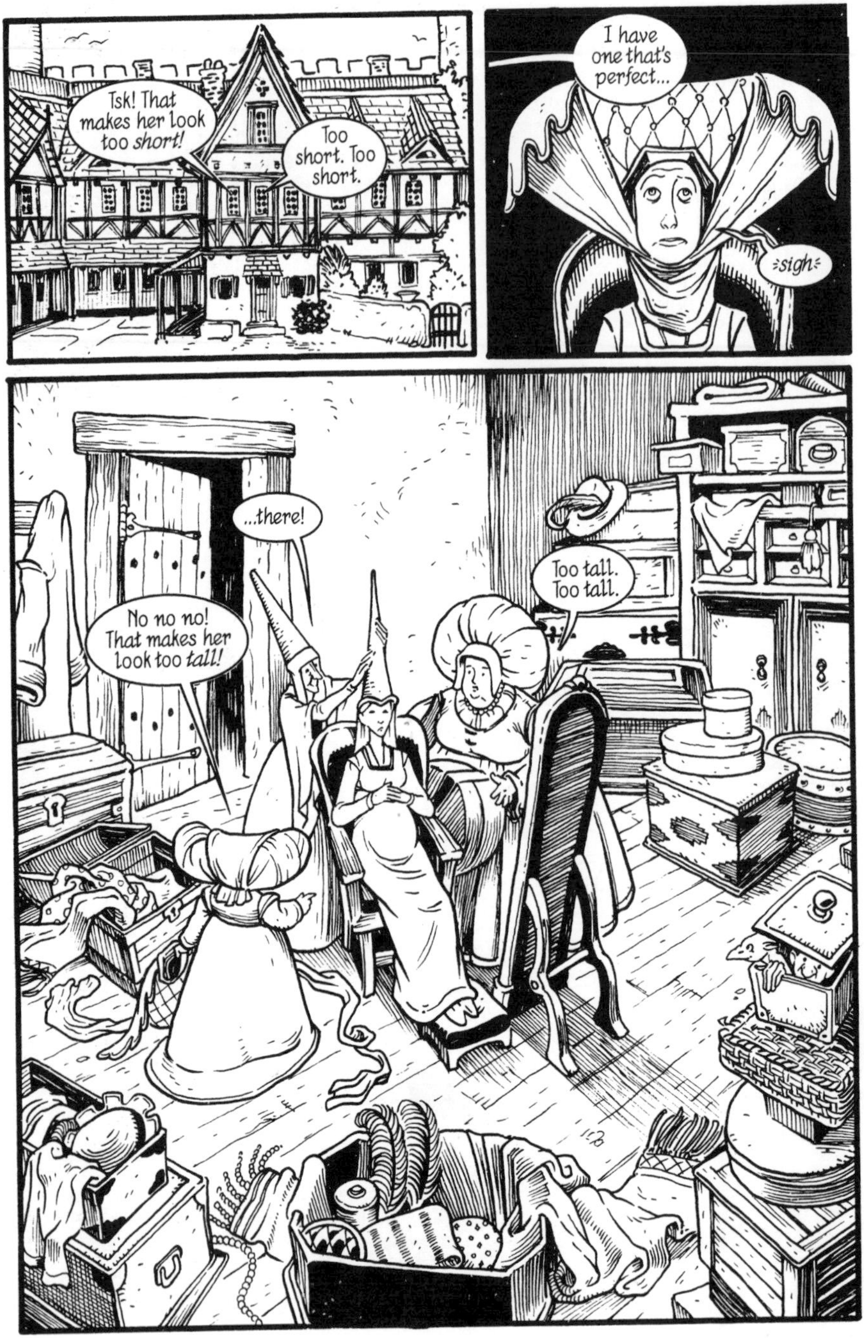
Tsk! That makes her look too *short!*
Too short. Too short.
I have one that's perfect...
sigh
...there!
No no no! That makes her look too *tall!*
Too tall. Too tall.

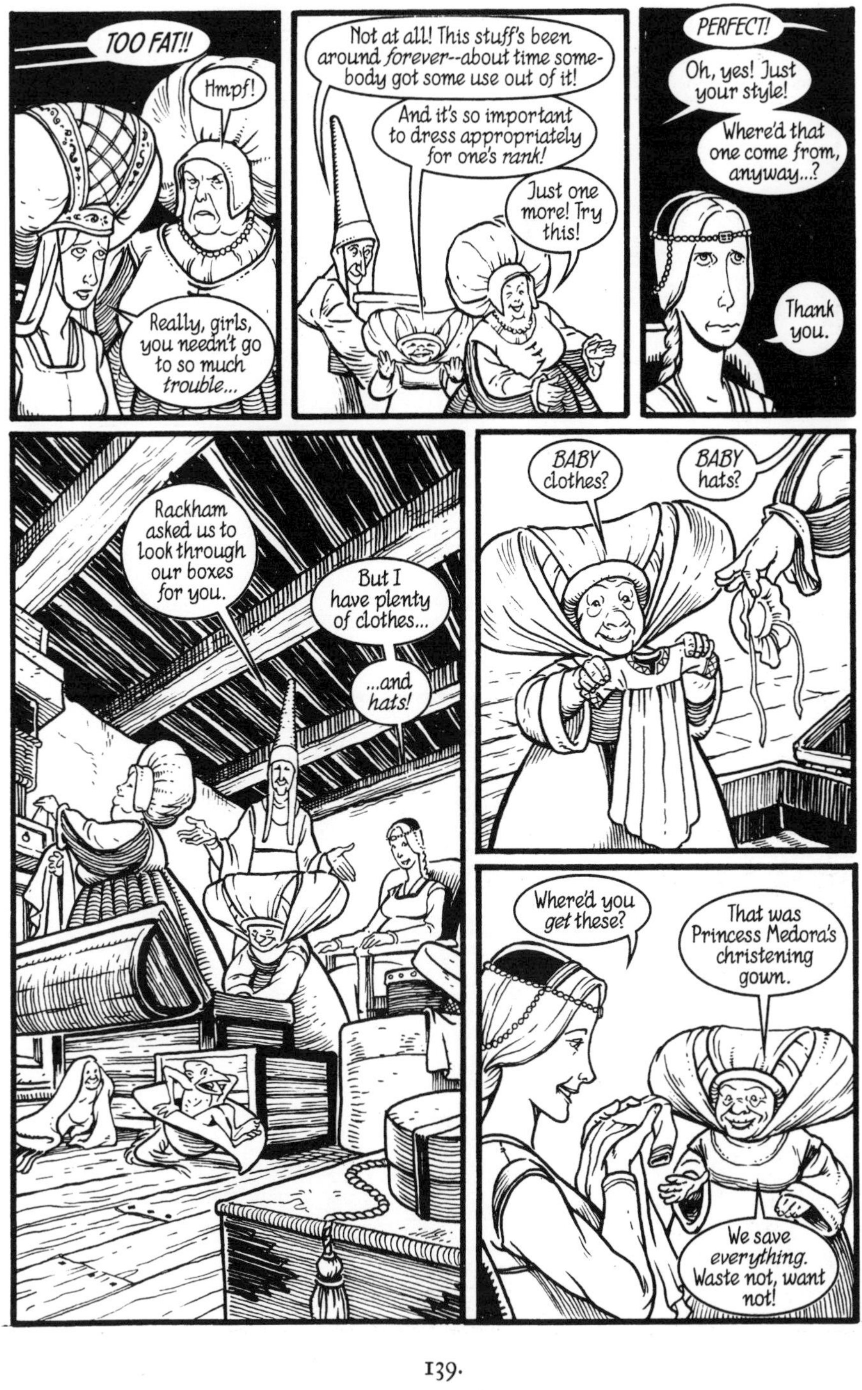
TOO FAT!!
Hmpf!
Really, girls, you needn't go to so much *trouble*...
Not at all! This stuff's been around *forever*--about time somebody got some use out of it!
And it's so important to dress appropriately for one's *rank!*
Just one more! Try this!
PERFECT!
Oh, yes! Just your style!
Where'd that one come from, anyway...?
Thank you.
Rackham asked us to look through our boxes for you.
But I have plenty of clothes...
...and *hats!*
BABY clothes?
BABY hats?
Where'd you *get* these?
That was Princess Medora's christening gown.
We save *everything.* Waste not, want not!

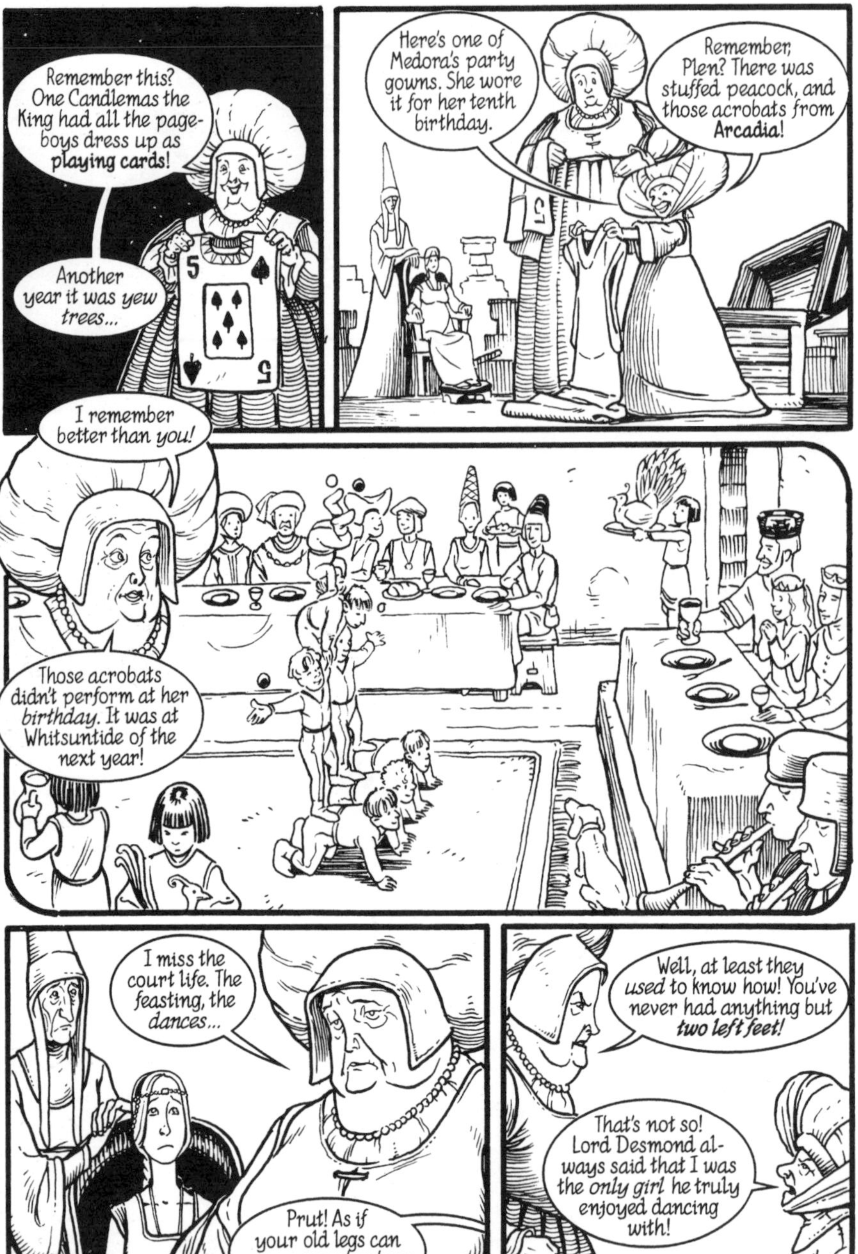
Remember this? One Candlemas the King had all the page-boys dress up as playing cards!
Another year it was yew trees...
Here's one of Medora's party gowns. She wore it for her tenth birthday.
Remember, Plen? There was stuffed peacock, and those acrobats from Arcadia!
I remember better than you!
Those acrobats didn't perform at her birthday. It was at Whitsuntide of the next year!
I miss the court life. The feasting, the dances...
Prut! As if your old legs can even remember how to dance!
Well, at least they used to know how! You've never had anything but two left feet!
That's not so! Lord Desmond always said that I was the only girl he truly enjoyed dancing with!

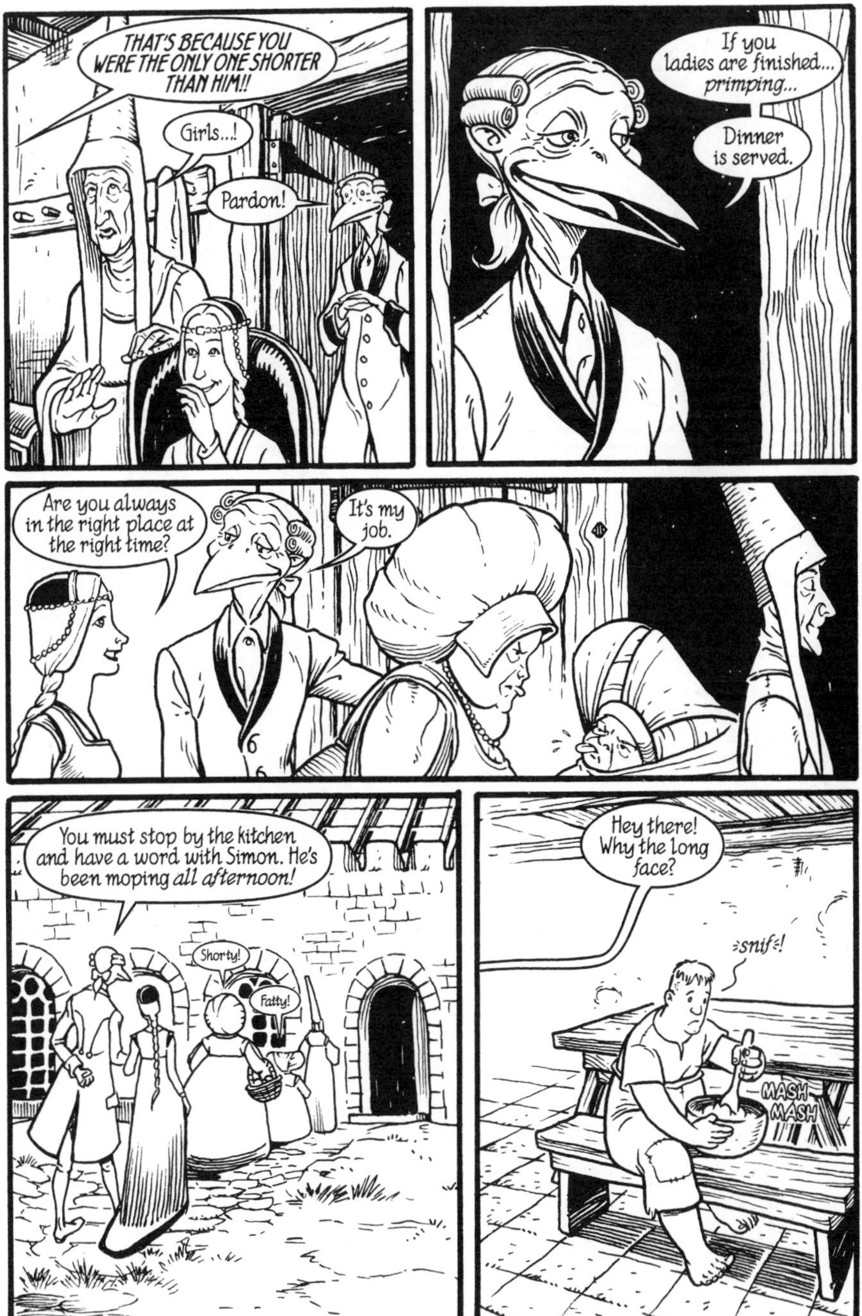
THAT'S BECAUSE YOU WERE THE ONLY ONE SHORTER THAN HIM!!
Girls...!
Pardon!
If you ladies are finished... *primping...*
Dinner is served.
Are you always in the right place at the right time?
It's my job.
You must stop by the kitchen and have a word with Simon. He's been moping *all afternoon!*
Shorty!
Fatty!
Hey there! Why the long face?
snif!
MASH MASH

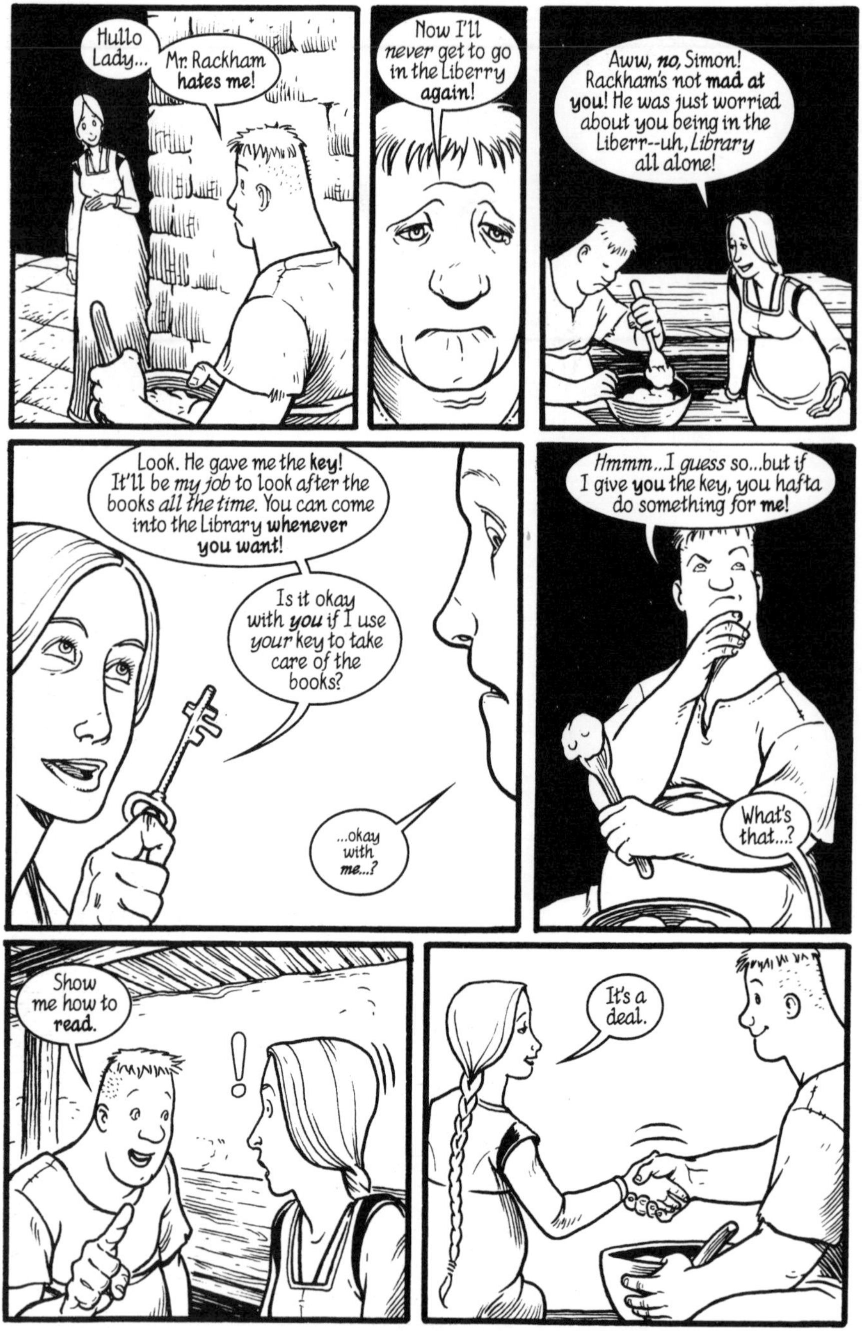
Hullo Lady...
Mr. Rackham hates me!
Now I'll never get to go in the Liberry again!
Aww, no, Simon! Rackham's not mad at you! He was just worried about you being in the Liberr--uh, Library all alone!
Look. He gave me the key! It'll be my job to look after the books all the time. You can come into the Library whenever you want!
Is it okay with you if I use your key to take care of the books?
...okay with me...?
Hmmm...I guess so...but if I give you the key, you hafta do something for me!
What's that...?
Show me how to read.
!
It's a deal.

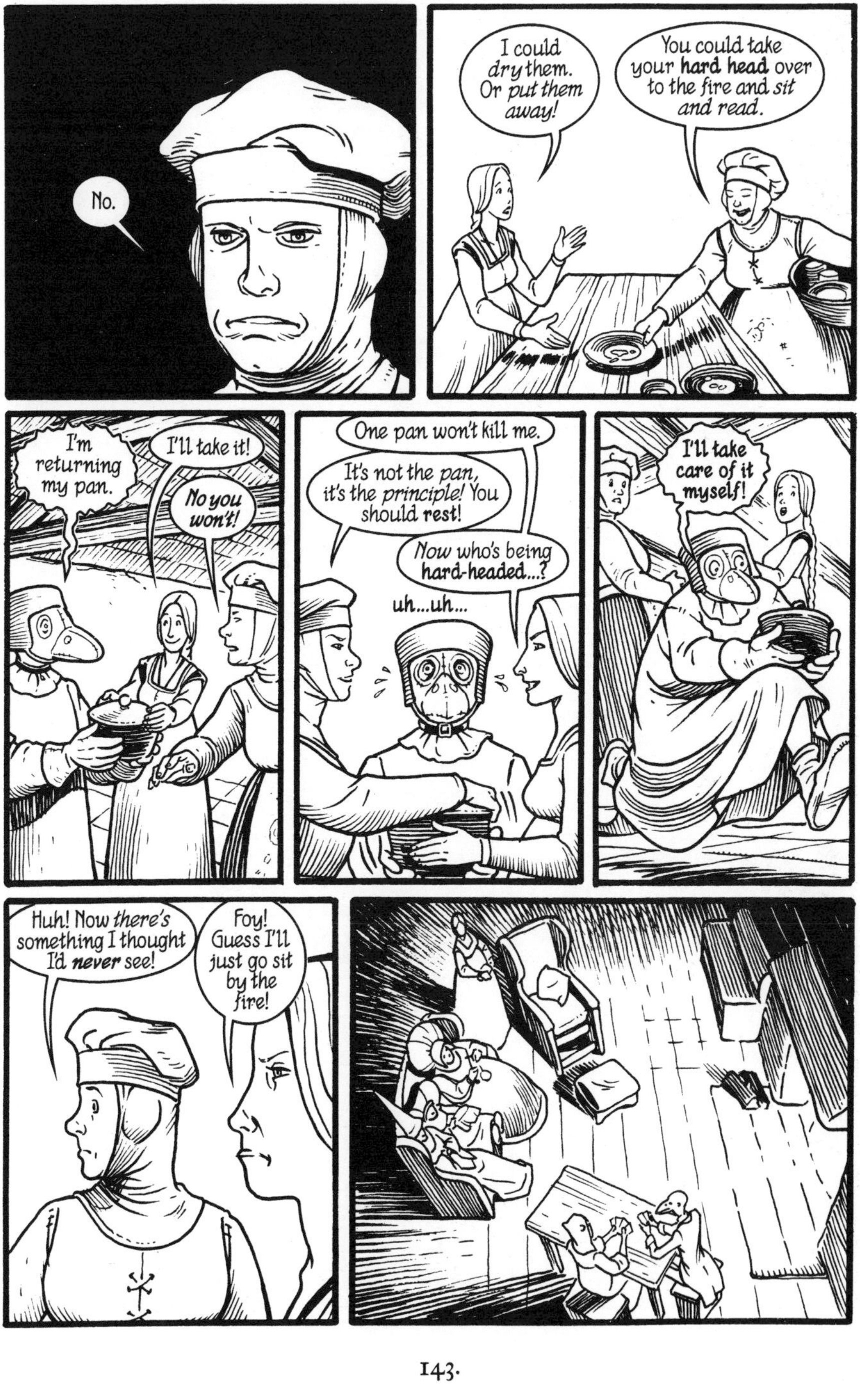
No.
I could *dry* them. Or *put them* away!
You could take your **hard head** over to the fire and *sit* and *read*.
I'm returning my pan.
I'll take it!
No you won't!
One pan won't kill me.
It's not the *pan*, it's the *principle*! You should **rest**!
uh...uh...
Now who's being **hard-headed...?**
I'll take care of it myself!
Huh! Now *there's* something I thought I'd ***never*** see!
Foy! Guess I'll just go sit by the fire!

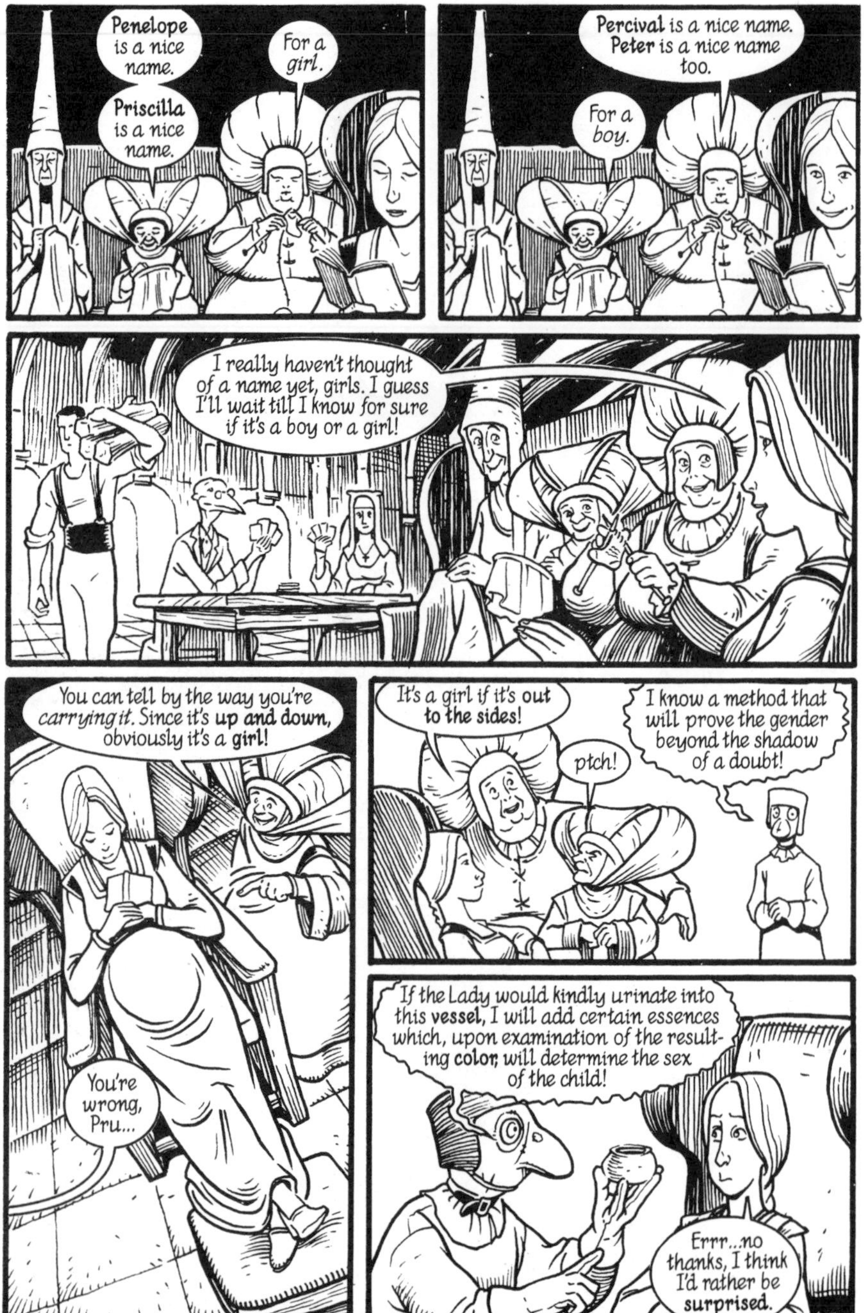
Penelope is a nice name.
For a girl.
Priscilla is a nice name.
Percival is a nice name. Peter is a nice name too.
For a boy.
I really haven't thought of a name yet, girls. I guess I'll wait till I know for sure if it's a boy or a girl!
You can tell by the way you're carrying it. Since it's up and down, obviously it's a girl!
You're wrong, Pru...
It's a girl if it's out to the sides!
ptch!
I know a method that will prove the gender beyond the shadow of a doubt!
If the Lady would kindly urinate into this vessel, I will add certain essences which, upon examination of the resulting color, will determine the sex of the child!
Errr...no thanks, I think I'd rather be surprised.

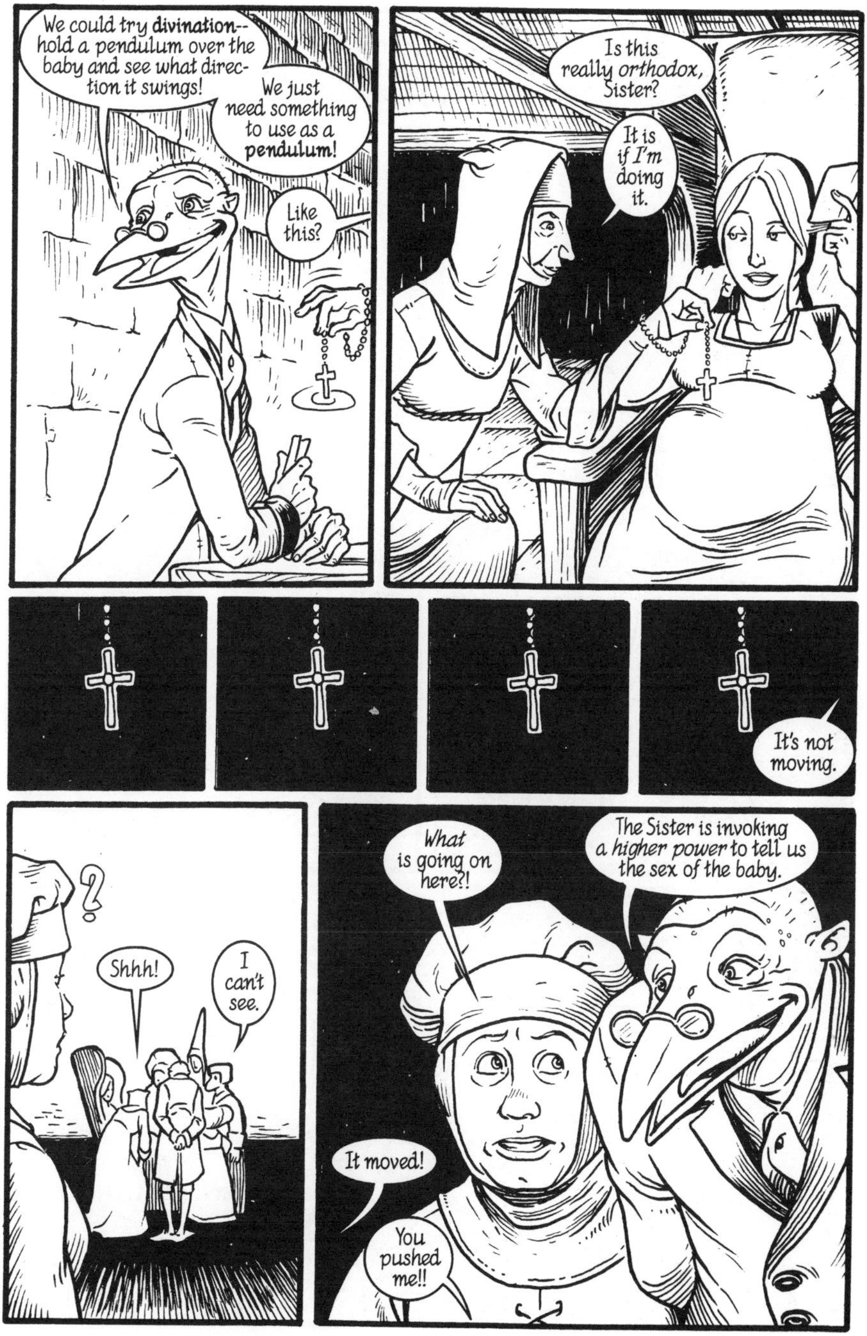
We could try **divination**--hold a pendulum over the baby and see what direction it swings!
We just need something to use as a **pendulum**!
Like this?
Is this really *orthodox*, Sister?
It is if *I'm* doing it.
It's not moving.
Shhh!
I can't see.
What is going on here?!
The Sister is invoking a *higher power* to tell us the sex of the baby.
It moved!
You pushed me!!

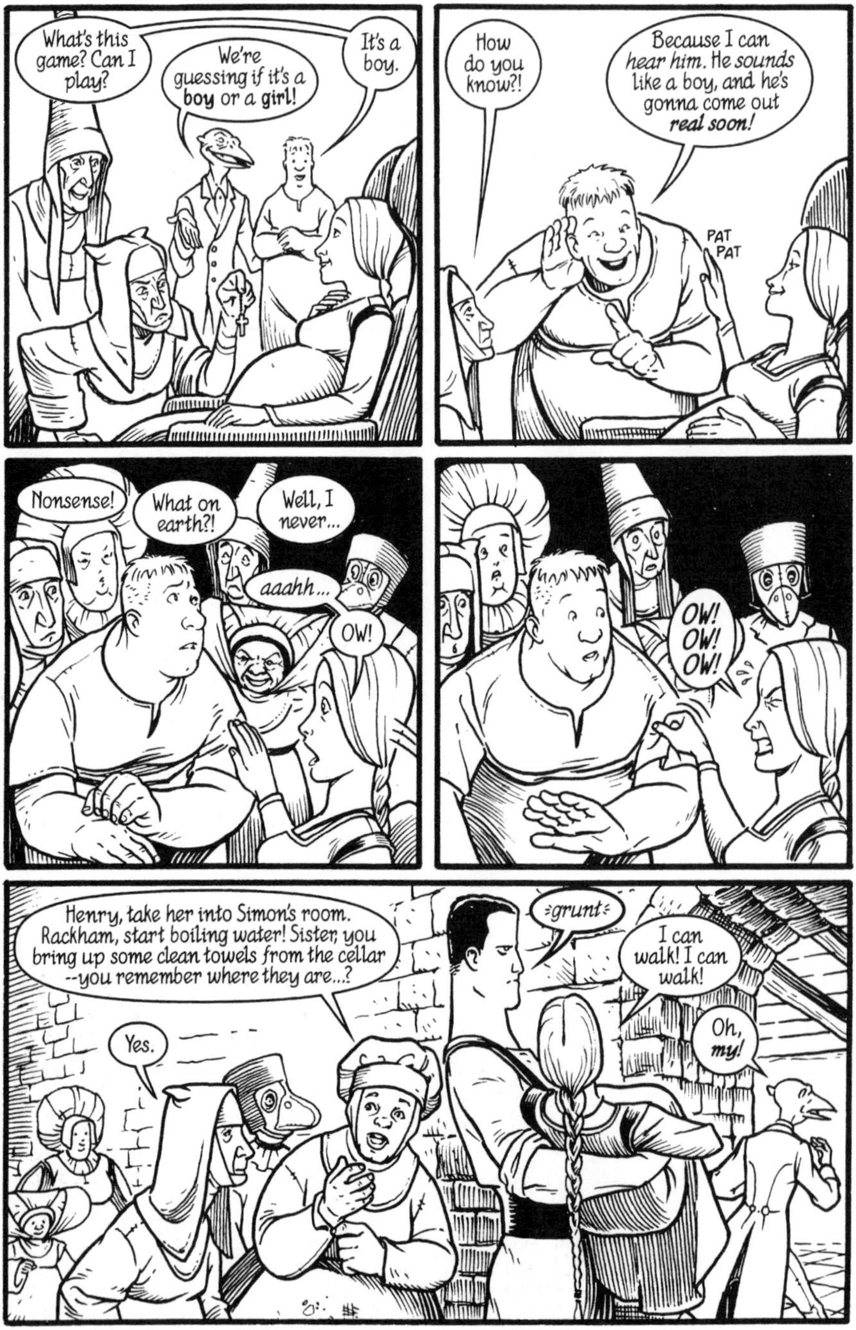

What's this game? Can I play?
We're guessing if it's a **boy** or a **girl**!
It's a boy.
How do you know?!
Because I can *hear him*. He *sounds* like a boy, and he's gonna come out ***real soon!***
PAT PAT
Nonsense!
What on earth?!
Well, I never...
aaahh...
OW!
OW! OW! OW!
Henry, take her into Simon's room. Rackham, start boiling water! Sister, you bring up some clean towels from the cellar --you remember where they are...?
grunt
I can walk! I can walk!
Yes.
Oh, *my!*

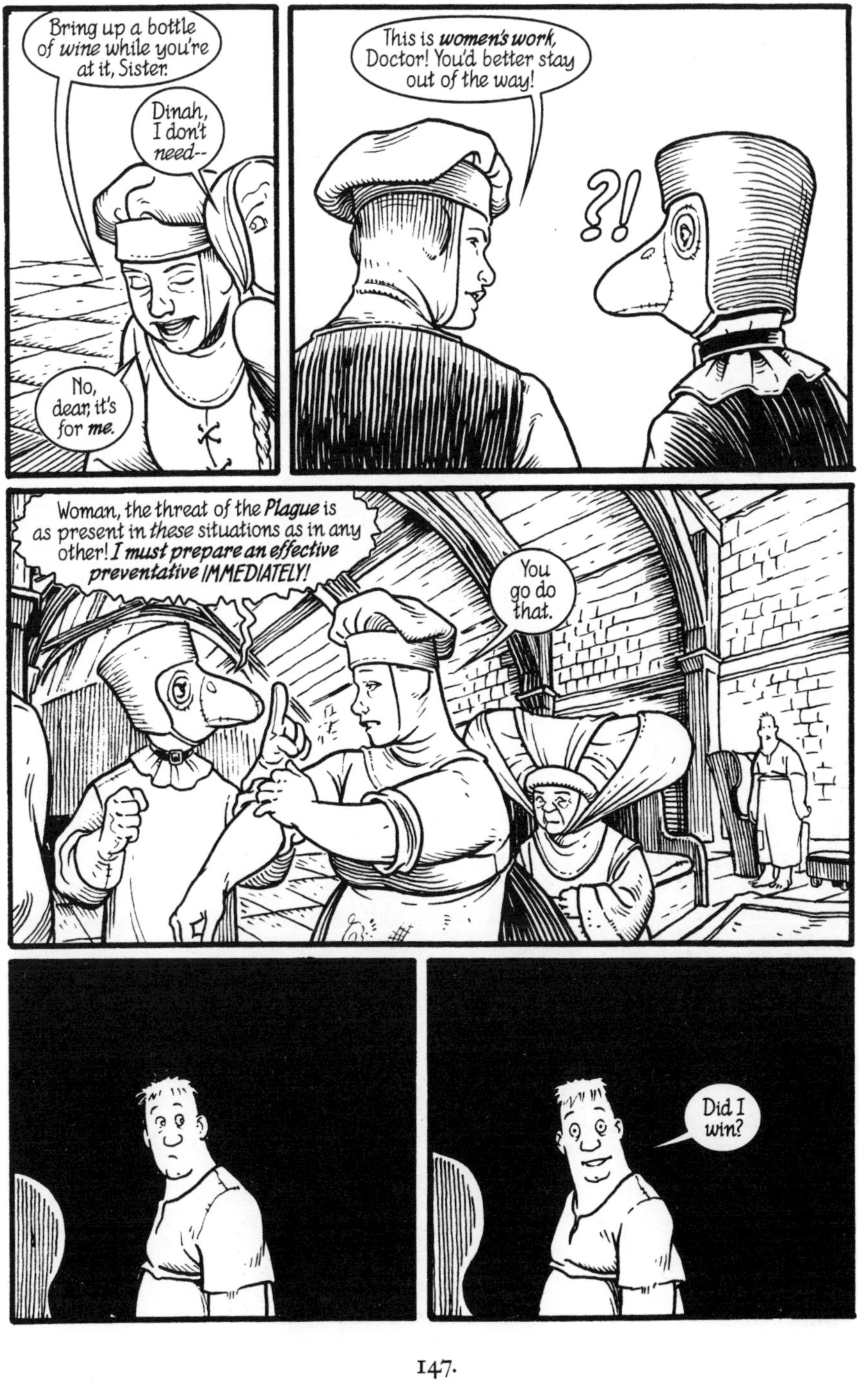
Bring up a bottle of *wine* while you're at it, Sister.
Dinah, I don't need--
No, dear, it's for **me**.
This is ***women's work***, Doctor! You'd better stay out of the way!
?!
Woman, the threat of the *Plague* is as present in *these* situations as in any other! ***I must prepare an effective preventative*** IMMEDIATELY!
You go do that.
Did I win?

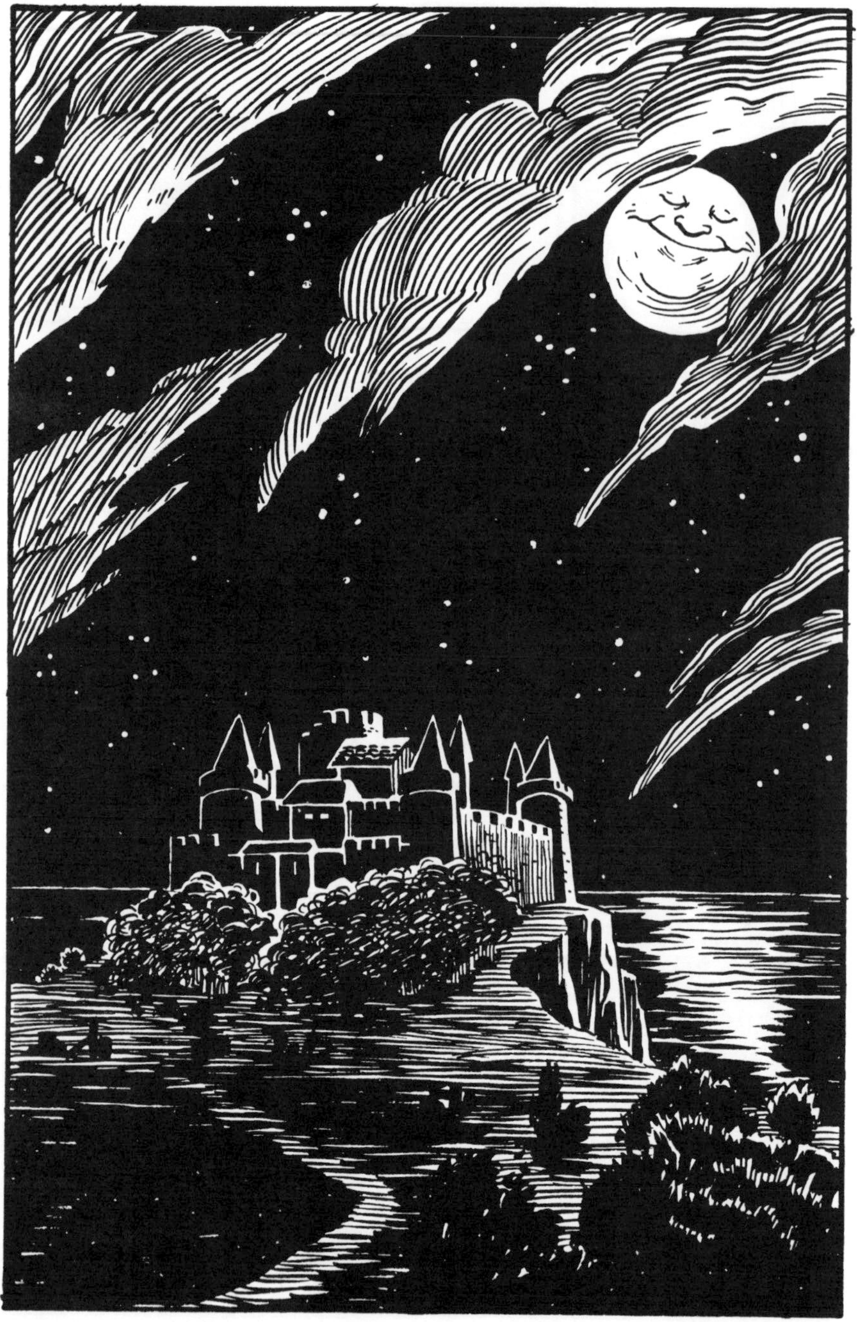

Chapter 7.

· THE CAGED HEART ·

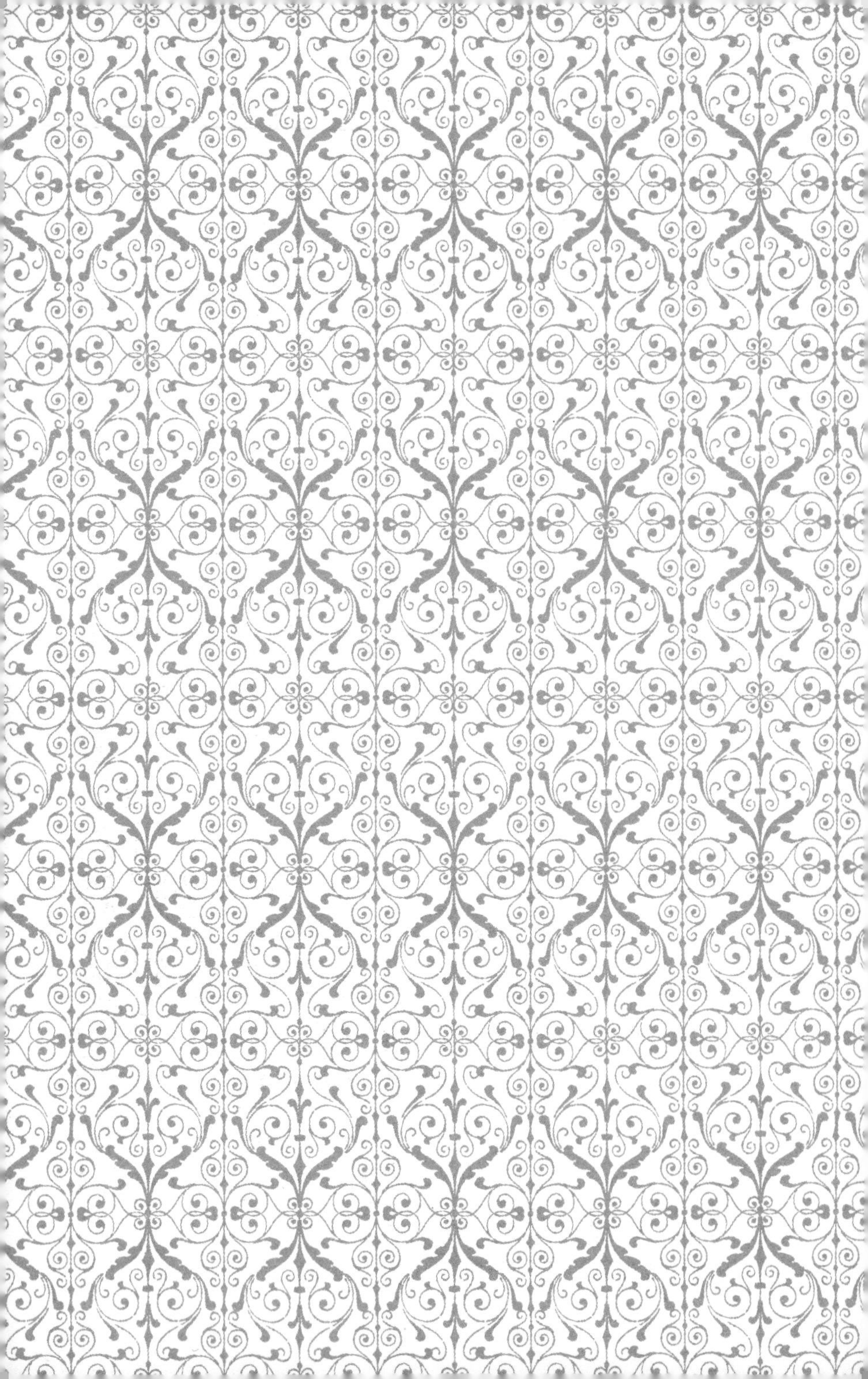

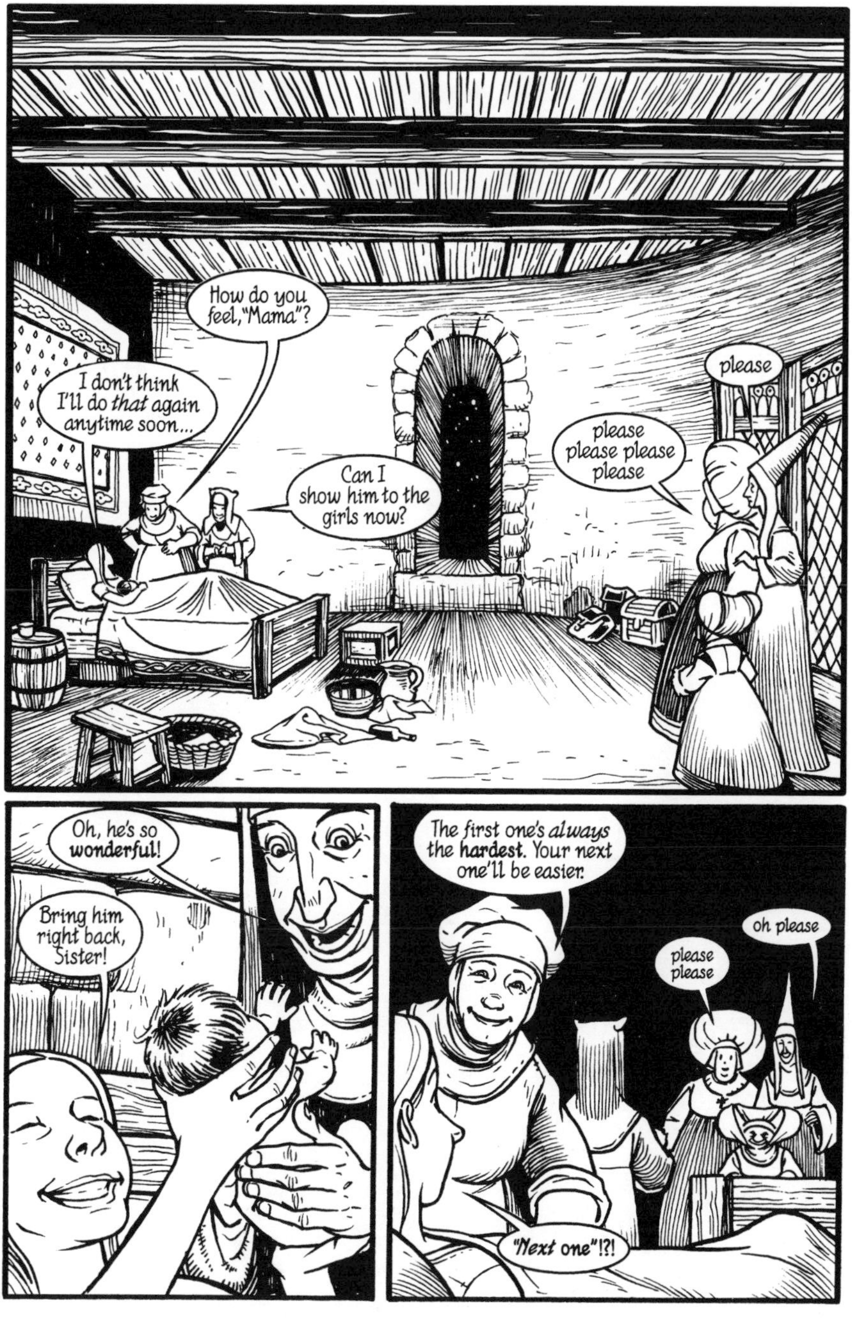
How do you feel, "Mama"?
I don't think I'll do *that* again anytime soon...
Can I show him to the girls now?
please
please please please please
Oh, he's so **wonderful**!
Bring him right back, Sister!
The first one's *always* the **hardest**. Your next one'll be easier.
please please
oh please
"*Next* one"!?!

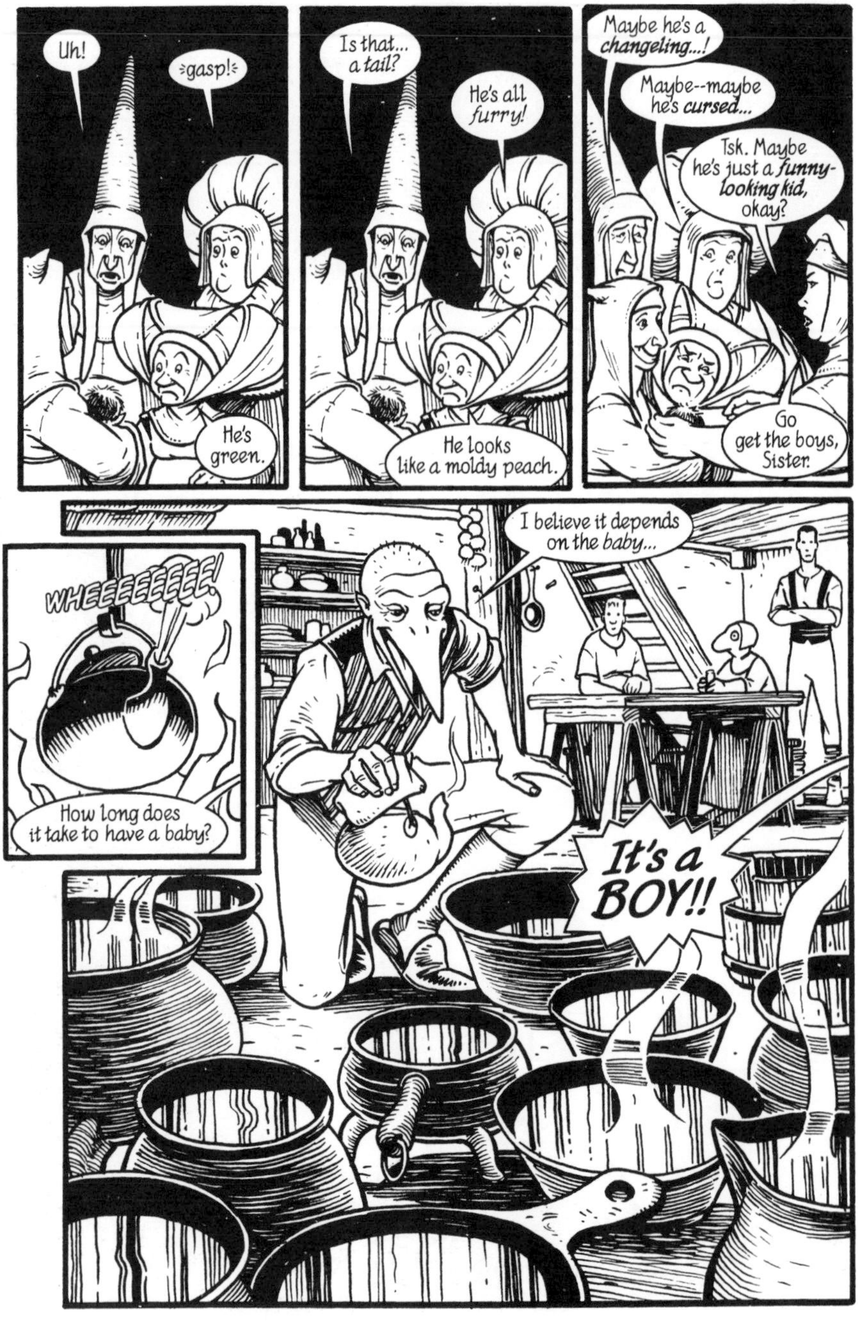
Uh!
gasp!
He's green.
Is that... a tail?
He's all furry!
He looks like a moldy peach.
Maybe he's a changeling...!
Maybe--maybe he's cursed...
Tsk. Maybe he's just a funny-looking kid, okay?
Go get the boys, Sister.
WHEEEEEEEEE!
How long does it take to have a baby?
I believe it depends on the baby...
It's a BOY!!

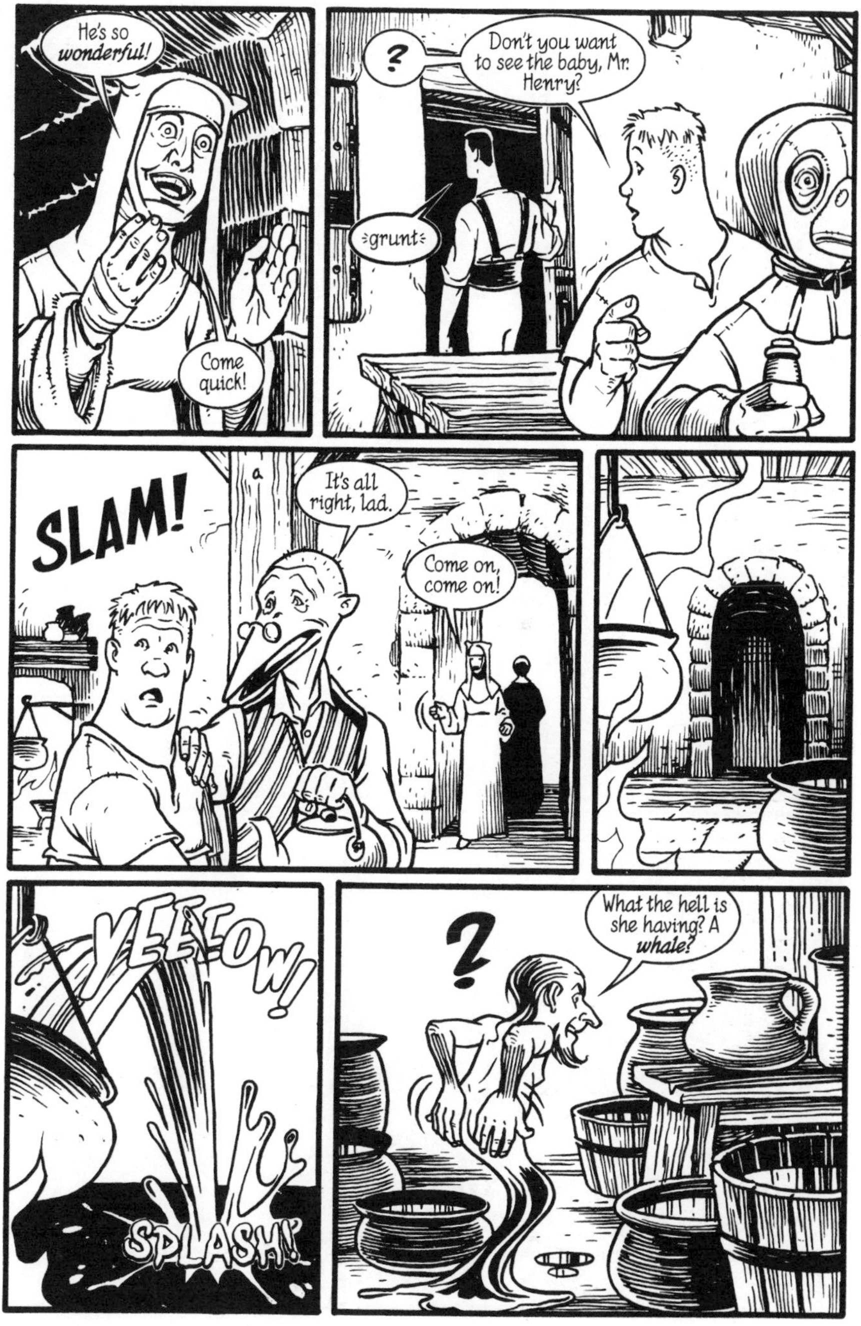
He's so *wonderful!*
Come quick!
?
Don't you want to see the baby, Mr. Henry?
grunt
SLAM!
It's all right, lad.
Come on, come on!
YEEEOW!
SPLASH!
?
What the hell is she having? A *whale?*

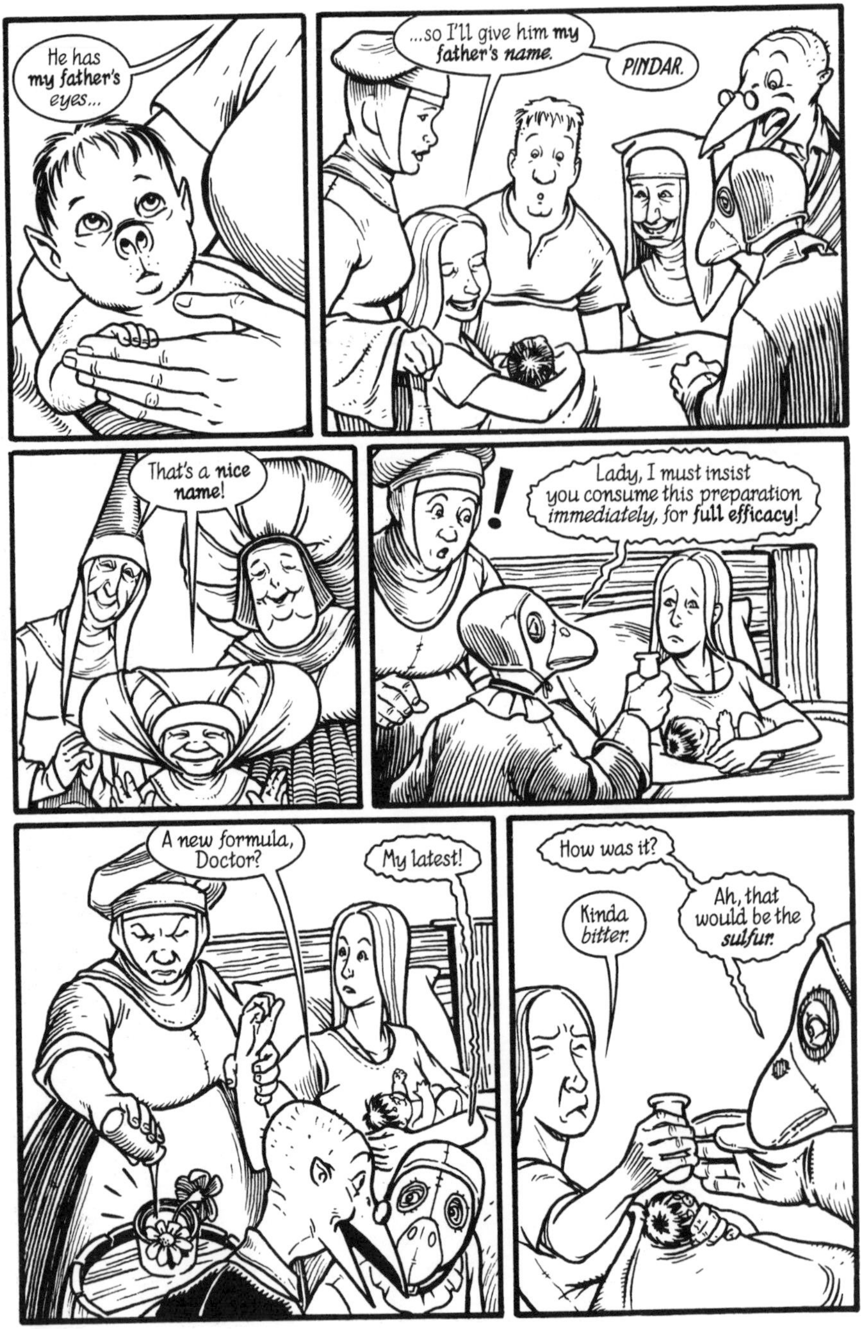
He has **my father's** eyes...
...so I'll give him **my father's *name*.**
PINDAR.
That's a **nice name**!
!
Lady, I must insist you consume this preparation *immediately*, for **full efficacy**!
A new formula, Doctor?
My latest!
How was it?
Kinda *bitter.*
Ah, that would be the ***sulfur.***

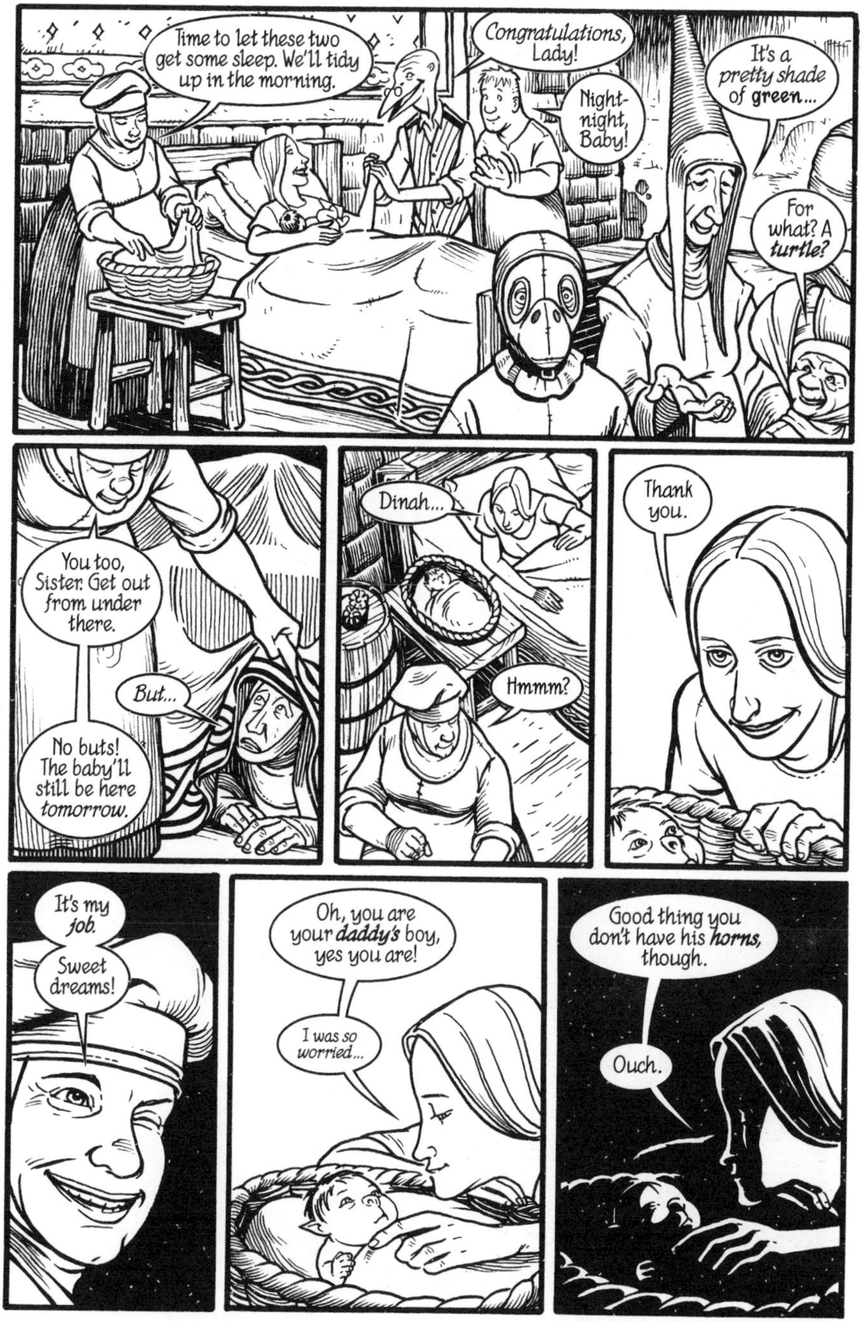
Time to let these two get some sleep. We'll tidy up in the morning.
Congratulations, Lady!
Night-night, Baby!
It's a pretty shade of **green**...
For what? A *turtle?*
You too, Sister. Get out from under there.
But...
No buts! The baby'll still be here *tomorrow.*
Dinah...
Hmmm?
Thank you.
It's my *job.*
Sweet dreams!
Oh, you are your *daddy's* boy, yes you are!
I was so worried...
Good thing you don't have his *horns,* though.
Ouch.

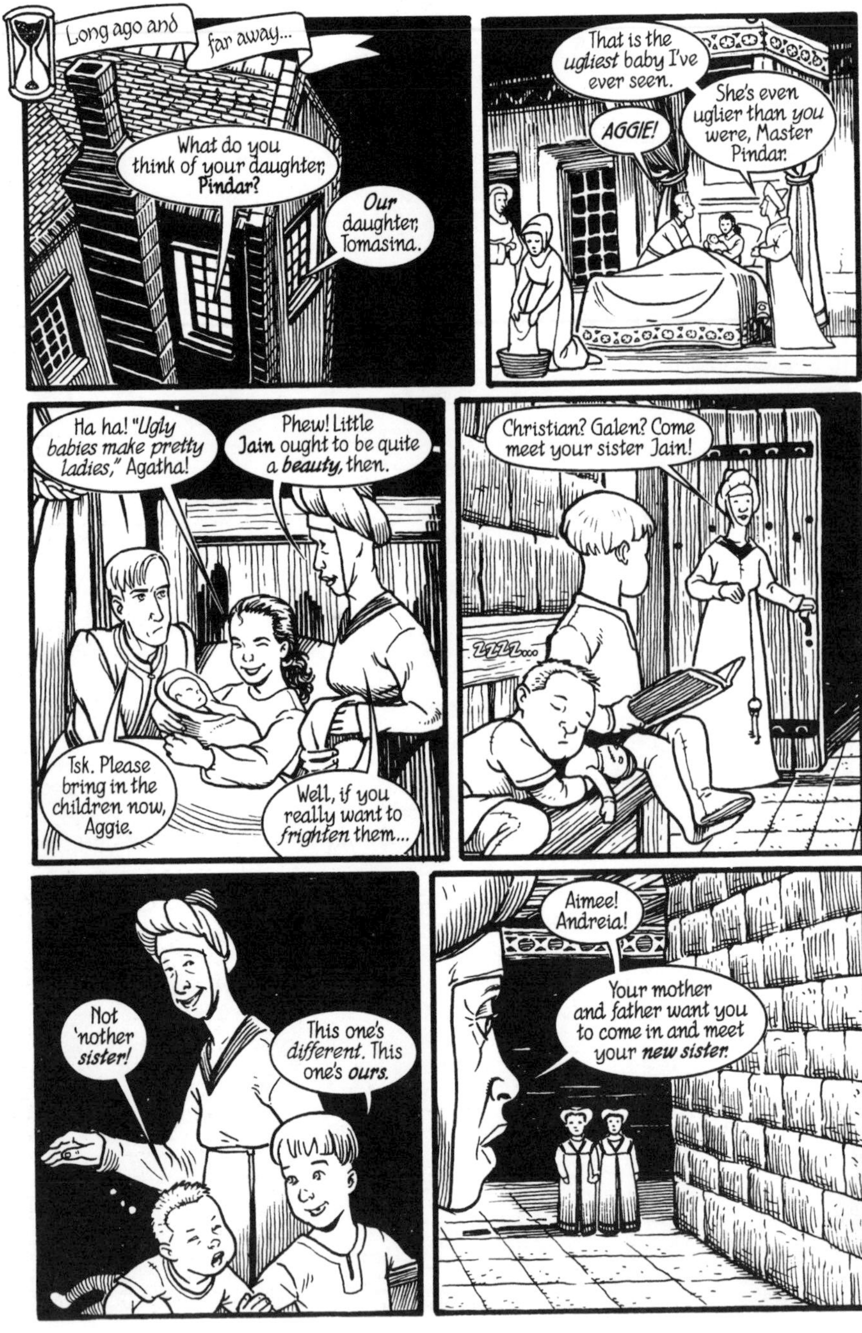
Long ago and
far away...
What do you think of your daughter, Pindar?
Our daughter, Tomasina.
That is the ugliest baby I've ever seen.
AGGIE!
She's even uglier than you were, Master Pindar.
Ha ha! "Ugly babies make pretty ladies," Agatha!
Phew! Little Jain ought to be quite a beauty, then.
Tsk. Please bring in the children now, Aggie.
Well, if you really want to frighten them...
Christian? Galen? Come meet your sister Jain!
ZZZZ...
Not 'nother sister!
This one's different. This one's ours.
Aimee! Andreia!
Your mother and father want you to come in and meet your new sister.

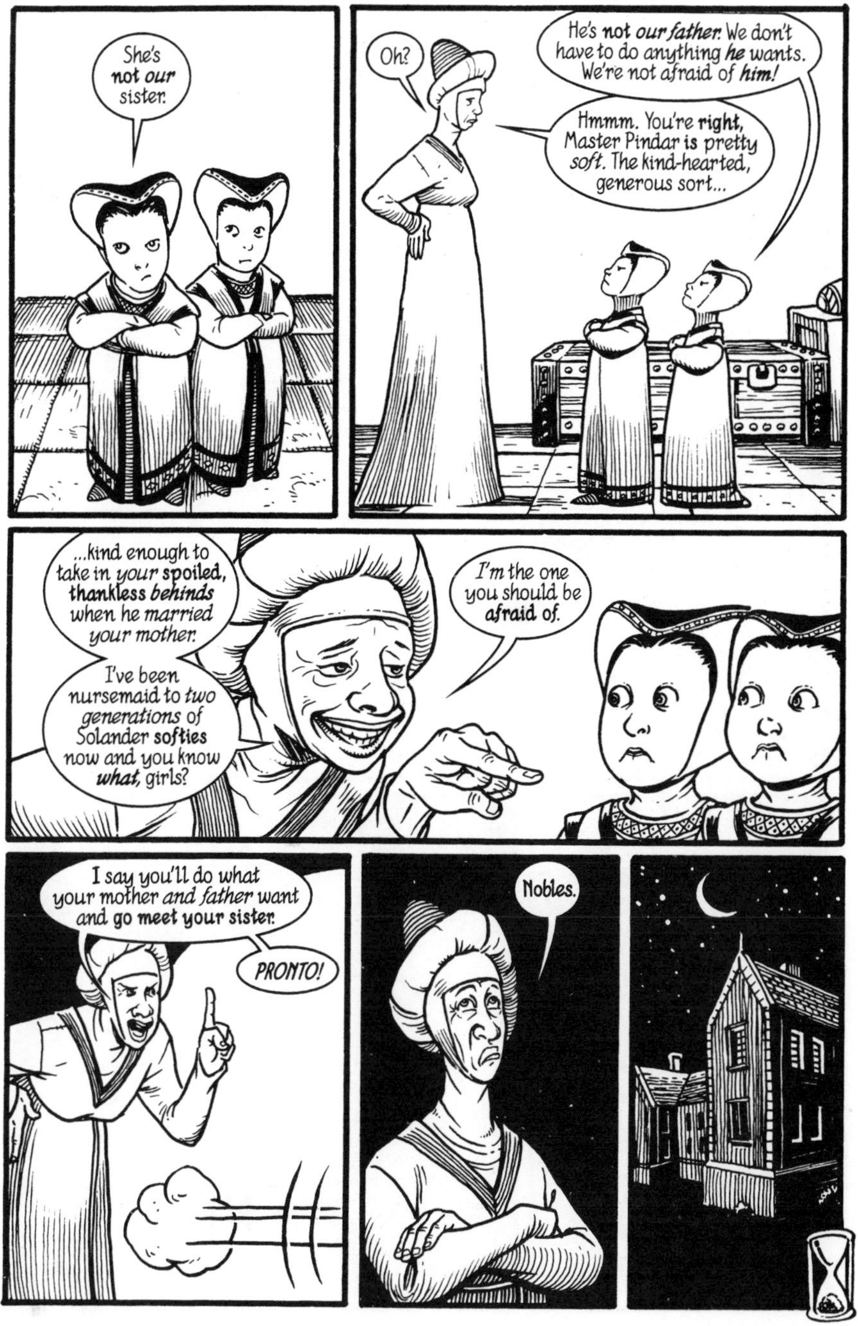
She's **not our** sister.
Oh?
He's **not our father.** We don't have to do anything ***he*** wants. We're not afraid of ***him!***
Hmmm. You're **right,** Master Pindar **is** pretty *soft*. The kind-hearted, generous sort...
...kind enough to take in *your* **spoiled, thankless *behinds*** when he married your mother.
I've been nursemaid to *two generations* of Solander **softies** now and you know ***what,*** girls?
I'm the one you should be **afraid of.**
I say you'll do *what* your mother *and father* want and **go meet your sister.**
PRONTO!
Nobles.

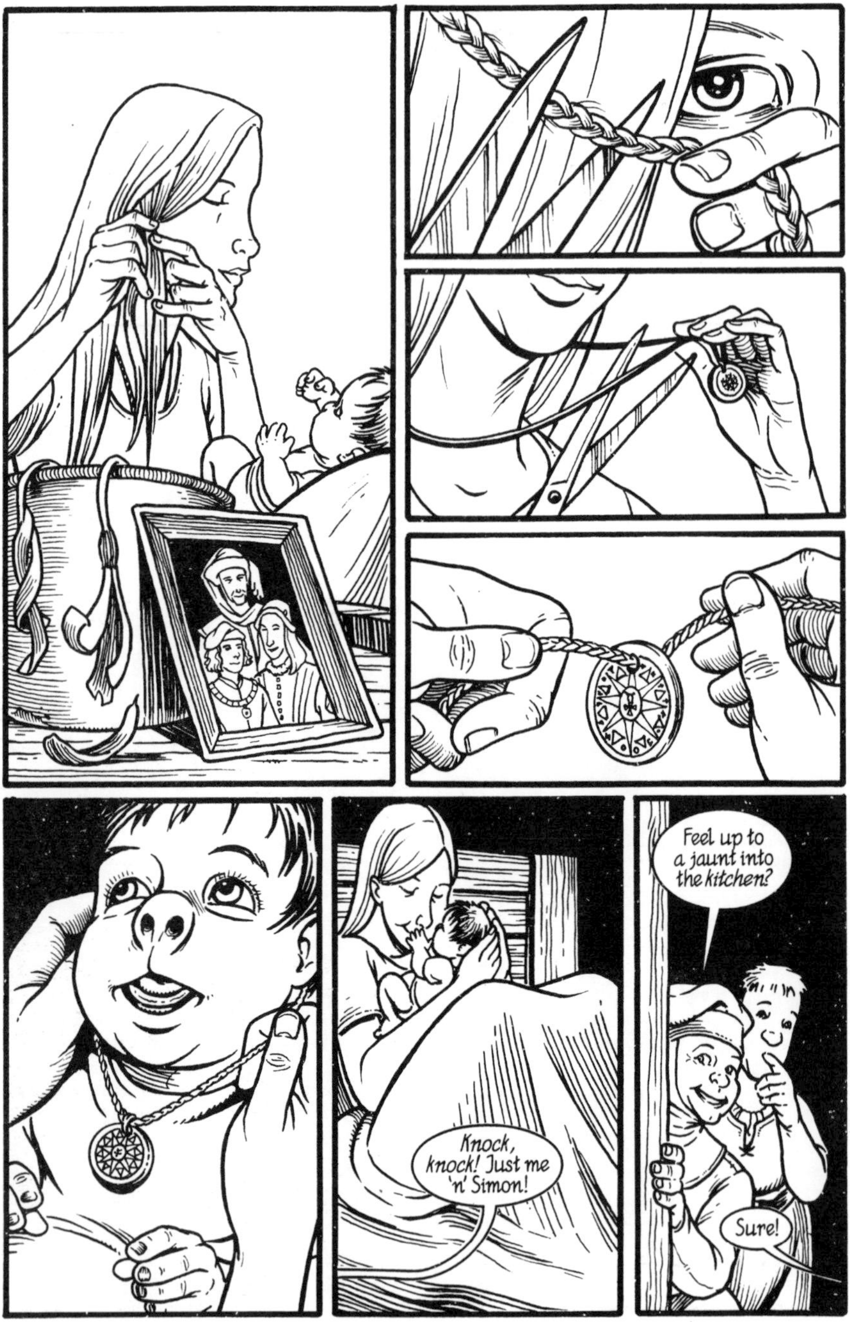
Knock, knock! Just me 'n' Simon!
Feel up to a jaunt into the kitchen?
Sure!

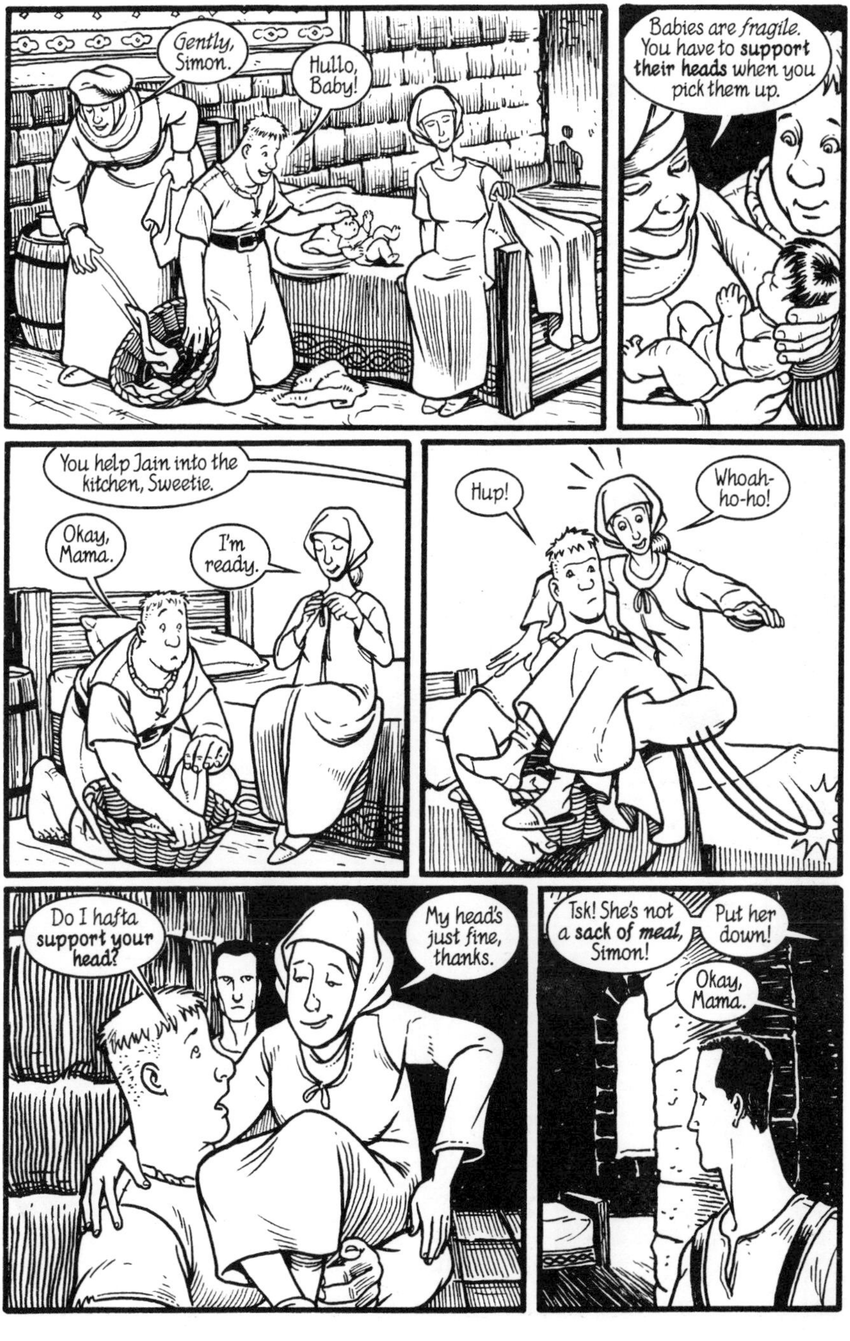
Gently, Simon.
Hullo, Baby!
Babies are *fragile.* You have to **support their heads** when you pick them up.
You help Jain into the kitchen, Sweetie.
Okay, Mama.
I'm ready.
Hup!
Whoah-ho-ho!
Do I hafta **support your head?**
My head's just fine, thanks.
Tsk! She's not a **sack of *meal,*** Simon!
Put her down!
Okay, Mama.

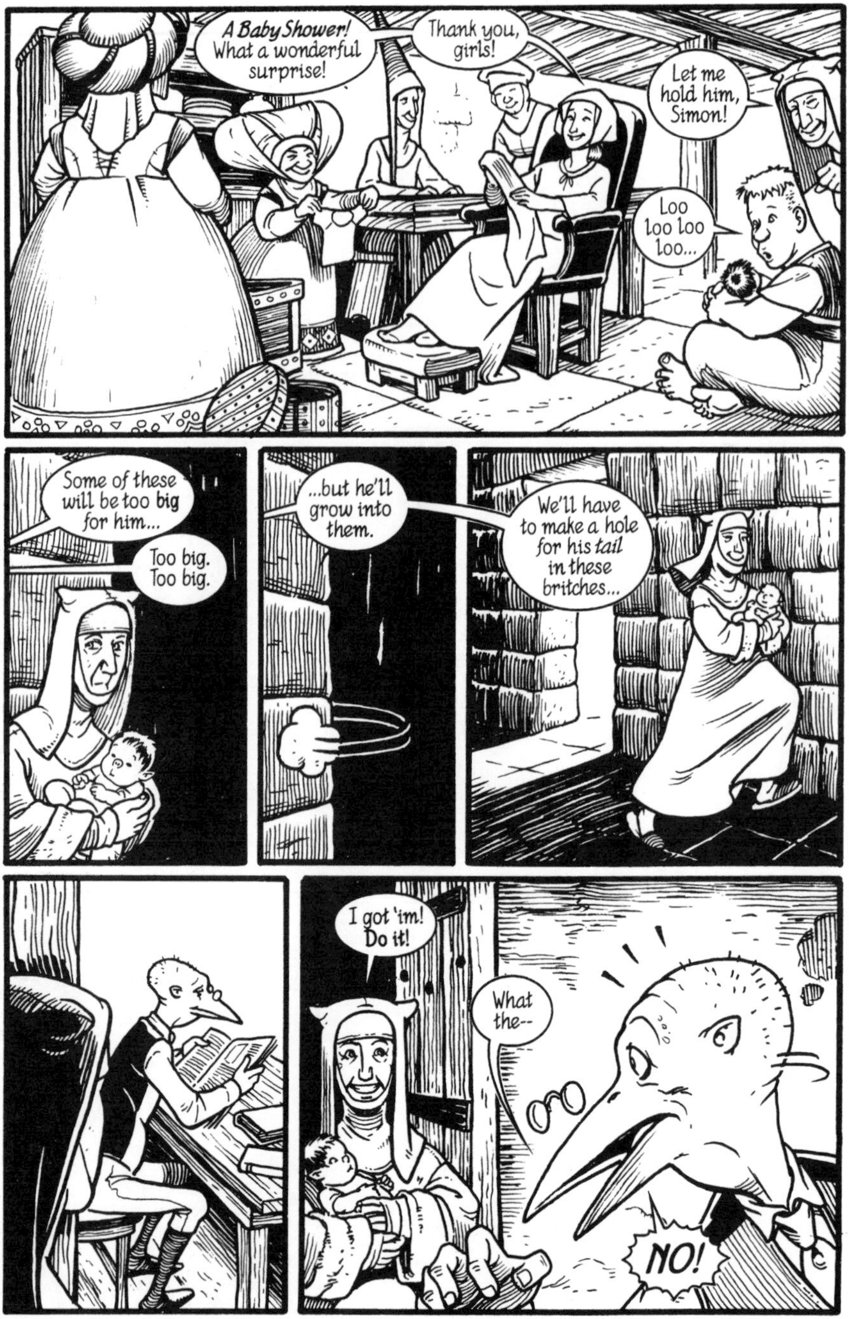
A Baby Shower! What a wonderful surprise!
Thank you, girls!
Let me hold him, Simon!
Loo loo loo loo...
Some of these will be too big for him...
Too big. Too big.
...but he'll grow into them.
We'll have to make a hole for his tail in these britches...
I got 'im! Do it!
What the--
NO!

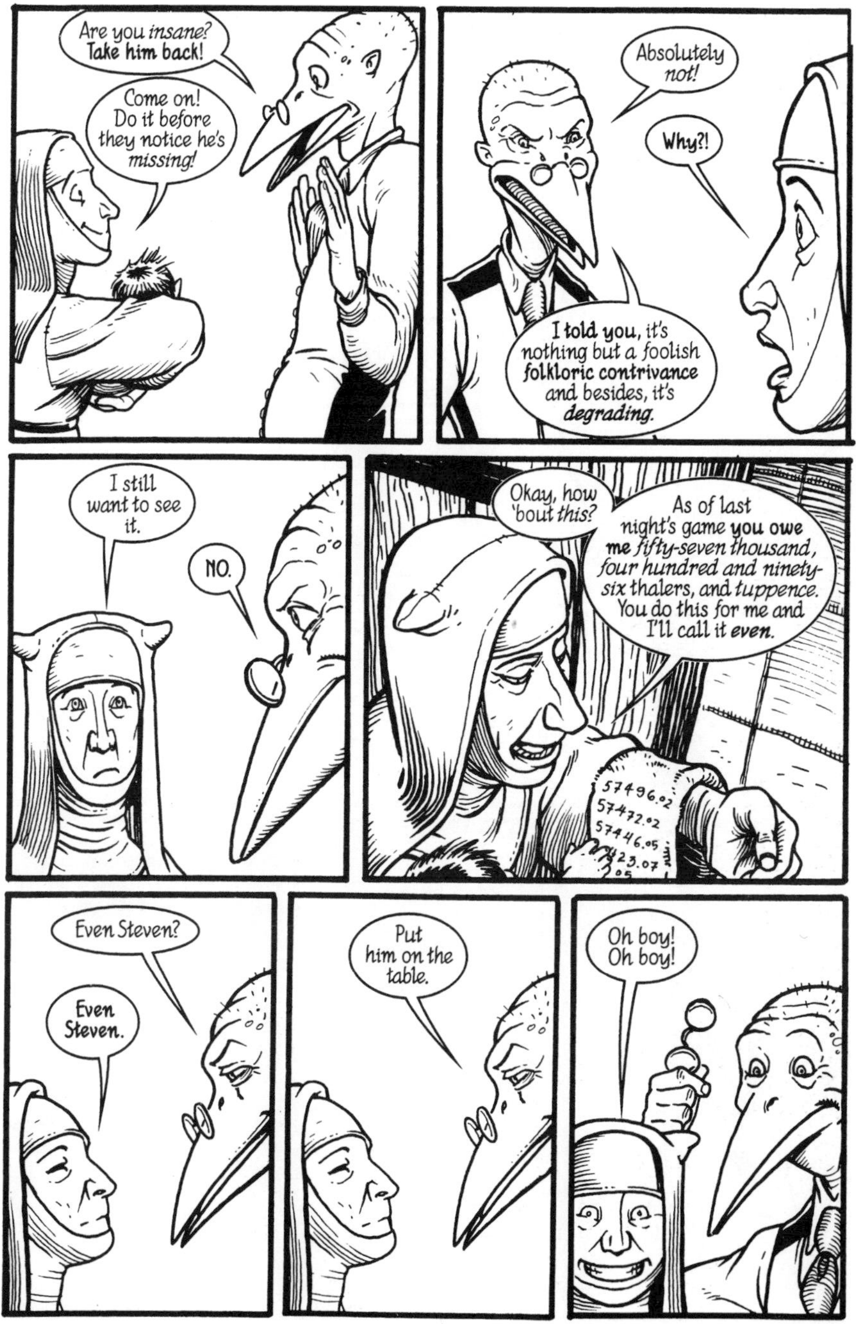
Are you *insane?* **Take him back!**
Come on! Do it before they notice he's *missing!*
Absolutely *not!*
Why?!
I told you, it's nothing but a foolish **folkloric contrivance** and besides, it's ***degrading***.
I still want to see it.
NO.
Okay, how 'bout *this?*
As of last night's game **you owe me** *fifty-seven thousand, four hundred and ninety-six thalers,* and *tuppence.* You do this for me and I'll call it ***even***.
57496.02
57472.02
57446.05
Even Steven?
Even Steven.
Put him on the table.
Oh boy! Oh boy!

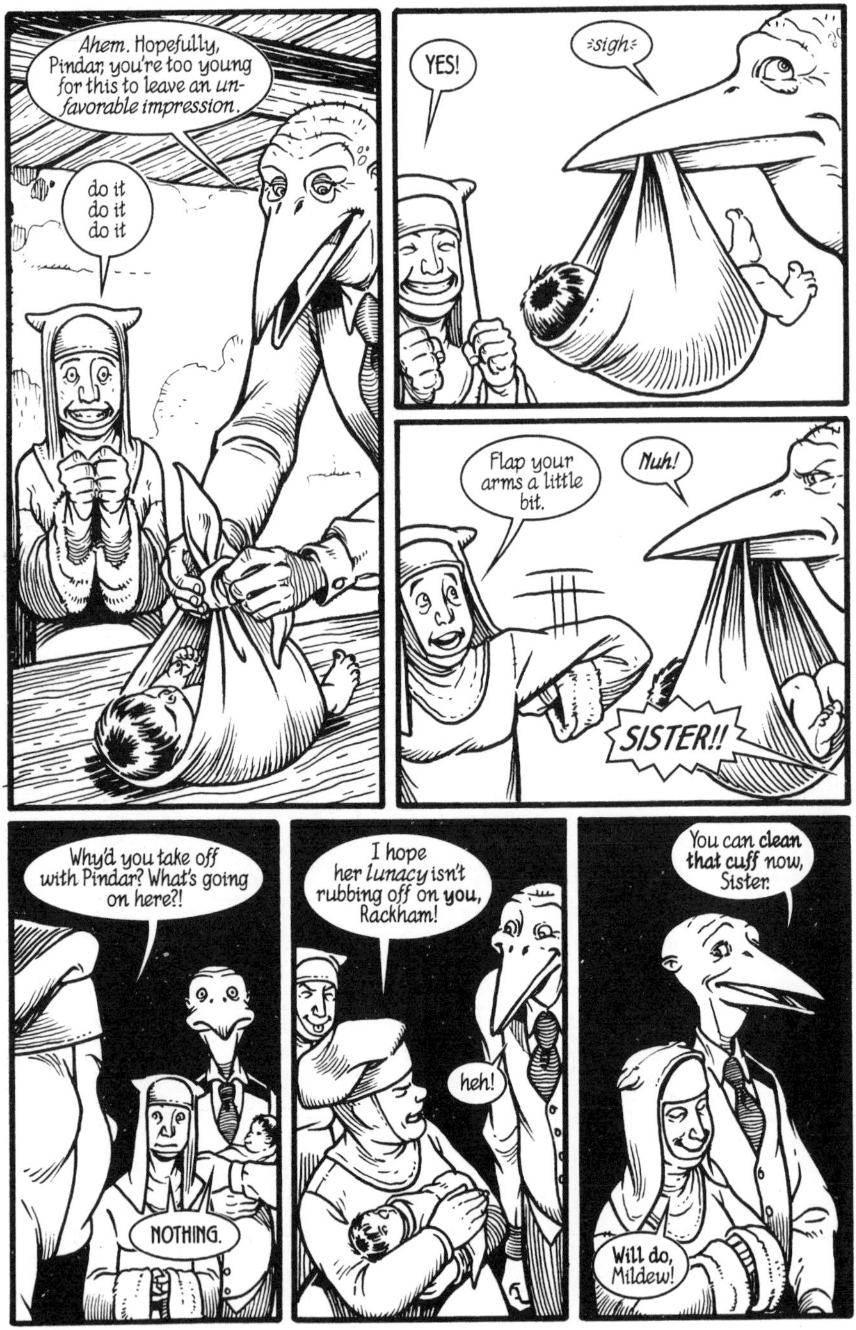
Ahem. Hopefully, Pindar, you're too young for this to leave an unfavorable impression.
do it do it do it
YES!
sigh
Flap your arms a little bit.
Nuh!
SISTER!!
Why'd you take off with Pindar? What's going on here?!
NOTHING.
I hope her lunacy isn't rubbing off on you, Rackham!
heh!
You can clean that cuff now, Sister.
Will do, Mildew!

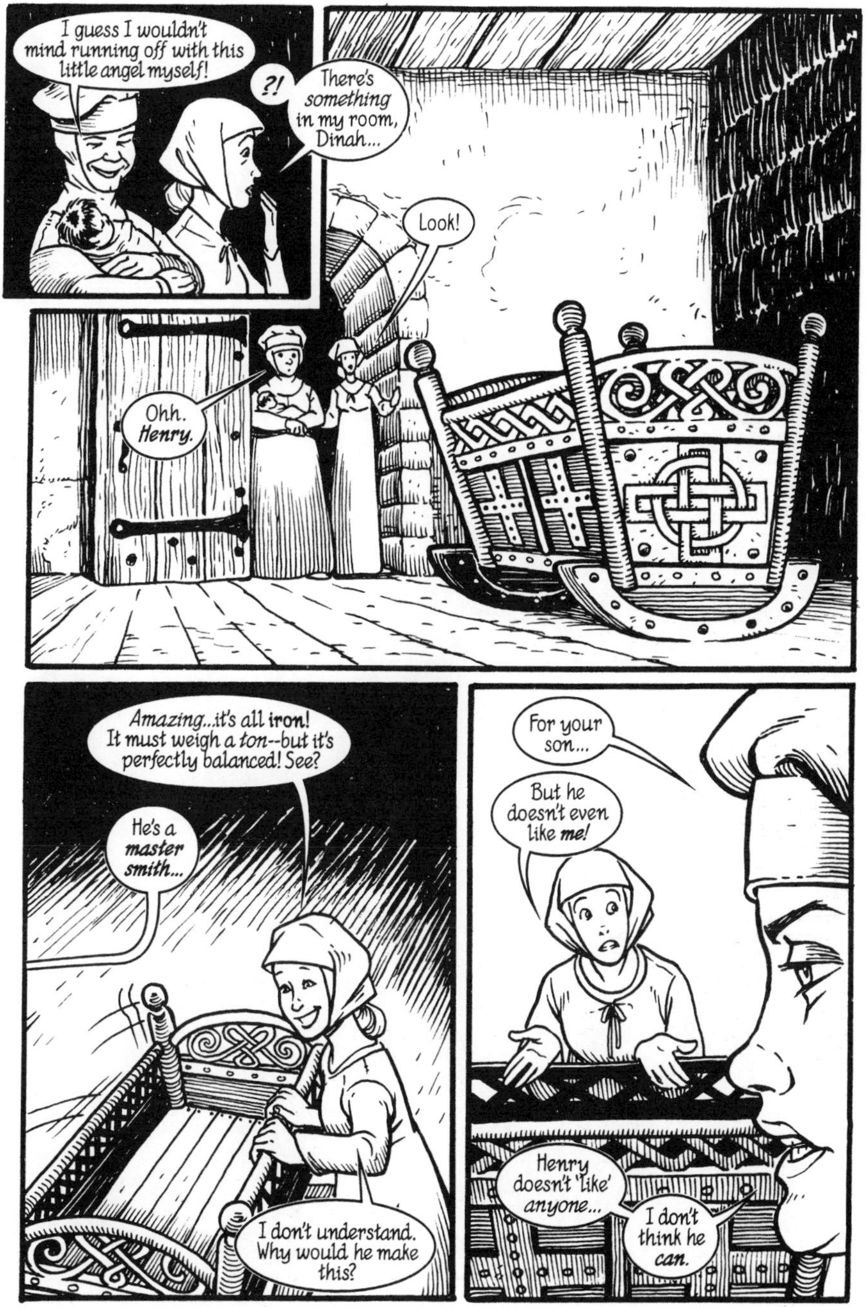
I guess I wouldn't mind running off with this little angel myself!
?!
There's *something* in my room, Dinah...
Look!
Ohh. *Henry.*
Amazing...it's all **iron**! It must weigh a *ton*--but it's perfectly balanced! See?
He's a ***master smith...***
I don't understand. Why would he make this?
For your son...
But he doesn't even like ***me!***
Henry doesn't 'like' *anyone*...
I don't think he ***can.***

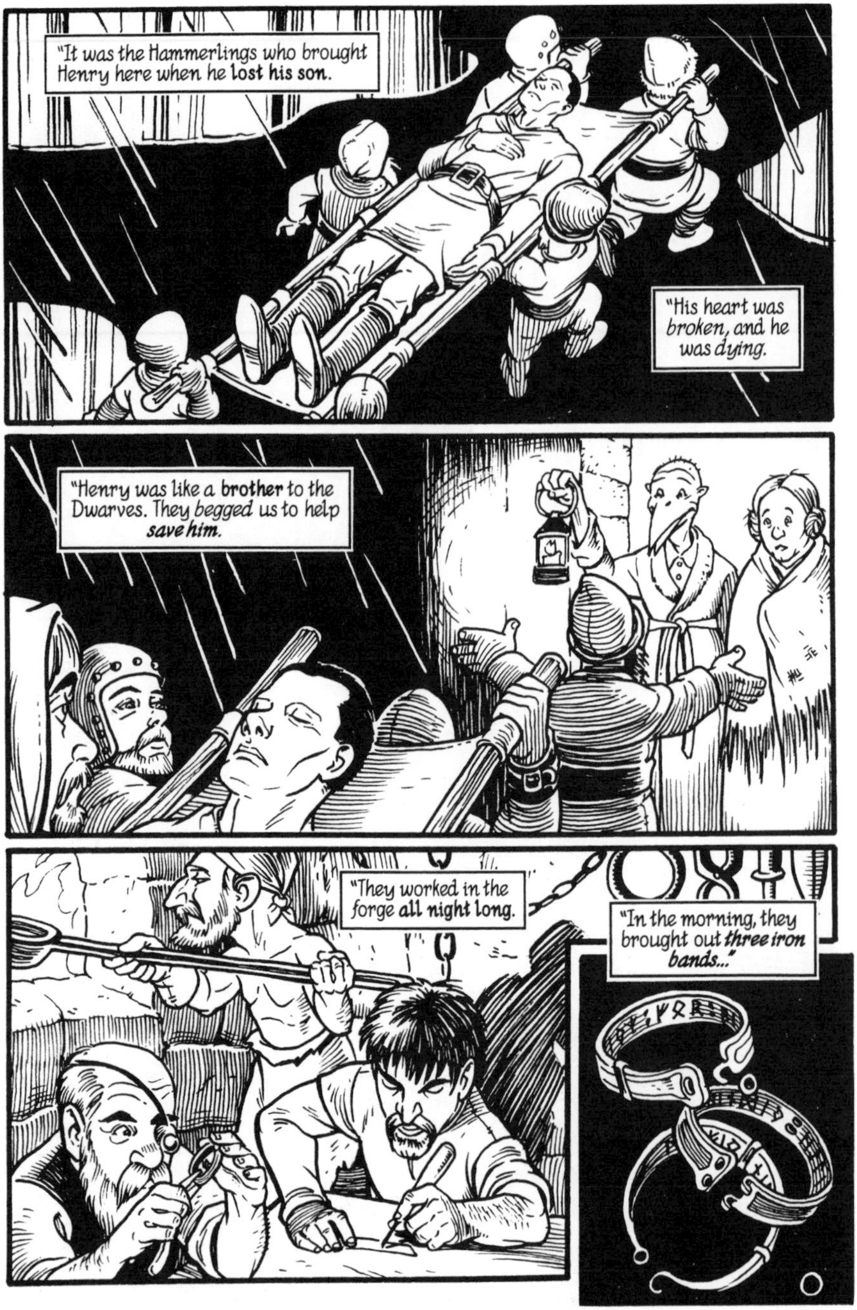
"It was the Hammerlings who brought Henry here when he lost his son.
"His heart was broken, and he was dying.
"Henry was like a brother to the Dwarves. They begged us to help save him.
"They worked in the forge all night long.
"In the morning, they brought out three iron bands..."

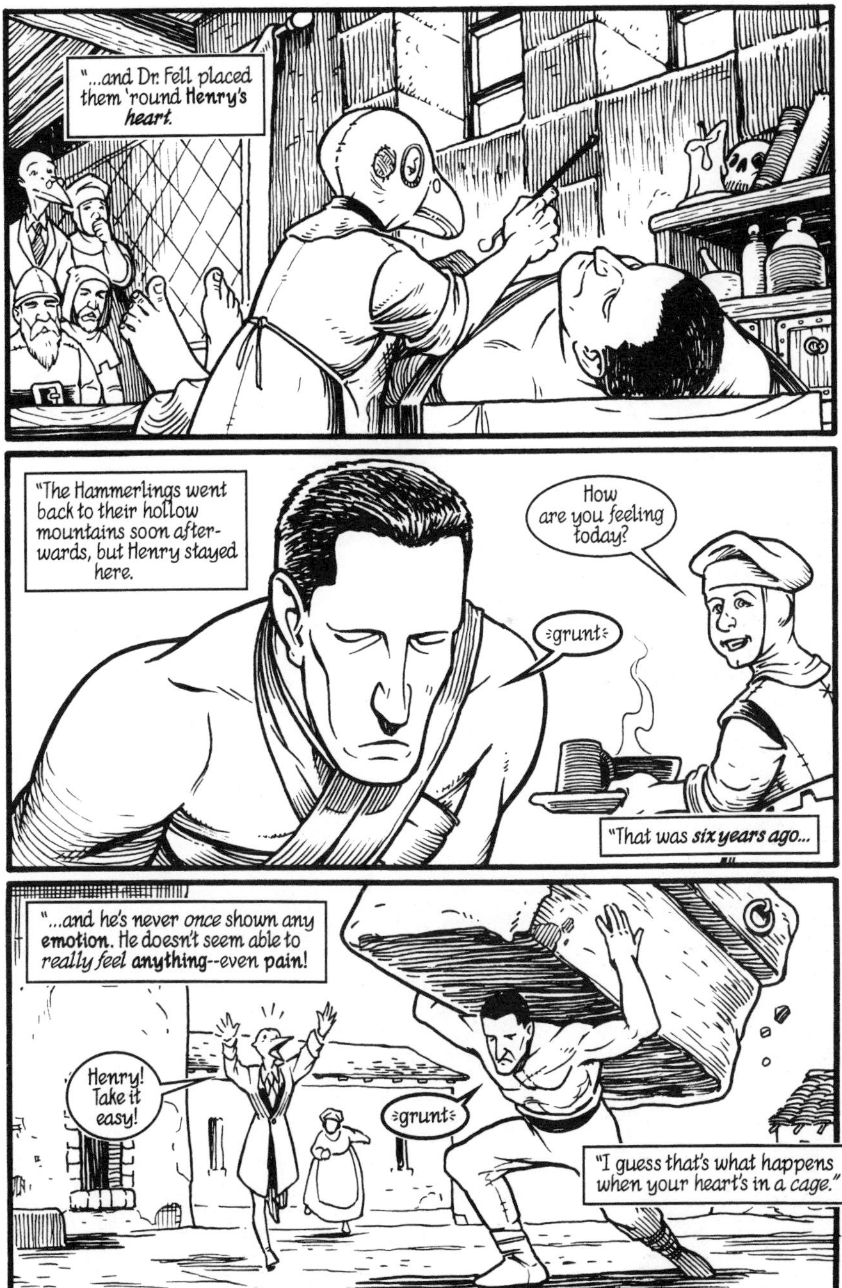
"...and Dr. Fell placed them 'round Henry's heart.
"The Hammerlings went back to their hollow mountains soon afterwards, but Henry stayed here.
How are you feeling today?
grunt
"That was six years ago...
"...and he's never once shown any emotion. He doesn't seem able to really feel anything--even pain!
Henry! Take it easy!
grunt
"I guess that's what happens when your heart's in a cage."

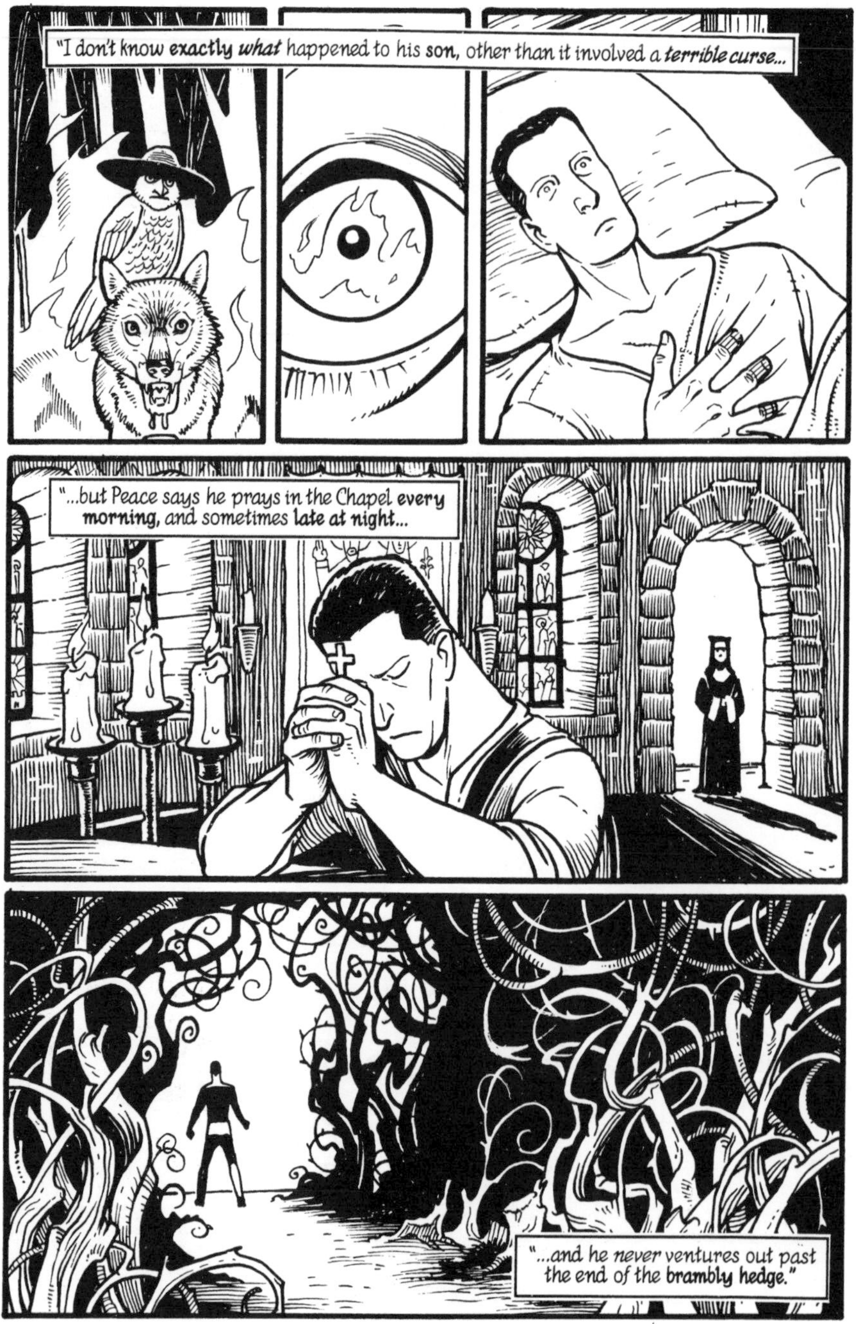
"I don't know **exactly** ***what*** happened to his **son**, other than it involved a ***terrible curse...***
"...but Peace says he prays in the Chapel **every morning**, and sometimes **late at night...**
"...and he *never* ventures out past the end of the **brambly hedge.**"

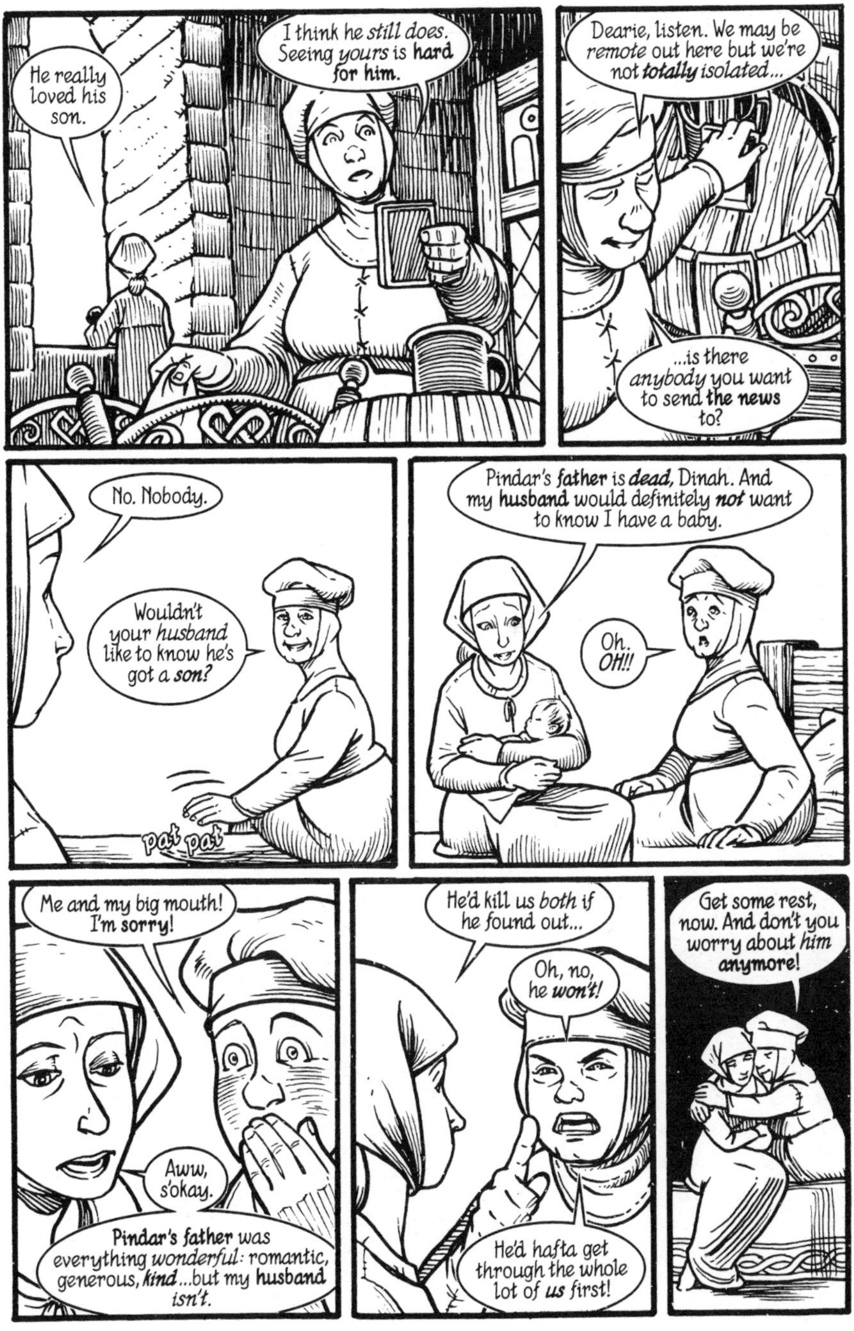
He really loved his son.
I think he *still does.* Seeing *yours* is **hard for him.**
Dearie, listen. We may be *remote* out here but we're not ***totally*** *isolated...*
...is there *anybody* you want to send **the news** to?
No. Nobody.
Wouldn't your *husband* like to know he's got a ***son?***
pat pat
Pindar's **father** is ***dead,*** Dinah. And my **husband** would definitely ***not*** want to know I have a baby.
Oh. *OH!!*
Me and my big mouth! I'm **sorry**!
Aww, s'okay.
Pindar's father was everything *wonderful*: romantic, generous, ***kind***...but my **husband** *isn't.*
He'd kill us *both* if he found out...
Oh, no, he ***won't!***
He'd hafta get through the whole lot of ***us*** first!
Get some rest, now. And don't you worry about *him* **anymore**!

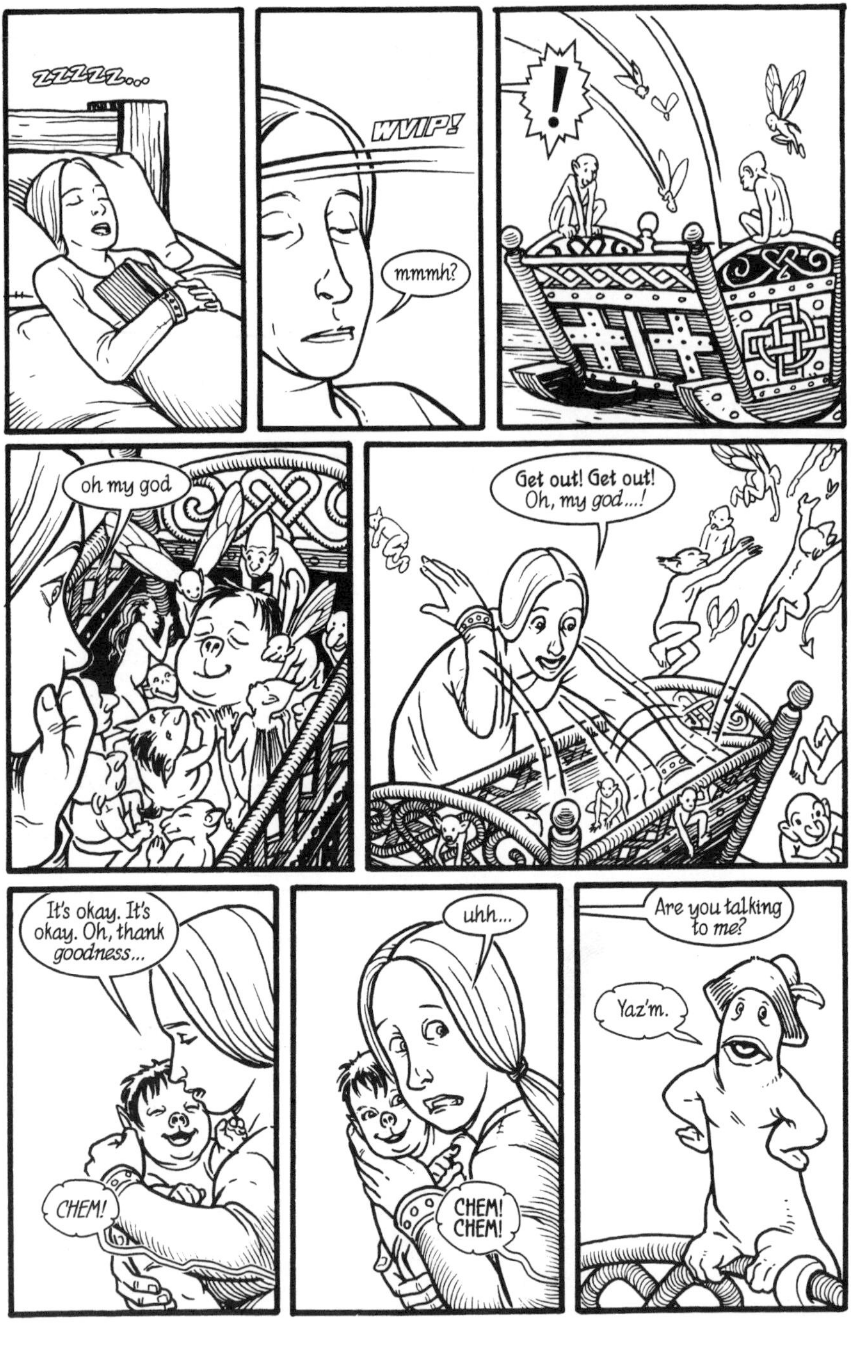
ZZZZZ...
WVIP!
mmmh?
!
oh my god
Get out! Get out! Oh, my god...!
It's okay. It's okay. Oh, thank goodness...
CHEM!
uhh...
CHEM! CHEM!
Are you talking to me?
Yaz'm.

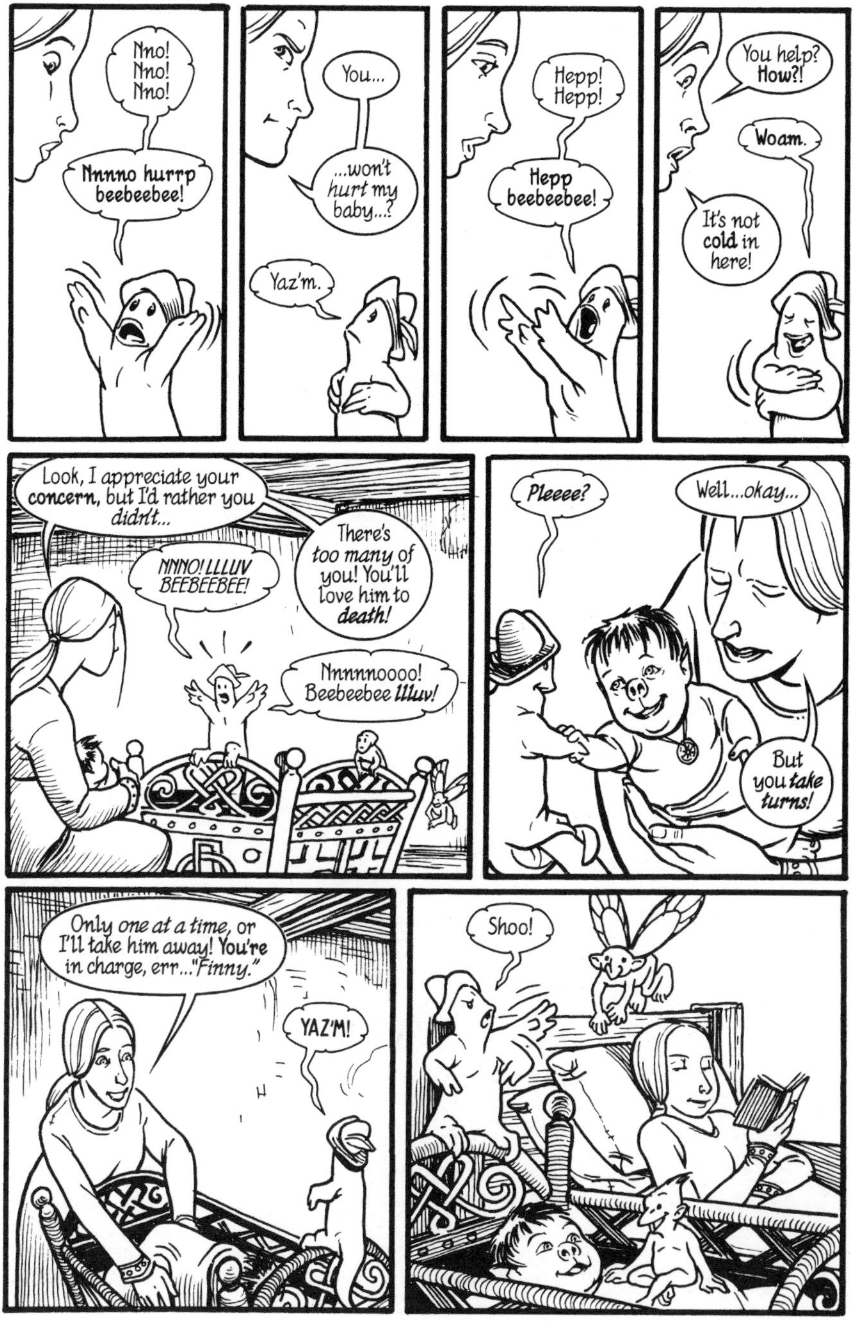
Nno!
Nno!
Nno!
Nnnno hurrp beebeebee!
You...
...won't hurt my baby...?
Yaz'm.
Hepp!
Hepp!
Hepp beebeebee!
You help? How?!
Woam.
It's not cold in here!
Look, I appreciate your concern, but I'd rather you didn't...
NNNO! LLLUV BEEBEEBEE!
There's too many of you! You'll love him to death!
Nnnnnoooo! Beebeebee llluv!
Pleeee?
Well...okay...
But you take turns!
Only one at a time, or I'll take him away! You're in charge, err..."Finny."
YAZ'M!
Shoo!

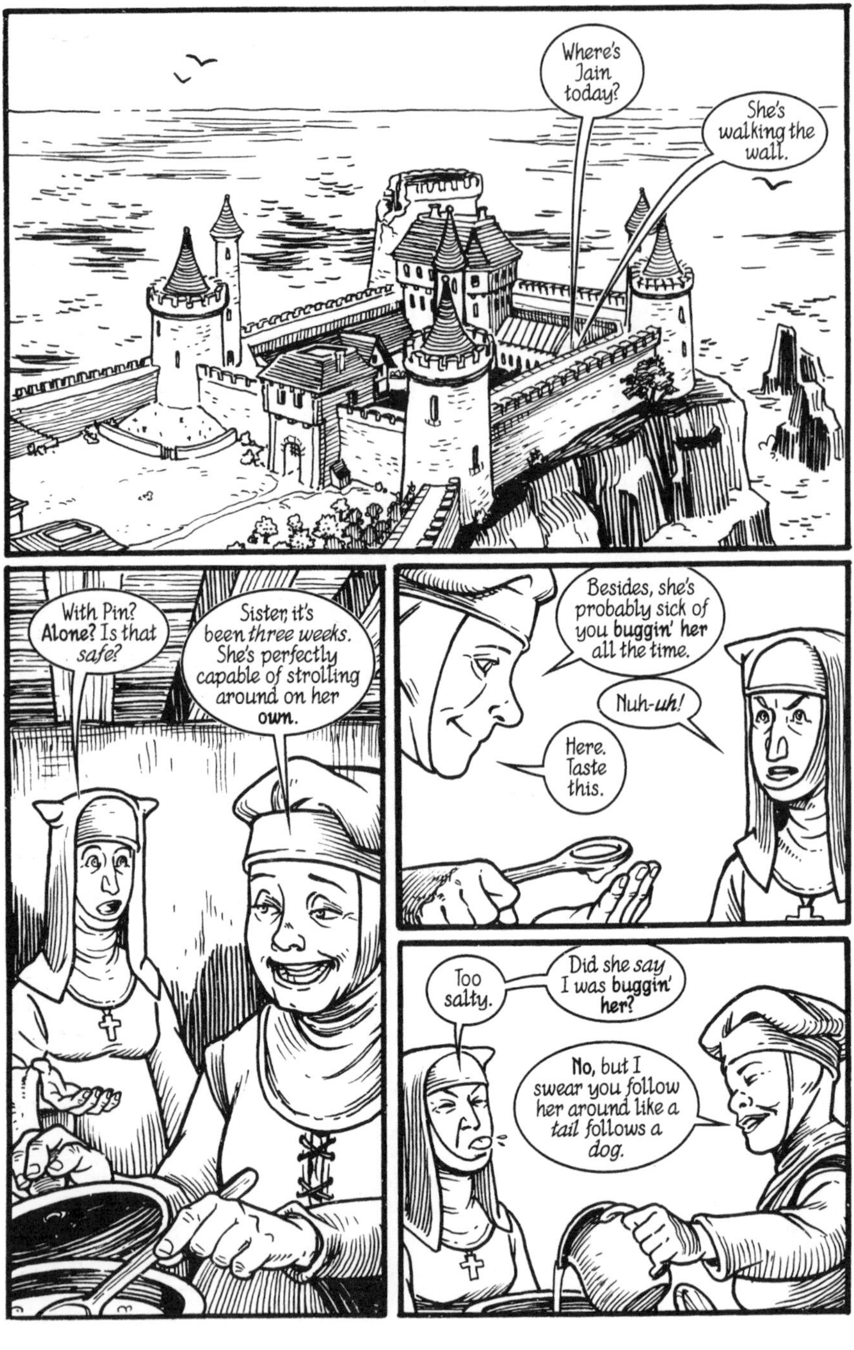
Where's Jain today?
She's walking the wall.
With Pin? **Alone?** Is that *safe?*
Sister, it's been *three weeks.* She's perfectly capable of strolling around on her **own**.
Besides, she's probably sick of you **buggin' her** all the time.
Nuh-*uh!*
Here. Taste this.
Too salty.
Did she *say* I was **buggin' her?**
No, but I swear you follow her around like a *tail* follows a dog.

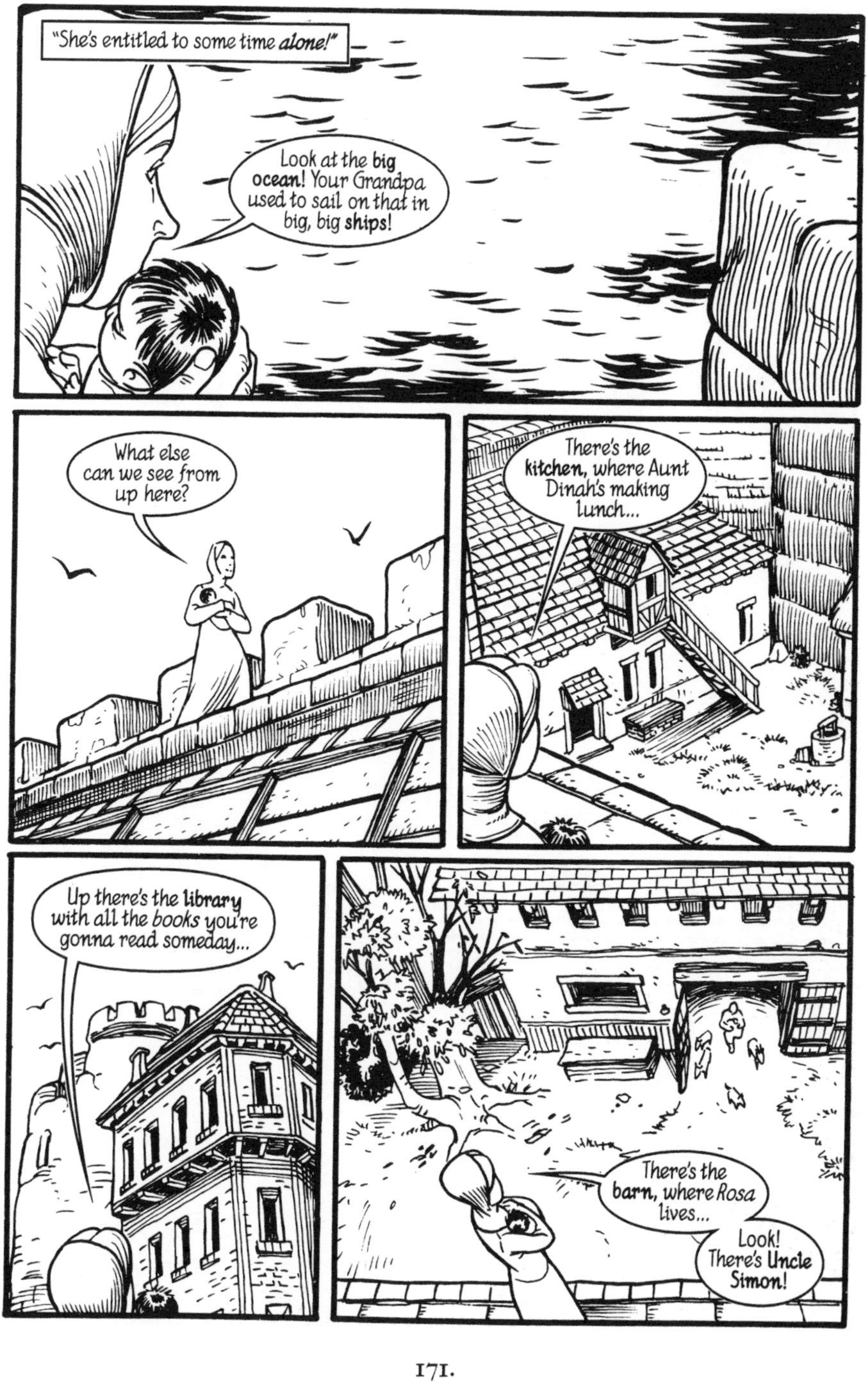
"She's entitled to some time *alone!*"
Look at the **big ocean**! Your Grandpa used to sail on that in big, big **ships**!
What else can we see from up here?
There's the **kitchen**, where Aunt Dinah's making lunch...
Up there's the **library** with all the *books* you're gonna read someday...
There's the **barn**, where *Rosa* lives...
Look! There's **Uncle Simon**!

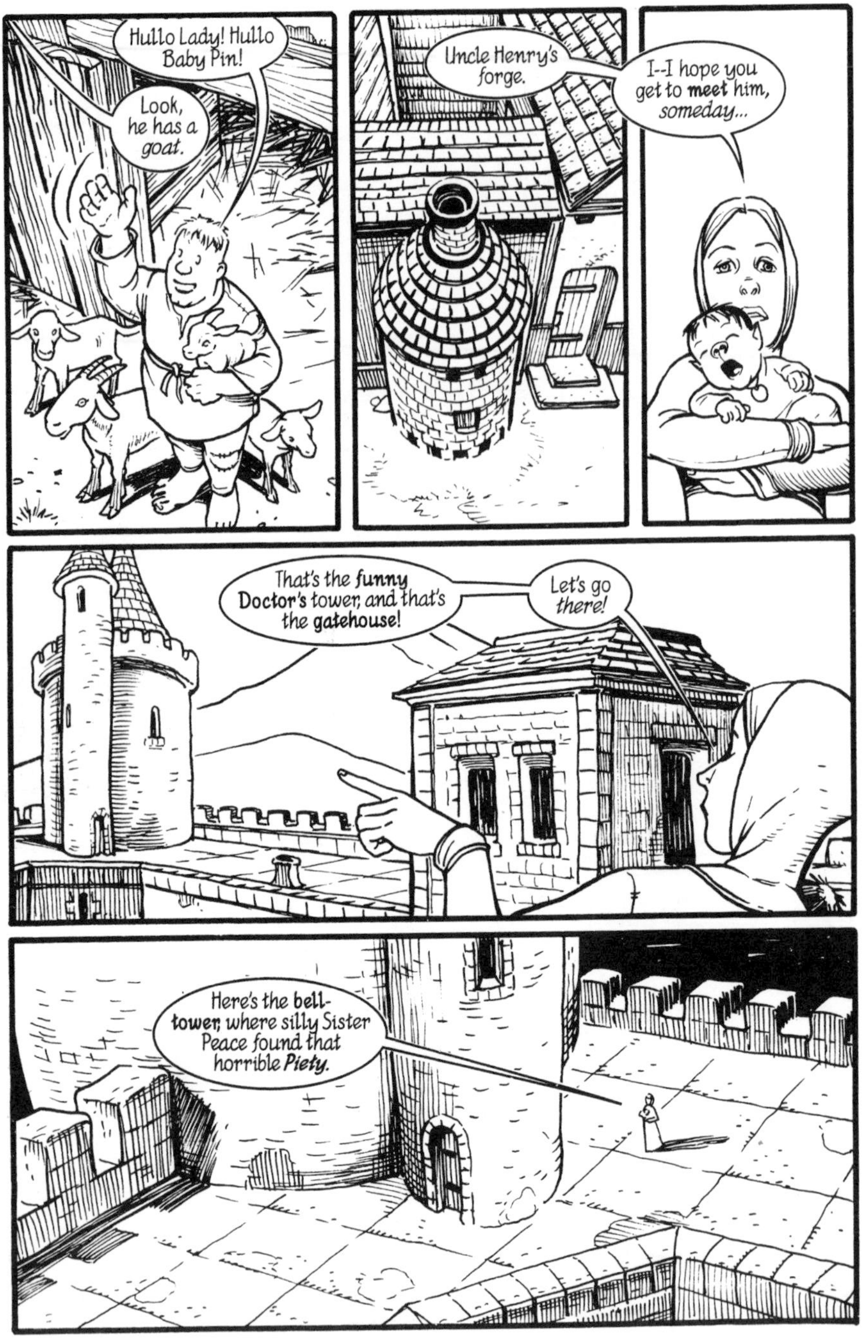
Hullo Lady! Hullo Baby Pin!
Look, he has a goat.
Uncle Henry's forge.
I--I hope you get to meet him, someday...
That's the funny Doctor's tower, and that's the gatehouse!
Let's go there!
Here's the bell-tower, where silly Sister Peace found that horrible Piety.

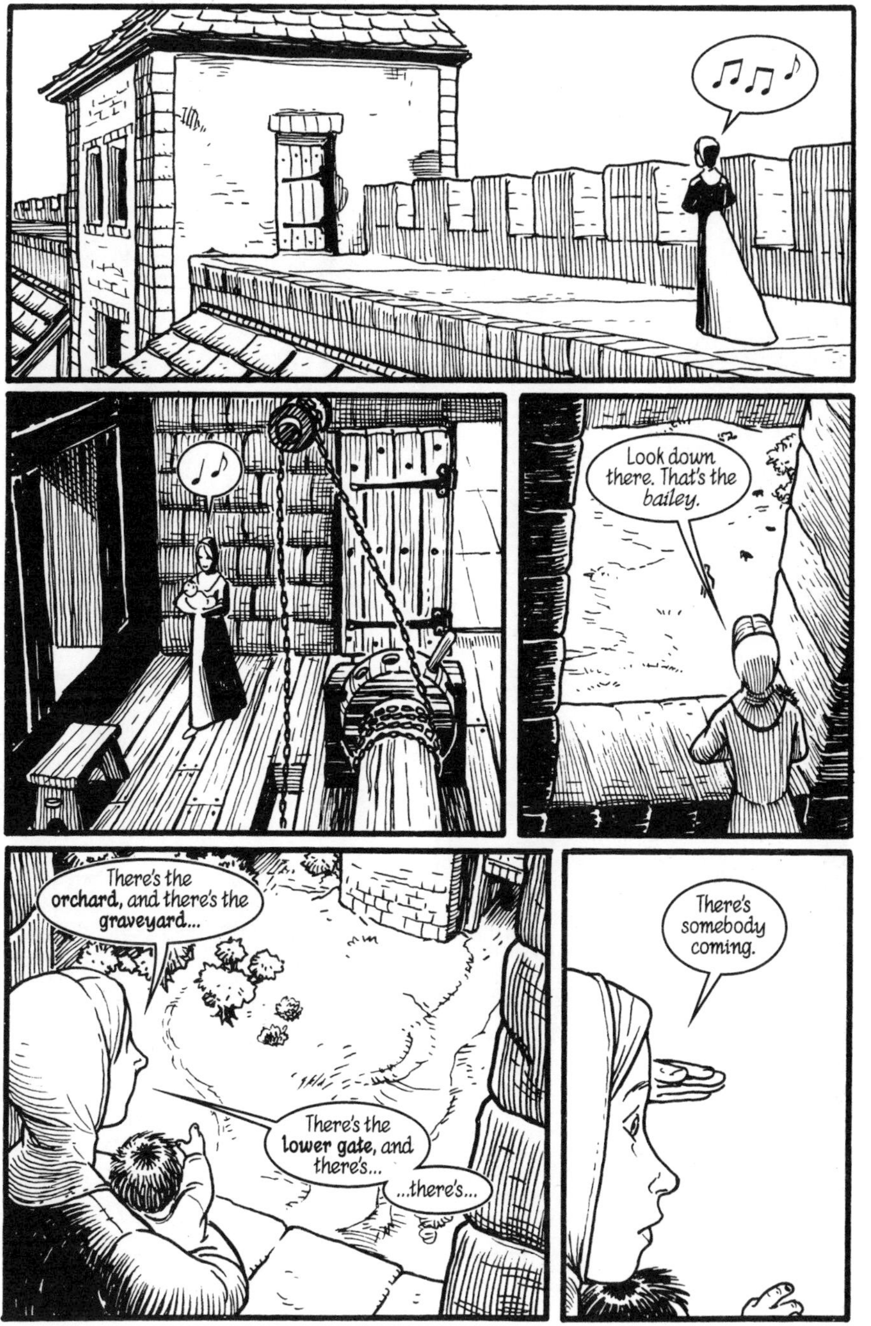
♫♫♪
♪♪
Look down there. That's the *bailey.*
There's the **orchard**, and there's the **graveyard**...
There's the **lower gate**, and there's...
...there's...
There's somebody coming.

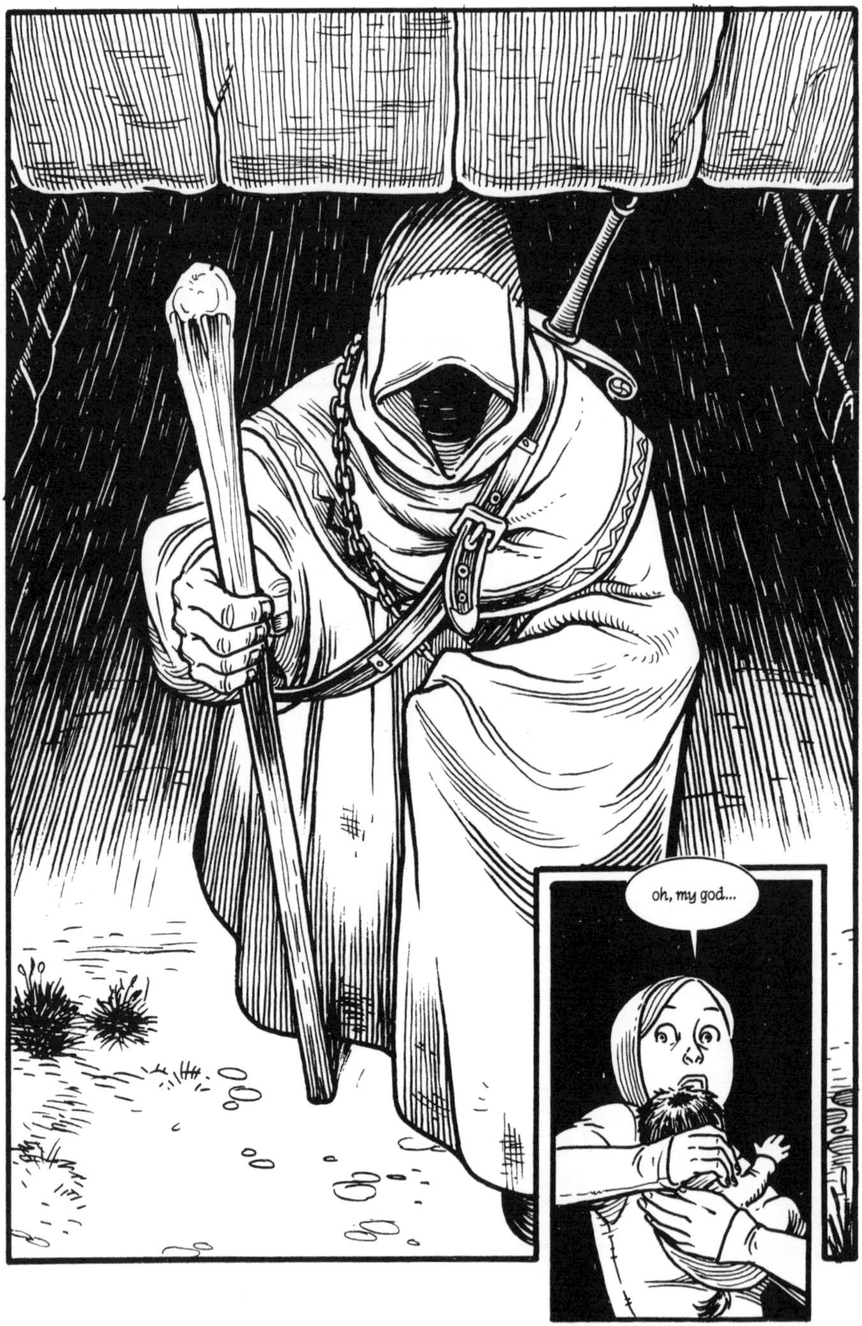
oh, my god...

Chapter 8.

· CAVALIER ·

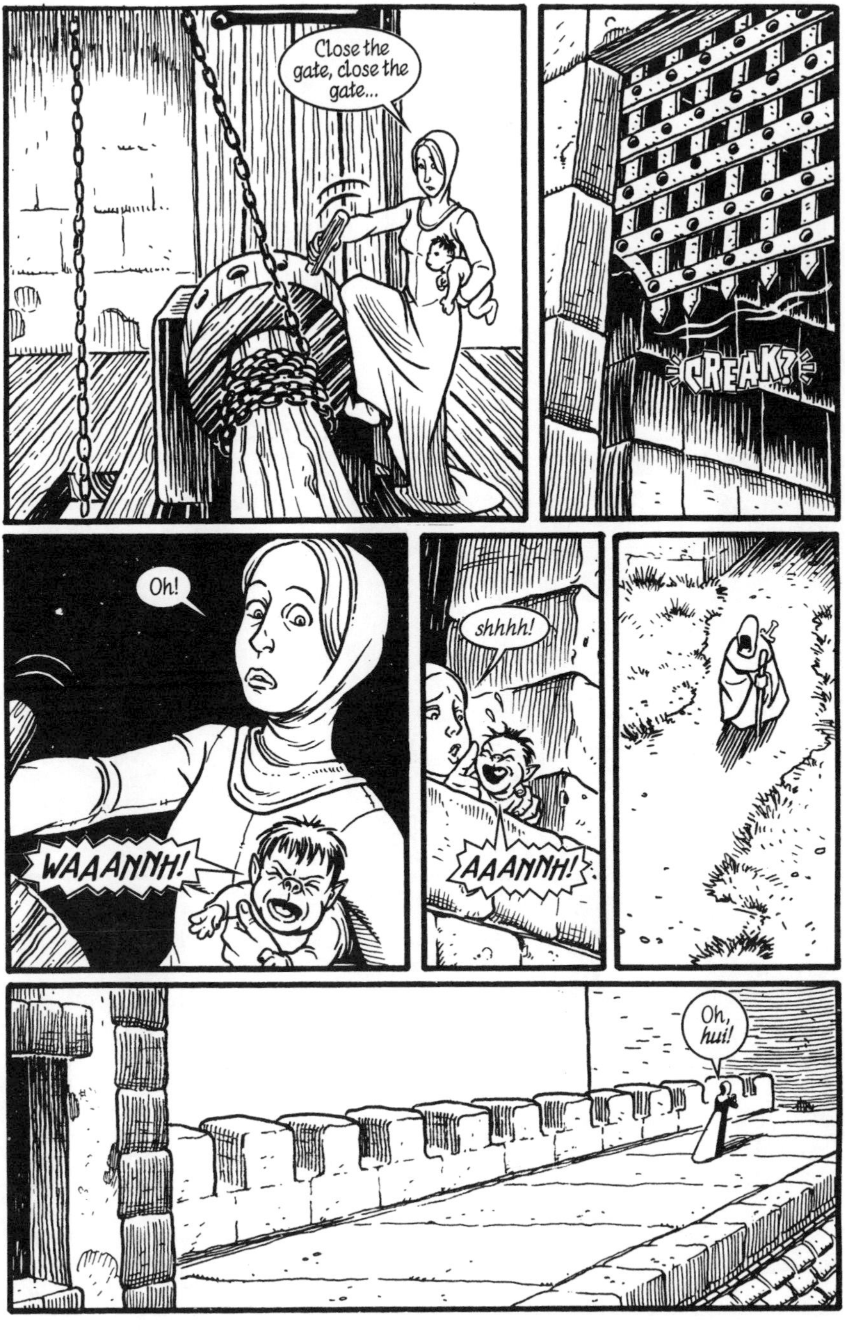
Close the gate, close the gate...
CREAK?
Oh!
WAAANNH!
shhhh!
AAANNH!
Oh, hui!

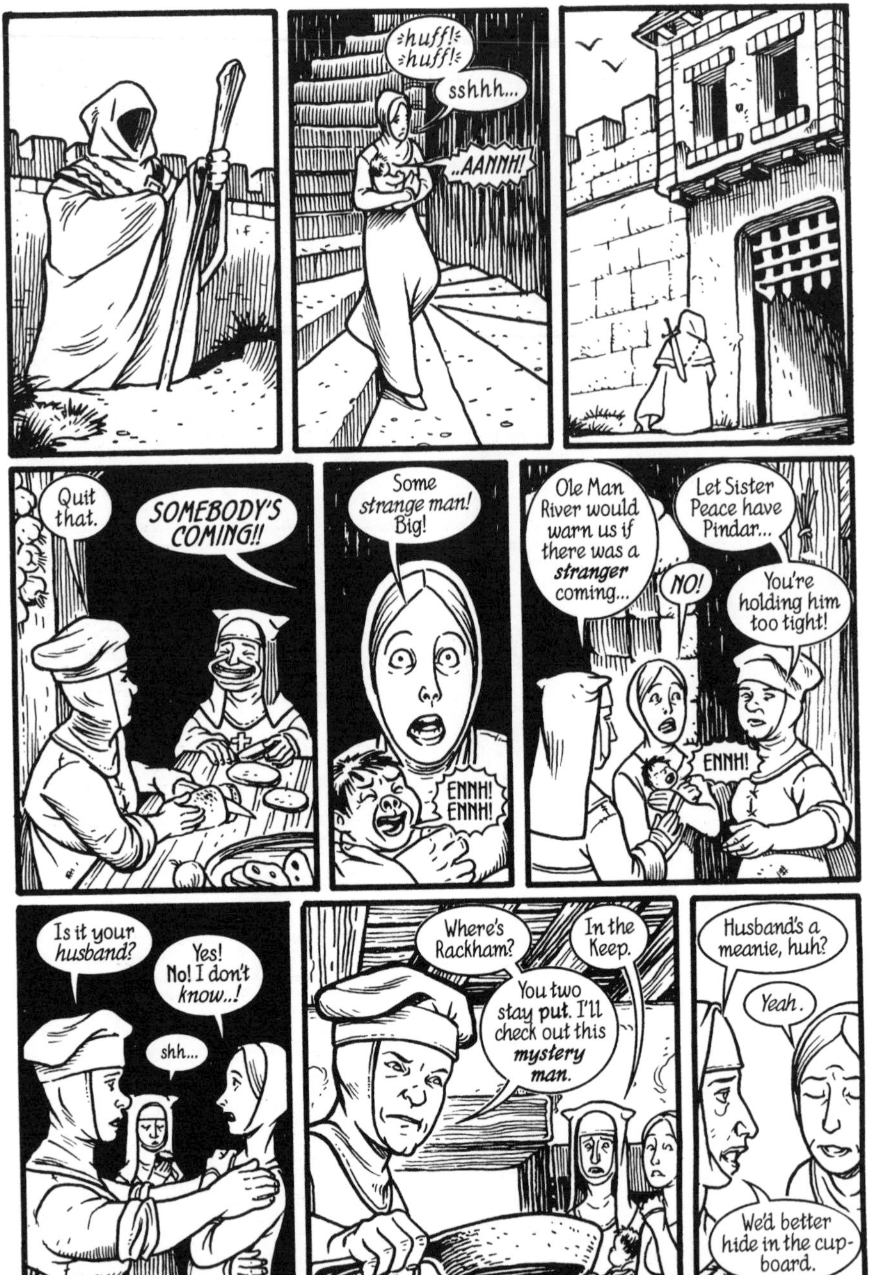
huff! huff!
sshhh...
..AANNH!
Quit that.
SOMEBODY'S COMING!!
Some strange man! Big!
ENNH! ENNH!
Ole Man River would warn us if there was a stranger coming...
Let Sister Peace have Pindar...
NO!
You're holding him too tight!
ENNH!
Is it your husband?
Yes! No! I don't know..!
shh...
Where's Rackham?
In the Keep.
You two stay put. I'll check out this mystery man.
Husband's a meanie, huh?
Yeah.
We'd better hide in the cupboard.

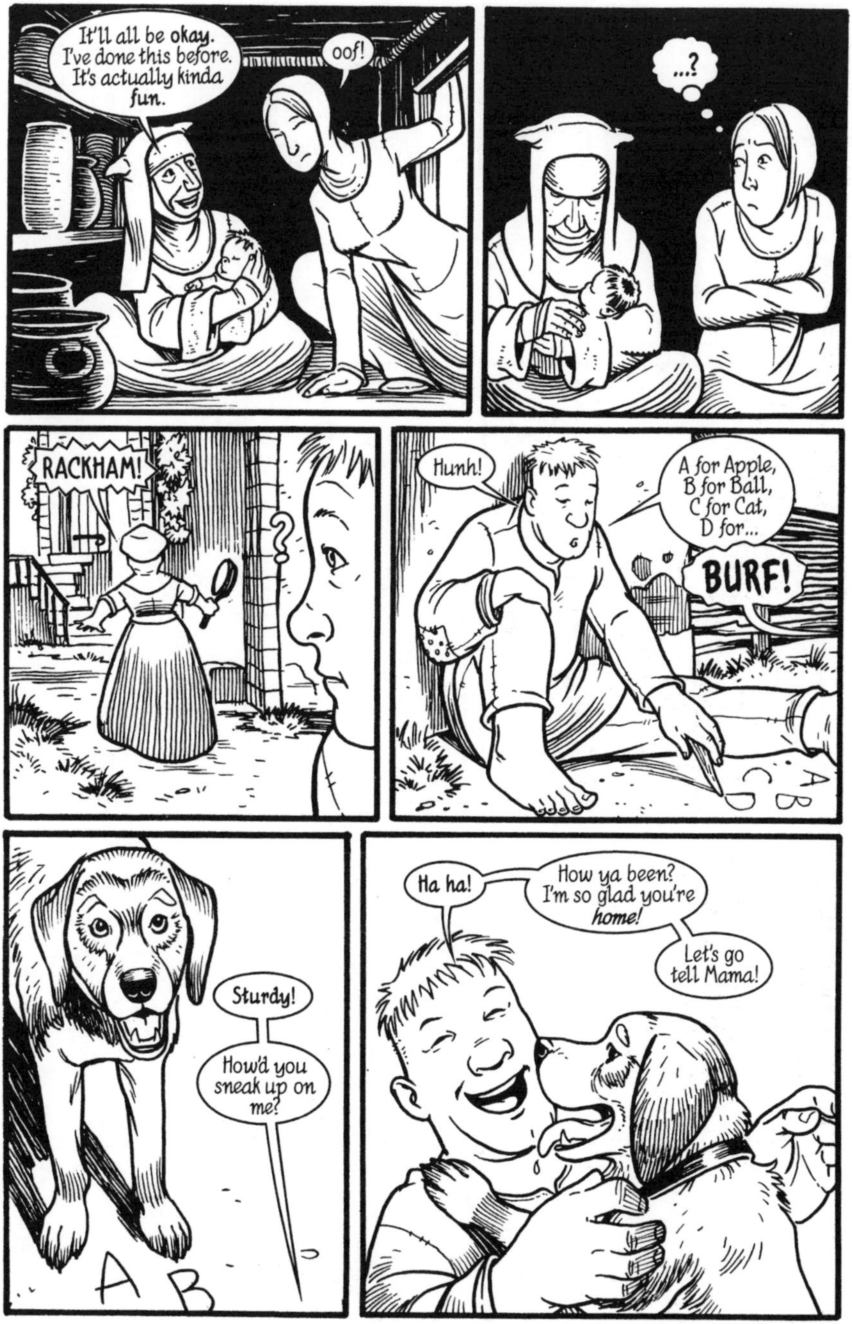
It'll all be **okay.** I've done this before. It's actually kinda **fun.**
oof!
...?
RACKHAM!
?
Hunh!
A for Apple, B for Ball, C for Cat, D for...
BURF!
Sturdy!
How'd you sneak up on me?
Ha ha!
How ya been? I'm so glad you're ***home!***
Let's go tell Mama!

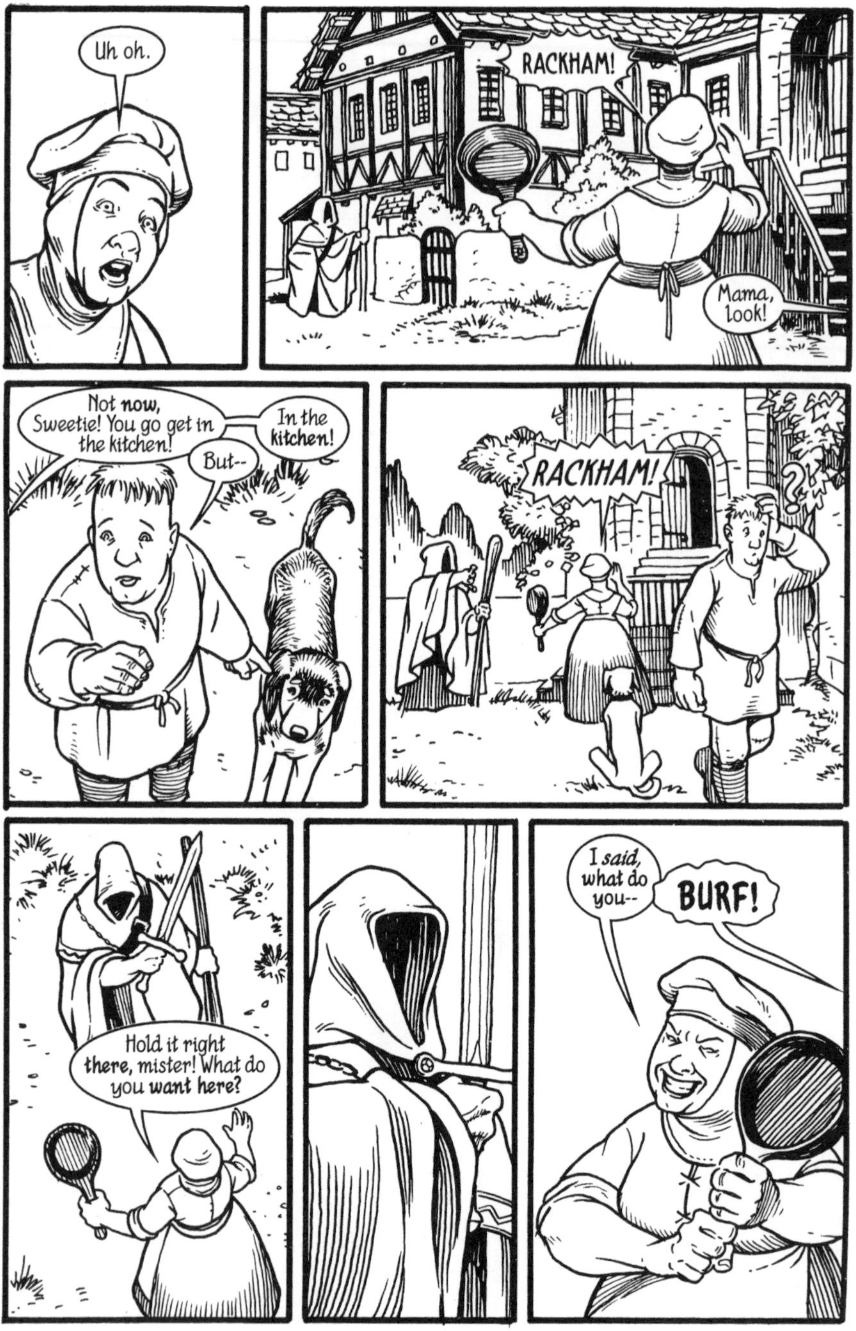
Uh oh.
RACKHAM!
Mama, look!
Not now, Sweetie! You go get in the kitchen!
In the kitchen!
But--
RACKHAM!
Hold it right there, mister! What do you want here?
I said, what do you--
BURF!

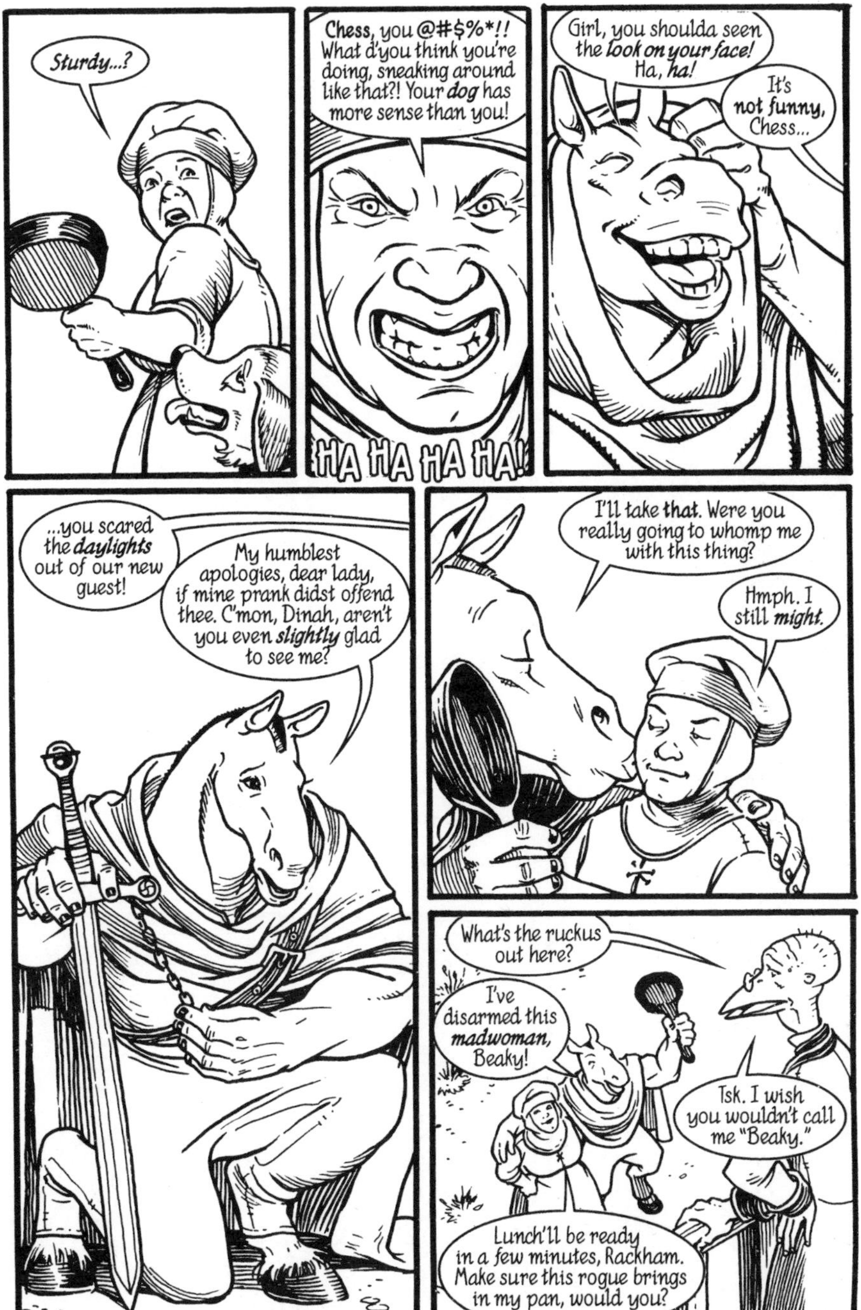
Sturdy...?
Chess, you @#$%*!! What d'you think you're doing, sneaking around like that?! Your dog has more sense than you!
HA HA HA HA!
Girl, you shoulda seen the look on your face! Ha, ha!
It's not funny, Chess...
...you scared the daylights out of our new guest!
My humblest apologies, dear lady, if mine prank didst offend thee. C'mon, Dinah, aren't you even slightly glad to see me?
I'll take that. Were you really going to whomp me with this thing?
Hmph. I still might.
What's the ruckus out here?
I've disarmed this madwoman, Beaky!
Tsk. I wish you wouldn't call me "Beaky."
Lunch'll be ready in a few minutes, Rackham. Make sure this rogue brings in my pan, would you?

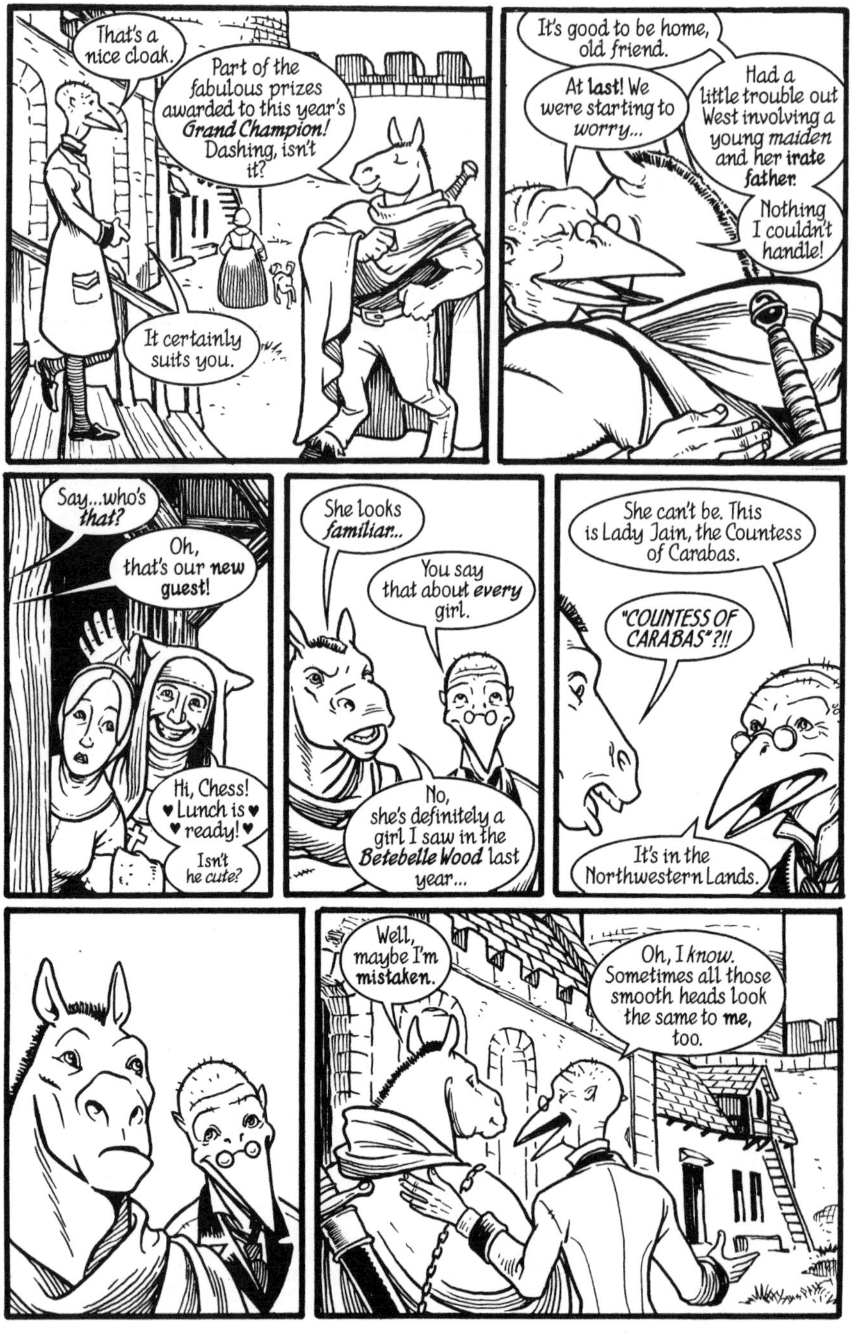
That's a nice cloak.
Part of the fabulous prizes awarded to this year's *Grand Champion!* Dashing, isn't it?
It certainly suits you.
It's good to be home, old friend.
At **last**! We were starting to *worry*...
Had a little trouble out West involving a young *maiden* and her **irate father**.
Nothing I couldn't handle!
Say...who's *that?*
Oh, that's our **new guest**!
Hi, Chess! ♥ Lunch is ♥ ♥ ready! ♥
Isn't he cute?
She looks *familiar*...
You say that about *every* girl.
No, she's definitely a girl I saw in the ***Betebelle Wood*** last year...
She can't be. This is Lady Jain, the Countess of Carabas.
"COUNTESS OF CARABAS"?!!
It's in the Northwestern Lands.
Well, maybe I'm **mistaken**.
Oh, I *know*. Sometimes all those smooth heads look the same to **me**, too.

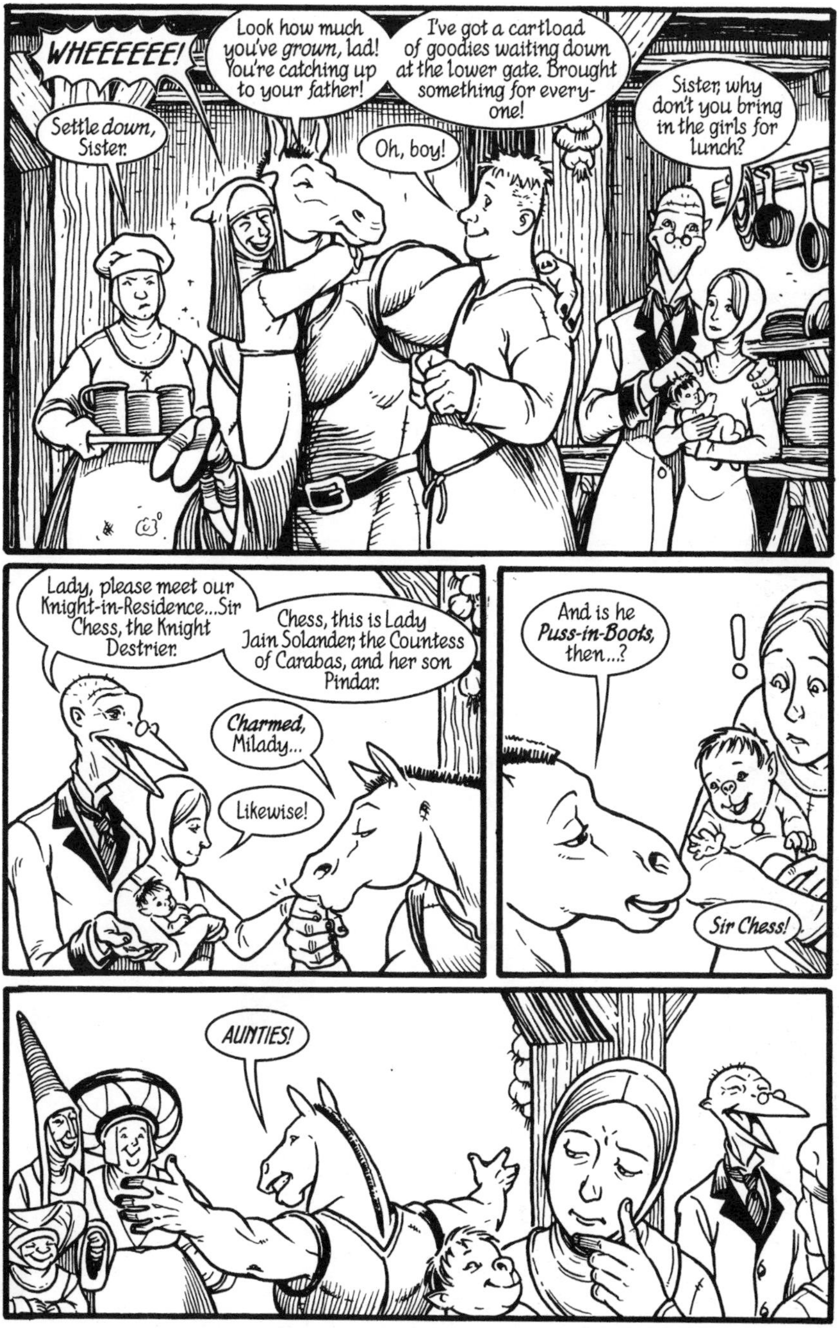
WHEEEEEEE!
Settle down, Sister.
Look how much you've grown, lad! You're catching up to your father!
I've got a cartload of goodies waiting down at the lower gate. Brought something for every-one!
Oh, boy!
Sister, why don't you bring in the girls for lunch?
Lady, please meet our Knight-in-Residence...Sir Chess, the Knight Destrier.
Chess, this is Lady Jain Solander, the Countess of Carabas, and her son Pindar.
Charmed, Milady...
Likewise!
And is he Puss-in-Boots, then...?
!
Sir Chess!
AUNTIES!

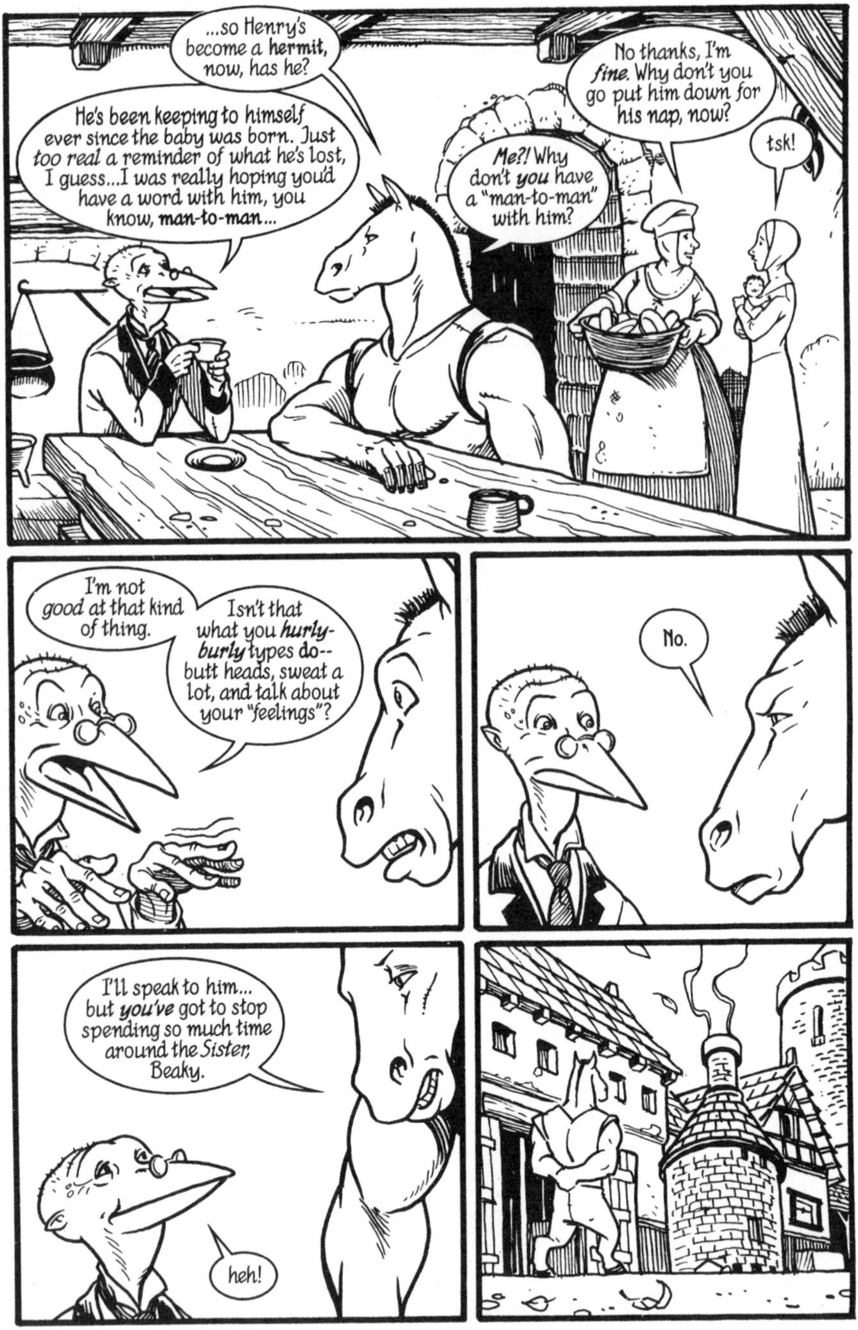
...so Henry's become a hermit, now, has he?
He's been keeping to himself ever since the baby was born. Just too real a reminder of what he's lost, I guess...I was really hoping you'd have a word with him, you know, man-to-man...
No thanks, I'm fine. Why don't you go put him down for his nap, now?
Me?! Why don't you have a "man-to-man" with him?
tsk!
I'm not good at that kind of thing.
Isn't that what you hurly-burly types do-- butt heads, sweat a lot, and talk about your "feelings"?
No.
I'll speak to him... but you've got to stop spending so much time around the Sister, Beaky.
heh!

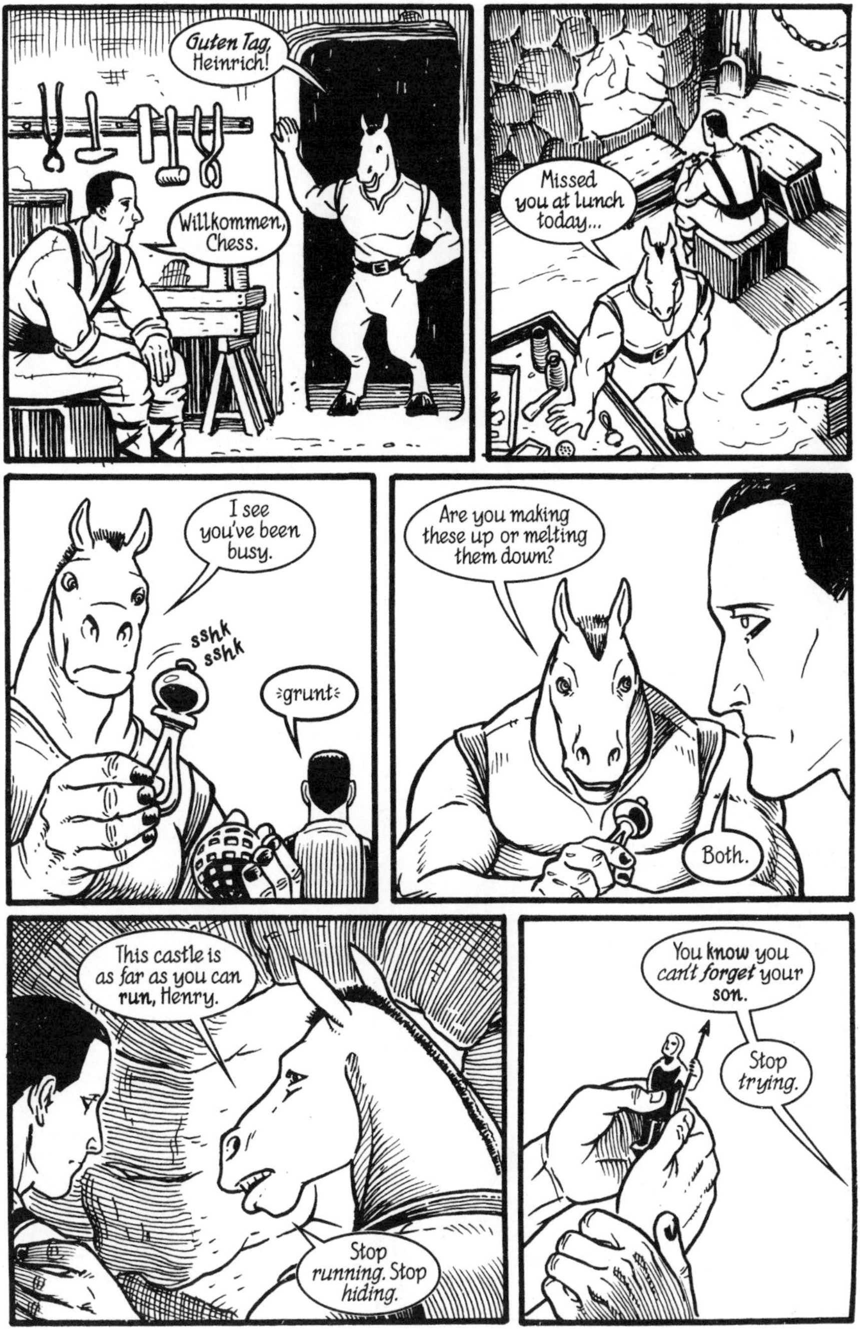
Guten Tag, Heinrich!
Willkommen, Chess.
Missed you at lunch today...
I see you've been busy.
sshk sshk
grunt
Are you making these up or melting them down?
Both.
This castle is as far as you can run, Henry.
Stop running. Stop hiding.
You know you can't forget your son.
Stop trying.

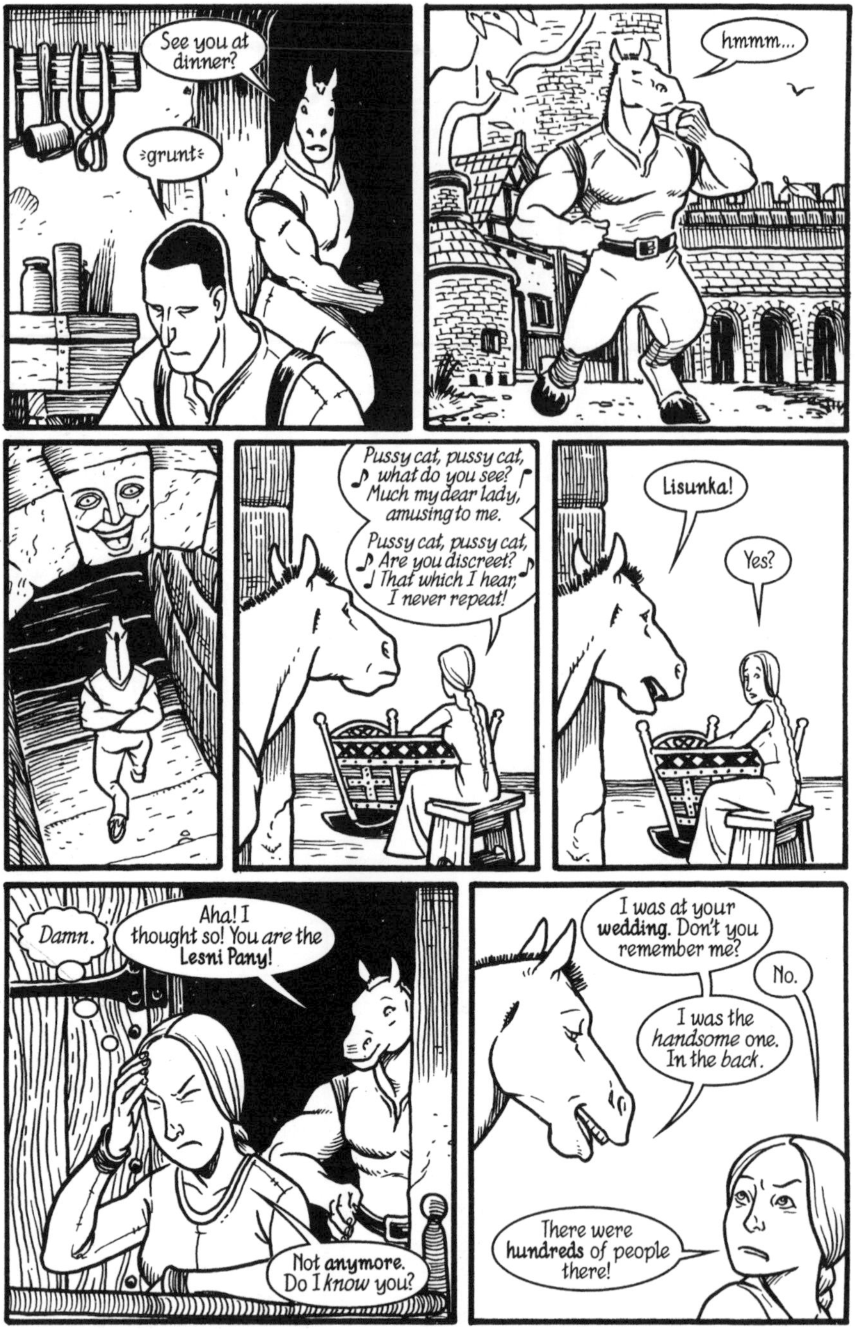
See you at dinner?
grunt
hmmm...
Pussy cat, pussy cat, what do you see? Much my dear lady, amusing to me.
Pussy cat, pussy cat, Are you discreet? That which I hear, I never repeat!
Lisunka!
Yes?
Damn.
Aha! I thought so! You *are* the **Lesni Pany**!
Not **anymore**. Do I *know* you?
I was at your **wedding**. Don't you remember me?
No.
I was the *handsome* one. In the *back*.
There were **hundreds** of people there!

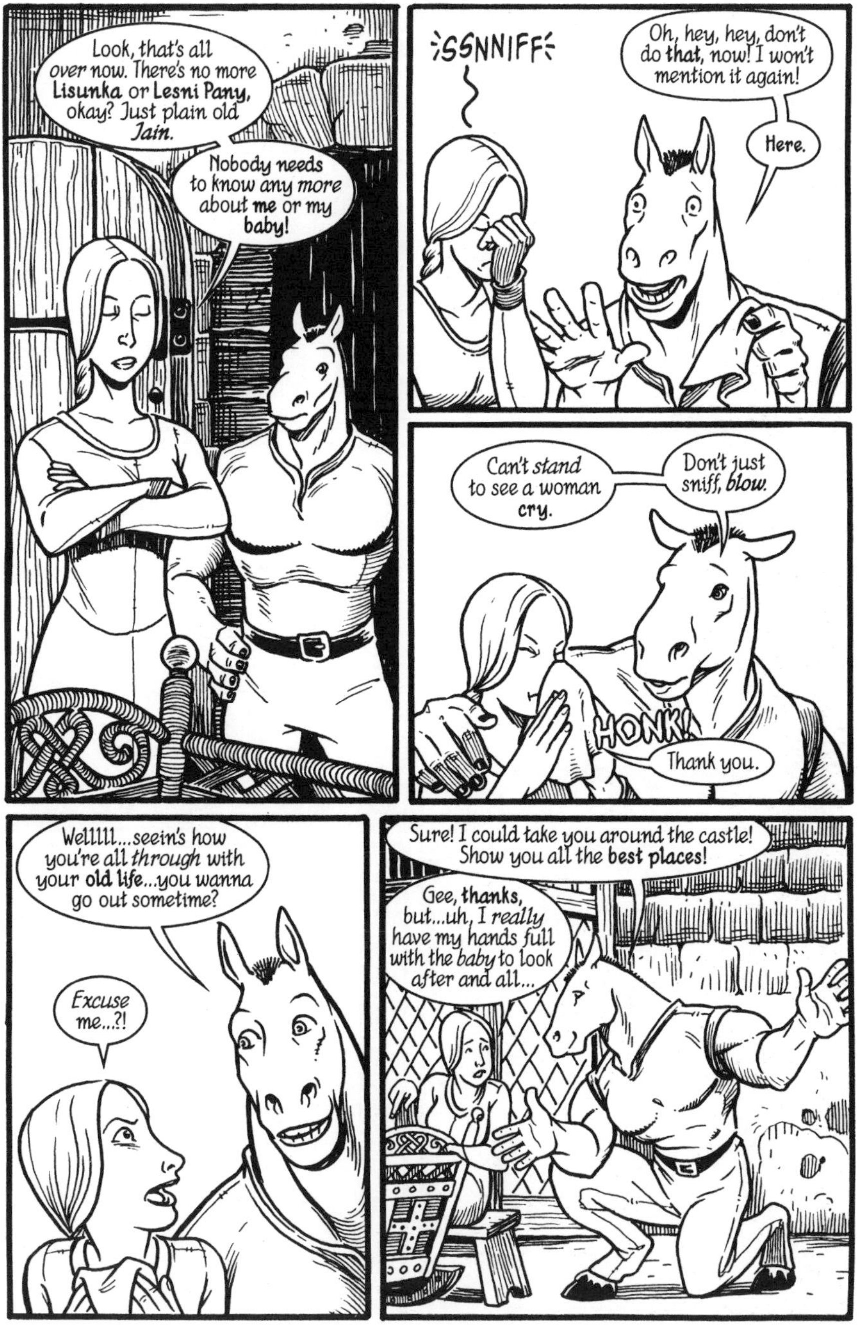
Look, that's all over now. There's no more Lisunka or Lesni Pany, okay? Just plain old Jain.
Nobody needs to know any more about me or my baby!
SSNNIFF
Oh, hey, hey, don't do that, now! I won't mention it again!
Here.
Can't stand to see a woman cry.
Don't just sniff, blow.
HONK!
Thank you.
Wellllll...seein's how you're all through with your old life...you wanna go out sometime?
Excuse me...?!
Sure! I could take you around the castle! Show you all the best places!
Gee, thanks, but...uh, I really have my hands full with the baby to look after and all...

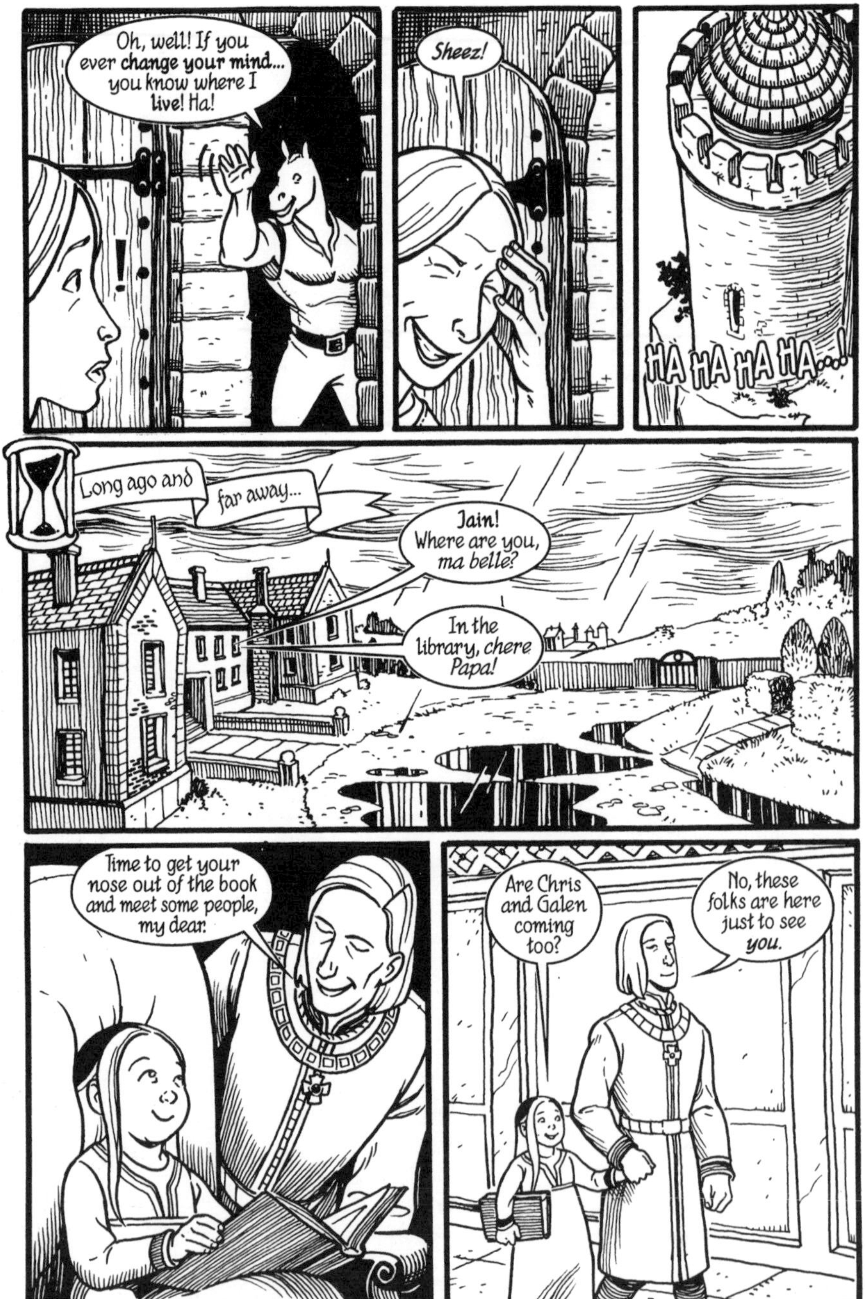
Oh, well! If you ever change your mind... you know where I live! Ha!
!
Sheez!
HA HA HA HA...!
Long ago and far away...
Jain! Where are you, ma belle?
In the library, chere Papa!
Time to get your nose out of the book and meet some people, my dear.
Are Chris and Galen coming too?
No, these folks are here just to see you.

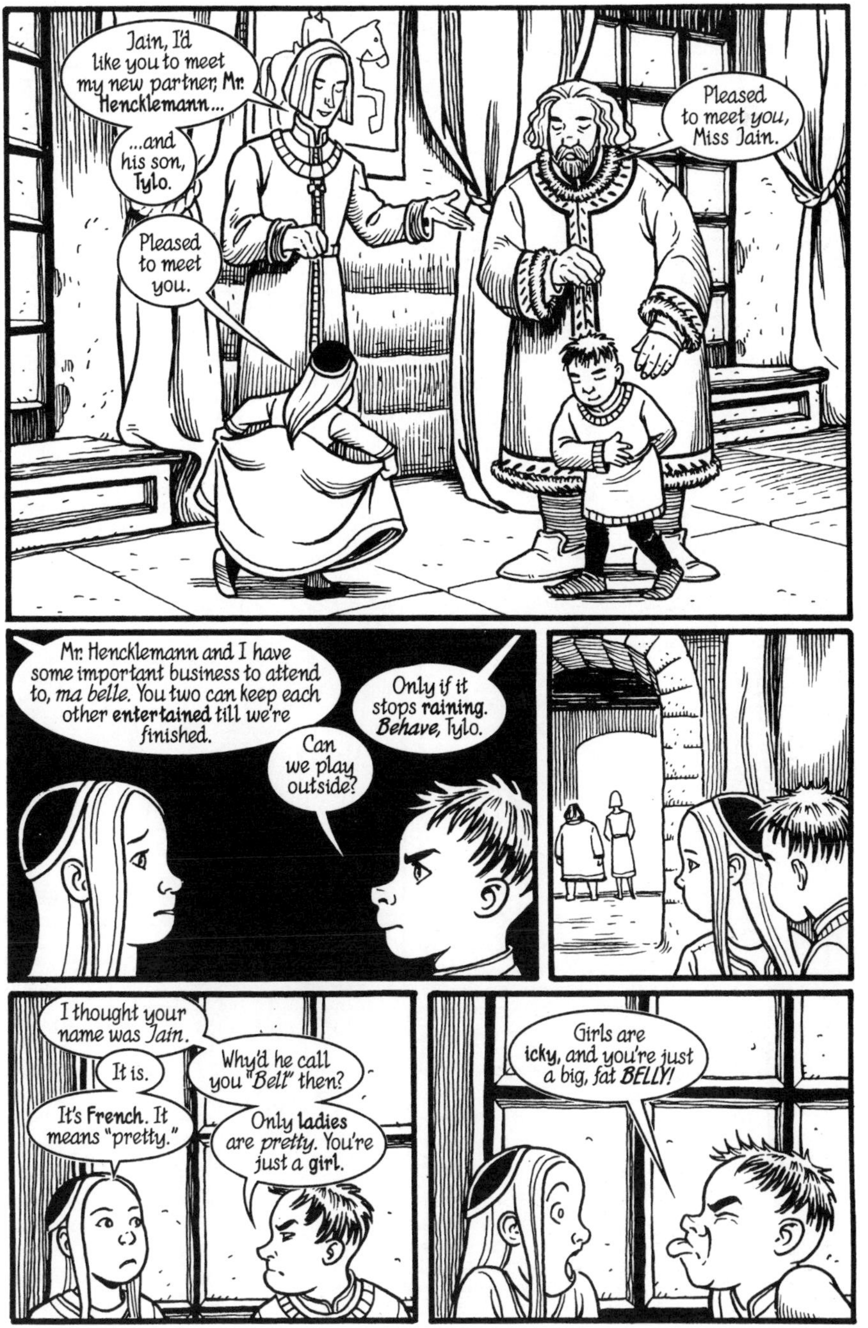
Jain, I'd like you to meet my new partner, Mr. Hencklemann...
...and his son, Tylo.
Pleased to meet you, Miss Jain.
Pleased to meet you.
Mr. Hencklemann and I have some important business to attend to, ma belle. You two can keep each other entertained till we're finished.
Can we play outside?
Only if it stops raining. Behave, Tylo.
I thought your name was Jain.
It is.
Why'd he call you "Bell" then?
It's French. It means "pretty."
Only ladies are pretty. You're just a girl.
Girls are icky, and you're just a big, fat BELLY!

My people drew up new papers adding the conditions you requested. I *know* you don't approve of **arranged marriages**, Solander, but it's so **crucial** to strengthening **business ties...**

Arranged marriages are for **Royals,** Hencklemann. *Blue Bloods.*

Ah, but one day the **Merchant** class *will* be the ruling class, my friend! Mark my words!

Probably not in **our** lifetimes, Hencklemann.

Which is *exactly* why we need to cement things **now,** to insure strong futures for both of our businesses! Err... and our **families,** too, of course!

SWSSH

Ha! Missed!

My late wife Tomasina-- Iain's *mother*...her first marriage was arranged. She was so *unhappy...*

Ah, yes. The infamous "Black Duke." He certainly came to a *disgraceful* end. You were a *saint* to take in his **children** as well...

Well, the Duke's family took the girls away from 'Sina when they were babies. She wanted to get to know them again...but she never got the *chance.* The girls insisted on returning to the Court and their "real family" after she passed away...

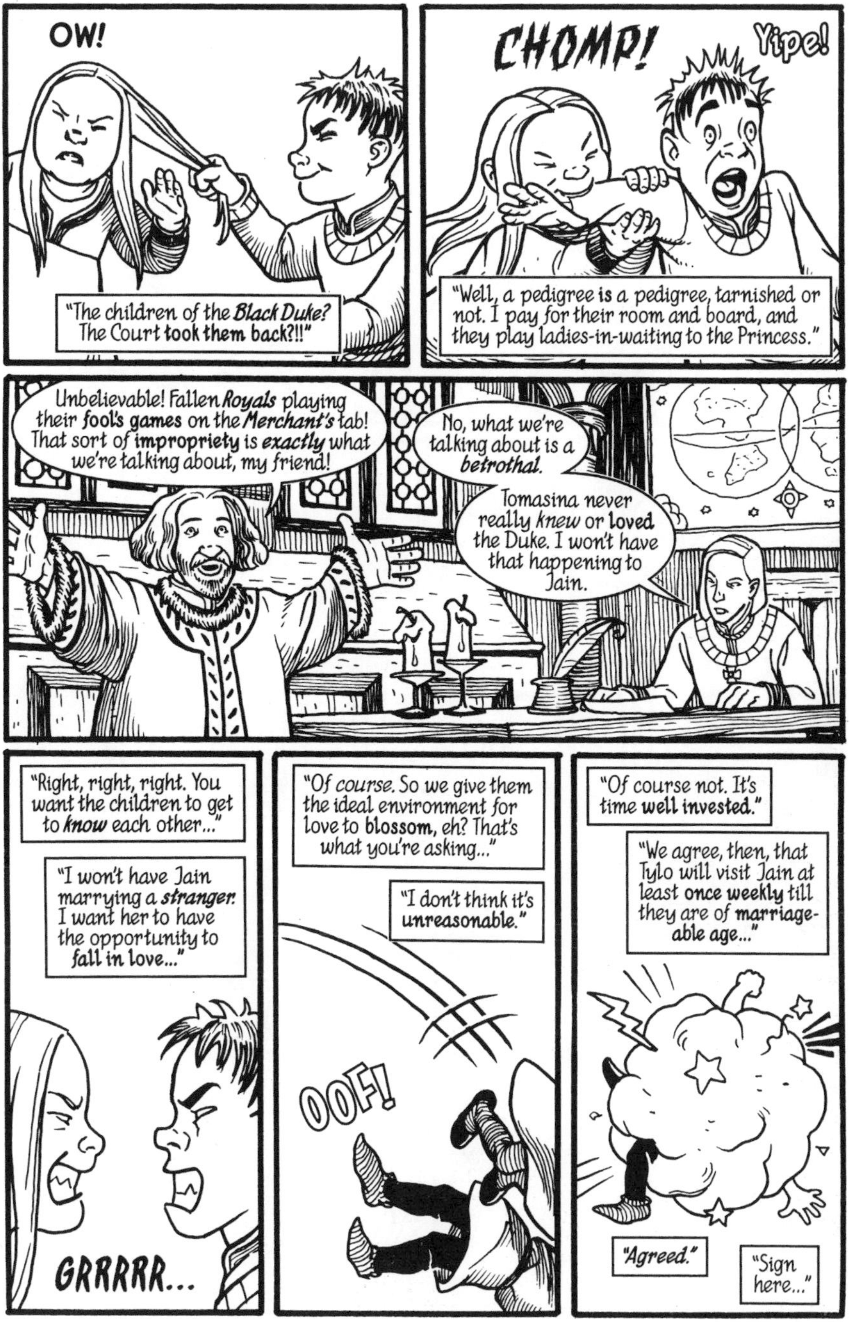
OW!
"The children of the Black Duke? The Court took them back?!!"
CHOMP!
Yipe!
"Well, a pedigree is a pedigree, tarnished or not. I pay for their room and board, and they play ladies-in-waiting to the Princess."
Unbelievable! Fallen Royals playing their fool's games on the Merchant's tab! That sort of impropriety is exactly what we're talking about, my friend!
No, what we're talking about is a betrothal.
Tomasina never really knew or loved the Duke. I won't have that happening to Jain.
"Right, right, right. You want the children to get to know each other..."
"I won't have Jain marrying a stranger. I want her to have the opportunity to fall in love..."
GRRRRR...
"Of course. So we give them the ideal environment for love to blossom, eh? That's what you're asking..."
"I don't think it's unreasonable."
OOF!
"Of course not. It's time well invested."
"We agree, then, that Tylo will visit Jain at least once weekly till they are of marriage-able age..."
"Agreed."
"Sign here..."

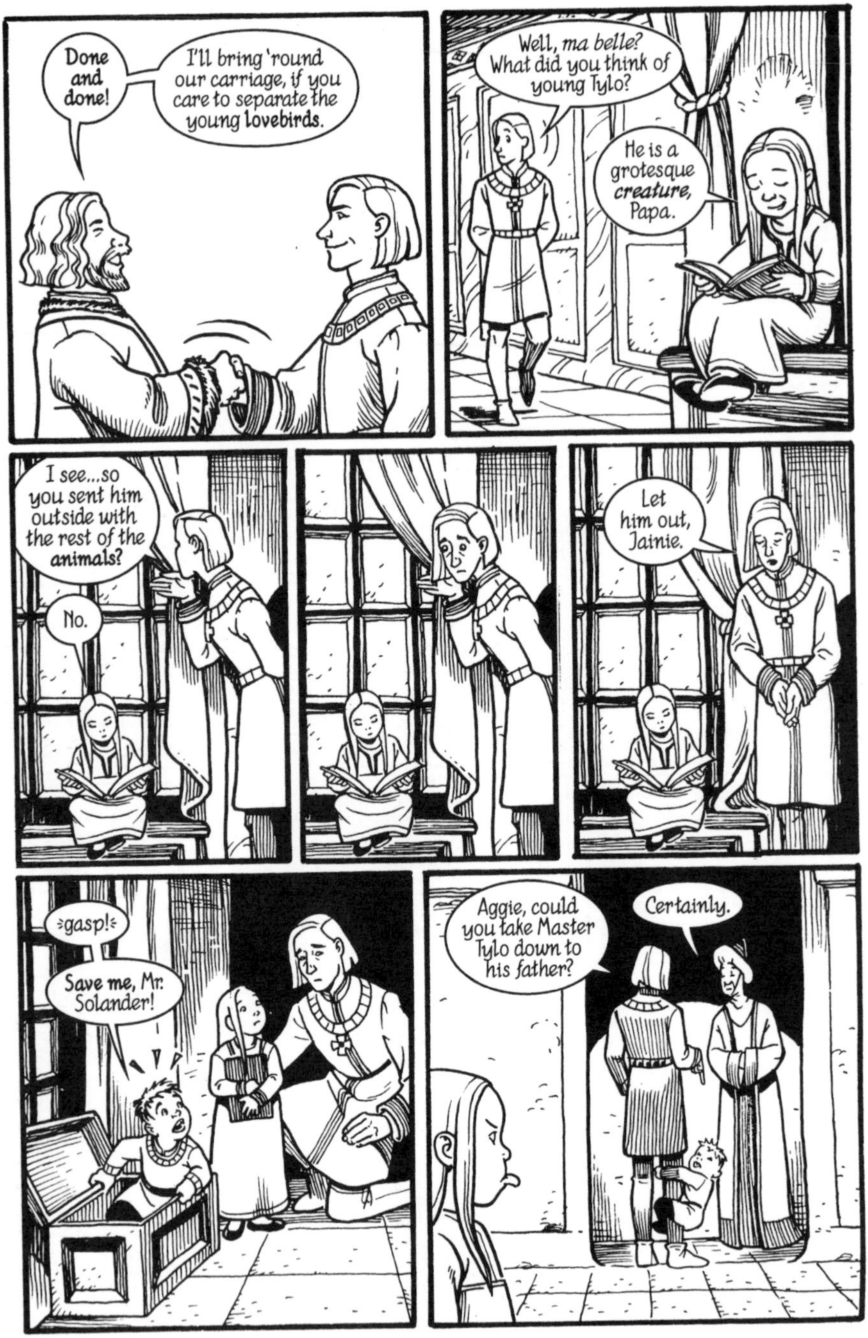
Done and done!
I'll bring 'round our carriage, if you care to separate the young lovebirds.
Well, ma belle? What did you think of young Tylo?
He is a grotesque creature, Papa.
I see...so you sent him outside with the rest of the animals?
No.
Let him out, Jainie.
gasp!
Save me, Mr. Solander!
Aggie, could you take Master Tylo down to his father?
Certainly.

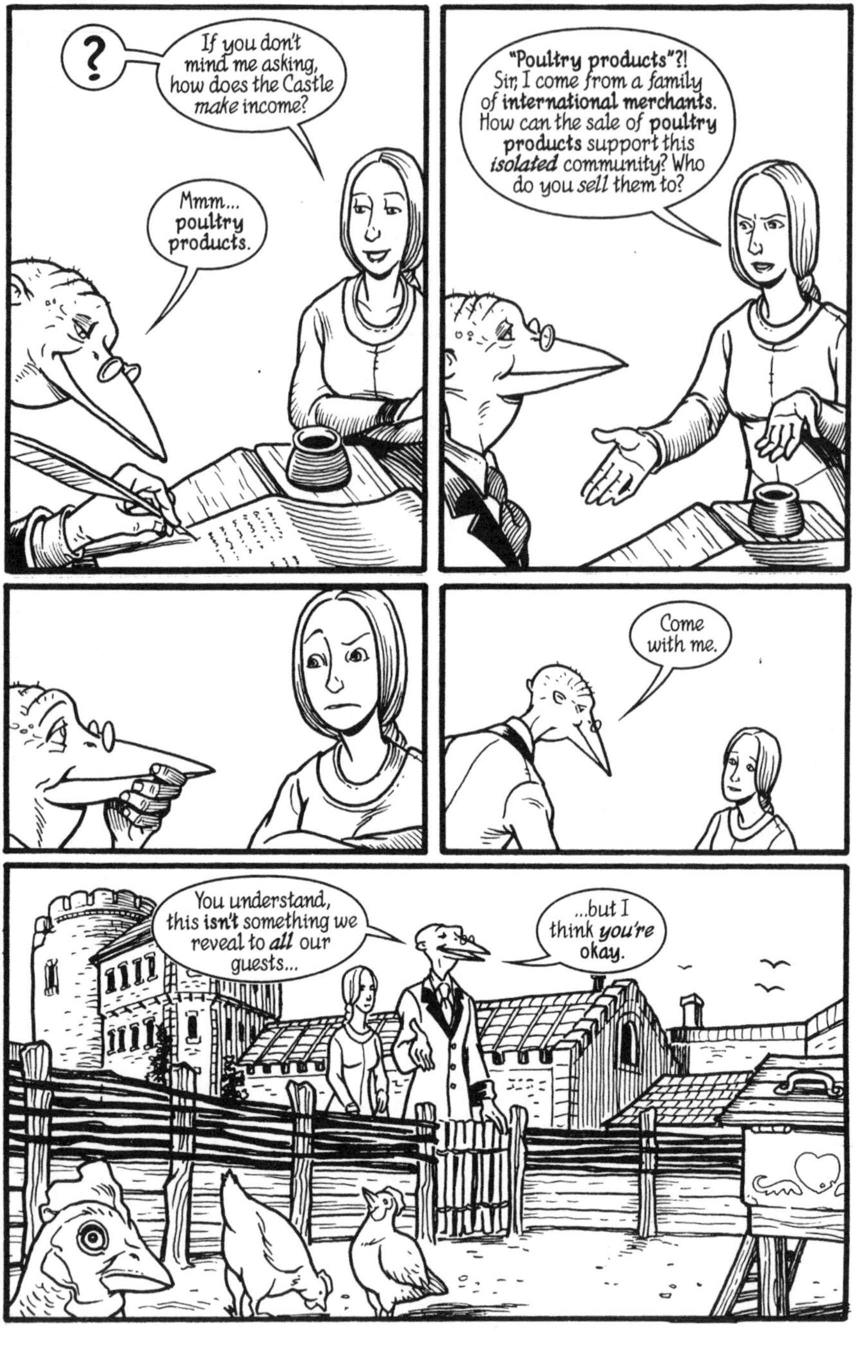
?
If you don't mind me asking, how does the Castle *make* income?
Mmm... **poultry products.**
"Poultry products"?! Sir, I come from a family of **international merchants.** How can the sale of **poultry products** support this ***isolated*** community? Who do you ***sell*** them to?
Come with me.
You understand, this **isn't** something we reveal to ***all*** our guests...
...but I think ***you're*** **okay.**

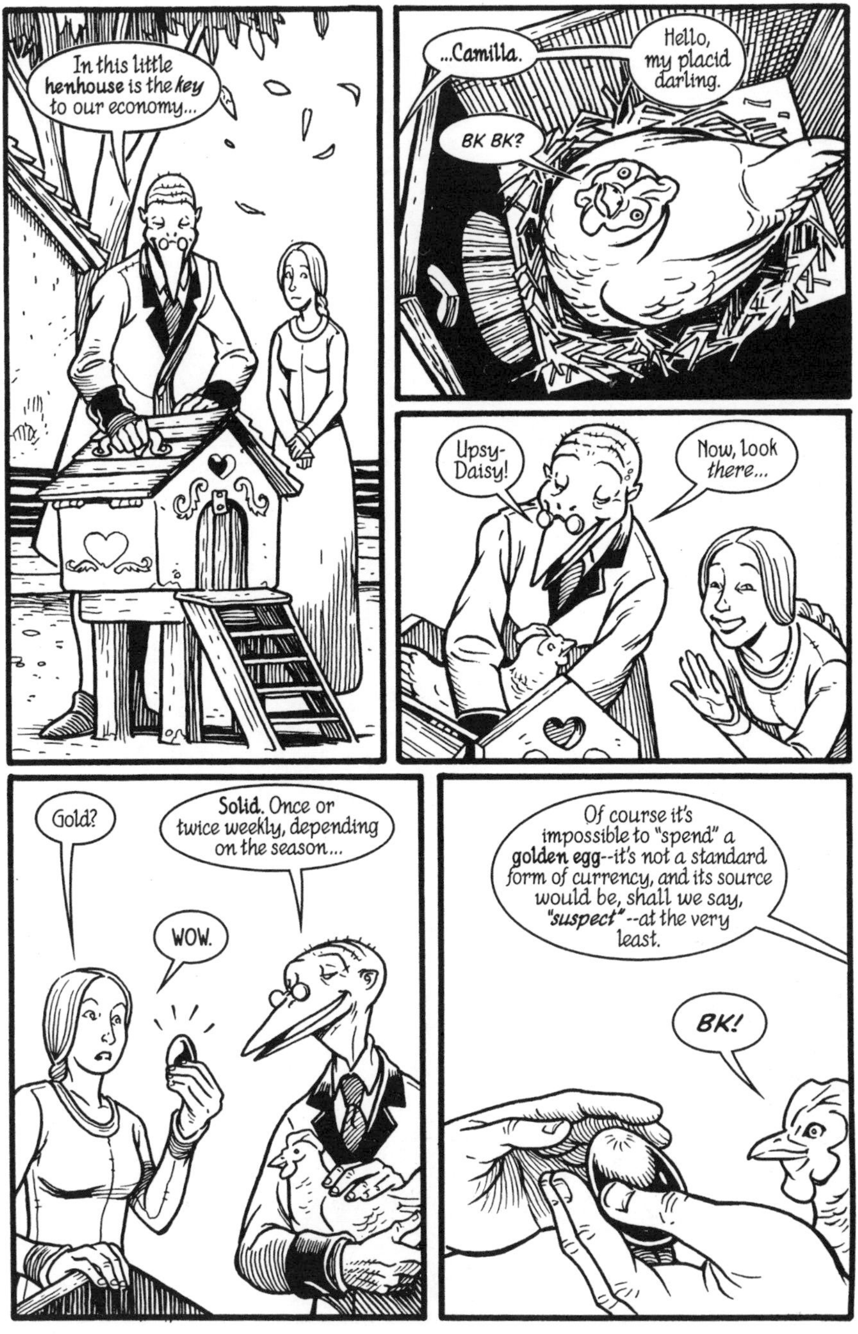
In this little **henhouse** is the ***key*** to our economy...
...**Camilla.**
Hello, my placid darling.
BK BK?
Upsy-Daisy!
Now, look *there*...
Gold?
Solid. Once or twice weekly, depending on the season...
WOW.
Of course it's impossible to "spend" a **golden egg**--it's not a standard form of currency, and its source would be, shall we say, ***"suspect"***--at the very least.
BK!

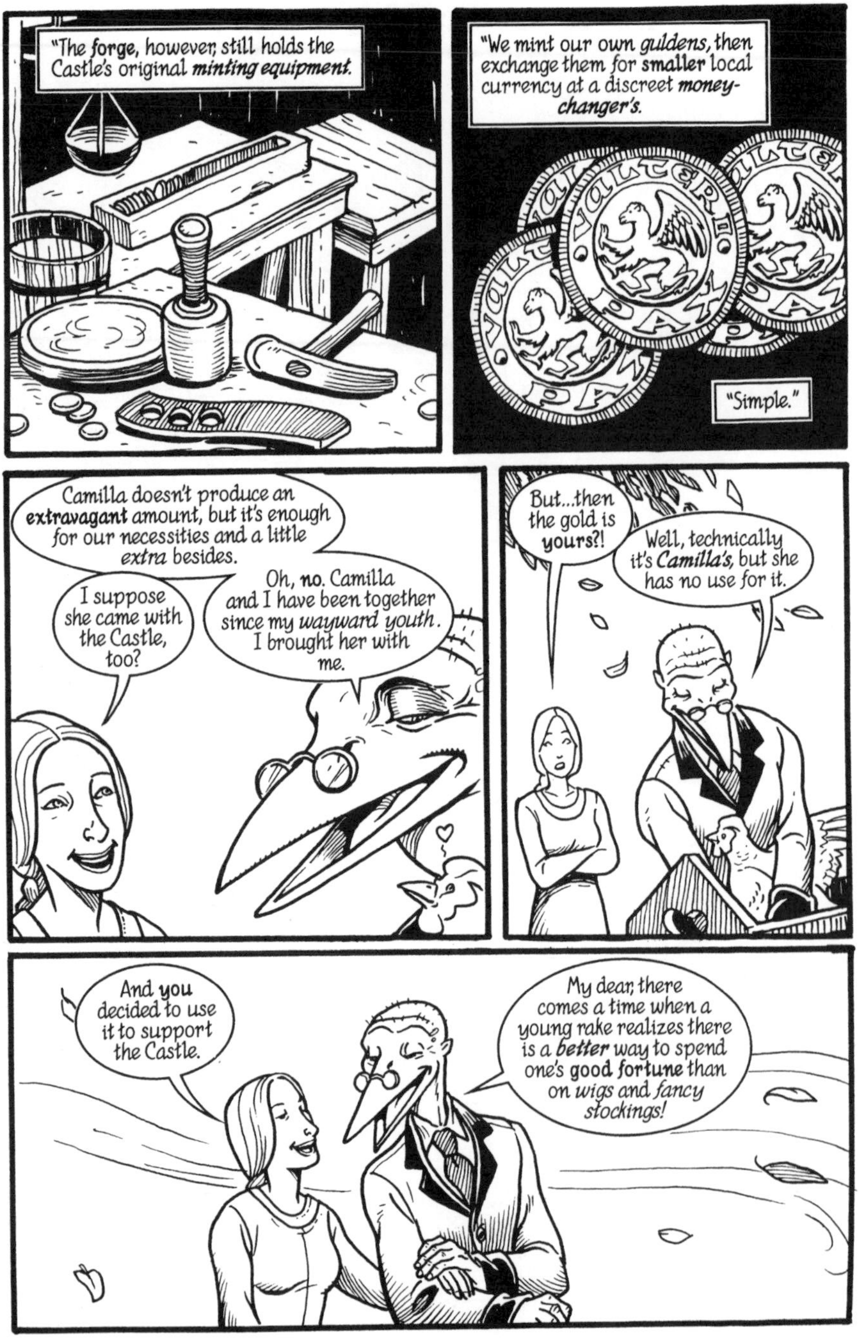
"The forge, however, still holds the Castle's original minting equipment.
"We mint our own guldens, then exchange them for smaller local currency at a discreet money-changer's.
"Simple."
Camilla doesn't produce an extravagant amount, but it's enough for our necessities and a little extra besides.
I suppose she came with the Castle, too?
Oh, no. Camilla and I have been together since my wayward youth. I brought her with me.
But...then the gold is yours?!
Well, technically it's Camilla's, but she has no use for it.
And you decided to use it to support the Castle.
My dear, there comes a time when a young rake realizes there is a better way to spend one's good fortune than on wigs and fancy stockings!

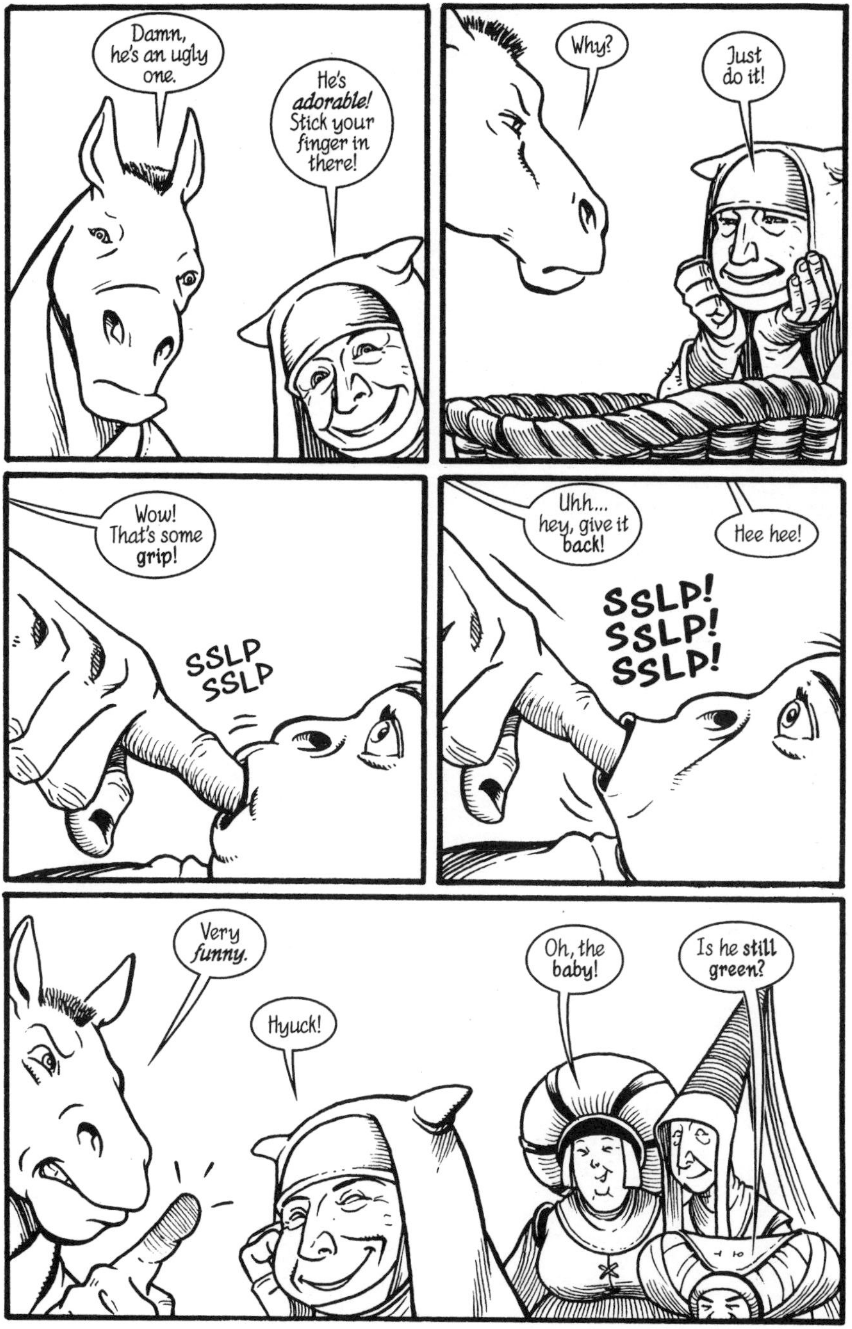
Damn, he's an ugly one.
He's *adorable!* Stick your finger in there!
Why?
Just do it!
Wow! That's some **grip!**
SSLP SSLP
Uhh... hey, give it back!
Hee hee!
SSLP! SSLP! SSLP!
Very *funny.*
Hyuck!
Oh, the **baby!**
Is he **still green?**

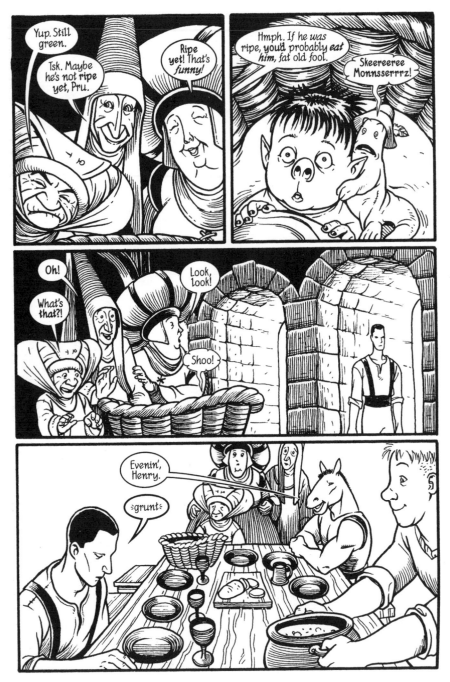

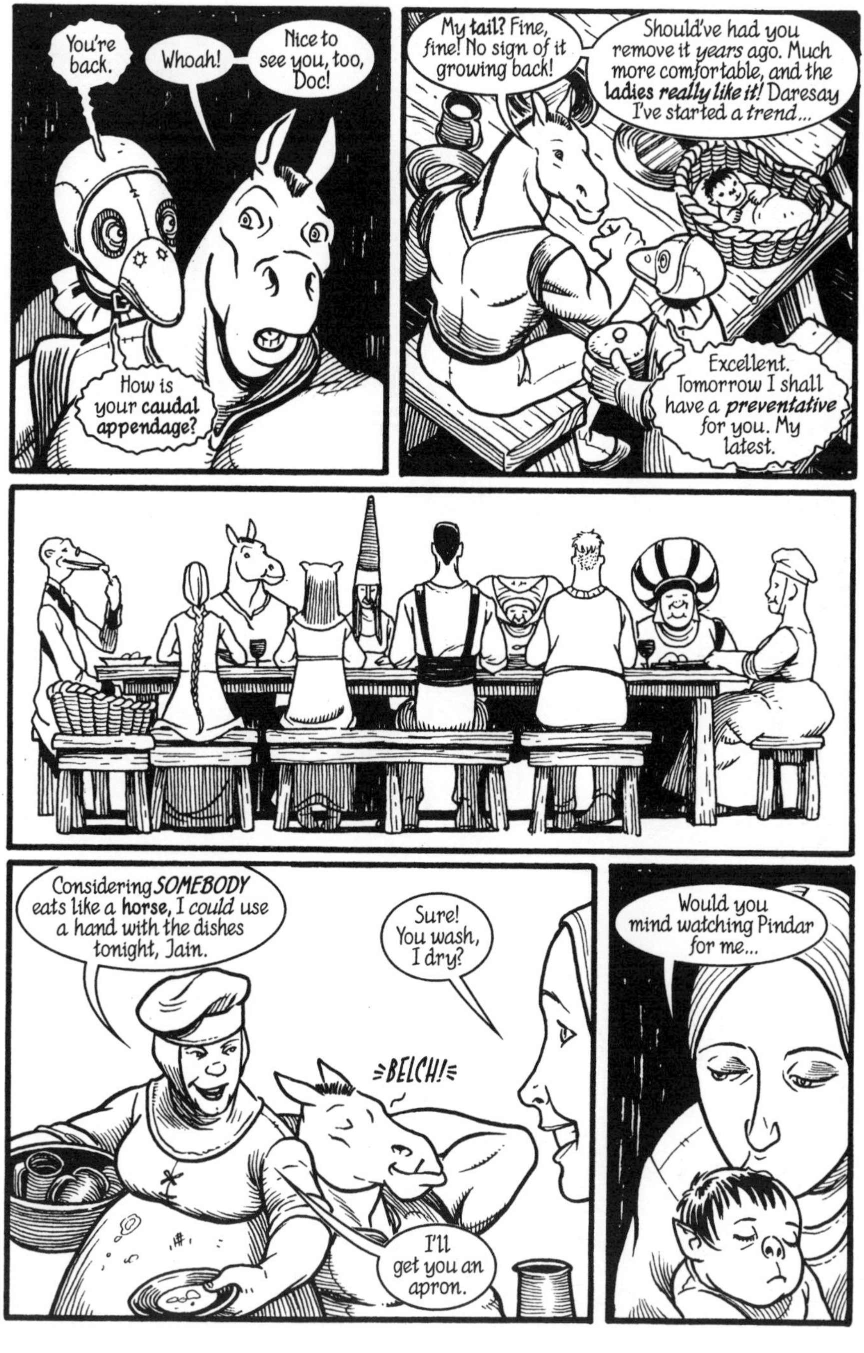
You're back.
Whoah!
Nice to see you, too, Doc!
How is your **caudal appendage?**
My **tail?** Fine, fine! No sign of it growing back!
Should've had you remove it *years* ago. Much more comfortable, and the **ladies *really like it!*** Daresay I've started a *trend*...
Excellent. Tomorrow I shall have a ***preventative*** for you. My latest.
Considering ***SOMEBODY*** eats like a **horse**, I *could* use a hand with the dishes tonight, Jain.
Sure! You wash, I dry?
BELCH!
I'll get you an apron.
Would you mind watching Pindar for me...

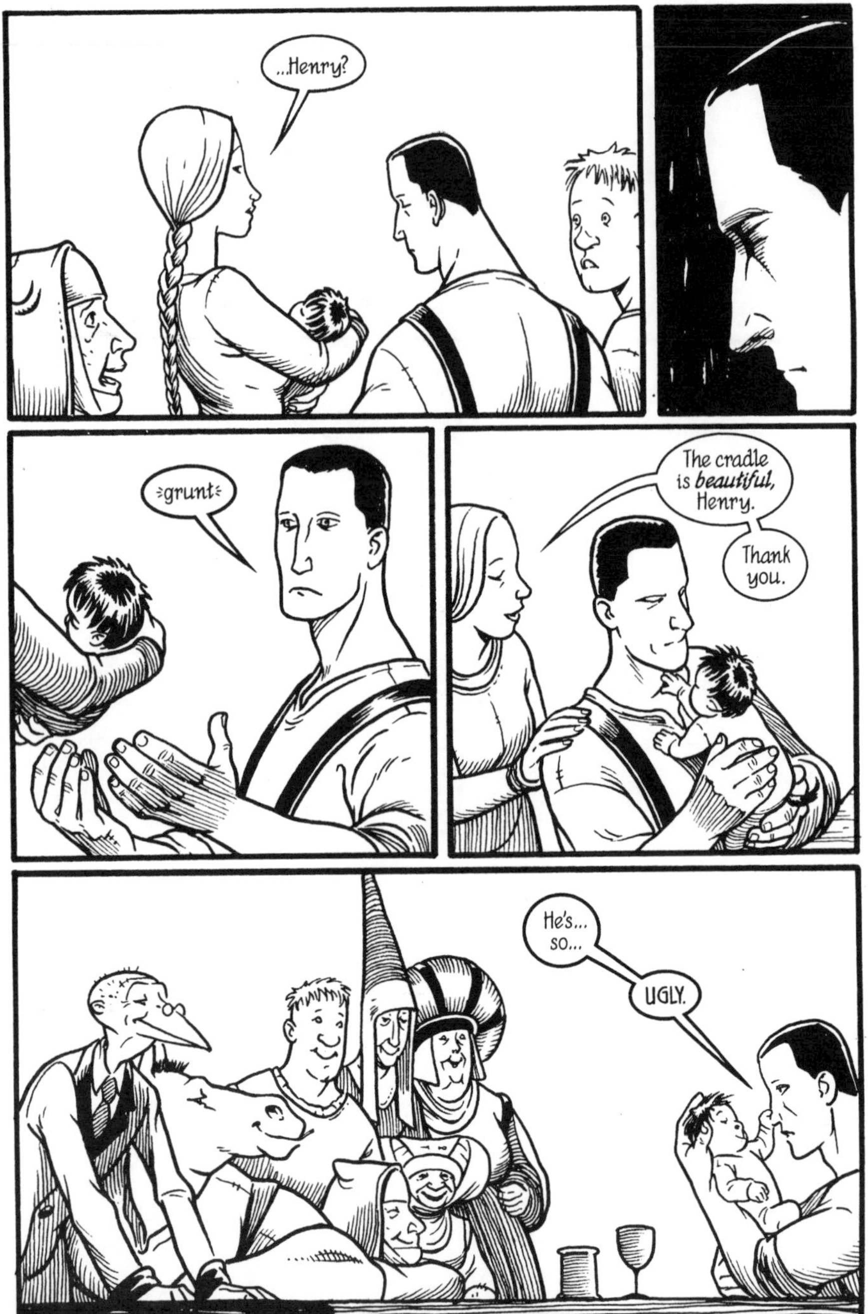
...Henry?
≈grunt≈
The cradle is *beautiful,* Henry.
Thank you.
He's... so...
UGLY.

Chapter 9.

· CITY MOUSE, COUNTRY MOUSE PT. I ·

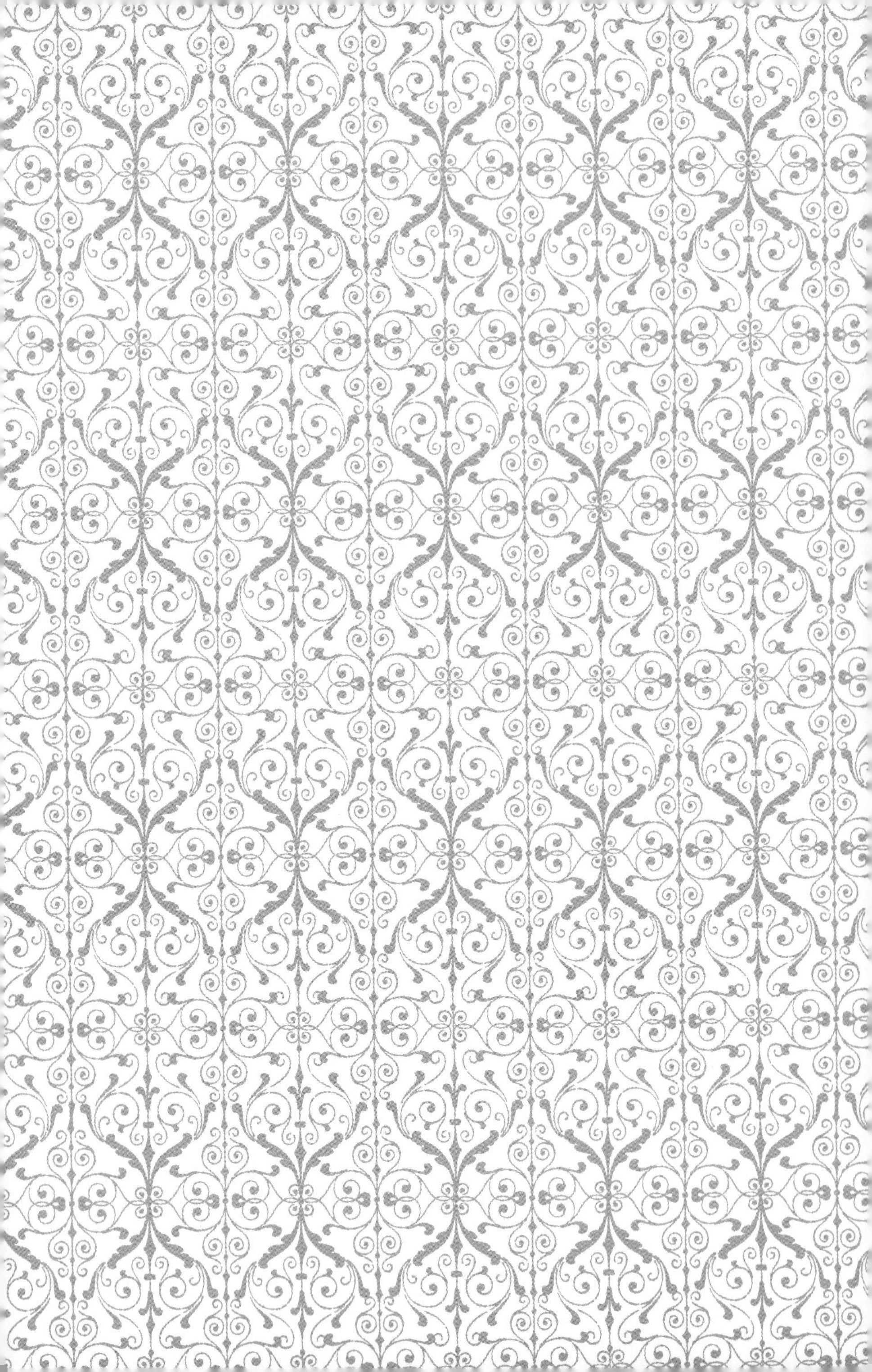

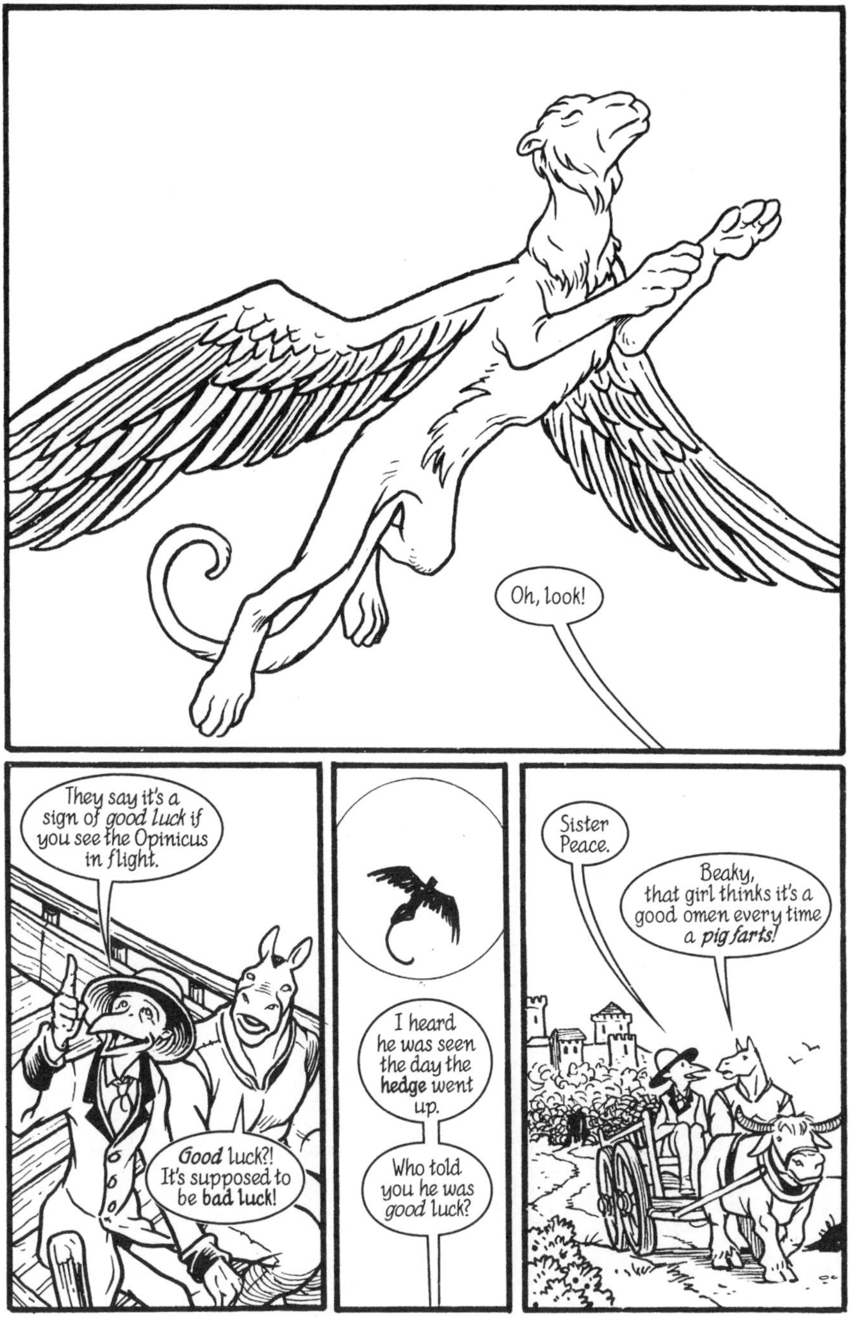
Oh, look!
They say it's a sign of *good luck* if you see the Opinicus in flight.
Good luck?! It's supposed to be **bad luck**!
I heard he was seen the day the **hedge** went up.
Who told you he was *good* luck?
Sister Peace.
Beaky, that girl thinks it's a good omen every time a ***pig farts!***

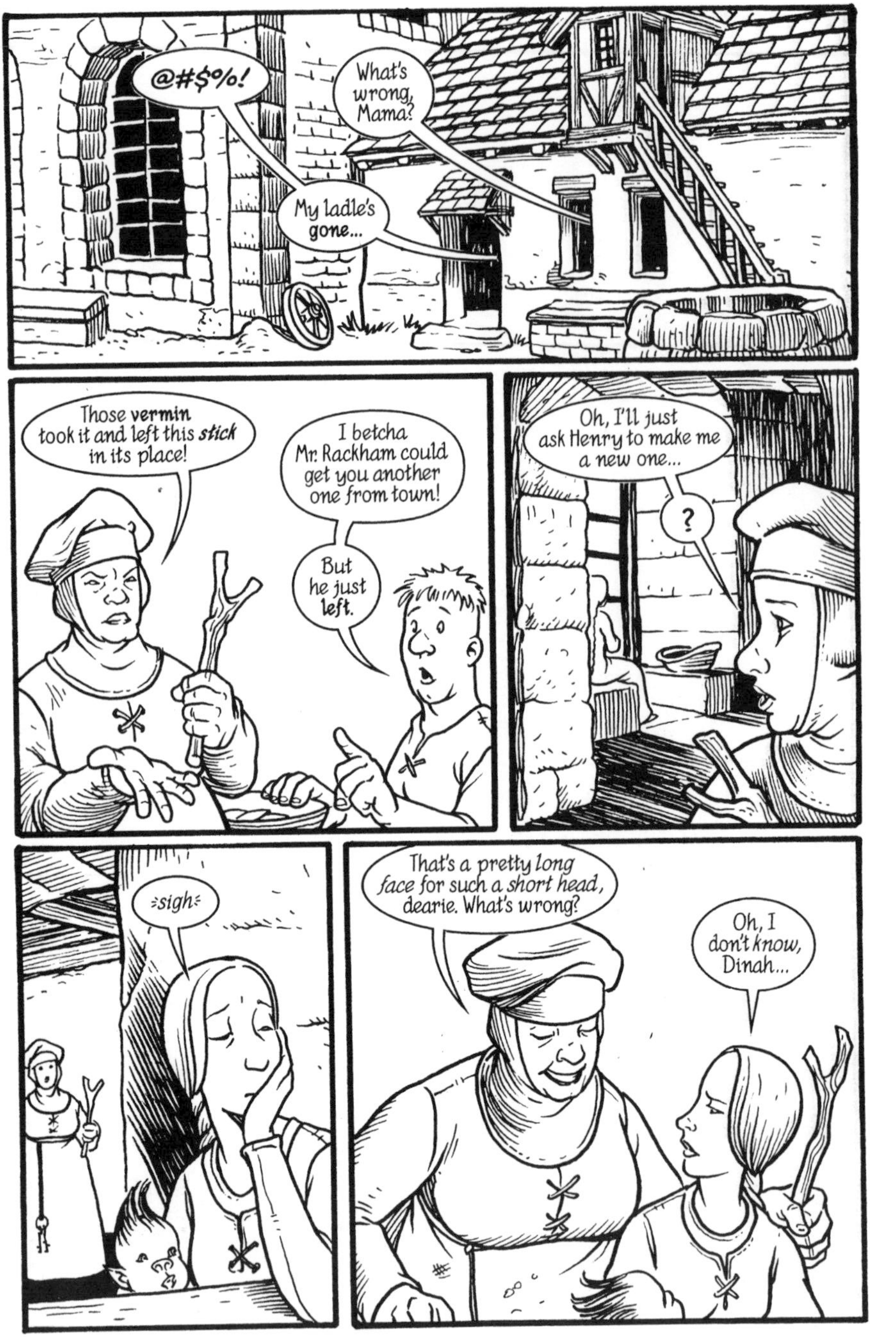
@#$%!
What's wrong, Mama?
My ladle's gone...
Those vermin took it and left this stick in its place!
I betcha Mr. Rackham could get you another one from town!
But he just left.
Oh, I'll just ask Henry to make me a new one...
?
sigh
That's a pretty long face for such a short head, dearie. What's wrong?
Oh, I don't know, Dinah...

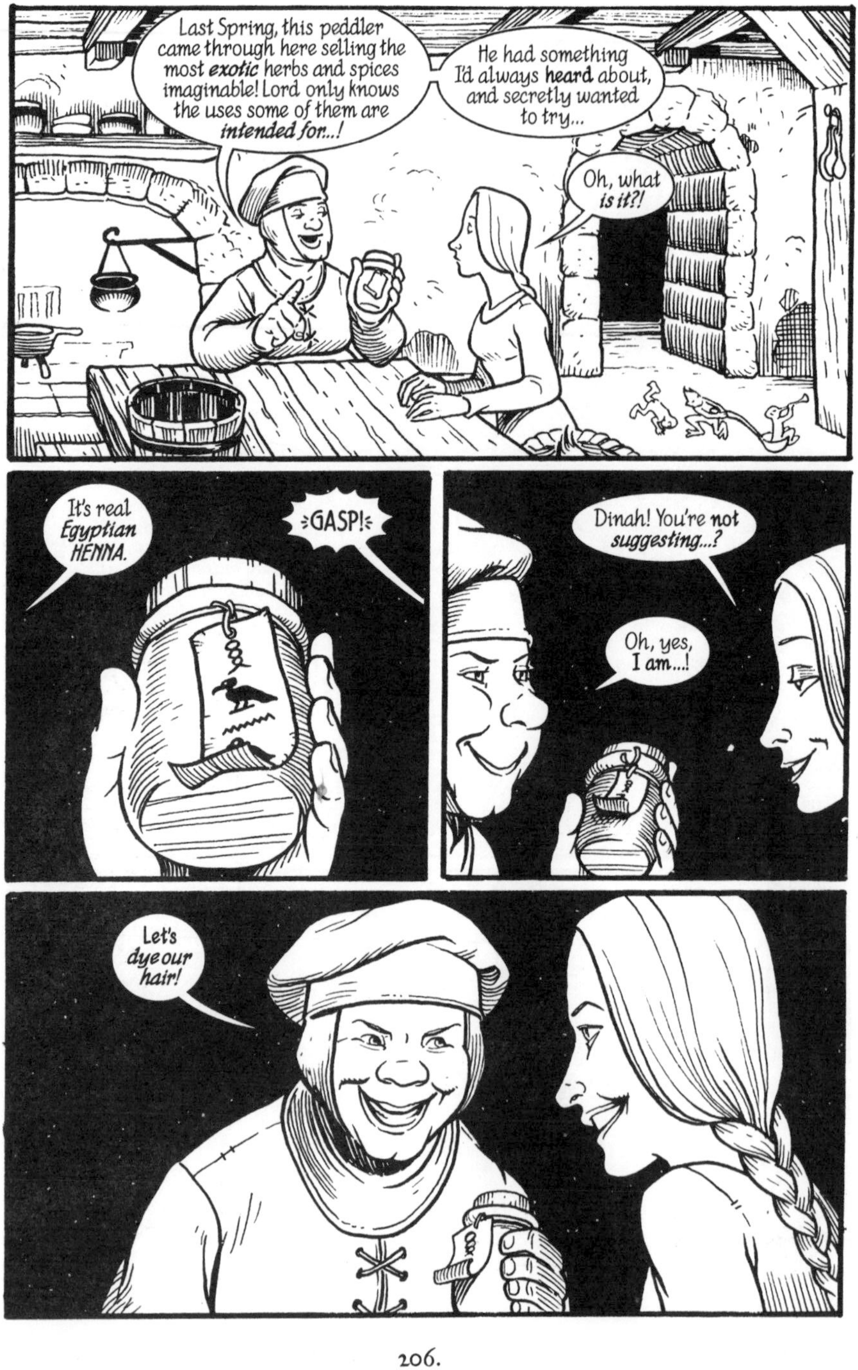
Last Spring, this peddler came through here selling the most *exotic* herbs and spices imaginable! Lord only knows the uses some of them are *intended for*...!
He had something I'd always **heard** about, and secretly wanted to try...
Oh, what *is it?!*
It's real *Egyptian HENNA.*
GASP!
Dinah! You're **not** *suggesting...?*
Oh, yes, **I am**...!
Let's *dye our hair!*

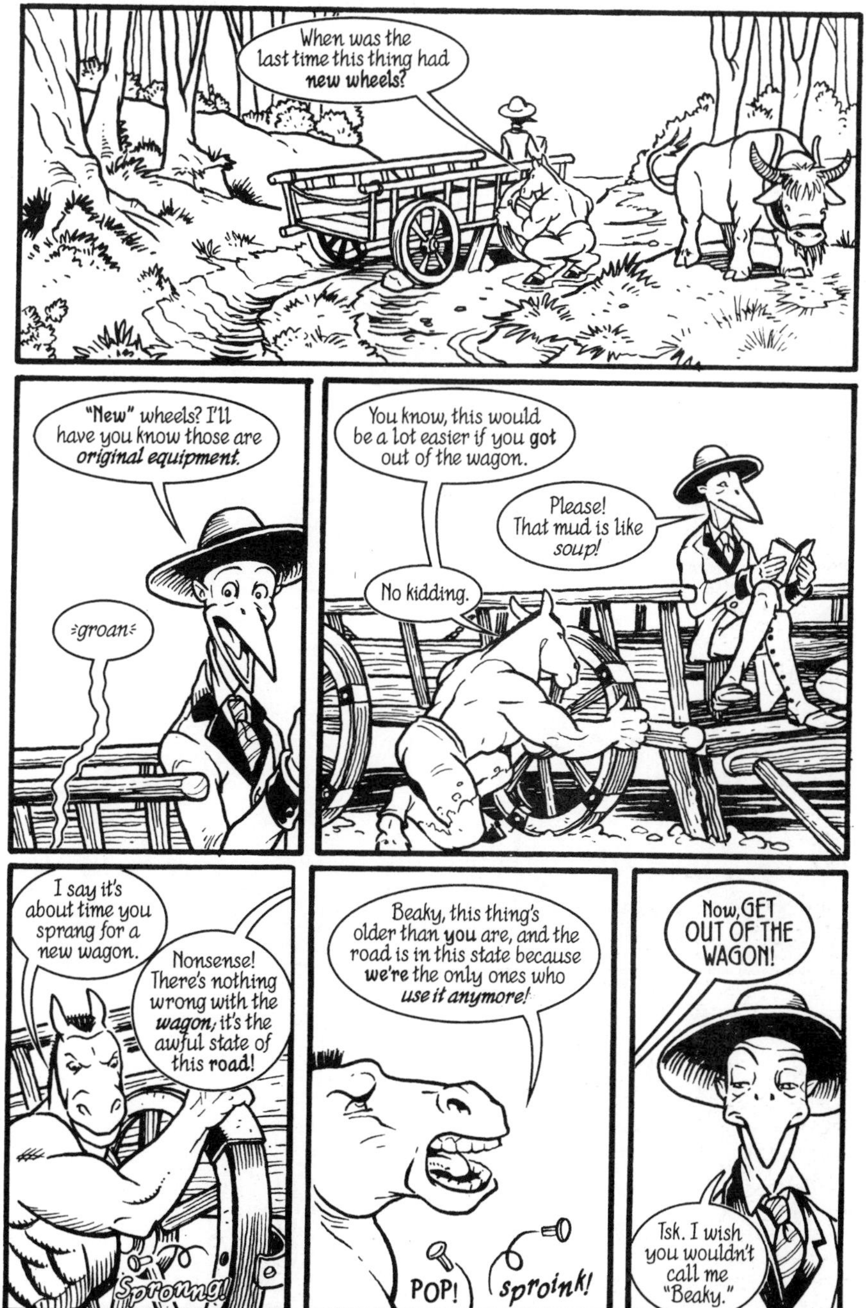
When was the last time this thing had **new wheels?**
"**New**" wheels? I'll have you know those are ***original equipment.***
groan
You know, this would be a lot easier if you **got** out of the wagon.
Please! That mud is like *soup!*
No kidding.
I say it's about time you sprang for a new wagon.
Nonsense! There's nothing wrong with the ***wagon;*** it's the awful state of this **road!**
Spronng!
Beaky, this thing's older than **you** are, and the road is in this state because **we're** the only ones who ***use it anymore!***
POP!
sproink!
Now, GET OUT OF THE WAGON!
Tsk. I wish you wouldn't call me "Beaky."

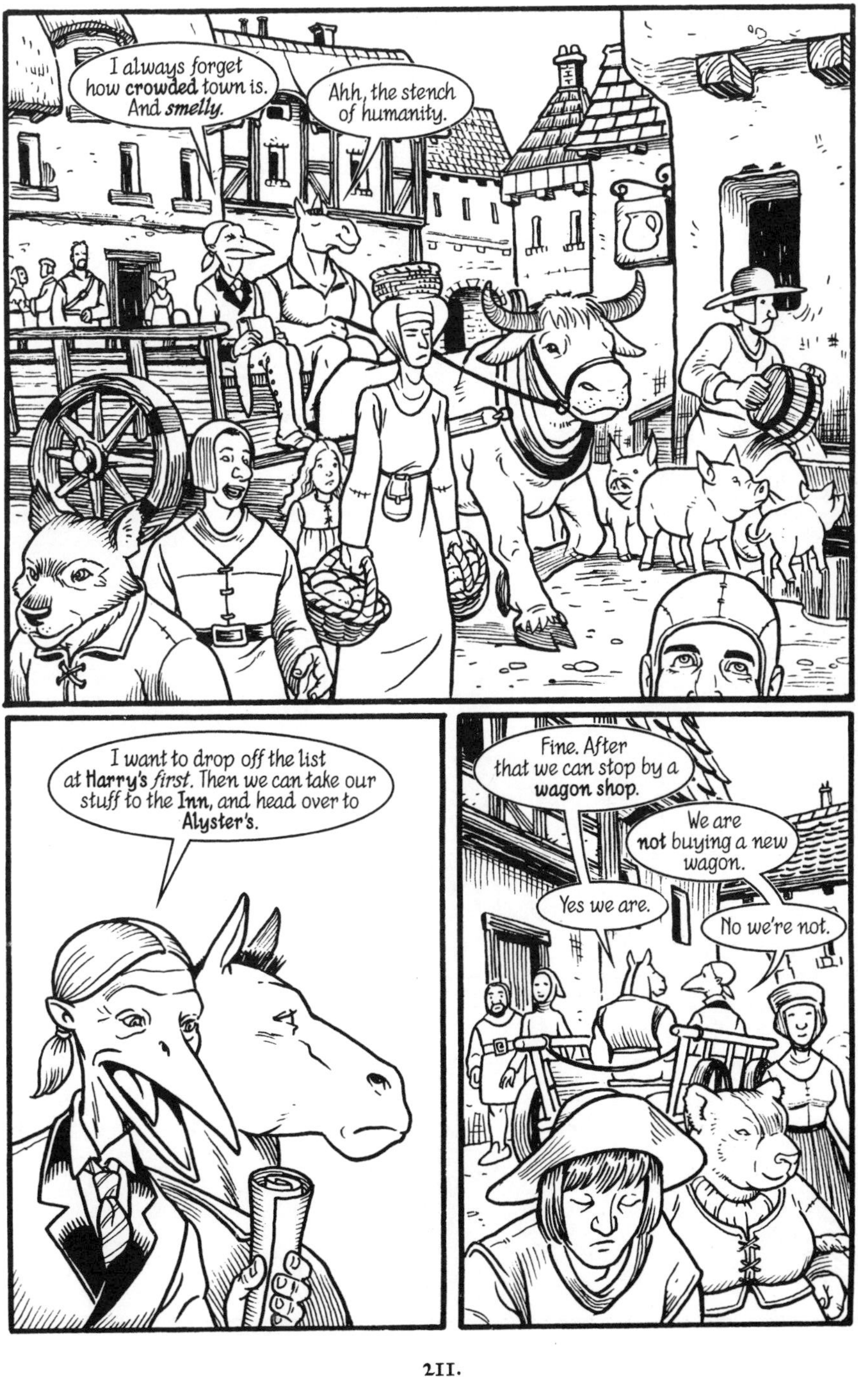
I always forget how **crowded** town is. And ***smelly***.
Ahh, the stench of humanity.
I want to drop off the list at **Harry's** *first*. Then we can take our stuff to the **Inn**, and head over to **Alyster's**.
Fine. After that we can stop by a **wagon shop**.
We are **not** buying a new wagon.
Yes we are.
No we're not.

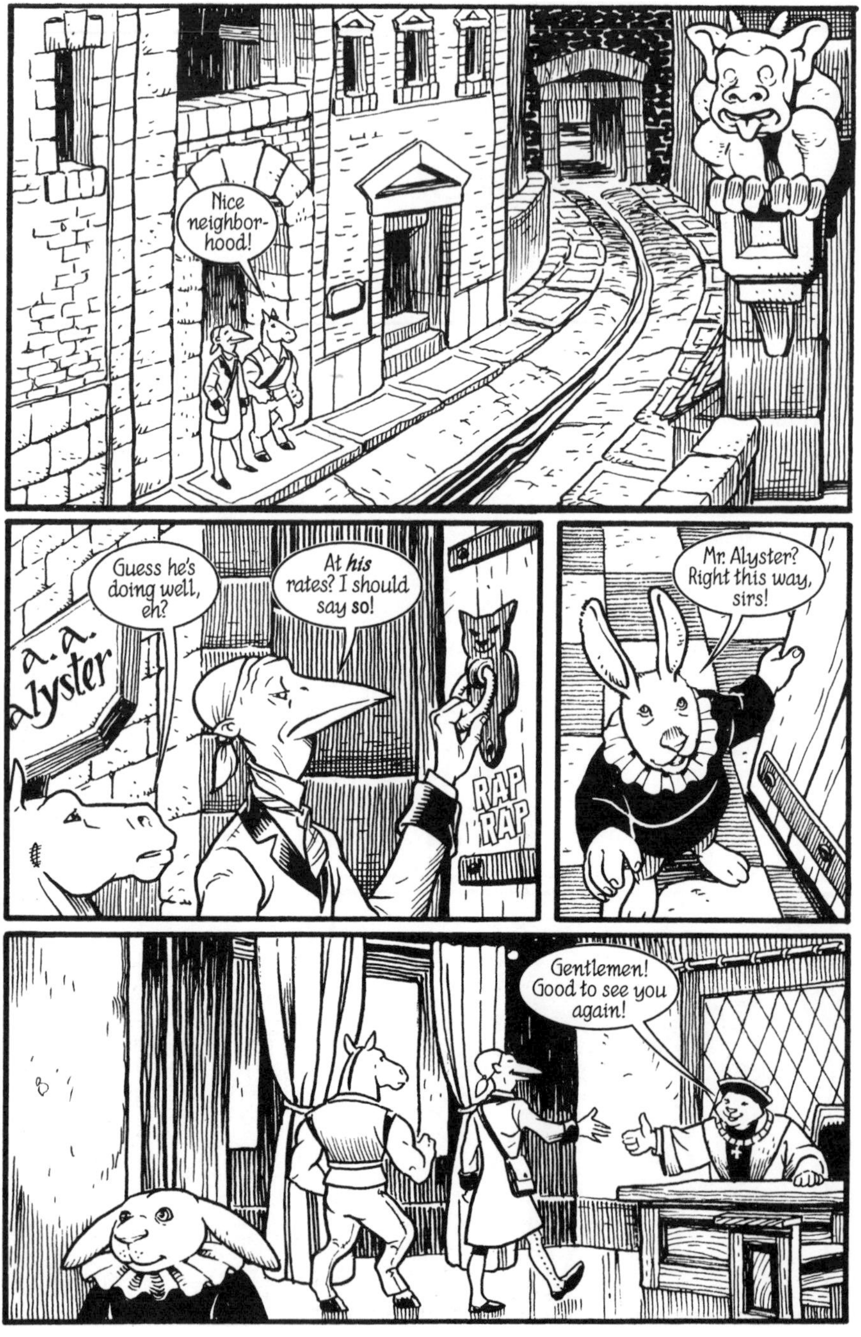
Nice neighbor-hood!
Guess he's doing well, eh?
At *his* rates? I should say so!
a. a. Alyster
RAP RAP
Mr. Alyster? Right this way, sirs!
Gentlemen! Good to see you again!

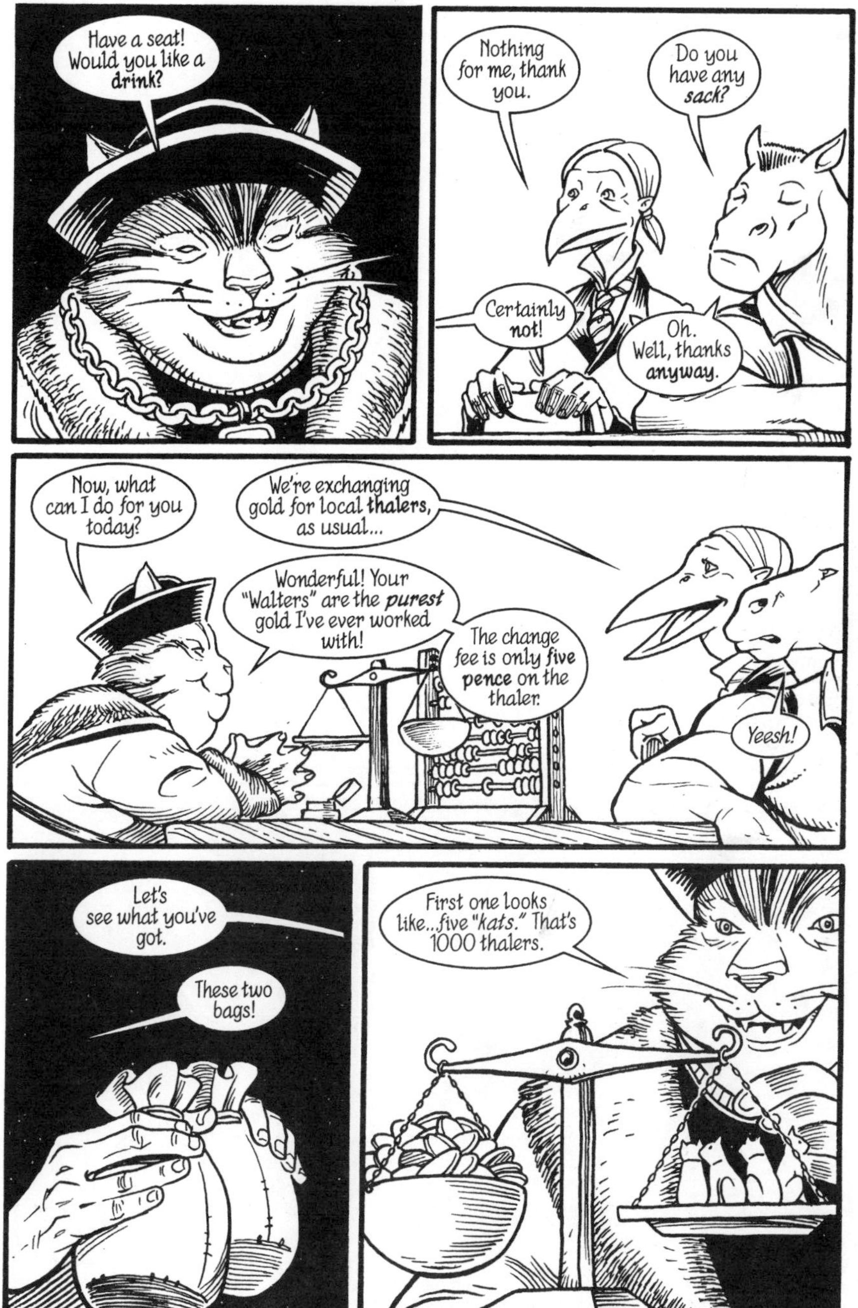
Have a seat! Would you like a **drink?**
Nothing for me, thank you.
Do you have any *sack?*
Certainly **not!**
Oh. Well, thanks **anyway.**
Now, what can I do for you today?
We're exchanging gold for local **thalers,** as usual...
Wonderful! Your "Walters" are the ***purest*** gold I've ever worked with!
The change fee is only **five pence** on the thaler.
Yeesh!
Let's see what you've got.
These two bags!
First one looks like...five "*kats.*" That's 1000 thalers.

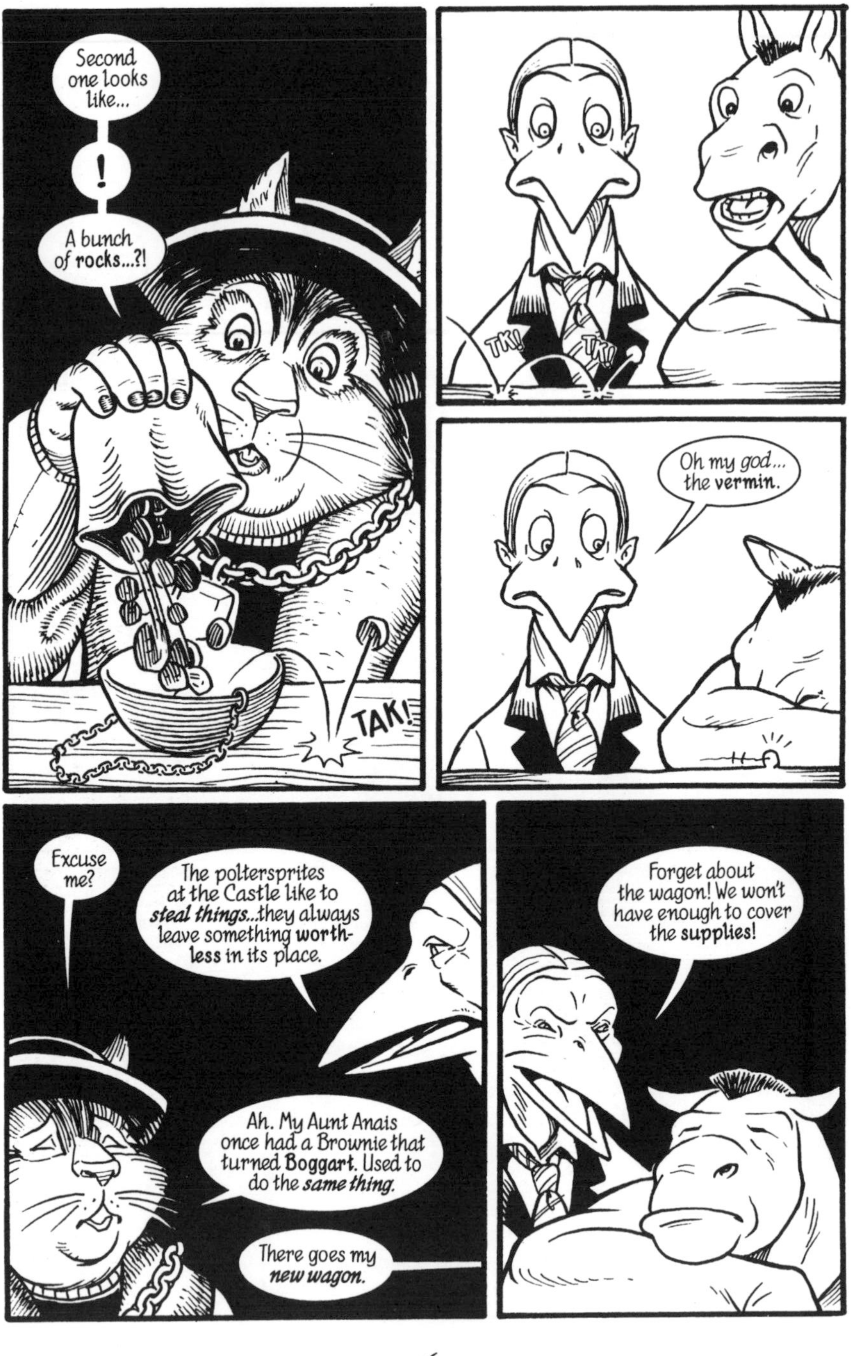
Second one looks like...
!
A bunch of **rocks**...?!
TAK!
TK!
TK!
Oh my god... the **vermin**.
Excuse me?
The poltersprites at the Castle like to ***steal things***...they always leave something **worthless** in its place.
Ah. My Aunt Anais once had a Brownie that turned **Boggart**. Used to do the ***same thing***.
There goes my ***new wagon***.
Forget about the wagon! We won't have enough to cover the **supplies**!

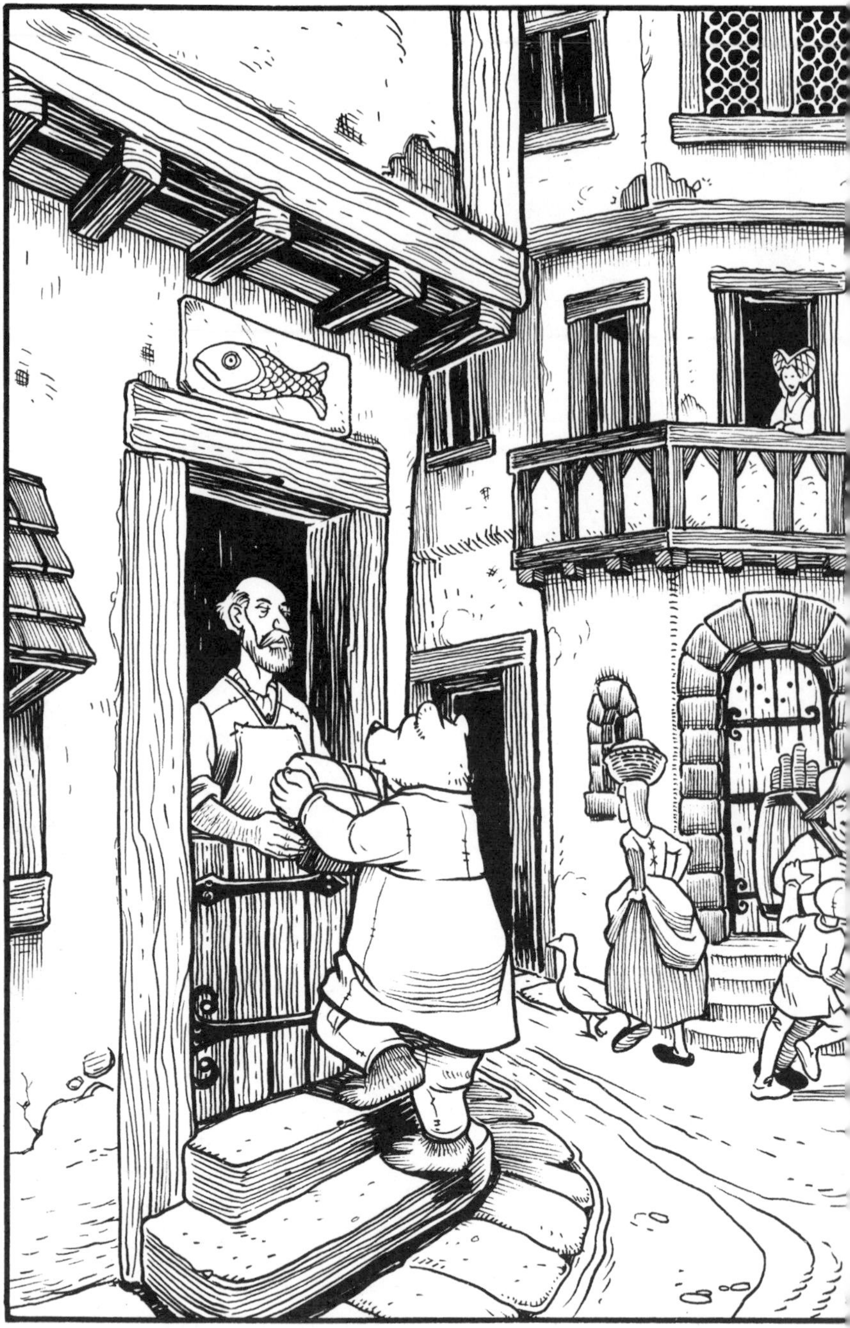

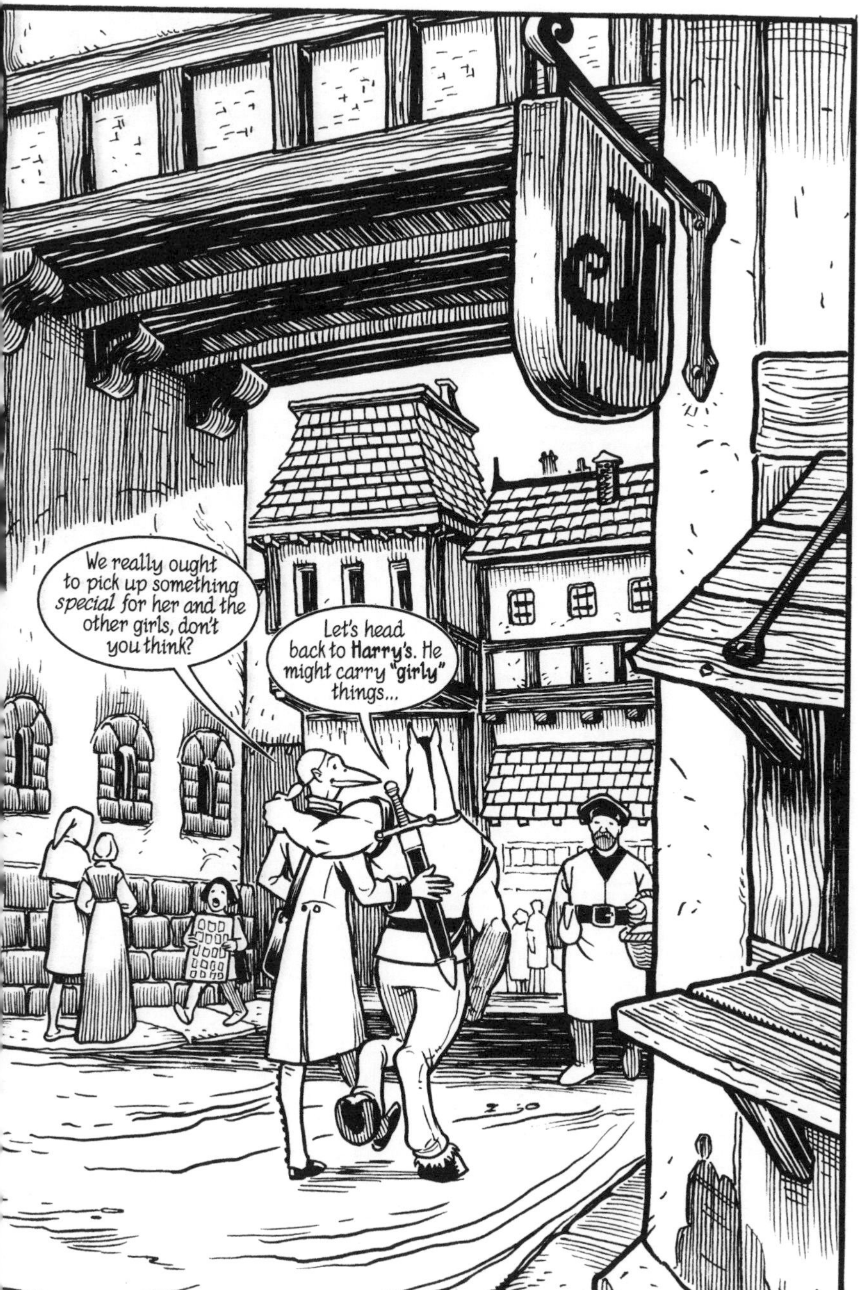
We really ought to pick up something *special* for her and the other girls, don't you think?
Let's head back to **Harry's**. He might carry **"girly"** things...

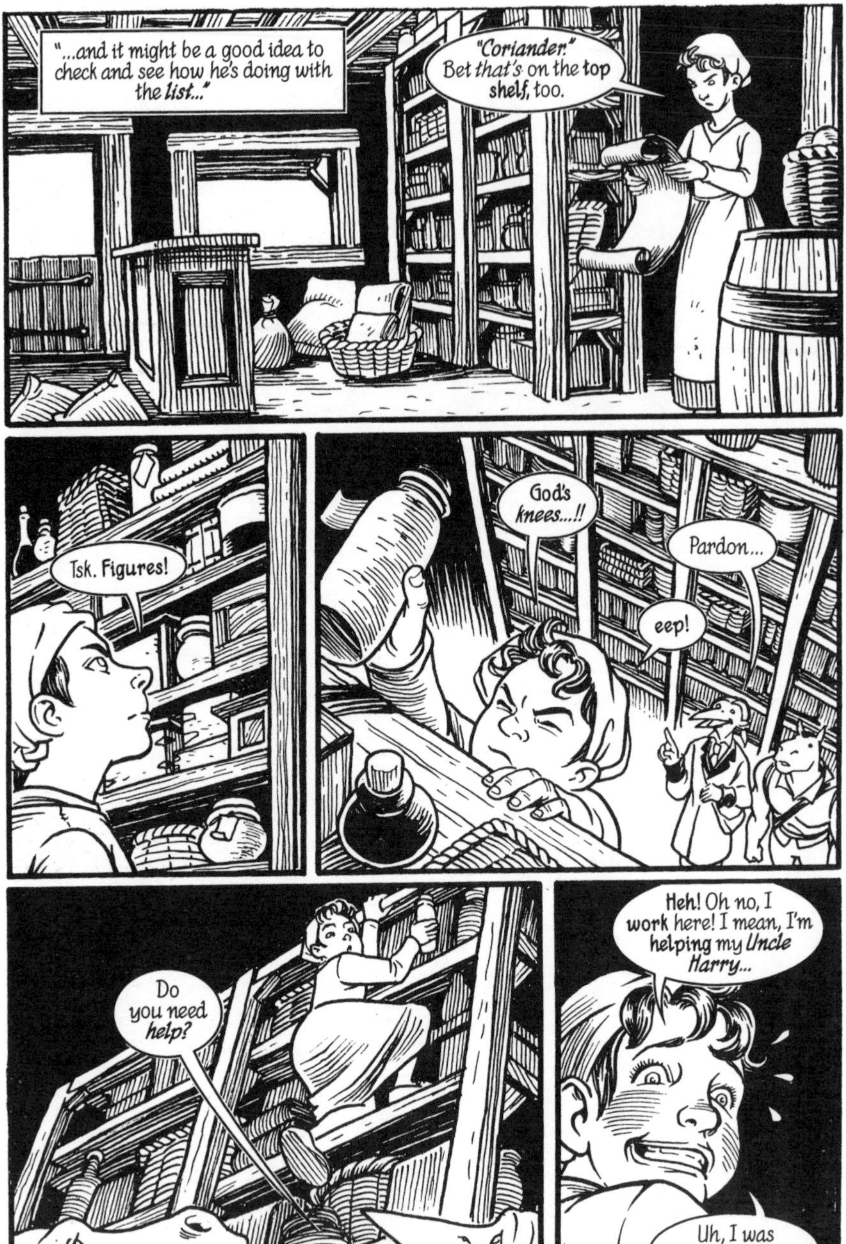
"...and it might be a good idea to check and see how he's doing with the *list*..."
"*Coriander*." Bet *that's* on the **top shelf**, too.
Tsk. **Figures!**
God's *knees*...!!
Pardon...
eep!
Do you need *help?*
Heh! Oh no, I **work** here! I mean, I'm **helping** my *Uncle Harry*...
Uh, I was just coming **down** now.

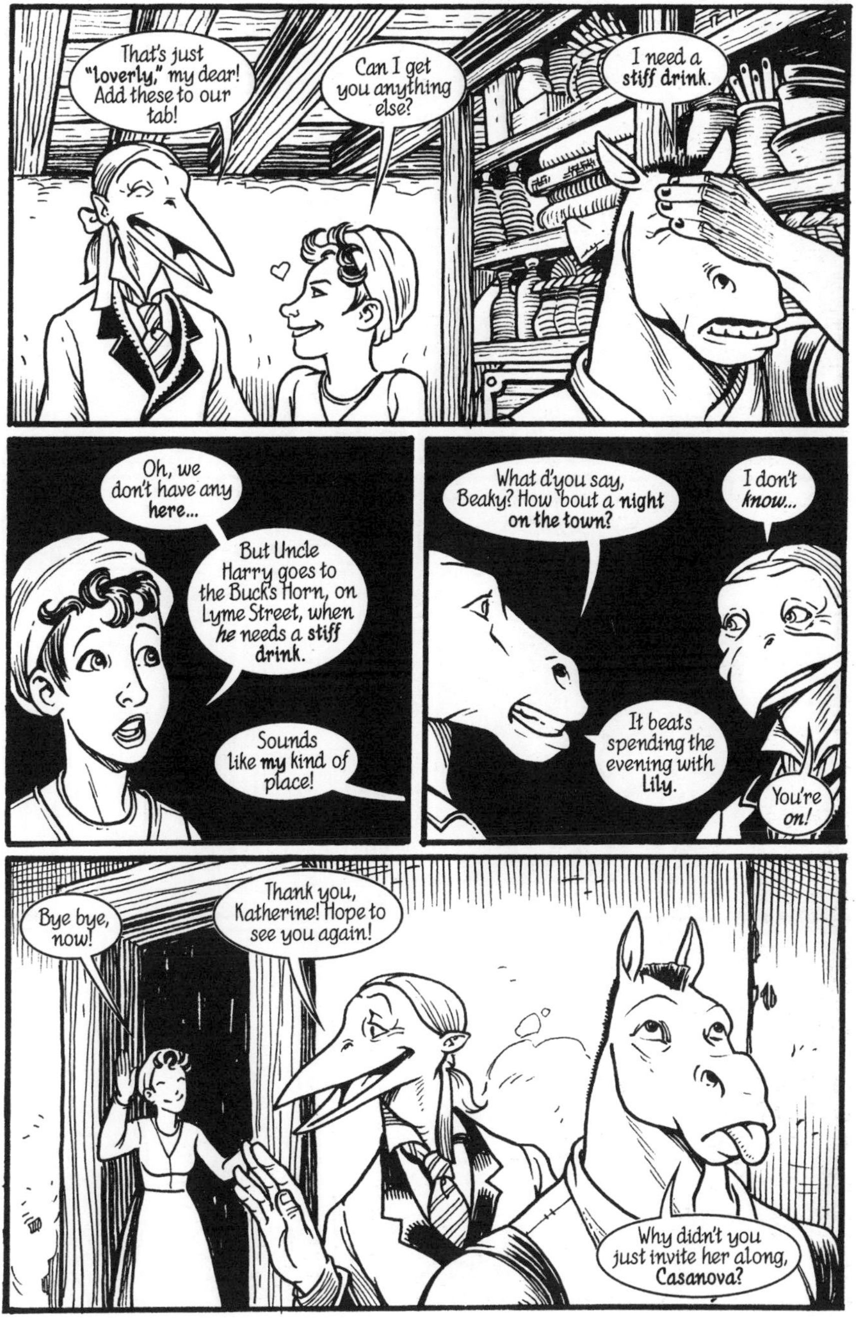
That's just "loverly," my dear! Add these to our tab!
Can I get you anything else?
I need a stiff drink.
Oh, we don't have any here...
But Uncle Harry goes to the Buck's Horn, on Lyme Street, when he needs a stiff drink.
Sounds like my kind of place!
What d'you say, Beaky? How 'bout a night on the town?
I don't know...
It beats spending the evening with Lily.
You're on!
Bye bye, now!
Thank you, Katherine! Hope to see you again!
Why didn't you just invite her along, Casanova?

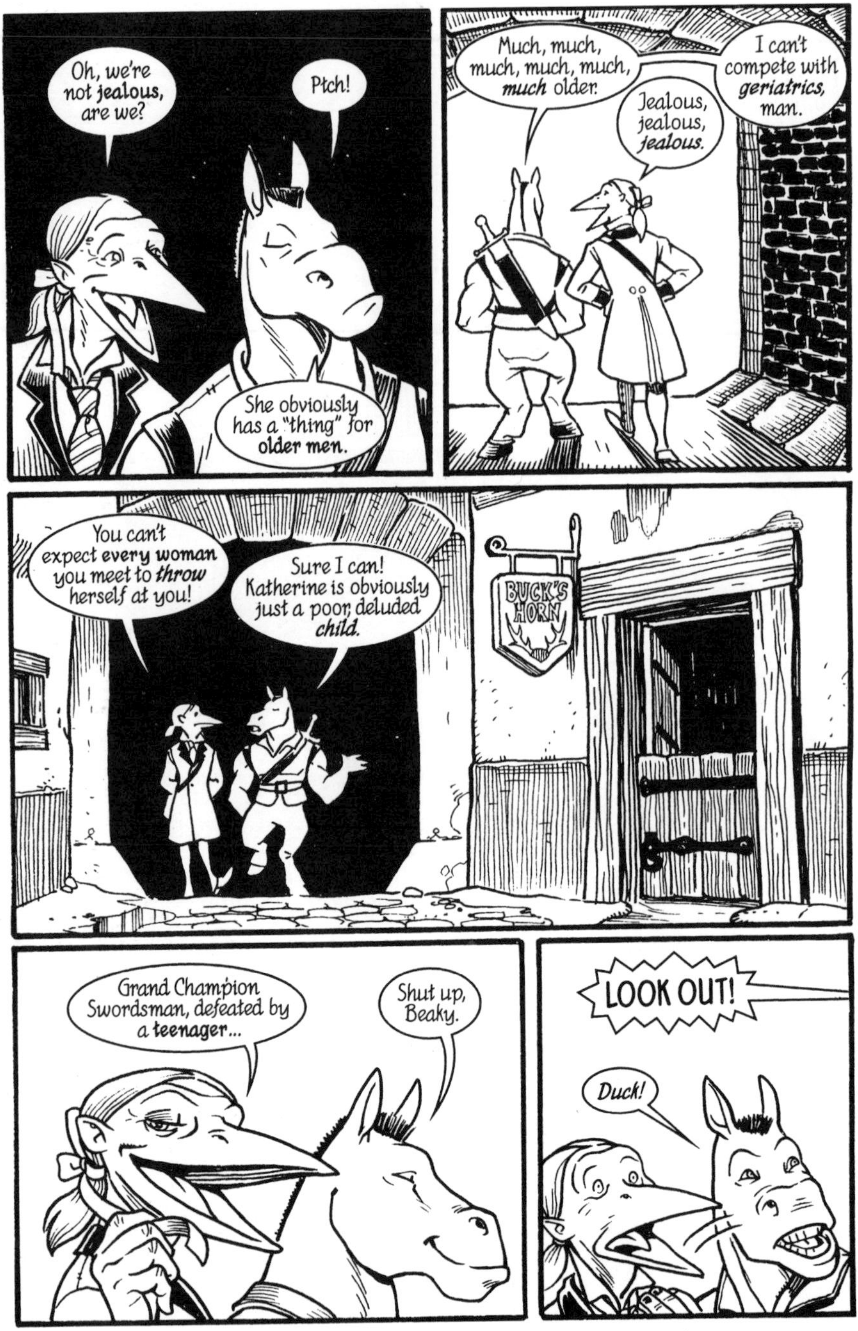
Oh, we're not jealous, are we?
Ptch!
She obviously has a "thing" for older men.
Much, much, much, much, much, much older.
Jealous, jealous, jealous.
I can't compete with geriatrics, man.
You can't expect every woman you meet to throw herself at you!
Sure I can! Katherine is obviously just a poor, deluded child.
BUCK'S HORN
Grand Champion Swordsman, defeated by a teenager...
Shut up, Beaky.
LOOK OUT!
Duck!

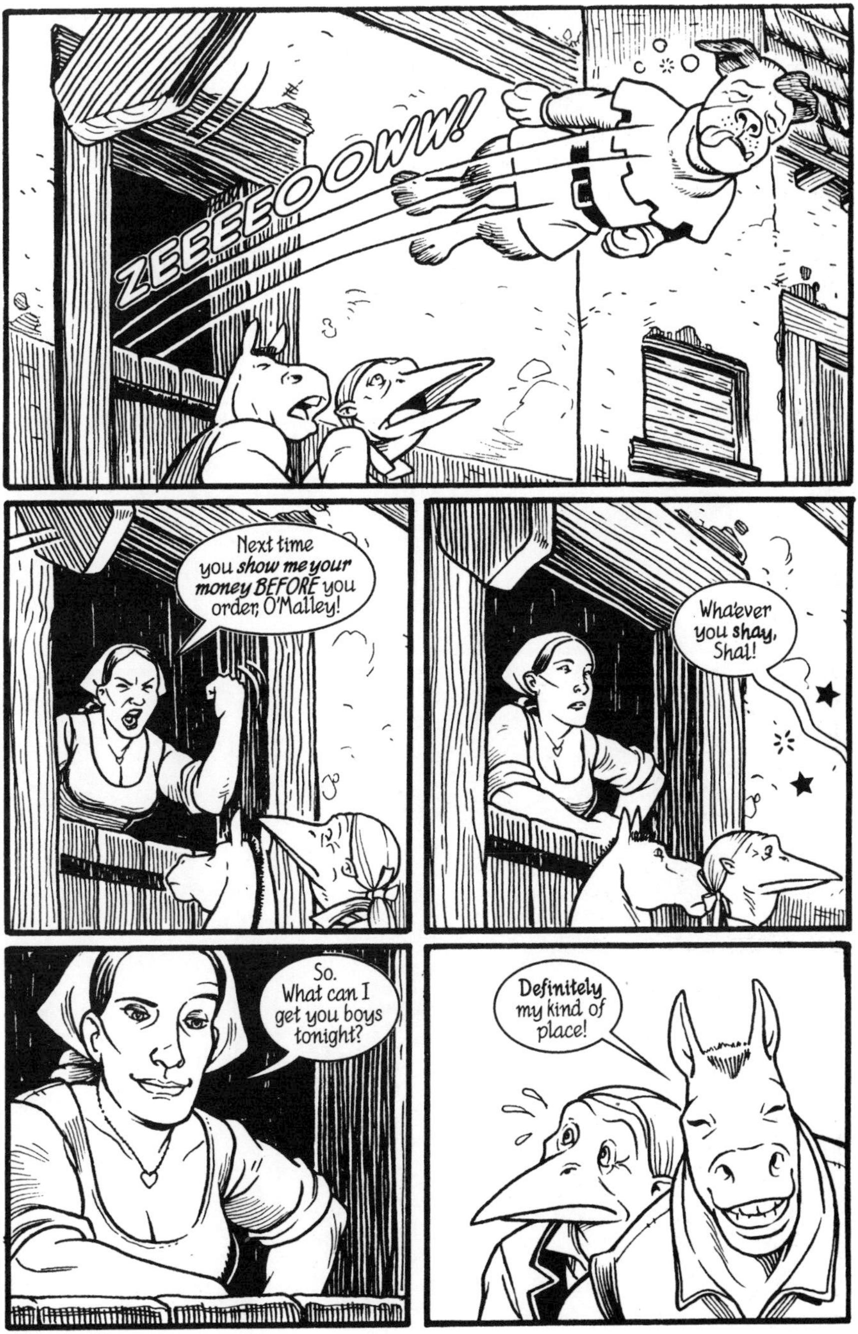
ZEEEEOOOWW!
Next time you show me your money BEFORE you order, O'Malley!
Wha'ever you shay, Shal!
So. What can I get you boys tonight?
Definitely my kind of place!

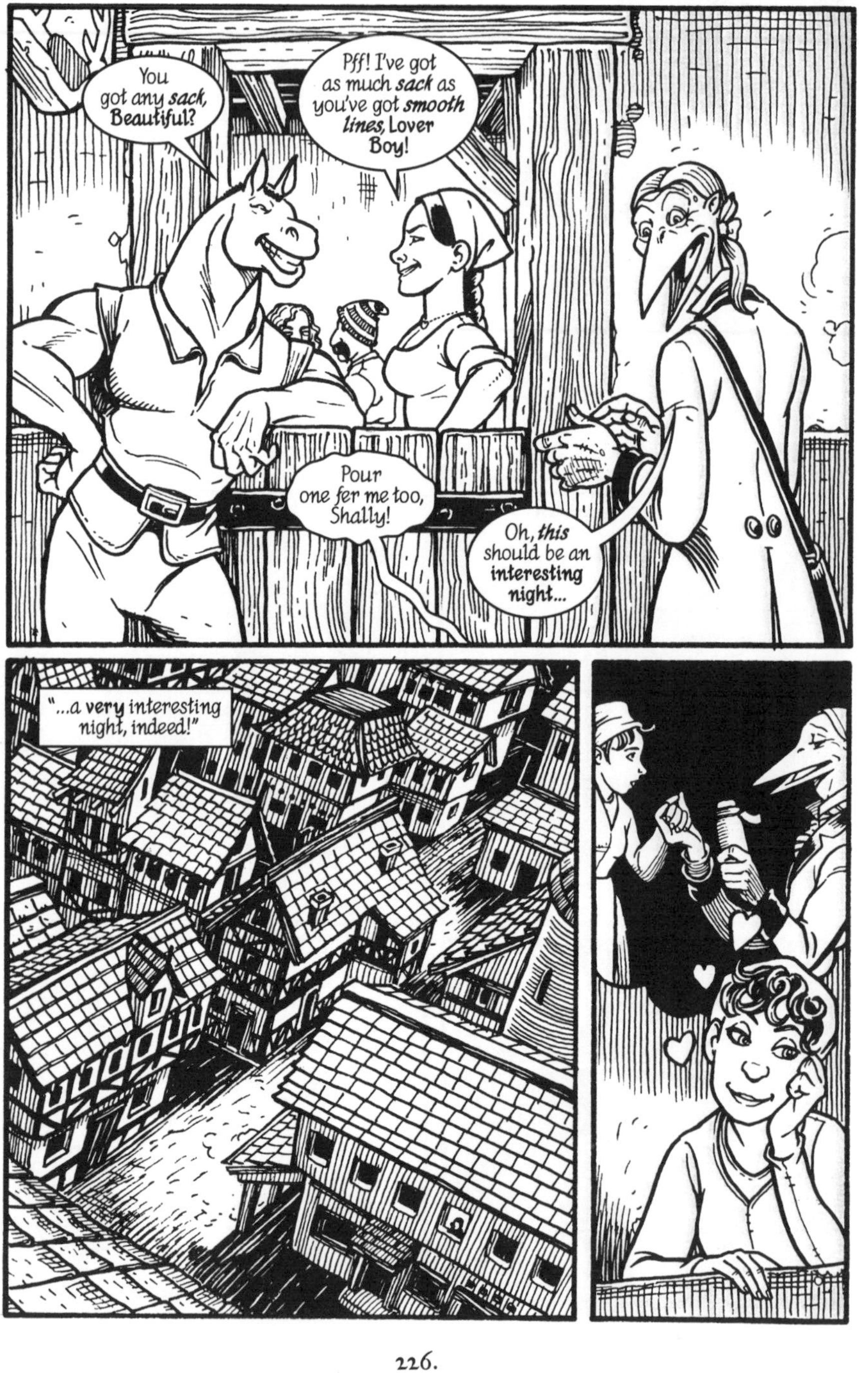
You got any *sack*, Beautiful?
Pff! I've got as much *sack* as you've got *smooth lines*, Lover Boy!
Pour one fer me too, Shally!
Oh, *this* should be an **interesting night...**
"...a **very** interesting night, indeed!"

Chapter 10.

· CITY MOUSE, COUNTRY MOUSE PT. 2 ·

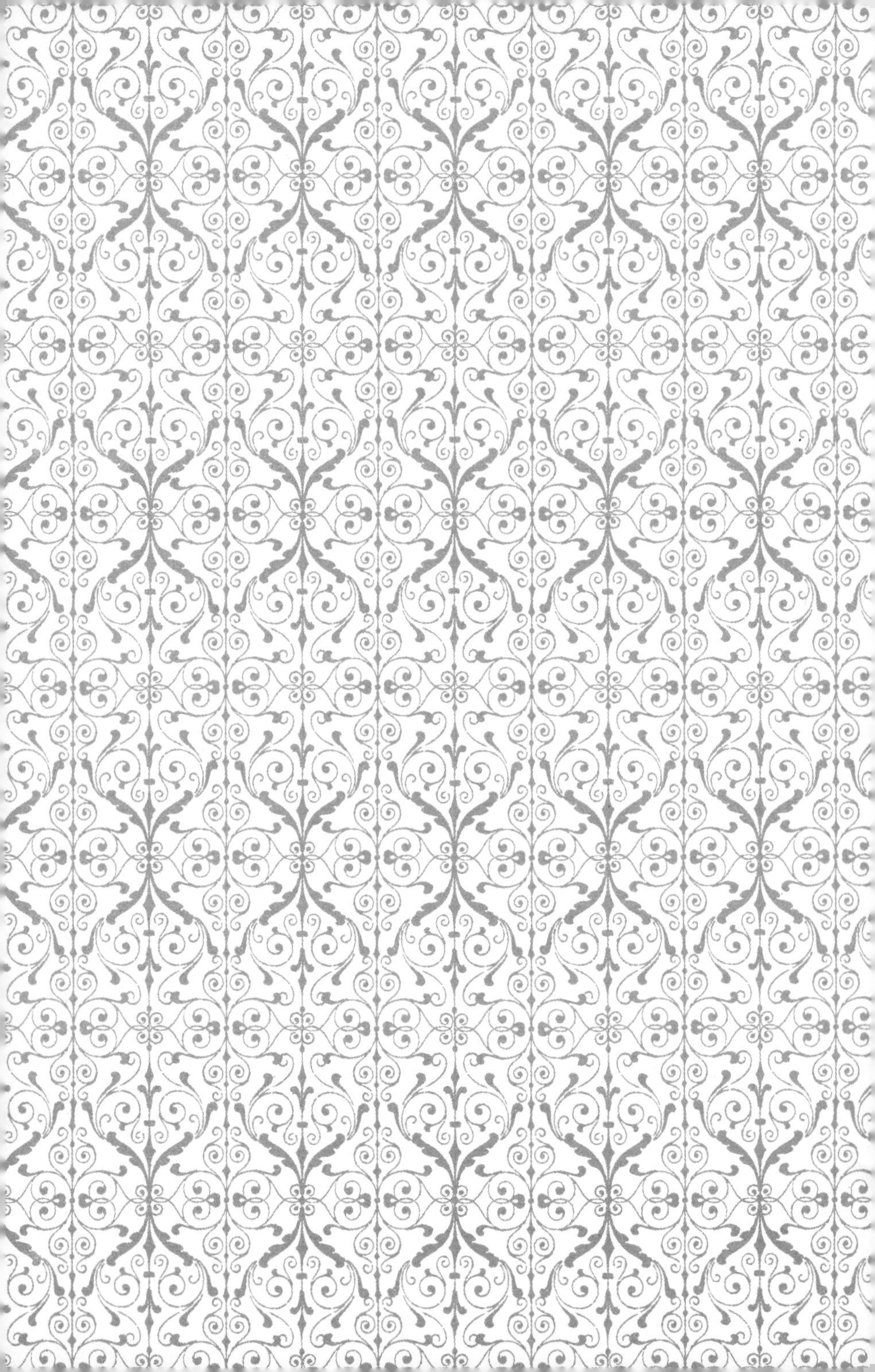

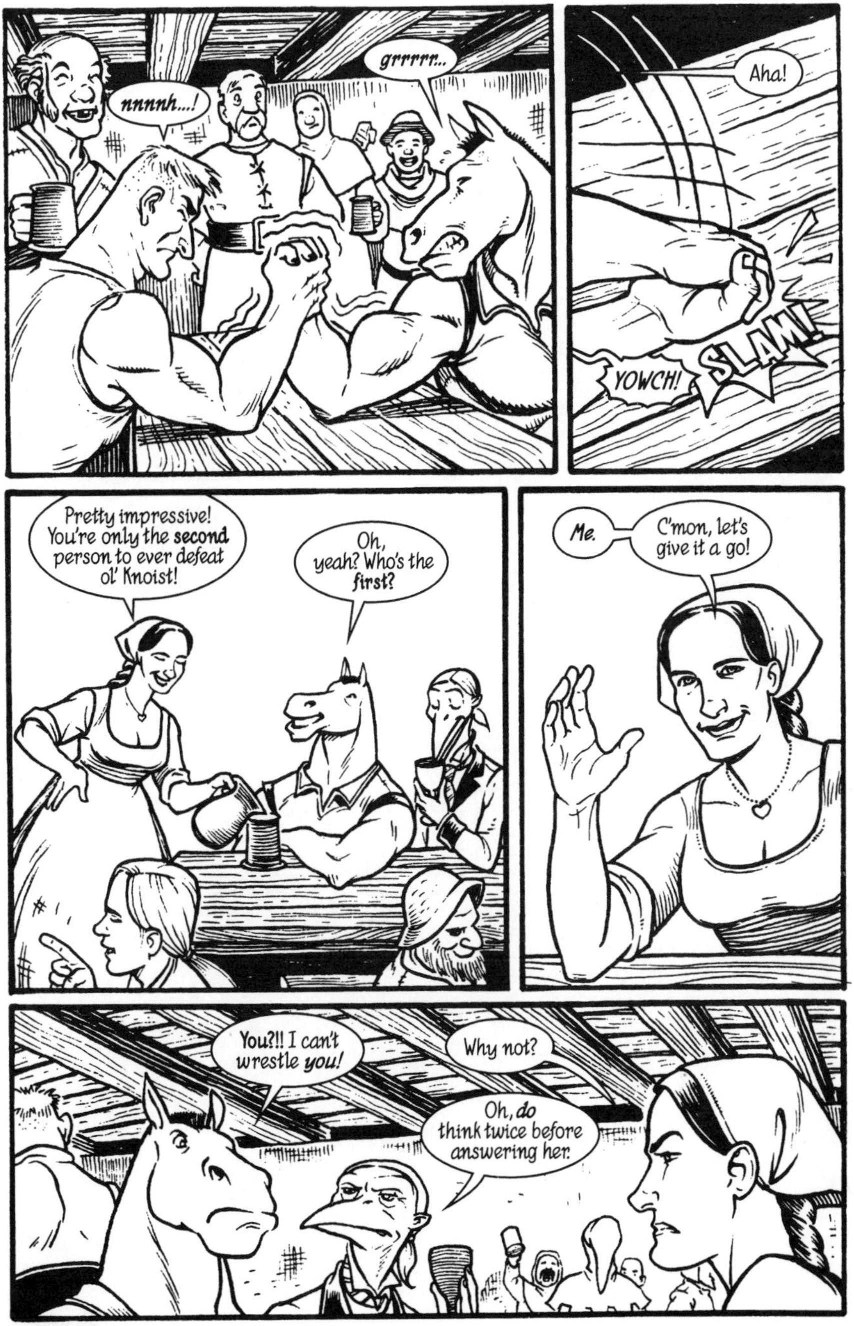
grrrrr...
nnnnh...!
Aha!
SLAM!
YOWCH!
Pretty impressive! You're only the **second** person to ever defeat ol' Knoist!
Oh, yeah? Who's the **first**?
Me.
C'mon, let's give it a go!
You?!! I can't wrestle *you*!
Why not?
Oh, *do* think twice before answering her.

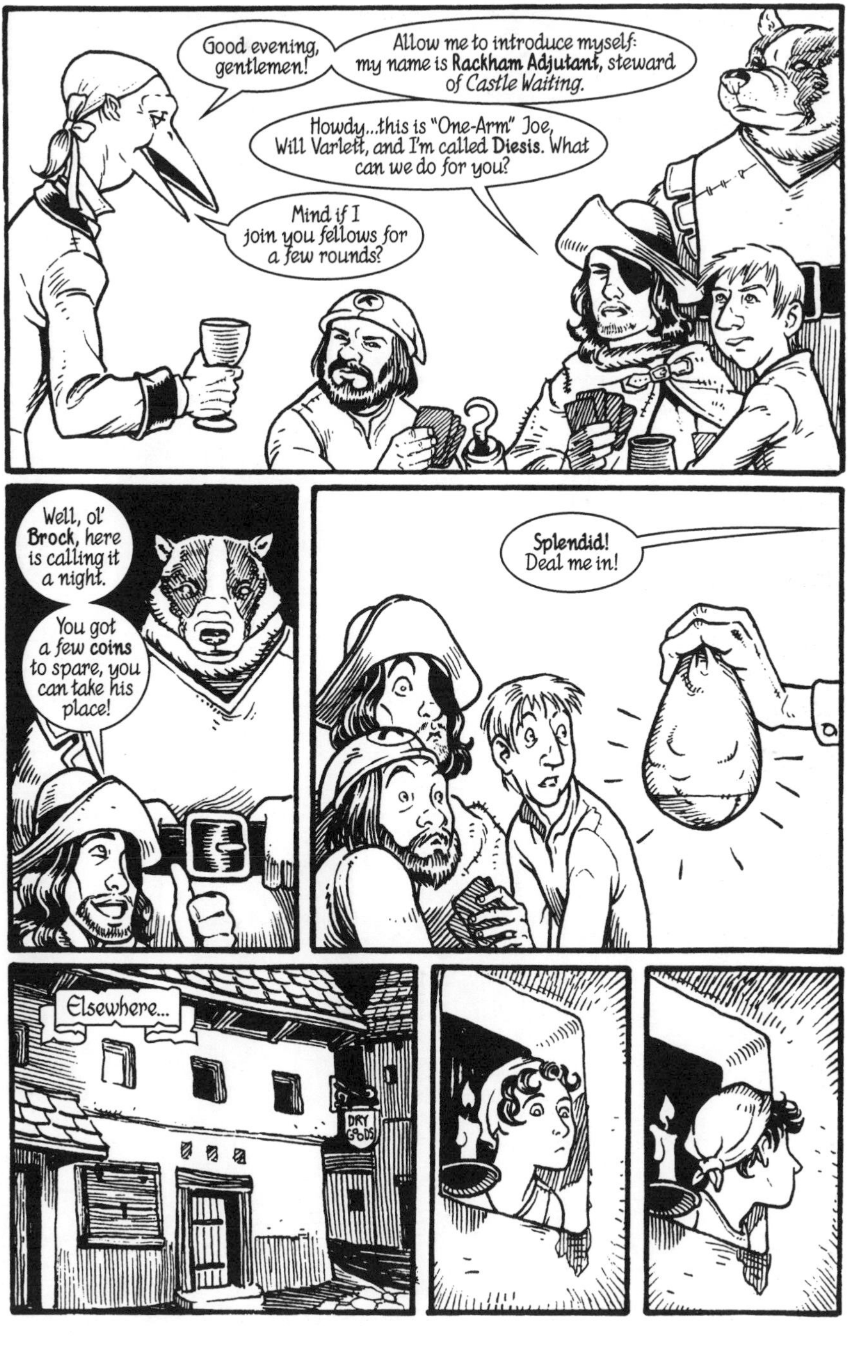

Good evening, gentlemen!
Allow me to introduce myself: my name is Rackham Adjutant, steward of Castle Waiting.
Mind if I join you fellows for a few rounds?
Howdy...this is "One-Arm" Joe, Will Varlett, and I'm called Diesis. What can we do for you?
Well, ol' Brock, here is calling it a night.
You got a few coins to spare, you can take his place!
Splendid! Deal me in!
Elsewhere...
DRY GOODS

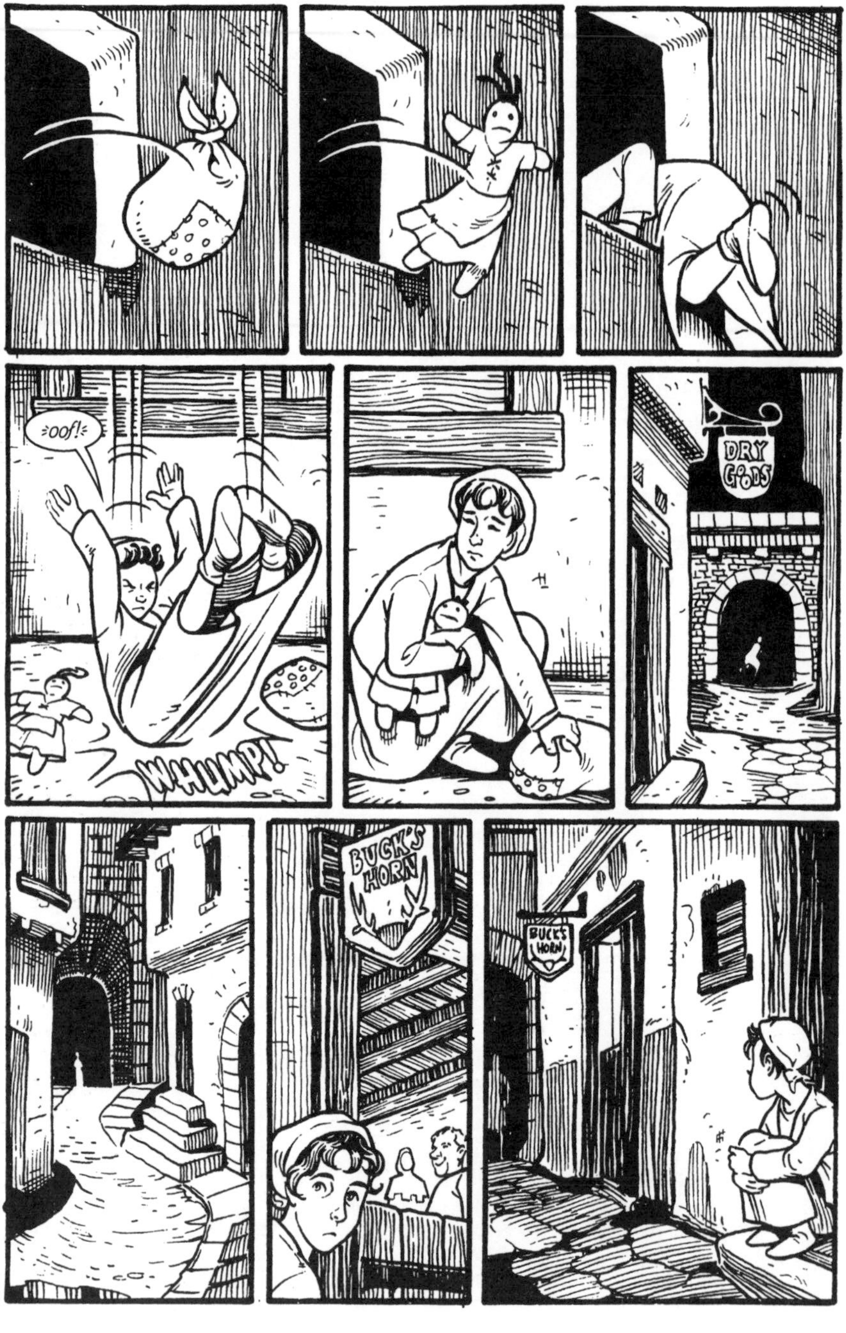
oof!
WHUMP!
DRY GOODS
BUCK'S HORN
BUCK'S HORN

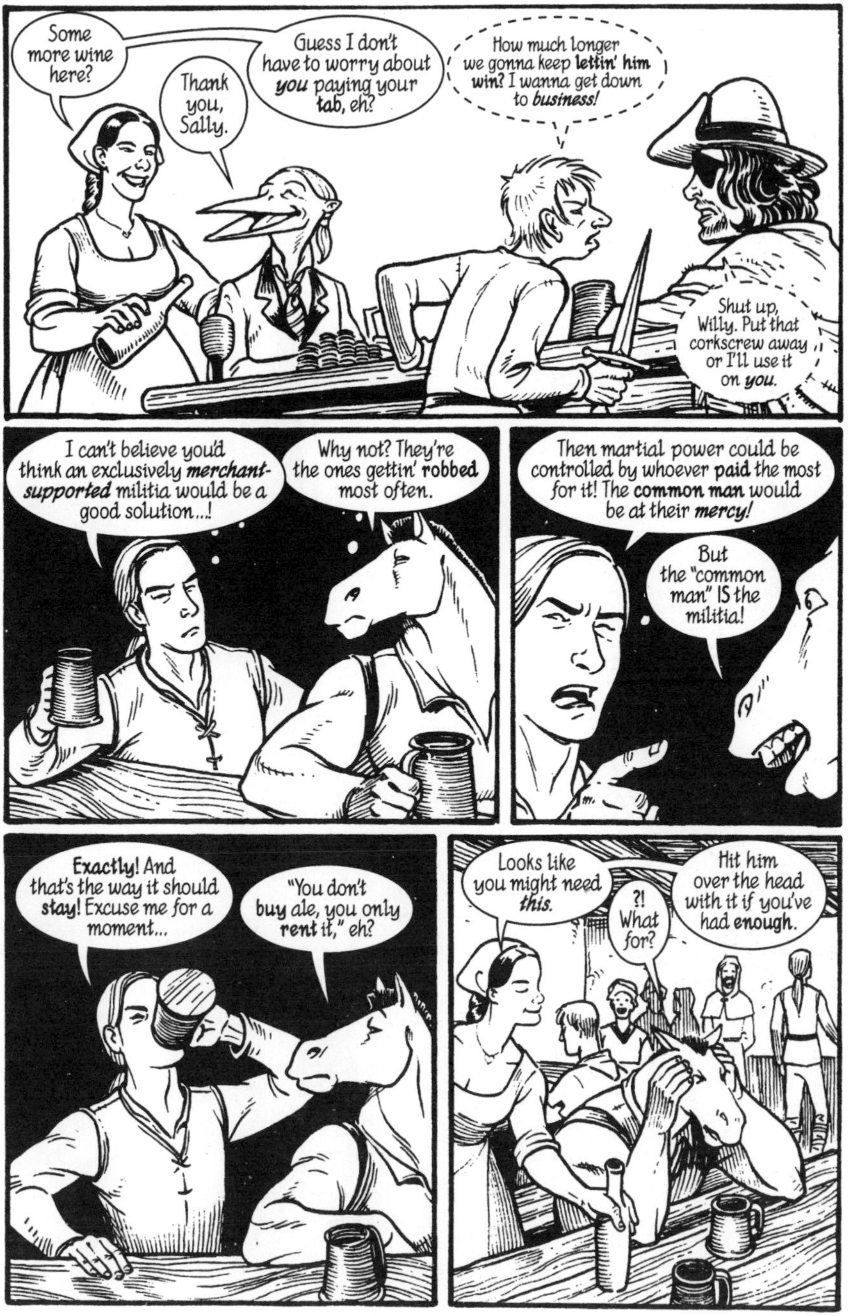
Some more wine here?
Thank you, Sally.
Guess I don't have to worry about **you** paying your **tab**, eh?
How much longer we gonna keep **lettin' him win?** I wanna get down to **business!**
Shut up, Willy. Put that corkscrew away or I'll use it on **you**.
I can't believe you'd think an exclusively **merchant-supported** militia would be a good solution...!
Why not? They're the ones gettin' **robbed** most often.
Then martial power could be controlled by whoever **paid** the most for it! The **common man** would be at their **mercy!**
But the "common man" IS the militia!
Exactly! And that's the way it should **stay**! Excuse me for a moment...
"You don't **buy** ale, you only **rent** it," eh?
Looks like you might need **this**.
?! What for?
Hit him over the head with it if you've had **enough**.

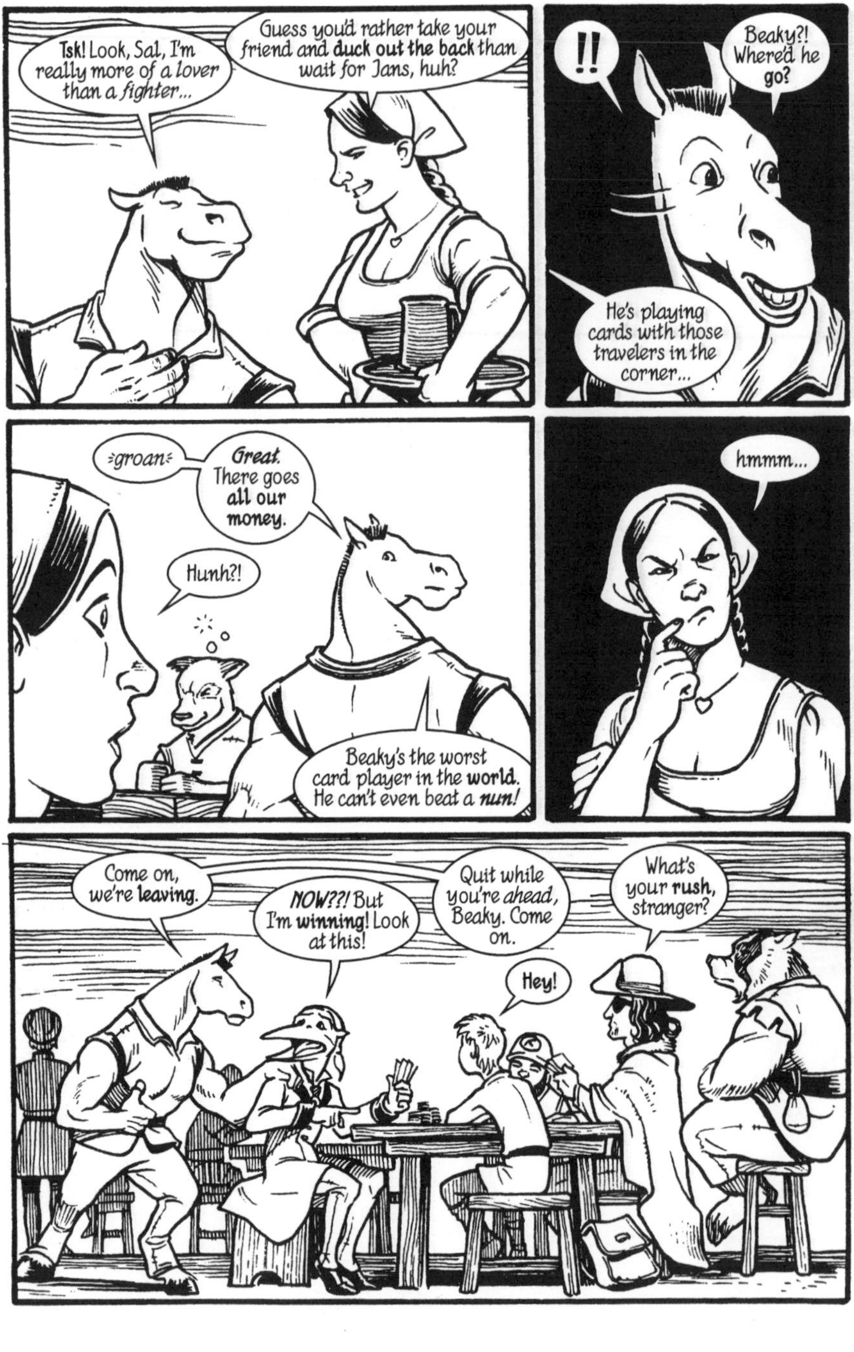
Tsk! Look, Sal, I'm really more of a *lover* than a *fighter*...
Guess you'd rather take your friend and **duck out the back** than wait for Jans, huh?
!!
Beaky?! Where'd he **go?**
He's playing cards with those travelers in the corner...
groan
Great. There goes **all our money.**
Hunh?!
Beaky's the worst card player in the **world**. He can't even beat a ***nun!***
hmmm...
Come on, we're **leaving**.
NOW??! But I'm **winning**! Look at this!
Quit while you're *ahead*, Beaky. Come on.
Hey!
What's your **rush**, stranger?

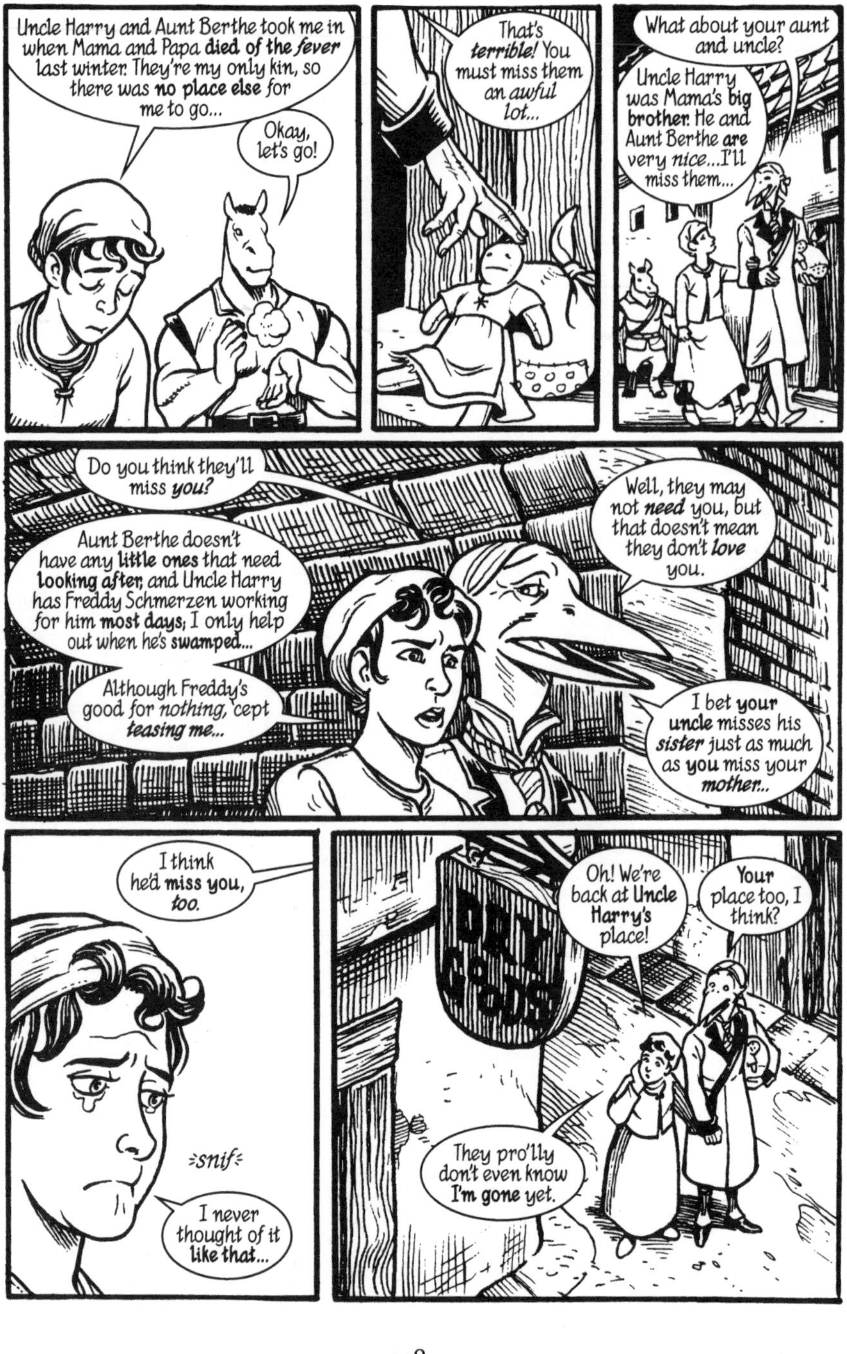
Uncle Harry and Aunt Berthe took me in when Mama and Papa **died of the *fever*** last winter. They're my only kin, so there was **no place else** for me to go...
Okay, let's go!
That's ***terrible!*** You must miss them an *awful* lot...
What about your aunt and uncle?
Uncle Harry was Mama's **big brother.** He and Aunt Berthe **are** very *nice*...I'll miss them...
Do you think they'll miss ***you?***
Aunt Berthe doesn't have any **little ones** that need **looking after,** and Uncle Harry has Freddy Schmerzen working for him **most days;** I only help out when he's **swamped...**
Although Freddy's good for *nothing,* 'cept ***teasing me...***
Well, they may not ***need*** you, but that doesn't mean they don't ***love*** you.
I bet **your uncle** misses his ***sister*** just as much as **you** miss your ***mother...***
I think he'd **miss you, *too.***
snif
I never thought of it **like that...**
DRY GOODS
Oh! We're back at **Uncle Harry's** place!
Your place too, I think?
They pro'lly don't even know **I'm gone** yet.

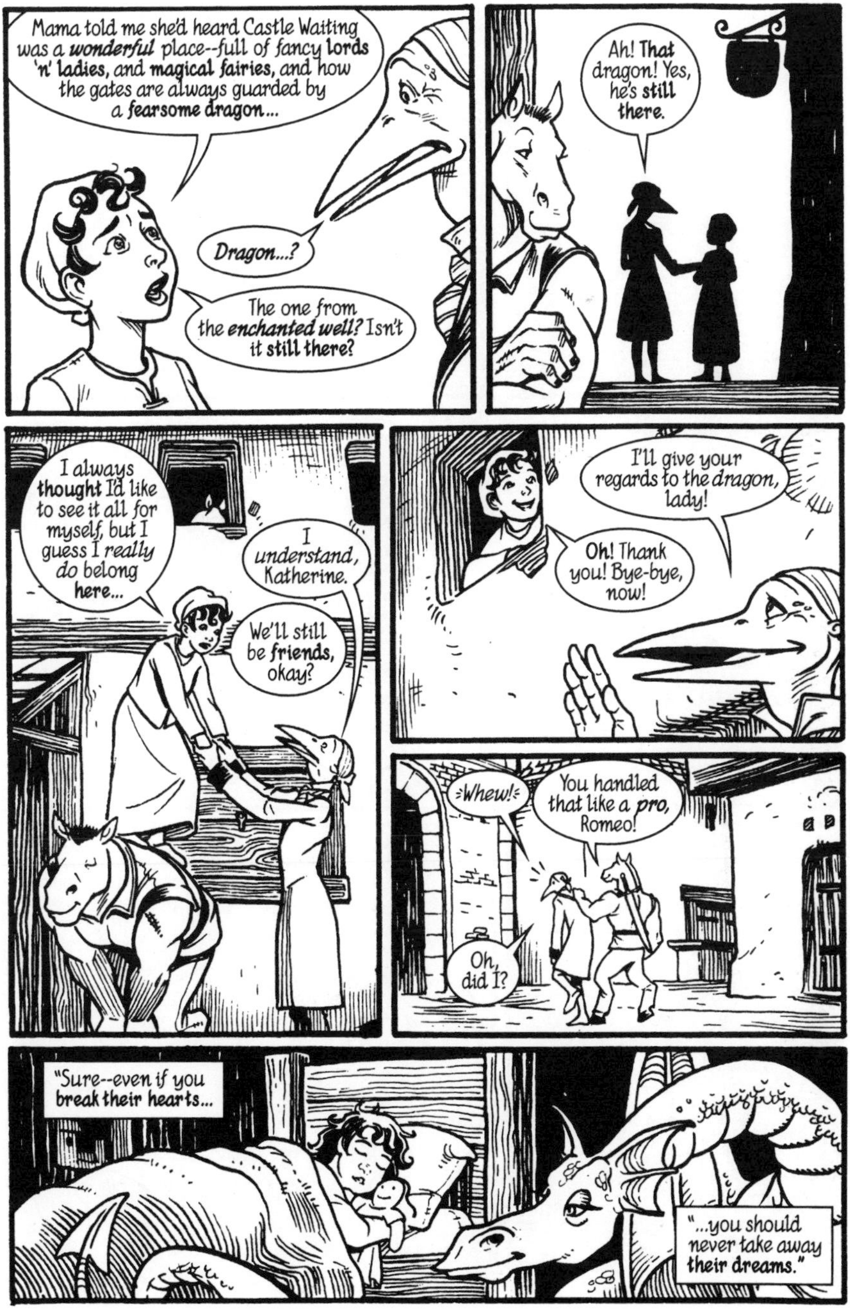
Mama told me she'd heard Castle Waiting was a **wonderful** place--full of fancy **lords 'n' ladies,** and **magical fairies,** and how the gates are always guarded by a **fearsome dragon...**
Dragon...?
The one from the **enchanted well?** Isn't it **still there?**
Ah! **That** dragon! Yes, he's **still there.**
I always **thought** I'd like to see it all for myself, but I guess I *really* do belong **here...**
I *understand,* Katherine.
We'll still be **friends,** okay?
I'll give your regards to the *dragon,* lady!
Oh! Thank you! Bye-bye, now!
Whew!
You handled that like a *pro,* Romeo!
Oh, did I?
"Sure--even if you **break their hearts...**
"...you should never take away **their dreams."**

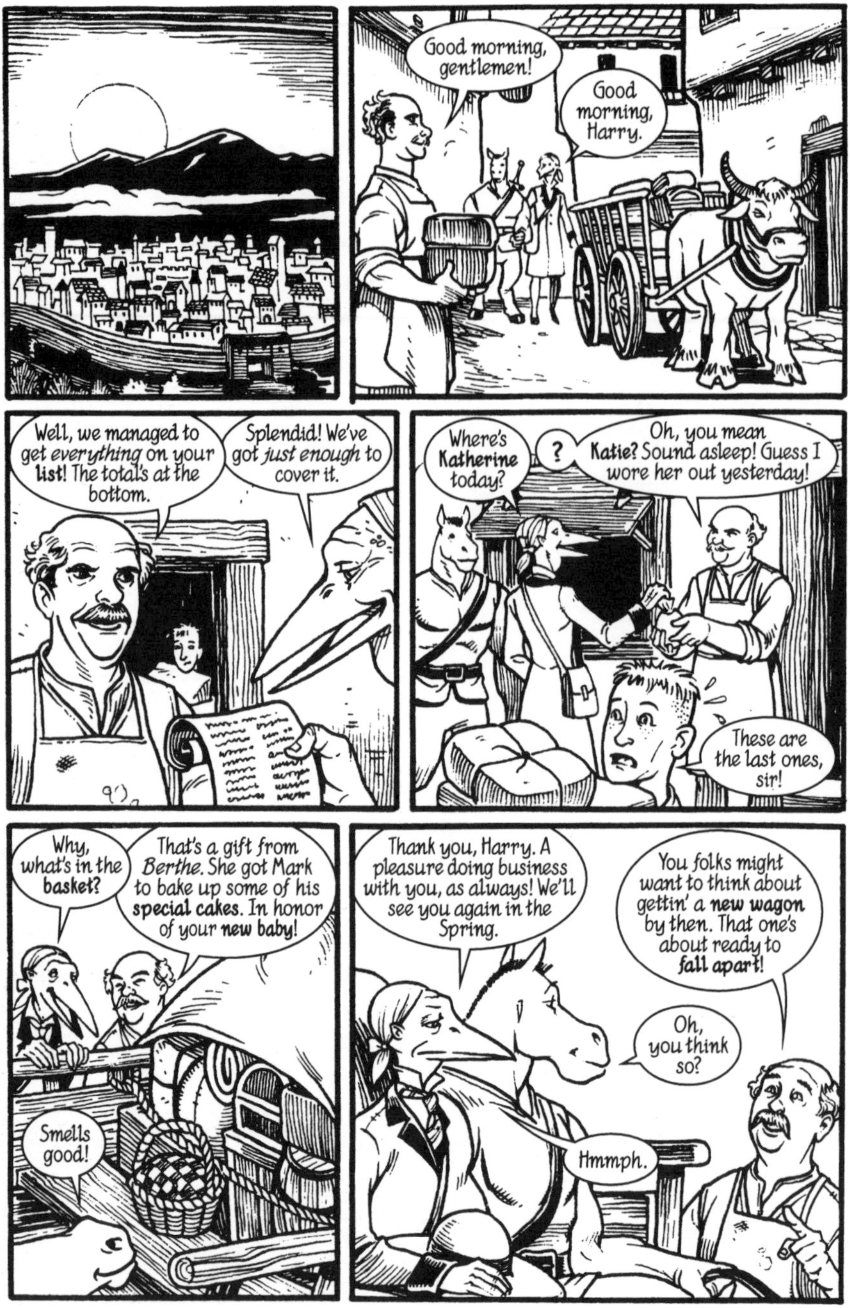
Good morning, gentlemen!
Good morning, Harry.
Well, we managed to get *everything* on your **list**! The total's at the bottom.
Splendid! We've got *just enough* to cover it.
Where's **Katherine** today?
?
Oh, you mean **Katie**? Sound asleep! Guess I wore her out yesterday!
These are the last ones, sir!
Why, what's in the **basket**?
That's a gift from *Berthe*. She got Mark to bake up some of his **special cakes**. In honor of your **new baby**!
Smells good!
Thank you, Harry. A pleasure doing business with you, as always! We'll see you again in the Spring.
You folks might want to think about gettin' a **new wagon** by then. That one's about ready to **fall apart**!
Oh, you think so?
Hmmph.

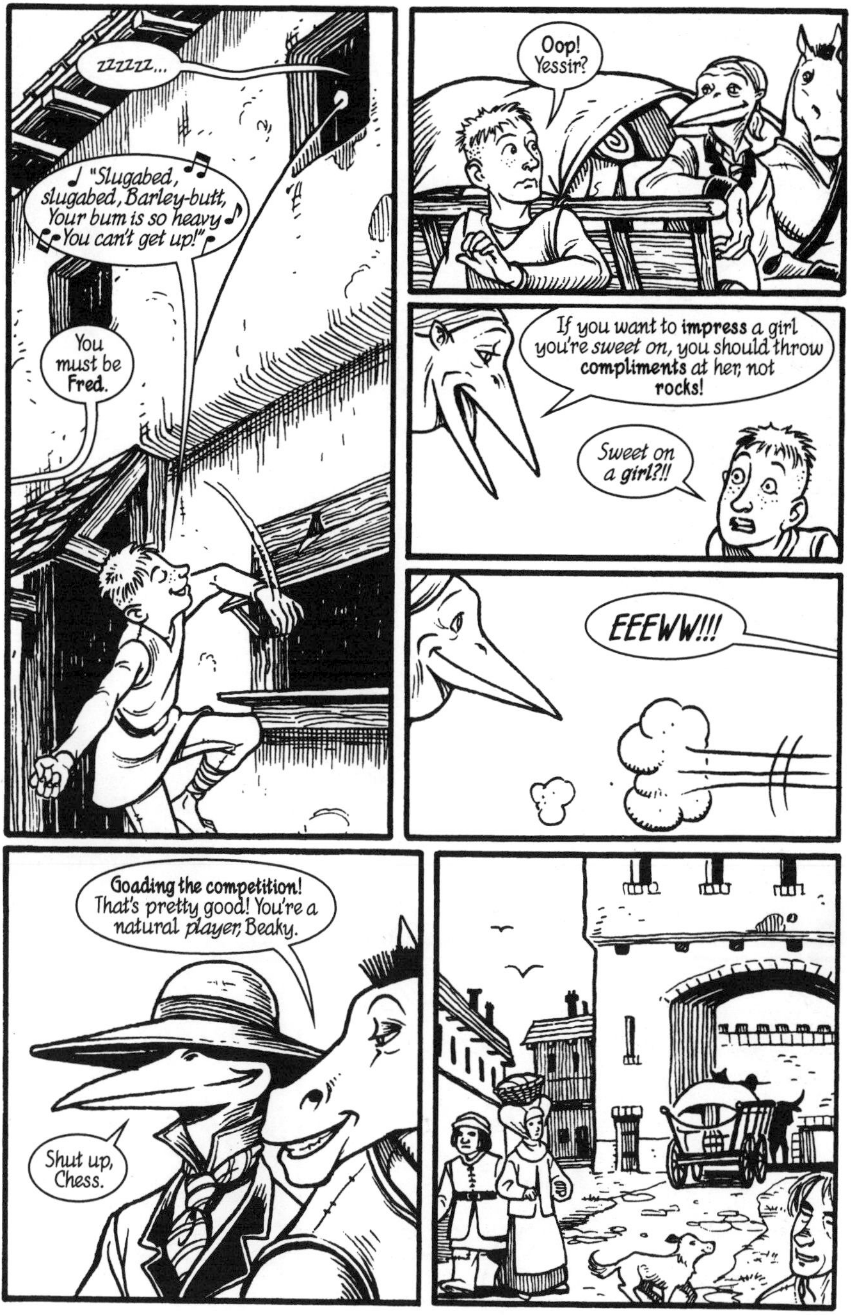
zzzzzz...
"Slugabed, slugabed, Barley-butt, Your bum is so heavy You can't get up!"
You must be Fred.
Oop! Yessir?
If you want to impress a girl you're sweet on, you should throw compliments at her, not rocks!
Sweet on a girl?!!
EEEWW!!!
Goading the competition! That's pretty good! You're a natural player, Beaky.
Shut up, Chess.

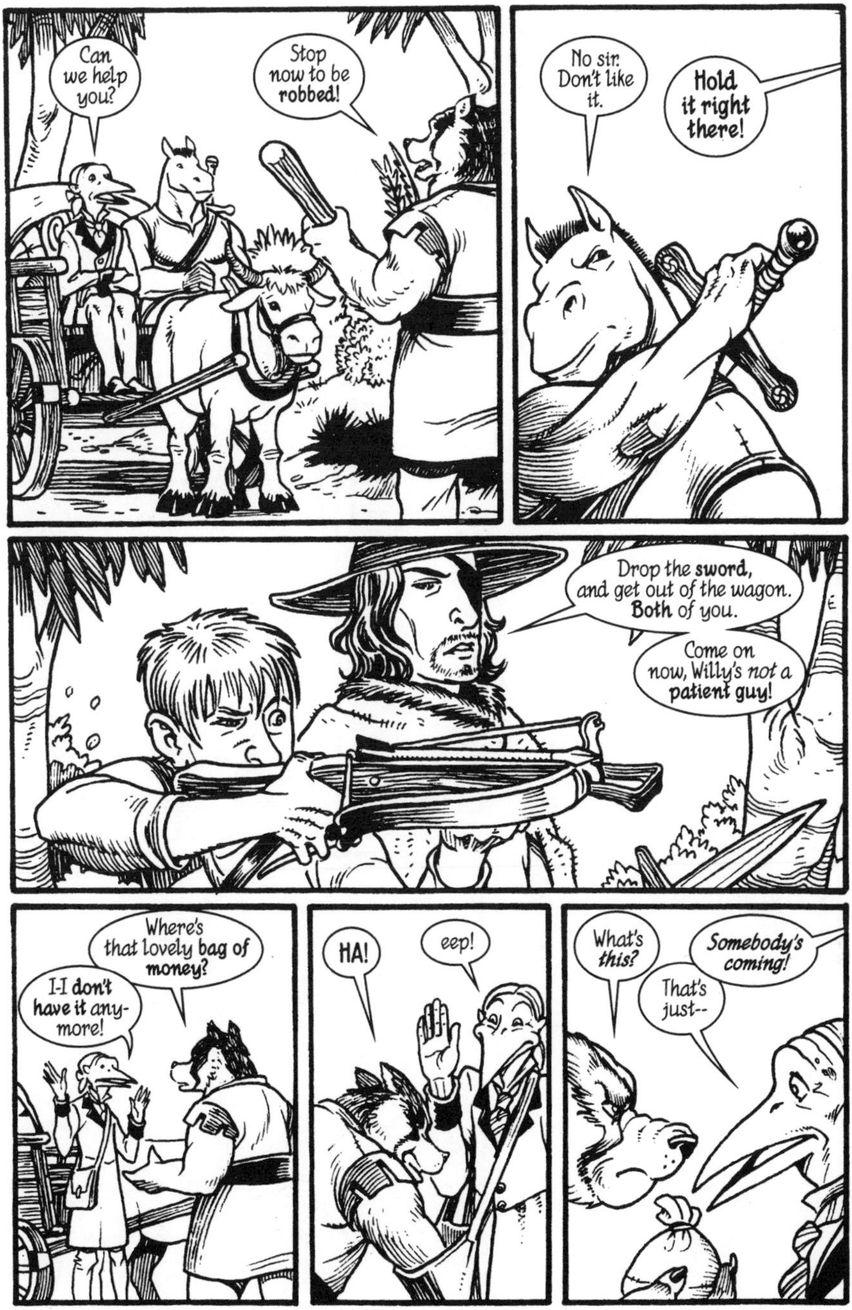
Can we help you?
Stop now to be **robbed**!
No sir. Don't like it.
Hold it right there!
Drop the **sword**, and get out of the wagon. **Both** of you.
Come on now, Willy's *not* a **patient guy**!
Where's that lovely **bag of money?**
I-I **don't have it** any-more!
HA!
eep!
What's *this?*
Somebody's coming!
That's just--

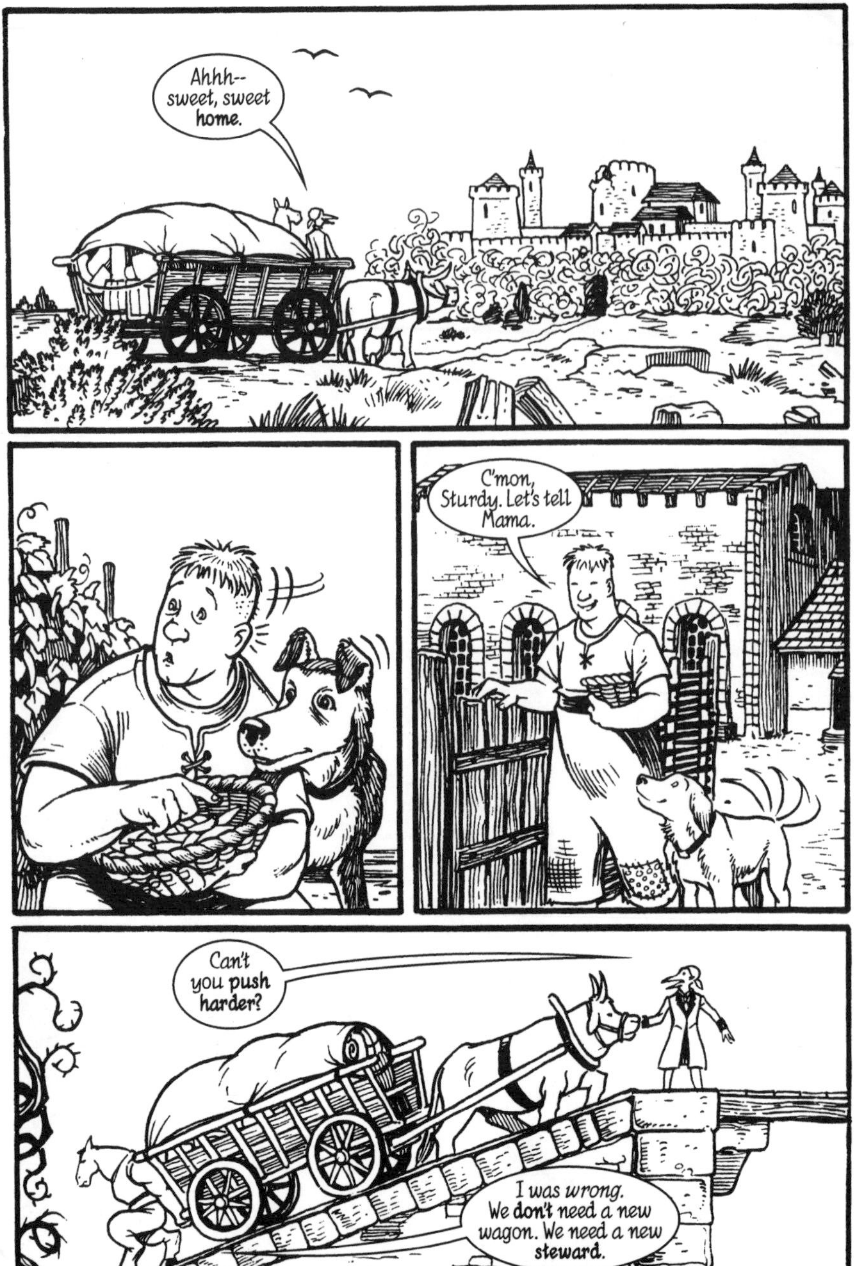
Ahhh--
sweet, sweet
home.
C'mon,
Sturdy. Let's tell
Mama.
Can't
you **push**
harder?
I was *wrong.*
We **don't** need a new
wagon. We need a new
steward.

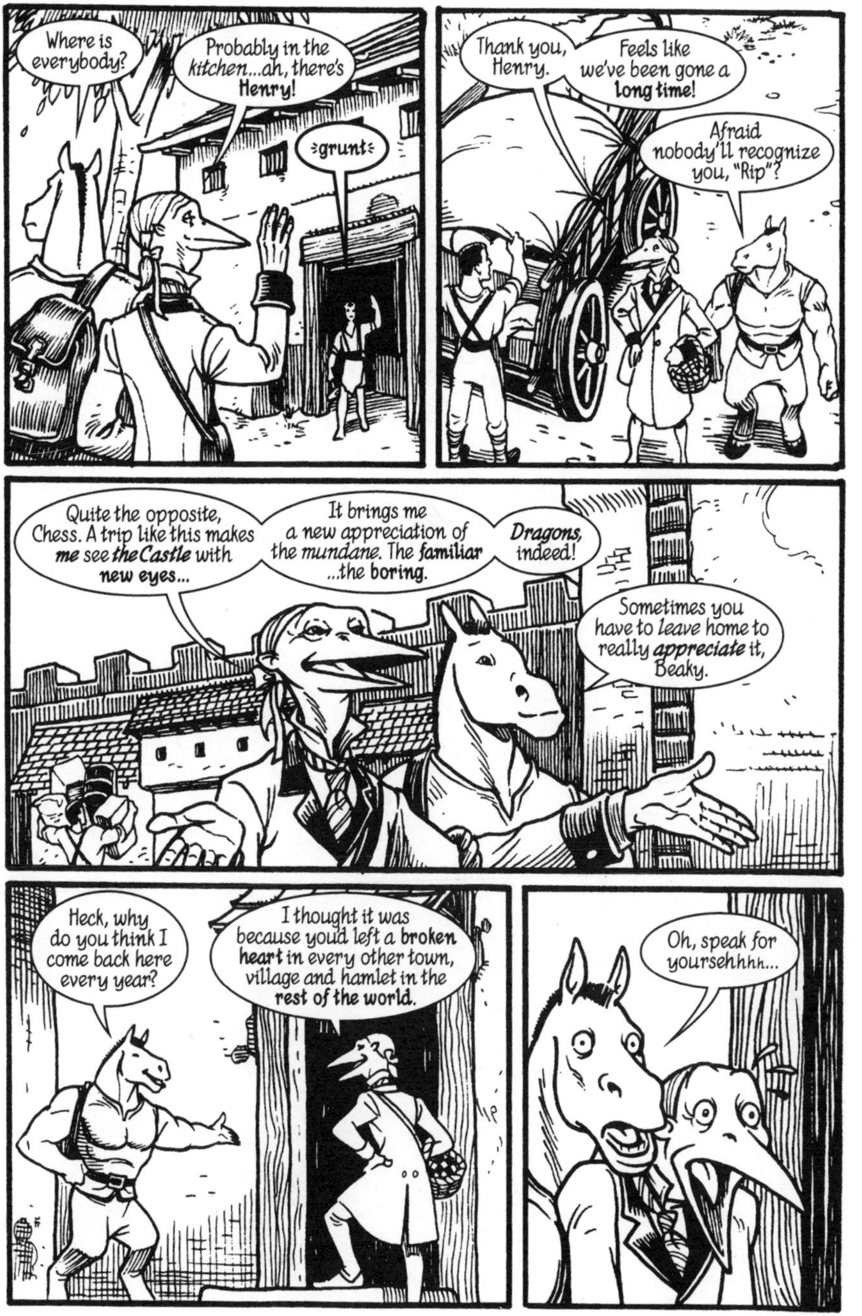
Where is everybody?
Probably in the kitchen...ah, there's **Henry!**
grunt
Thank you, Henry.
Feels like we've been gone a **long time!**
Afraid nobody'll recognize you, "Rip"?
Quite the opposite, Chess. A trip like this makes ***me*** see ***the Castle*** with **new eyes...**
It brings me a new appreciation of the *mundane*. The **familiar** ...the **boring**.
Dragons, indeed!
Sometimes you have to *leave* home to really ***appreciate*** it, Beaky.
Heck, why do you think I come back here every year?
I thought it was because you'd left a **broken heart** in every other town, village and hamlet in the **rest of the world.**
Oh, speak for yoursehhhh...

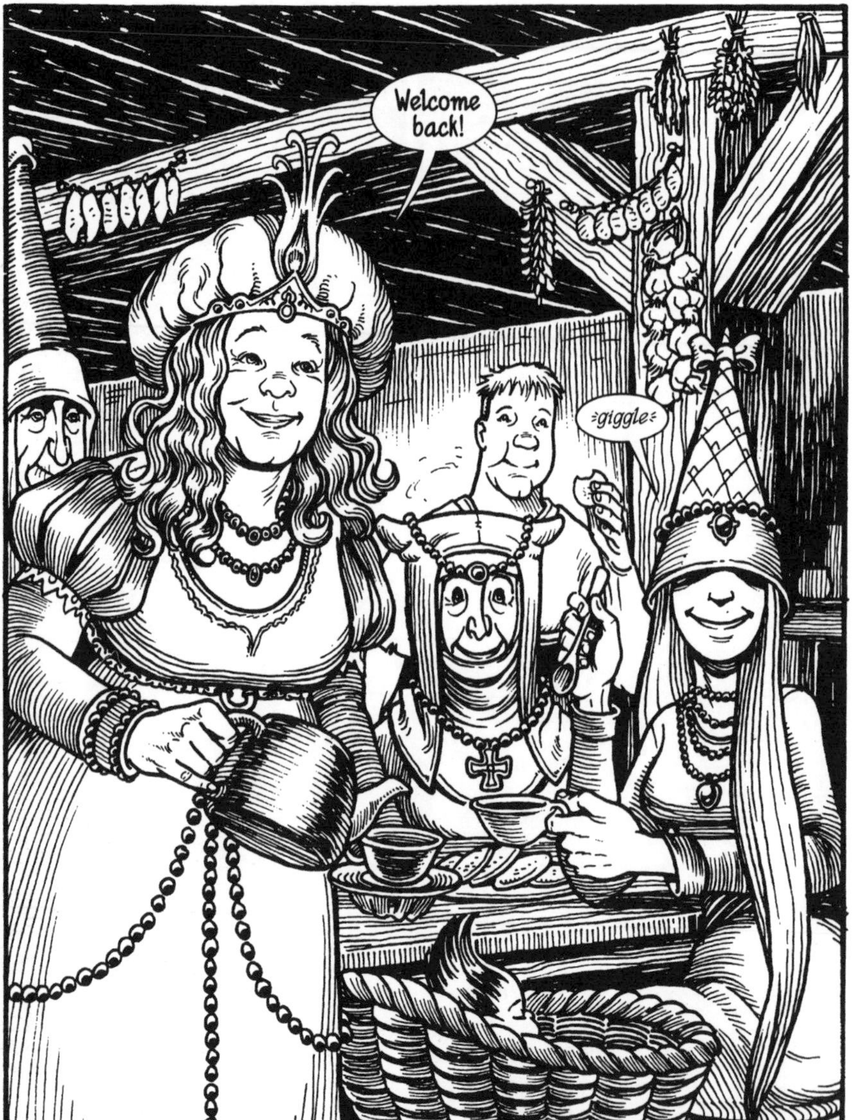
Welcome back!
giggle

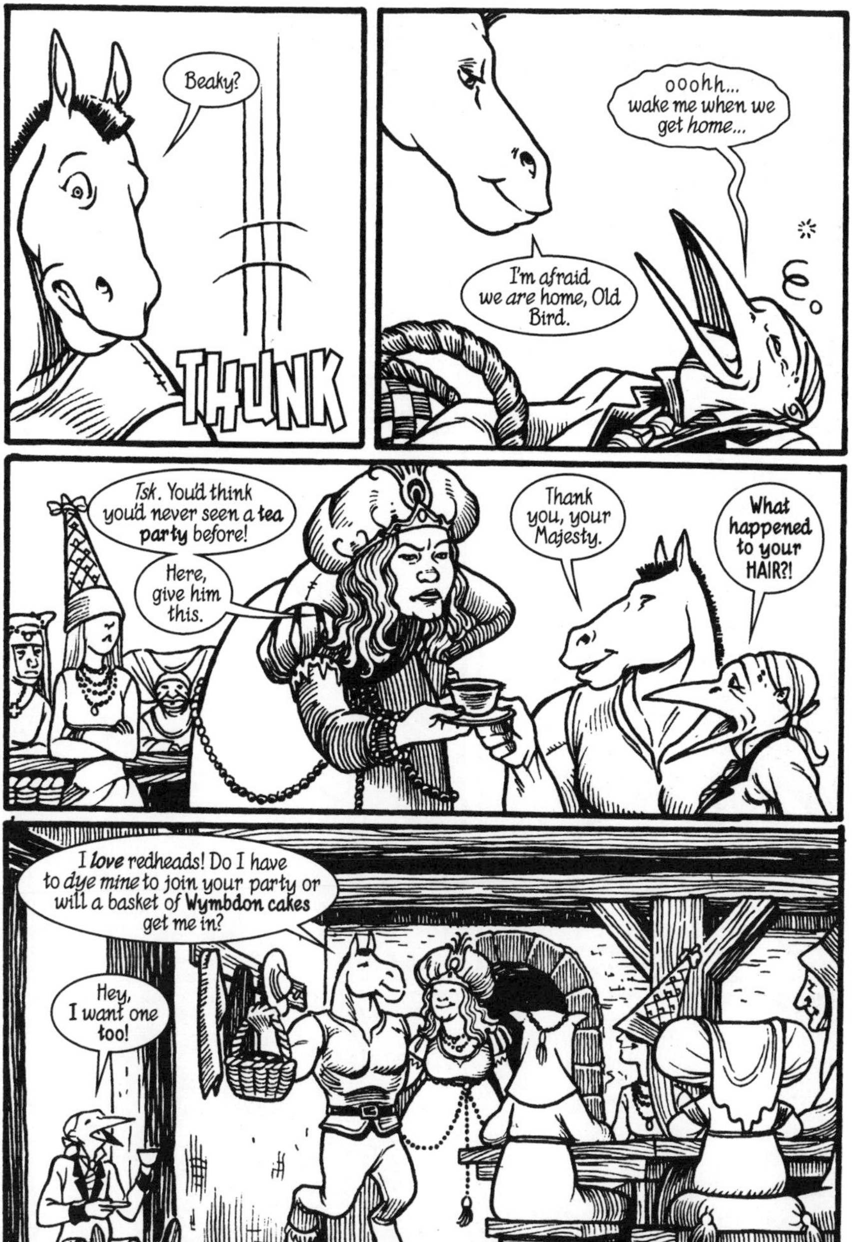
Beaky?
THUNK
oooh h...
wake me when we
get *home*...
I'm afraid
we *are* home, Old
Bird.
Tsk. You'd think
you'd never seen a **tea**
party before!
Here,
give him
this.
Thank
you, your
Majesty.
What
happened
to your
HAIR?!
I **love** redheads! Do I have
to *dye mine* to join your party or
will a basket of **Wymbdon cakes**
get me in?
Hey,
I want one
too!

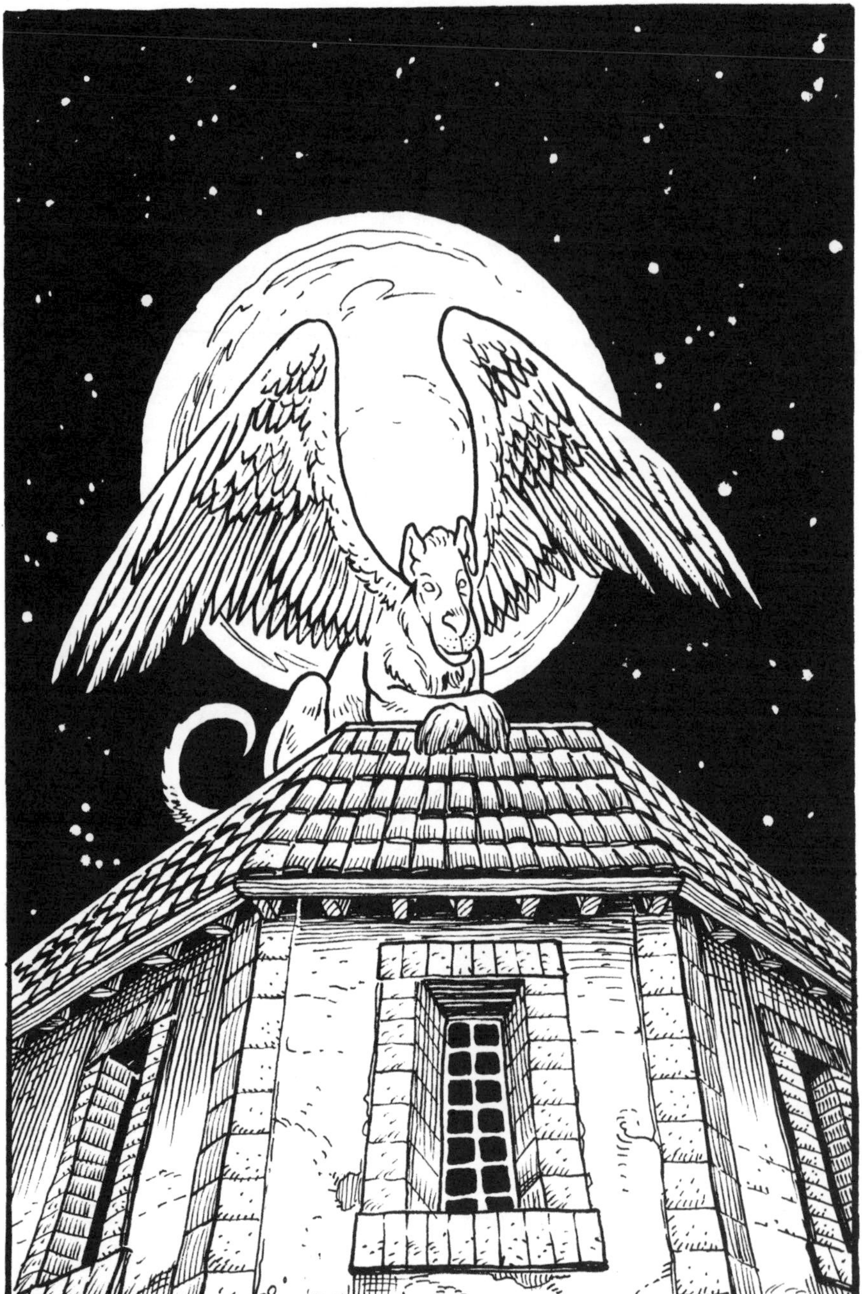

Chapter 11.

· HOOK, LINE, AND SINKER ·

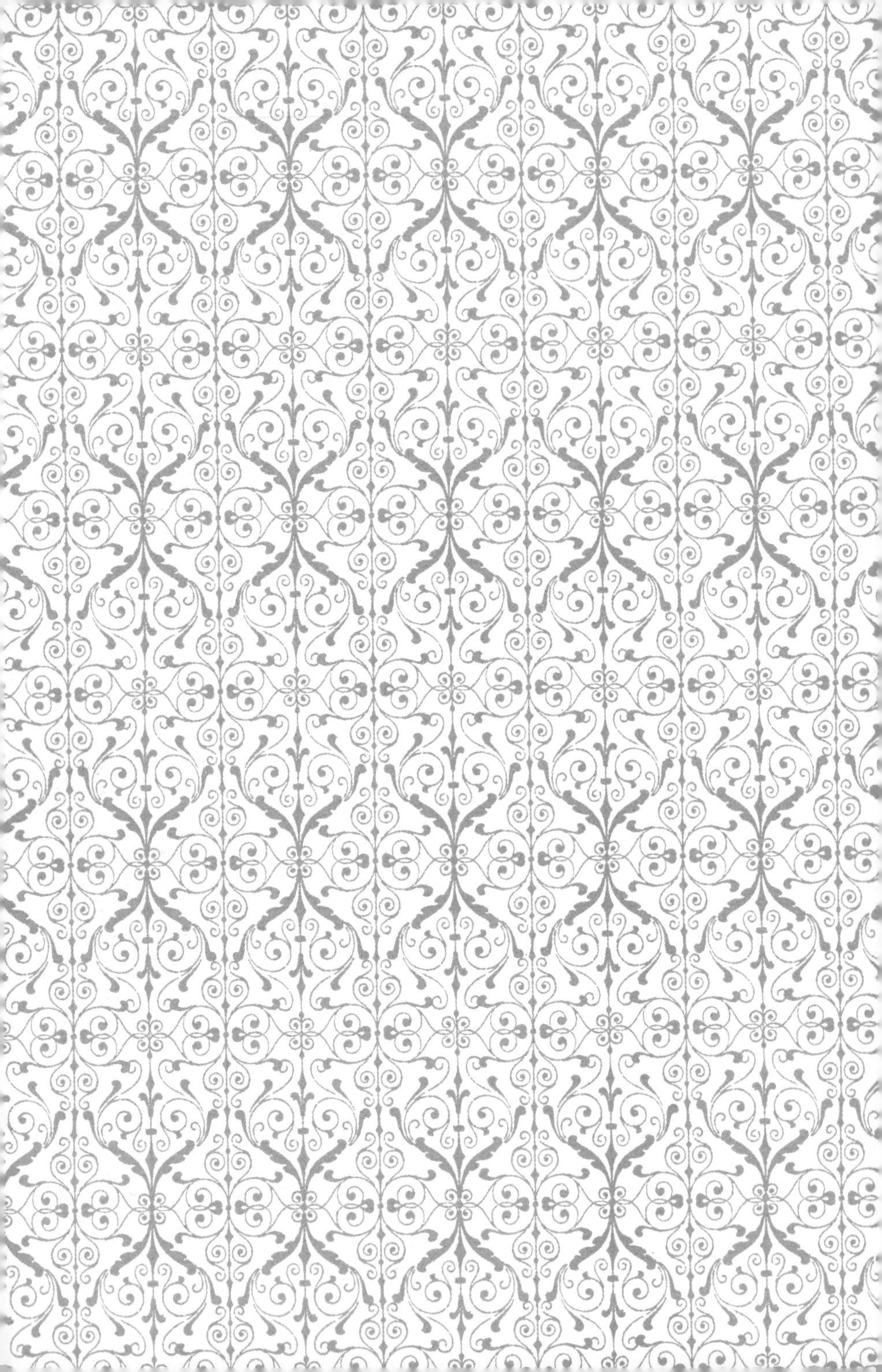

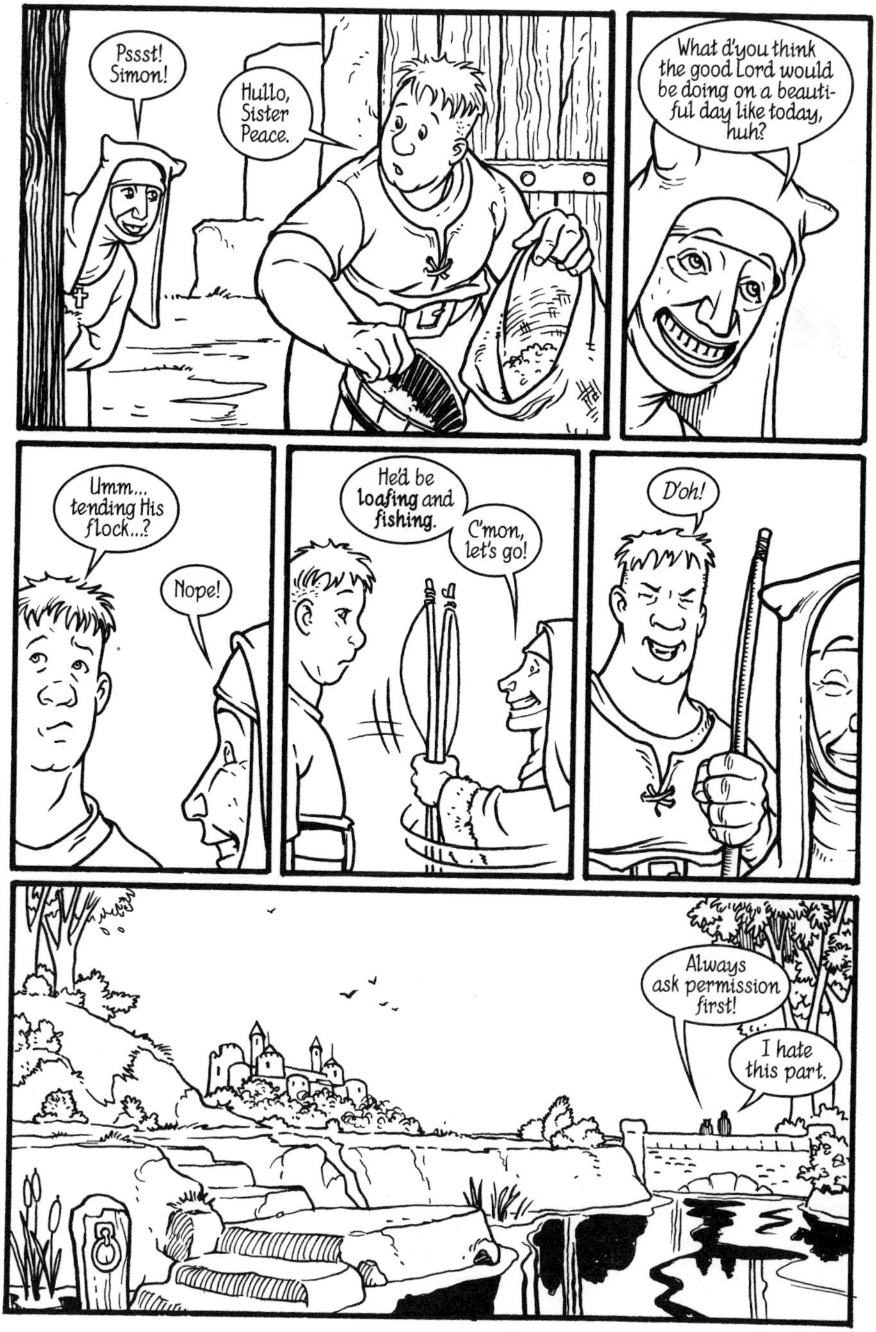
Pssst! Simon!
Hullo, Sister Peace.
What d'you think the good Lord would be doing on a beautiful day like today, huh?
Umm... tending His flock...?
Nope!
He'd be **loafing** and **fishing**.
C'mon, let's go!
D'oh!
Always ask permission first!
I hate this part.

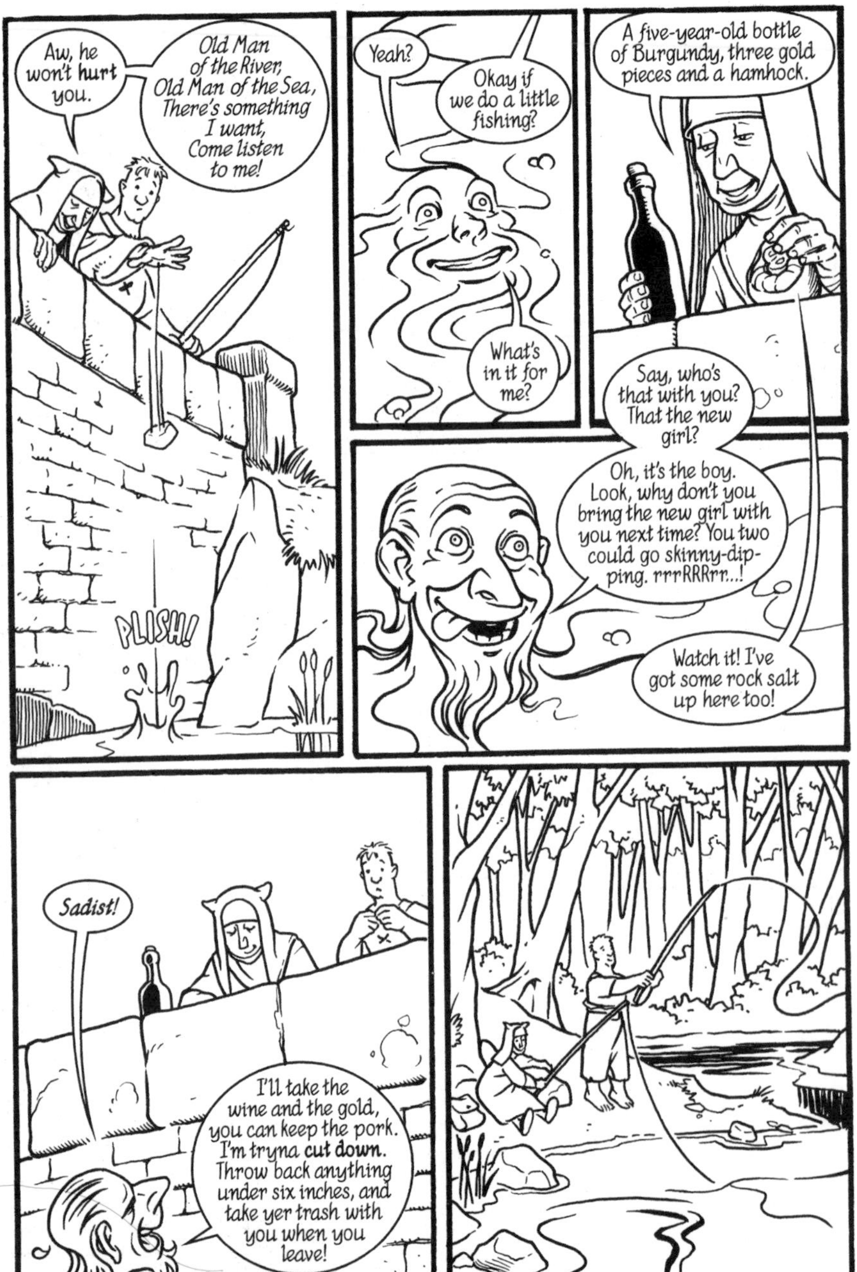
Aw, he won't **hurt** you.
Old Man of the River, Old Man of the Sea, There's something I want, Come listen to me!
PLISH!
Yeah?
Okay if we do a little fishing?
What's in it for me?
A five-year-old bottle of Burgundy, three gold pieces and a hamhock.
Say, who's that with you? That the new girl?
Oh, it's the boy. Look, why don't you bring the new girl with you next time? You two could go skinny-dipping. rrrRRRrr...!
Watch it! I've got some rock salt up here too!
Sadist!
I'll take the wine and the gold, you can keep the pork. I'm tryna **cut down**. Throw back anything under six inches, and take yer trash with you when you leave!

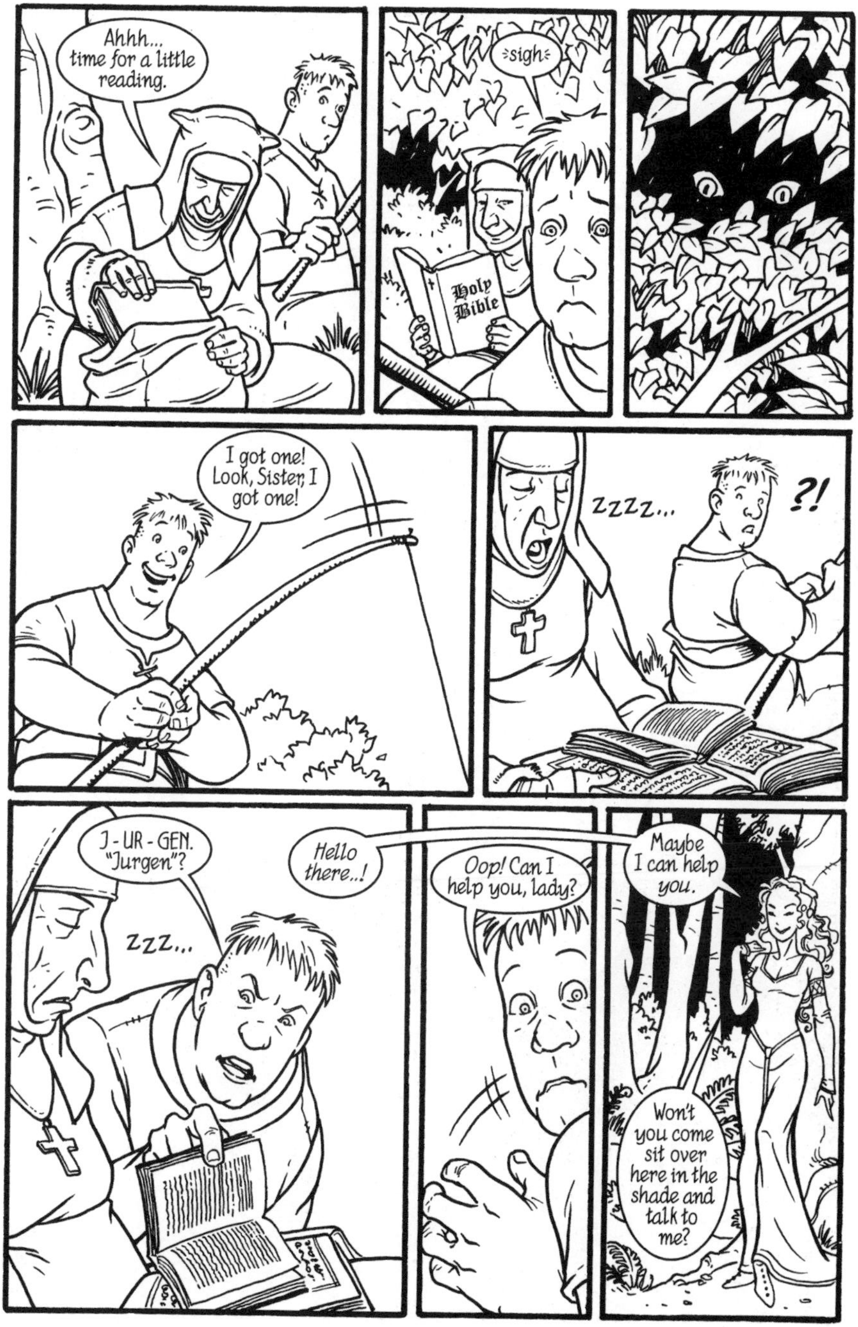
Ahhh... time for a little reading.
sigh
Holy Bible
I got one! Look, Sister, I got one!
ZZZZ...
?!
J-UR-GEN. "Jurgen"?
ZZZ...
Hello there...!
Oop! Can I help you, lady?
Maybe I can help you.
Won't you come sit over here in the shade and talk to me?

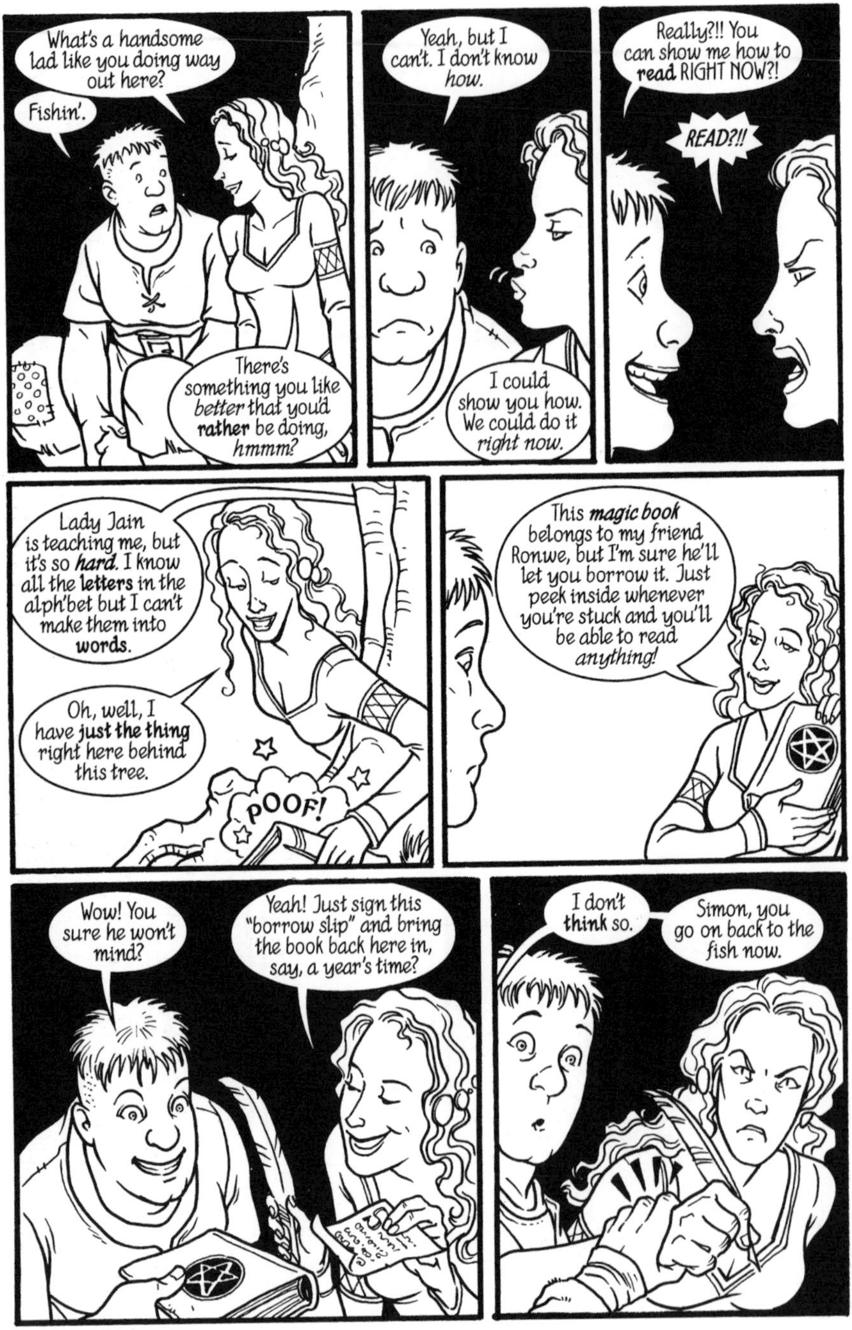
What's a handsome lad like you doing way out here?
Fishin'.
There's something you like better that you'd rather be doing, hmmm?
Yeah, but I can't. I don't know how.
I could show you how. We could do it right now.
Really?!! You can show me how to read RIGHT NOW?!
READ?!!
Lady Jain is teaching me, but it's so hard. I know all the letters in the alph'bet but I can't make them into words.
Oh, well, I have just the thing right here behind this tree.
POOF!
This magic book belongs to my friend Ronwe, but I'm sure he'll let you borrow it. Just peek inside whenever you're stuck and you'll be able to read anything!
Wow! You sure he won't mind?
Yeah! Just sign this "borrow slip" and bring the book back here in, say, a year's time?
I don't think so.
Simon, you go on back to the fish now.

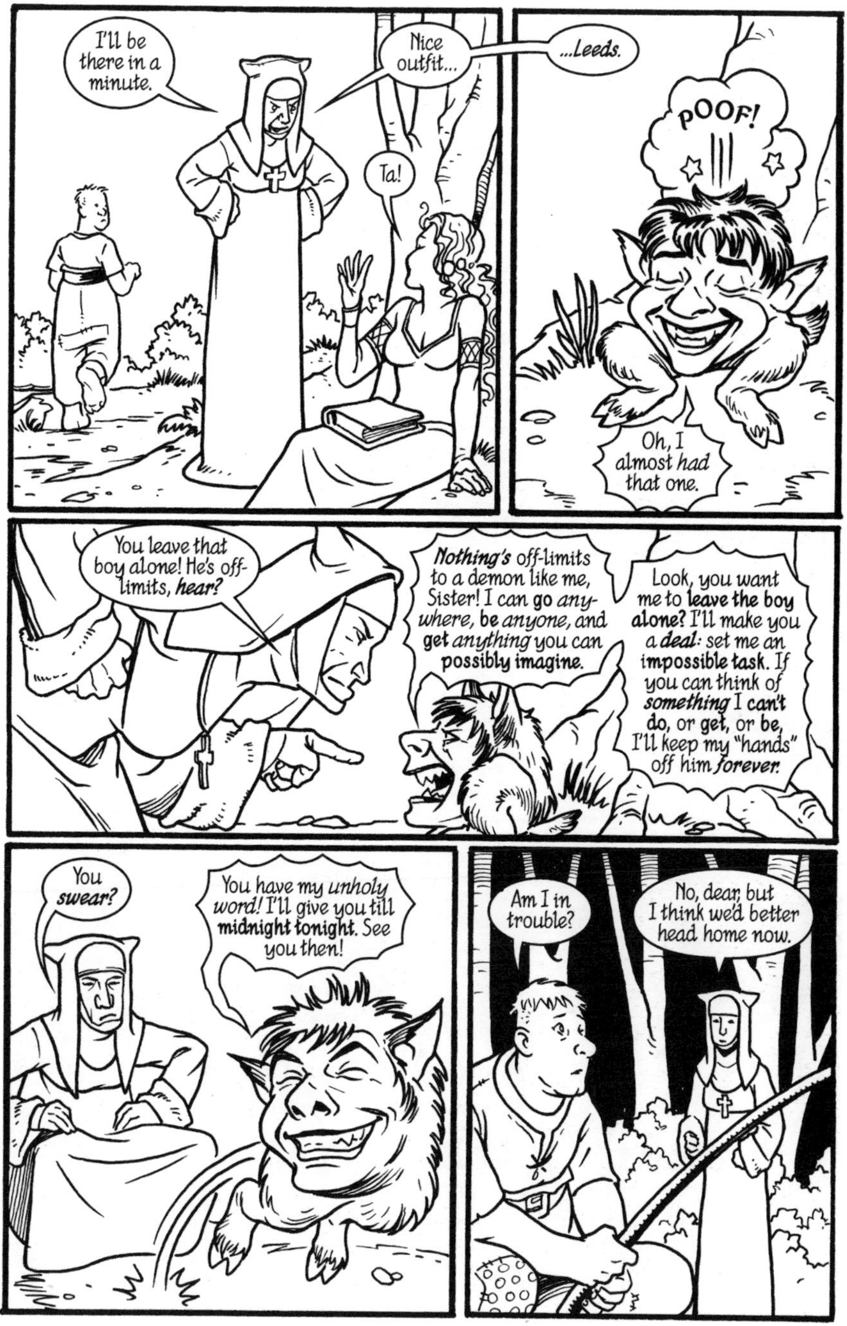
I'll be there in a minute.
Nice outfit...
...Leeds.
Ta!
POOF!
Oh, I almost had that one.
You leave that boy alone! He's off-limits, hear?
Nothing's off-limits to a demon like me, Sister! I can go anywhere, be anyone, and get anything you can possibly imagine.
Look, you want me to leave the boy alone? I'll make you a deal: set me an impossible task. If you can think of something I can't do, or get, or be, I'll keep my "hands" off him forever.
You swear?
You have my unholy word! I'll give you till midnight tonight. See you then!
Am I in trouble?
No, dear, but I think we'd better head home now.

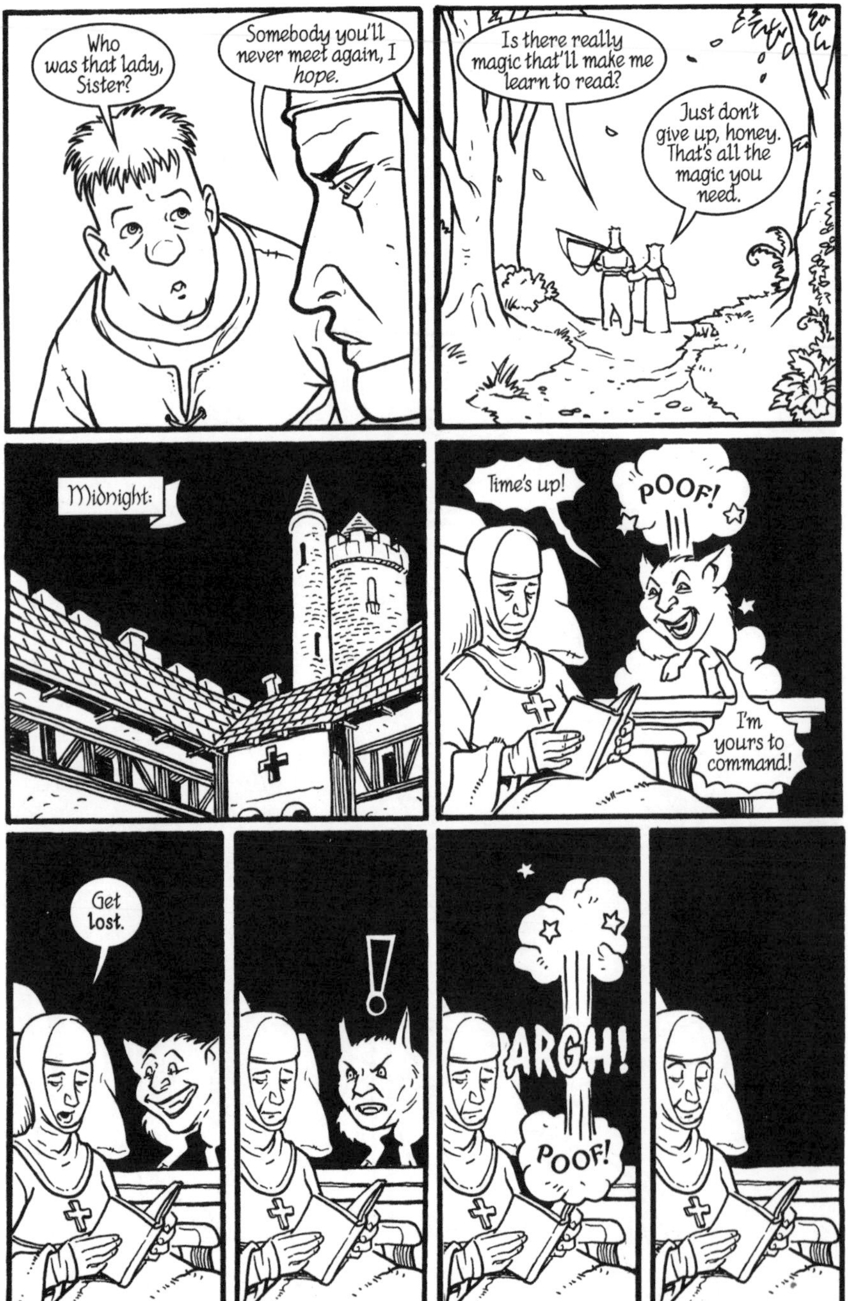
Who was that lady, Sister?
Somebody you'll never meet again, I hope.
Is there really magic that'll make me learn to read?
Just don't give up, honey. That's all the magic you need.
Midnight:
Time's up!
POOF!
I'm yours to command!
Get lost.
!
ARGH!
POOF!

Chapter 12.

· SWEET TEMPTATIONS ·

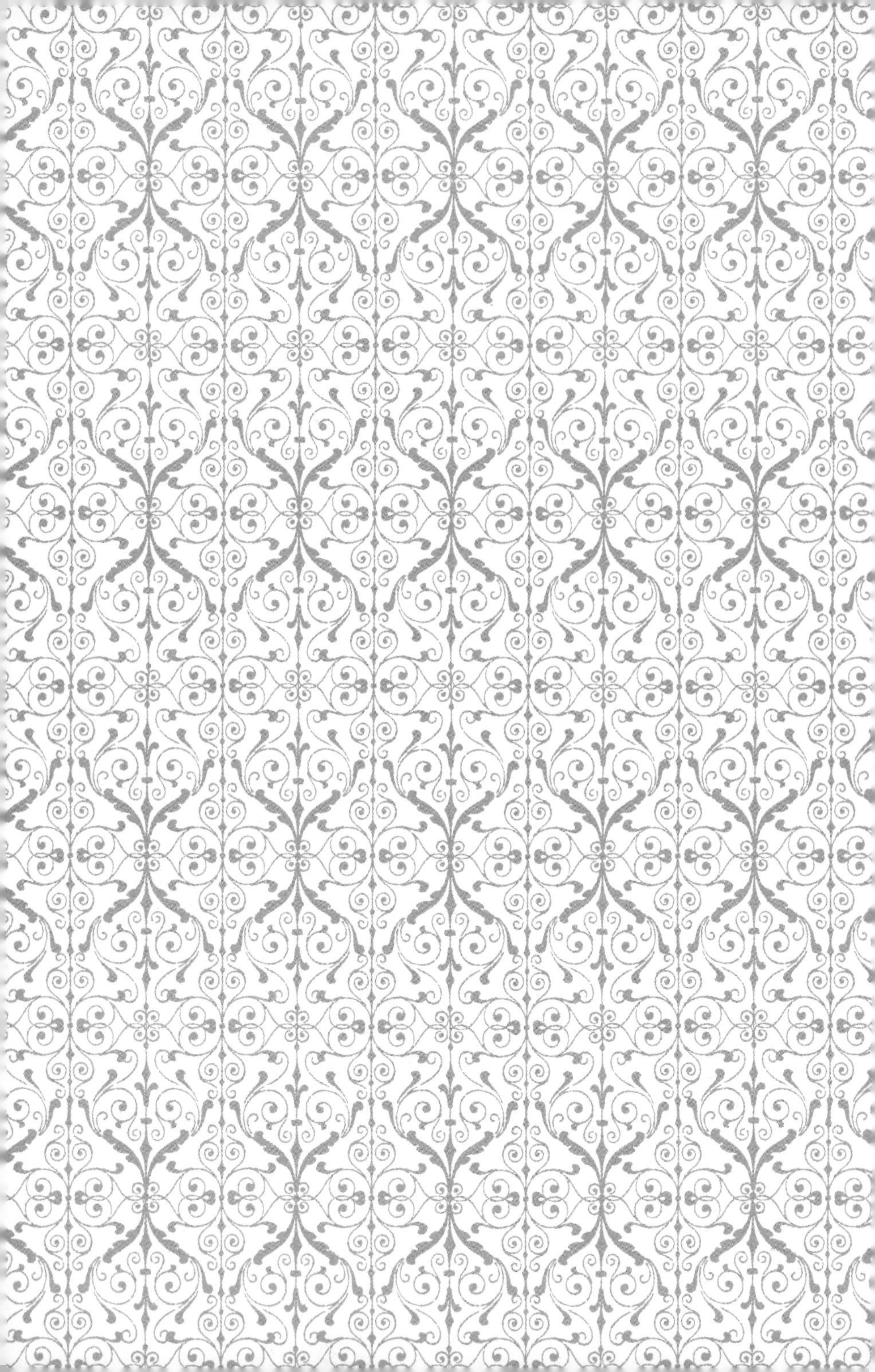

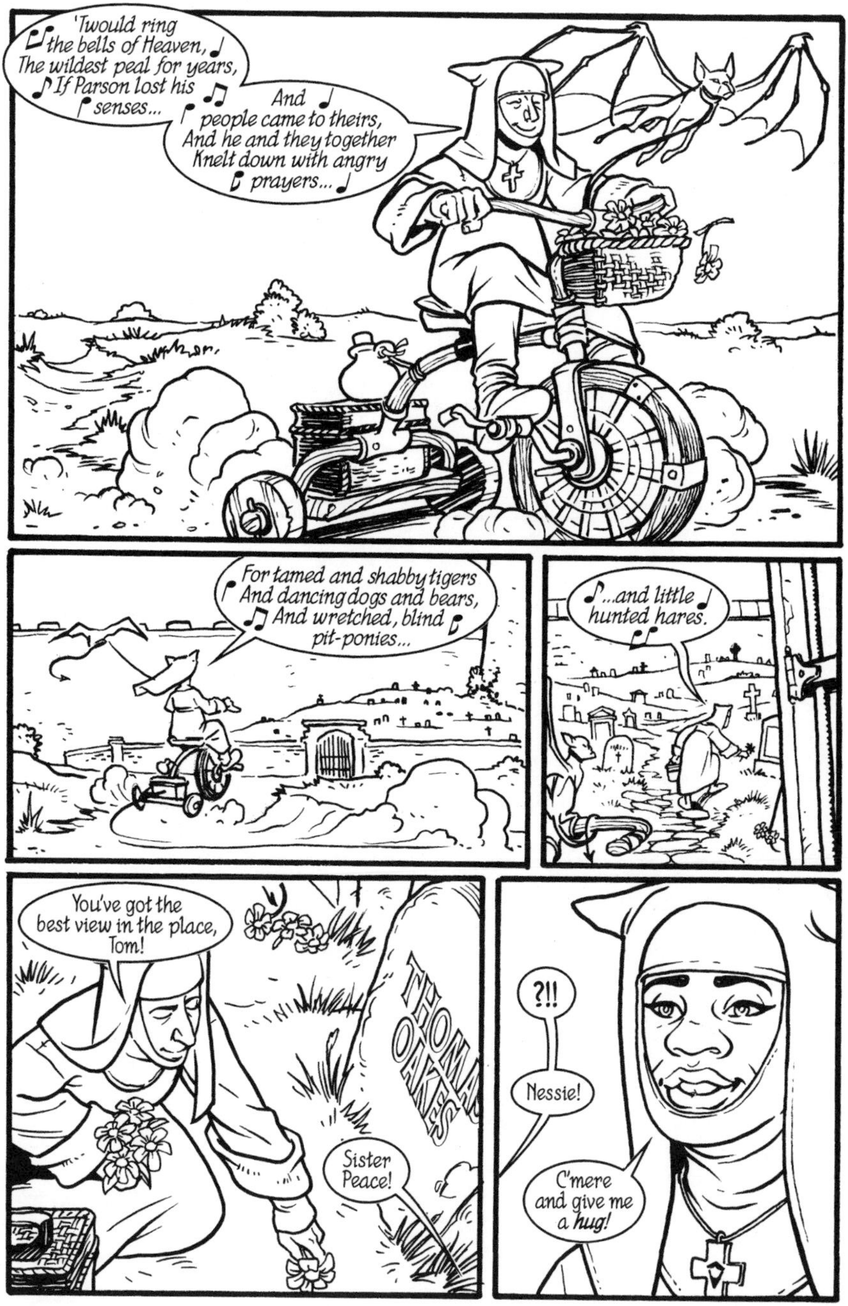
'Twould ring the bells of Heaven, The wildest peal for years, If Parson lost his senses...
And people came to theirs, And he and they together Knelt down with angry prayers...
For tamed and shabby tigers And dancing dogs and bears, And wretched, blind pit-ponies...
...and little hunted hares.
You've got the best view in the place, Tom!
THOMAS OAKES
Sister Peace!
?!!
Nessie!
C'mere and give me a hug!

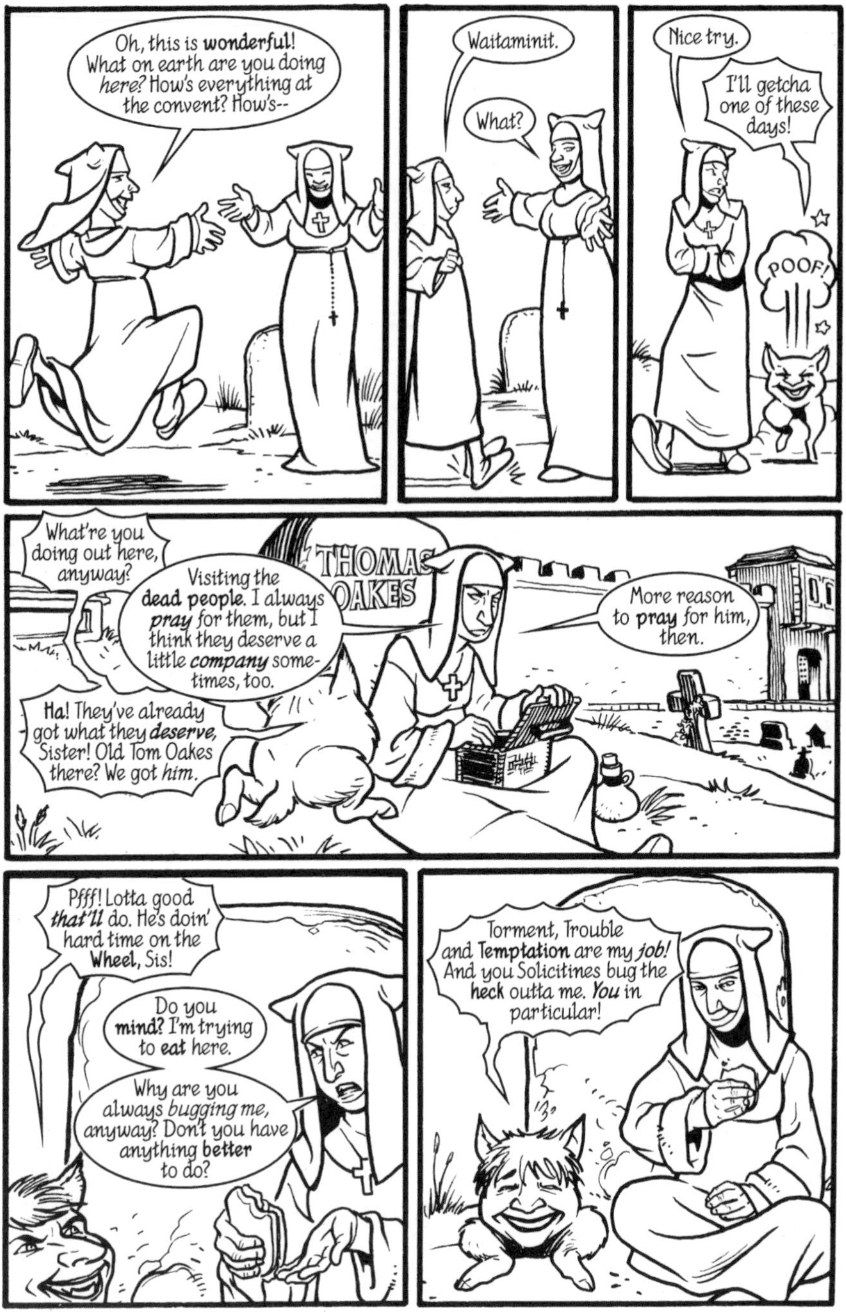

Oh, this is **wonderful!** What on earth are you doing *here?* How's everything at the convent? How's--
Waitaminit.
What?
Nice try.
I'll getcha one of these days!
POOF!
What're you doing out here, anyway?
THOMAS OAKES
Visiting the **dead people.** I always ***pray*** for them, but I think they deserve a little ***company*** sometimes, too.
Ha! They've already got what they ***deserve,*** Sister! Old Tom Oakes there? We got *him.*
More reason to **pray** for him, then.
Pfff! Lotta good ***that'll*** do. He's doin' hard time on the **Wheel,** Sis!
Do you **mind?** I'm trying to **eat** here.
Why are you always *bugging me,* anyway? Don't you have anything **better** to do?
Torment, Trouble and **Temptation** are my *job!* And you Solicitines bug the **heck** outta me. ***You*** in particular!

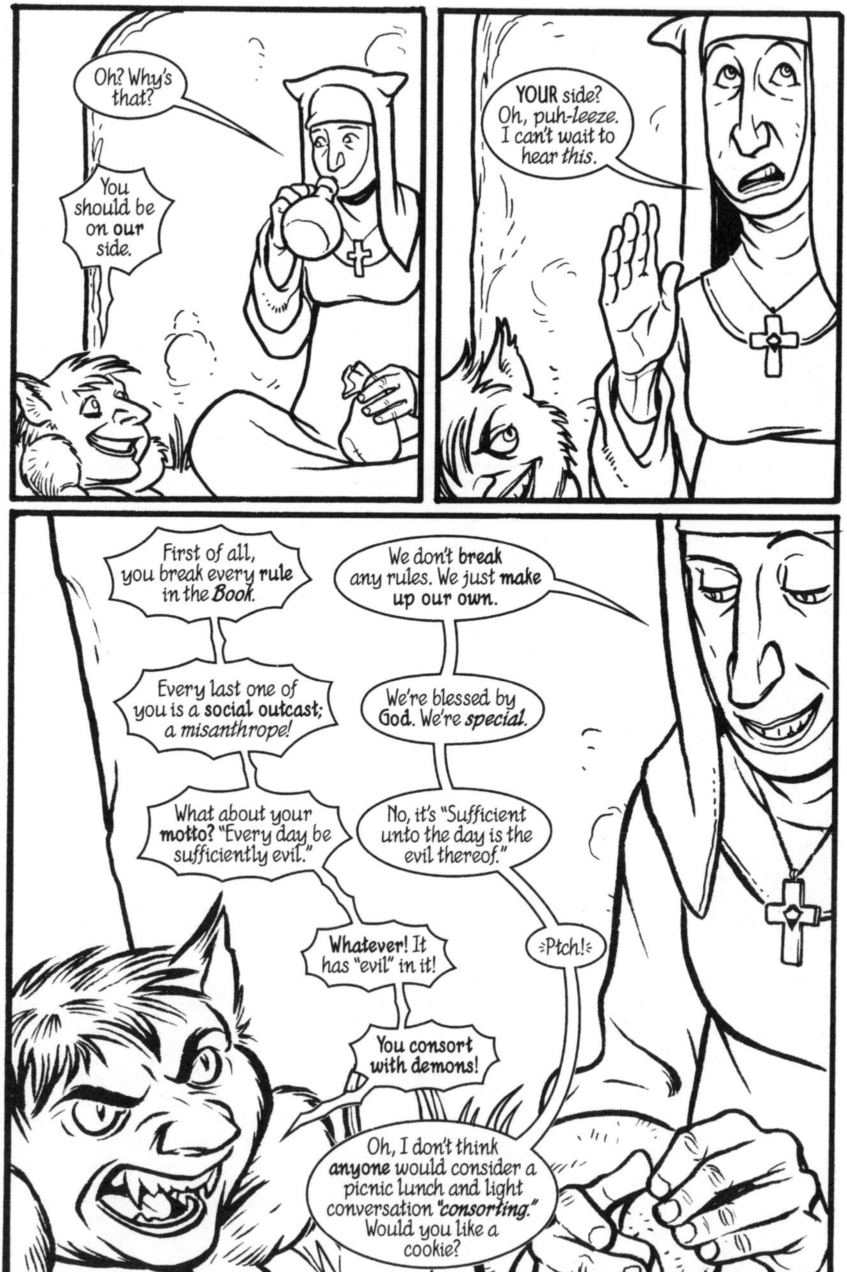
Oh? Why's that?
You should be on **our** side.
YOUR side? Oh, puh-*leeze*. I can't wait to hear *this*.
First of all, you break every **rule** in the ***Book***.
We don't **break** any rules. We just **make up our own**.
Every last one of you is a **social outcast;** a *misanthrope!*
We're blessed by **God**. We're ***special***.
What about your **motto?** "Every day be sufficiently evil."
No, it's "Sufficient unto the day is the evil thereof."
Whatever! It has "evil" in it!
Ptch!
You consort with demons!
Oh, I don't think **anyone** would consider a picnic lunch and light conversation ***"consorting."*** Would you like a cookie?

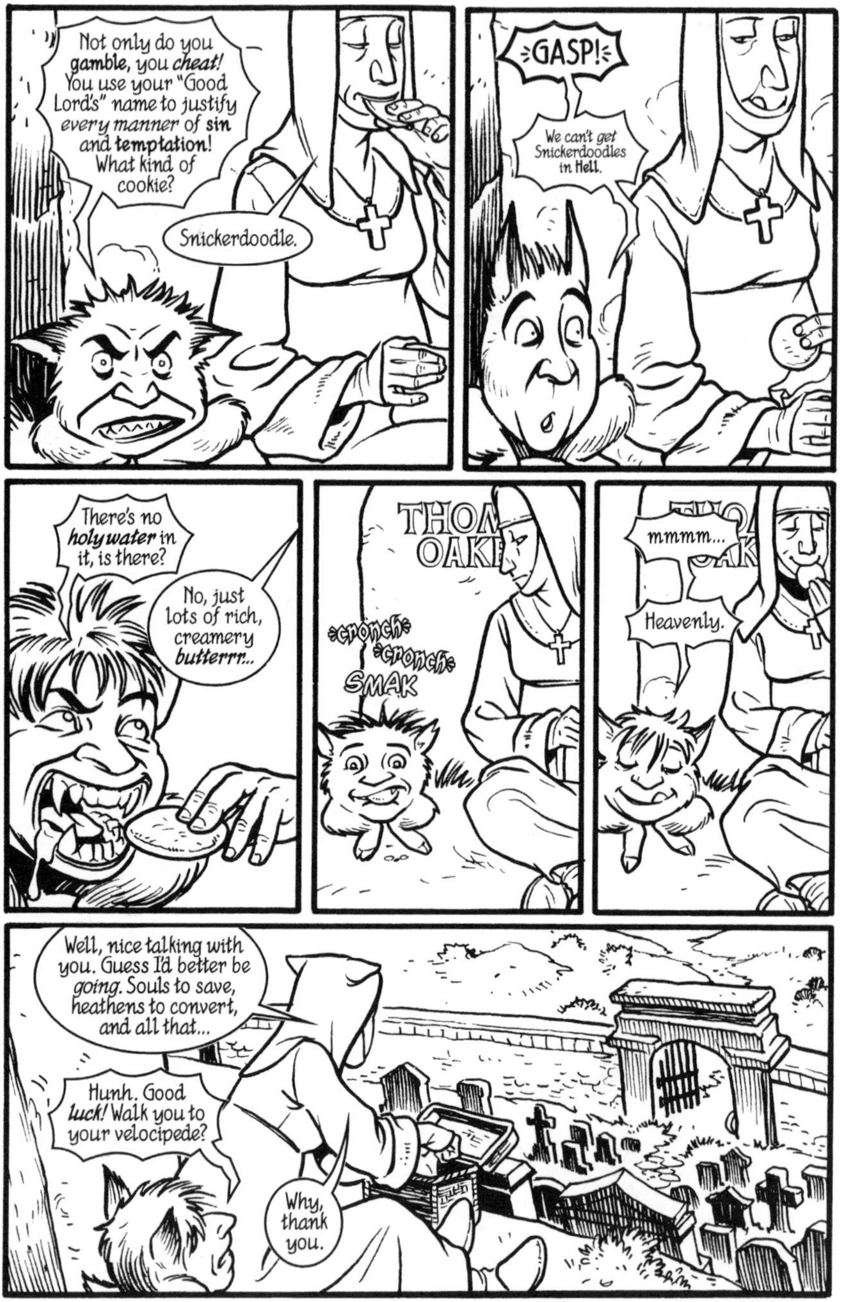
Not only do you gamble, you cheat! You use your "Good Lord's" name to justify every manner of sin and temptation! What kind of cookie?
Snickerdoodle.
GASP!
We can't get Snickerdoodles in Hell.
There's no holy water in it, is there?
No, just lots of rich, creamery butterrr...
THOM OAKE
cronch cronch
SMAK
mmmm...
Heavenly.
Well, nice talking with you. Guess I'd better be going. Souls to save, heathens to convert, and all that...
Hunh. Good luck! Walk you to your velocipede?
Why, thank you.

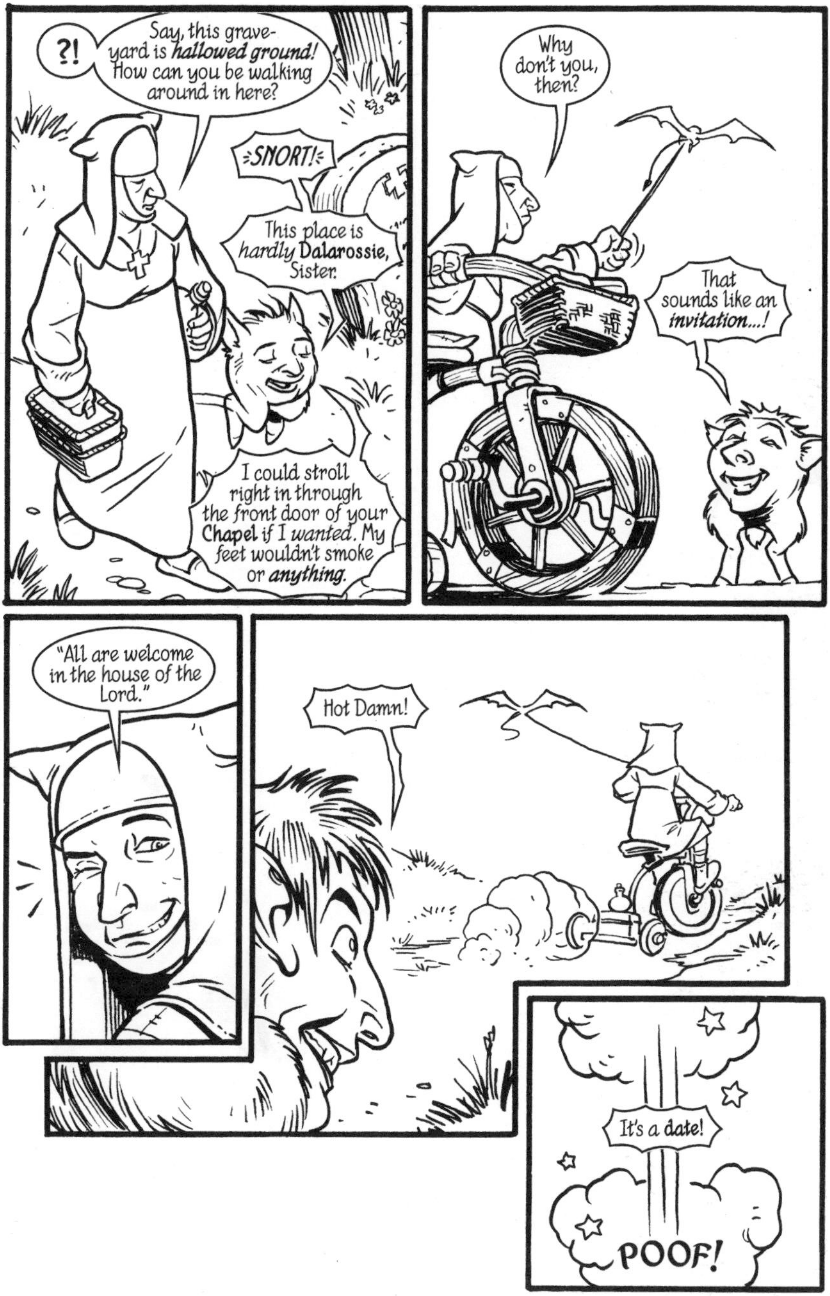
?!
Say, this graveyard is **hallowed ground!** How can you be walking around in here?
SNORT!
This place is *hardly* **Dalarossie**, Sister.
I could stroll right in through the front door of your **Chapel** if I *wanted*. My feet wouldn't smoke or ***anything.***
Why don't you, then?
That sounds like an ***invitation...!***
"All are welcome in the house of the Lord."
Hot Damn!
It's a **date!**
POOF!

Chapter 13.

· SOLICITINE PT. I ·

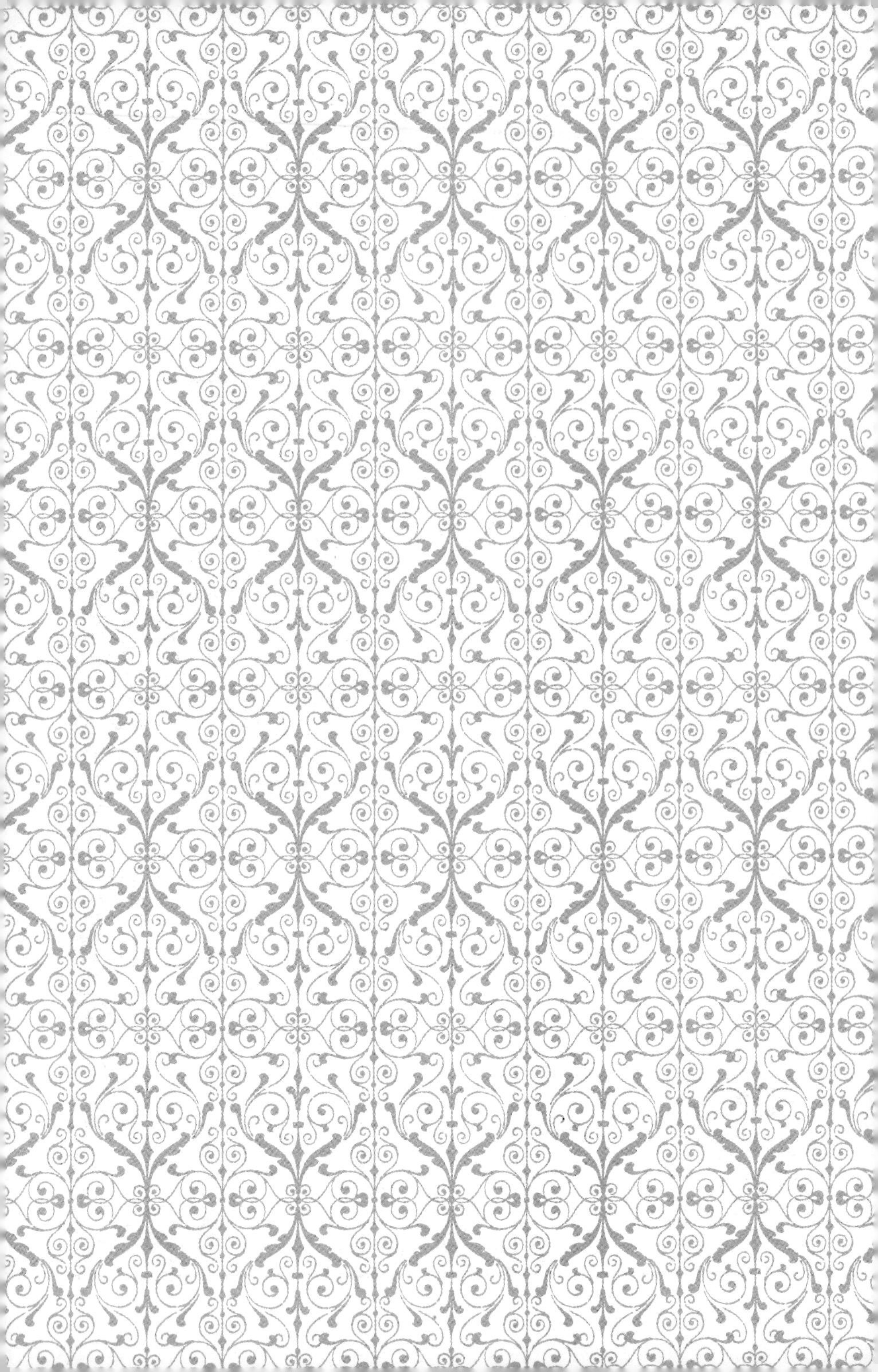

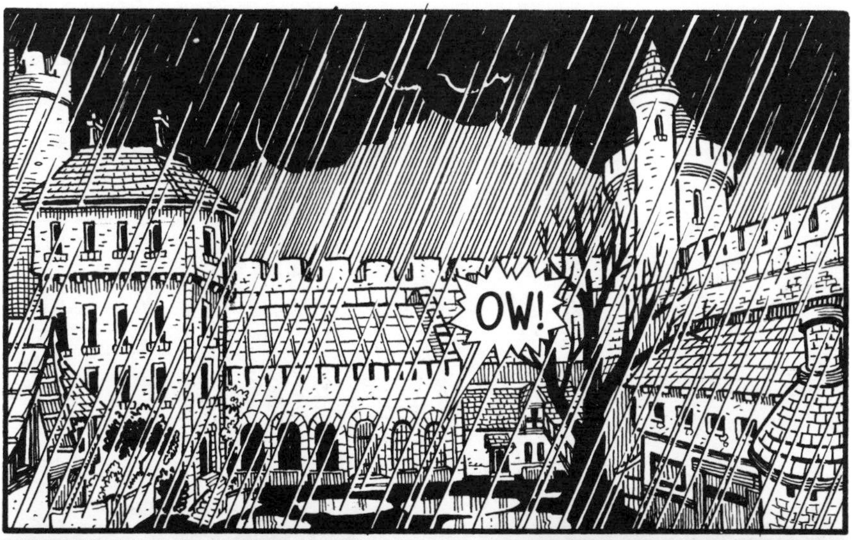
OW!

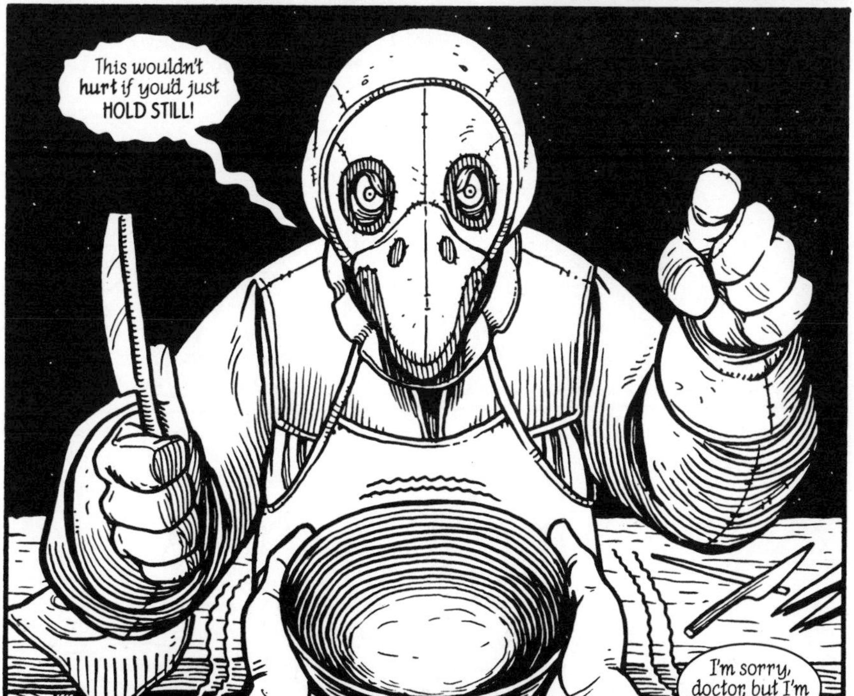
This wouldn't **hurt** *if you'd just* HOLD STILL!
I'm sorry, doctor, but I'm s-scared...

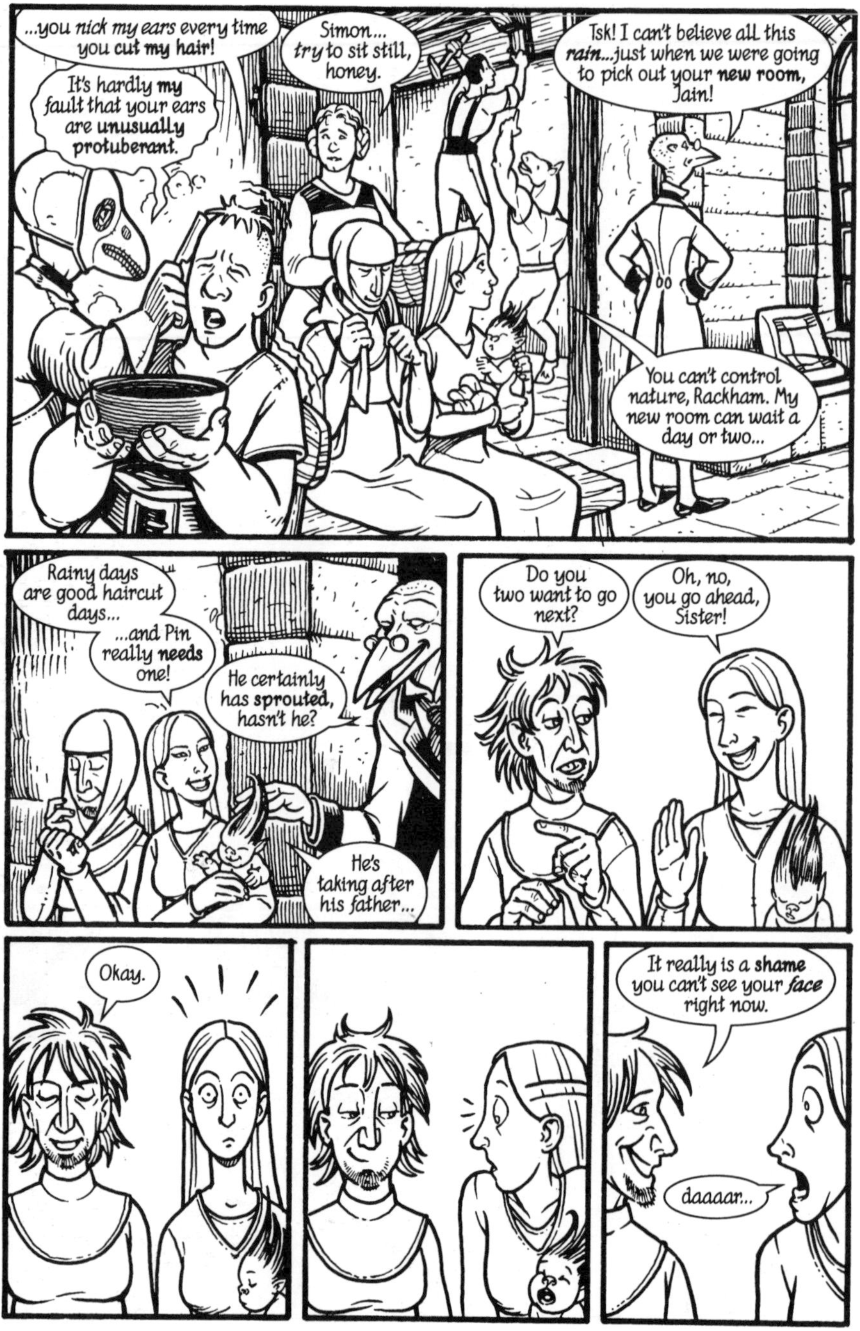
...you nick my ears every time you cut my hair!
It's hardly my fault that your ears are unusually protuberant.
Simon... try to sit still, honey.
Tsk! I can't believe all this rain...just when we were going to pick out your new room, Jain!
You can't control nature, Rackham. My new room can wait a day or two...
Rainy days are good haircut days...
...and Pin really needs one!
He certainly has sprouted, hasn't he?
He's taking after his father...
Do you two want to go next?
Oh, no, you go ahead, Sister!
Okay.
It really is a shame you can't see your face right now.
daaaar...

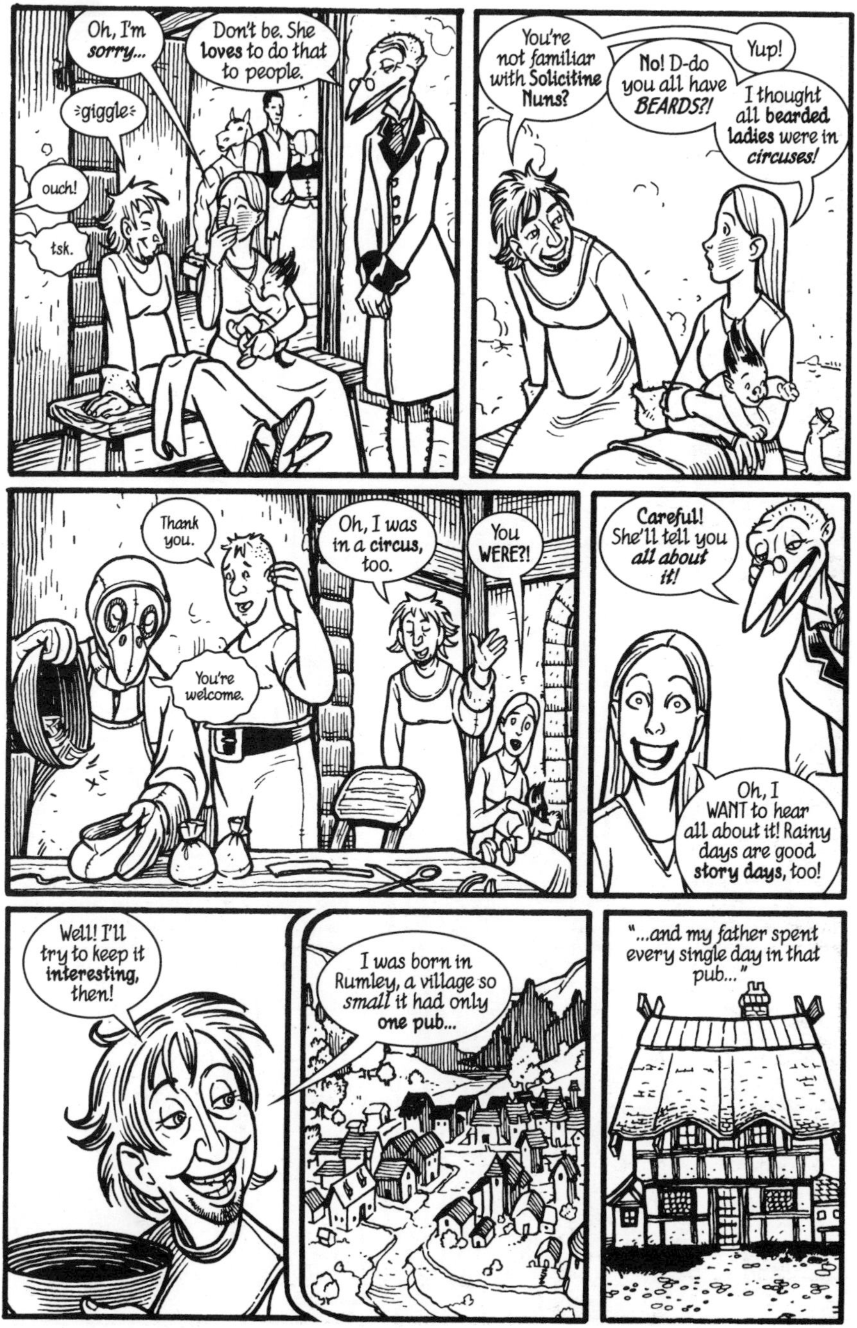
Oh, I'm *sorry...*
Don't be. She **loves** to do that to people.
giggle
ouch!
tsk.
You're *not familiar with* **Solicitine Nuns?**
No! D-do you all have ***BEARDS?!***
Yup!
I thought all **bearded ladies** were in ***circuses!***
Thank you.
You're welcome.
Oh, I was in a **circus,** too.
You **WERE?!**
Careful! She'll tell you ***all about it!***
Oh, I WANT to hear all about it! Rainy days are good **story days,** too!
Well! I'll try to keep it **interesting,** then!
I was born in Rumley, a village so *small* it had only **one pub...**
"...and my father spent every single day in that pub..."

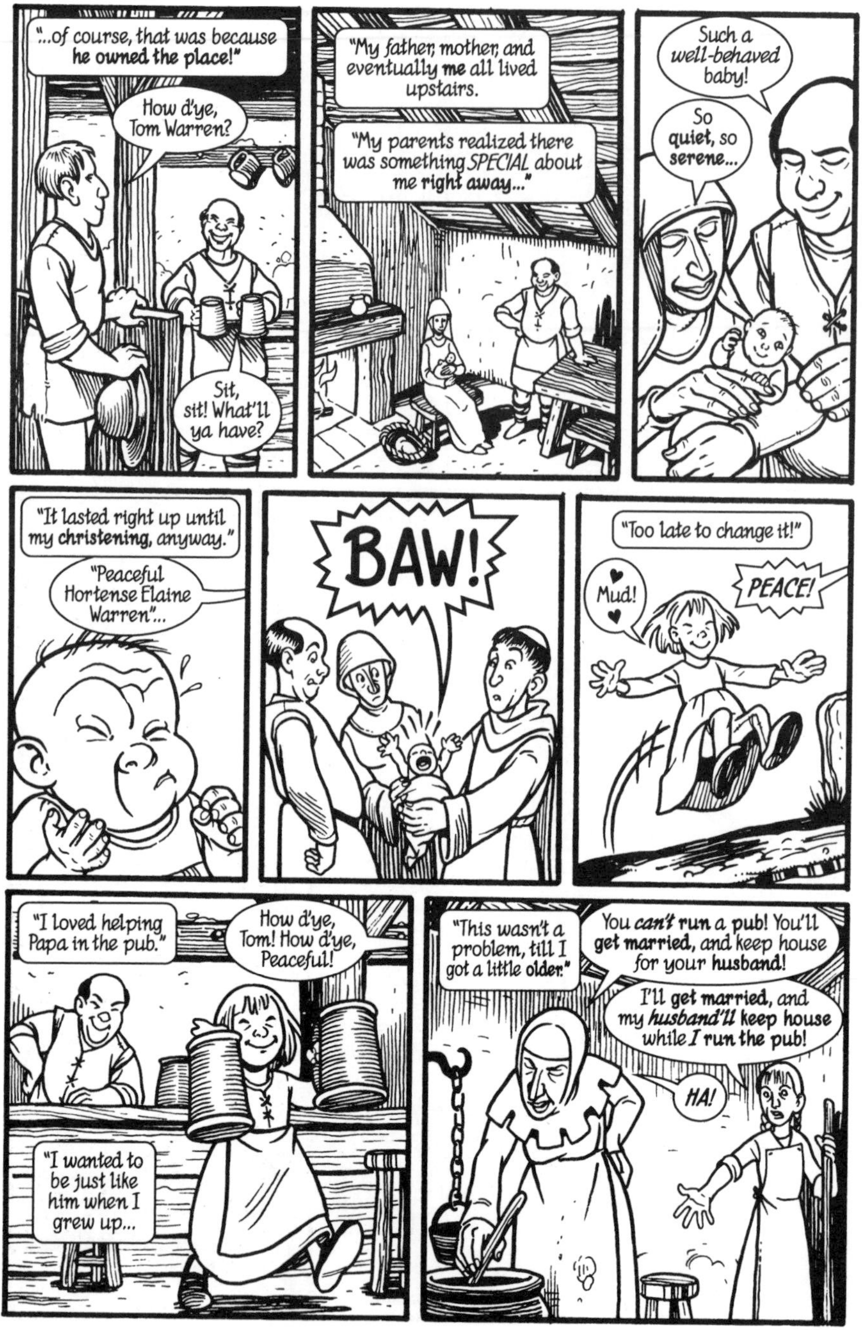
"...of course, that was because he owned the place!"
How d'ye, Tom Warren?
Sit, sit! What'll ya have?
"My father, mother, and eventually me all lived upstairs.
"My parents realized there was something SPECIAL about me right away..."
Such a well-behaved baby!
So quiet, so serene...
"It lasted right up until my christening, anyway."
"Peaceful Hortense Elaine Warren"...
BAW!
"Too late to change it!"
Mud!
PEACE!
"I loved helping Papa in the pub."
How d'ye, Tom! How d'ye, Peaceful!
"I wanted to be just like him when I grew up...
"This wasn't a problem, till I got a little older."
You can't run a pub! You'll get married, and keep house for your husband!
I'll get married, and my husband'll keep house while I run the pub!
HA!

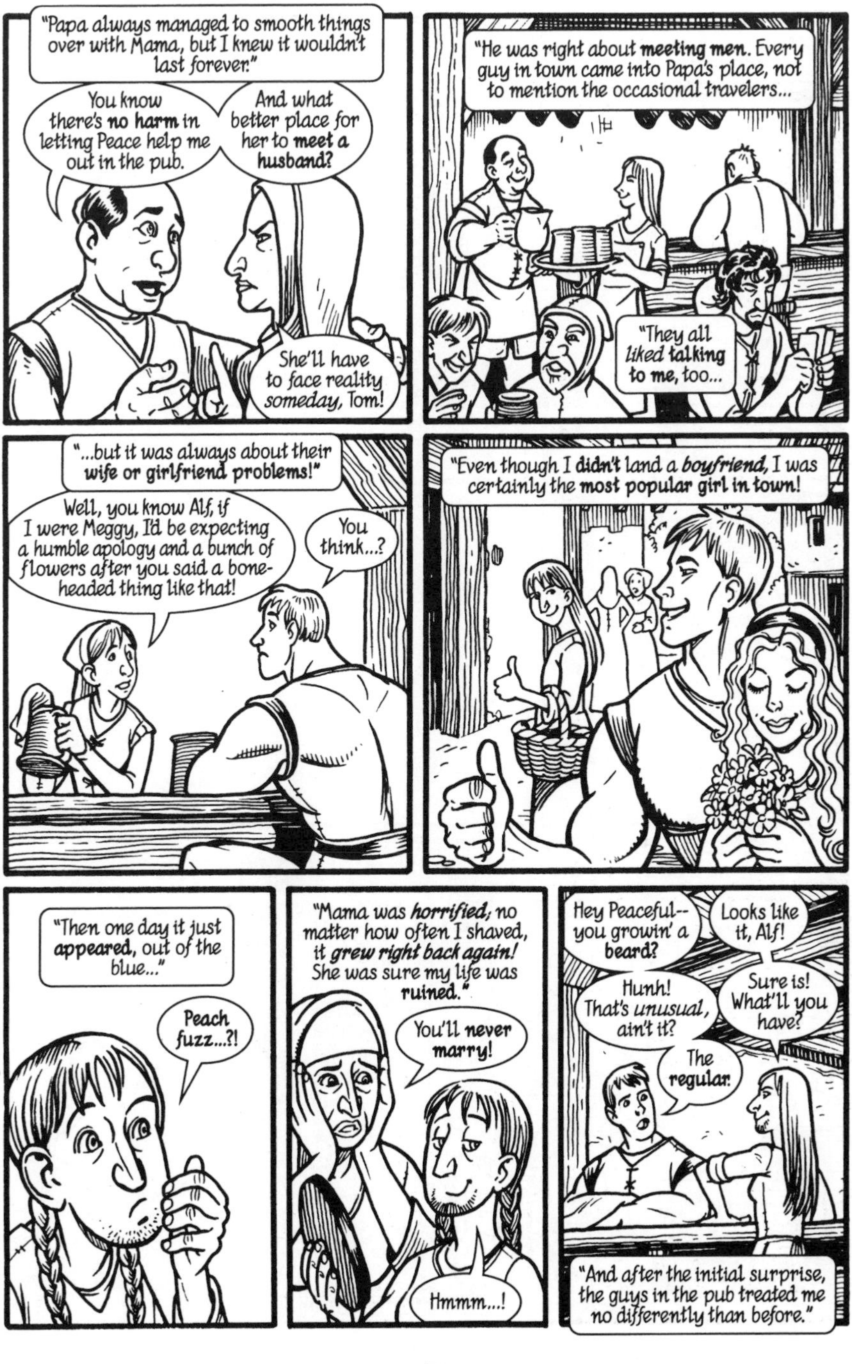
"Papa always managed to smooth things over with Mama, but I knew it wouldn't last forever."
You know there's **no harm** in letting Peace help me out in the pub.
And what better place for her to **meet a husband?**
She'll have to face reality someday, Tom!
"He was right about **meeting men**. Every guy in town came into Papa's place, not to mention the occasional travelers...
"They all *liked* **talking to me**, too...
"...but it was always about their **wife or girlfriend problems!**"
Well, you know Alf, if I were Meggy, I'd be expecting a humble apology and a bunch of flowers after you said a bone-headed thing like that!
You think...?
"Even though I **didn't** land a ***boyfriend***, I was certainly the **most popular girl in town**!
"Then one day it just **appeared**, out of the blue..."
Peach fuzz...?!
"Mama was ***horrified***; no matter how often I shaved, it ***grew right back again!*** She was sure my life was **ruined**."
You'll **never marry**!
Hmmm...!
Hey Peaceful-- you growin' a **beard?**
Looks like it, Alf!
Hunh! That's *unusual*, ain't it?
Sure is! What'll you have?
The **regular**.
"And after the initial surprise, the guys in the pub treated me no differently than before."

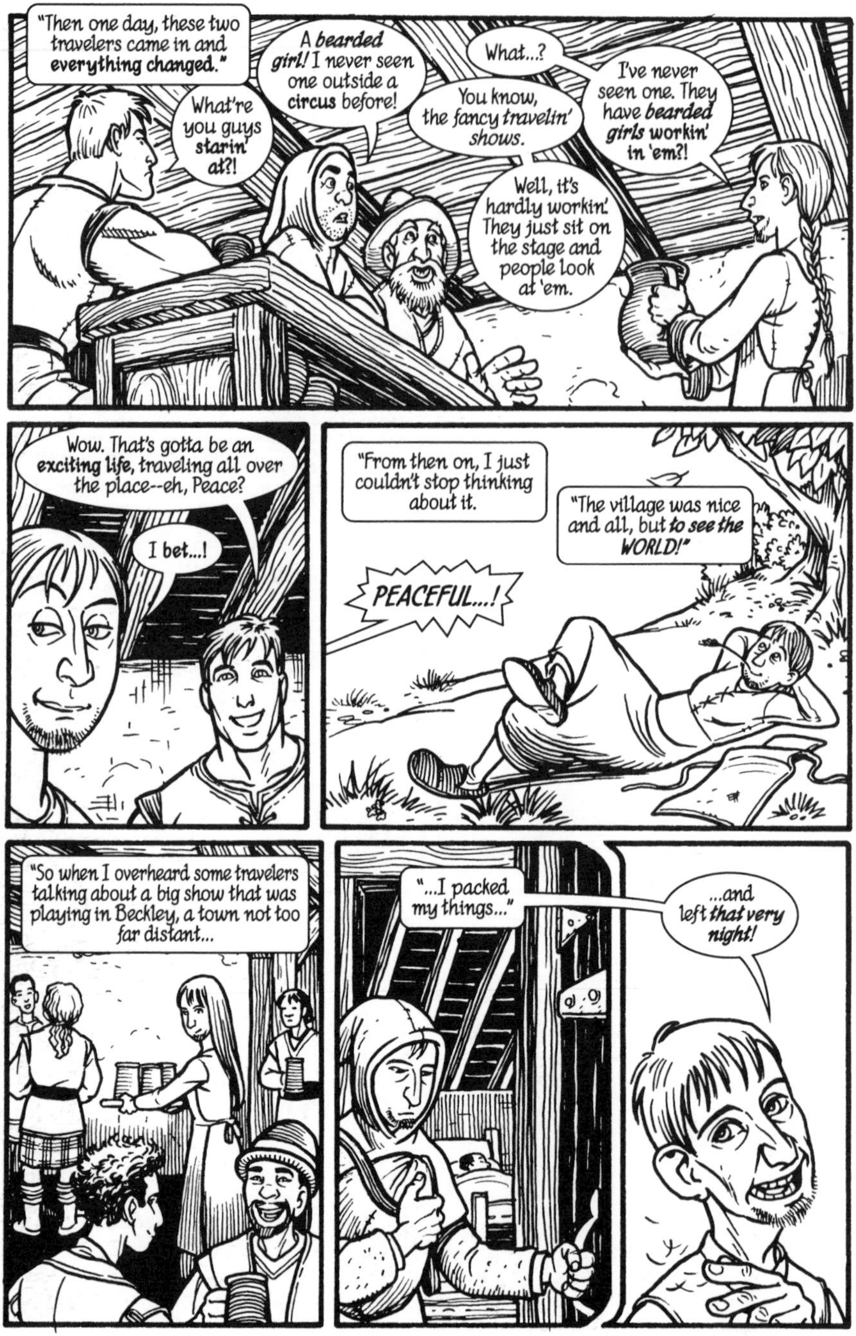
"Then one day, these two travelers came in and **everything changed.**"
What're you guys **starin'** at?!
A ***bearded girl!*** I never seen one outside a **circus** before!
What...?
You know, the fancy *travelin'* shows.
I've never seen one. They have ***bearded girls*** **workin'** in 'em?!
Well, it's hardly workin'. They just sit on the stage and people look at 'em.
Wow. That's gotta be an **exciting life**, traveling all over the place--eh, Peace?
I bet...!
"From then on, I just couldn't stop thinking about it.
"The village was nice and all, but ***to see the WORLD!"***
PEACEFUL...!
"So when I overheard some travelers talking about a big show that was playing in Beckley, a town not too far distant...
"...I packed my things..."
...and left ***that very night!***

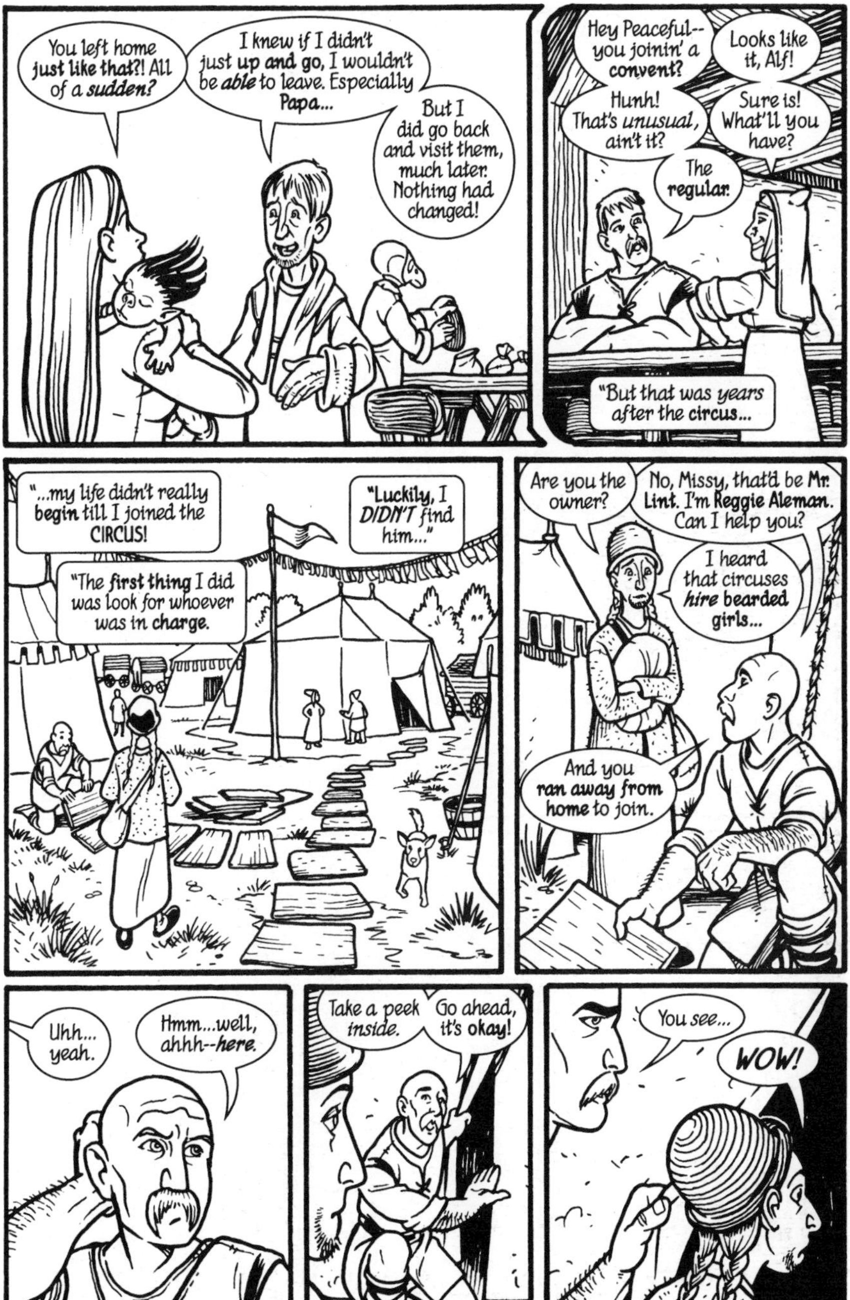
You left home just like that?! All of a sudden?
I knew if I didn't just up and go, I wouldn't be able to leave. Especially Papa...
But I did go back and visit them, much later. Nothing had changed!
Hey Peaceful-- you joinin' a convent?
Looks like it, Alf!
Hunh! That's unusual, ain't it?
Sure is! What'll you have?
The regular.
"But that was years after the circus...
"...my life didn't really begin till I joined the CIRCUS!
"Luckily, I DIDN'T find him..."
"The first thing I did was look for whoever was in charge.
Are you the owner?
No, Missy, that'd be Mr. Lint. I'm Reggie Aleman. Can I help you?
I heard that circuses hire bearded girls...
And you ran away from home to join.
Uhh... yeah.
Hmm...well, ahhh--here.
Take a peek inside.
Go ahead, it's okay!
You see...
WOW!

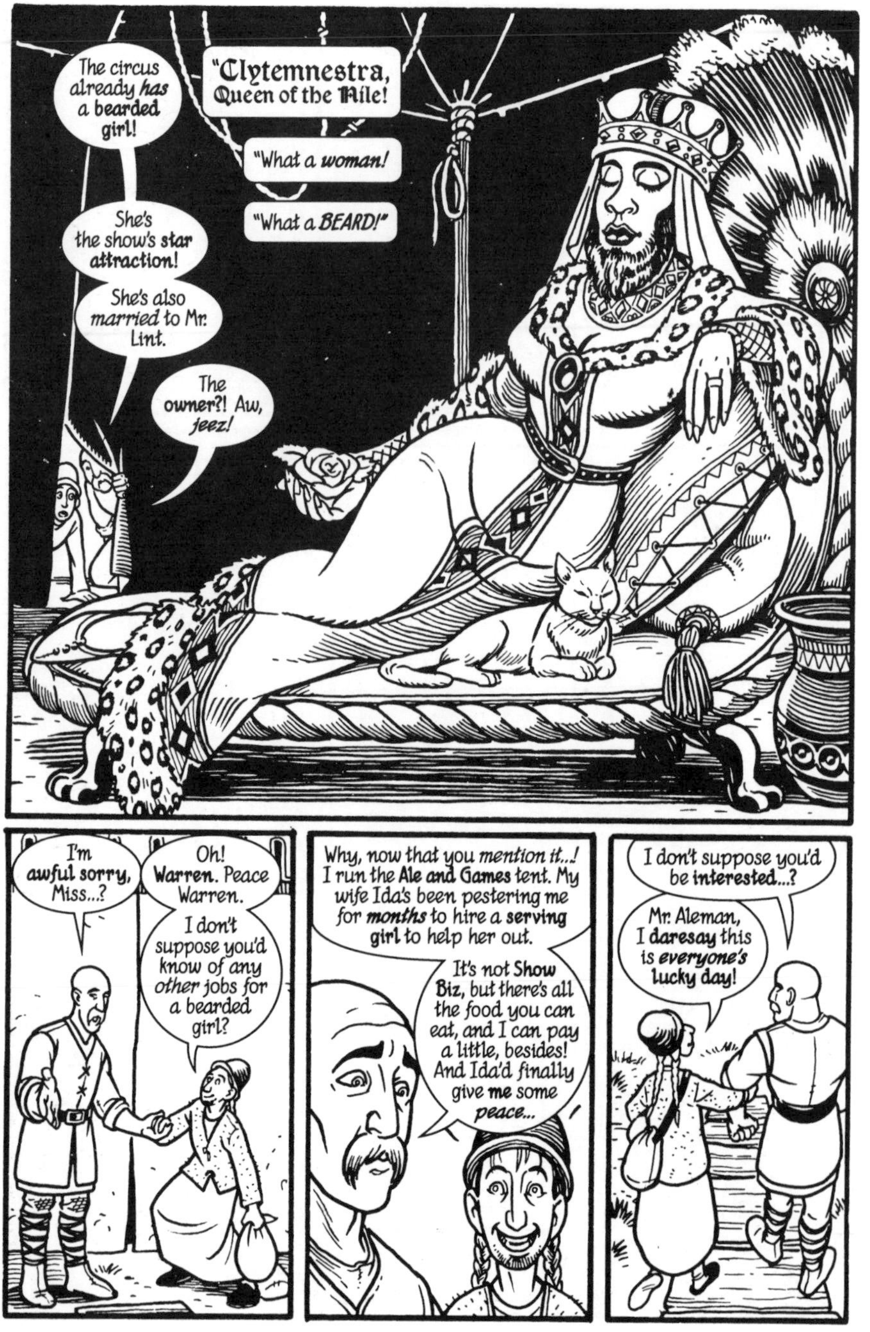
"Clytemnestra, Queen of the Nile!
"What a woman!
"What a BEARD!"
The circus already has a bearded girl!
She's the show's star attraction!
She's also married to Mr. Lint.
The owner?! Aw, jeez!
I'm awful sorry, Miss...?
Oh! Warren. Peace Warren.
I don't suppose you'd know of any other jobs for a bearded girl?
Why, now that you mention it...! I run the Ale and Games tent. My wife Ida's been pestering me for months to hire a serving girl to help her out.
It's not Show Biz, but there's all the food you can eat, and I can pay a little, besides! And Ida'd finally give me some peace...
I don't suppose you'd be interested...?
Mr. Aleman, I daresay this is everyone's lucky day!

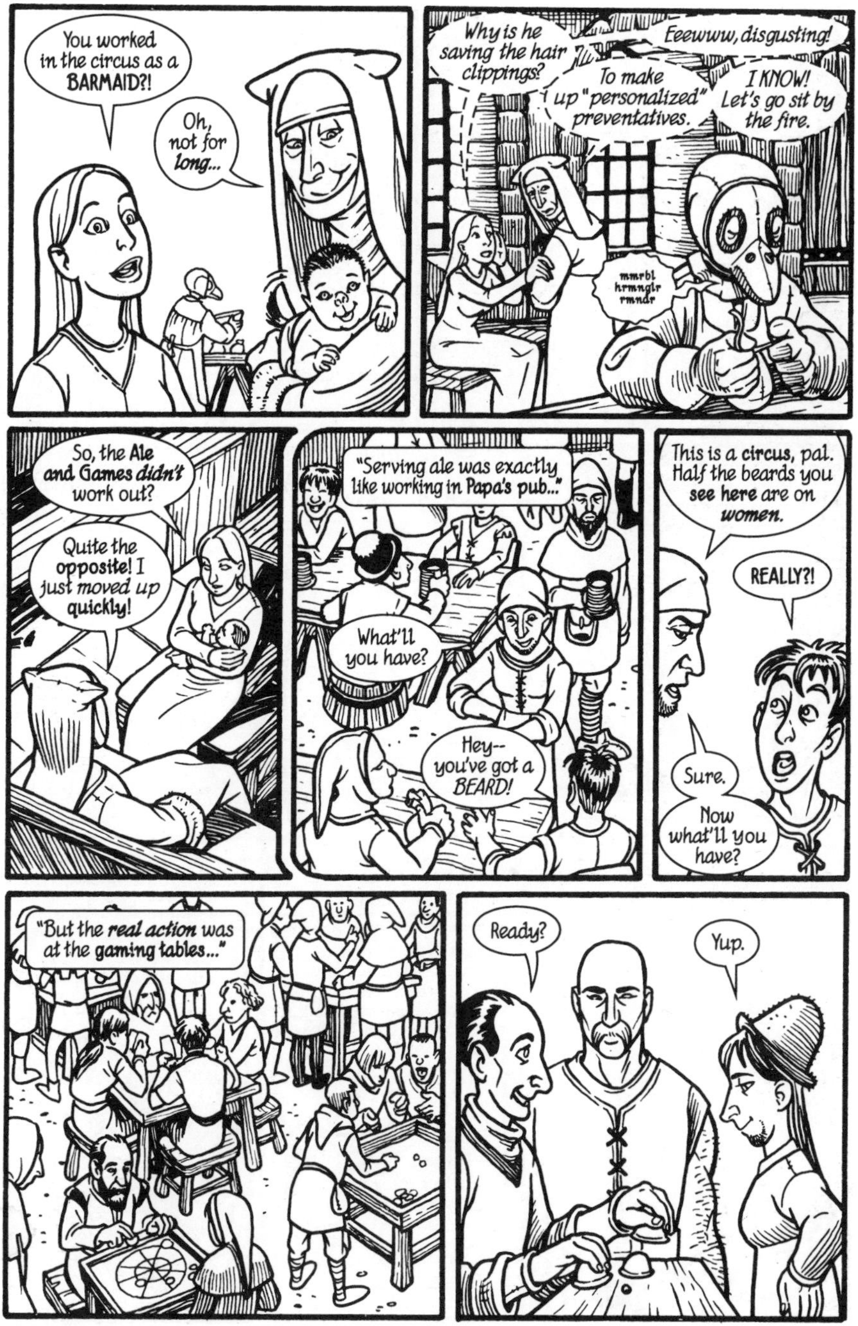
You worked in the circus as a BARMAID?!
Oh, not for long...
Why is he saving the hair clippings?
Eeewww, disgusting!
To make up "personalized" preventatives.
I KNOW! Let's go sit by the fire.
mmrbl hrmnglr rmndr
So, the Ale and Games didn't work out?
Quite the opposite! I just moved up quickly!
"Serving ale was exactly like working in Papa's pub..."
What'll you have?
Hey-- you've got a BEARD!
This is a circus, pal. Half the beards you see here are on women.
REALLY?!
Sure.
Now what'll you have?
"But the real action was at the gaming tables..."
Ready?
Yup.

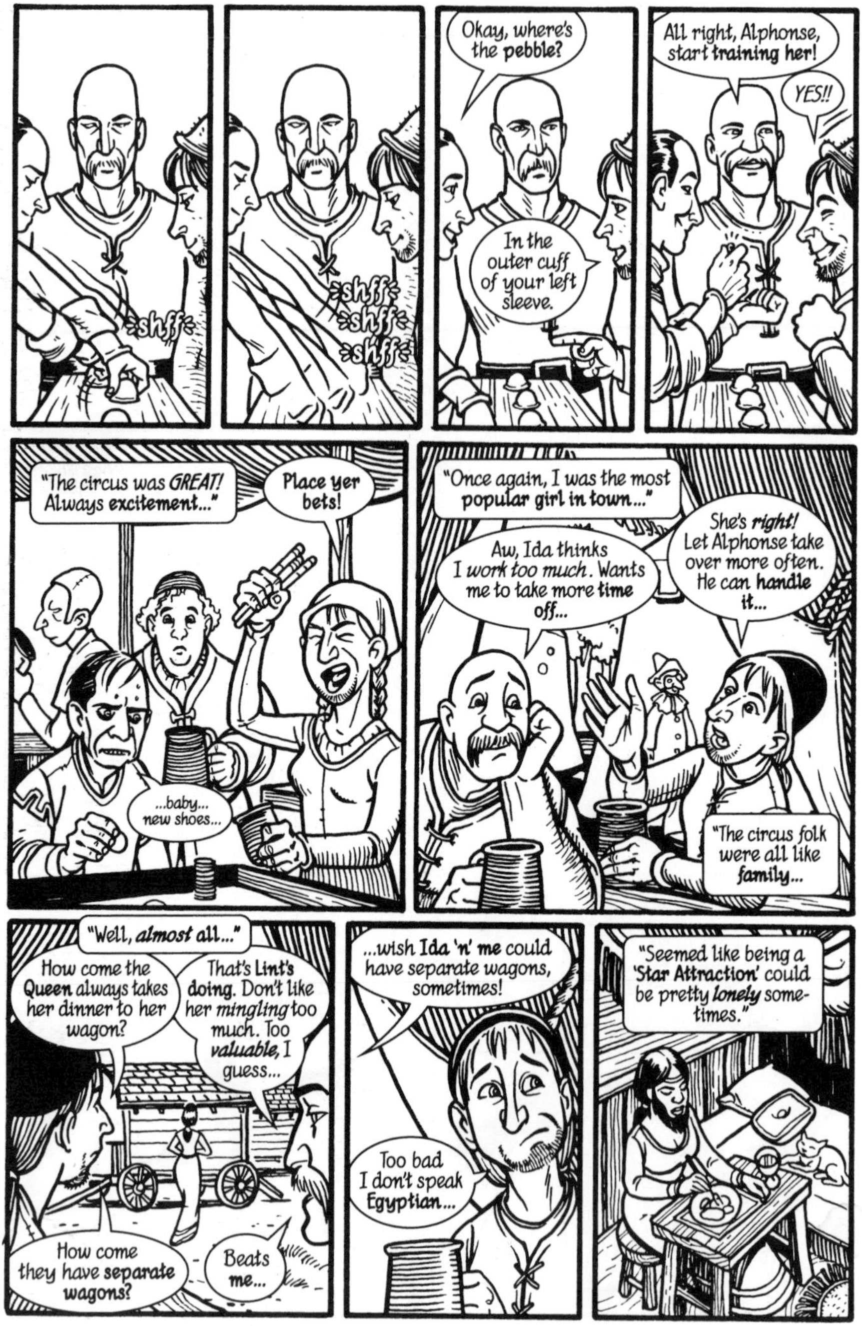
shff
shff
shff
shff
Okay, where's the pebble?
In the outer cuff of your left sleeve.
All right, Alphonse, start training her!
YES!!
"The circus was GREAT! Always excitement..."
Place yer bets!
...baby... new shoes...
"Once again, I was the most popular girl in town..."
Aw, Ida thinks I work too much. Wants me to take more time off...
She's right! Let Alphonse take over more often. He can handle it...
"The circus folk were all like family...
"Well, almost all..."
How come the Queen always takes her dinner to her wagon?
That's Lint's doing. Don't like her mingling too much. Too valuable, I guess...
How come they have separate wagons?
Beats me...
...wish Ida 'n' me could have separate wagons, sometimes!
Too bad I don't speak Egyptian...
"Seemed like being a 'Star Attraction' could be pretty lonely sometimes."

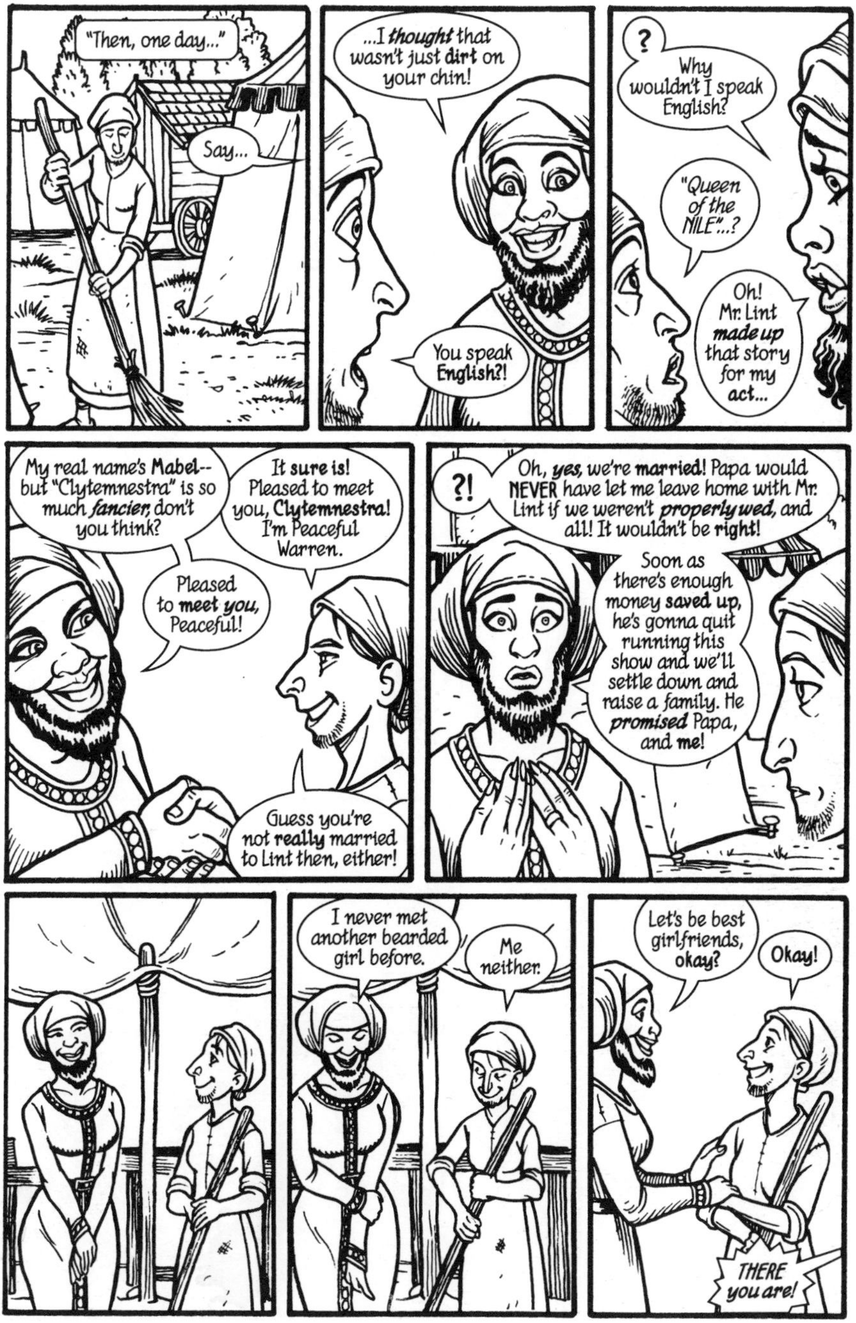
"Then, one day..."
Say...
...I thought that wasn't just dirt on your chin!
You speak English?!
?
Why wouldn't I speak English?
"Queen of the NILE"...?
Oh! Mr. Lint made up that story for my act...
My real name's Mabel-- but "Clytemnestra" is so much fancier, don't you think?
It sure is! Pleased to meet you, Clytemnestra! I'm Peaceful Warren.
Pleased to meet you, Peaceful!
Guess you're not really married to Lint then, either!
?!
Oh, yes, we're married! Papa would NEVER have let me leave home with Mr. Lint if we weren't properly wed, and all! It wouldn't be right!
Soon as there's enough money saved up, he's gonna quit running this show and we'll settle down and raise a family. He promised Papa, and me!
I never met another bearded girl before.
Me neither.
Let's be best girlfriends, okay?
Okay!
THERE you are!

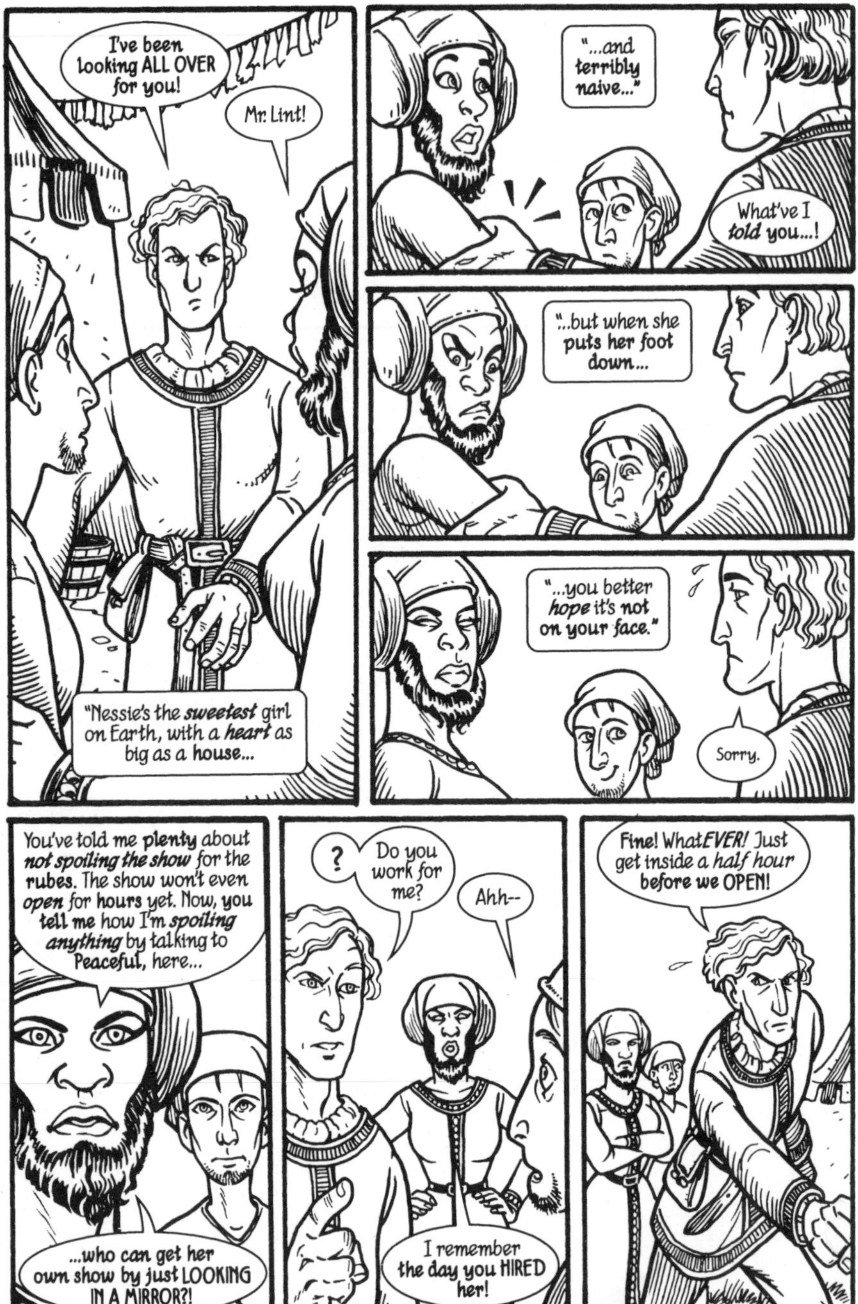
I've been looking ALL OVER for you!
Mr. Lint!
"Nessie's the sweetest girl on Earth, with a heart as big as a house...
"...and terribly naive..."
What've I told you...!
"...but when she puts her foot down...
"...you better hope it's not on your face."
Sorry.
You've told me plenty about not spoiling the show for the rubes. The show won't even open for hours yet. Now, you tell me how I'm spoiling anything by talking to Peaceful, here...
...who can get her own show by just LOOKING IN A MIRROR?!
?
Do you work for me?
Ahh--
I remember the day you HIRED her!
Fine! WhatEVER! Just get inside a half hour before we OPEN!

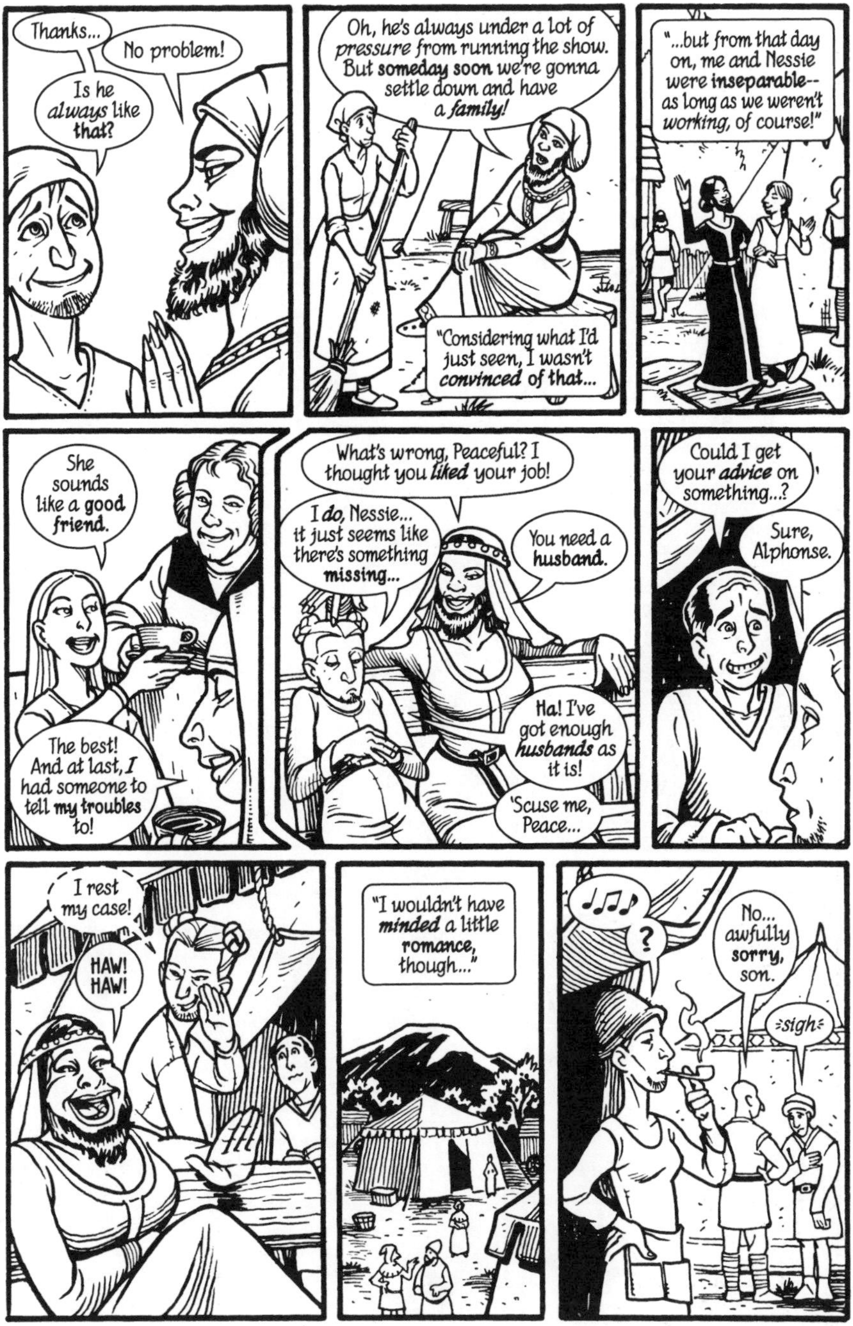
Thanks...
No problem!
Is he *always* like **that?**
Oh, he's always under a lot of *pressure* from running the show. But **someday soon** we're gonna settle down and have a ***family!***
"Considering what I'd just seen, I wasn't ***convinced*** of that...
"...but from that day on, me and Nessie were **inseparable**-- as long as we weren't *working,* of course!"
She sounds like a **good friend.**
The best! And at last, ***I*** had someone to tell **my troubles** to!
What's wrong, Peaceful? I thought you ***liked*** your job!
I ***do,*** Nessie... it just seems like there's something **missing...**
You need a **husband.**
Ha! I've got enough ***husbands*** as it is!
'Scuse me, Peace...
Could I get your ***advice*** on something...?
Sure, Alphonse.
I rest my case!
HAW! HAW!
"I wouldn't have ***minded*** a little **romance,** though..."
♪♪♪
?
No... awfully **sorry,** son.
sigh

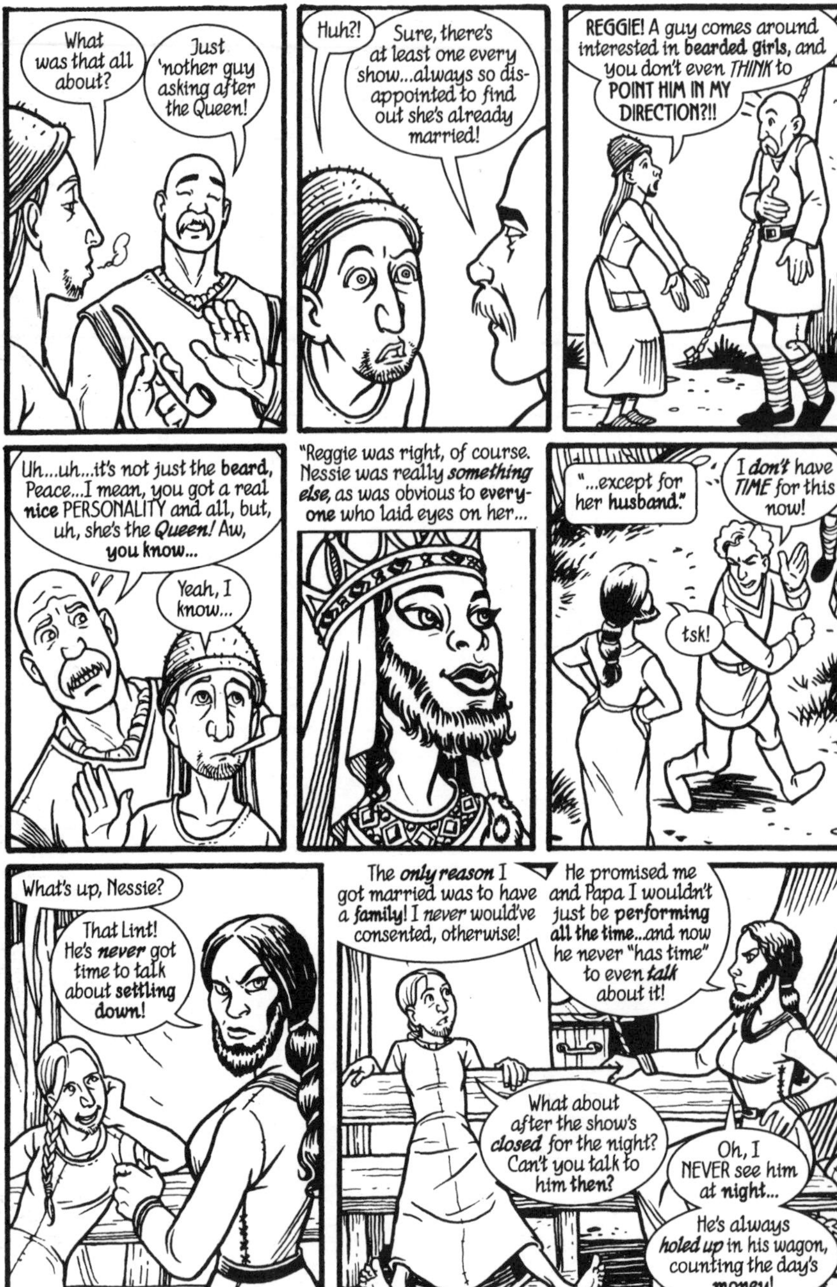
What was that all about?
Just 'nother guy asking after the Queen!
Huh?!
Sure, there's at least one every show...always so disappointed to find out she's already married!
REGGIE! A guy comes around interested in bearded girls, and you don't even THINK to POINT HIM IN MY DIRECTION?!!
Uh...uh...it's not just the beard, Peace...I mean, you got a real nice PERSONALITY and all, but, uh, she's the Queen! Aw, you know...
Yeah, I know...
"Reggie was right, of course. Nessie was really something else, as was obvious to everyone who laid eyes on her...
"...except for her husband."
I don't have TIME for this now!
tsk!
What's up, Nessie?
That Lint! He's never got time to talk about settling down!
The only reason I got married was to have a family! I never would've consented, otherwise!
He promised me and Papa I wouldn't just be performing all the time...and now he never "has time" to even talk about it!
What about after the show's closed for the night? Can't you talk to him then?
Oh, I NEVER see him at night...
He's always holed up in his wagon, counting the day's money!

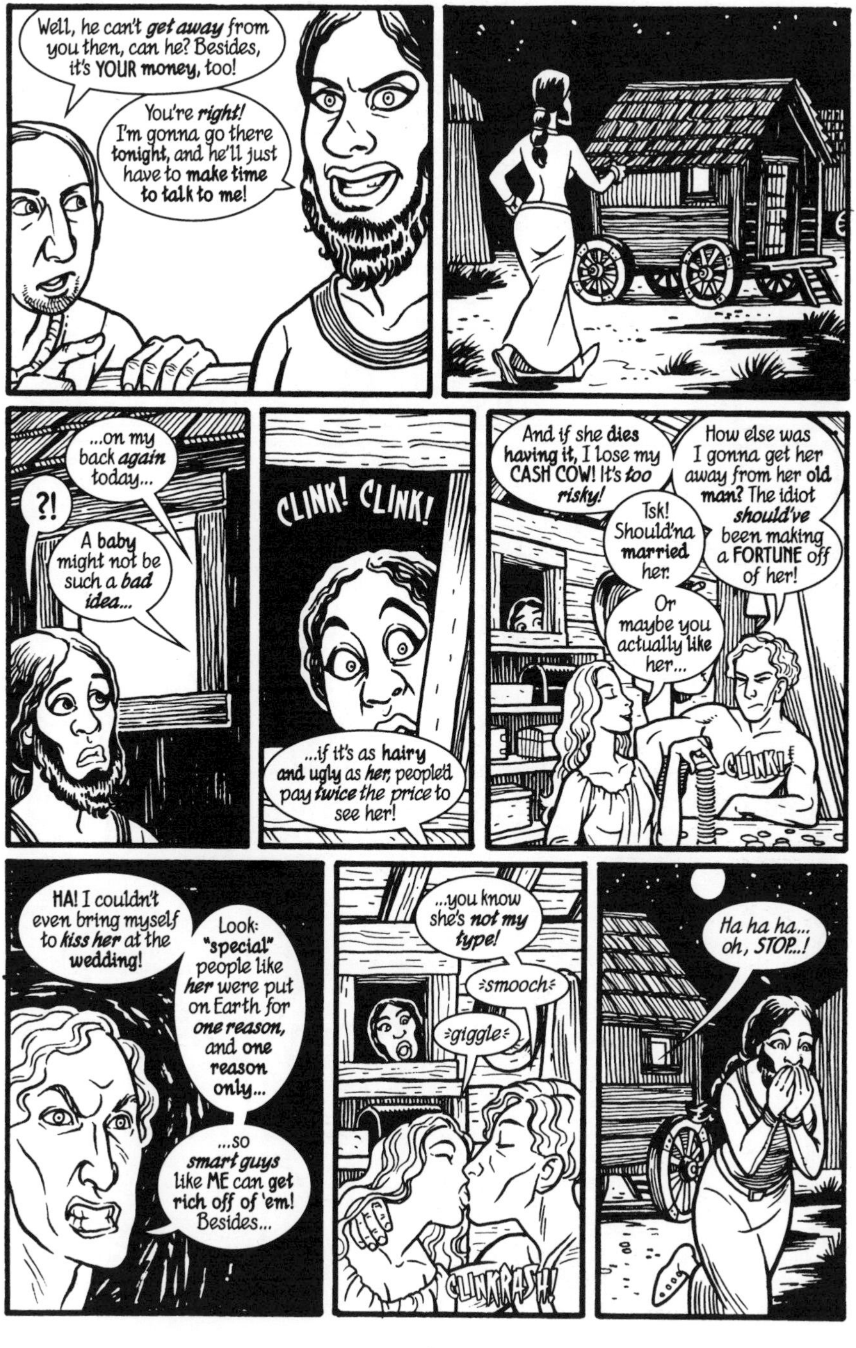
Well, he can't get away from you then, can he? Besides, it's YOUR money, too!
You're right! I'm gonna go there tonight, and he'll just have to make time to talk to me!
...on my back again today...
?!
A baby might not be such a bad idea...
CLINK! CLINK!
...if it's as hairy and ugly as her, people'd pay twice the price to see her!
And if she dies having it, I lose my CASH COW! It's too risky!
How else was I gonna get her away from her old man? The idiot should've been making a FORTUNE off of her!
Tsk! Should'na married her.
Or maybe you actually like her...
CLINK!
HA! I couldn't even bring myself to kiss her at the wedding!
Look: "special" people like her were put on Earth for one reason, and one reason only...
...so smart guys like ME can get rich off of 'em! Besides...
...you know she's not my type!
smooch
giggle
CLINKRASH!
Ha ha ha... oh, STOP...!

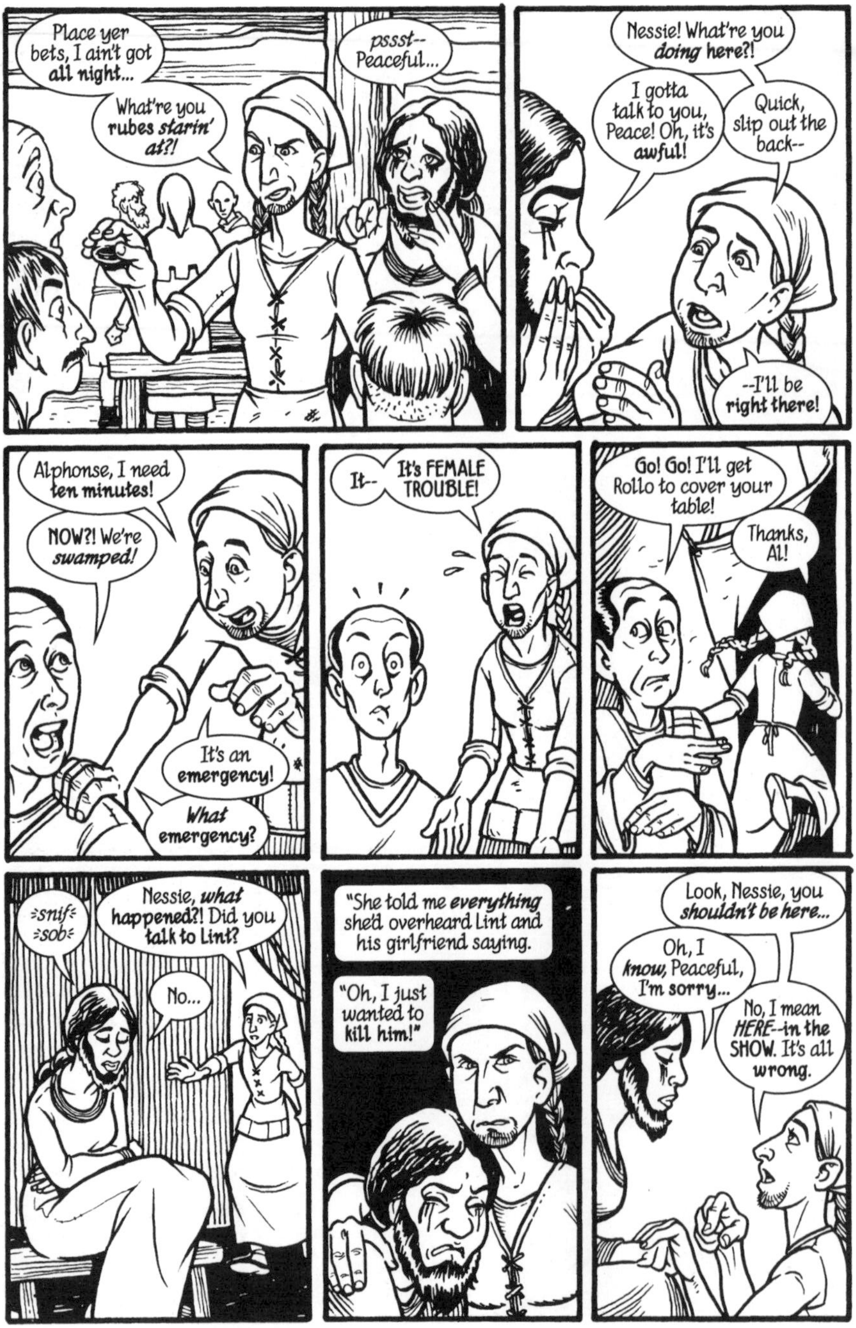
Place yer bets, I ain't got all night...
What're you rubes starin' at?!
pssst-- Peaceful...
Nessie! What're you doing here?!
I gotta talk to you, Peace! Oh, it's awful!
Quick, slip out the back--
--I'll be right there!
Alphonse, I need ten minutes!
NOW?! We're swamped!
It's an emergency!
What emergency?
It--
It's FEMALE TROUBLE!
Go! Go! I'll get Rollo to cover your table!
Thanks, Al!
snif sob
Nessie, what happened?! Did you talk to Lint?
No...
"She told me everything she'd overheard Lint and his girlfriend saying.
"Oh, I just wanted to kill him!"
Look, Nessie, you shouldn't be here...
Oh, I know, Peaceful, I'm sorry...
No, I mean HERE--in the SHOW. It's all wrong.

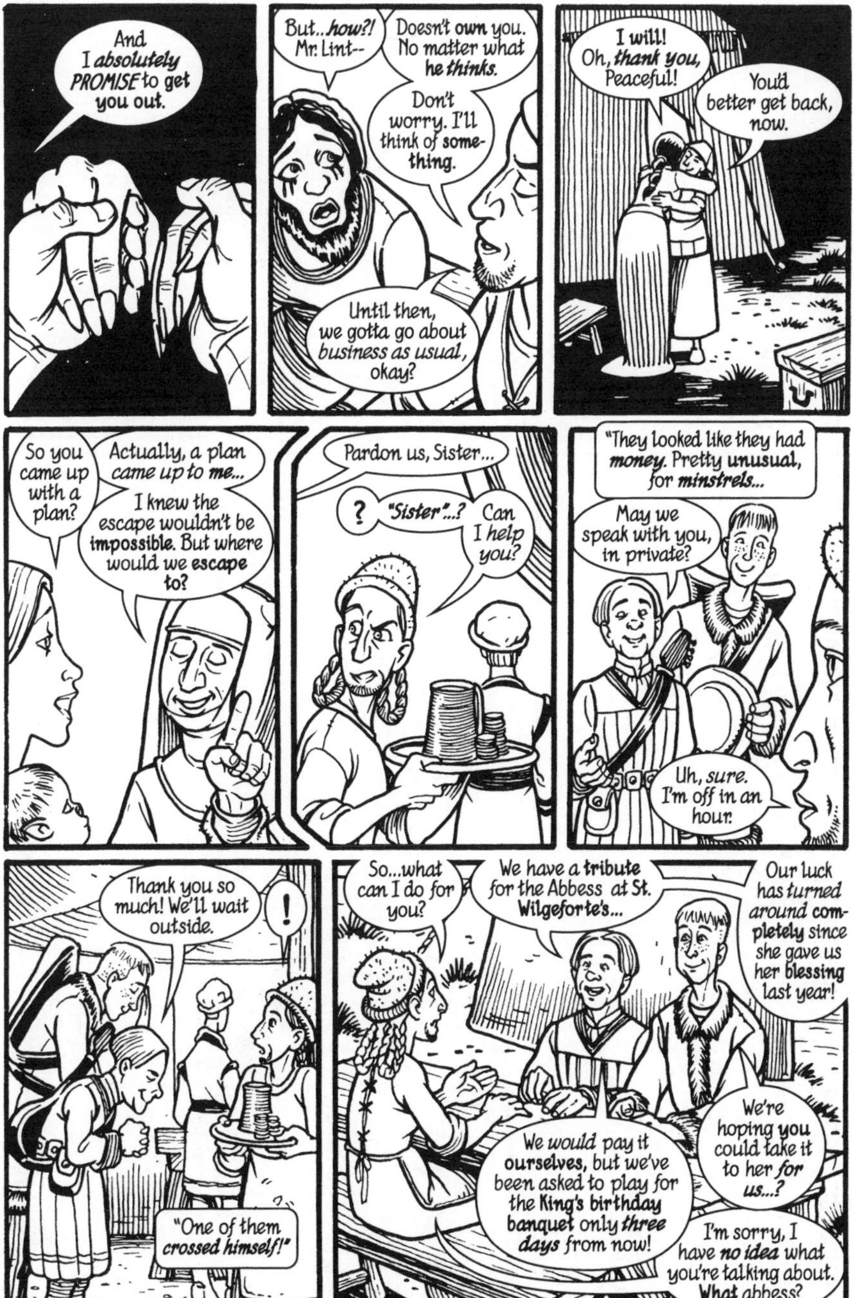
And I *absolutely* **PROMISE** to get you out.
But...**how?!** Mr. Lint--
Doesn't **own** you. No matter what **he thinks.**
Don't worry. I'll think of **some-thing.**
Until then, we gotta go about *business as usual,* okay?
I will! Oh, ***thank you,*** Peaceful!
You'd better get back, now.
So you came up with a plan?
Actually, a plan *came up to* **me...**
I knew the escape wouldn't be **impossible.** But where would we **escape to?**
Pardon us, Sister...
?
"Sister"...? Can I *help* you?
"They looked like they had ***money.*** Pretty **unusual,** for ***minstrels...***
May we speak with you, in private?
Uh, *sure.* I'm off in an hour.
Thank you so much! We'll wait outside.
!
"One of them ***crossed himself!"***
So...what can I do for you?
We have a **tribute** for the Abbess at St. **Wilgeforte's...**
Our luck has *turned around* **com-pletely** since she gave us her **blessing** last year!
We *would* pay it **ourselves,** but we've been asked to play for the **King's birthday banquet** only ***three days*** from now!
We're hoping **you** could take it to her ***for us...?***
I'm sorry, I have ***no idea*** what you're talking about. **What** abbess?

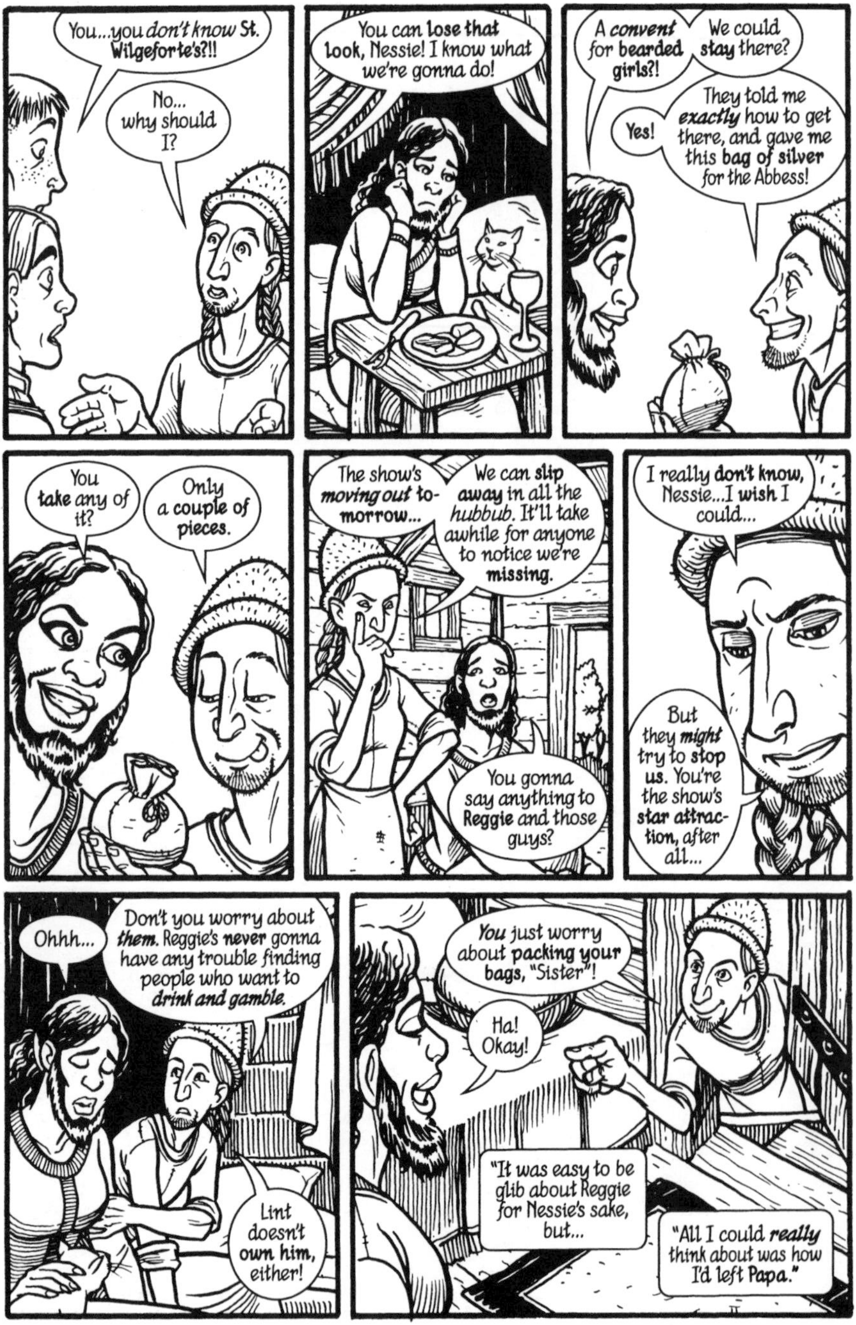
You...you *don't know* St. **Wilgeforte's?!!**
No... why should I?
You can **lose that look,** Nessie! I know what we're gonna do!
A ***convent*** for **bearded girls?!**
We could **stay** there?
Yes!
They told me ***exactly*** how to get there, and gave me this **bag of silver** for the Abbess!
You **take** any of it?
Only a **couple of pieces.**
The show's ***moving out*** to-**morrow...**
We can **slip away** in all the *hubbub*. It'll take awhile for anyone to notice we're **missing.**
You gonna say anything to **Reggie** and those guys?
I really **don't know,** Nessie...I **wish** I could...
But they ***might*** try to **stop us.** You're the show's **star attraction,** after all...
Ohhh...
Don't you worry about ***them***. Reggie's **never** gonna have any trouble finding people who want to ***drink and gamble.***
Lint doesn't **own him,** either!
You just worry about **packing your bags,** "Sister"!
Ha! Okay!
"It was easy to be glib about Reggie for Nessie's sake, but...
"All I could ***really*** think about was how I'd left **Papa.**"

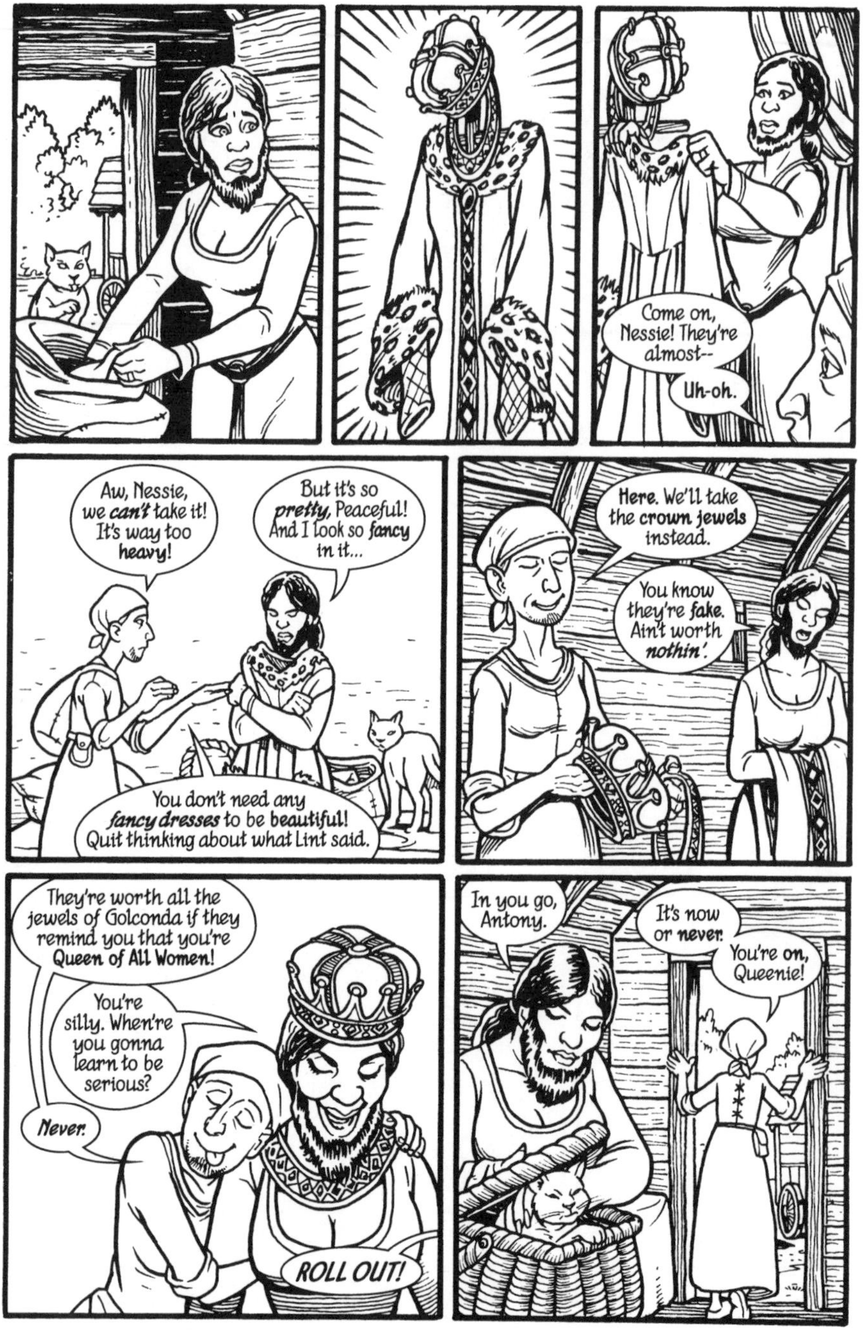
Come on, Nessie! They're almost--
Uh-oh.
Aw, Nessie, we **can't** take it! It's way too **heavy**!
But it's so ***pretty***, Peaceful! And I look so **fancy** in it...
You don't need any ***fancy dresses*** to be **beautiful**! Quit thinking about what Lint said.
Here. We'll take the **crown jewels** instead.
You know they're **fake**. Ain't worth ***nothin'***.
They're worth all the jewels of Golconda if they remind you that you're **Queen of All Women**!
You're silly. When're you gonna learn to be serious?
Never.
ROLL OUT!
In you go, Antony.
It's now or **never**.
You're **on**, Queenie!

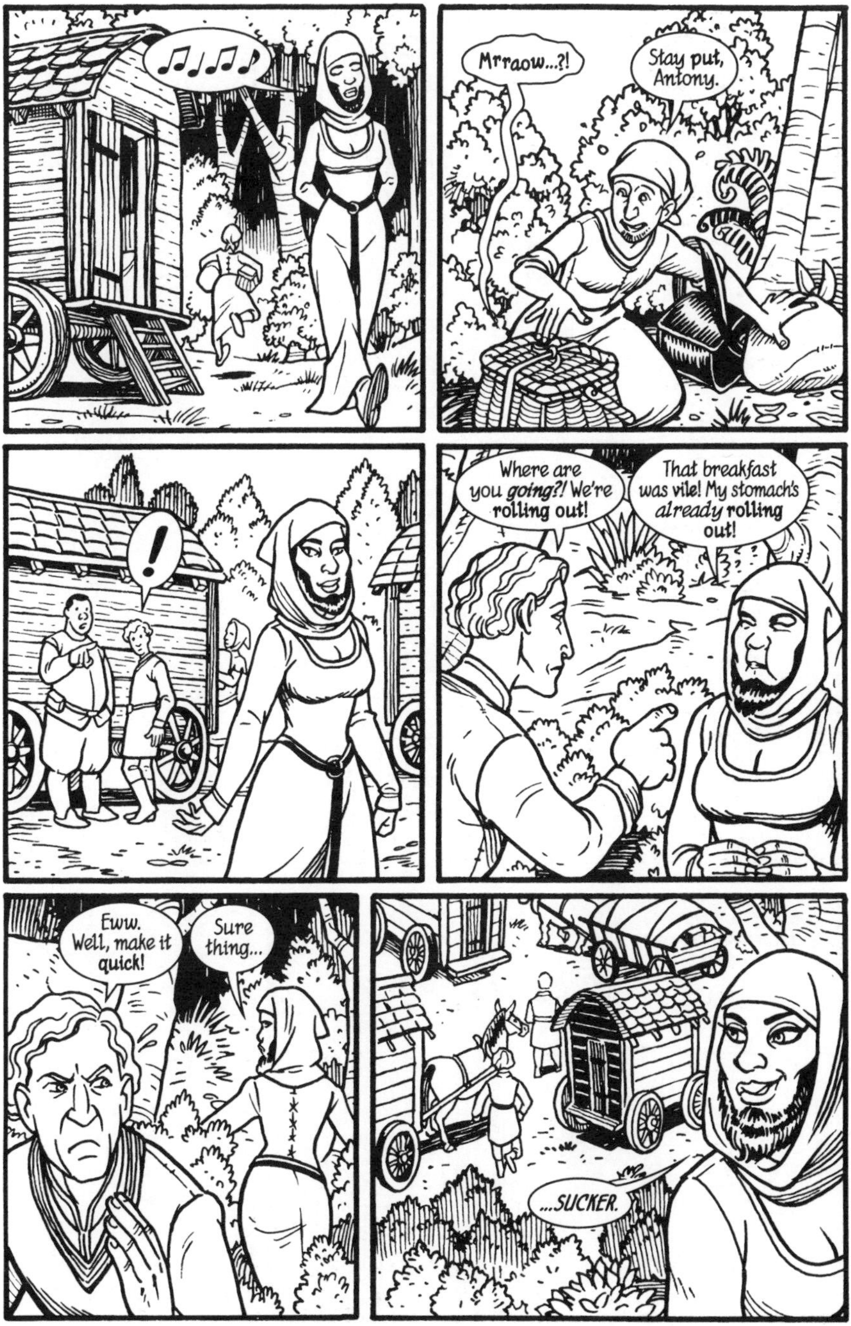

♫♩♫♪
Mrraow...?!
Stay put, Antony.
!
Where are you *going?!* We're **rolling out!**
That breakfast was vile! My stomach's *already* **rolling** out!
Eww. Well, make it **quick!**
Sure thing...
...SUCKER.

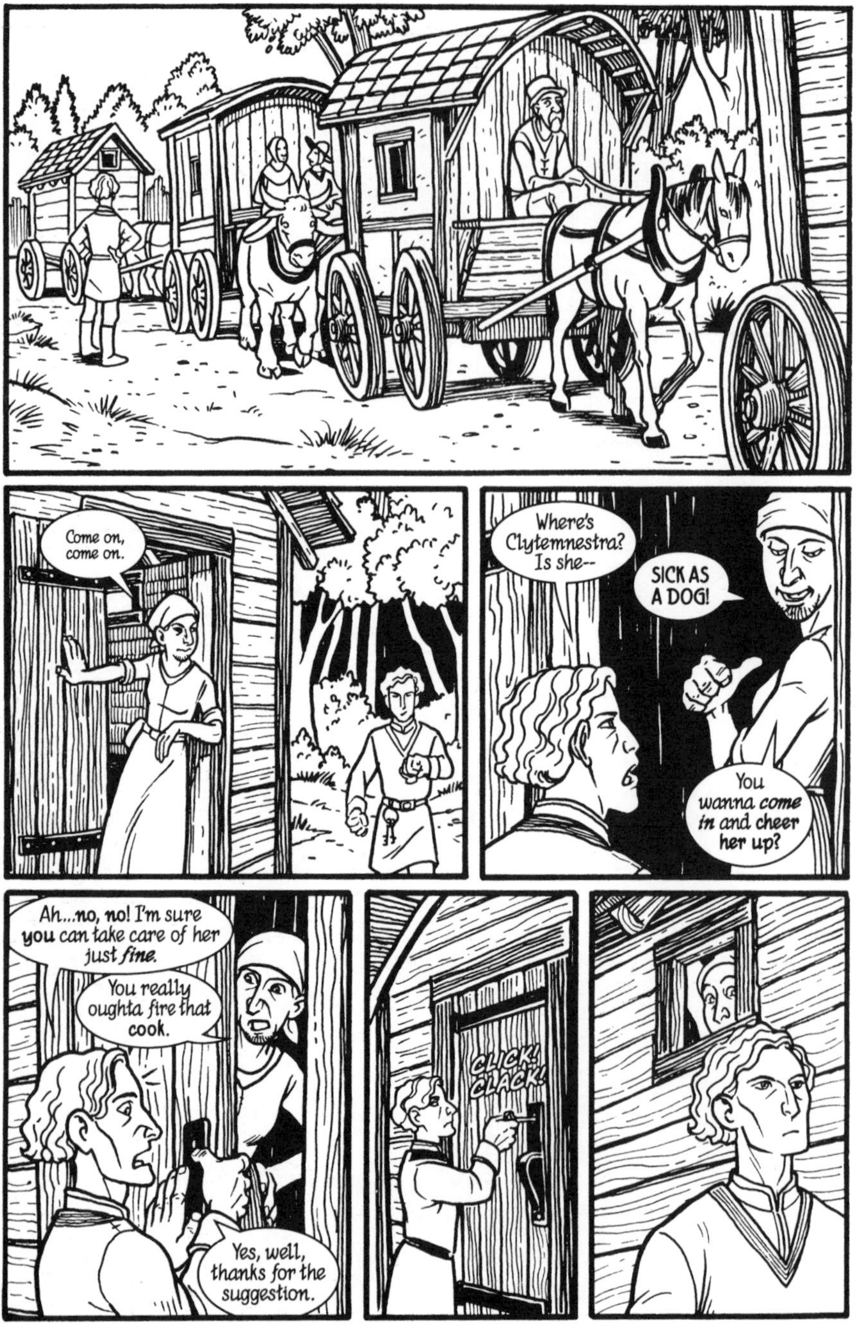
Come on, come on.
Where's Clytemnestra? Is she--
SICK AS A DOG!
You wanna *come in* and cheer her up?
Ah...**no, no**! I'm sure **you** can take care of her just ***fine***.
You really oughta fire that **cook**.
Yes, well, thanks for the suggestion.
CLICK! CLACK!

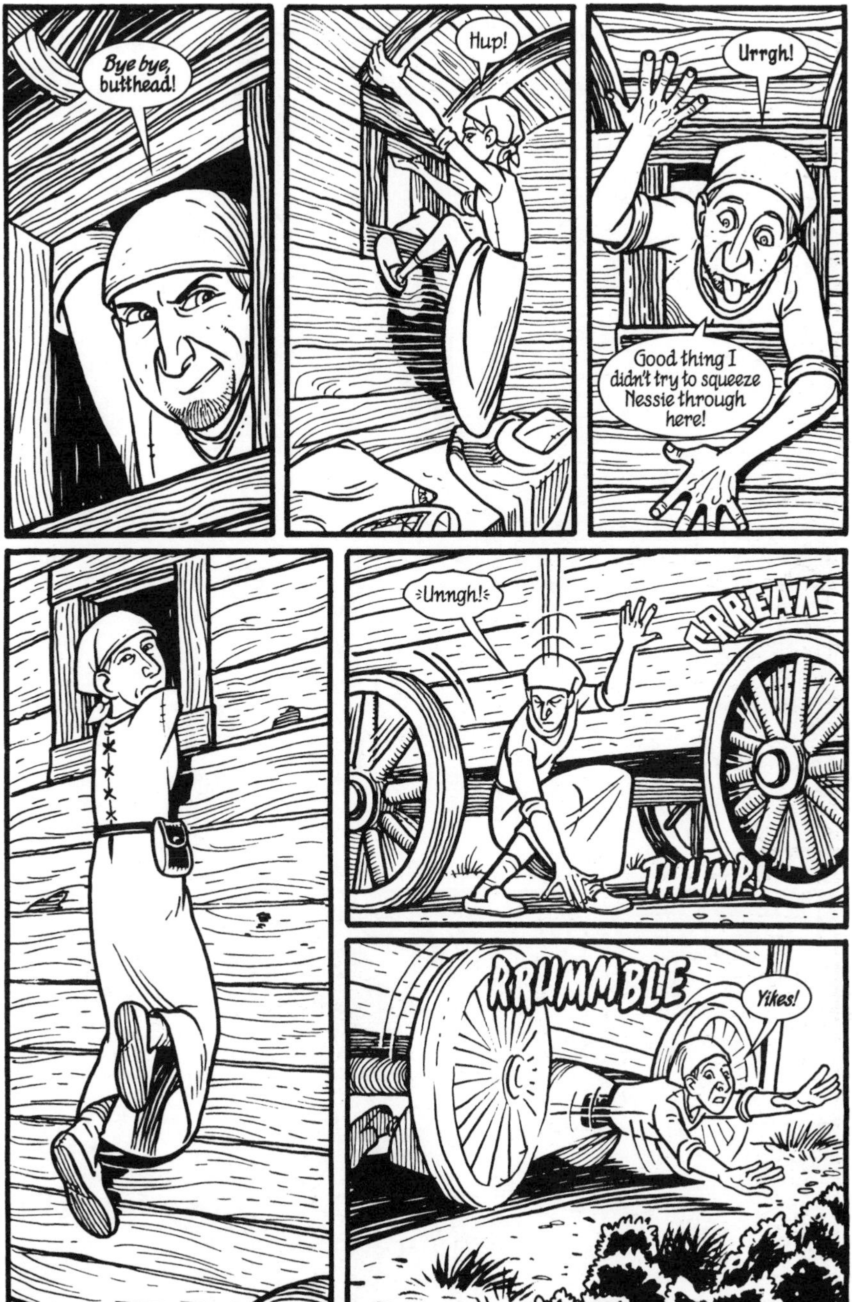
Bye bye, butthead!
Hup!
Urrgh!
Good thing I didn't try to squeeze Nessie through here!
Unngh!
CRREAK
THUMP!
RRUMMBLE
Yikes!

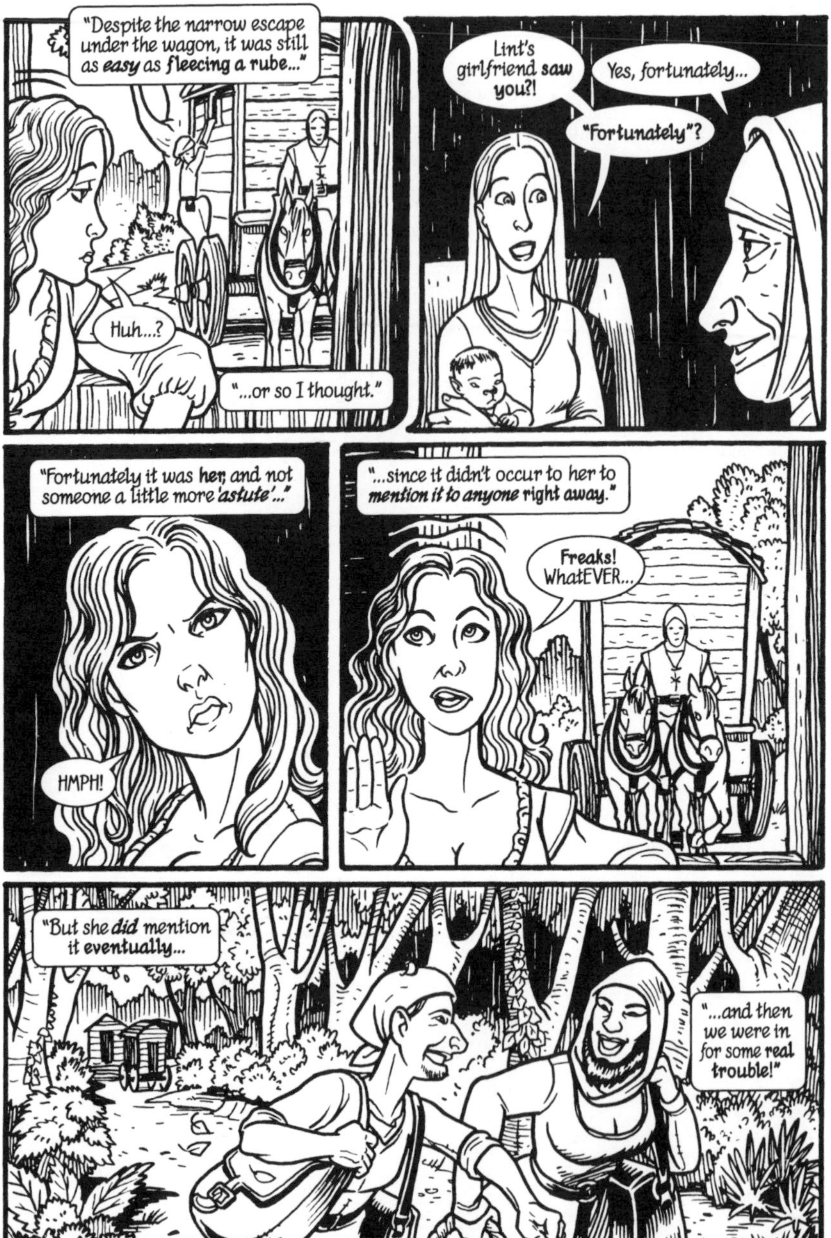
"Despite the narrow escape under the wagon, it was still as **easy** as **fleecing a rube**..."
Huh...?
"...or so I thought."
Lint's girlfriend **saw** you?!
Yes, fortunately...
"Fortunately"?
"Fortunately it was **her**, and not someone a little more **'astute'**..."
HMPH!
"...since it didn't occur to her to **mention it to anyone** right away."
Freaks! WhatEVER...
"But she **did** mention it **eventually**...
"...and then we were in for some **real trouble**!"

Chapter 14.

· SOLICITINE PT. 2 ·

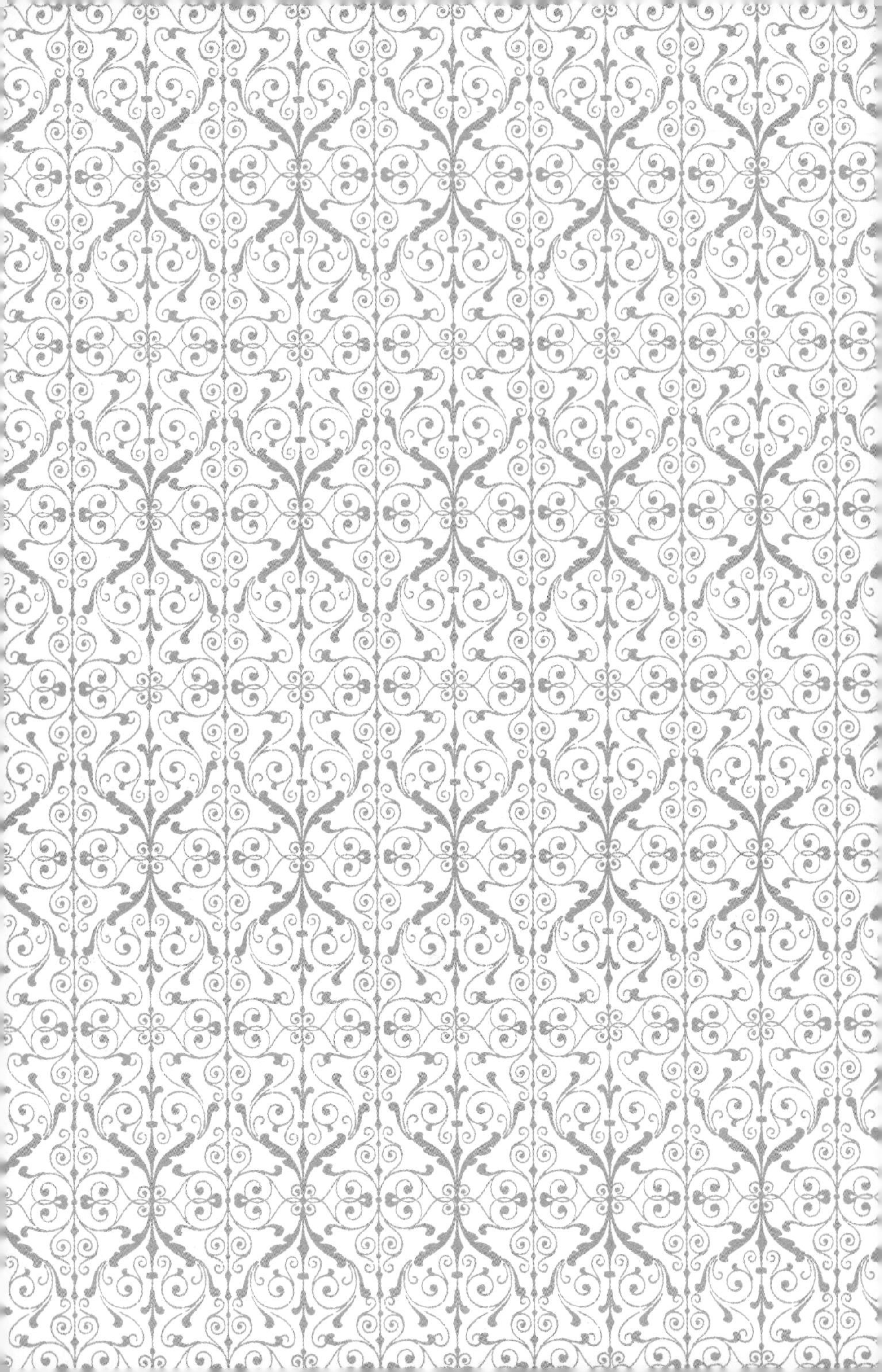

297.

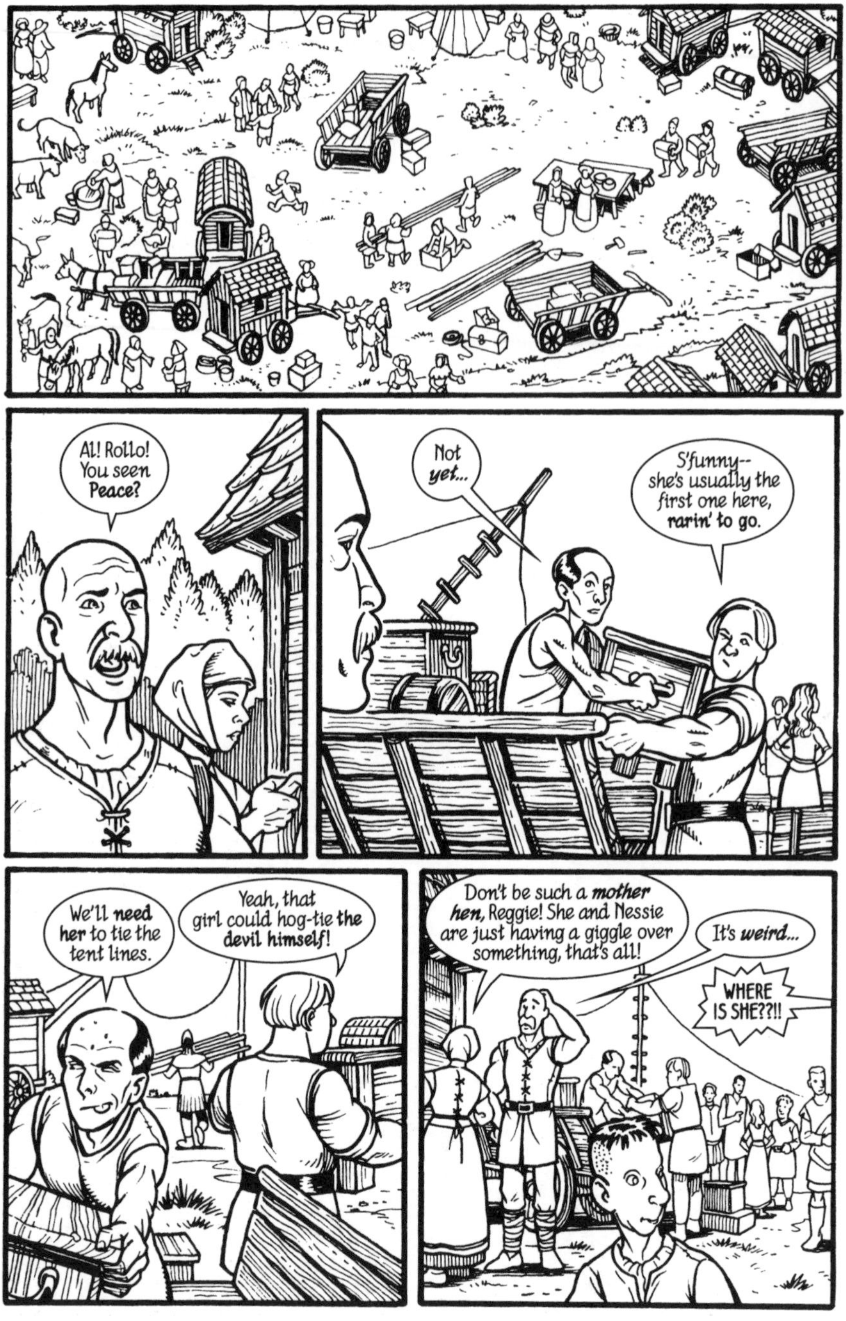
Al! Rollo! You seen Peace?
Not yet...
S'funny-- she's usually the first one here, rarin' to go.
We'll need her to tie the tent lines.
Yeah, that girl could hog-tie the devil himself!
Don't be such a mother hen, Reggie! She and Nessie are just having a giggle over something, that's all!
It's weird...
WHERE IS SHE??!!

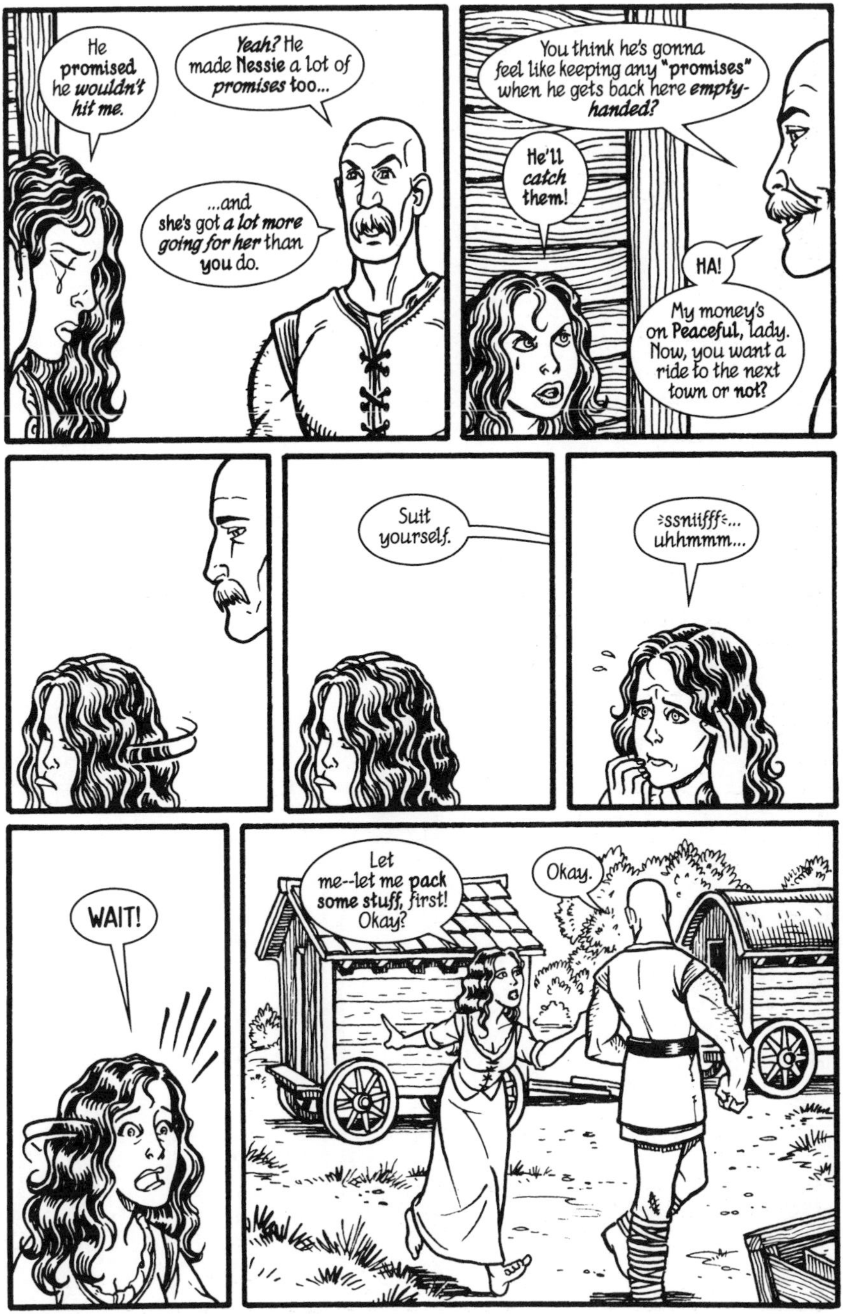
He promised he wouldn't hit me.
Yeah? He made Nessie a lot of promises too...
...and she's got a lot more going for her than you do.
You think he's gonna feel like keeping any "promises" when he gets back here empty-handed?
He'll catch them!
HA!
My money's on Peaceful, lady. Now, you want a ride to the next town or not?
Suit yourself.
ssniifff... uhhmmm...
WAIT!
Let me--let me pack some stuff, first! Okay?
Okay.

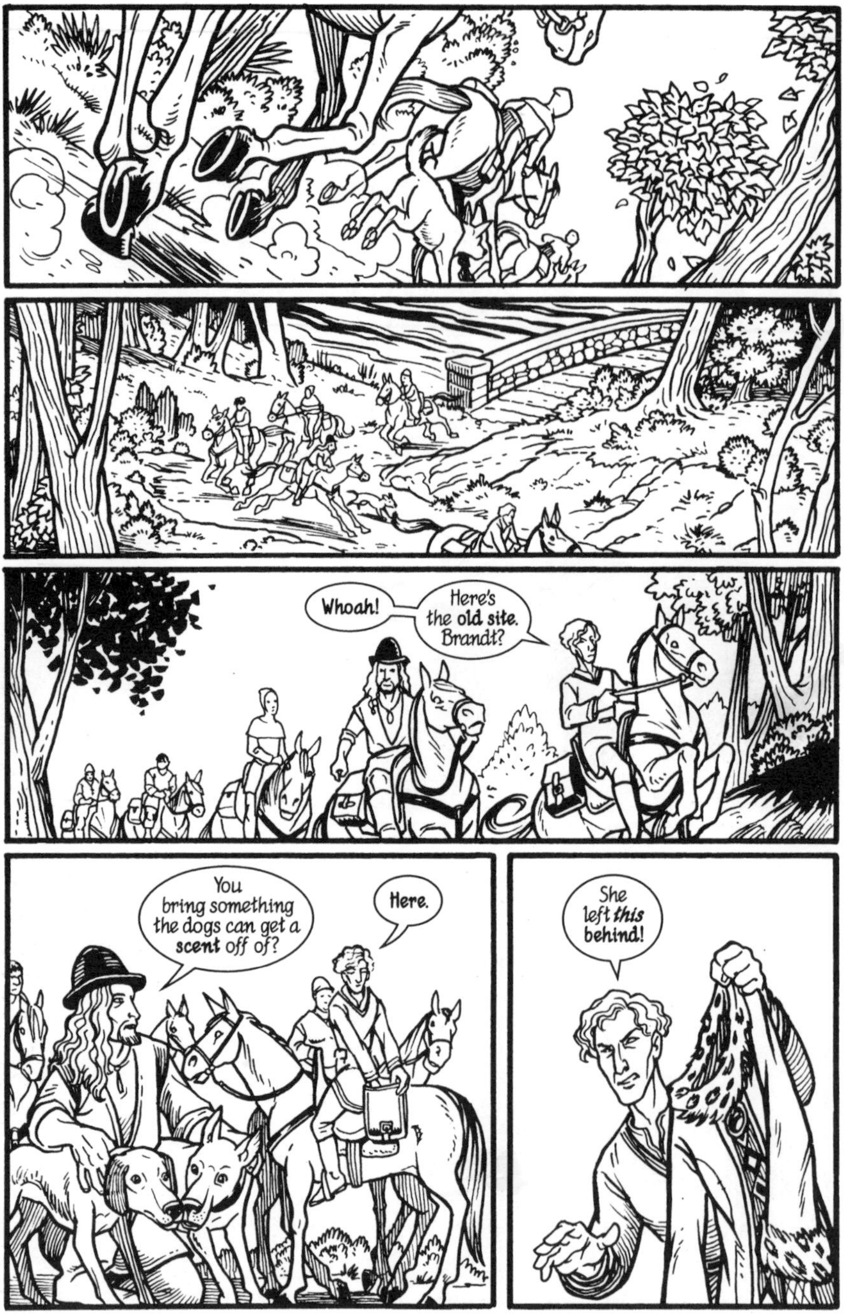
Whoah!
Here's the old site. Brandt?
You bring something the dogs can get a scent off of?
Here.
She left this behind!

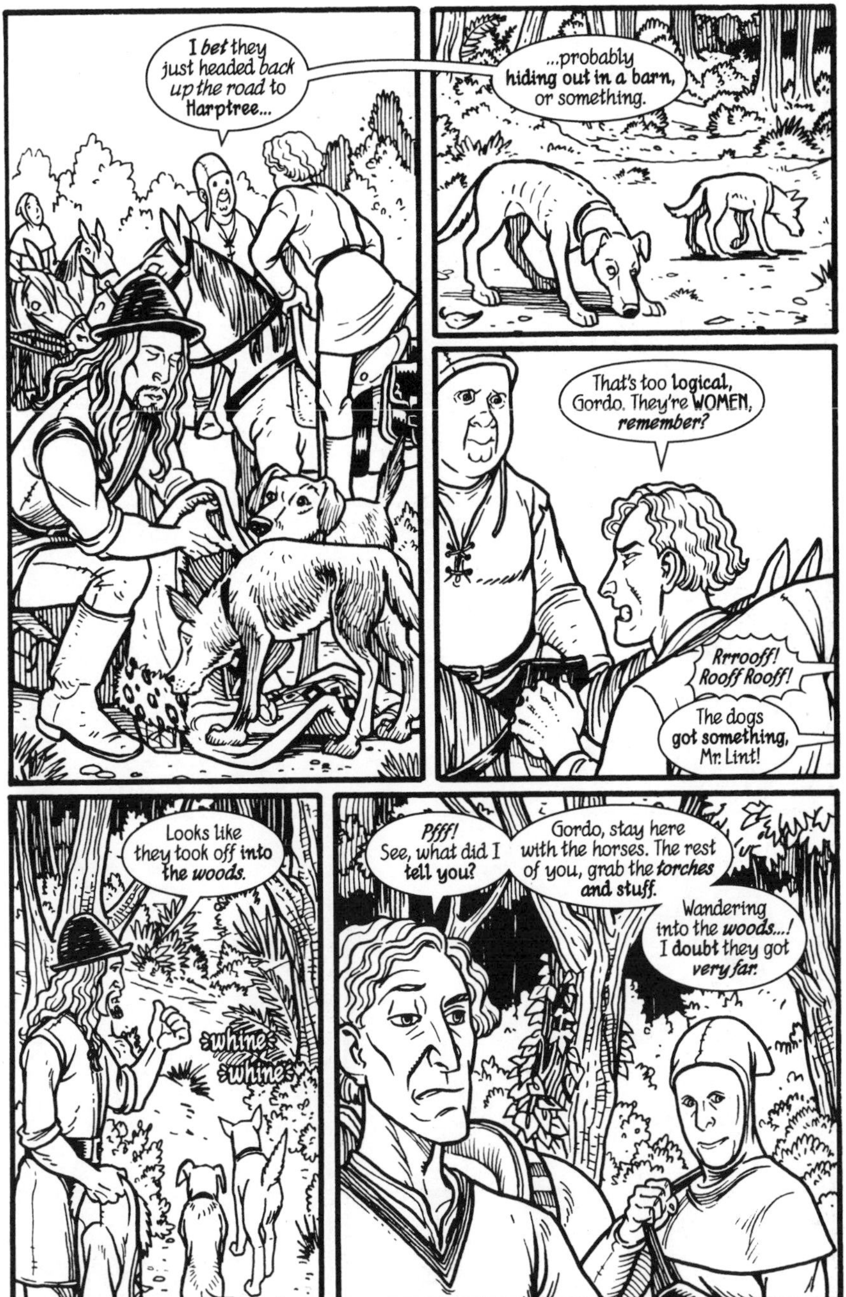
I *bet* they just headed back *up the road* to **Harptree...**
...probably **hiding out in a barn,** or something.
That's too **logical,** Gordo. They're **WOMEN,** ***remember?***
Rrrooff! Rooff Rooff!
The dogs **got something,** Mr. Lint!
Looks like they took off **into the *woods*.**
whine whine
Pfff! See, what did I **tell you?**
Gordo, stay here with the horses. The rest of you, grab the ***torches* and stuff.**
Wandering into the ***woods...!*** I **doubt** they got ***very far.***

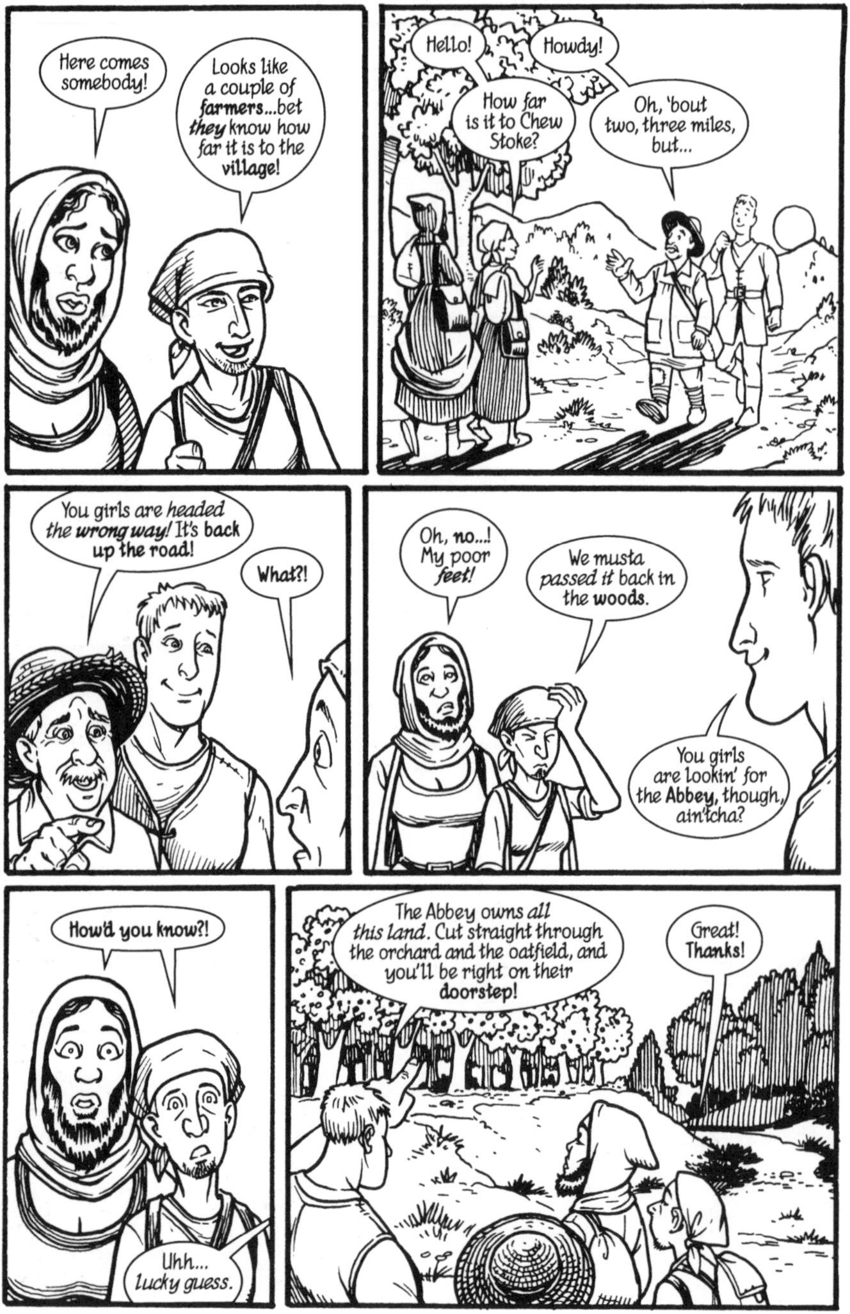
Here comes somebody!
Looks like a couple of **farmers**...bet ***they*** know how far it is to the **village**!
Hello!
Howdy!
How far is it to Chew Stoke?
Oh, 'bout two, three miles, but...
You girls are *headed* the ***wrong way***! It's **back up the road**!
What?!
Oh, **no**...! My poor ***feet***!
We musta *passed it* back in the **woods**.
You girls are lookin' for the **Abbey**, though, ain'tcha?
How'd you know?!
Uhh... *lucky guess.*
The Abbey owns *all this land*. Cut straight through the orchard and the oatfield, and you'll be right on their **doorstep**!
Great! **Thanks!**

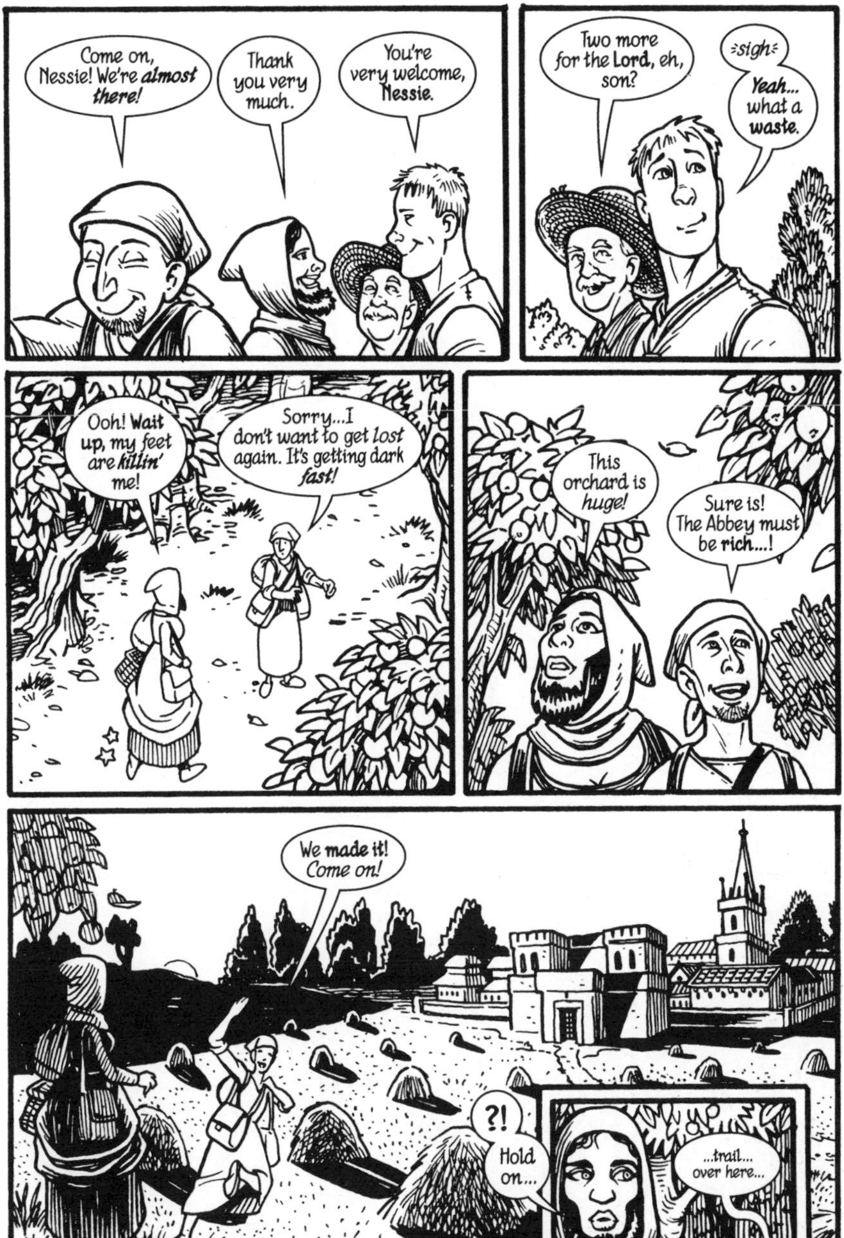
Come on, Nessie! We're *almost there!*
Thank you very much.
You're very welcome, **Nessie.**
Two more for the **Lord**, eh, son?
sigh
Yeah... what a **waste.**
Ooh! **Wait up**, my feet are ***killin'*** me!
Sorry...I don't want to get *lost* again. It's getting dark ***fast!***
This orchard is *huge!*
Sure is! The Abbey must be **rich...!**
We **made it!** *Come on!*
?!
Hold on...
...trail... over here...

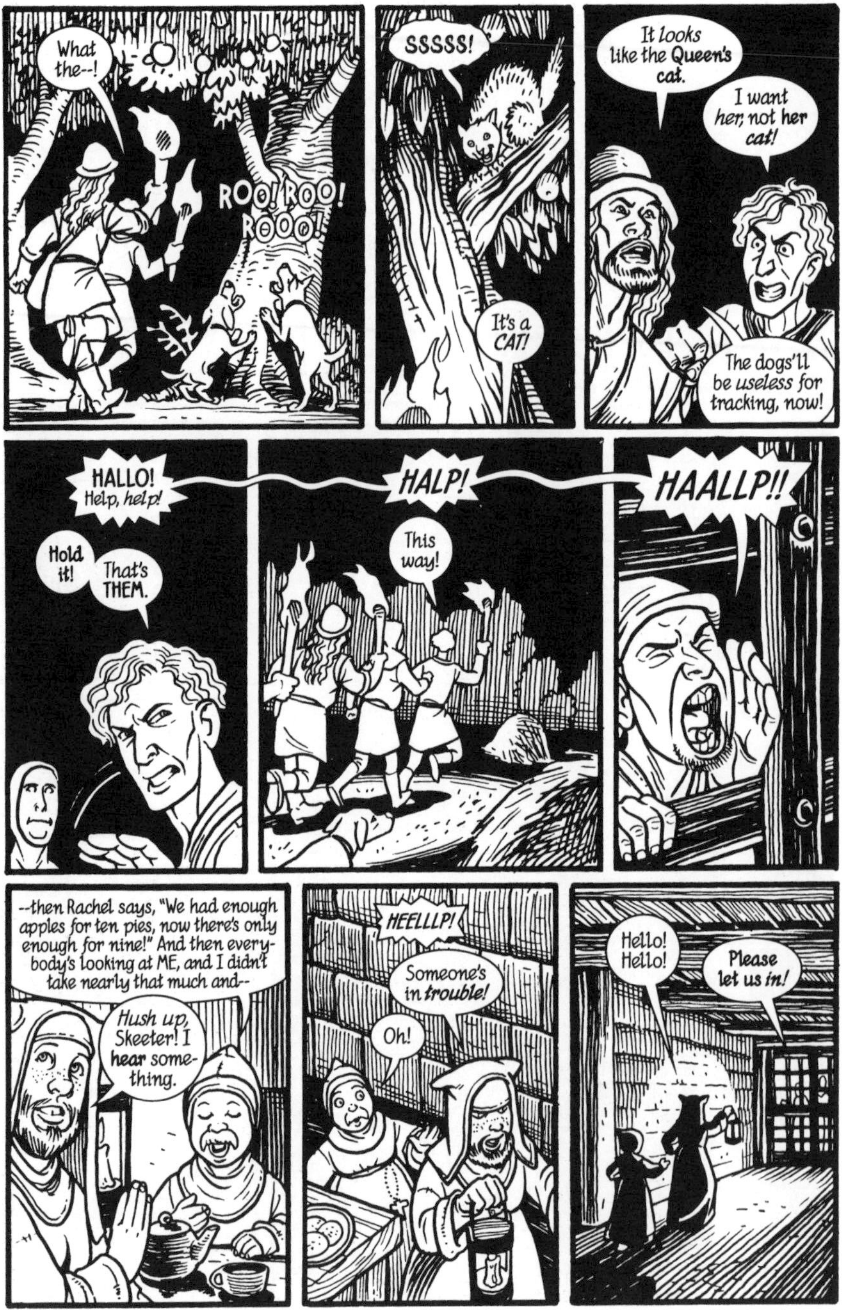
What the--!
ROO! ROO! ROOO!
SSSSS!
It's a CAT!
It looks like the Queen's cat.
I want her, not her cat!
The dogs'll be useless for tracking, now!
HALLO! Help, help!
HALP!
HAALLP!!
Hold it!
That's THEM.
This way!
--then Rachel says, "We had enough apples for ten pies, now there's only enough for nine!" And then everybody's looking at ME, and I didn't take nearly that much and--
Hush up, Skeeter! I hear something.
HEELLLP!
Someone's in trouble!
Oh!
Hello! Hello!
Please let us in!

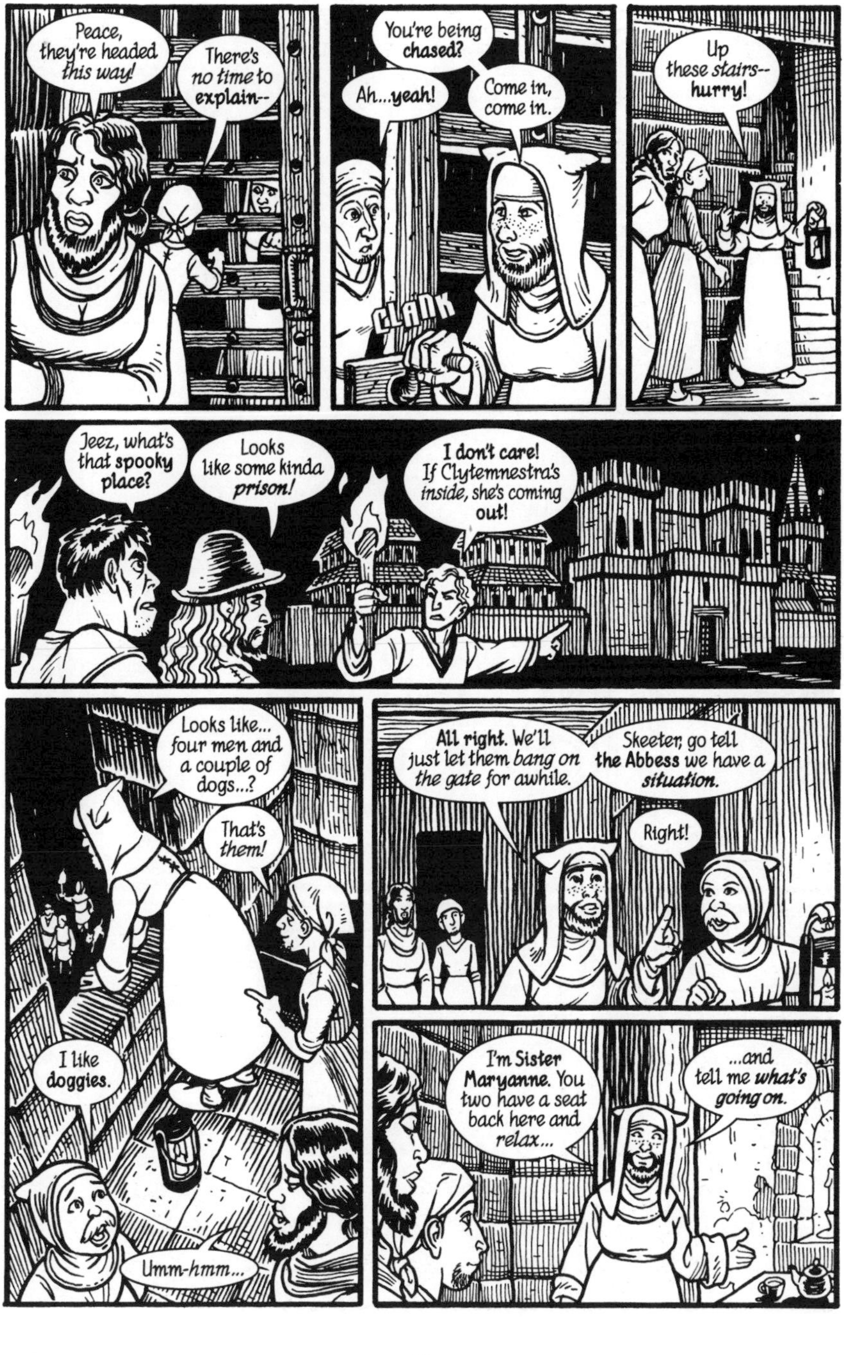
Peace, they're headed this way!
There's no time to explain--
You're being chased?
Ah...yeah!
Come in, come in.
CLANK
Up these stairs-- hurry!
Jeez, what's that spooky place?
Looks like some kinda prison!
I don't care! If Clytemnestra's inside, she's coming out!
Looks like... four men and a couple of dogs...?
That's them!
I like doggies.
Umm-hmm...
All right. We'll just let them bang on the gate for awhile.
Skeeter, go tell the Abbess we have a situation.
Right!
I'm Sister Maryanne. You two have a seat back here and relax...
...and tell me what's going on.

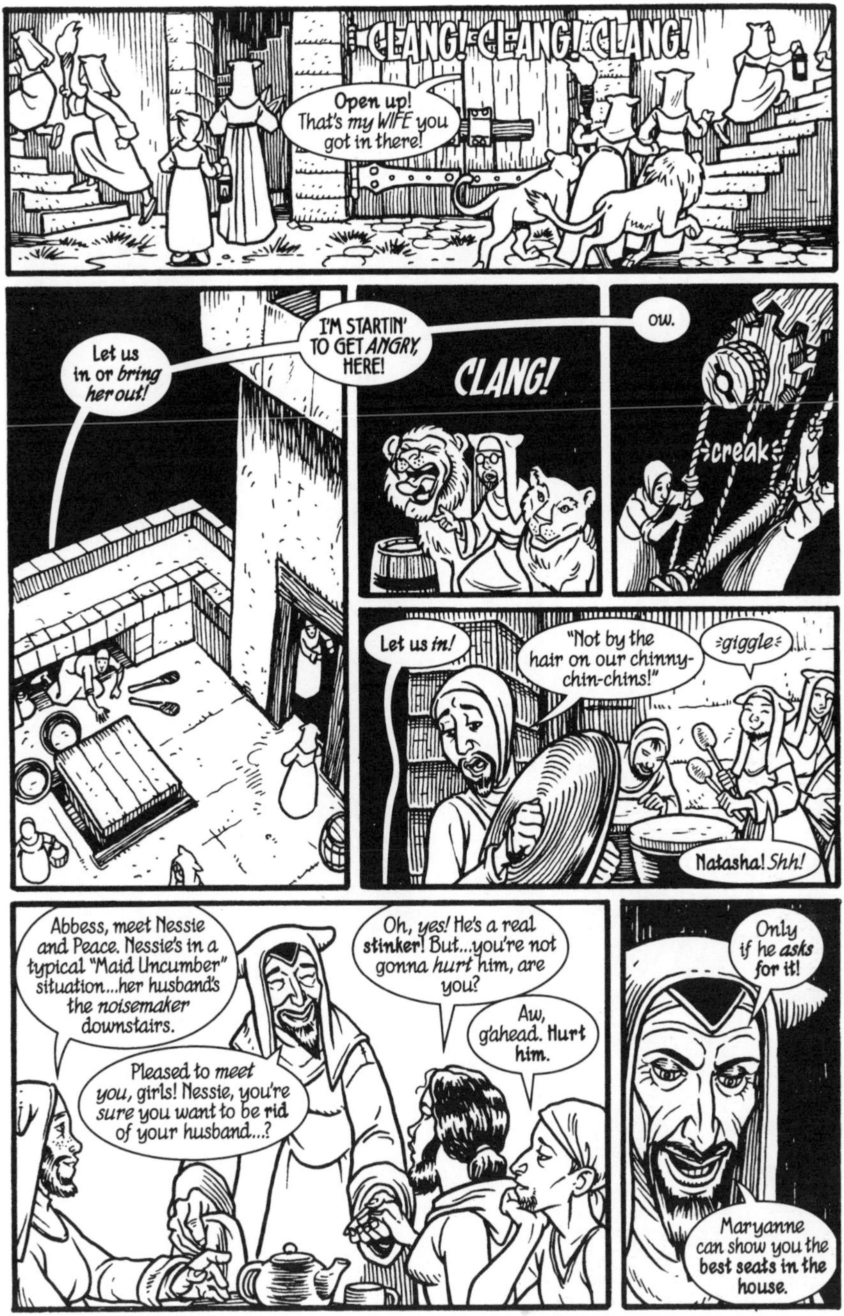
CLANG! CLANG! CLANG!
Open up! That's my *WIFE* you got in there!
Let us in or *bring her out!*
I'M STARTIN' TO GET *ANGRY*, HERE!
CLANG!
OW.
creak
Let us *in!*
"Not by the hair on our chinny-chin-chins!"
giggle
Natasha! *Shh!*
Abbess, meet Nessie and Peace. Nessie's in a typical "Maid Uncumber" situation...her husband's the *noisemaker* downstairs.
Pleased to *meet you*, girls! Nessie, you're *sure* you want to be **rid** of your husband...?
Oh, *yes!* He's a real **stinker**! But...you're not gonna *hurt* him, are you?
Aw, g'ahead. **Hurt him.**
Only if he *asks* for it!
Maryanne can show you the **best seats in the house.**

Chapter 15.

· SOLICITINE PT. 3 ·

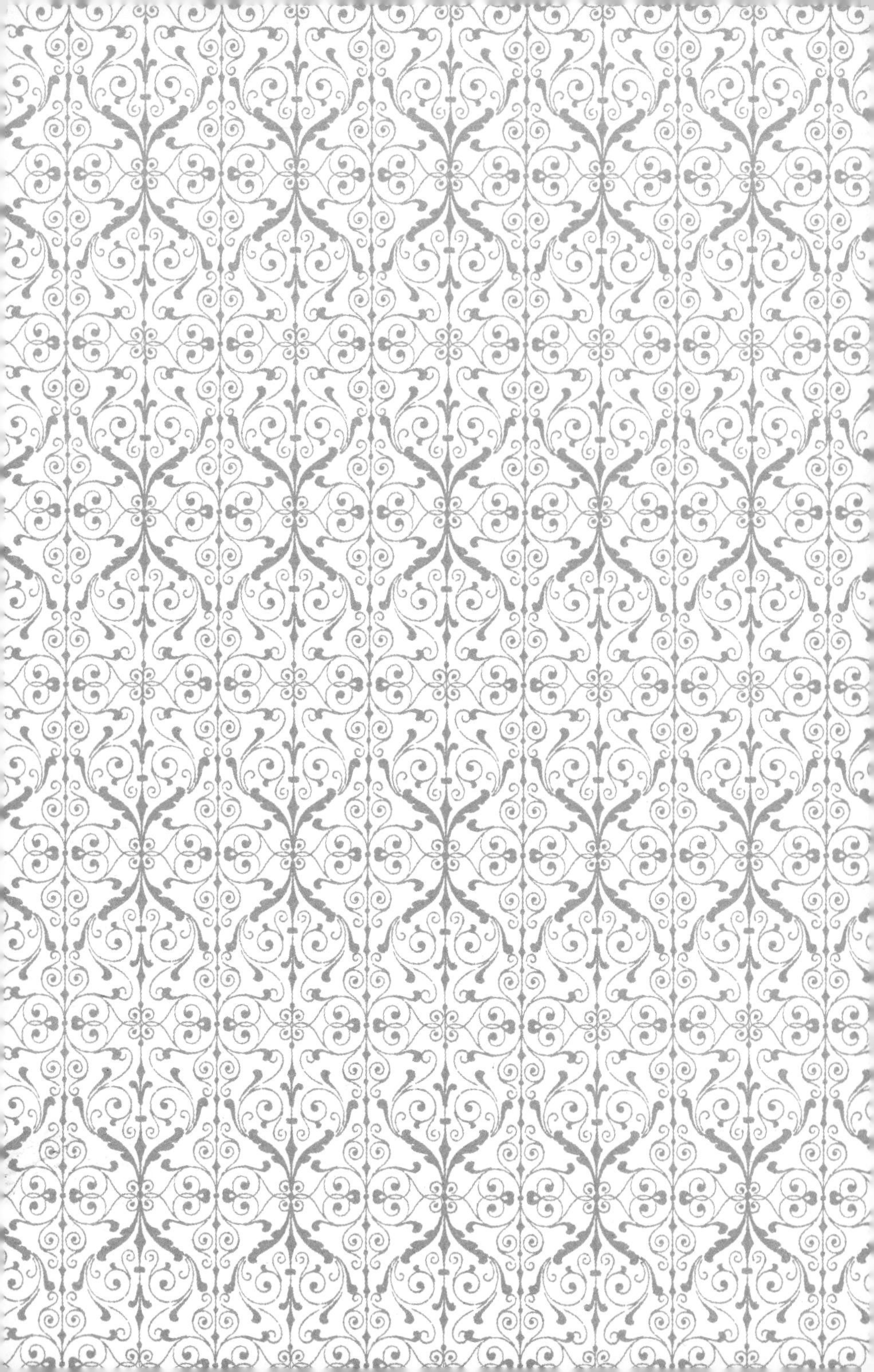

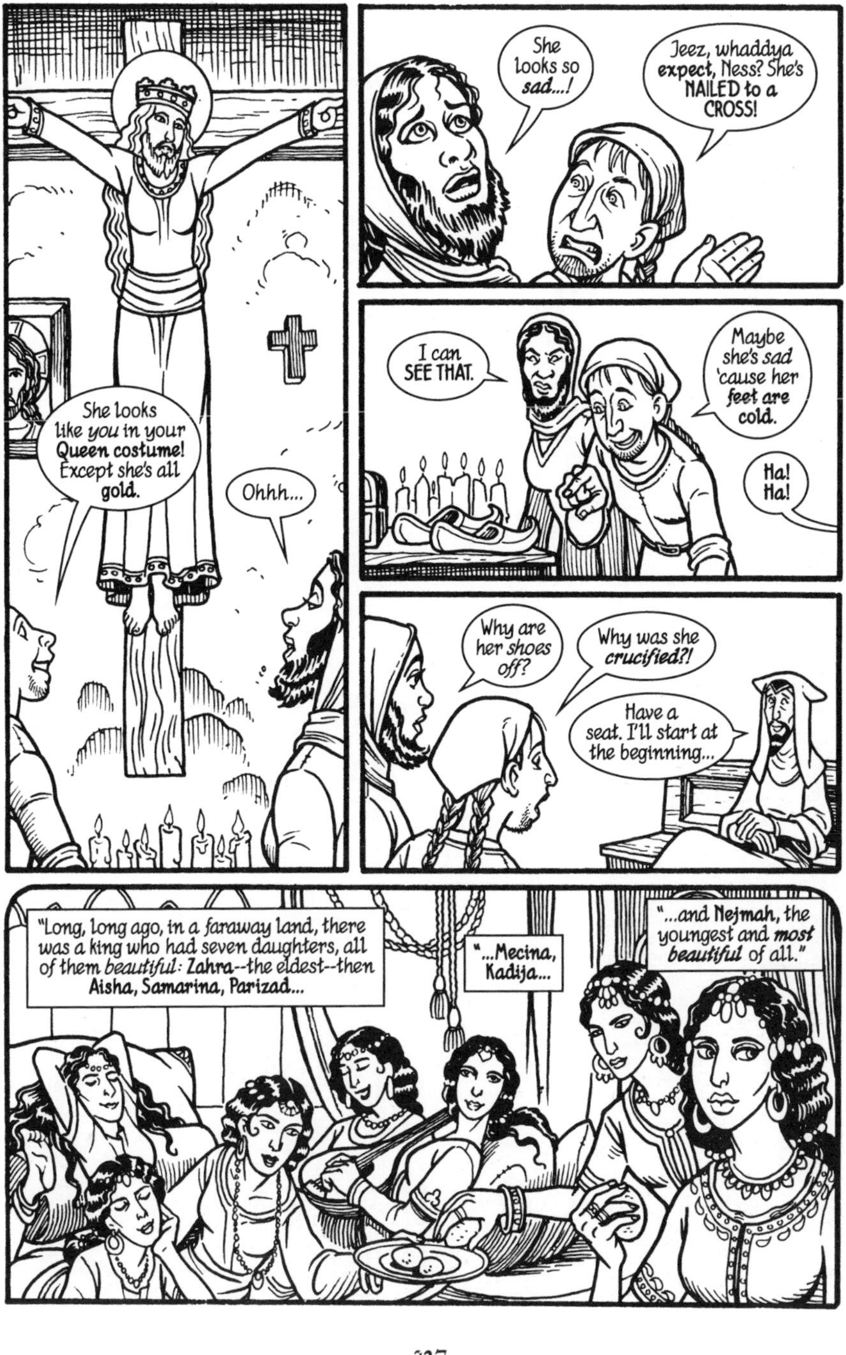
She looks like *you* in your **Queen costume**! Except she's all **gold**.
Ohhh...
She looks so *sad*...!
Jeez, whaddya **expect**, Ness? She's **NAILED to a CROSS!**
I can **SEE THAT.**
Maybe she's *sad* 'cause her *feet are* **cold.**
Ha! Ha!
Why are her *shoes* off?
Why was she *crucified?!*
Have a seat. I'll start at the beginning...
"Long, long ago, in a *faraway* land, there was a king who had seven daughters, all of them *beautiful*: **Zahra**--the eldest--then **Aisha, Samarina, Parizad...**
"...**Mecina, Kadija...**
"...and **Nejmah**, the youngest and ***most beautiful*** of all."

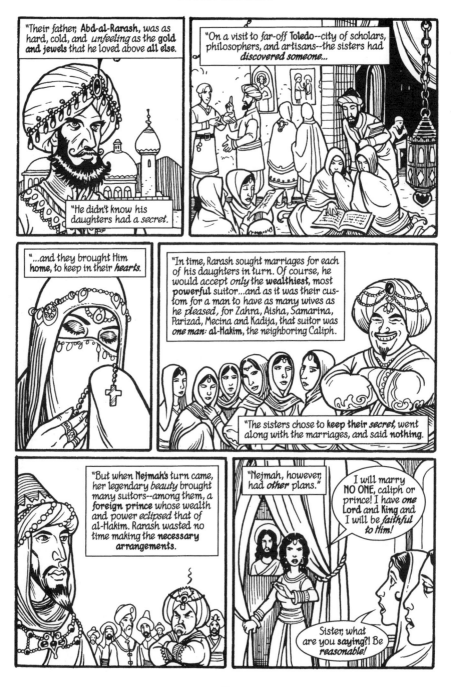

"Their father, **Abd-al-Rarash,** was as hard, cold, and *unfeeling* as the **gold and jewels** that he loved above all else.

"He didn't know his daughters had a *secret*.

"On a visit to far-off **Toledo**--city of scholars, philosophers, and artisans--the sisters had *discovered someone...*

"...and they brought Him home, to keep in their *hearts*.

"In time, Rarash sought marriages for each of his daughters in turn. Of course, he would accept *only* the **wealthiest**, most **powerful** suitor...and as it was their custom for a man to have as many wives as he *pleased*, for Zahra, Aisha, Samarina, Parizad, Mecina and Kadija, that suitor was *one man*: al-Hakim, the neighboring Caliph.

"The sisters chose to **keep their** *secret*, went along with the marriages, and said **nothing**.

"But when **Nejmah's** turn came, her legendary *beauty* brought many suitors--among them, a **foreign prince** whose wealth and power *eclipsed* that of al-Hakim. Rarash wasted no time making the **necessary arrangements.**

"Nejmah, however, had *other* plans."

I will marry **NO ONE,** caliph or prince! I have *one* Lord and King and I will be *faithful to Him!*

Sister, what are you *saying*?! Be *reasonable!*

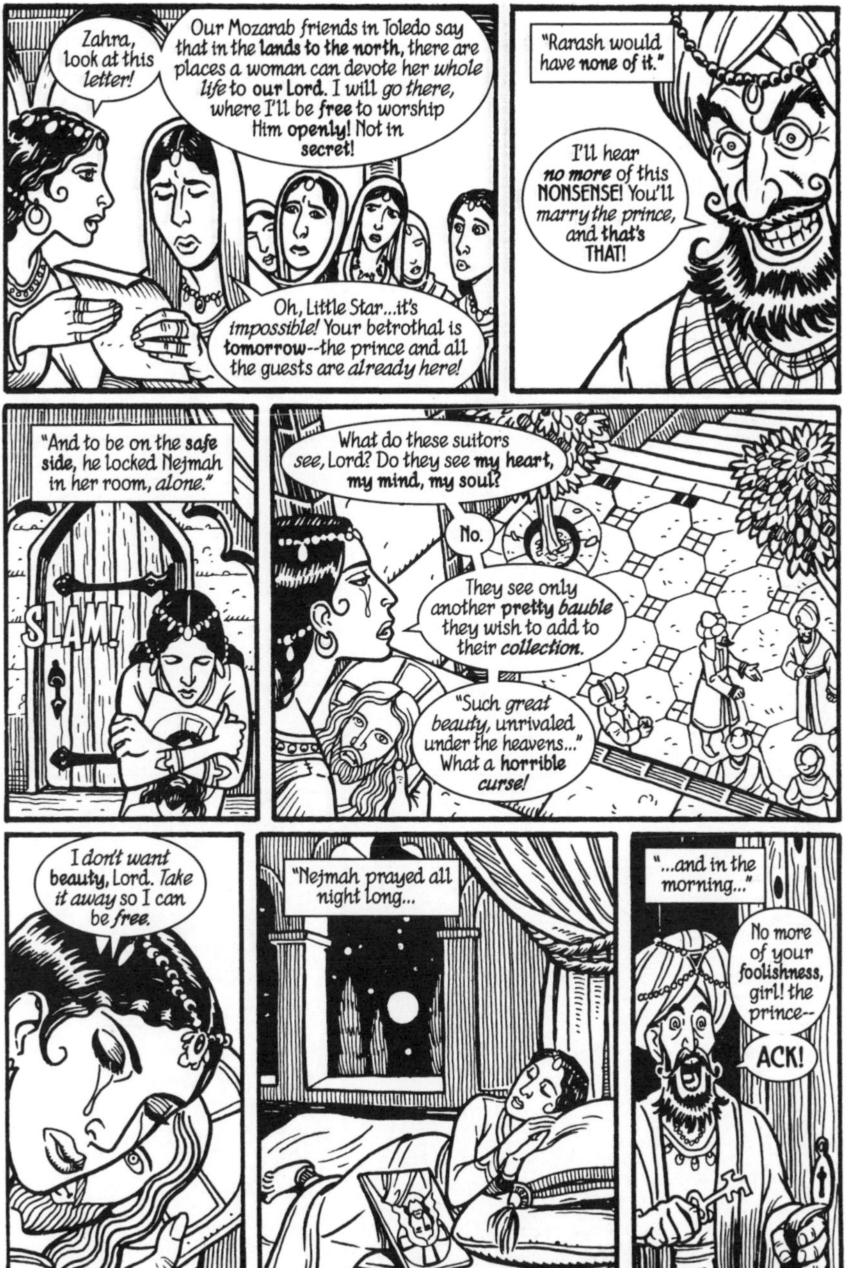
Zahra, look at this *letter!*
Our Mozarab *friends* in Toledo say that in the **lands to the north**, there are places a woman can devote her *whole life* to **our Lord**. I will *go there*, where I'll be **free** to worship Him **openly**! Not in **secret**!
Oh, Little Star...it's *impossible!* Your betrothal is **tomorrow**--the prince and all the guests are *already here!*
"Rarash would have **none of it.**"
I'll hear ***no more*** of this **NONSENSE!** You'll *marry the prince,* and **that's THAT!**
"And to be on the **safe side,** he locked Nejmah in her room, *alone."*
SLAM!
What do these suitors *see,* Lord? Do they see **my heart, my mind, my soul?**
No.
They see only another **pretty *bauble*** they wish to add to their ***collection.***
"Such *great beauty,* unrivaled under the heavens..." What a **horrible *curse!***
I *don't want* **beauty,** Lord. *Take it away* so I can be *free.*
"Nejmah prayed all night long...
"...and in the morning..."
No more of your **foolishness,** girl! the prince--
ACK!

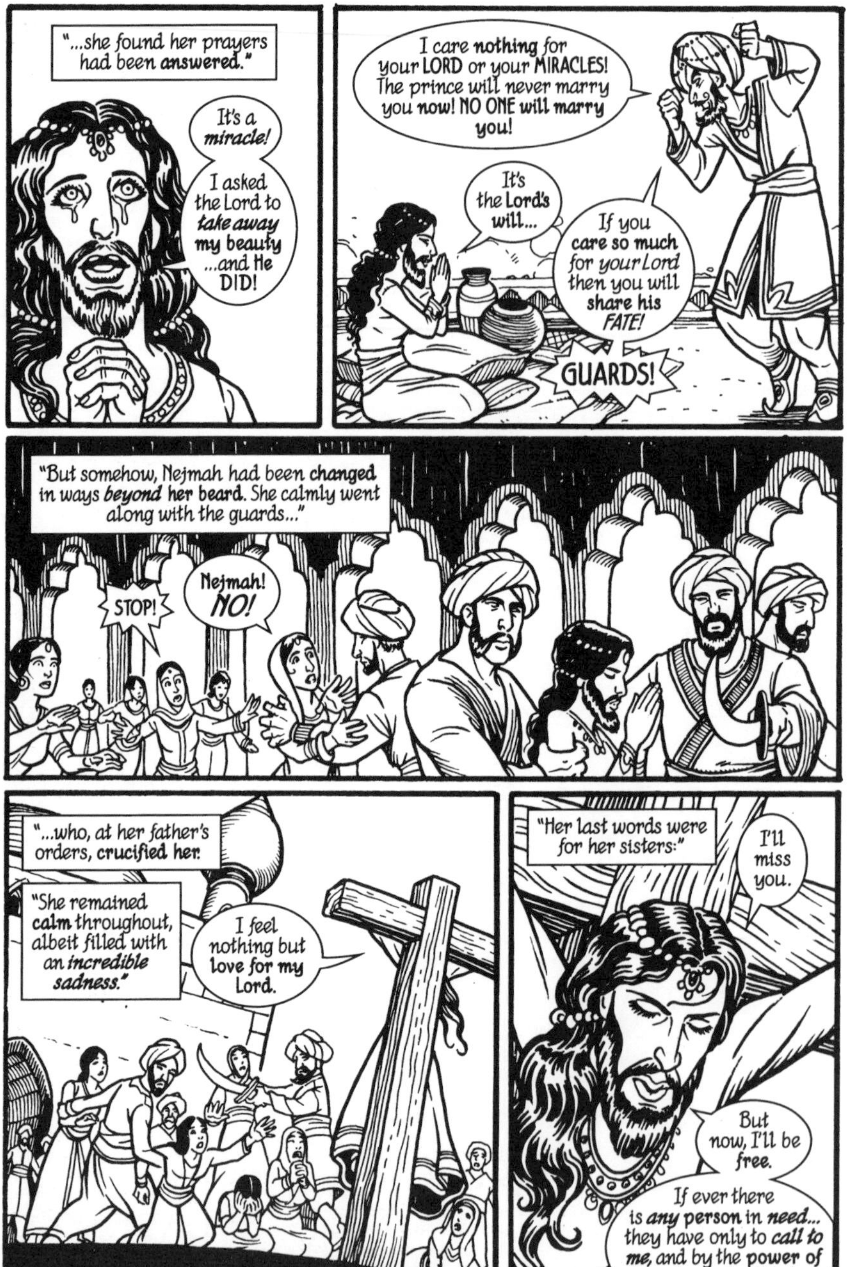
"...she found her prayers had been answered."
It's a miracle!
I asked the Lord to take away my beauty ...and He DID!
I care nothing for your LORD or your MIRACLES! The prince will never marry you now! NO ONE will marry you!
It's the Lord's will...
If you care so much for your Lord then you will share his FATE!
GUARDS!
"But somehow, Nejmah had been changed in ways beyond her beard. She calmly went along with the guards..."
STOP!
Nejmah! NO!
"...who, at her father's orders, crucified her.
"She remained calm throughout, albeit filled with an incredible sadness."
I feel nothing but love for my Lord.
"Her last words were for her sisters:"
I'll miss you.
But now, I'll be free.
If ever there is any person in need... they have only to call to me, and by the power of our Lord, I will help.

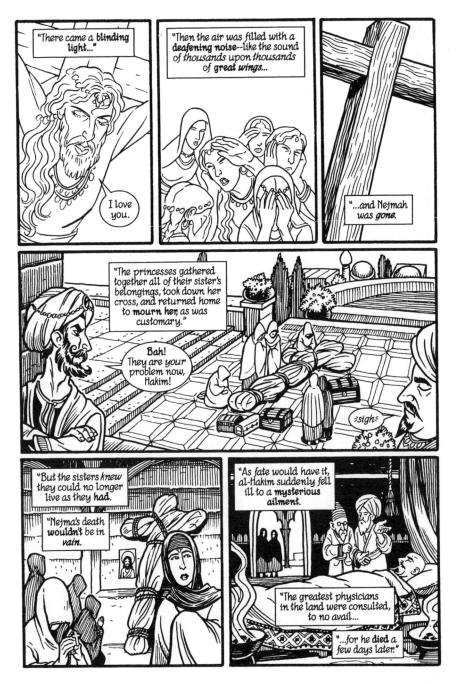

"There came a blinding light..."

I love you.

"Then the air was filled with a deafening noise--like the sound of *thousands* upon *thousands* of great *wings*...

"...and Nejmah was *gone*.

"The princesses gathered together all of their sister's belongings, took down her cross, and returned home to mourn her, as was customary."

Bah! They are *your* problem now, Hakim!

≈sigh≈

"But the sisters *knew* they could no longer live as they *had*.

"Nejma's death wouldn't be in vain.

"As fate would have it, al-Hakim suddenly fell ill to a mysterious ailment.

"The greatest physicians in the land were consulted, to no avail...

"...for he died a few days later."

"The sisters wasted no time.

"With the help of a few **trusted servants**--all of whom had converted, upon witnessing Nejmah's miracle--they packed up her relics, their belongings, and **all the caliph's gold**...

"And FLED.

"First to Toledo, where their friends helped the sisters find a guide to lead them **north**.

"In *every* land they passed through, the princesses spread the story of their martyred sister, determined that **Nejmah's miracle** would *not* die with her."

"On the *contrary*, her legend only **grew** as it *spread*!

"Monks in every land dutifully recorded those legends. Nejmah acquired a new name in every new land and language, **Wilge-forte**--or **"Holy Face"** among them.

"She also acquired a reputation as **Patron Saint** of *unhappily married and independent women*.

"No doubt her *sisters* had a hand in encouraging THAT.

Country folk believe, if a **wife** leaves an offering of a peck of OATS for the Saint, she'll use them to lure the husband's *horse*--presumably with *him* on it--straight to the Devil!

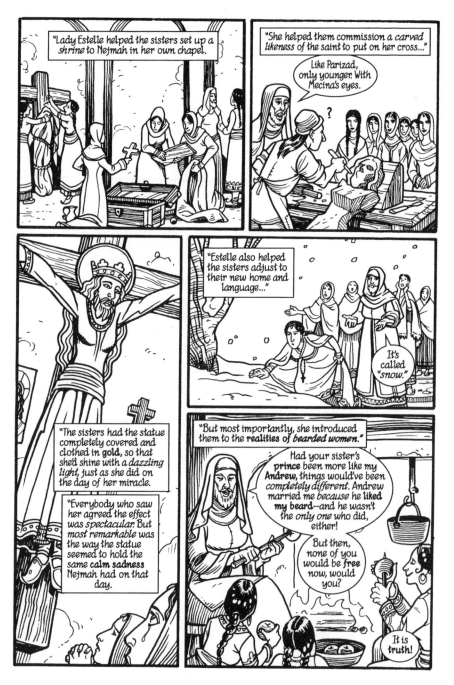

"Lady Estelle helped the sisters set up a *shrine* to Nejmah in her own chapel.

"She helped them commission *a carved likeness* of the saint to put on her cross..."

Like Parizad, only *younger*. With Mecina's eyes.

?

"The sisters had the statue completely covered and clothed in **gold**, so that she'd shine with a *dazzling light*, just as she did on the day of her miracle.

"Everybody who saw her agreed the effect was *spectacular*. But most remarkable was the way the statue seemed to hold the same **calm sadness** Nejmah had on that day.

"Estelle also helped the sisters adjust to their new home and language..."

It's called *"snow."*

"But most importantly, she introduced them to the **realities** of *bearded women*."

Had your sister's **prince** been more like my **Andrew**, things would've been *completely different*. Andrew married me because he **liked** my beard--and he wasn't the *only one* who did, either!

But then, none of you would be **free** now, would you?

It is **truth!**

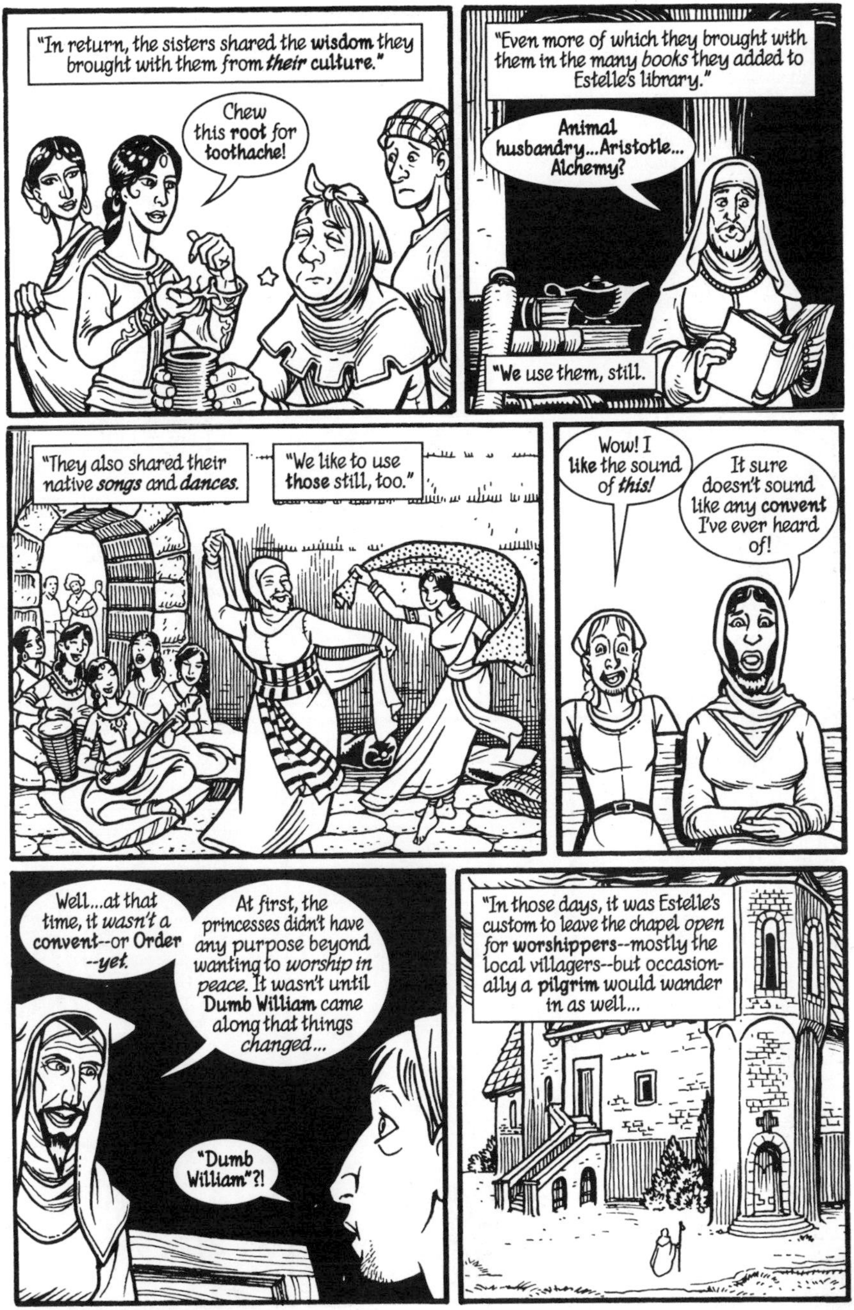
"In return, the sisters shared the **wisdom** they brought with them from ***their* culture.**"
Chew this **root** for toothache!
"Even more of which they brought with them in the many *books* they added to Estelle's library."
Animal husbandry...Aristotle... Alchemy?
"**We** use them, still.
"They also shared their native ***songs*** and ***dances***.
"We like to use **those** still, too."
Wow! I **like** the sound of ***this!***
It sure doesn't sound like any **convent** I've ever heard of!
Well...at that time, it *wasn't* a **convent**--or **Order** --***yet***.
At *first*, the princesses didn't have any purpose beyond wanting to *worship in peace*. It wasn't until **Dumb William** came along that things *changed*...
"Dumb William"?!
"In those days, it was Estelle's custom to leave the chapel *open* for **worshippers**--mostly the local villagers--but occasionally a **pilgrim** would wander in as well...

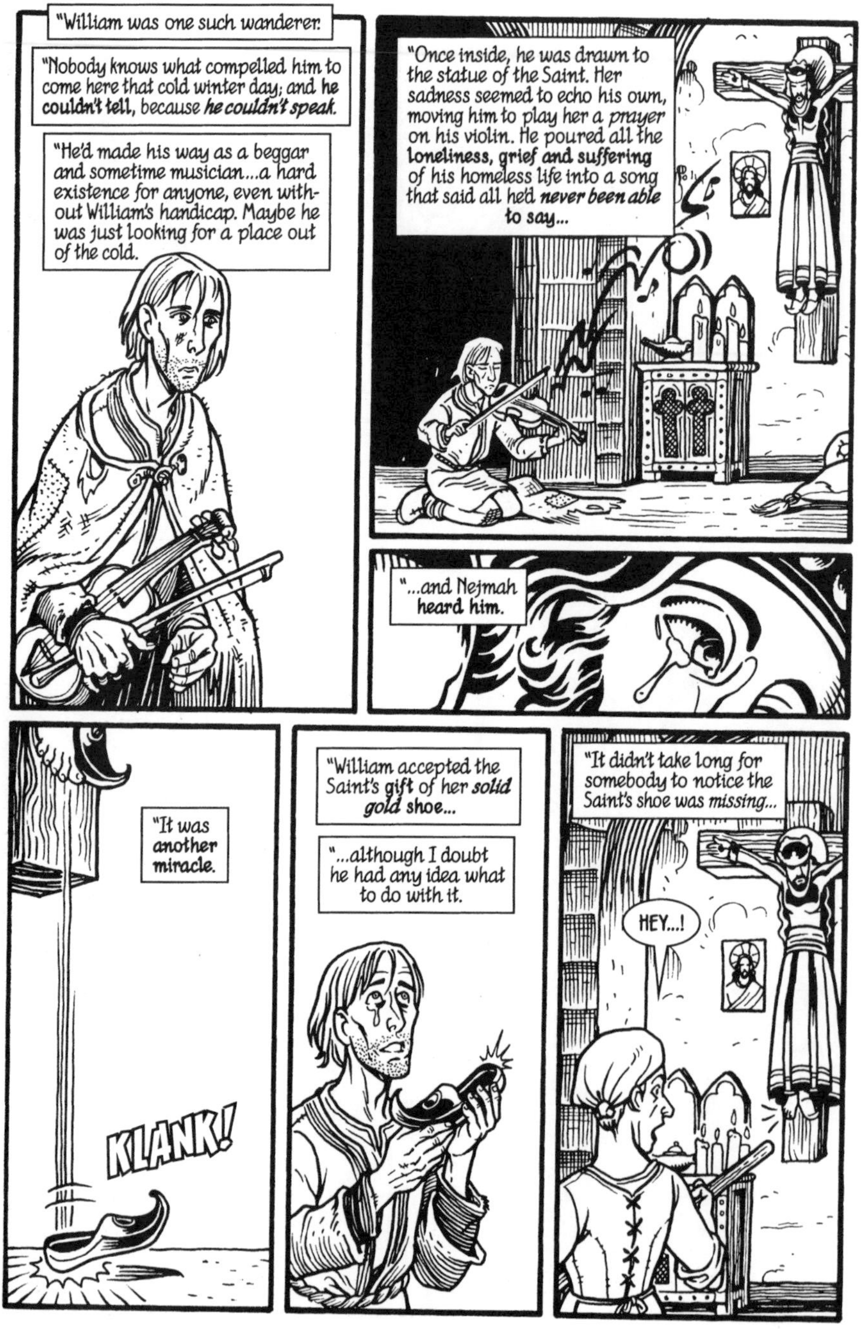
"William was one such wanderer.
"Nobody knows what compelled him to come here that cold winter day; and **he couldn't tell**, because ***he couldn't speak.***
"He'd made his way as a beggar and sometime musician...a hard existence for anyone, even without William's handicap. Maybe he was just looking for a place out of the cold.
"Once inside, he was drawn to the statue of the Saint. Her sadness seemed to echo his own, moving him to play her a *prayer* on his violin. He poured all the **loneliness, grief and suffering** of his homeless life into a song that said all he'd ***never been able* to say...**
"...and Nejmah **heard him.**
"It was **another miracle.**
KLANK!
"William accepted the Saint's **gift** of her ***solid gold*** **shoe...**
"...although I doubt he had any idea what to do with it.
"It didn't take long for somebody to notice the Saint's shoe was *missing*...
HEY...!

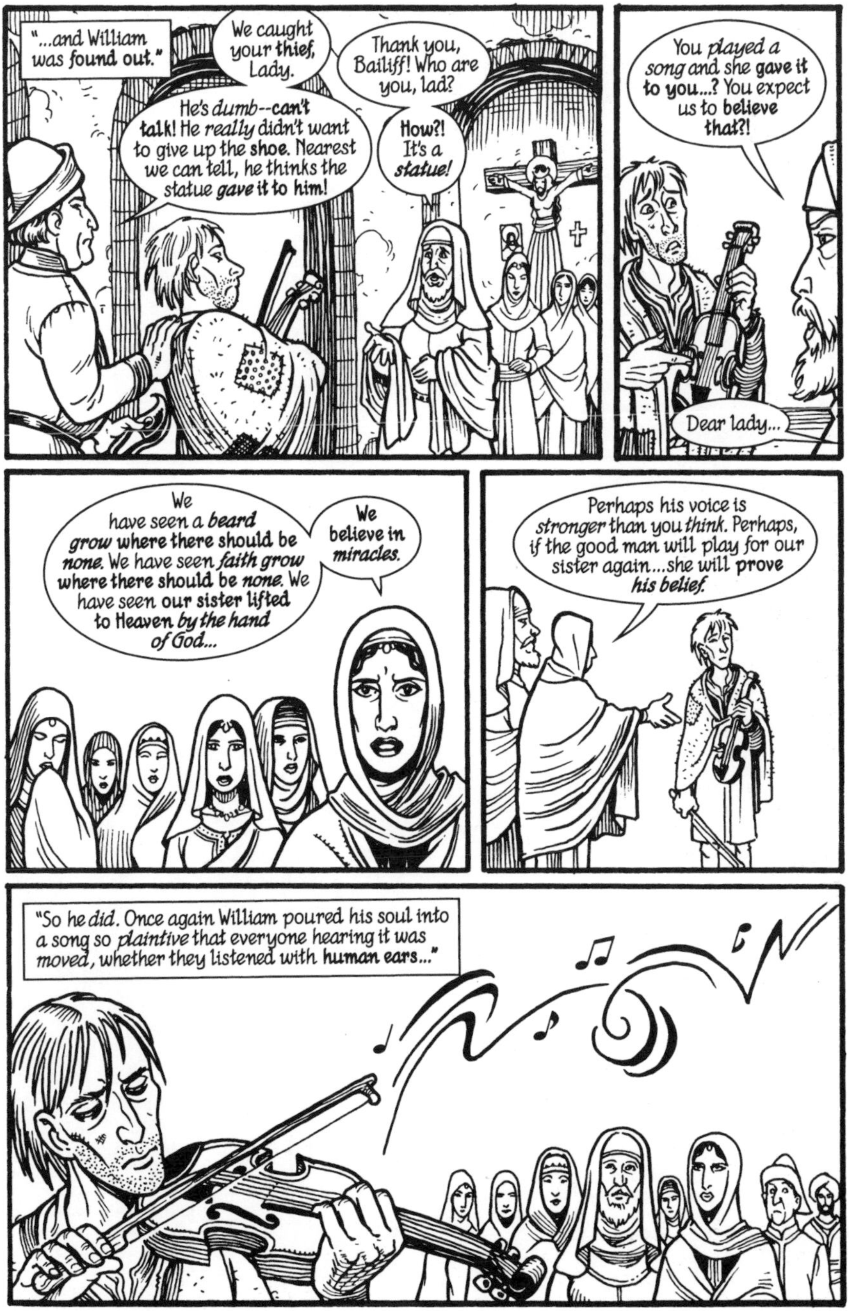
"...and William was **found out.**"
We caught your **thief**, Lady.
He's *dumb*--**can't talk**! He *really* didn't want to give up the **shoe**. Nearest we can tell, he thinks the statue ***gave* it to him**!
Thank you, Bailiff! Who are you, lad?
How?! It's a ***statue!***
You *played a song* and she **gave it to you**...? You expect us to **believe that?!**
Dear lady...
We have seen a ***beard grow*** **where there should be** ***none***. We have seen ***faith grow*** **where there should be** ***none***. We have seen **our sister lifted** to Heaven ***by the hand of God***...
We believe in *miracles*.
Perhaps his voice is *stronger* than you *think*. Perhaps, if the good man will play for our sister again...she will **prove *his belief*.**
"So he *did*. Once again William poured his soul into a song so *plaintive* that everyone hearing it was moved, whether they listened with **human ears**..."

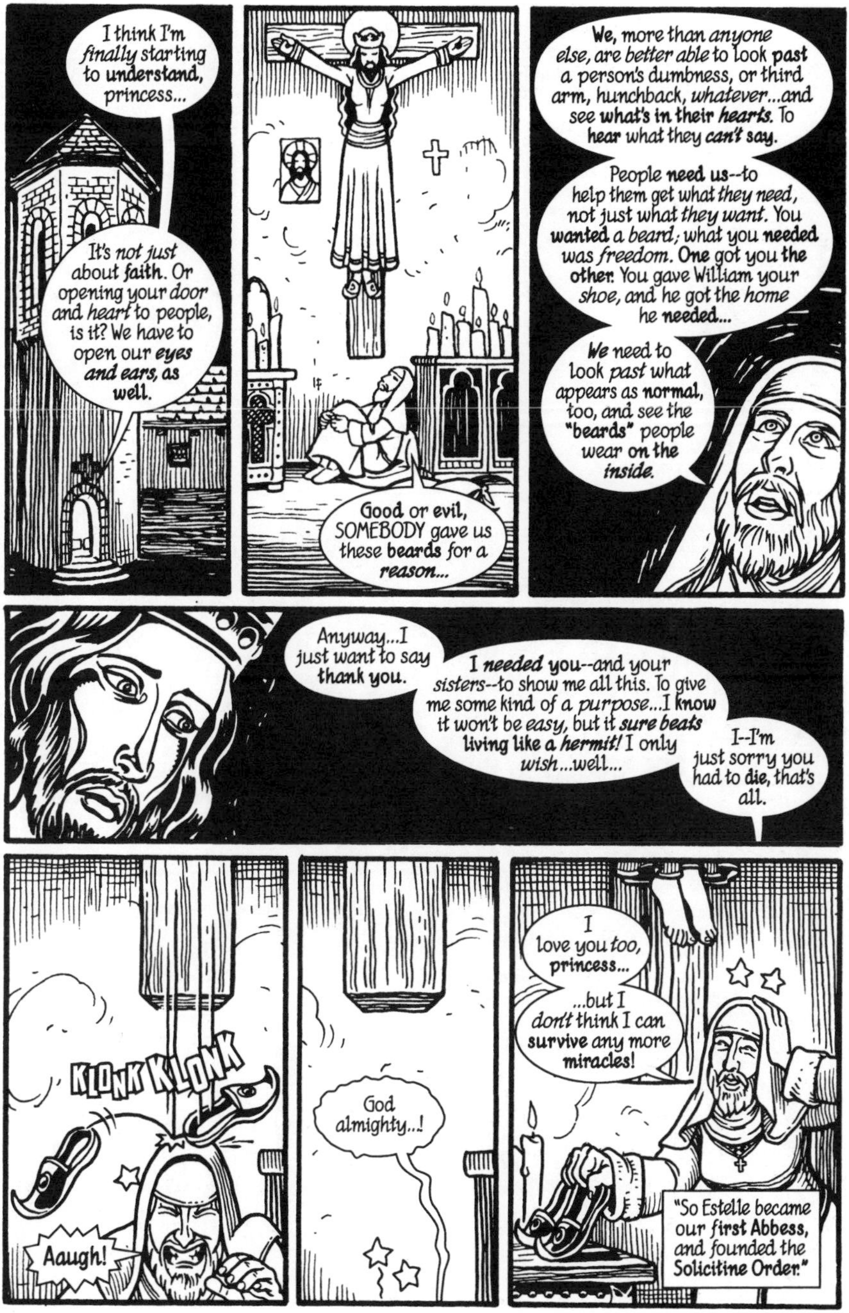
I think I'm *finally* starting to **understand,** princess...
It's *not just* about **faith.** Or opening your *door* and *heart* to people, is it? We have to open our ***eyes and ears,* as well.**
Good or evil, SOMEBODY gave us these **beards** for a ***reason...***
We, more than *anyone else,* are *better able* to look **past** a person's dumbness, or third arm, hunchback, *whatever*...and see **what's in their *hearts*.** To **hear** what they ***can't*** **say.**
People **need us**--to help them get what *they need,* not just what *they want.* You **wanted** a *beard;* what you **needed** was *freedom.* **One** got you **the other.** You gave William your *shoe,* and he got the *home* he **needed...**
We need to look *past* what appears as **normal,** too, and see the **"beards"** people wear **on the *inside*.**
Anyway...I just want to say **thank you.**
I ***needed*** **you**--and your *sisters*--to show me all this. To give me some kind of a *purpose*...I **know** it won't be *easy,* but it ***sure beats*** **living like a *hermit!*** I only *wish*...well...
I--I'm just sorry you had to **die,** that's all.
KLONK KLONK
Aaugh!
God almighty...!
I love you *too,* **princess...**
...but I *don't* think I can **survive** any more **miracles!**
"So Estelle became our *first* **Abbess,** and founded the **Solicitine Order."**

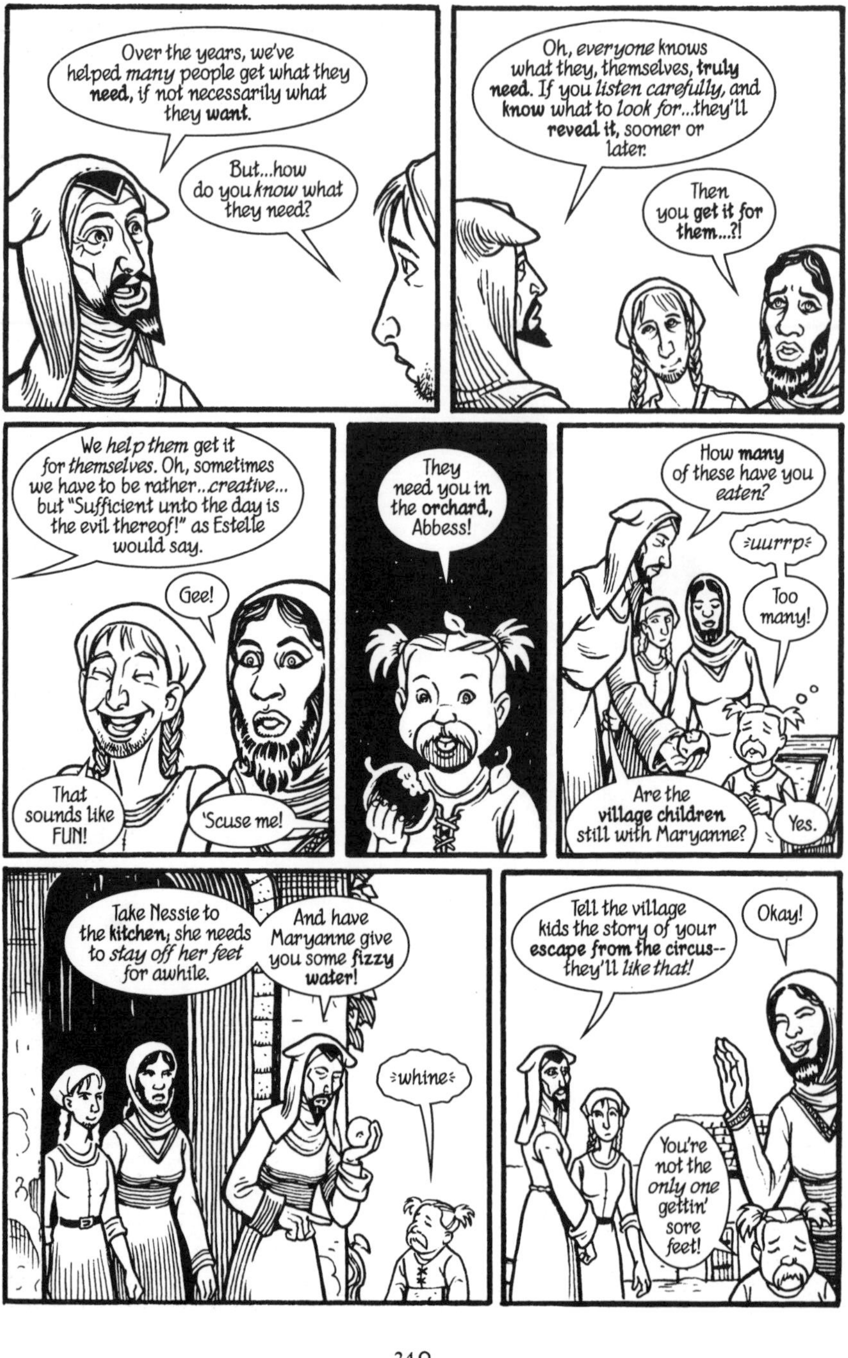
Over the years, we've helped *many* people get what they **need**, if not necessarily what they **want**.
But...how do you *know* what they need?
Oh, *everyone* knows what they, themselves, **truly need**. If you *listen carefully*, and **know** what to *look for*...they'll **reveal it**, sooner or later.
Then you **get it for them**...?!
We *help them* get it for *themselves*. Oh, sometimes we have to be rather...*creative*... but "Sufficient unto the day is the evil thereof!" as Estelle would say.
Gee!
That sounds like FUN!
'Scuse me!
They need you in the **orchard**, Abbess!
How **many** of these have you *eaten*?
uurrp
Too many!
Are the **village children** still with Maryanne?
Yes.
Take Nessie to the **kitchen**; she needs to *stay off her feet* for awhile.
And have Maryanne give you some **fizzy water**!
whine
Tell the village kids the story of your **escape from the circus**-- they'll *like that!*
Okay!
You're not the *only one* gettin' sore feet!

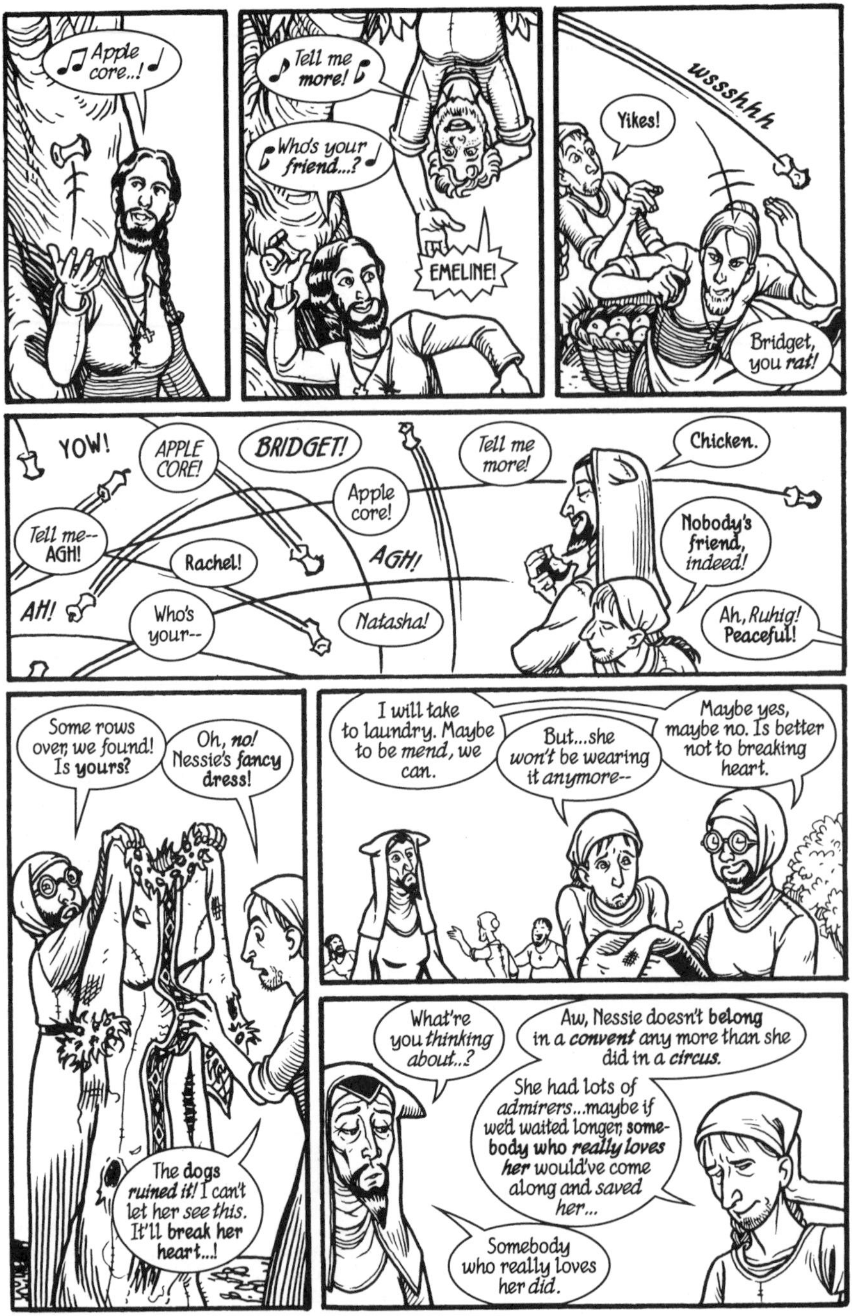
♫ Apple core...! ♩
♪ Tell me more! ♪
♪ Who's your friend...? ♩
EMELINE!
wssshhh
Yikes!
Bridget, you rat!
YOW!
APPLE CORE!
BRIDGET!
Tell me more!
Chicken.
Apple core!
Tell me-- AGH!
Nobody's friend, indeed!
Rachel!
AGH!
AH!
Who's your--
Natasha!
Ah, Ruhig! Peaceful!
Some rows over, we found! Is yours?
Oh, no! Nessie's fancy dress!
The dogs ruined it! I can't let her see this. It'll break her heart...!
I will take to laundry. Maybe to be mend, we can.
But...she won't be wearing it anymore--
Maybe yes, maybe no. Is better not to breaking heart.
What're you thinking about...?
Aw, Nessie doesn't belong in a convent any more than she did in a circus.
She had lots of admirers...maybe if we'd waited longer, somebody who really loves her would've come along and saved her...
Somebody who really loves her did.

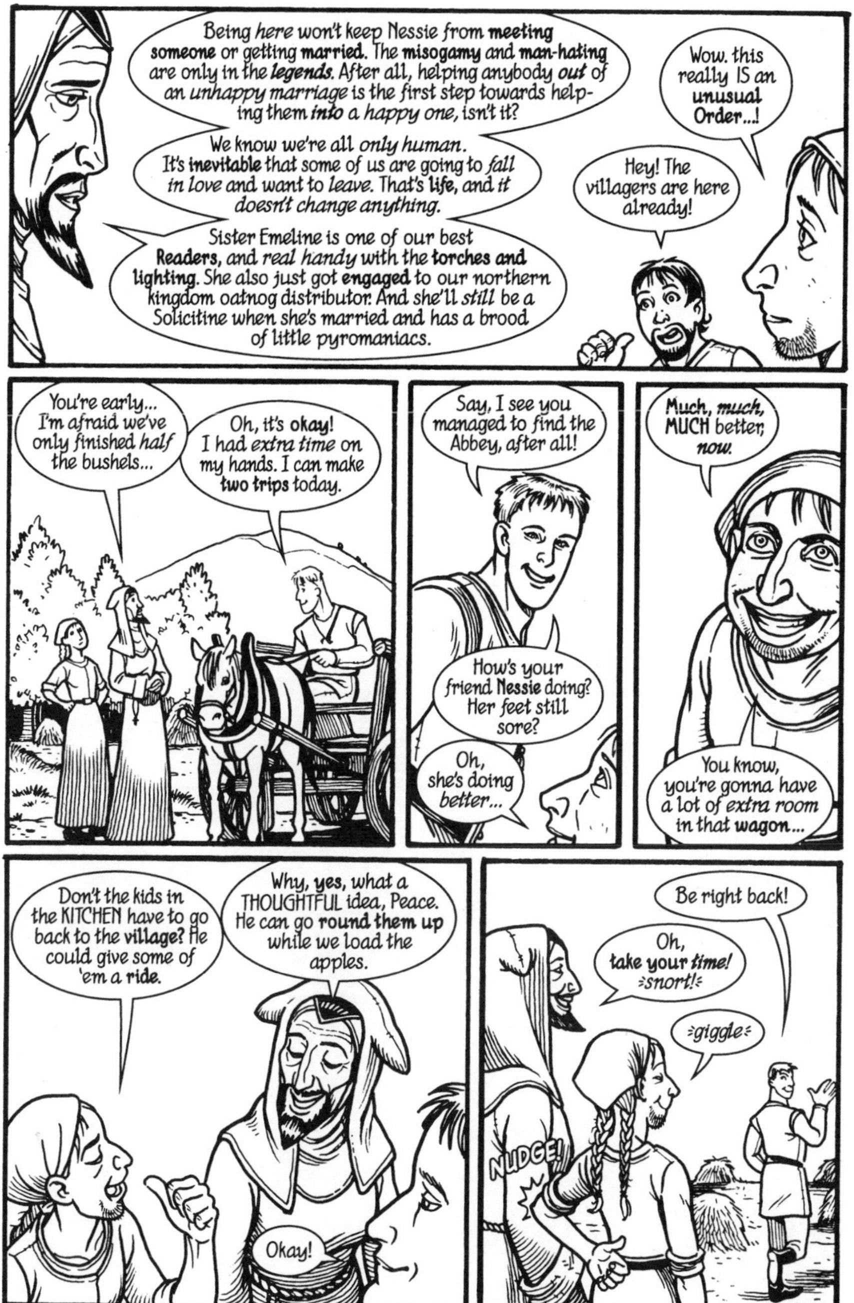
Being *here* won't keep Nessie *from* **meeting someone** or getting **married**. The **misogamy** and **man-hating** are only in the ***legends***. After all, helping anybody ***out*** of an *unhappy marriage* is the *first step towards help-ing* them ***into*** a *happy one*, isn't it?
We know we're all *only human*. It's **inevitable** that some of us are going to *fall in love* and want to *leave*. That's **life**, and *it doesn't change anything*.
Sister Emeline is one of our best **Readers**, and *real handy* with the **torches and lighting**. She also just got **engaged** to our northern kingdom oatnog distributor. And she'll *still* be a Solicitine when she's married and has a brood of little pyromaniacs.
Wow. this really IS an **unusual Order**...!
Hey! The villagers are here already!
You're early... I'm *afraid* we've only finished *half* the bushels...
Oh, it's **okay**! I had *extra time* on my hands. I can make **two trips** today.
Say, I see you managed to *find* the Abbey, *after* all!
How's your friend **Nessie** doing? Her *feet* still sore?
Oh, she's doing *better*...
Much, *much*, MUCH better, ***now***.
You know, you're gonna have a lot of *extra* room in that **wagon**...
Don't the kids in the KITCHEN have to go back to the **village**? He could give some of 'em a **ride**.
Why, **yes**, what a THOUGHTFUL idea, Peace. He can go **round them up** while we load the apples.
Okay!
Be right back!
Oh, **take your *time*!** *snort!*
giggle
NUDGE!

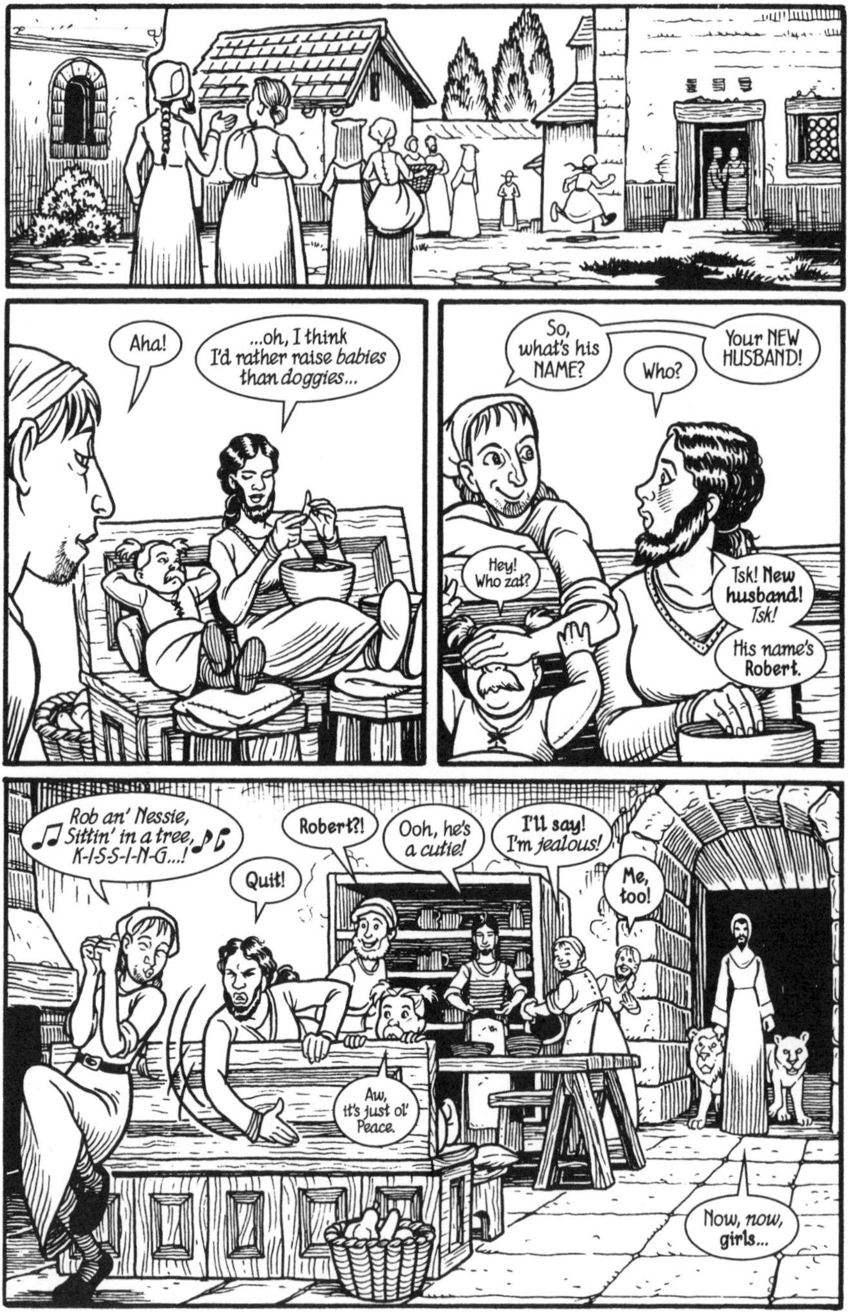
Aha!
...oh, I think I'd rather raise *babies* than *doggies*...
So, what's his NAME?
Who?
Your NEW HUSBAND!
Hey! Who zat?
Tsk! **New husband!** *Tsk!*
His name's **Robert.**
Rob an' Nessie, Sittin' in a tree, K-I-S-S-I-N-G...!
Quit!
Robert?!
Ooh, he's *a cutie!*
I'll say! I'm *jealous!*
Me, too!
Aw, it's just ol' Peace.
Now, now, **girls...**

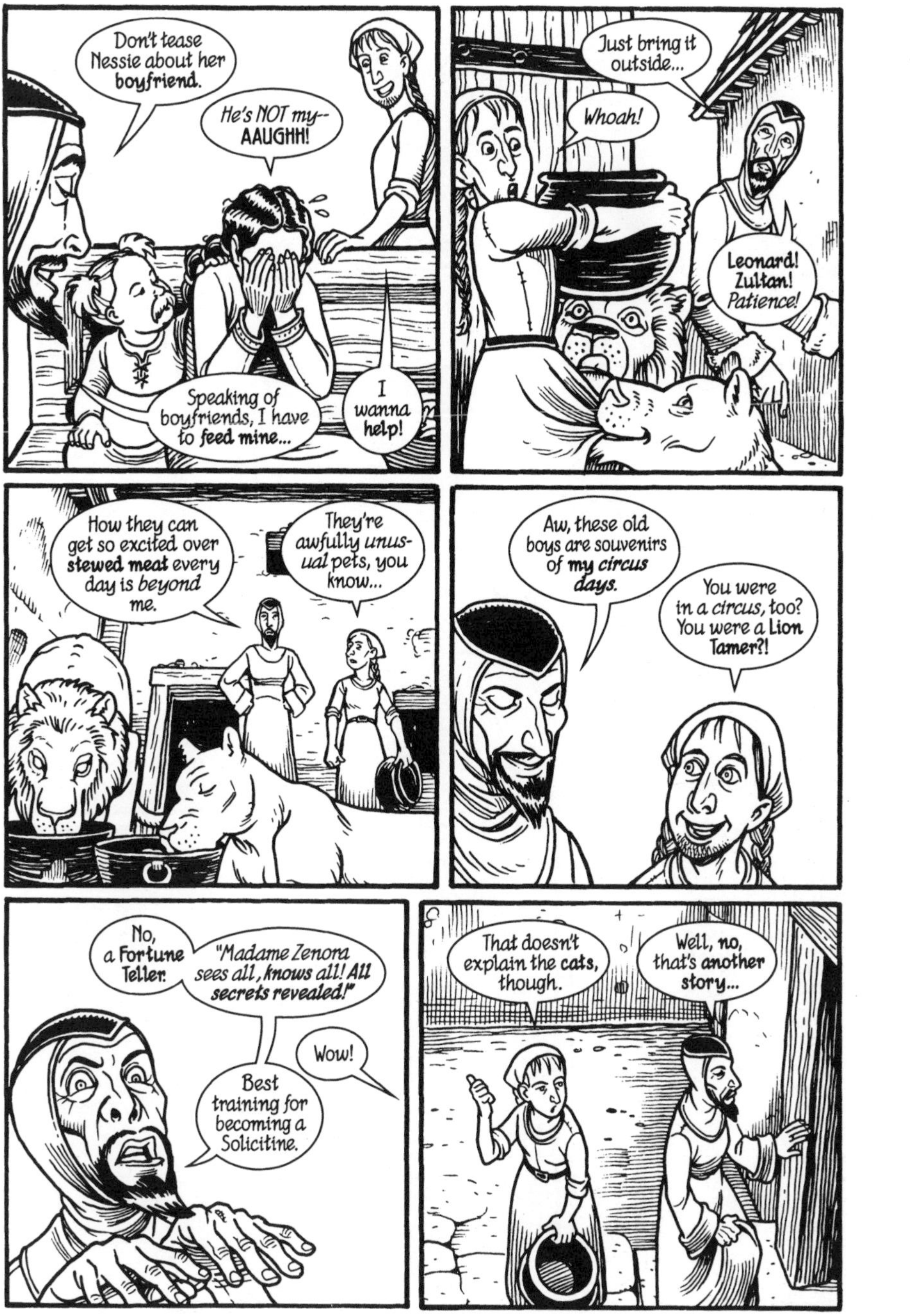
Don't tease Nessie about her **boyfriend**.
He's NOT my-- **AAUGHH!**
Speaking of boyfriends, I have to **feed mine...**
I wanna **help!**
Just bring it outside...
Whoah!
Leonard! Zultan! *Patience!*
How they can get so excited over **stewed meat** every day is *beyond* me.
They're awfully *unusual* pets, you know...
Aw, these old boys are souvenirs of **my *circus days.***
You were in a *circus,* too? You were a **Lion Tamer**?!
No, a **Fortune Teller.**
"Madame Zenora sees all, ***knows all! All secrets revealed!"***
Best training for becoming a Solicitine.
Wow!
That doesn't explain the **cats**, though.
Well, **no**, that's **another story...**

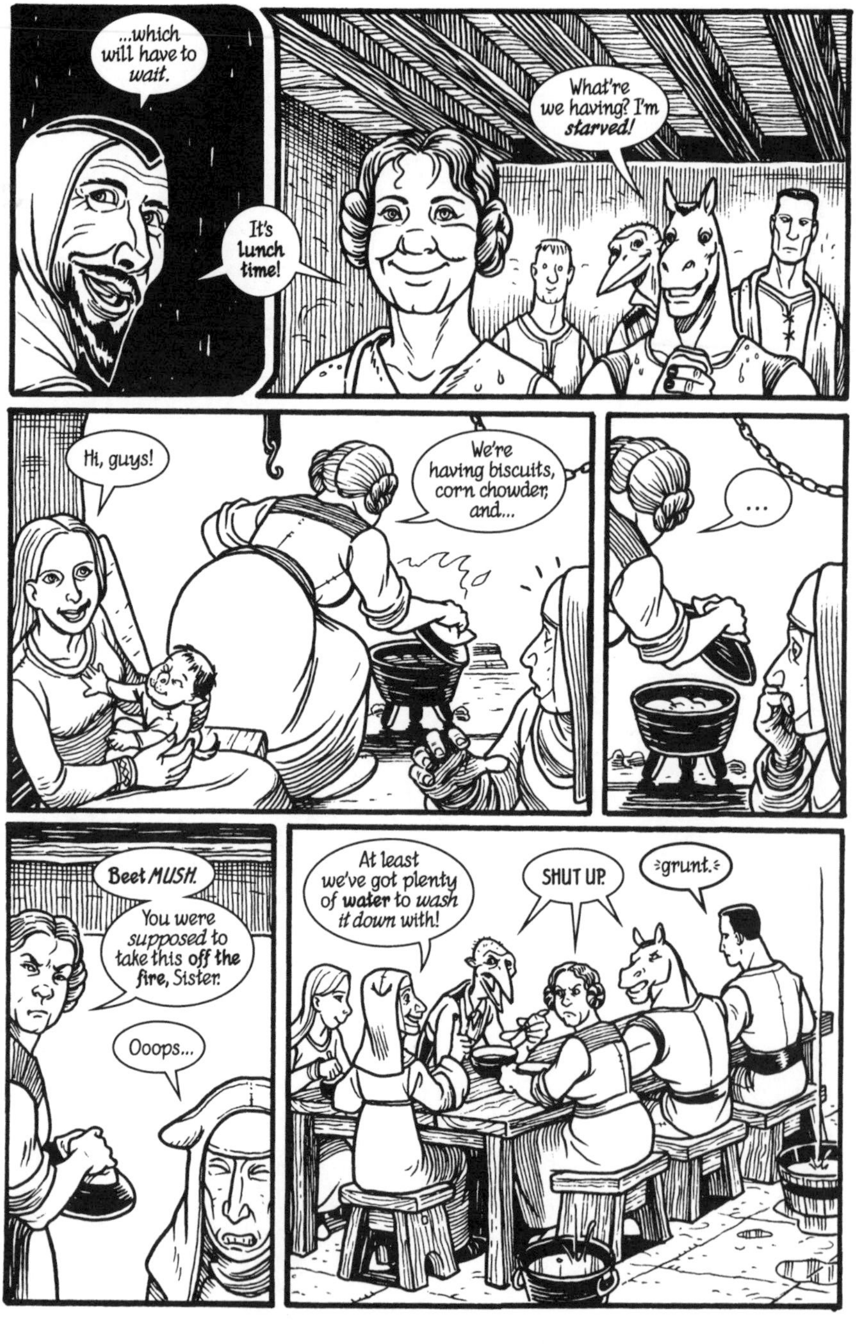
...which will have to *wait*.
It's **lunch time!**
What're we having? I'm ***starved!***
Hi, guys!
We're having biscuits, corn chowder, and...
...
Beet *MUSH.*
You were *supposed* to take this **off the fire,** Sister.
Ooops...
At least we've got plenty of **water** to *wash it down* with!
SHUT UP.
grunt.

Chapter 16.

· SOLICITINE PT. 4 ·

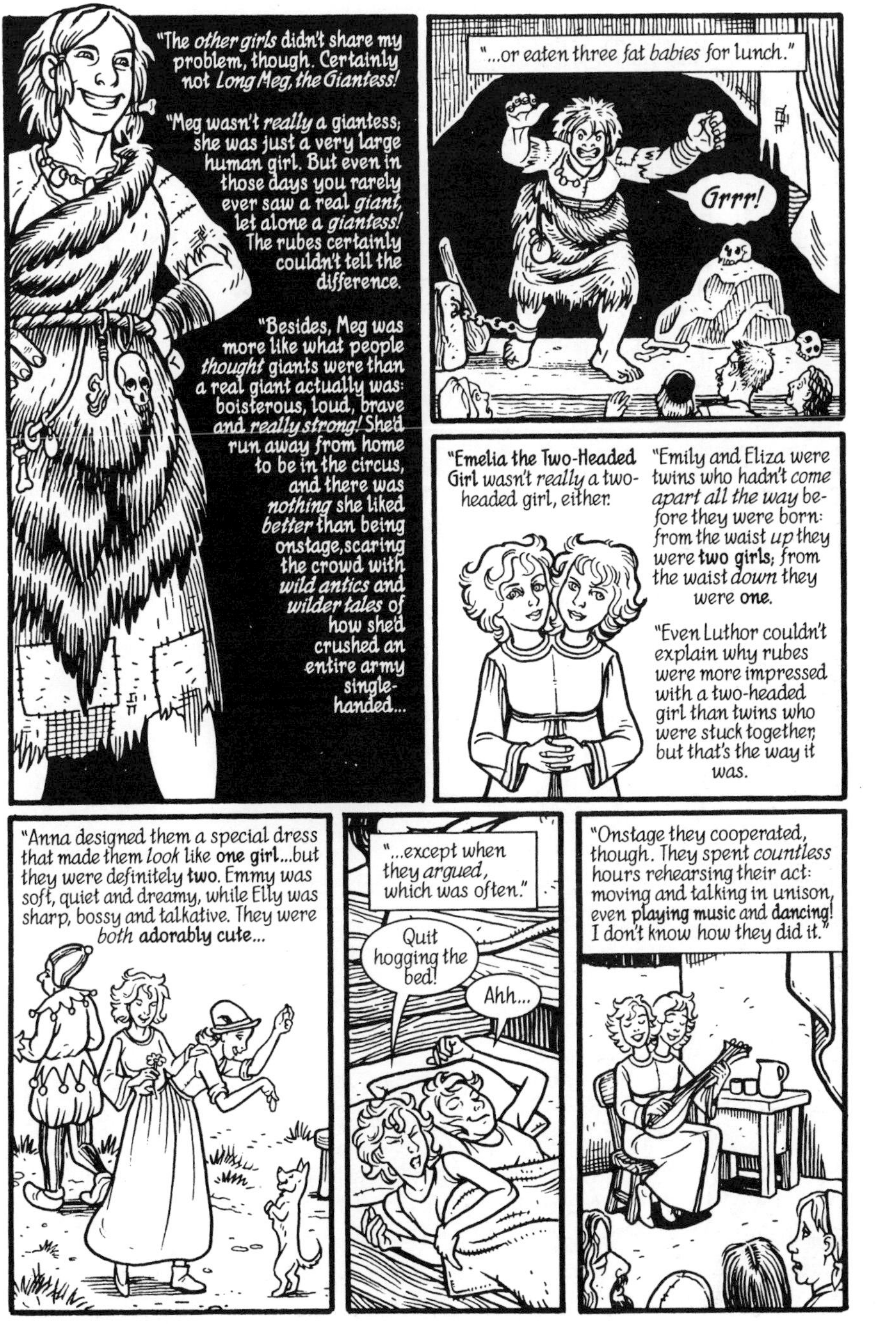
"The other girls didn't share my problem, though. Certainly not Long Meg, the Giantess!
"Meg wasn't really a giantess; she was just a very large human girl. But even in those days you rarely ever saw a real giant, let alone a giantess! The rubes certainly couldn't tell the difference.
"Besides, Meg was more like what people thought giants were than a real giant actually was: boisterous, loud, brave and really strong! She'd run away from home to be in the circus, and there was nothing she liked better than being onstage, scaring the crowd with wild antics and wilder tales of how she'd crushed an entire army single-handed...
"...or eaten three fat babies for lunch."
Grrr!
"Emelia the Two-Headed Girl wasn't really a two-headed girl, either.
"Emily and Eliza were twins who hadn't come apart all the way before they were born: from the waist up they were two girls; from the waist down they were one.
"Even Luthor couldn't explain why rubes were more impressed with a two-headed girl than twins who were stuck together, but that's the way it was.
"Anna designed them a special dress that made them look like one girl...but they were definitely two. Emmy was soft, quiet and dreamy, while Elly was sharp, bossy and talkative. They were both adorably cute...
"...except when they argued, which was often."
Quit hogging the bed!
Ahh...
"Onstage they cooperated, though. They spent countless hours rehearsing their act: moving and talking in unison, even playing music and dancing! I don't know how they did it."

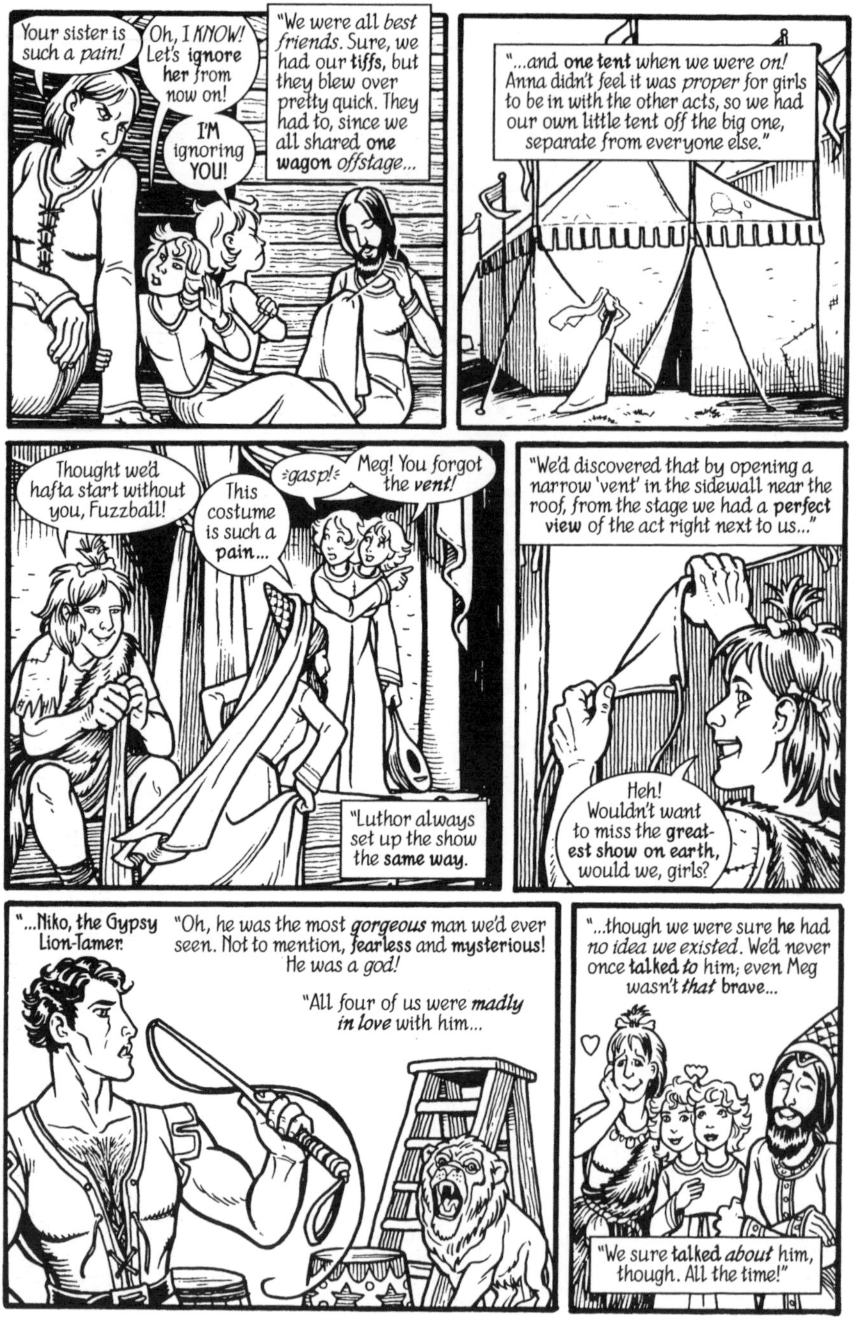
Your sister is such a *pain!*
Oh, I *KNOW!* Let's **ignore her** from now on!
I'M ignoring YOU!
"We were all *best friends*. Sure, we had our **tiffs**, but they blew over pretty quick. They had to, since we all shared **one wagon** *offstage*...
"...and **one tent** when we were *on!* Anna didn't feel it was *proper* for girls to be in with the other acts, so we had our own little tent off the big one, separate from everyone else."
Thought we'd hafta start without you, Fuzzball!
This costume is such a **pain**...
gasp!
Meg! You forgot the ***vent!***
"Luthor always set up the show the **same way**.
"We'd discovered that by opening a narrow 'vent' in the sidewall near the roof, from the stage we had a **perfect view** of the act right next to us..."
Heh! Wouldn't want to miss the **great-est show on earth**, would we, girls?
"...**Niko, the Gypsy Lion-Tamer.**
"Oh, he was the most ***gorgeous*** man we'd ever seen. Not to mention, ***fearless*** and **mysterious**! He was a *god!*
"All four of us were ***madly in love*** with him...
"...though we were sure **he** had *no idea we existed*. We'd never once **talked *to*** him; even Meg wasn't ***that*** **brave**...
"We sure **talked *about*** him, though. All the time!"

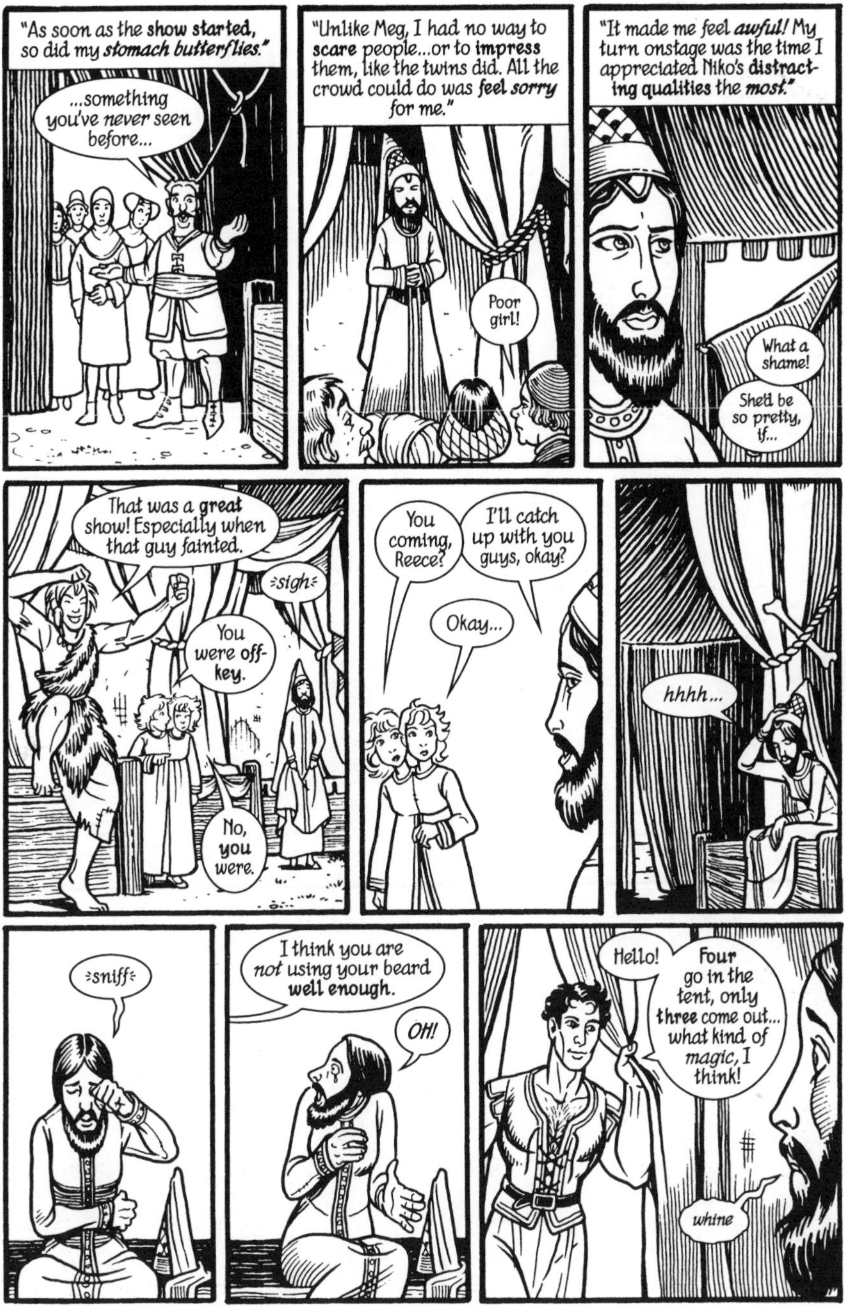
"As soon as the **show started**, so did my ***stomach butterflies.***"
...something you've *never* seen before...
"Unlike Meg, I had no way to **scare** people...or to **impress** them, like the twins did. All the crowd could do was ***feel sorry*** for me."
Poor girl!
"It made me feel ***awful!*** My turn onstage was the time I appreciated Niko's **distracting qualities** the ***most.***"
What a shame!
She'd be so pretty, if...
That was a **great** show! Especially when that guy fainted.
sigh
You were **off-key.**
No, **you** were.
You coming, Reece?
I'll catch up with you guys, okay?
Okay...
hhhh...
sniff
I think you are *not* using your beard **well enough**.
OH!
Hello!
Four go in the tent, only **three** come out... what kind of *magic*, I think!
whine

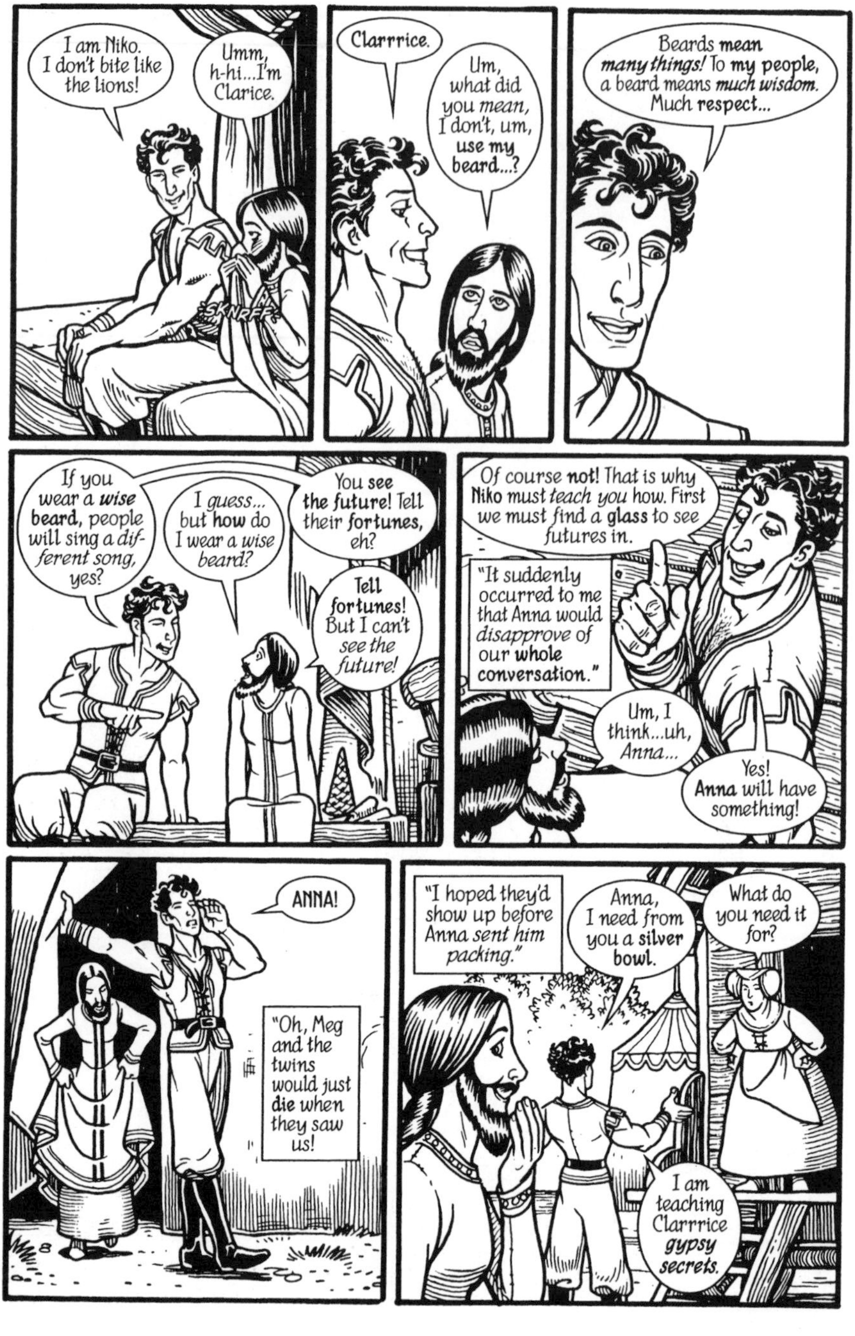
I am Niko. I don't bite like the lions!
Umm, h-hi...I'm Clarice.
SKNRFF
Clarrrice.
Um, what did you *mean*, I don't, um, **use my beard**...?
Beards **mean** ***many things!*** To **my people**, a beard means ***much wisdom***. Much **respect**...
If you wear a **wise beard**, people will sing a *different song*, yes?
I *guess*... but **how** do I wear a *wise beard?*
You **see the future!** Tell their **fortunes**, eh?
Tell fortunes! But I can't *see the future!*
Of course **not!** That is why **Niko** must *teach you* how. First we must *find* a **glass** to see futures in.
"It suddenly occurred to me that Anna would *disapprove* of our **whole conversation**."
Um, I think...uh, Anna...
Yes! **Anna** will have something!
ANNA!
"Oh, Meg and the twins would just **die** when they saw us!"
"I hoped they'd show up before Anna *sent him packing*."
Anna, I need from you a **silver bowl**.
What do you need it for?
I am teaching Clarrrice ***gypsy secrets***.

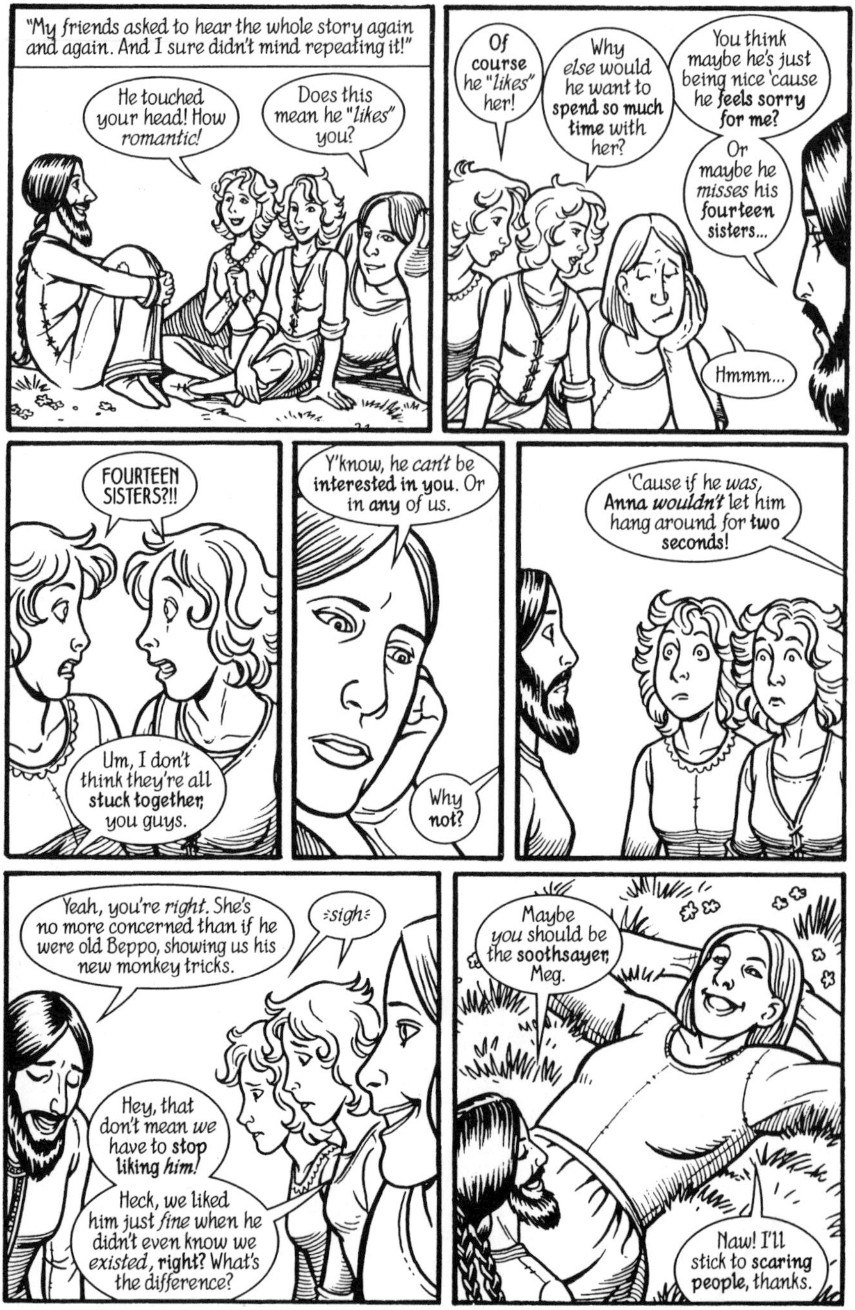
"My friends asked to hear the whole story again and again. And I sure didn't mind repeating it!"
He touched your head! How *romantic!*
Does this mean he "*likes*" you?
Of **course** he "*likes*" her!
Why *else* would he want to **spend so much time** with her?
You think maybe he's just being nice 'cause he **feels sorry for me?**
Or maybe he *misses* his **fourteen sisters...**
Hmmm...
FOURTEEN SISTERS?!!
Um, I don't think they're all **stuck together,** you guys.
Y'know, he *can't* be **interested in you.** Or in **any** of us.
Why **not?**
'Cause if he *was,* **Anna *wouldn't*** let him hang around for **two seconds!**
Yeah, you're *right.* She's no more concerned than if he were old Beppo, showing us his new monkey tricks.
sigh
Hey, that don't mean *we* have to **stop liking *him!***
Heck, we liked him just *fine* when he didn't even know we *existed,* **right?** What's the difference?
Maybe *you* should be the **soothsayer,** Meg.
Naw! I'll stick to **scaring people,** thanks.

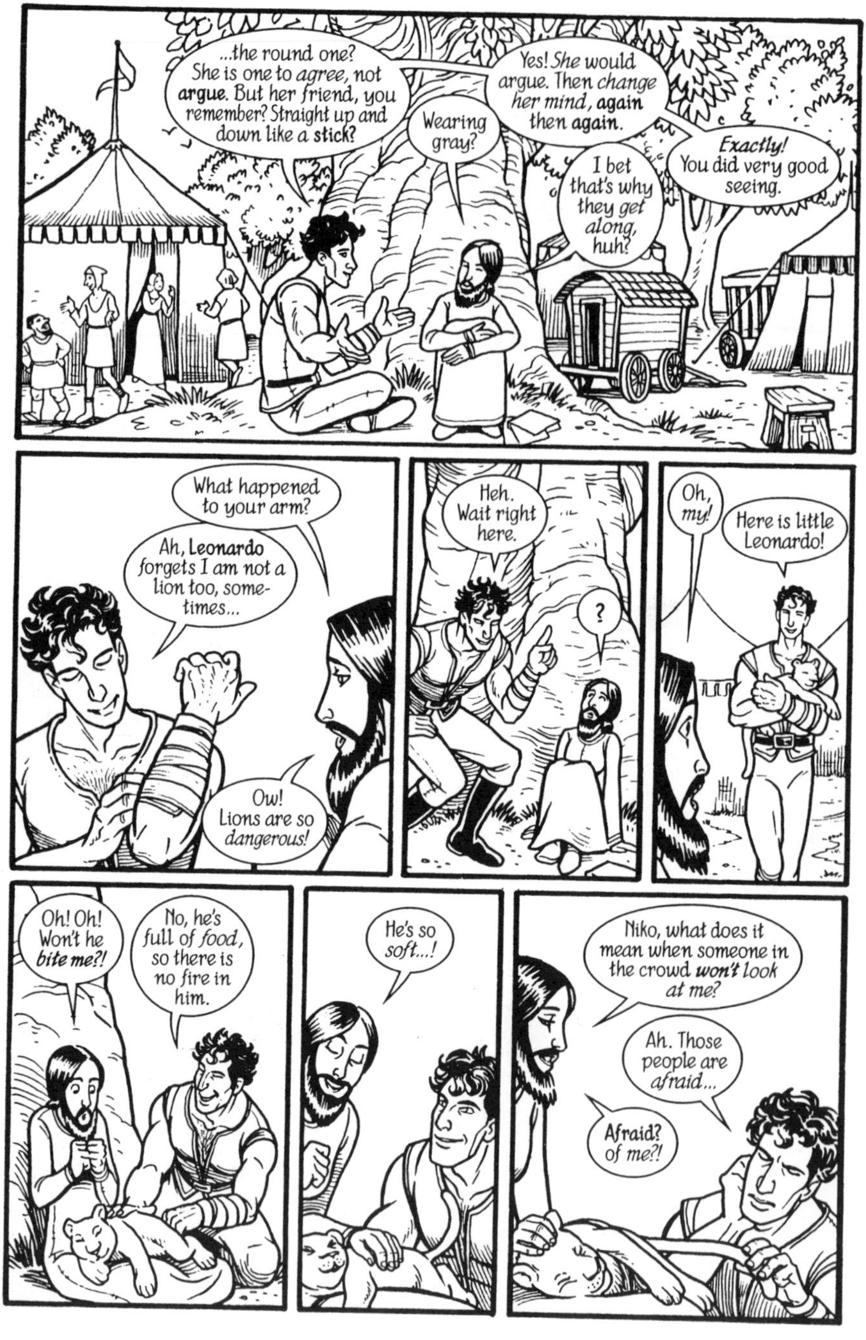
...the round one? She is one to *agree*, not **argue**. But her friend, you remember? Straight up and down like a **stick**?
Wearing gray?
Yes! *She* would argue. Then *change her mind*, **again** then **again**.
I bet that's why they *get along*, huh?
Exactly! You did very good seeing.
What happened to your arm?
Ah, **Leonardo** forgets I am not a lion too, some-times...
Ow! Lions are so *dangerous!*
Heh. Wait right here.
?
Oh, *my!*
Here is little Leonardo!
Oh! Oh! Won't he *bite me?!*
No, he's full of *food*, so there is no fire in him.
He's so *soft...!*
Niko, what does it mean when someone in the crowd *won't* look at me?
Ah. Those people are *afraid*...
Afraid? of *me?!*

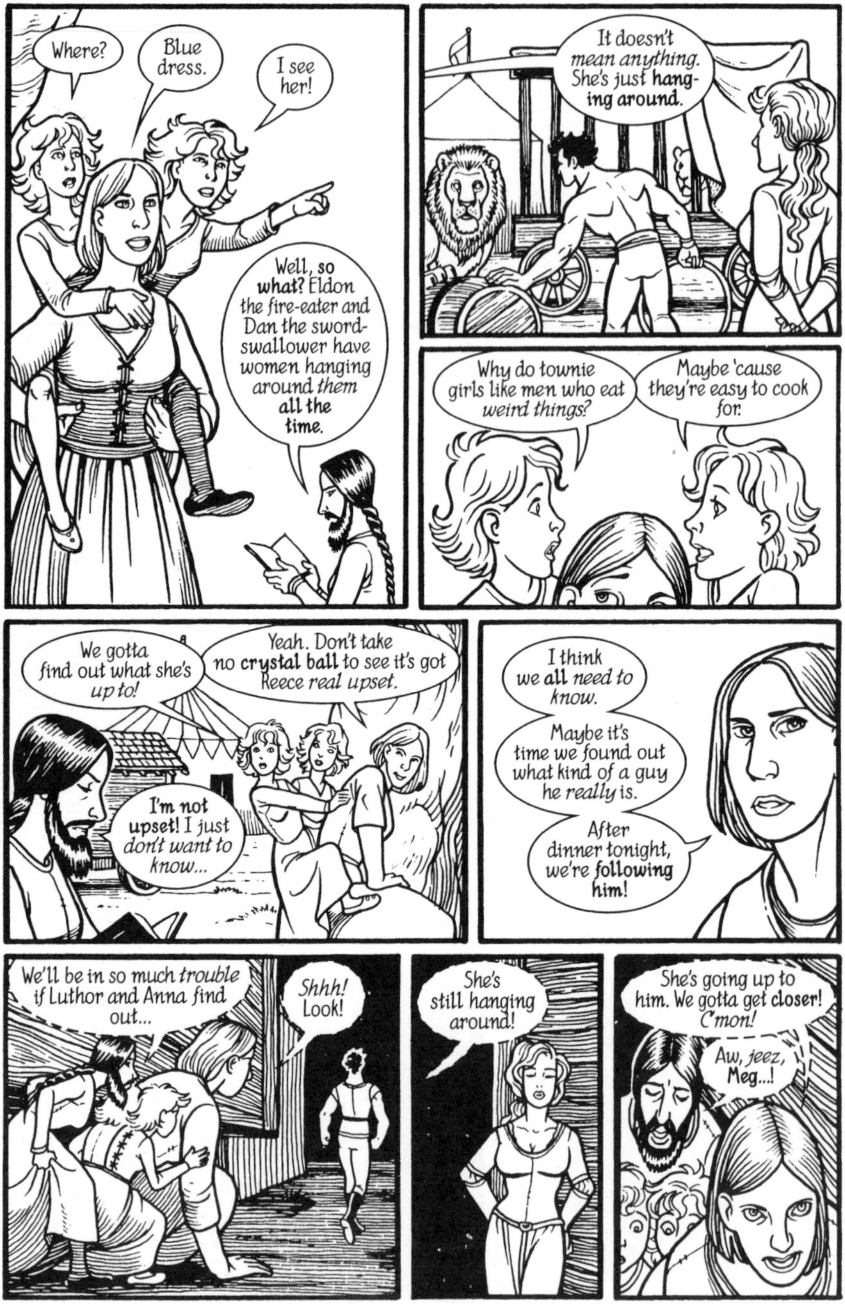
Where?
Blue dress.
I see her!
Well, so **what?** Eldon the fire-eater and Dan the sword-swallower have women hanging around *them* **all the time.**
It doesn't *mean anything.* She's just **hanging around.**
Why do townie girls like men who eat *weird things?*
Maybe 'cause they're easy to cook for.
We gotta find out what she's *up to!*
Yeah. Don't take no **crystal ball** to see it's got Reece *real upset.*
I'm not upset! I just *don't want to know...*
I think we **all** *need to know.*
Maybe it's time we found out what kind of a guy he *really* is.
After dinner tonight, we're **following him!**
We'll be in so much *trouble* if Luthor and Anna find out...
Shhh! Look!
She's still hanging around!
She's going up to him. We gotta get **closer!** *C'mon!*
Aw, *jeez,* **Meg...!**

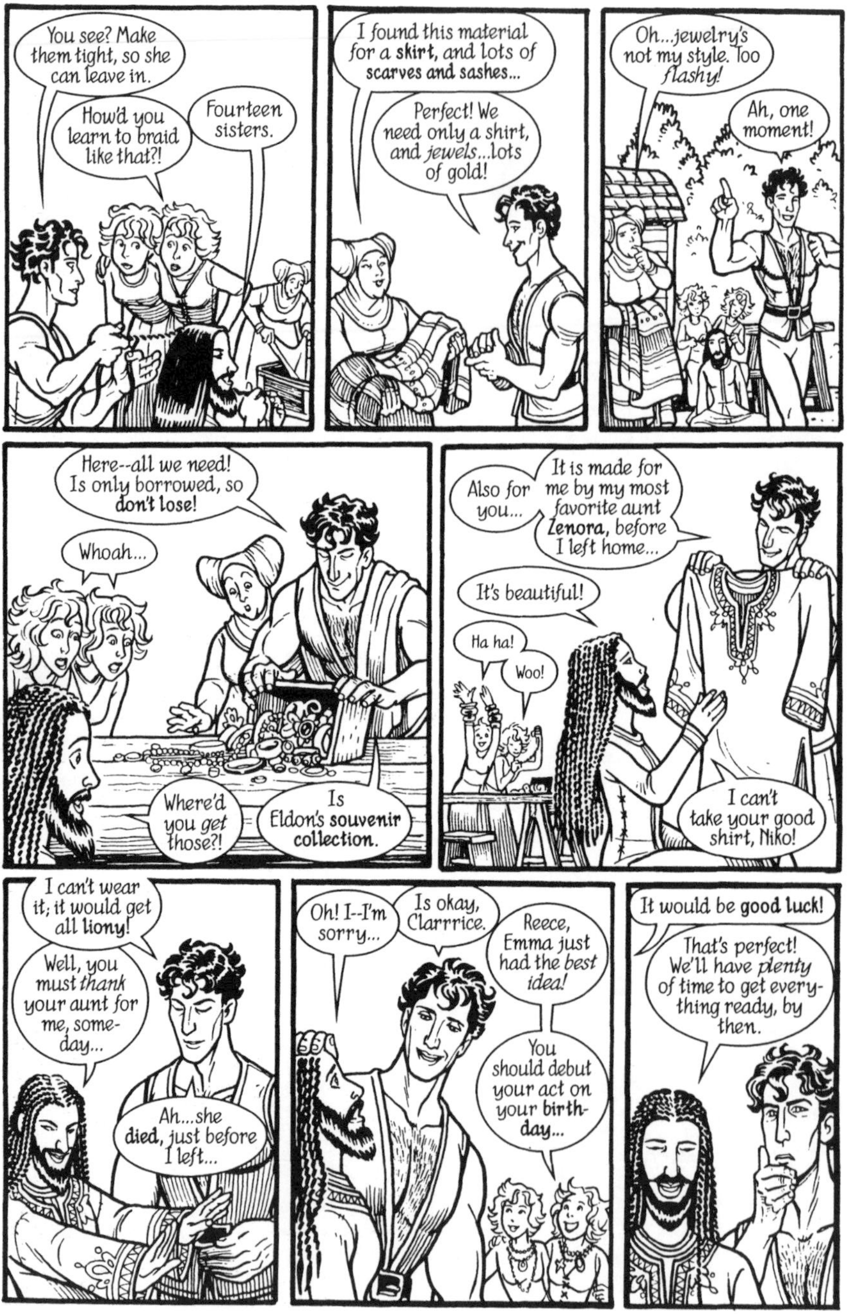
You see? Make them tight, so she can leave in.
How'd you learn to braid like that?!
Fourteen sisters.
I found this material for a **skirt**, and lots of **scarves and sashes**...
Perfect! We need only a shirt, and *jewels*...lots of gold!
Oh...jewelry's not my style. Too *flashy!*
Ah, one moment!
Here--all we need! Is only borrowed, so **don't lose!**
Whoah...
Where'd you *get* those?!
Is Eldon's **souvenir collection.**
Also for you...
It is made for me by my most *favorite* aunt **Zenora**, before I left home...
It's beautiful!
Ha ha!
Woo!
I can't take your good shirt, Niko!
I can't wear it; it would get all **liony!**
Well, you must *thank* your aunt for me, someday...
Ah...she **died**, just before I left...
Oh! I--I'm sorry...
Is okay, Clarrrice.
Reece, Emma just had the *best idea!*
You should debut your act on your **birthday**...
It would be **good luck!**
That's perfect! We'll have *plenty* of time to get everything ready, by then.

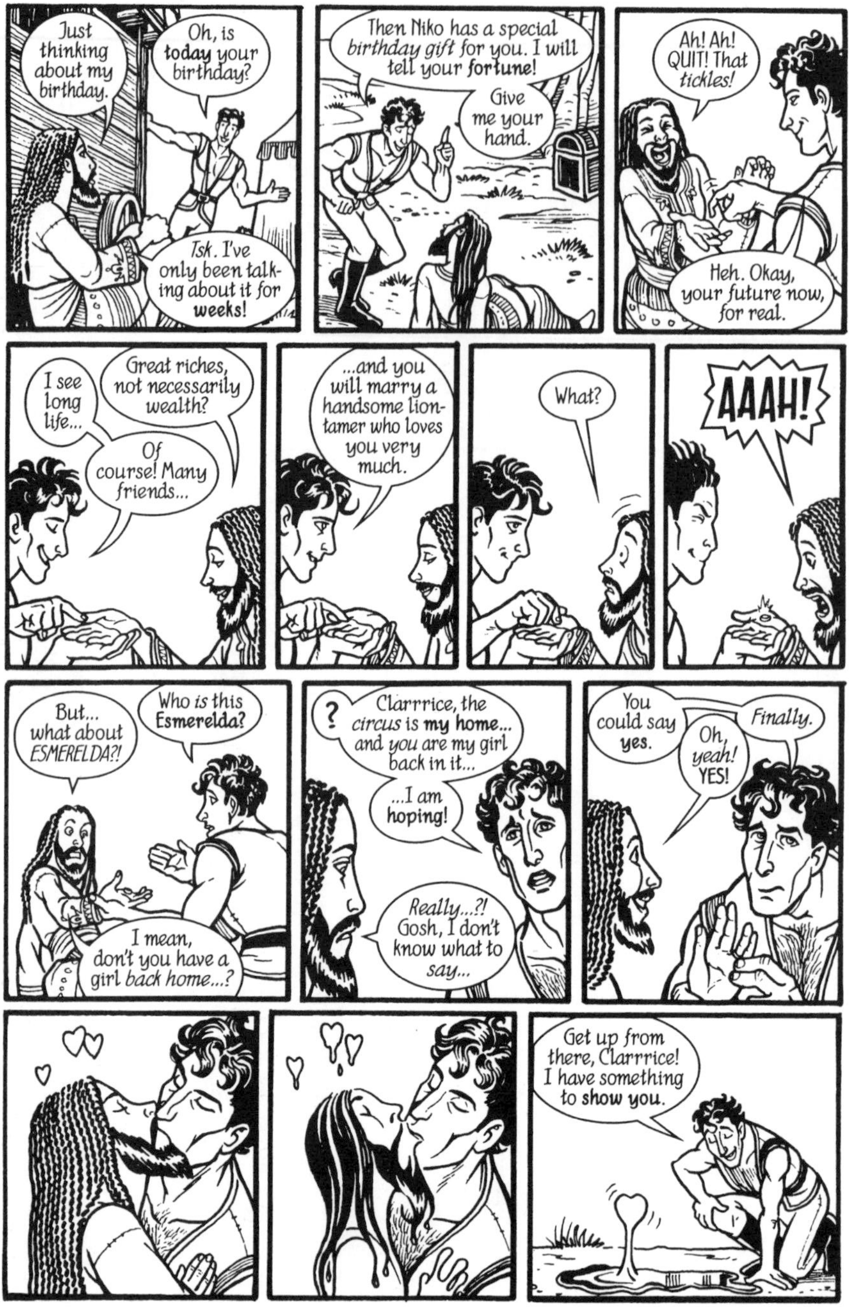
Just thinking about my birthday.
Oh, is **today** your birthday?
Tsk. I've only been talking about it for **weeks**!
Then Niko has a special *birthday gift* for you. I will tell your **fortune**!
Give me your hand.
Ah! Ah! QUIT! That *tickles*!
Heh. Okay, your *future* now, for real.
I see long life...
Great riches, not necessarily wealth?
Of course! Many friends...
...and you will marry a handsome lion-tamer who loves you very much.
What?
AAAH!
But... what about *ESMERELDA*?!
Who *is* this **Esmerelda?**
I mean, don't you have a girl *back home*...?
?
Clarrrice, the *circus* is **my home**... and *you* are my girl back in it...
...I am **hoping**!
Really...?! Gosh, I don't know what to say...
You could say **yes**.
Finally.
Oh, *yeah*! YES!
Get up from there, Clarrrice! I have something to **show you**.

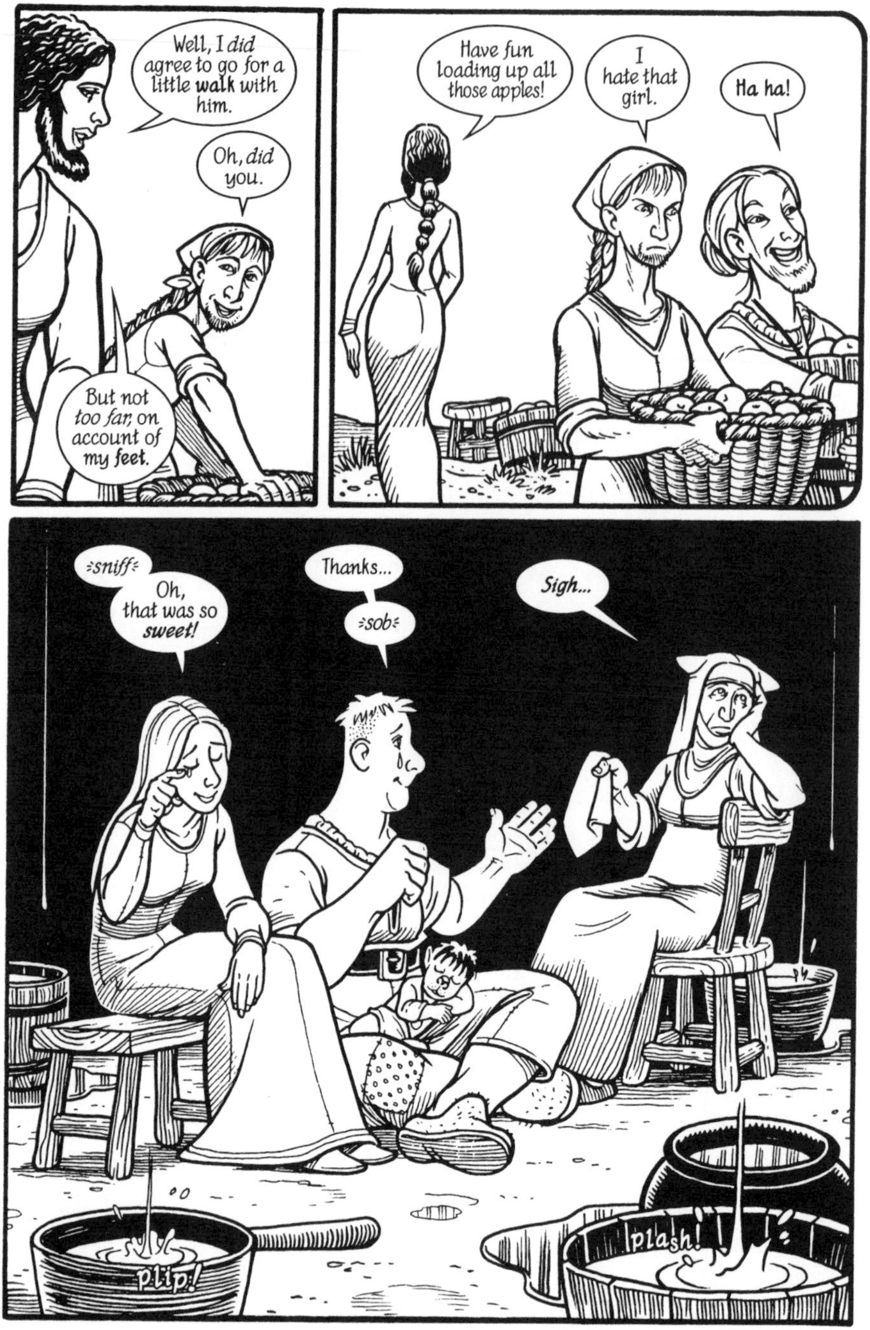
Well, I did agree to go for a little walk with him.
Oh, did you.
But not too far, on account of my feet.
Have fun loading up all those apples!
I hate that girl.
Ha ha!
sniff
Oh, that was so sweet!
Thanks...
sob
Sigh...
plip!
plash!

Chapter 17.

· SOLICITINE PT. 5 ·

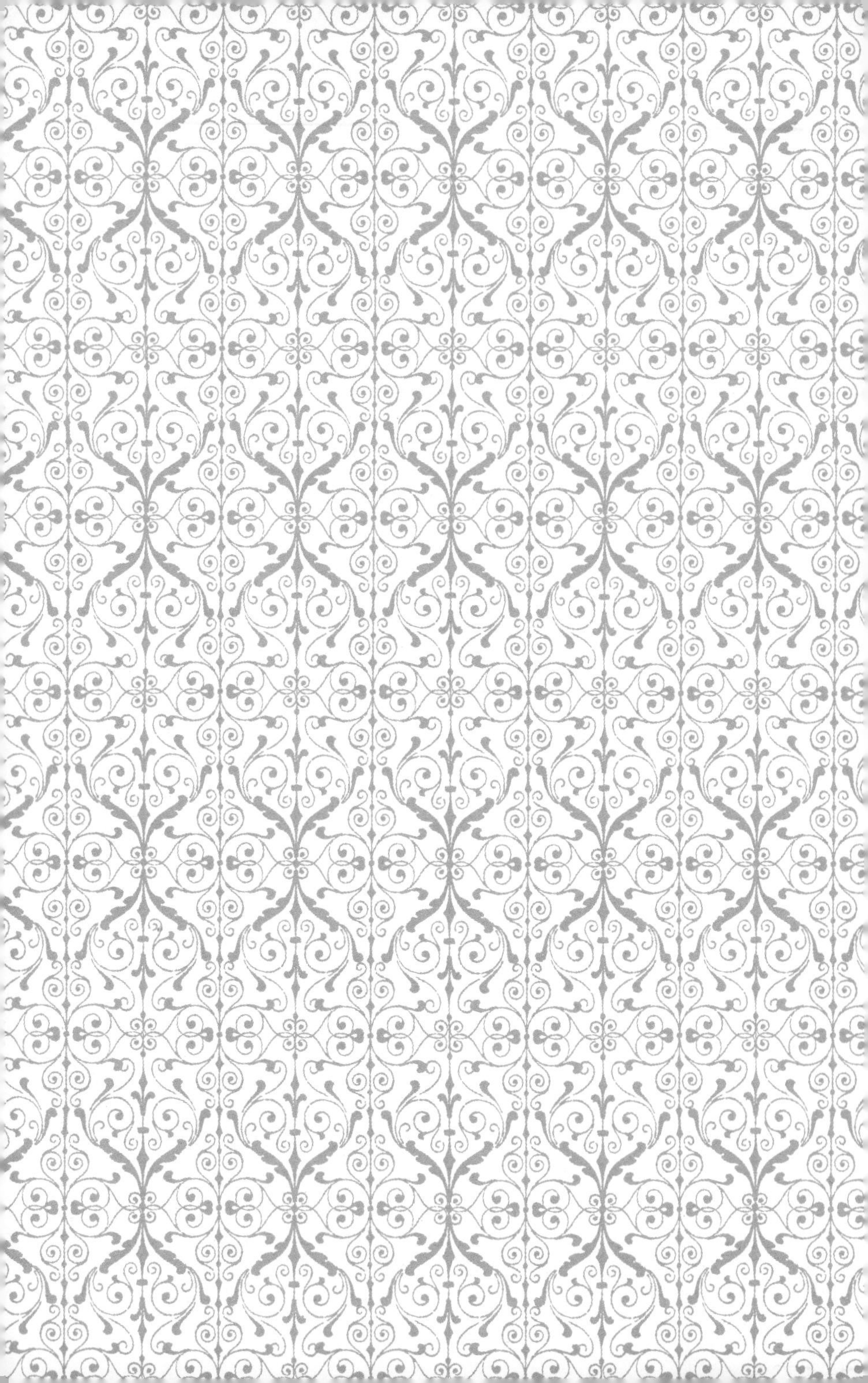

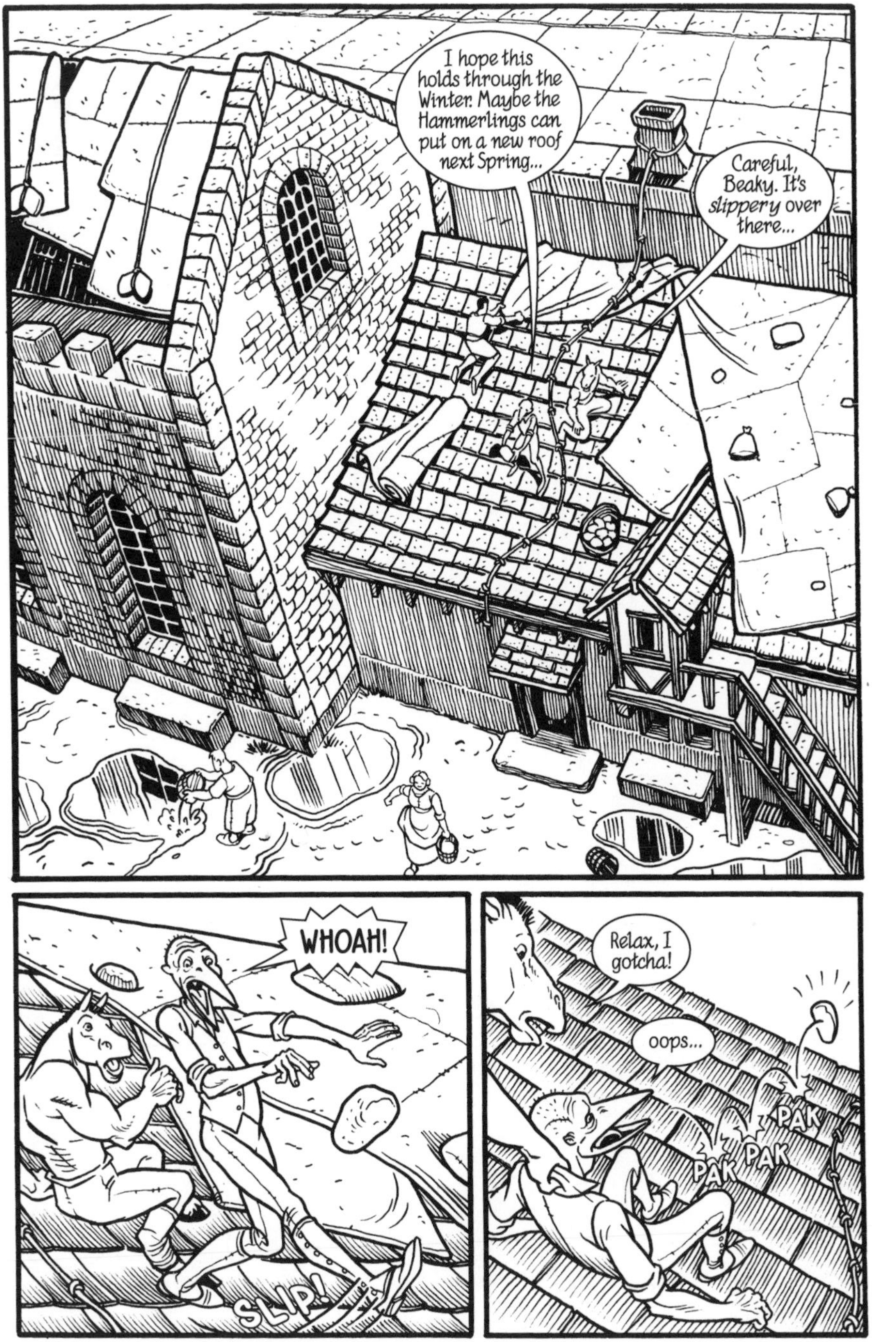
I hope this holds through the Winter. Maybe the Hammerlings can put on a new roof next Spring...
Careful, Beaky. It's *slippery* over there...
WHOAH!
SLIP!
Relax, I gotcha!
oops...
PAK
PAK
PAK

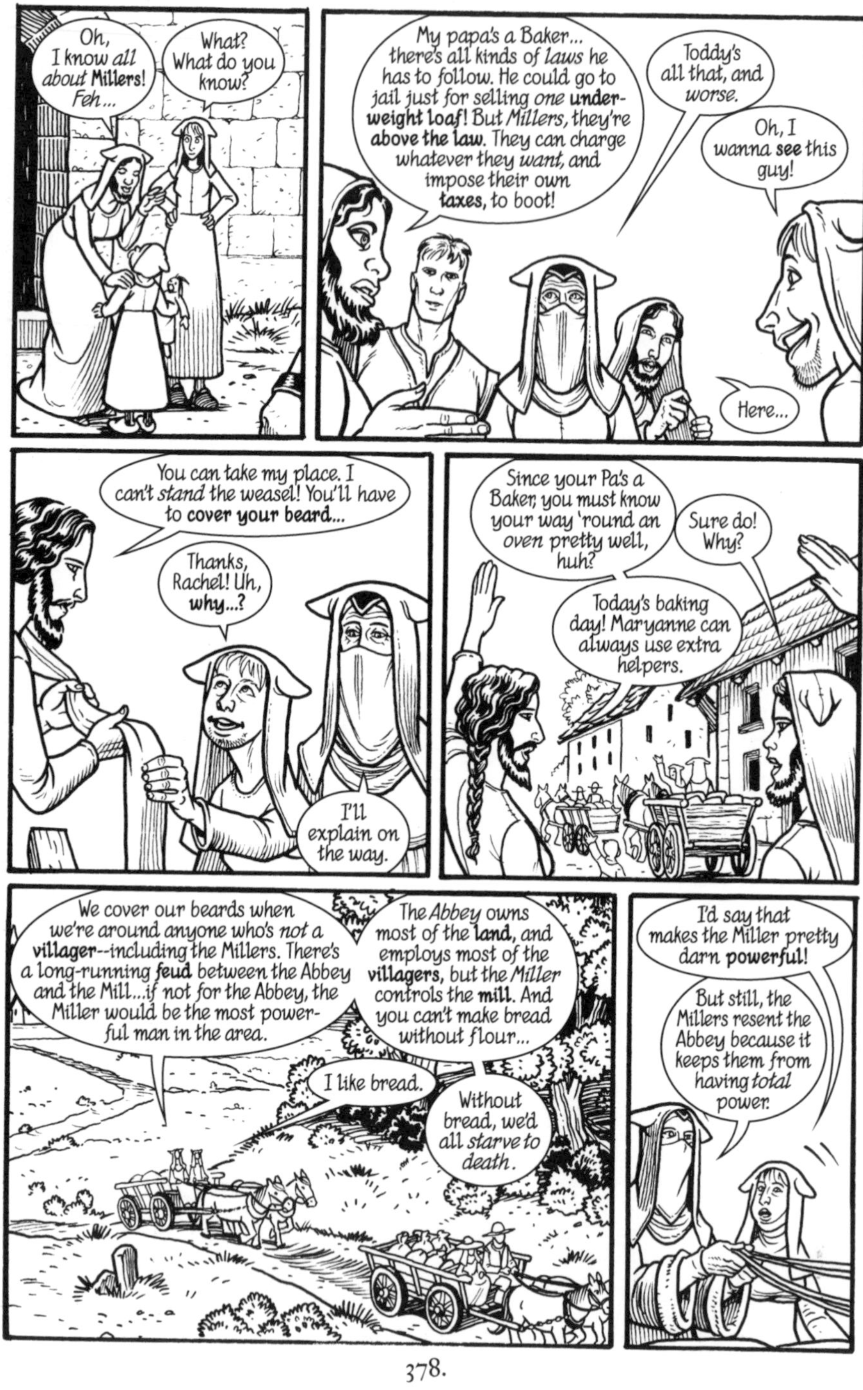
Oh, I know *all about* **Millers**! *Feh*...
What? What do you know?
My papa's a Baker... there's all kinds of *laws* he has to follow. He could go to jail just for selling *one* **under-weight loaf**! But *Millers*, they're **above the law**. They can charge whatever they *want*, and impose their own **taxes**, to boot!
Toddy's all that, and *worse*.
Oh, I wanna **see** this guy!
Here...
You can take my place. I can't *stand* the weasel! You'll have to **cover your beard**...
Thanks, Rachel! Uh, **why**...?
I'll explain on the way.
Since your Pa's a Baker, you must know your way 'round an *oven* pretty well, huh?
Sure do! Why?
Today's baking day! Maryanne can always use extra helpers.
We cover our beards when we're around anyone who's *not* a **villager**--including the Millers. There's a long-running **feud** between the Abbey and the Mill...*if* not for the Abbey, the Miller would be the most powerful man in the area.
The *Abbey* owns most of the **land**, and employs most of the **villagers**, but the *Miller* controls the **mill**. And you can't make bread without flour...
I like bread.
Without bread, we'd all *starve* to *death*.
I'd *say* that makes the Miller pretty darn **powerful**!
But still, the Millers resent the Abbey because it keeps them from having *total* power.

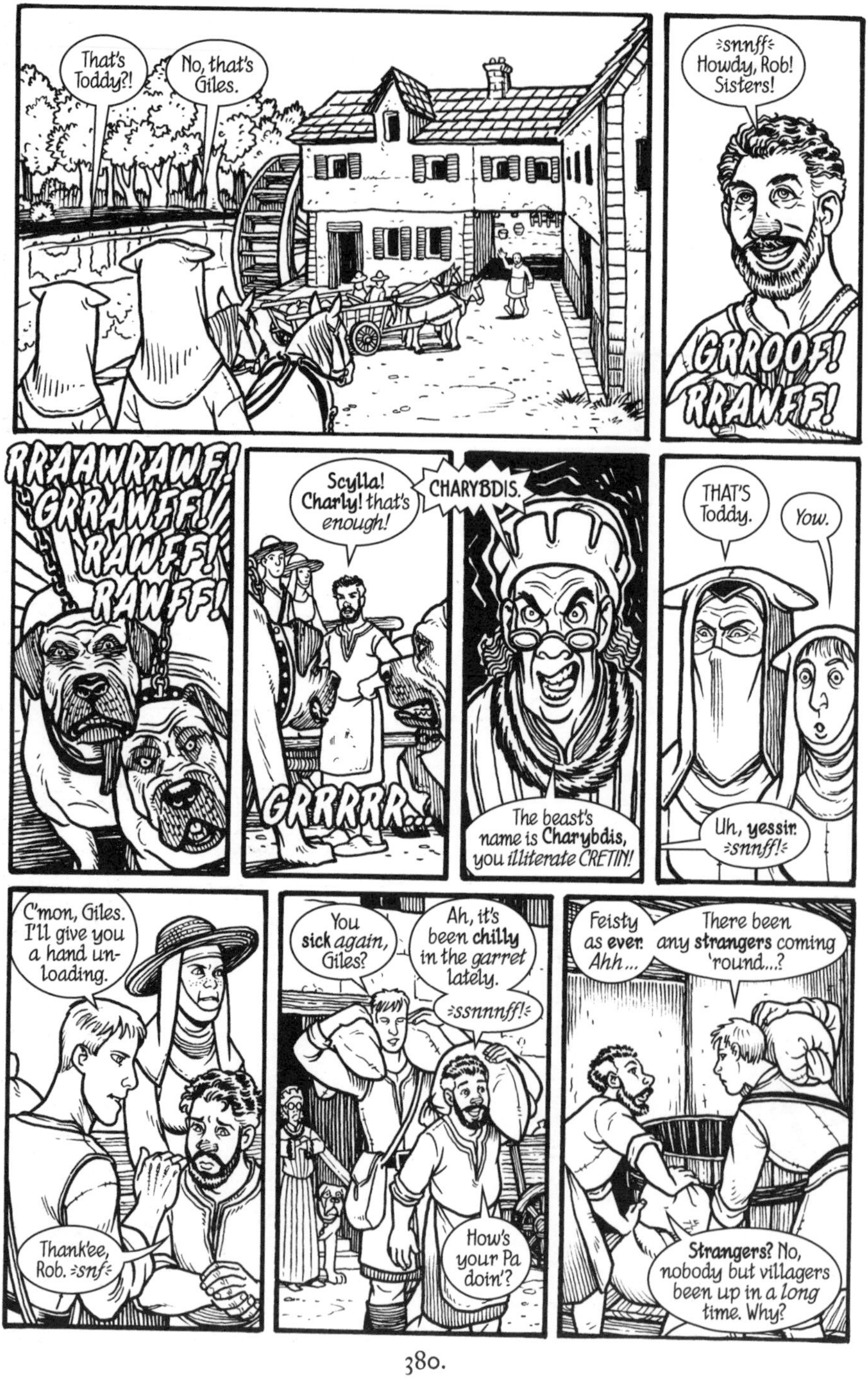
That's Toddy?!
No, that's Giles.
=snnff= Howdy, Rob! Sisters!
GRROOF! RRAWFF!
RRAAWRAWF! GRRAWFF! RAWFF! RAWFF!
Scylla! Charly! that's enough!
GRRRRR...
CHARYBDIS.
The beast's name is Charybdis, you illiterate CRETIN!
THAT'S Toddy.
You.
Uh, yessir. =snnff!=
C'mon, Giles. I'll give you a hand unloading.
Thank'ee, Rob. =snf=
You sick again, Giles?
Ah, it's been chilly in the garret lately.
=ssnnnff!=
How's your Pa doin'?
Feisty as ever. Ahh...
There been any strangers coming 'round...?
Strangers? No, nobody but villagers been up in a long time. Why?

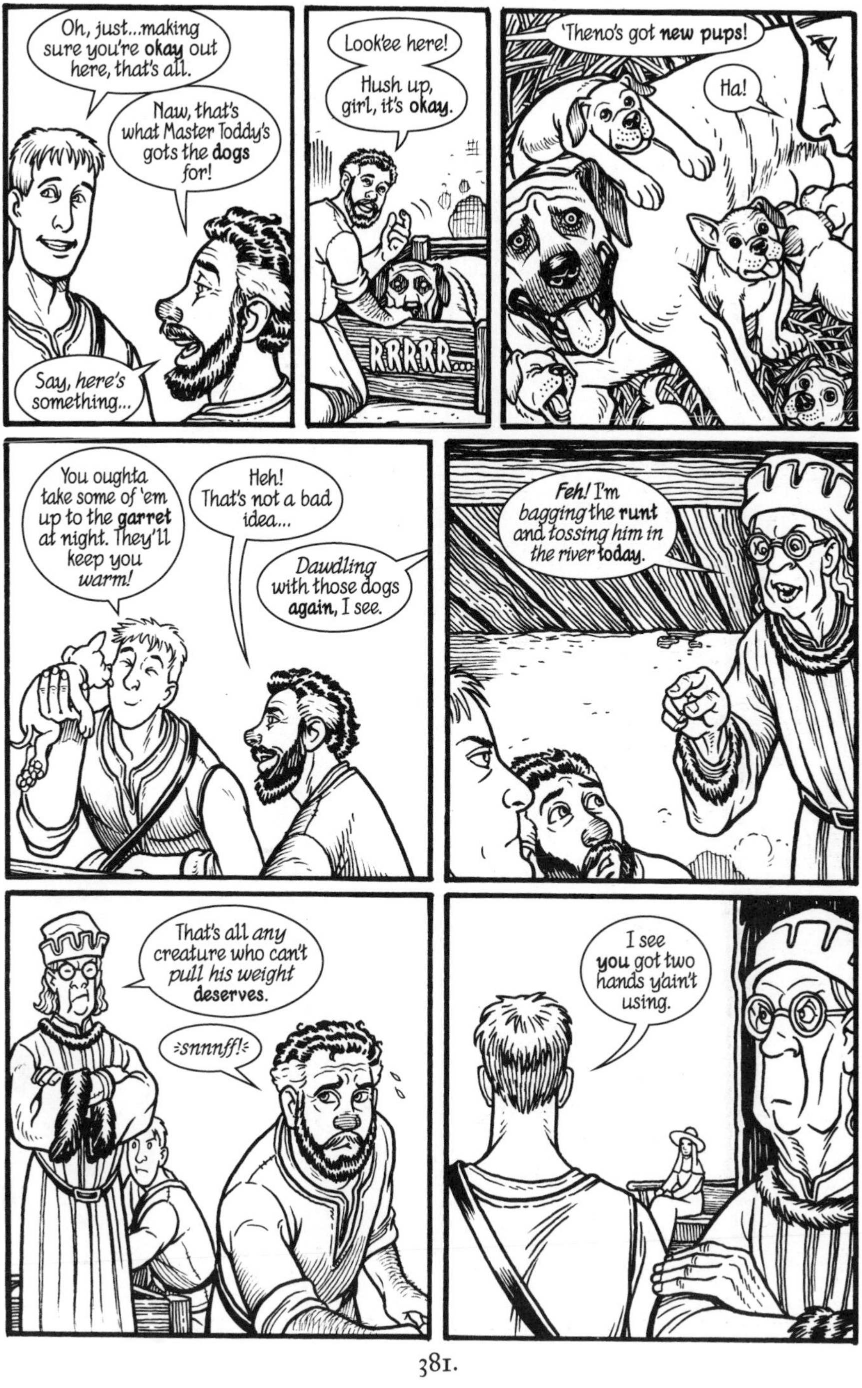
Oh, just...making sure you're **okay** out here, that's all.
Naw, that's what Master Toddy's gots the **dogs** for!
Say, here's something...
Look'ee here!
Hush up, girl, it's **okay**.
RRRRR...
'Theno's got **new pups**!
Ha!
You oughta take some of 'em up to the **garret** at night. They'll keep you *warm!*
Heh! That's not a bad idea...
Dawdling with those dogs **again**, I see.
Feh! I'm *bagging* the **runt** *and tossing him in the river* **today**.
That's all *any* creature who *can't pull his weight* **deserves**.
snnnff!
I see **you** got two hands y'ain't using.

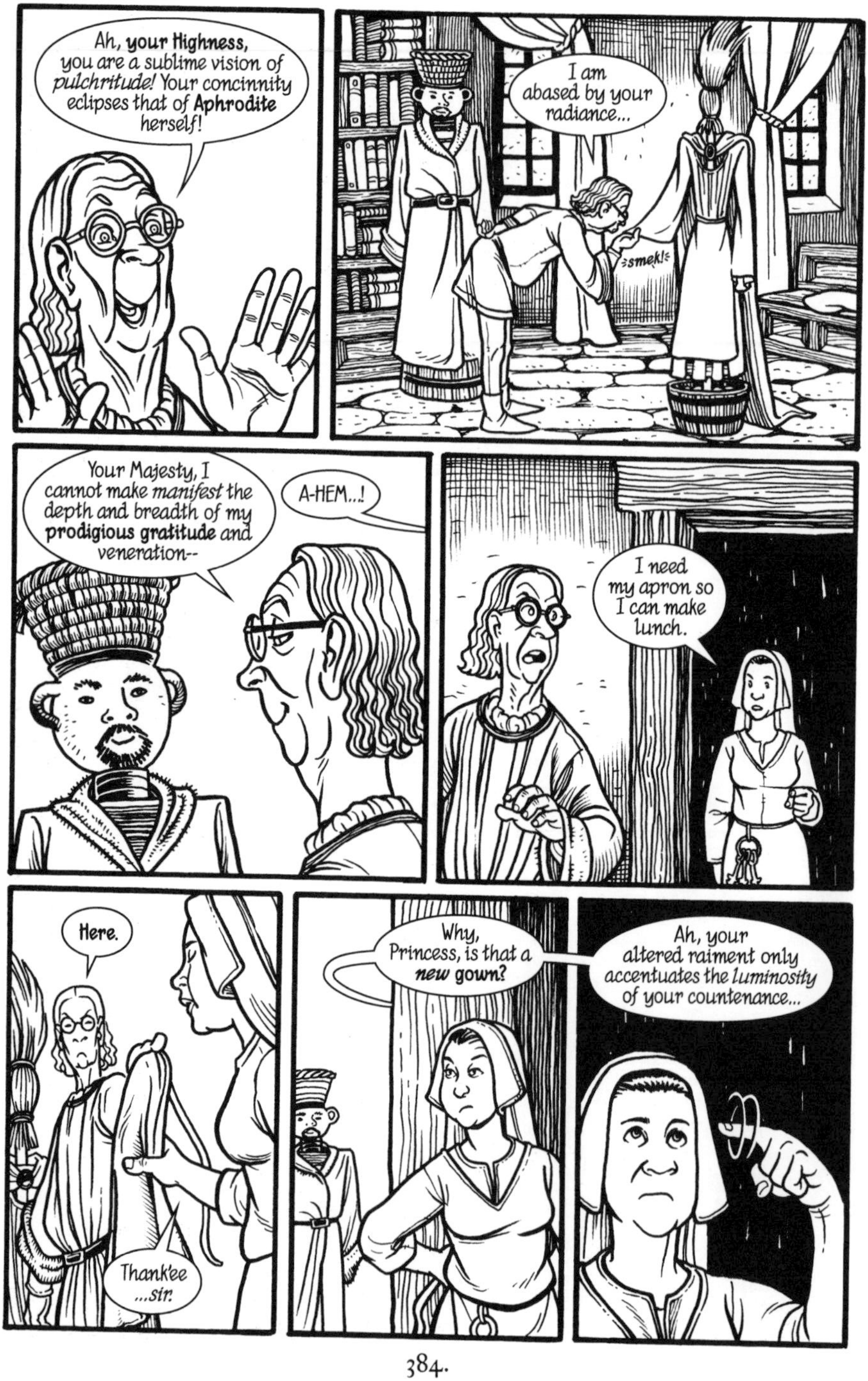
Ah, your Highness, you are a sublime vision of pulchritude! Your concinnity eclipses that of Aphrodite herself!
I am abased by your radiance...
smek!
Your Majesty, I cannot make manifest the depth and breadth of my prodigious gratitude and veneration--
A-HEM...!
I need my apron so I can make lunch.
Here.
Thank'ee ...sir.
Why, Princess, is that a new gown?
Ah, your altered raiment only accentuates the luminosity of your countenance...

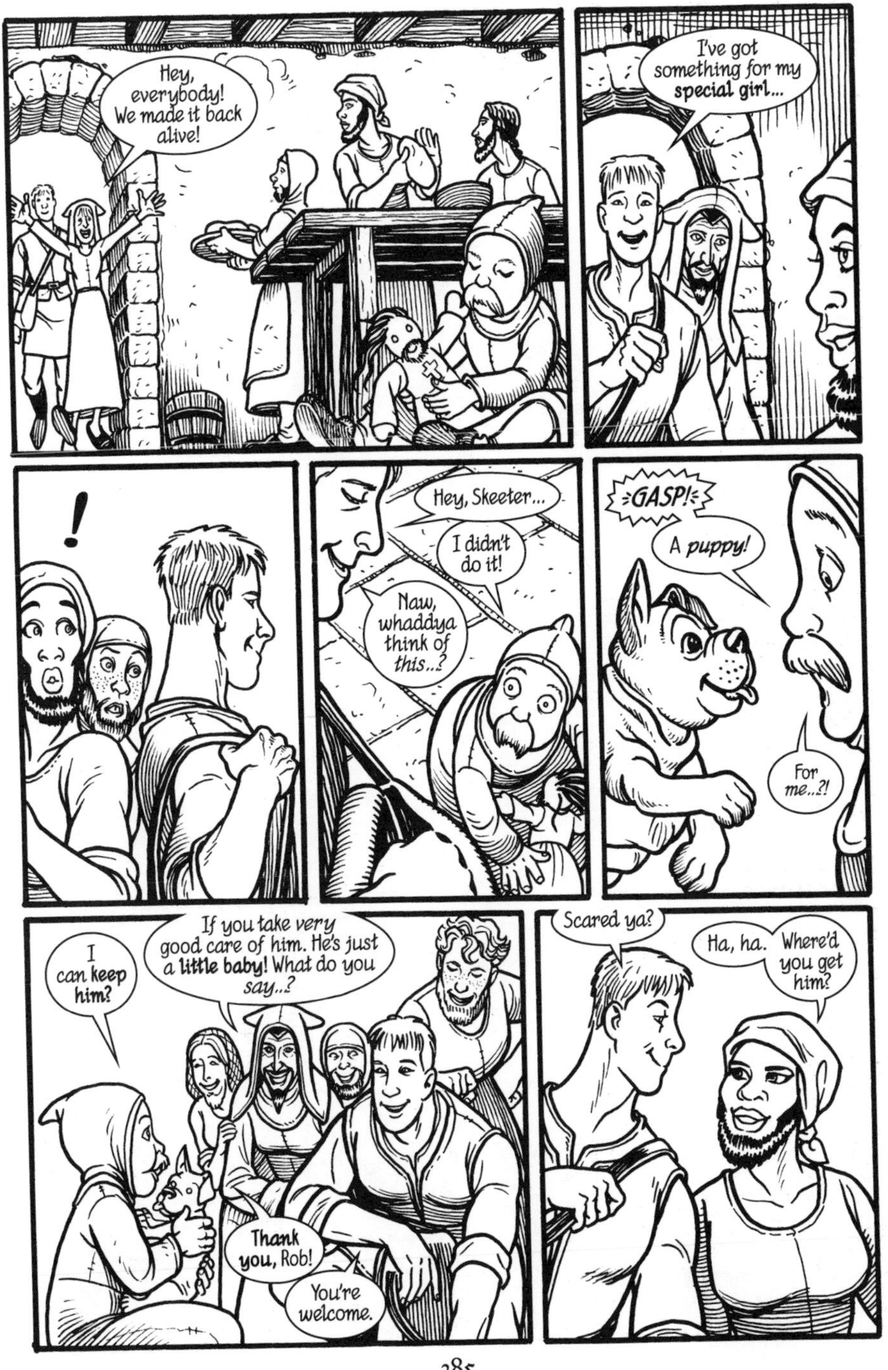
Hey, everybody! We made it back alive!
I've got something for my **special girl**...
!
Hey, Skeeter...
I didn't do it!
Naw, whaddya think of *this*...?
GASP!
A *puppy!*
For *me*...?!
I can **keep** him?
If you take *very* good care of him. He's just a **little baby!** What do you *say*...?
Thank you, Rob!
You're welcome.
Scared ya?
Ha, ha.
Where'd you get him?

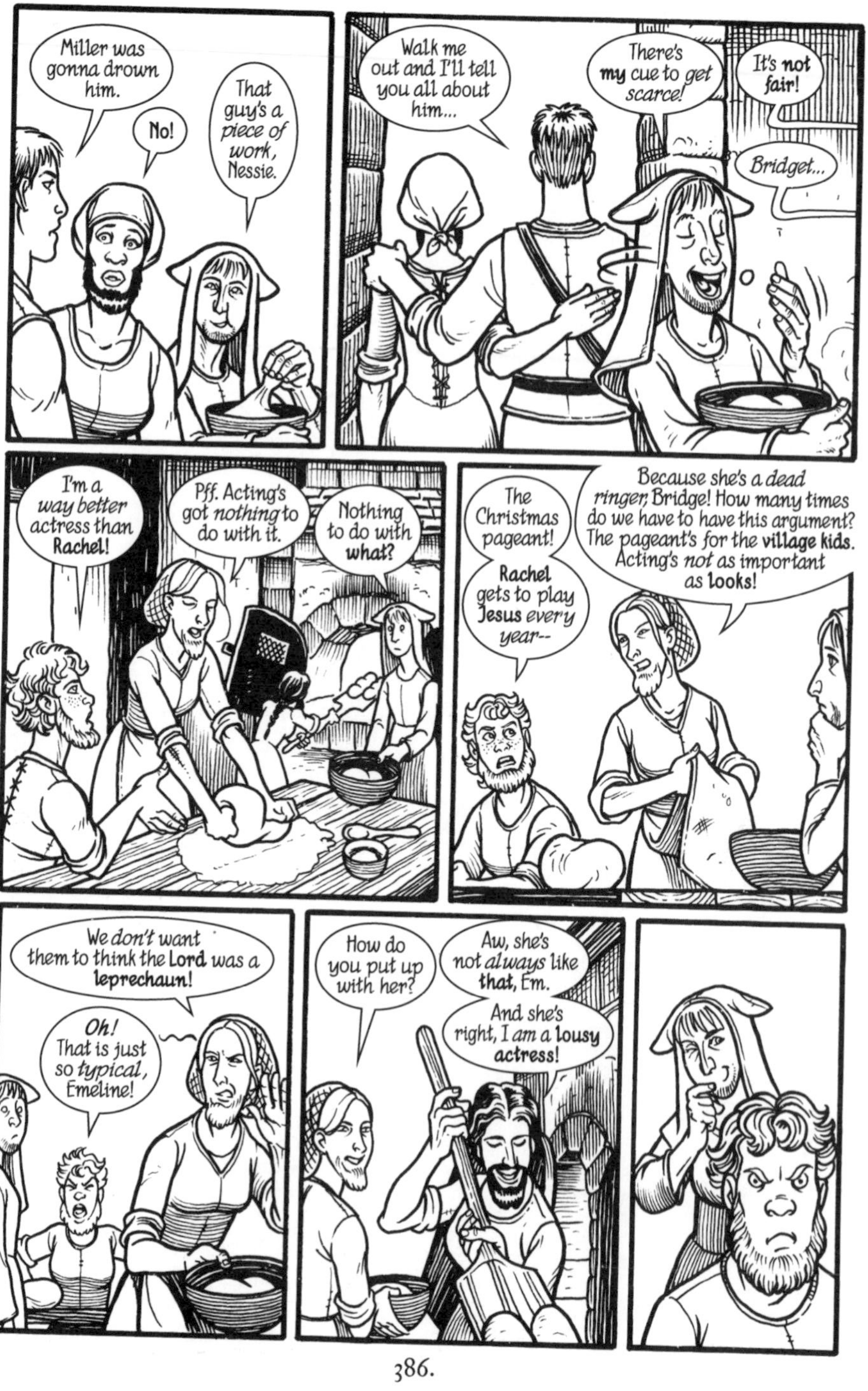
Miller was gonna drown him.
No!
That guy's a *piece of work*, Nessie.
Walk me out and I'll tell you all about him...
There's **my** cue to *get scarce!*
It's **not fair!**
Bridget...
I'm a *way better* actress than **Rachel!**
Pff. Acting's got *nothing* to do with it.
Nothing to do with **what?**
The Christmas pageant!
Rachel gets to play **Jesus** *every year--*
Because she's a *dead ringer*, Bridge! How many times do we have to have this argument? The pageant's for the **village kids**. Acting's *not* as important as **looks!**
We *don't want* them to think the **Lord** was a **leprechaun!**
Oh! That is just so *typical*, Emeline!
How do you put up with her?
Aw, she's not *always* like **that**, Em.
And she's right, I *am* a **lousy actress!**

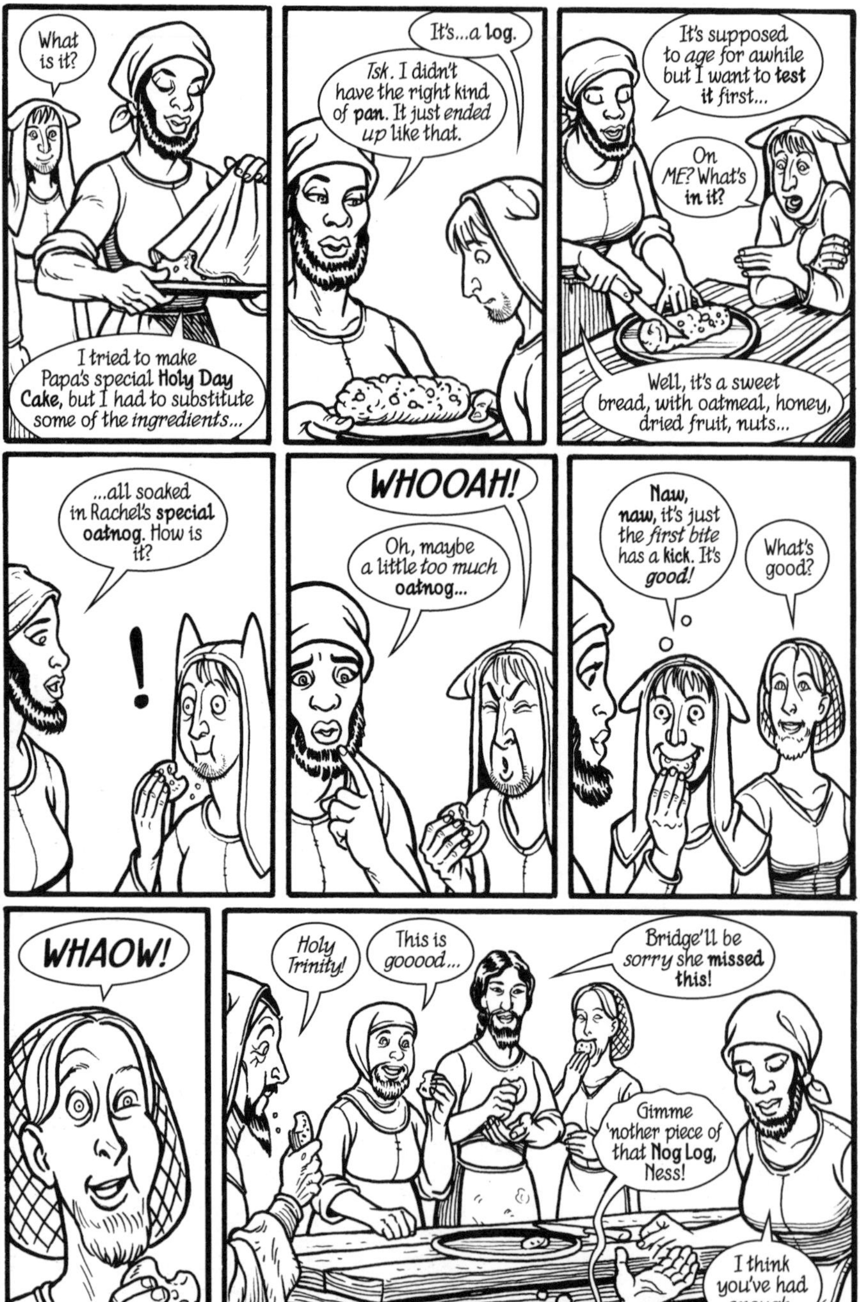
What is it?
I tried to make Papa's special **Holy Day Cake,** but I had to substitute some of the *ingredients...*
It's...a **log.**
Tsk. I didn't have the right kind of **pan**. It just *ended up* like that.
It's supposed to *age* for awhile but I want to **test it** first...
On *ME?* What's **in it?**
Well, it's a sweet bread, with oatmeal, honey, dried fruit, nuts...
...all soaked in Rachel's **special oatnog**. How is it?
!
WHOOAH!
Oh, maybe a little *too much* **oatnog...**
Naw, naw, it's just the *first bite* has a **kick**. It's ***good!***
What's good?
WHAOW!
Holy Trinity!
This is *gooood...*
Bridge'll be *sorry* she **missed this!**
Gimme 'nother piece of that **Nog Log,** Ness!
I think you've had *enough*.

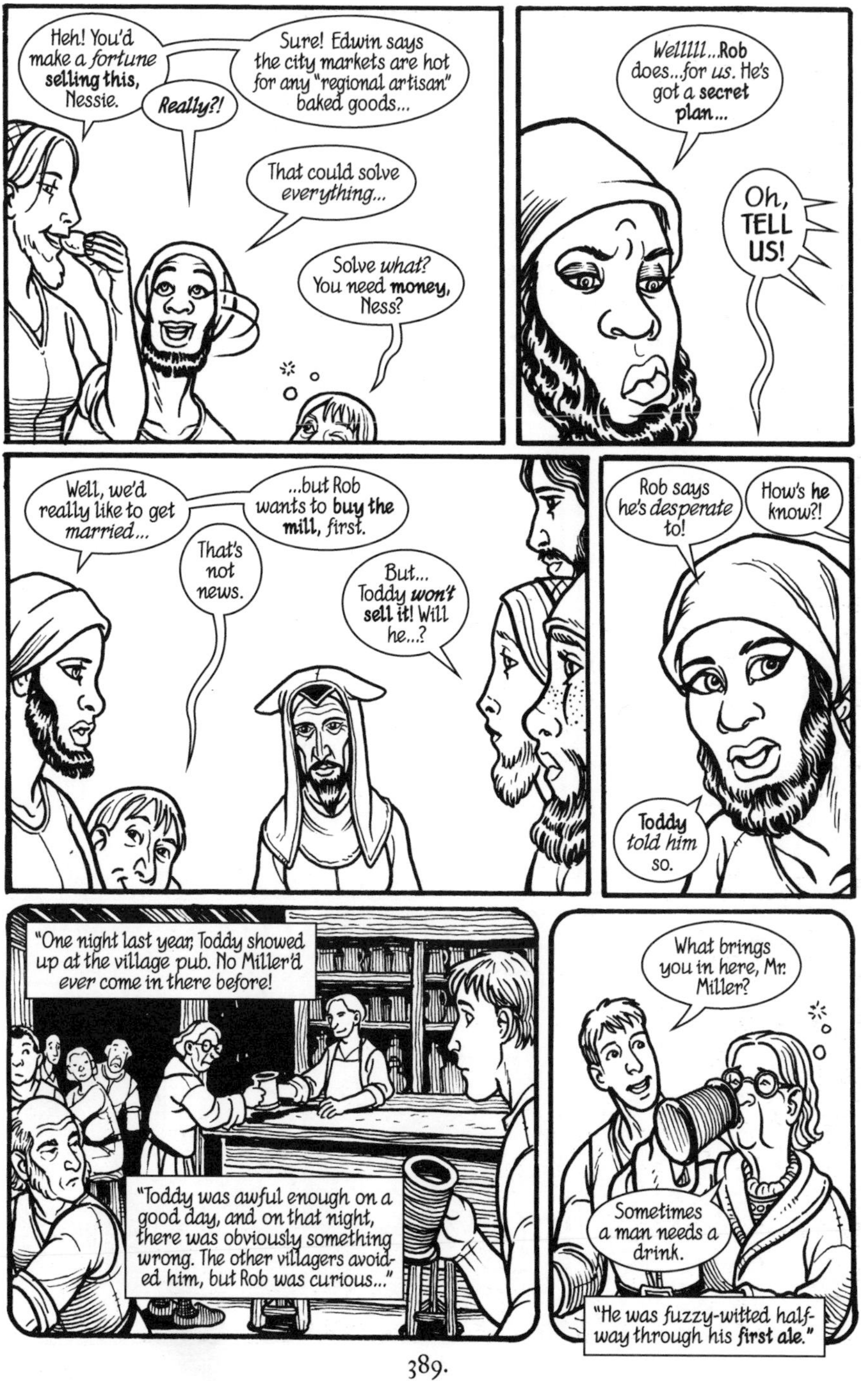
Heh! You'd make a *fortune* **selling this,** Nessie.
Sure! Edwin says the city markets are hot for any "regional artisan" baked goods...
Really?!
That could solve *everything...*
Solve *what?* You need **money,** Ness?
Welllll...**Rob** does...for *us*. He's got a **secret plan...**
Oh, **TELL US!**
Well, we'd really like to get *married...*
...but Rob wants to **buy the mill,** *first.*
That's not news.
But... Toddy ***won't*** **sell it**! Will he...?
Rob says he's *desperate* to!
How's **he** know?!
Toddy *told him* so.
"One night last year, Toddy showed up at the village pub. No Miller'd *ever* come in there before!
"Toddy was awful enough on a good day, and on that night, there was obviously something wrong. The other villagers avoided him, but Rob was curious..."
What brings you in here, Mr. Miller?
Sometimes a man needs a drink.
"He was fuzzy-witted halfway through his **first ale.**"

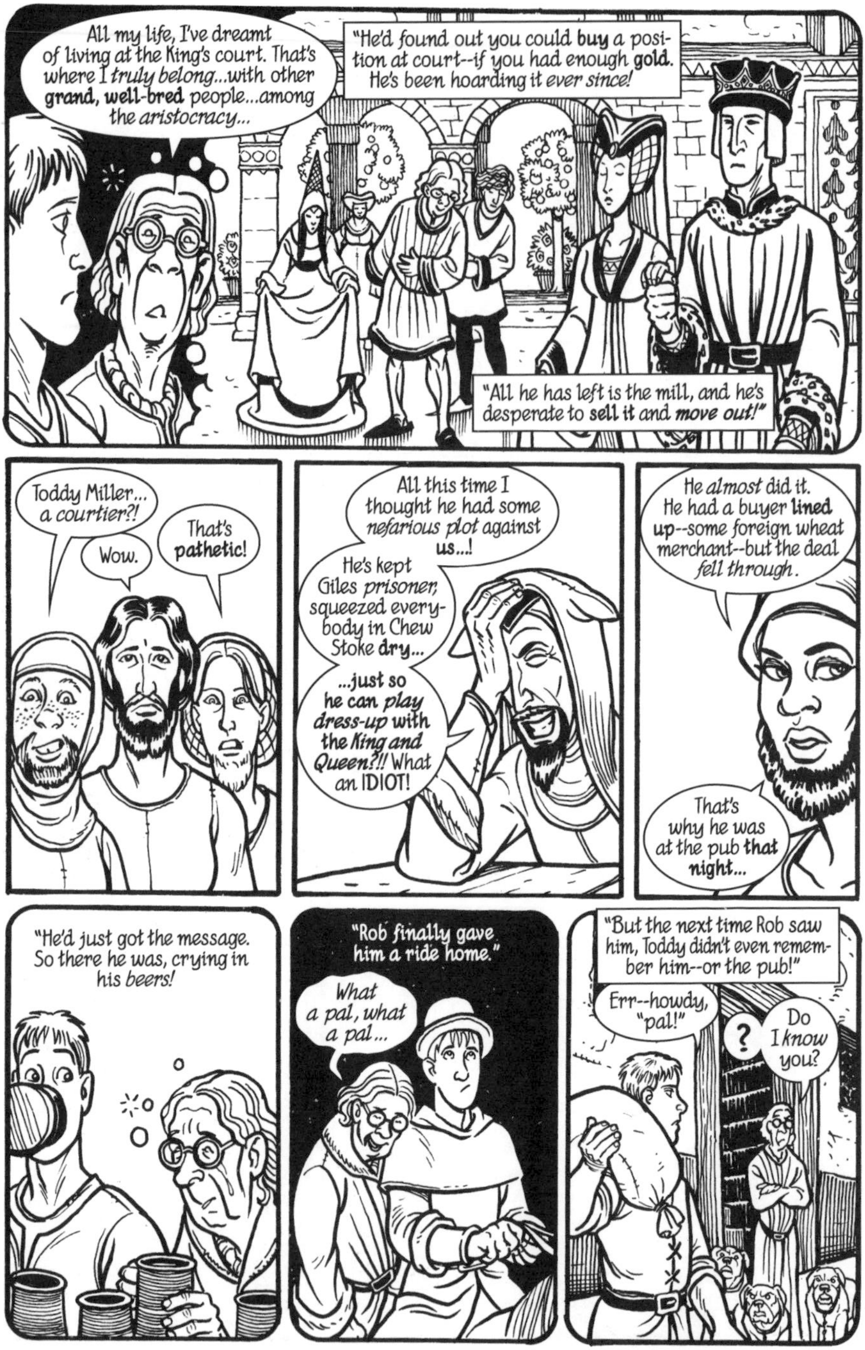
All my life, I've dreamt of living at the King's court. That's where I *truly belong*...with other **grand, well-bred** people...among the *aristocracy*...
"He'd found out you could **buy** a position at court--if you had enough **gold**. He's been hoarding it *ever since!*
"All he has left is the mill, and he's desperate to **sell it** and ***move out!***"
Toddy Miller... a *courtier?!*
Wow.
That's **pathetic**!
All this time I thought he had some *nefarious plot* against **us**...!
He's kept Giles *prisoner*, squeezed everybody in Chew Stoke **dry**...
...just so he can *play dress-up* with the *King and Queen?!!* What an IDIOT!
He *almost* did it. He had a buyer **lined up**--some foreign wheat merchant--but the deal *fell through*.
That's why he was at the pub **that night...**
"He'd just got the message. So there he was, crying in his *beers!*
"Rob *finally* gave him a ride home."
What a pal, what a pal...
"But the next time Rob saw him, Toddy didn't even remember him--or the pub!"
Err--howdy, "pal!"
?
Do I *know* you?

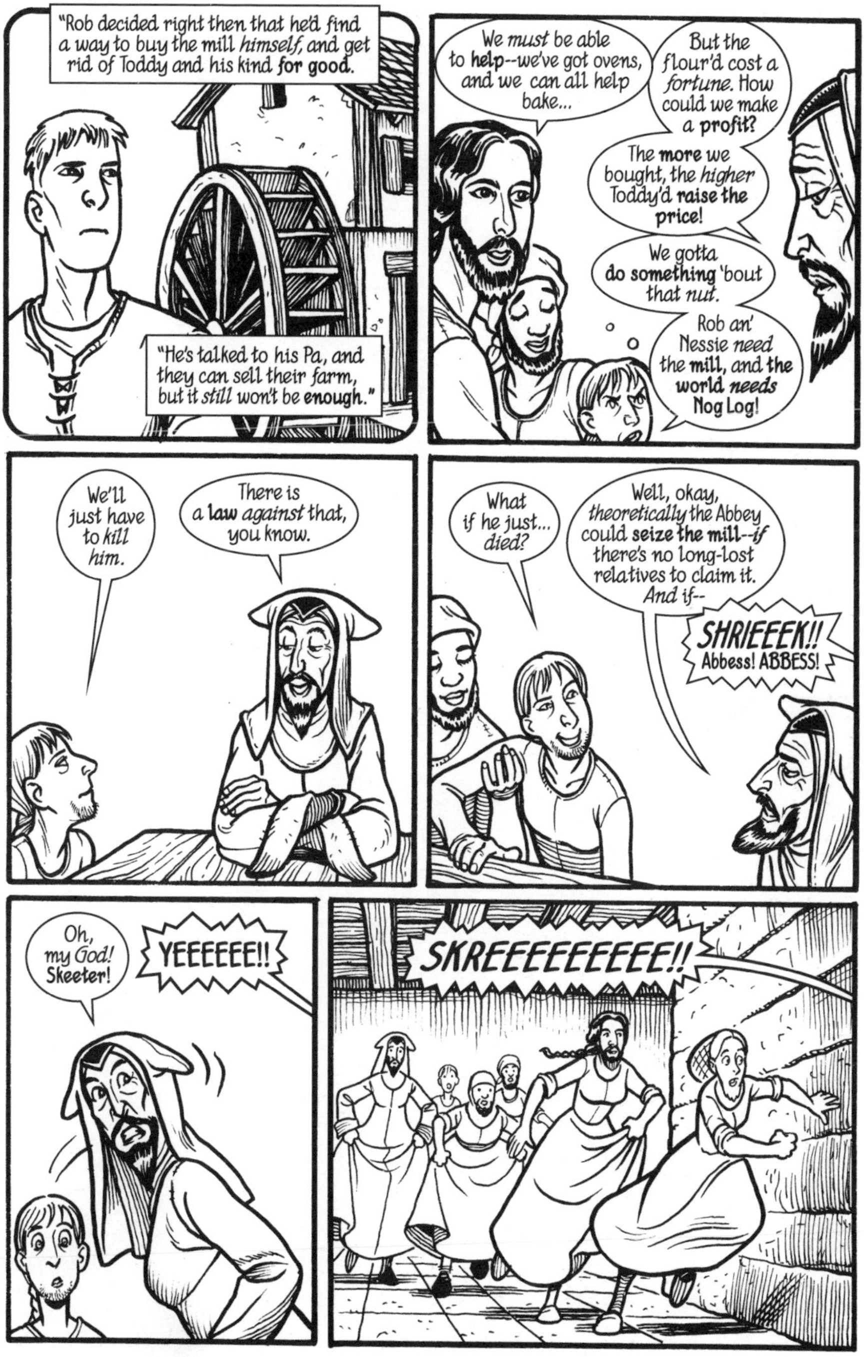
"Rob decided right then that he'd find a way to buy the mill *himself,* and get rid of Toddy and his kind **for good**.
"He's talked to his Pa, and they can sell their *farm,* but it *still* won't be **enough.**"
We *must* be able to **help**--we've got ovens, and we can all help bake...
But the flour'd cost a *fortune.* How could we make a **profit?**
The **more** we bought, the *higher* Toddy'd **raise the price!**
We gotta **do something** 'bout that *nut.*
Rob an' Nessie *need* the **mill,** and **the world** ***needs*** **Nog Log!**
We'll just have to *kill him.*
There is a **law** *against* that, you know.
What if he just... *died?*
Well, okay, *theoretically* the Abbey could **seize the mill**--*if* there's no long-lost relatives to claim it. *And if*--
SHRIEEEK!! Abbess! ABBESS!
Oh, my God! **Skeeter!**
YEEEEEE!!
SKREEEEEEEEEEE!!

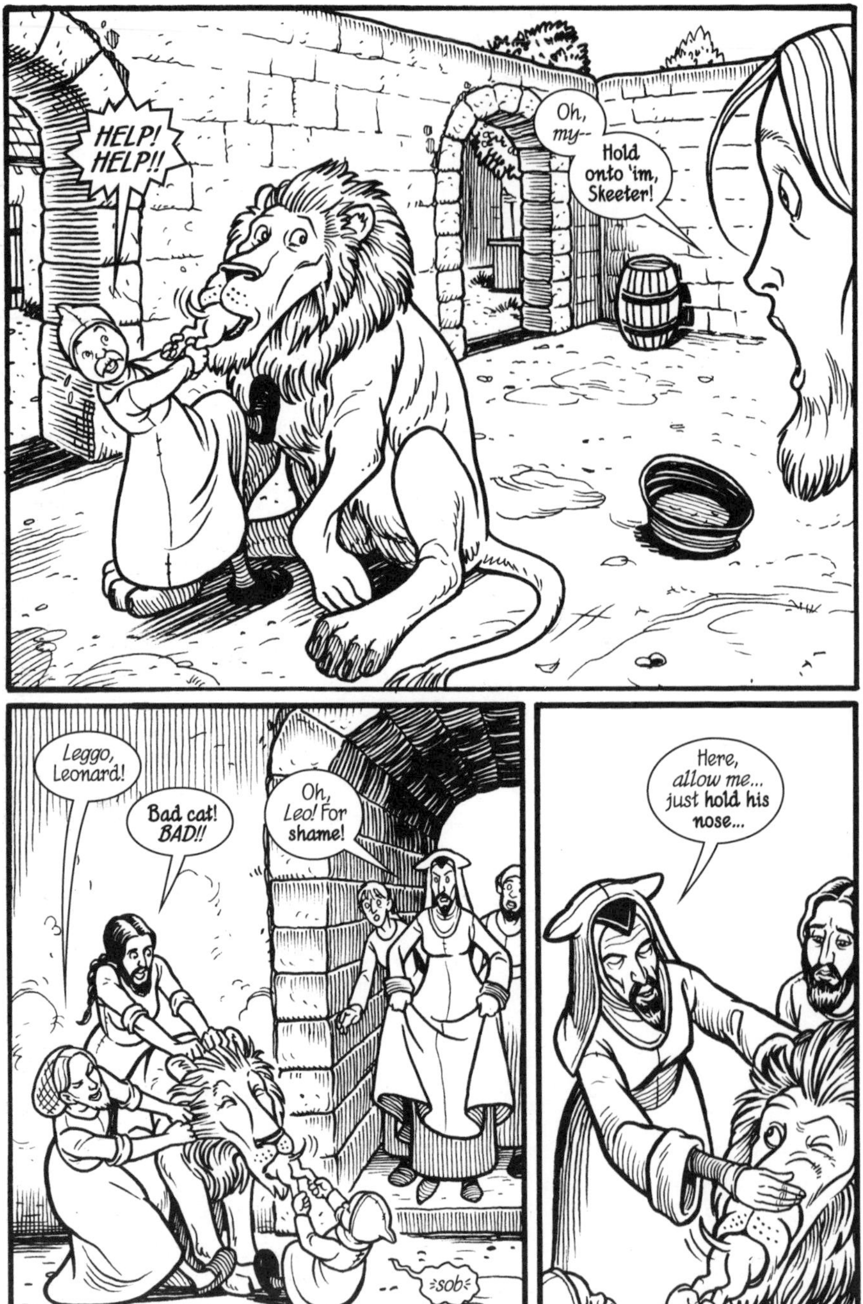
HELP! HELP!!
Oh, my--
Hold onto 'im, Skeeter!
Leggo, Leonard!
Bad cat! BAD!!
Oh, Leo! For shame!
sob
Here, allow me... just hold his nose...

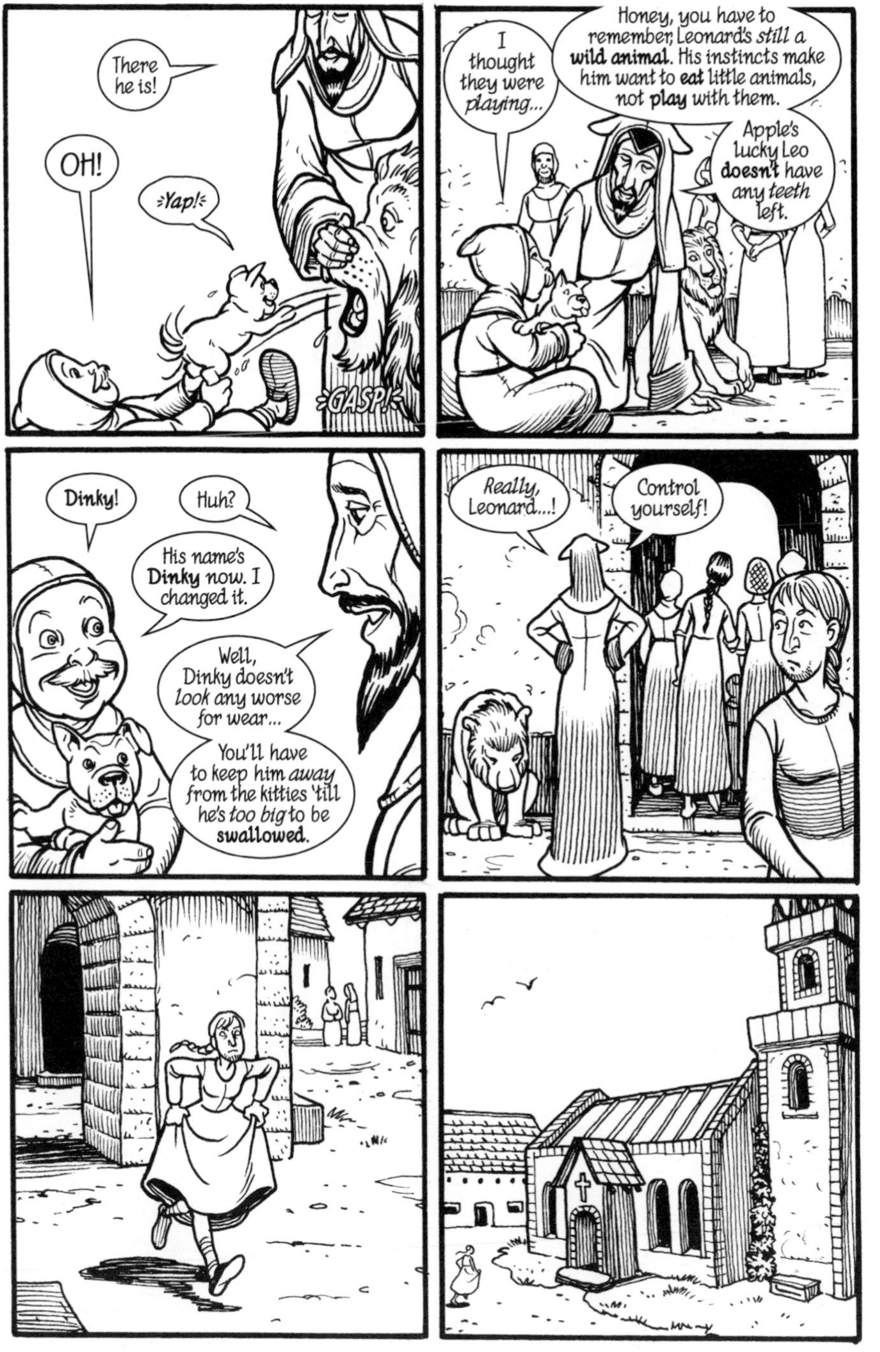
There he is!
OH!
Yap!
GASP!
I thought they were *playing*...
Honey, you have to remember, Leonard's *still* a **wild animal**. His instincts make him want to **eat** little animals, not **play** with them.
Apple's lucky Leo **doesn't** have any *teeth* left.
Dinky!
Huh?
His name's **Dinky** now. I changed it.
Well, Dinky doesn't *look* any worse for wear...
You'll have to keep him *away* from the kitties 'till he's *too big* to be **swallowed**.
Really, Leonard...!
Control yourself!

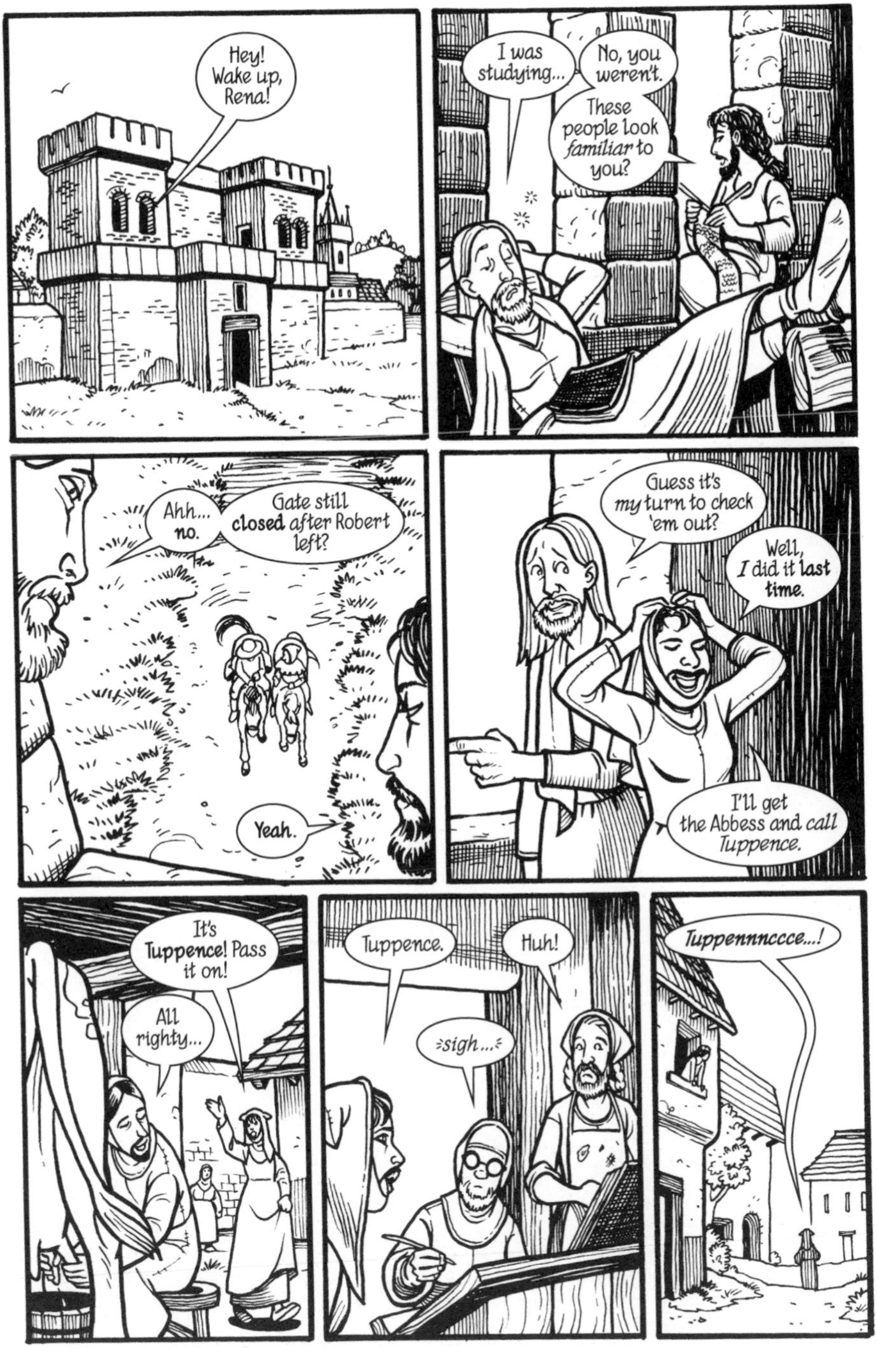
Hey! Wake up, Rena!
I was studying...
No, you weren't.
These people look *familiar* to you?
Ahh... **no.**
Gate still **closed** *after* Robert left?
Yeah.
Guess it's *my* turn to check 'em out?
Well, *I* did it **last time.**
I'll get the Abbess and call *Tuppence.*
It's **Tuppence!** Pass it on!
All righty...
Tuppence.
Huh!
sigh...
Tuppennnccce...!

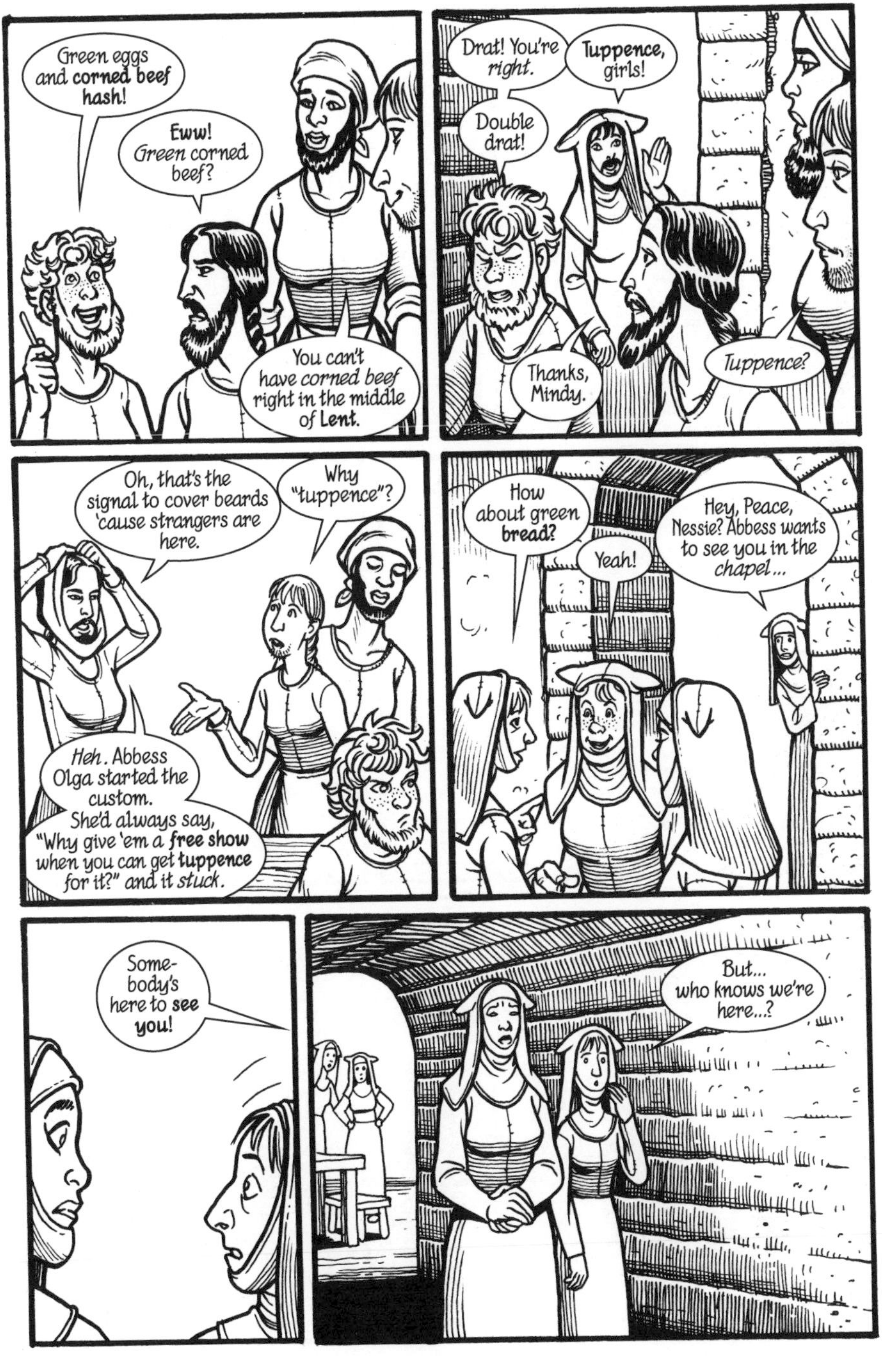
Green eggs and **corned beef hash!**
Eww! *Green* corned beef?
You can't have *corned beef* right in the middle of **Lent**.
Drat! You're *right*.
Double drat!
Tuppence, girls!
Thanks, Mindy.
Tuppence?
Oh, that's the signal to cover beards 'cause strangers are here.
Why "tuppence"?
Heh. Abbess Olga started the custom. She'd always say, "Why give 'em a **free show** when you can get **tuppence** for it?" and it *stuck*.
How about green **bread?**
Yeah!
Hey, Peace, Nessie? Abbess wants to see you in the *chapel*...
Some-body's here to **see you!**
But... who knows we're here...?

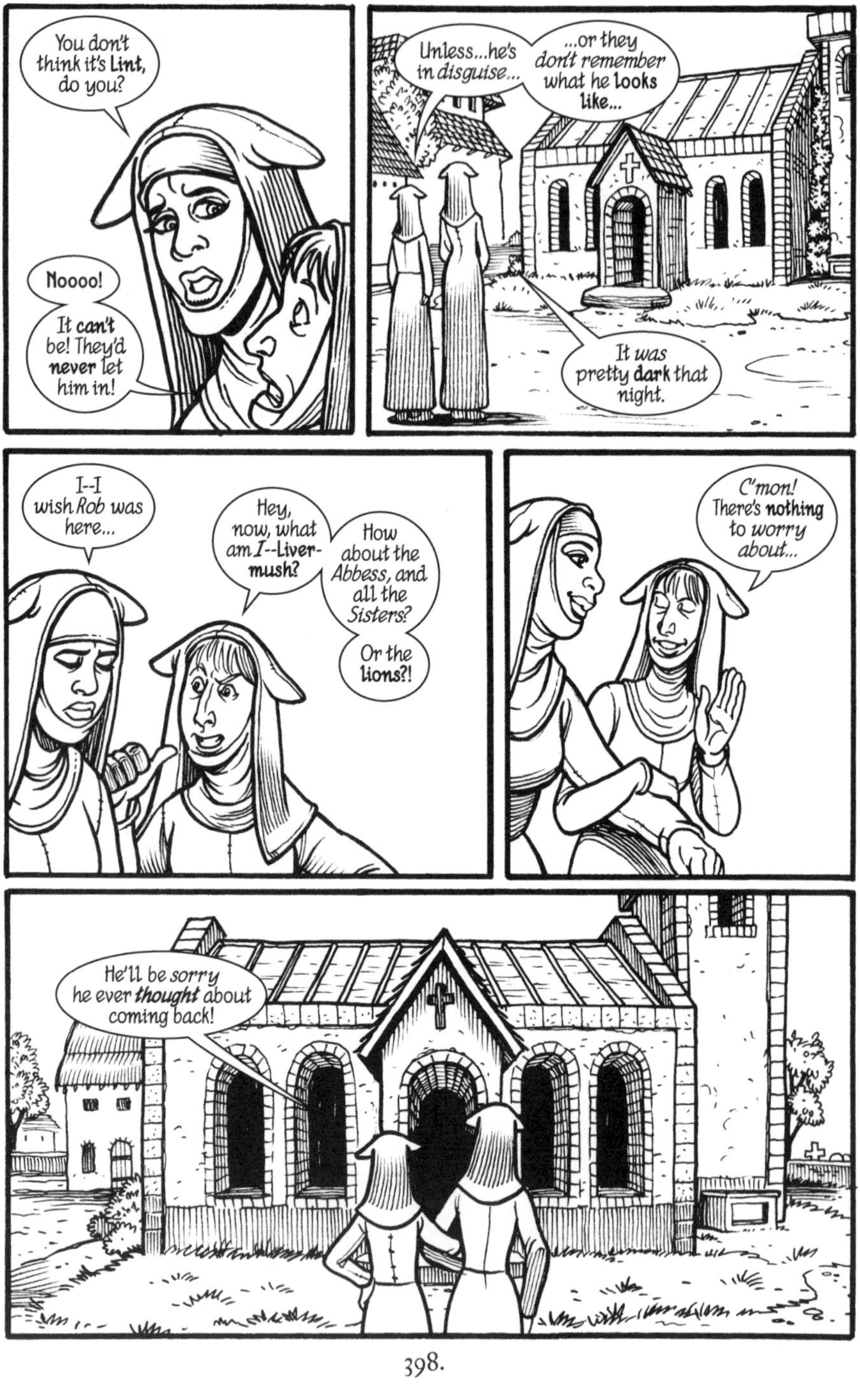
You don't think it's **Lint,** do you?
Noooo!
It **can't** be! They'd **never** let him in!
Unless...he's in *disguise*...
...or they *don't remember* what he **looks like...**
It *was* pretty **dark** that night.
I--I wish *Rob* was here...
Hey, now, what am *I*--**Liver-mush?**
How about the *Abbess,* and all the *Sisters?*
Or the **lions?!**
C'mon! There's **nothing** to *worry* about...
He'll be *sorry* he ever ***thought*** about coming back!

Chapter 18.

· SOLICITINE PT. 6 ·

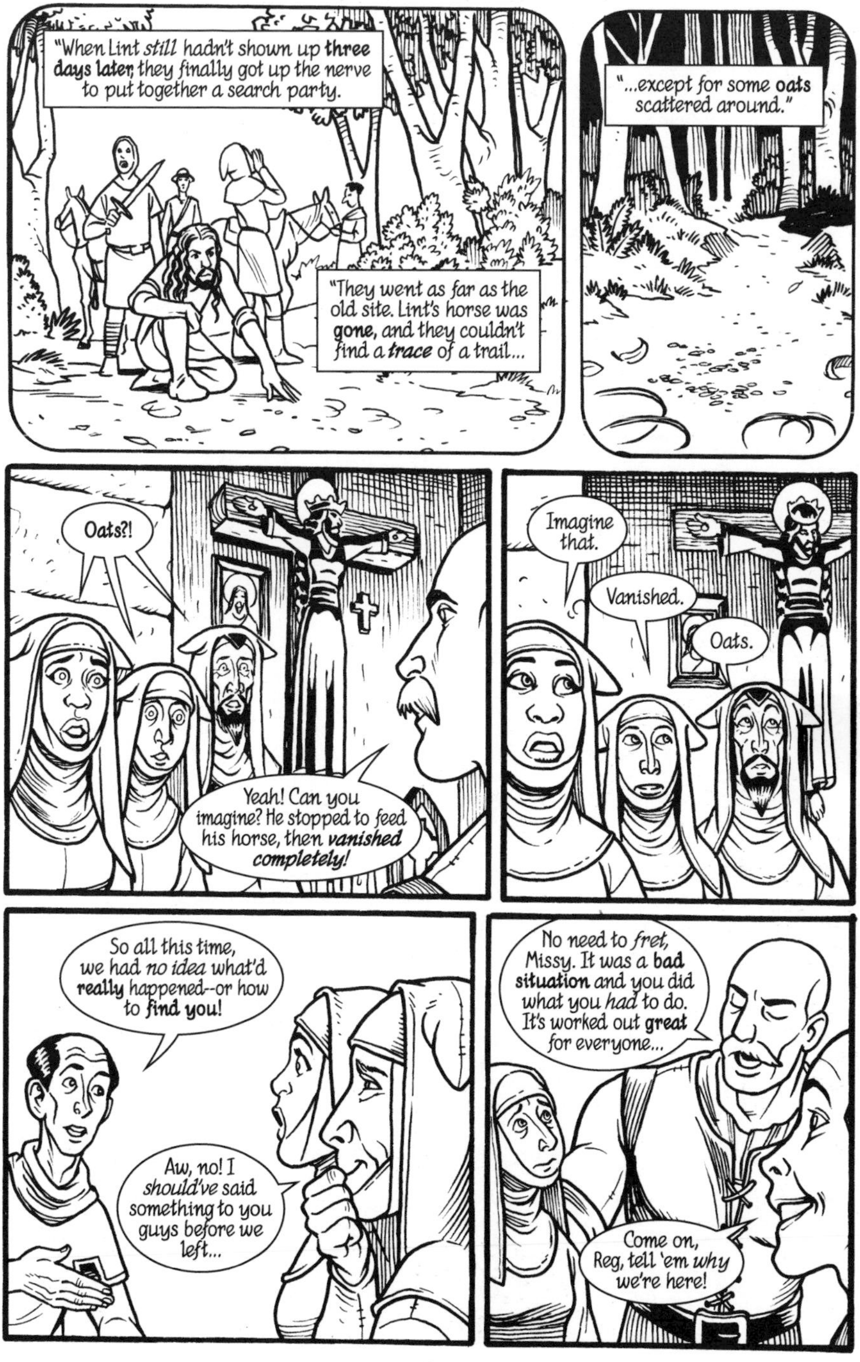
"When Lint still hadn't shown up three days later, they finally got up the nerve to put together a search party.
"They went as far as the old site. Lint's horse was gone, and they couldn't find a trace of a trail...
"...except for some oats scattered around."
Oats?!
Yeah! Can you imagine? He stopped to feed his horse, then vanished completely!
Imagine that.
Vanished.
Oats.
So all this time, we had no idea what'd really happened--or how to find you!
Aw, no! I should've said something to you guys before we left...
No need to fret, Missy. It was a bad situation and you did what you had to do. It's worked out great for everyone...
Come on, Reg, tell 'em why we're here!

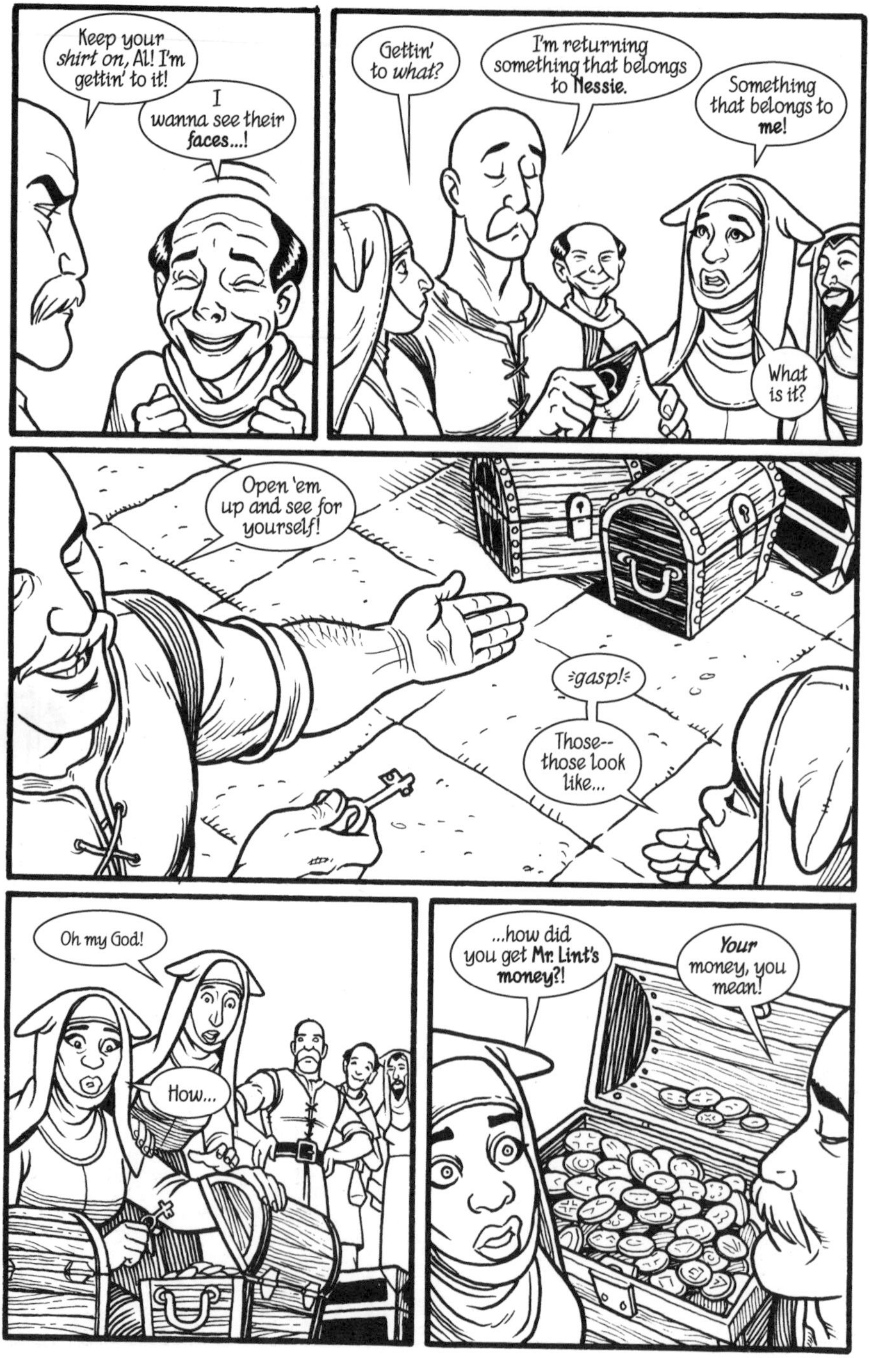
Keep your *shirt on*, Al! I'm gettin' to it!
I wanna see their **faces**...!
Gettin' to *what?*
I'm returning something that belongs to **Nessie.**
Something that belongs to **me!**
What is it?
Open 'em up and see for yourself!
gasp!
Those-- those look like...
Oh my God!
How...
...how did you get **Mr. Lint's money?!**
Your money, you mean!

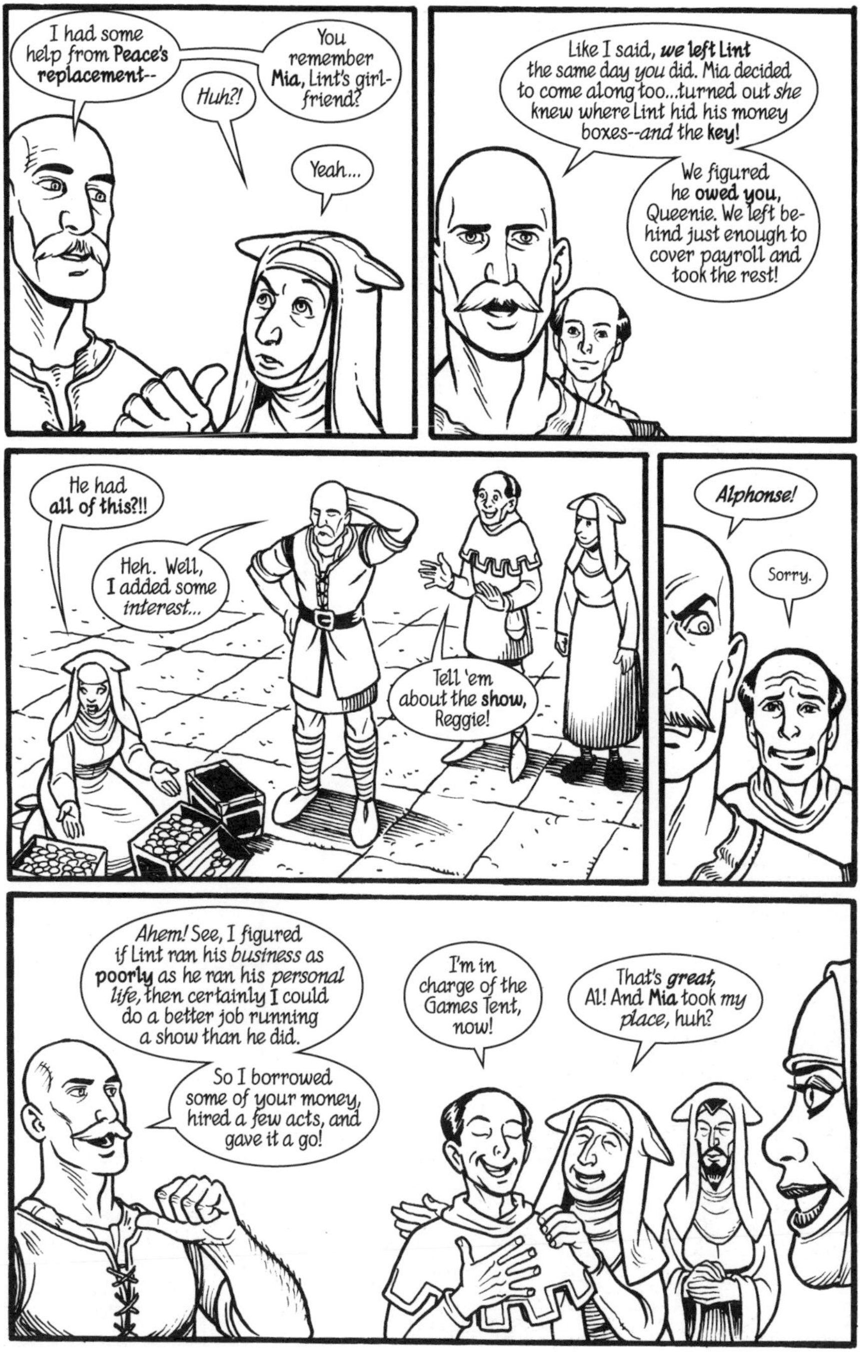
I had some help from **Peace's replacement**--
You remember **Mia**, Lint's girl-friend?
Huh?!
Yeah...
Like I said, ***we left Lint*** the same day *you* did. Mia decided to come along too...turned out *she* knew where Lint hid his money boxes--*and* the **key!**
We figured he **owed you**, Queenie. We left behind just enough to cover payroll and took the rest!
He had **all of this?!!**
Heh. Well, I added some *interest...*
Tell 'em about the **show**, Reggie!
Alphonse!
Sorry.
Ahem! See, I figured if Lint ran his *business* as **poorly** as he ran his *personal life*, then certainly I could do a better job running a show than he did.
So I borrowed some of your money, hired a few acts, and gave it a go!
I'm in charge of the Games Tent, now!
That's ***great***, Al! And **Mia** took *my place*, huh?

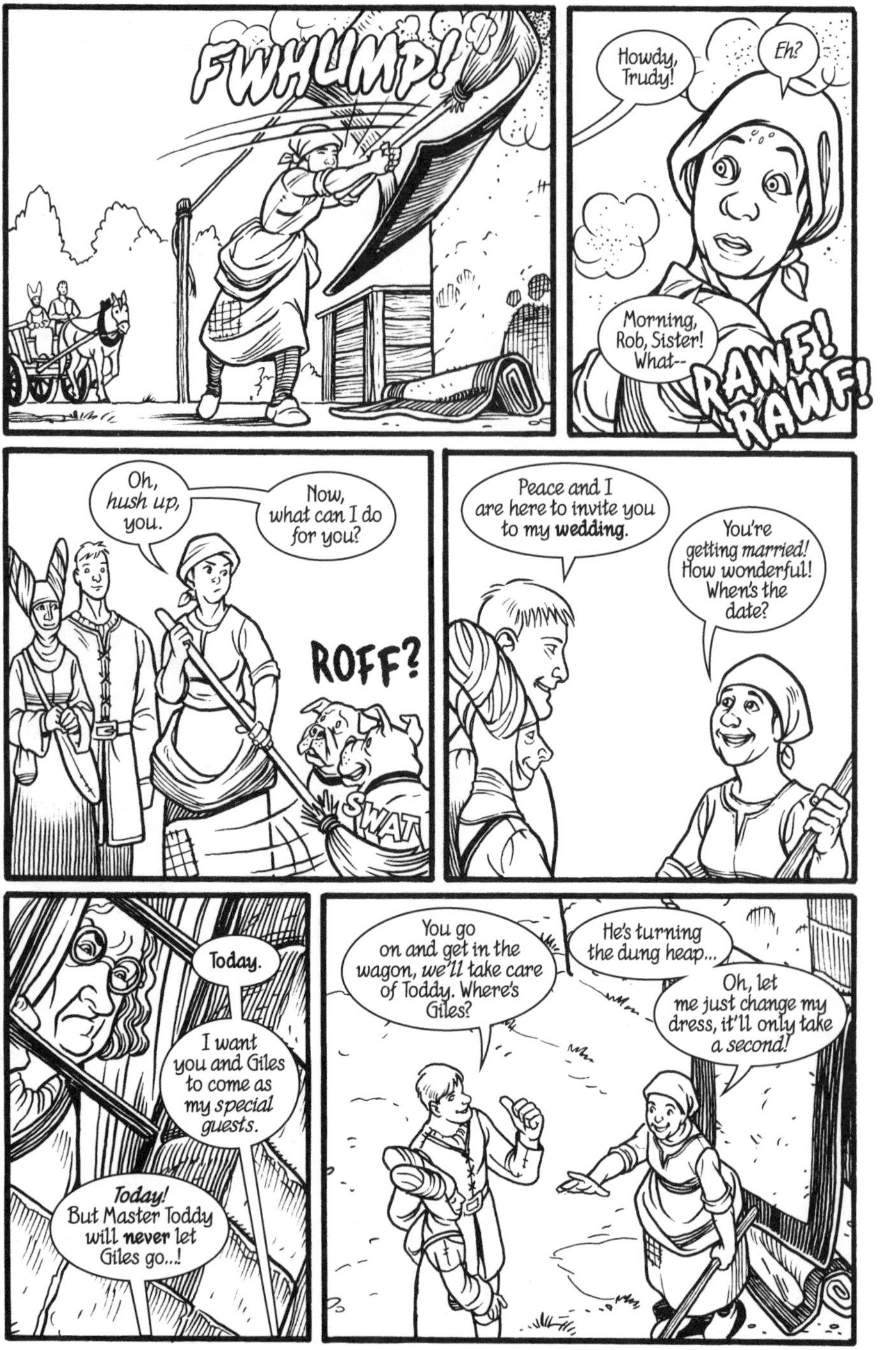
FWHUMP!
Howdy, Trudy!
Eh?
Morning, Rob, Sister! What--
RAWF! RAWF!
Oh, *hush up,* you.
Now, what can I do for you?
ROFF?
SWAT
Peace and I are here to invite you to my **wedding**.
You're getting *married!* How wonderful! When's the date?
Today.
I want you and Giles to come as my *special guests.*
Today! But Master Toddy will **never** let Giles go...!
You go on and get in the wagon, *we'll* take care of Toddy. Where's Giles?
He's turning the dung heap...
Oh, let me just change my dress, it'll only take *a second!*

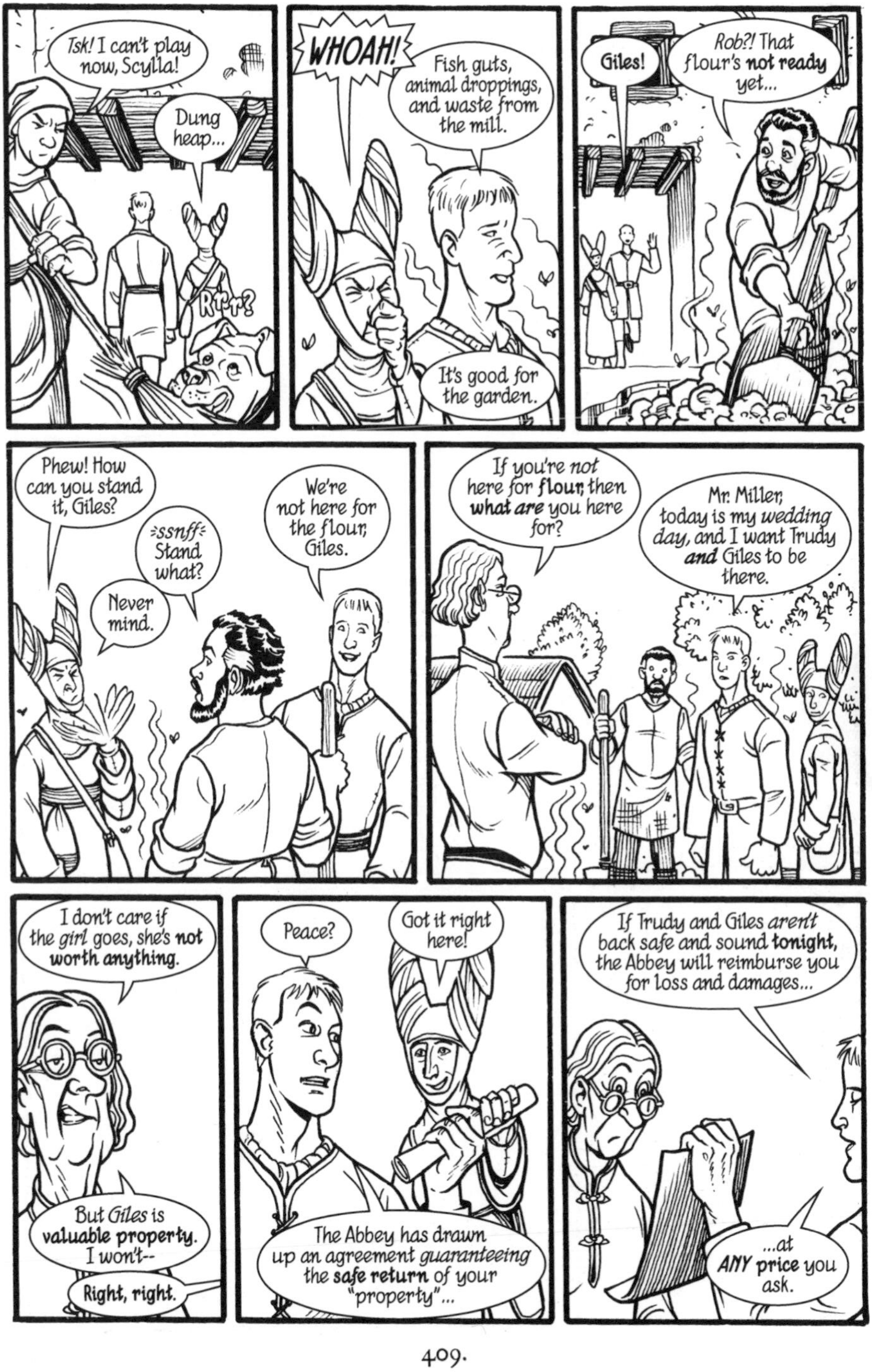
Tsk! I can't play now, Scylla!
Dung heap...
Rrr?
WHOAH!
Fish guts, animal droppings, and waste from the mill.
It's good for the garden.
Giles!
Rob?! That flour's **not ready** yet...
Phew! How can you stand it, Giles?
ssnff Stand what?
Never mind.
We're not here for the flour, Giles.
If you're *not* here for **flour**, then **what are** you here for?
Mr. Miller, today is my *wedding day*, and I want Trudy **and** Giles to be there.
I don't care if the *girl* goes, she's **not worth anything**.
But *Giles* is **valuable property**. I won't--
Right, right.
Peace?
Got it right here!
The Abbey has drawn up an agreement *guaranteeing* the **safe return** of your "property"...
If Trudy and Giles *aren't* back safe and sound **tonight**, the Abbey will reimburse you for loss and damages...
...at **ANY price** you ask.

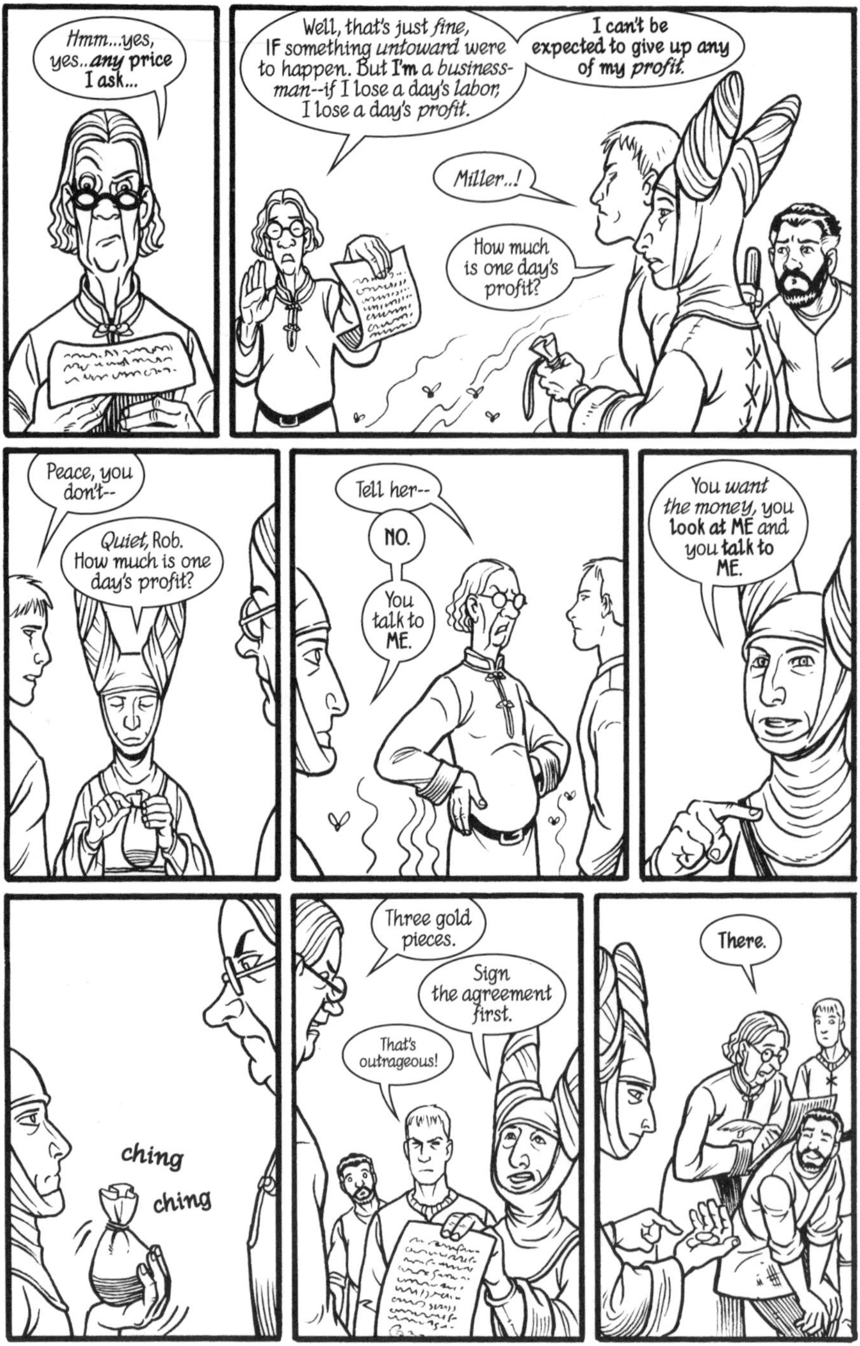

Hmm...yes, yes..any price I ask...
Well, that's just fine, IF something untoward were to happen. But I'm a businessman--if I lose a day's labor, I lose a day's profit.
I can't be expected to give up any of my profit.
Miller..!
How much is one day's profit?
Peace, you don't--
Quiet, Rob. How much is one day's profit?
Tell her--
NO.
You talk to ME.
You want the money, you look at ME and you talk to ME.
ching
ching
Three gold pieces.
Sign the agreement first.
That's outrageous!
There.

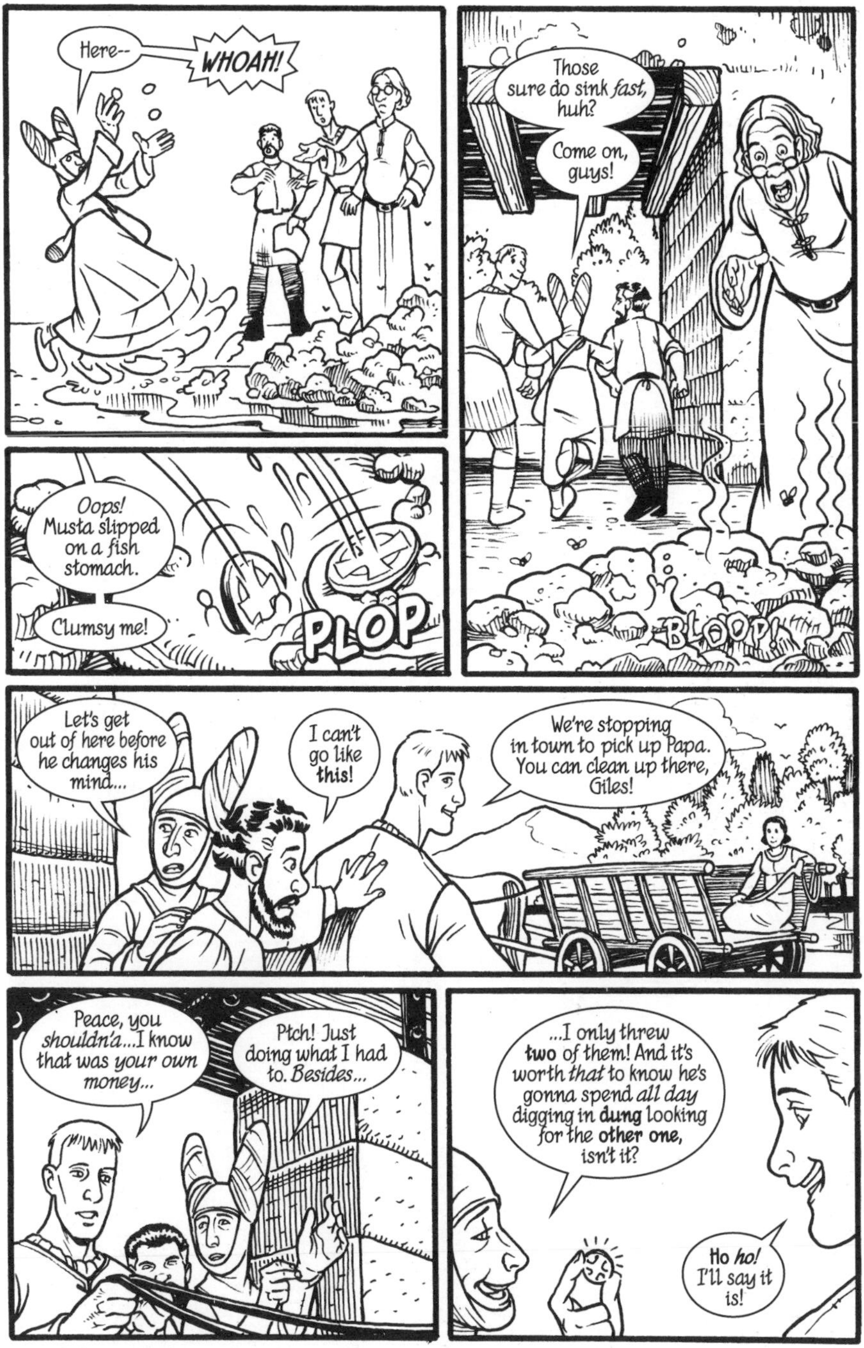

Here--
WHOAH!
Those sure do sink *fast*, huh?
Come on, guys!
Oops! Musta slipped on a fish stomach.
Clumsy me!
PLOP
BLOOP!
Let's get out of here before he changes his mind...
I can't go like **this**!
We're stopping in town to pick up Papa. You can clean up there, Giles!
Peace, you *shouldn'a*...I know that was *your own* money...
Ptch! Just doing what I had to. *Besides...*
...I only threw **two** of them! And it's worth *that* to know he's gonna spend *all day* digging in **dung** looking for the **other one**, isn't it?
Ho *ho!* I'll say it is!

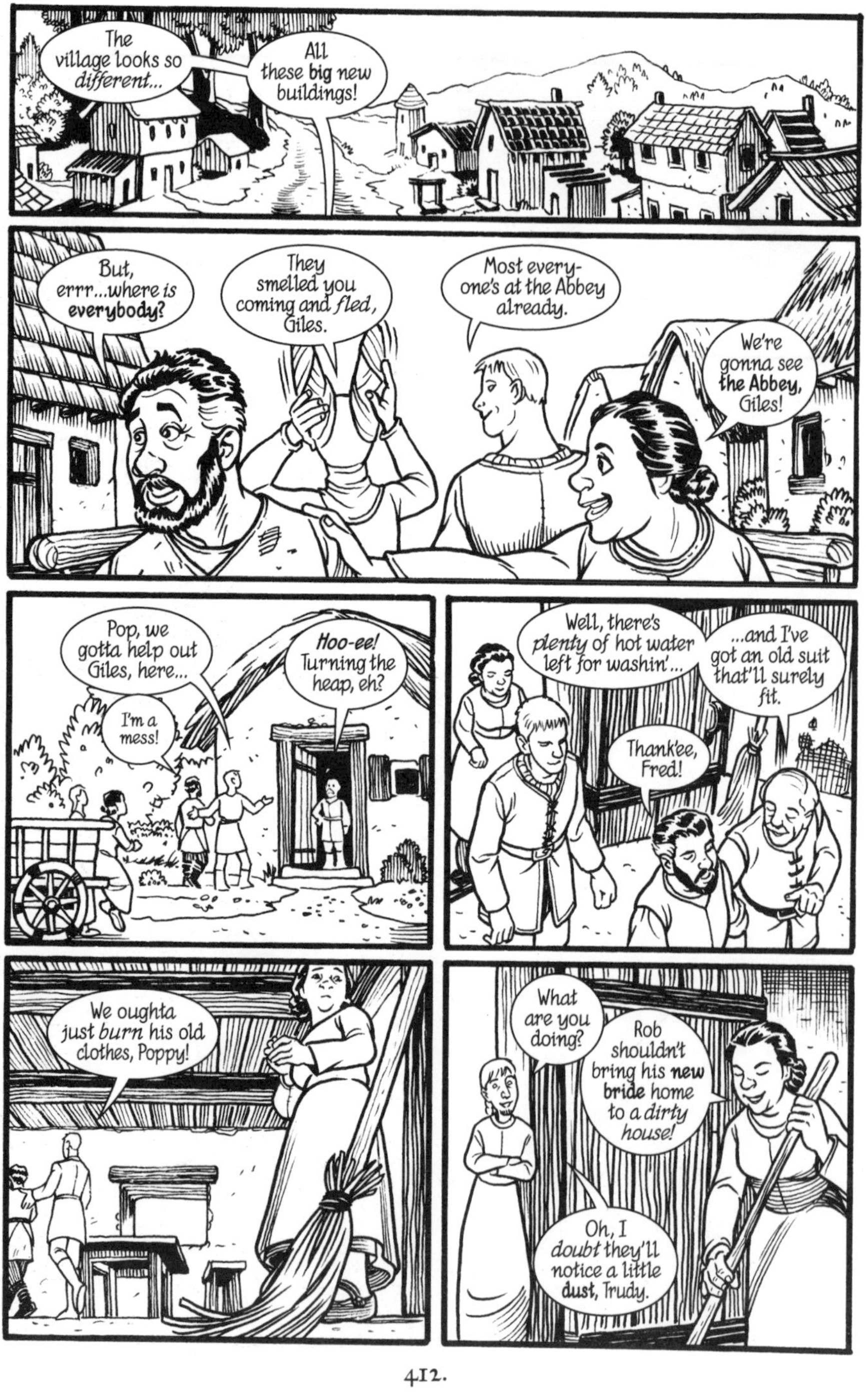
The village looks so *different*...
All these **big** new buildings!
But, errr...where *is* **everybody?**
They smelled you coming and *fled*, Giles.
Most every-one's at the Abbey already.
We're gonna see **the Abbey,** Giles!
Pop, we gotta help out Giles, here...
I'm a mess!
Hoo-ee! Turning the heap, eh?
Well, there's *plenty* of hot water left for washin'...
...and I've got an old suit that'll surely fit.
Thank'ee, Fred!
We oughta just *burn* his old clothes, Poppy!
What are you doing?
Rob shouldn't bring his **new bride** home to a *dirty house!*
Oh, I *doubt* they'll notice a little **dust**, Trudy.

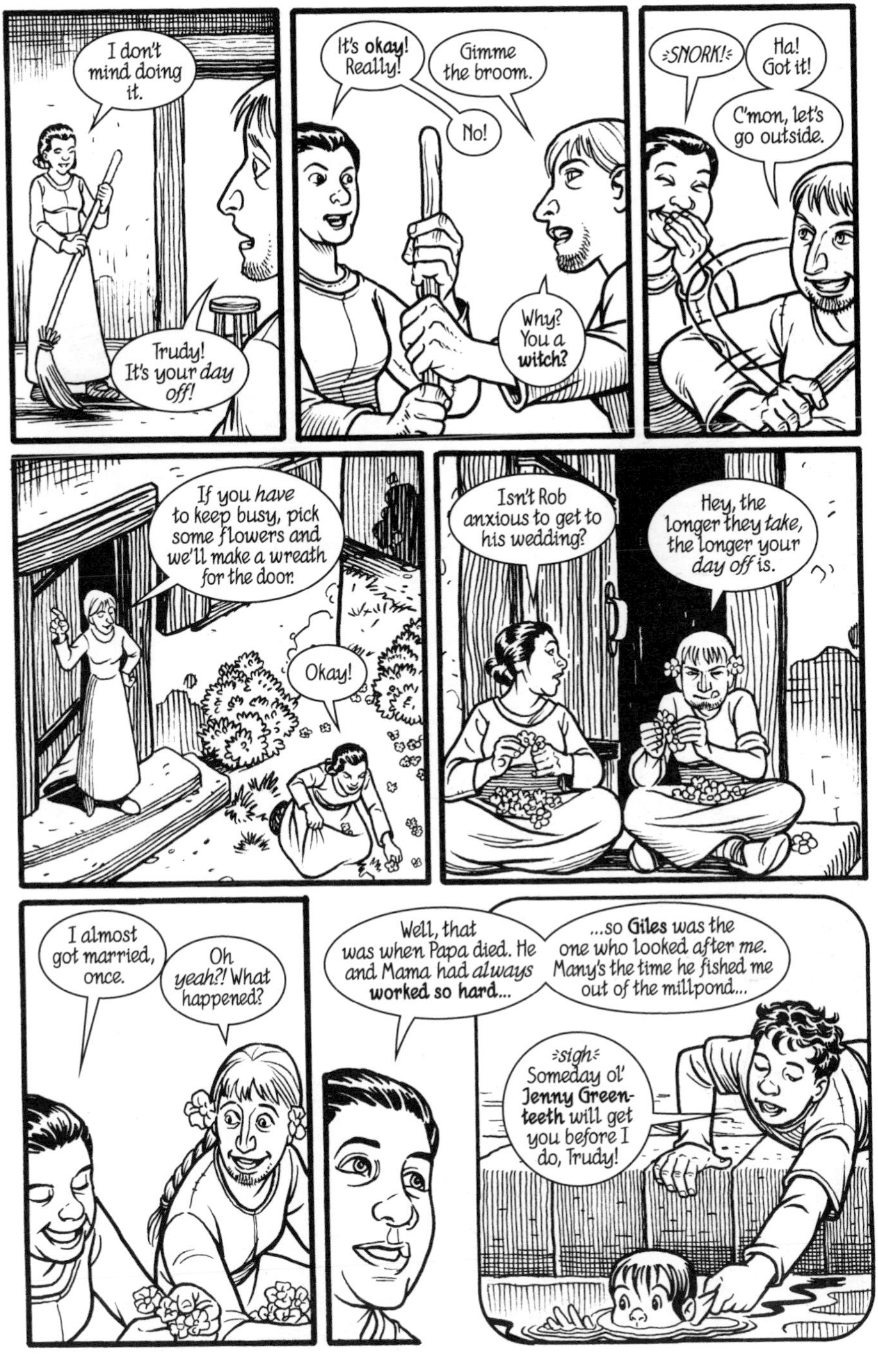
I don't mind doing it.
Trudy! It's your *day off!*
It's **okay!** Really!
Gimme the broom.
No!
Why? You a **witch?**
SNORK!
Ha! Got it!
C'mon, let's go outside.
If you *have* to keep busy, pick some flowers and we'll make a wreath for the door.
Okay!
Isn't Rob anxious to get to his wedding?
Hey, the longer they *take,* the longer your *day off* is.
I almost got married, once.
Oh *yeah?!* What happened?
Well, that was when Papa died. He and Mama had *always* **worked so hard...**
...so **Giles** was the one who looked *after me.* Many's the time he fished me out of the millpond...
sigh
Someday ol' **Jenny Greenteeth** will get you before I do, Trudy!

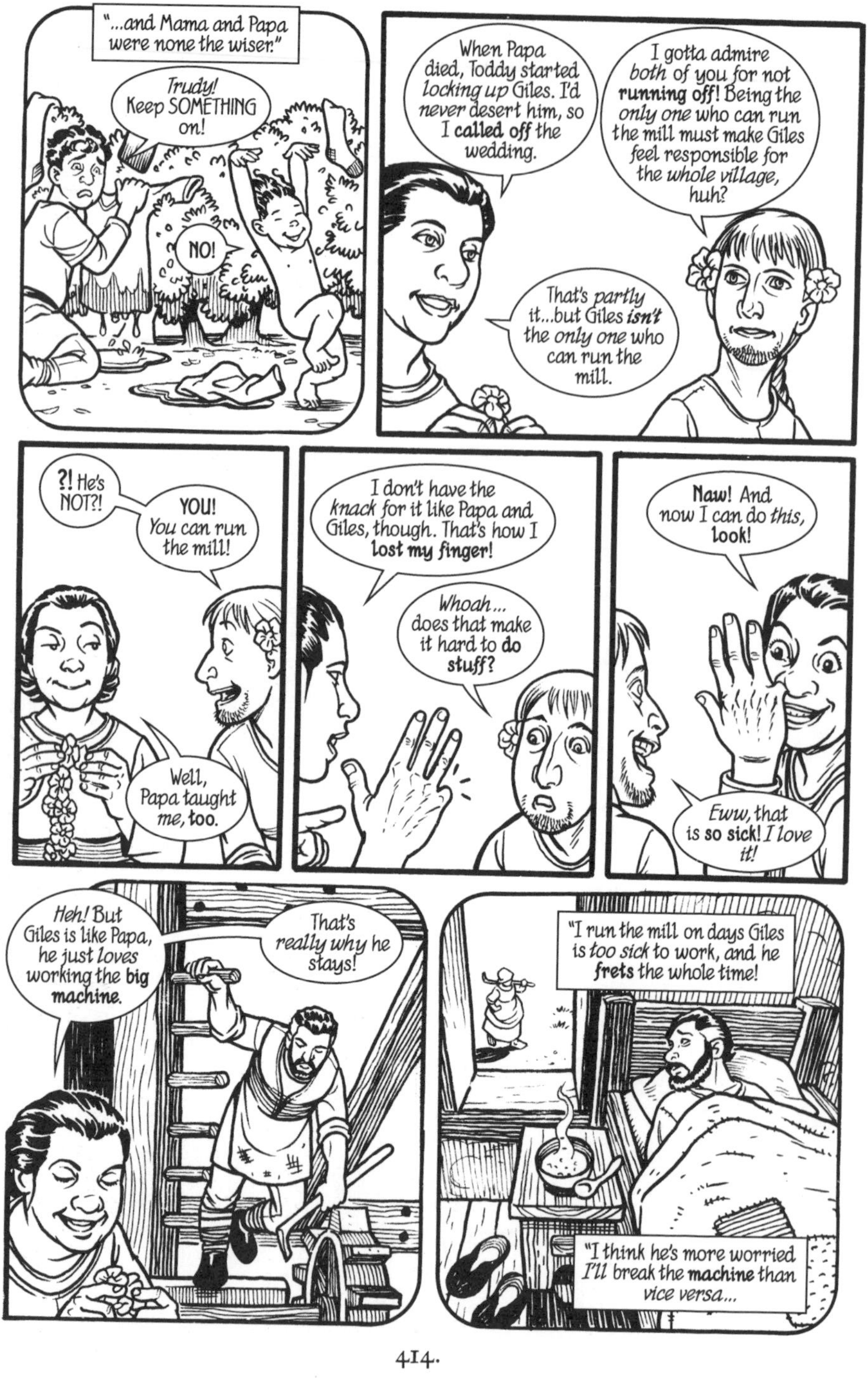
"...and Mama and Papa were none the wiser."
Trudy! Keep SOMETHING on!
NO!
When Papa died, Toddy started *locking up* Giles. I'd *never* desert him, so I **called off** the wedding.
I gotta admire *both* of you for not **running off**! Being the *only one* who can run the mill must make Giles feel responsible for the *whole village*, huh?
That's *partly* it...but Giles ***isn't*** the *only one* who can run the mill.
?! He's NOT?!
YOU! *You* can run the mill!
Well, Papa taught me, **too**.
I don't have the *knack* for it like Papa and Giles, though. That's how I **lost my finger**!
Whoah... does that make it hard to **do stuff?**
Naw! And now I can do *this,* **look!**
Eww, that is **so sick!** *I love it!*
Heh! But Giles is like Papa, he just *loves* working the **big machine.**
That's *really why* he stays!
"I run the mill on days Giles is *too sick* to work, and he **frets** the whole time!
"I think he's more worried *I'll* break the **machine** than *vice versa...*

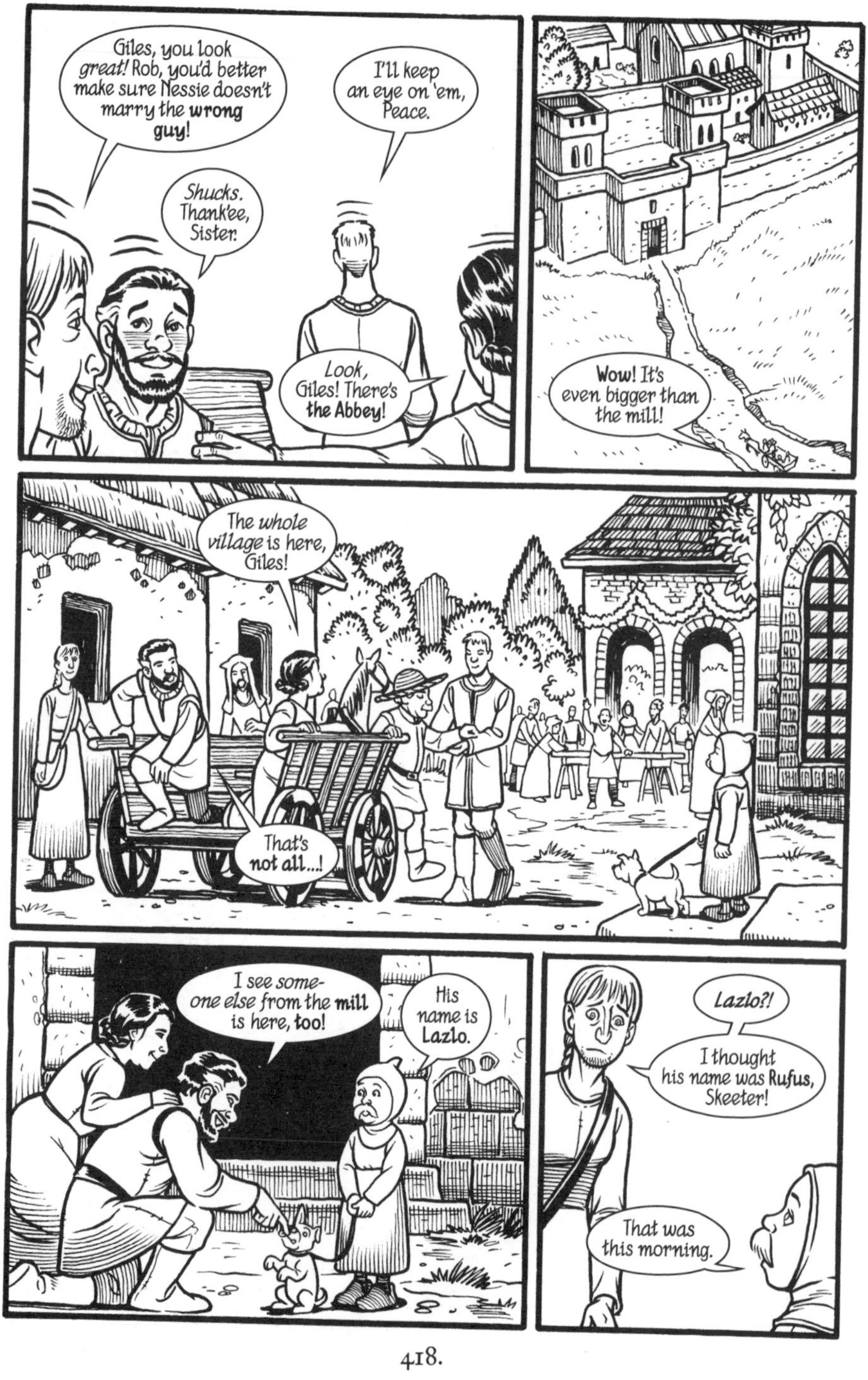
Giles, you look *great!* Rob, you'd better make sure Nessie doesn't marry the **wrong guy**!
Shucks. Thank'ee, Sister.
I'll keep an eye on 'em, Peace.
Look, Giles! There's **the Abbey**!
Wow! It's even bigger than the mill!
The *whole village* is here, Giles!
That's **not all**...!
I see *some-one else* from the **mill** is here, **too**!
His name is **Lazlo.**
Lazlo?!
I thought his name was **Rufus**, Skeeter!
That was this morning.

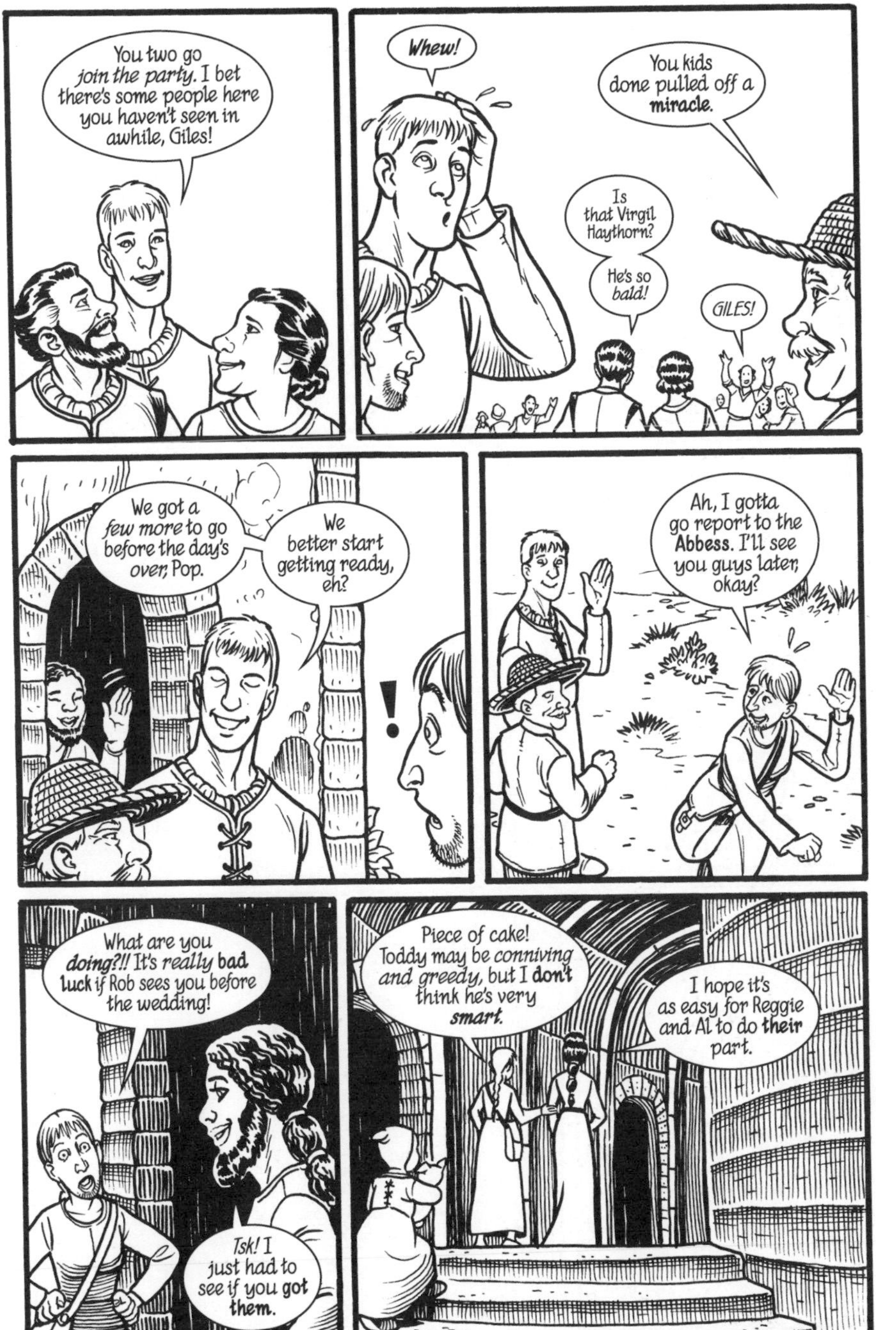
You two go *join the party*. I bet there's some people here you haven't seen in awhile, Giles!
Whew!
You kids done pulled off a **miracle**.
Is that Virgil Haythorn?
He's so *bald!*
GILES!
We got a *few more* to go before the day's *over*, Pop.
We better start getting ready, eh?
!
Ah, I gotta go report to the **Abbess**. I'll see you guys later, okay?
What are you *doing?!!* It's *really* **bad luck** if Rob sees you before the wedding!
Tsk! I just had to see if you **got them**.
Piece of cake! Toddy may be *conniving and greedy*, but I **don't** think he's very ***smart***.
I hope it's as easy for Reggie and Al to do **their** part.

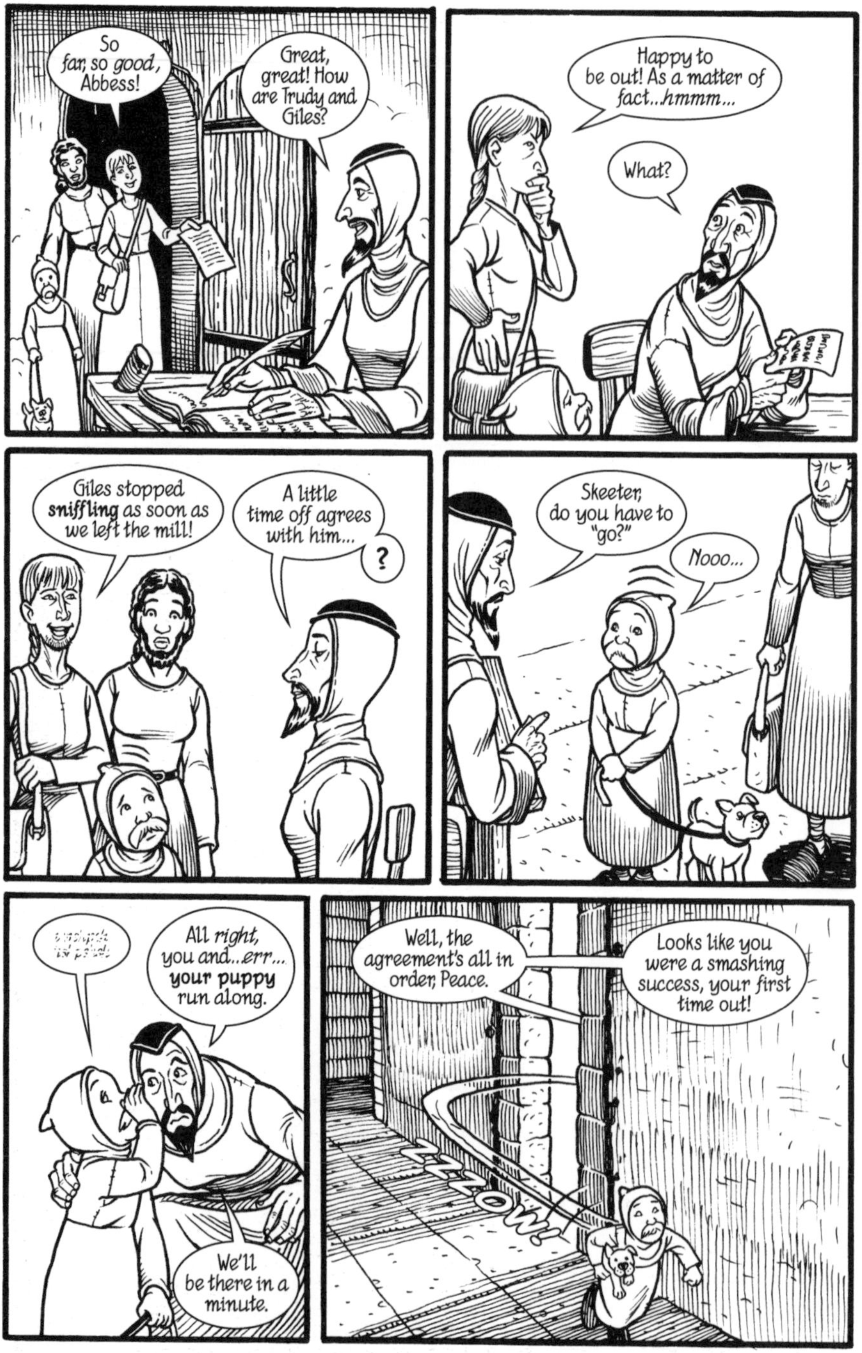
So far, so *good*, Abbess!
Great, great! How are Trudy and Giles?
Happy to be out! As a matter of fact...*hmmm*...
What?
Giles stopped **sniffling** as soon as we left the mill!
A little time off agrees with him...
?
Skeeter, do you have to "go?"
Nooo...
All *right*, you and...*err*... **your puppy** run along.
We'll be there in a minute.
Well, the agreement's all in order, Peace.
Looks like you were a smashing success, your first time out!
ZZZOOM!

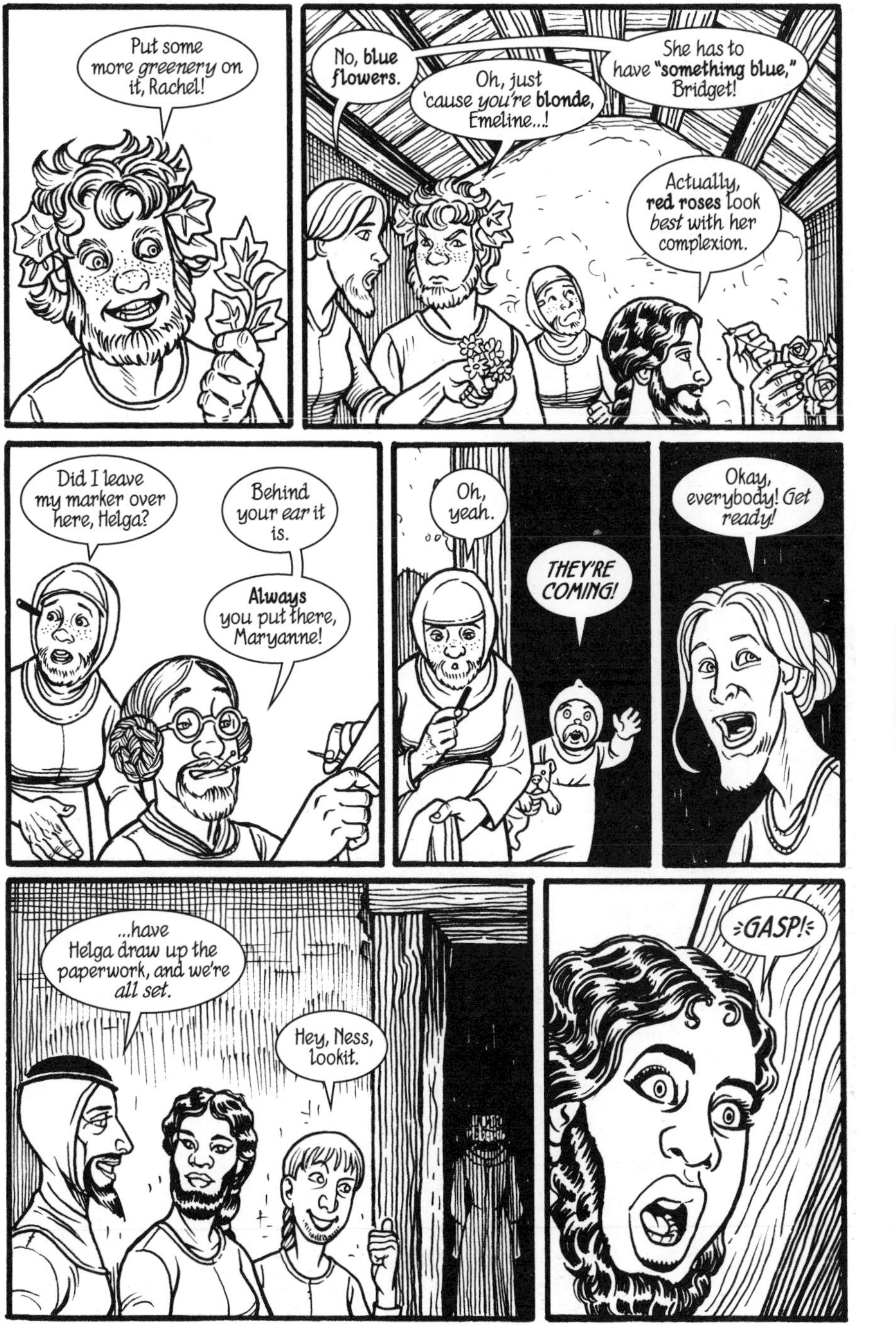
Put some more *greenery* on it, Rachel!
No, **blue flowers.**
Oh, just 'cause *you're* **blonde,** Emeline...!
She has to have **"something blue,"** Bridget!
Actually, **red roses** look *best* with her complexion.
Did I leave my marker over here, Helga?
Behind your *ear* it is.
Always you put there, Maryanne!
Oh, yeah.
THEY'RE COMING!
Okay, everybody! *Get ready!*
...have Helga draw up the paperwork, and we're *all set*.
Hey, Ness, lookit.
GASP!

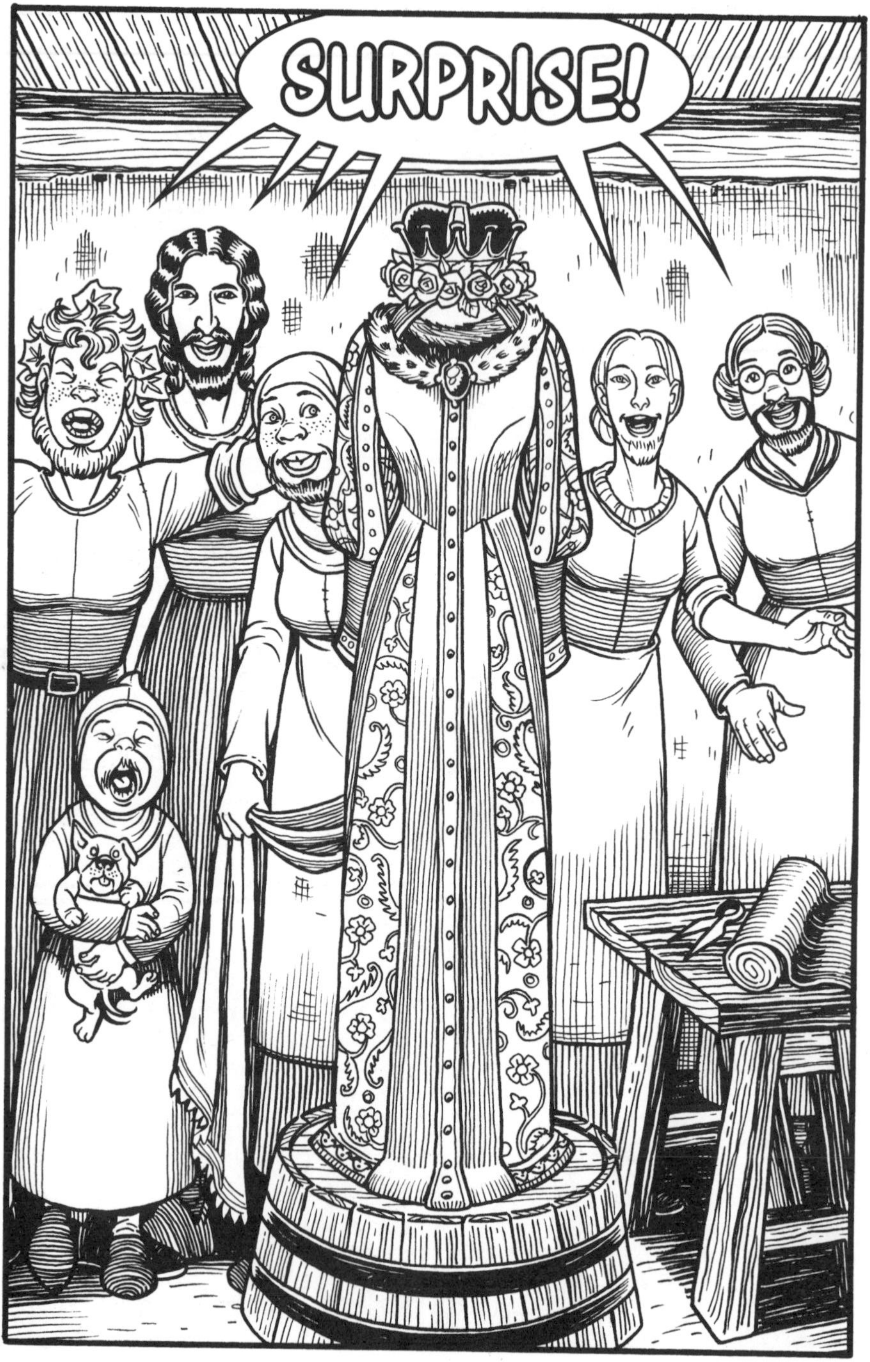
SURPRISE!

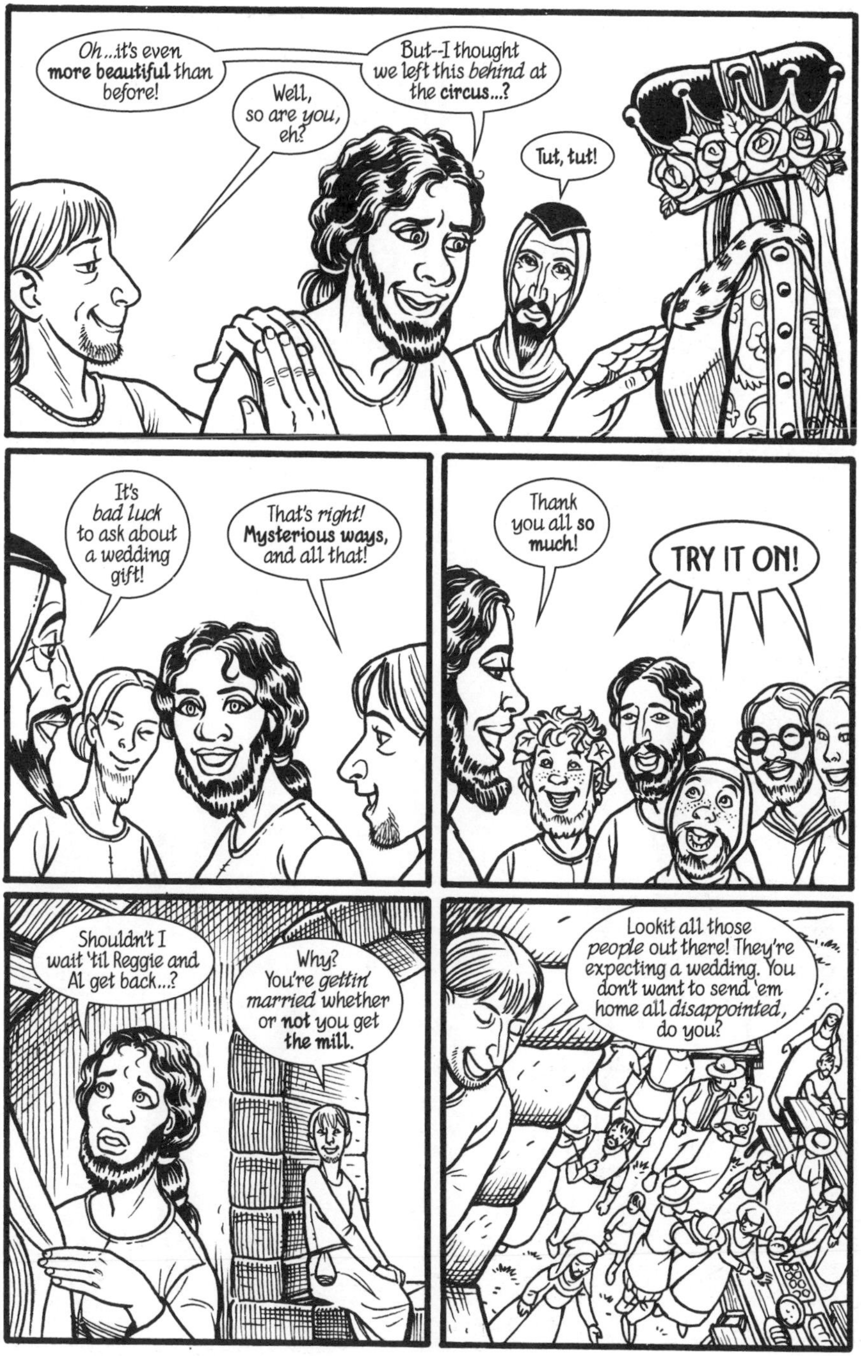
Oh...it's even more beautiful than before!
Well, so are you, eh?
But--I thought we left this behind at the circus...?
Tut, tut!
It's bad luck to ask about a wedding gift!
That's right! Mysterious ways, and all that!
Thank you all so much!
TRY IT ON!
Shouldn't I wait 'til Reggie and Al get back...?
Why? You're gettin' married whether or not you get the mill.
Lookit all those people out there! They're expecting a wedding. You don't want to send 'em home all disappointed, do you?

Chapter 19.

· SOLICITINE PT. 7 ·

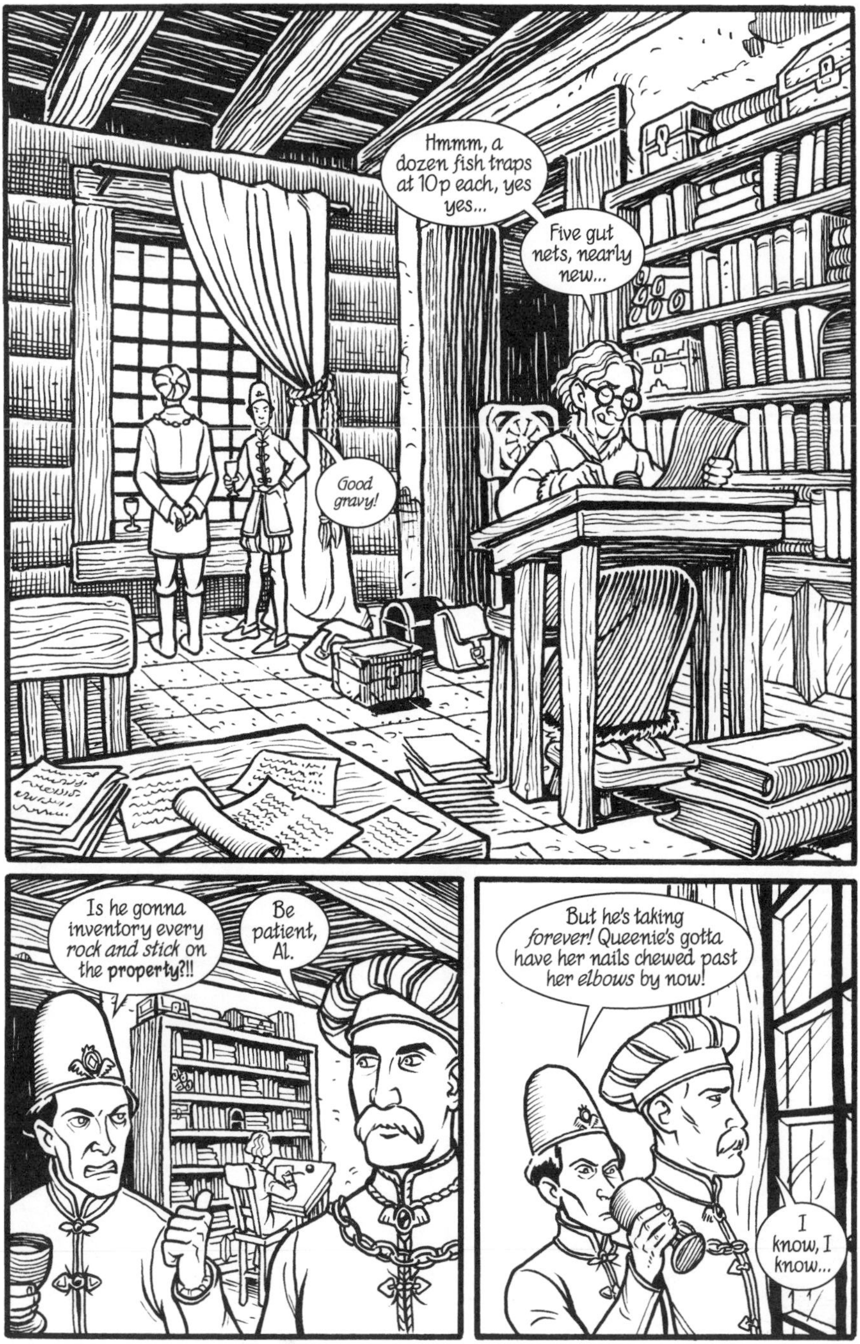
Hmmm, a dozen fish traps at 10p each, yes yes...
Five gut nets, nearly new...
Good gravy!
Is he gonna inventory every *rock and stick* on the **property**?!!
Be patient, Al.
But he's taking *forever!* Queenie's gotta have her nails chewed past her *elbows* by now!
I know, I know...

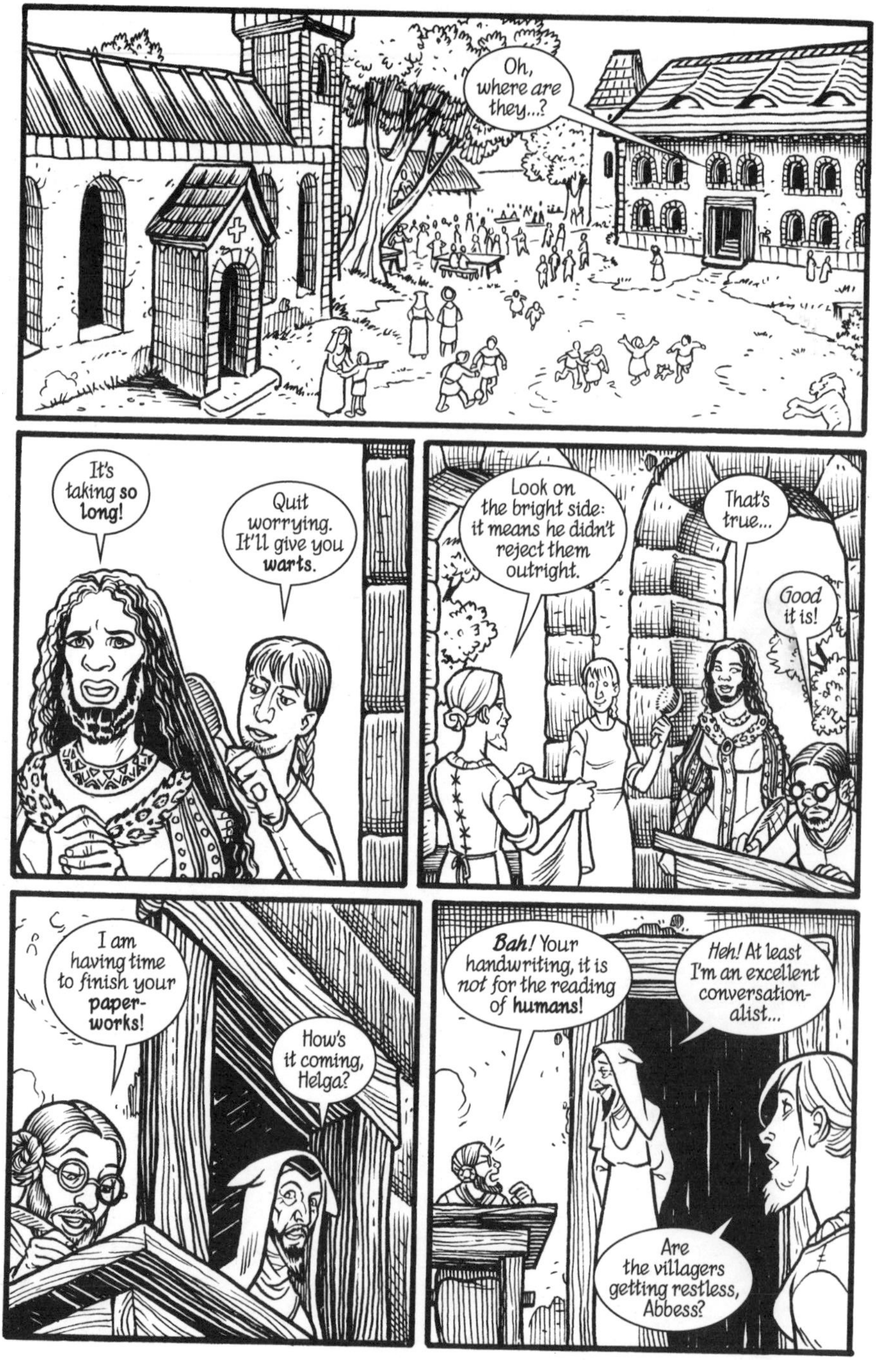
Oh, where are they...?
It's taking so long!
Quit worrying. It'll give you warts.
Look on the bright side: it means he didn't reject them outright.
That's true...
Good it is!
I am having time to finish your paper-works!
How's it coming, Helga?
Bah! Your handwriting, it is not for the reading of humans!
Heh! At least I'm an excellent conversation-alist...
Are the villagers getting restless, Abbess?

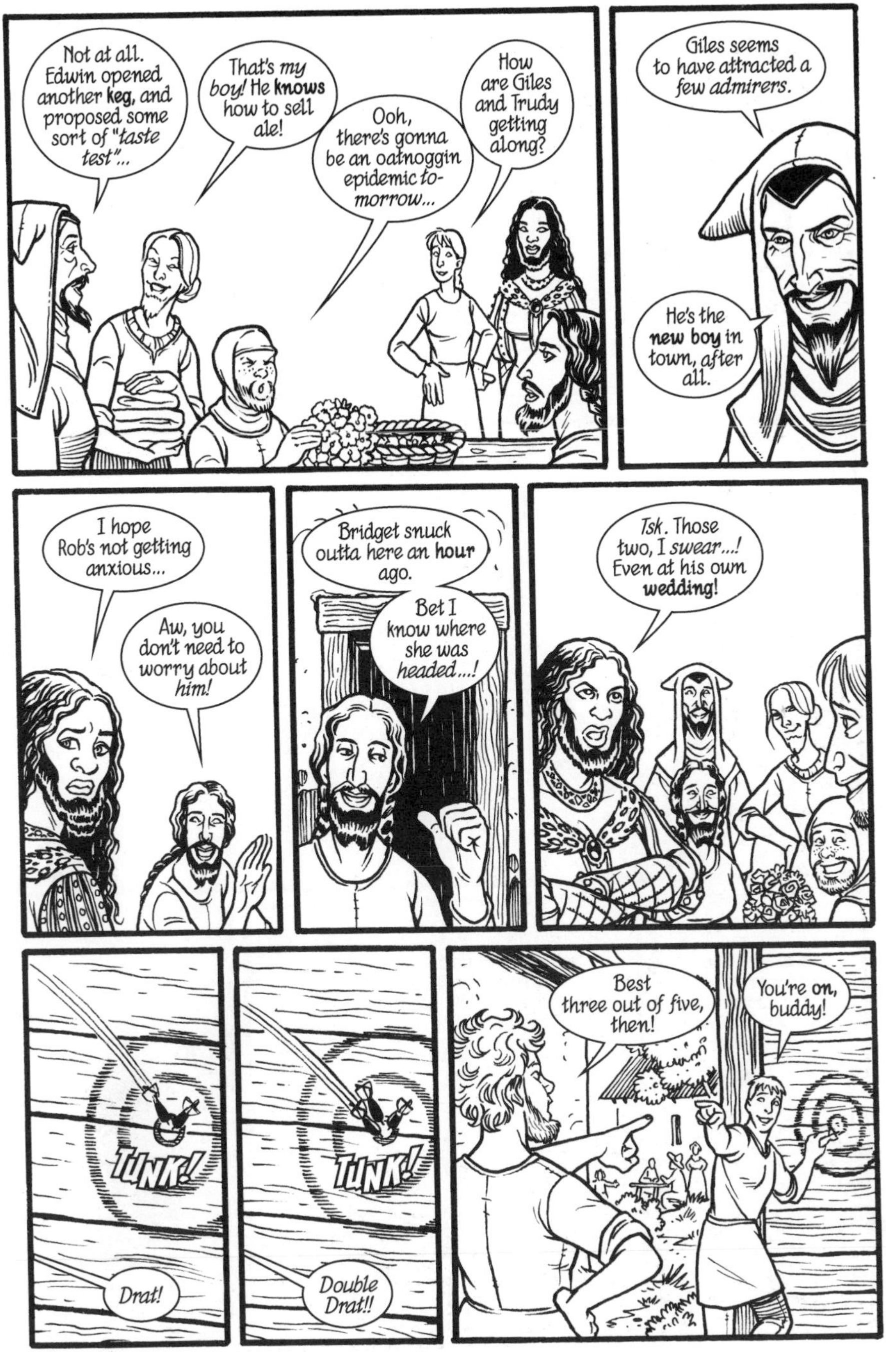
Not at all. Edwin opened another **keg**, and proposed some sort of "*taste test*"...
That's *my boy!* He **knows** how to sell ale!
Ooh, there's gonna be an oatnoggin epidemic to-morrow...
How are Giles and Trudy getting along?
Giles seems to have attracted a few *admirers*.
He's the **new boy** in town, after all.
I hope Rob's not getting anxious...
Aw, you don't need to worry about *him!*
Bridget snuck outta here an **hour** ago.
Bet I know where she was *headed*...!
Tsk. Those two, I *swear*...! Even at his own **wedding**!
TUNK!
Drat!
TUNK!
Double Drat!!
Best three out of five, then!
You're **on**, buddy!

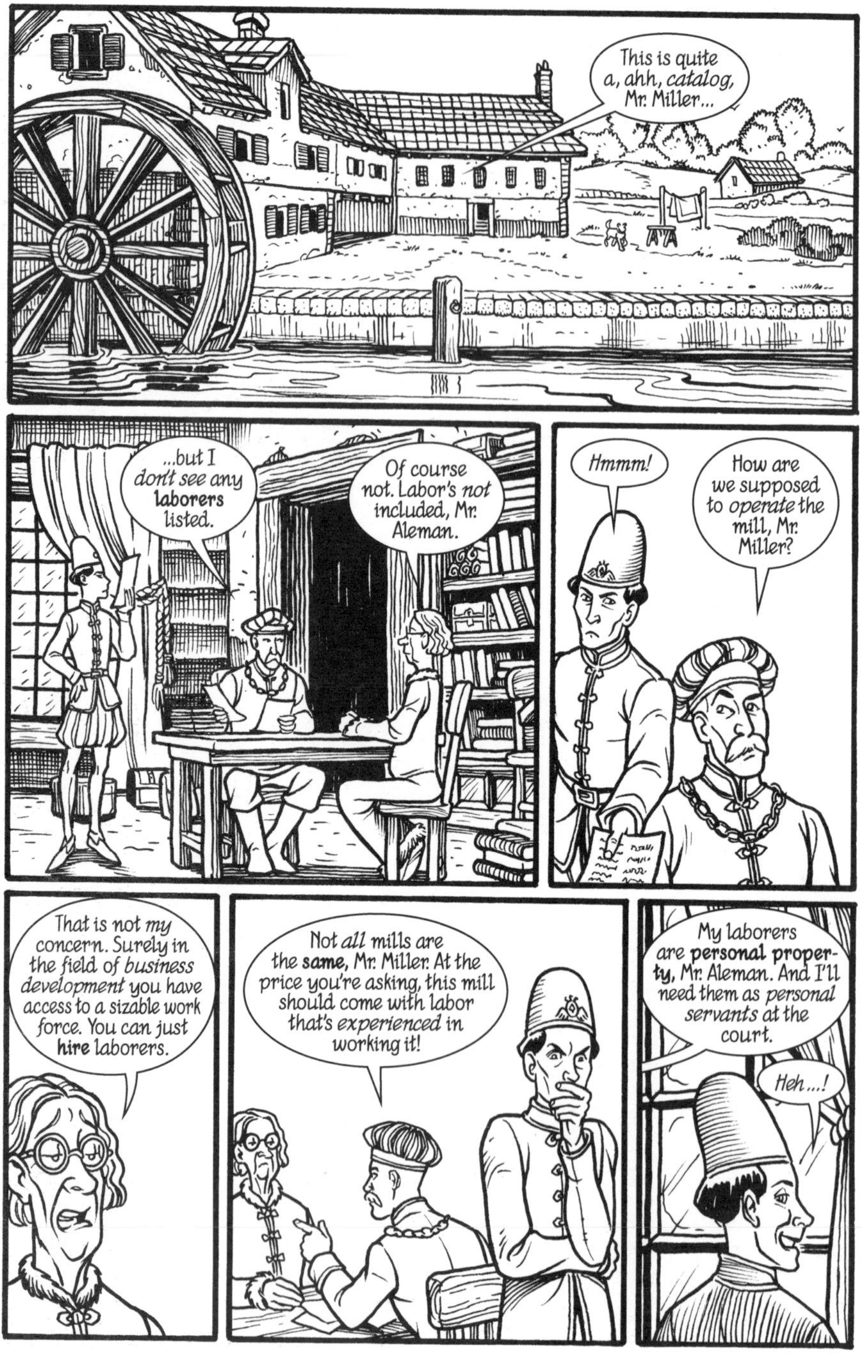
This is quite a, ahh, *catalog*, Mr. Miller...
...but I *don't see* any **laborers** listed.
Of course not. Labor's *not* included, Mr. Aleman.
Hmmm!
How are we supposed to *operate* the mill, Mr. Miller?
That is not *my* concern. Surely in the field of *business development* you have access to a sizable work force. You can just **hire** laborers.
Not *all* mills are the **same,** Mr. Miller. At the price you're asking, this mill should come with labor that's *experienced* in working it!
My laborers are **personal property,** Mr. Aleman. And I'll need them as *personal servants* at the court.
Heh...!

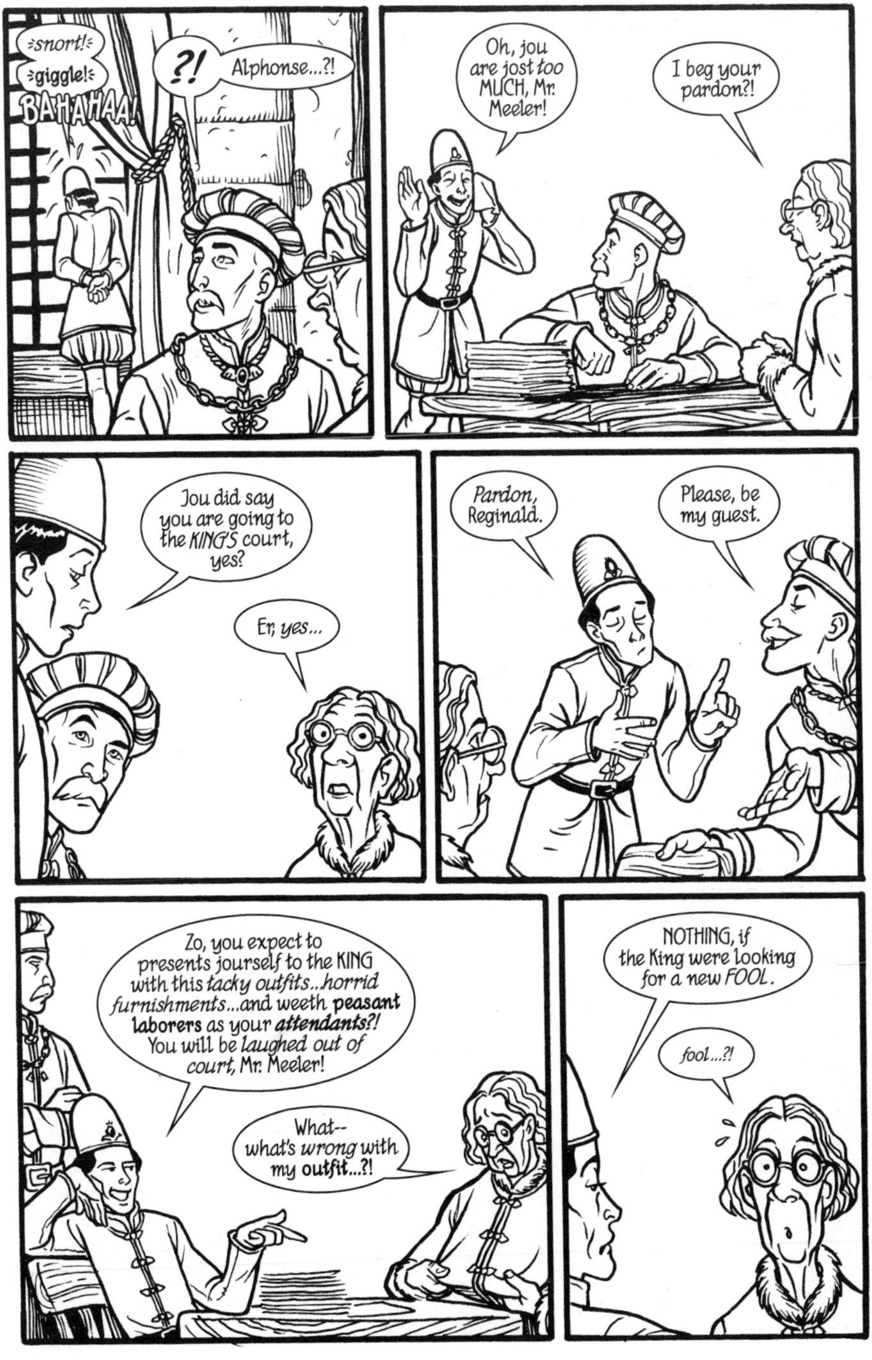
snort!
giggle!
BAHAHAA!
?!
Alphonse...?!
Oh, jou are jost *too* MUCH, Mr. Meeler!
I beg your pardon?!
Jou did say you are going to the *KING'S* court, yes?
Er, yes...
Pardon, Reginald.
Please, be my guest.
Zo, you expect to presents jourself to the KING with this *tacky outfits...horrid furnishments*...and weeth **peasant laborers** as your ***attendants?!*** You will be *laughed out of court,* Mr. Meeler!
What-- what's *wrong* with my **outfit**...?!
NOTHING, if the King were looking for a new *FOOL*.
fool...?!

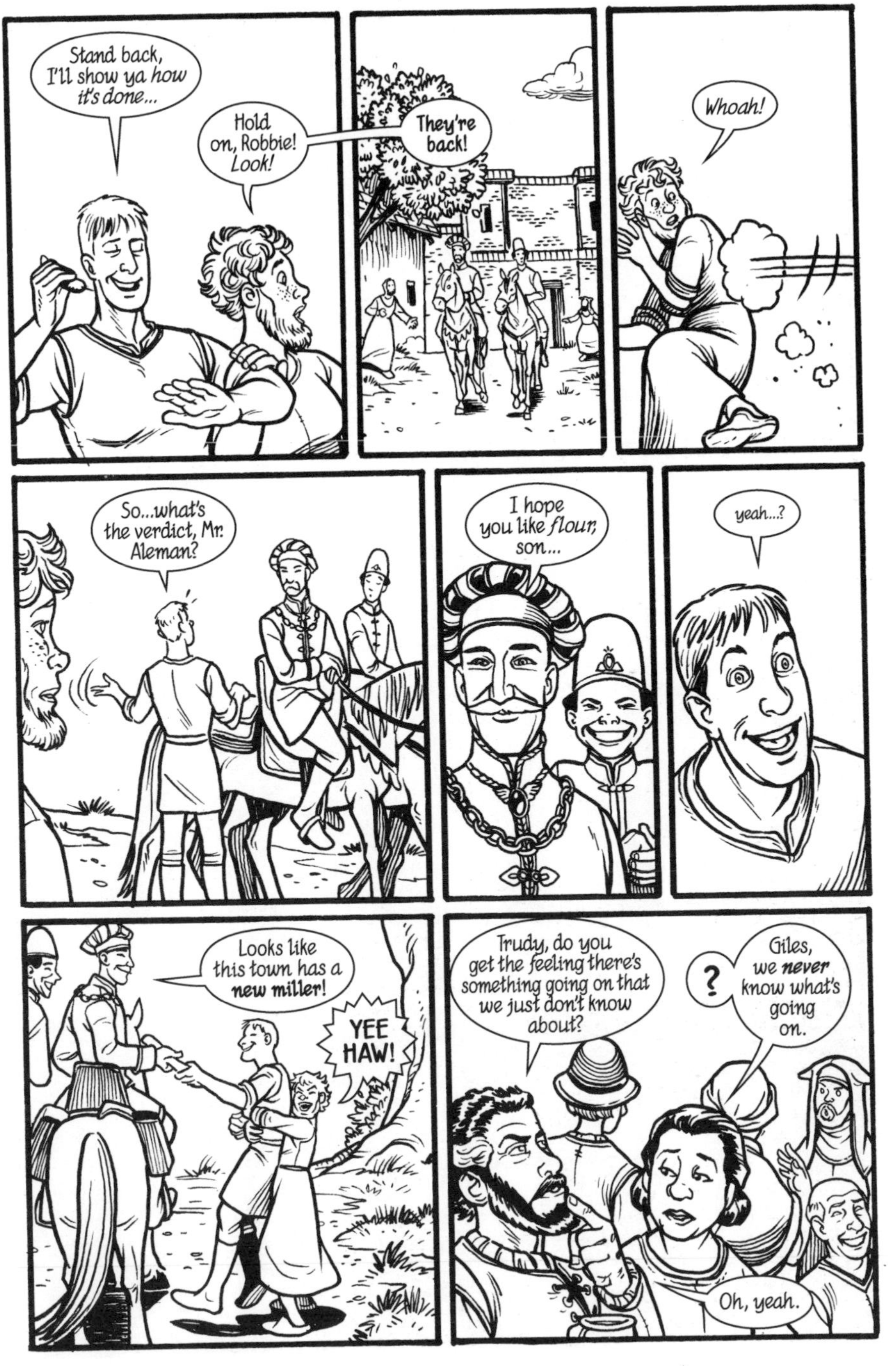
Stand back, I'll show ya how it's done...
Hold on, Robbie! Look!
They're back!
Whoah!
So...what's the verdict, Mr. Aleman?
I hope you like flour, son...
yeah...?
Looks like this town has a new miller!
YEE HAW!
Trudy, do you get the feeling there's something going on that we just don't know about?
?
Giles, we never know what's going on.
Oh, yeah.

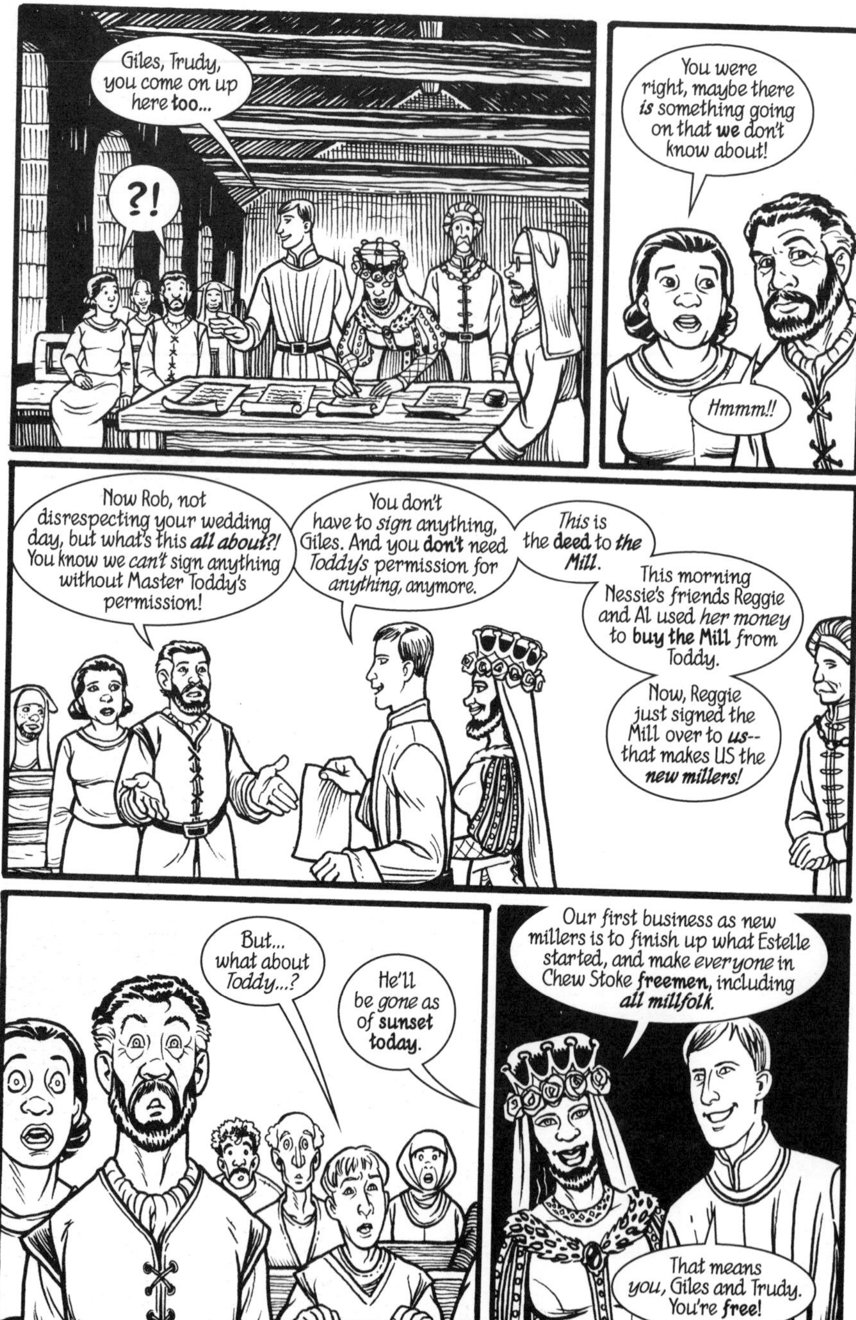
Giles, Trudy, you come on up here **too...**
?!
You were right, maybe there *is* something going on that **we** don't know about!
Hmmm!!
Now Rob, not disrespecting your wedding day, but what's this ***all about?!*** You know we *can't* sign anything without Master Toddy's permission!
You don't have to *sign* anything, Giles. And you **don't** need *Toddy's* permission for *anything, anymore.*
This is the **deed** to ***the Mill.***
This morning Nessie's friends Reggie and Al used *her money* to **buy the Mill** from Toddy.
Now, Reggie just signed the Mill over to ***us***-- that makes US the ***new millers!***
But... what about *Toddy...?*
He'll be *gone* as of **sunset today.**
Our first business as new millers is to finish up what Estelle started, and make *everyone* in Chew Stoke ***freemen,*** including ***all millfolk.***
That means *you*, Giles and Trudy. You're ***free!***

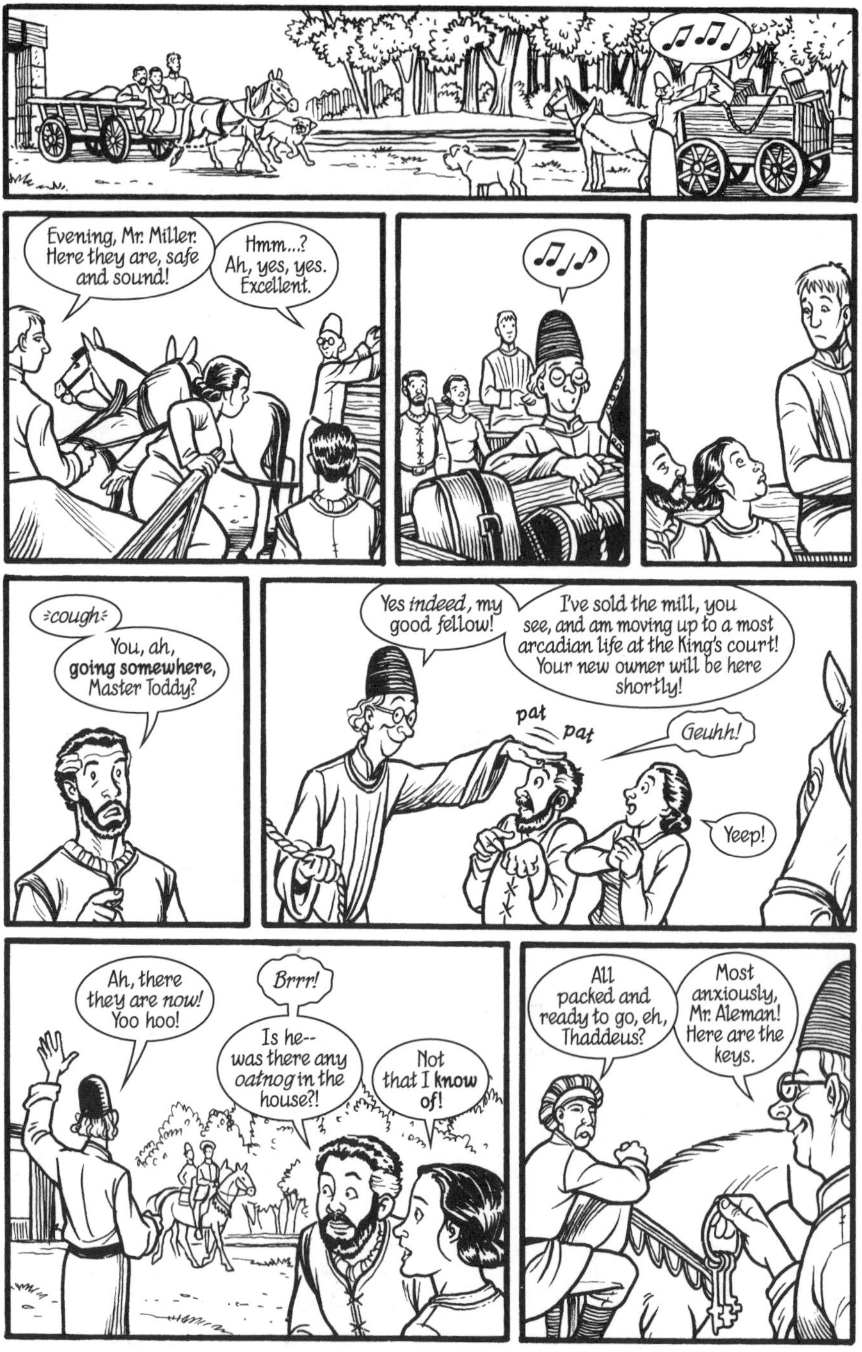
Evening, Mr. Miller. Here they are, safe and sound!
Hmm...? Ah, yes, yes. Excellent.
cough
You, ah, **going somewhere,** Master Toddy?
Yes *indeed*, my good fellow!
I've sold the mill, you see, and am moving up to a most arcadian life at the King's court! Your new owner will be here shortly!
pat pat
Geuhh!
Yeep!
Ah, there they are *now!* Yoo hoo!
Brrr!
Is he-- was there any *oatnog* in the house?!
Not that I **know of!**
All packed and ready to go, eh, Thaddeus?
Most anxiously, Mr. Aleman! Here are the keys.

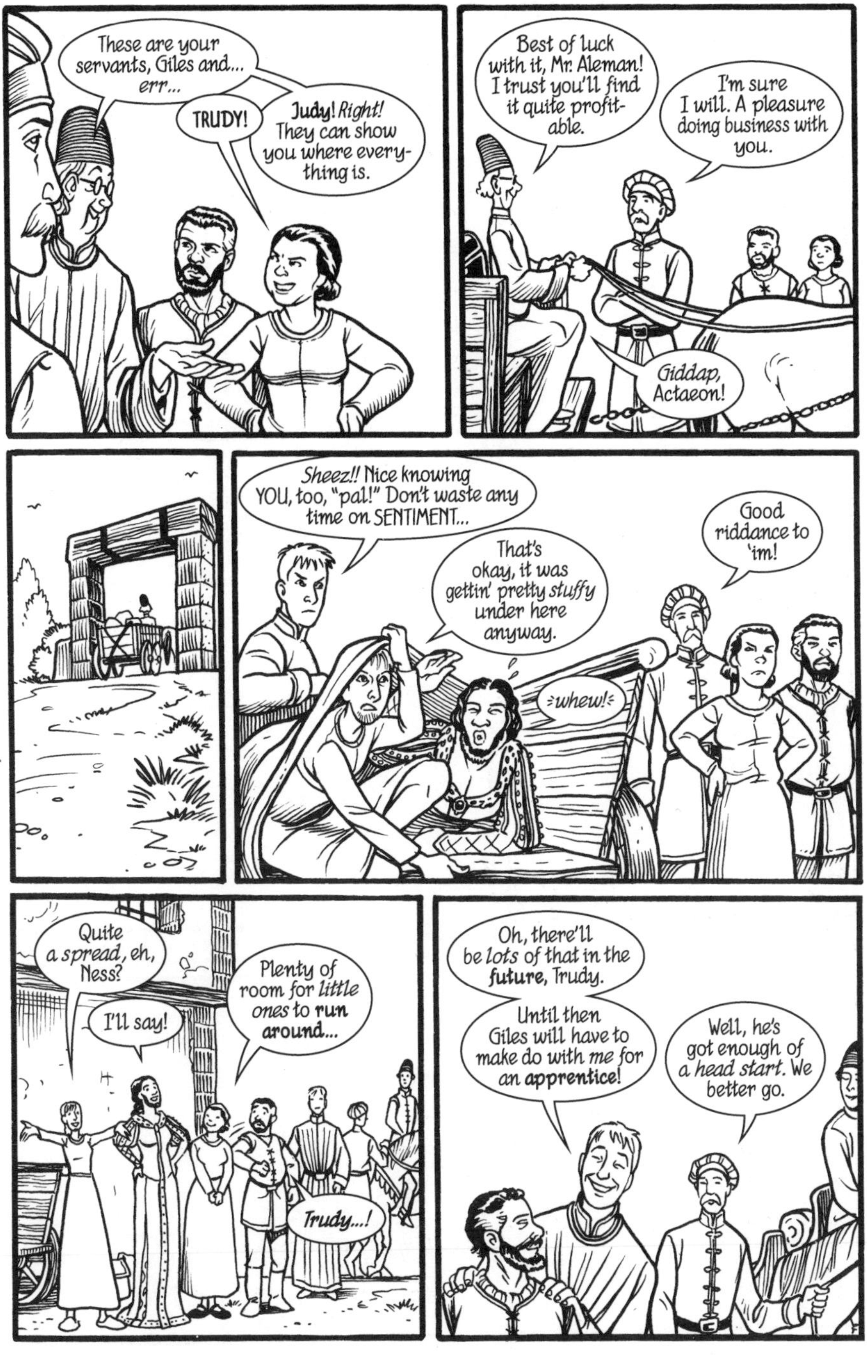
These are your servants, Giles and... err...
TRUDY!
Judy! *Right!* They can show you where everything is.
Best of luck with it, Mr. Aleman! I trust you'll find it quite profitable.
I'm sure I will. A pleasure doing business with you.
Giddap, Actaeon!
Sheez!! Nice knowing YOU, too, "*pal!*" Don't waste any time on SENTIMENT...
That's okay, it was gettin' pretty *stuffy* under here anyway.
whew!
Good riddance to 'im!
Quite a *spread*, eh, Ness?
I'll say!
Plenty of room for *little ones* to **run around**...
Trudy...!
Oh, there'll be *lots* of that in the **future**, Trudy.
Until then Giles will have to make do with *me* for an **apprentice**!
Well, he's got enough of a *head start*. We better go.

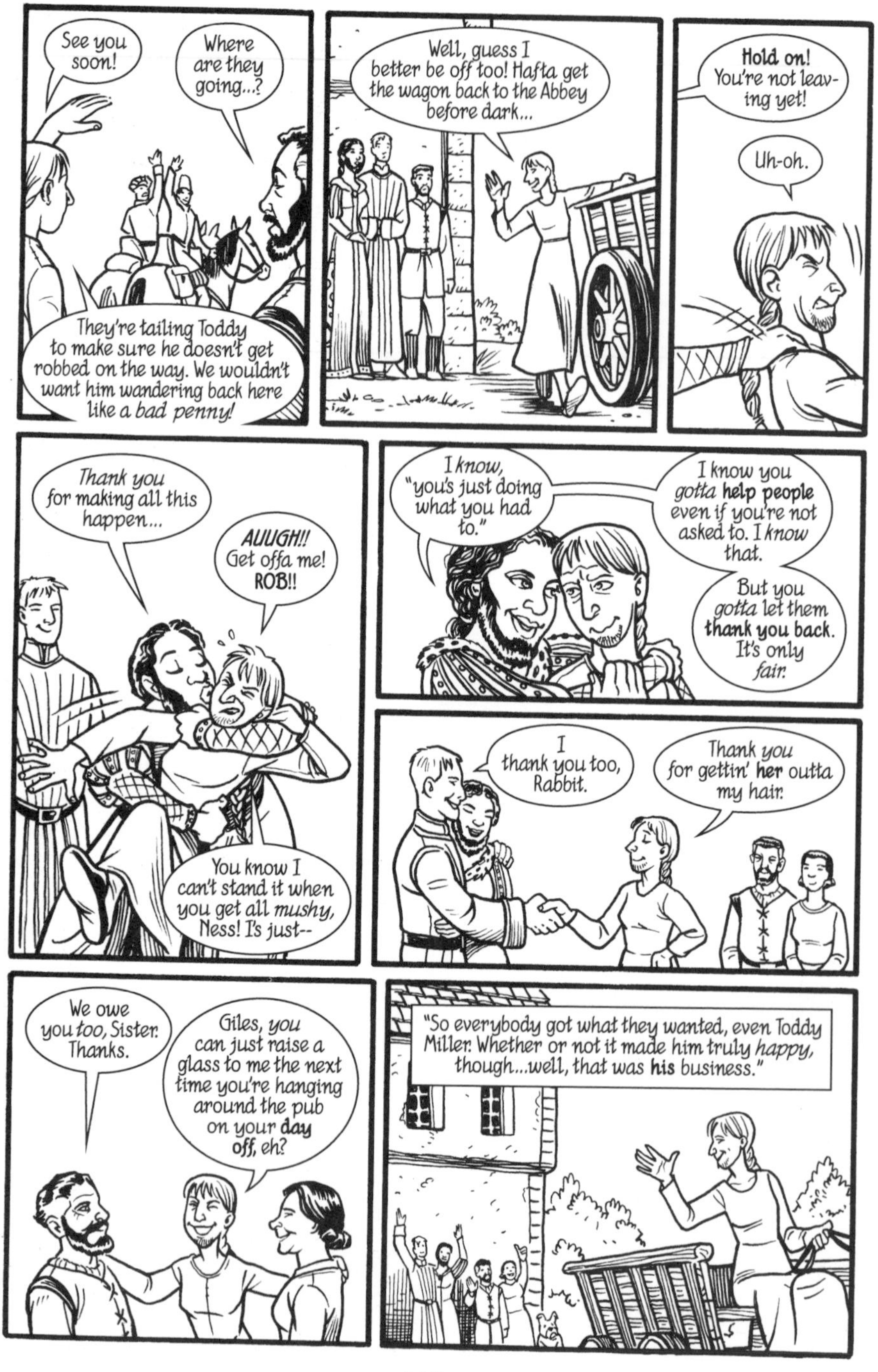
See you soon!
Where are they going...?
They're tailing Toddy to make sure he doesn't get robbed on the way. We wouldn't want him wandering back here like a *bad penny!*
Well, guess I better be off too! Hafta get the wagon back to the Abbey before dark...
Hold on! You're not leaving yet!
Uh-oh.
Thank you for making all this happen...
AUUGH!! Get offa me! **ROB!!**
You know I can't stand it when you get all *mushy,* Ness! I's just--
I *know,* "you's just doing what you had to."
I know you *gotta* **help people** even if you're not asked to. I *know* that.
But you *gotta* let them **thank you back**. It's only *fair.*
I thank you too, Rabbit.
Thank *you* for gettin' **her** outta my hair.
We owe you *too*, Sister. Thanks.
Giles, *you* can just raise a glass to me the next time you're hanging around the pub on your **day off**, eh?
"So everybody got what they wanted, even Toddy Miller. Whether or not it made him truly *happy,* though...well, that was **his** business."

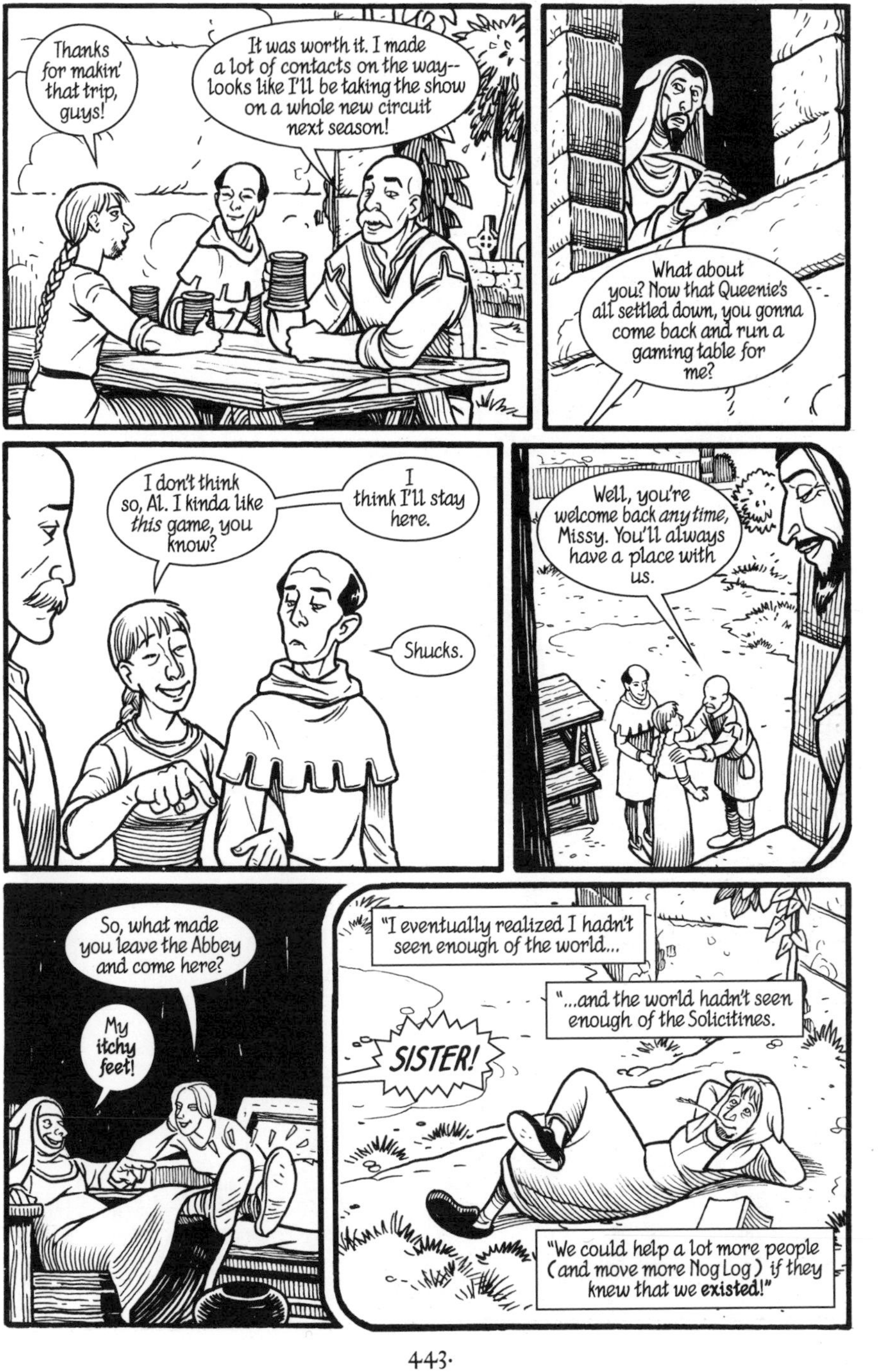
Thanks for makin' that trip, guys!
It was worth it. I made a lot of contacts on the way-- looks like I'll be taking the show on a whole new circuit next season!
What about you? Now that Queenie's all settled down, you gonna come back and run a gaming table for me?
I don't think so, Al. I kinda like *this* game, you know?
I think I'll stay here.
Shucks.
Well, you're welcome back *any time*, Missy. You'll always have a place with us.
So, what made you leave the Abbey and come here?
My itchy feet!
"I eventually realized I hadn't seen enough of the world...
"...and the world hadn't seen enough of the Solicitines.
SISTER!
"We could help a lot more people (and move more Nog Log) if they knew that we **existed!**"

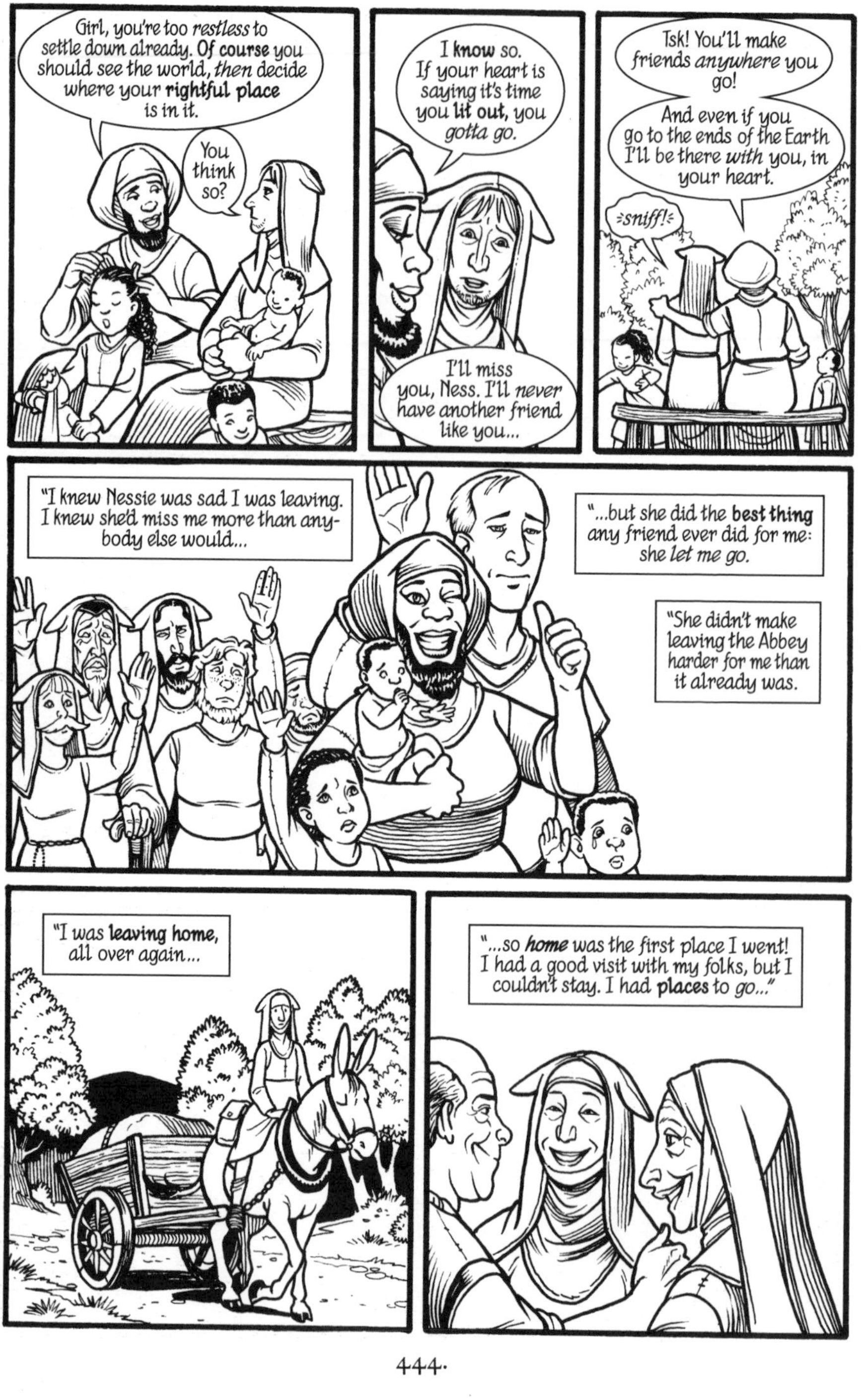
Girl, you're too restless to settle down already. Of course you should see the world, then decide where your rightful place is in it.
You think so?
I know so. If your heart is saying it's time you lit out, you gotta go.
I'll miss you, Ness. I'll never have another friend like you...
Tsk! You'll make friends anywhere you go!
And even if you go to the ends of the Earth I'll be there with you, in your heart.
sniff!
"I knew Nessie was sad I was leaving. I knew she'd miss me more than anybody else would...
"...but she did the best thing any friend ever did for me: she let me go.
"She didn't make leaving the Abbey harder for me than it already was.
"I was leaving home, all over again...
"...so home was the first place I went! I had a good visit with my folks, but I couldn't stay. I had places to go..."

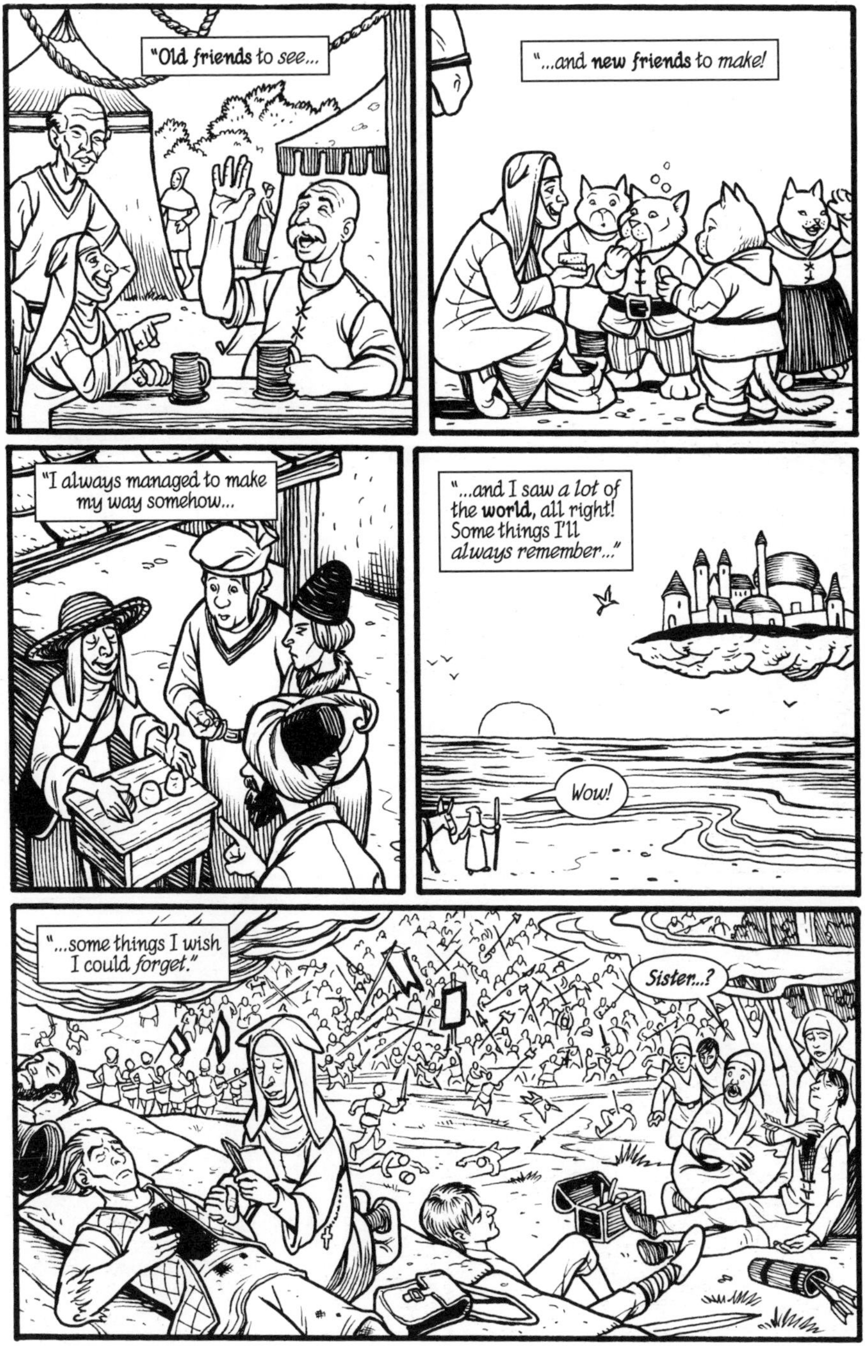
"Old friends to see...
"...and new friends to make!
"I always managed to make my way somehow...
"...and I saw a lot of the world, all right! Some things I'll always remember..."
Wow!
"...some things I wish I could forget."
Sister...?

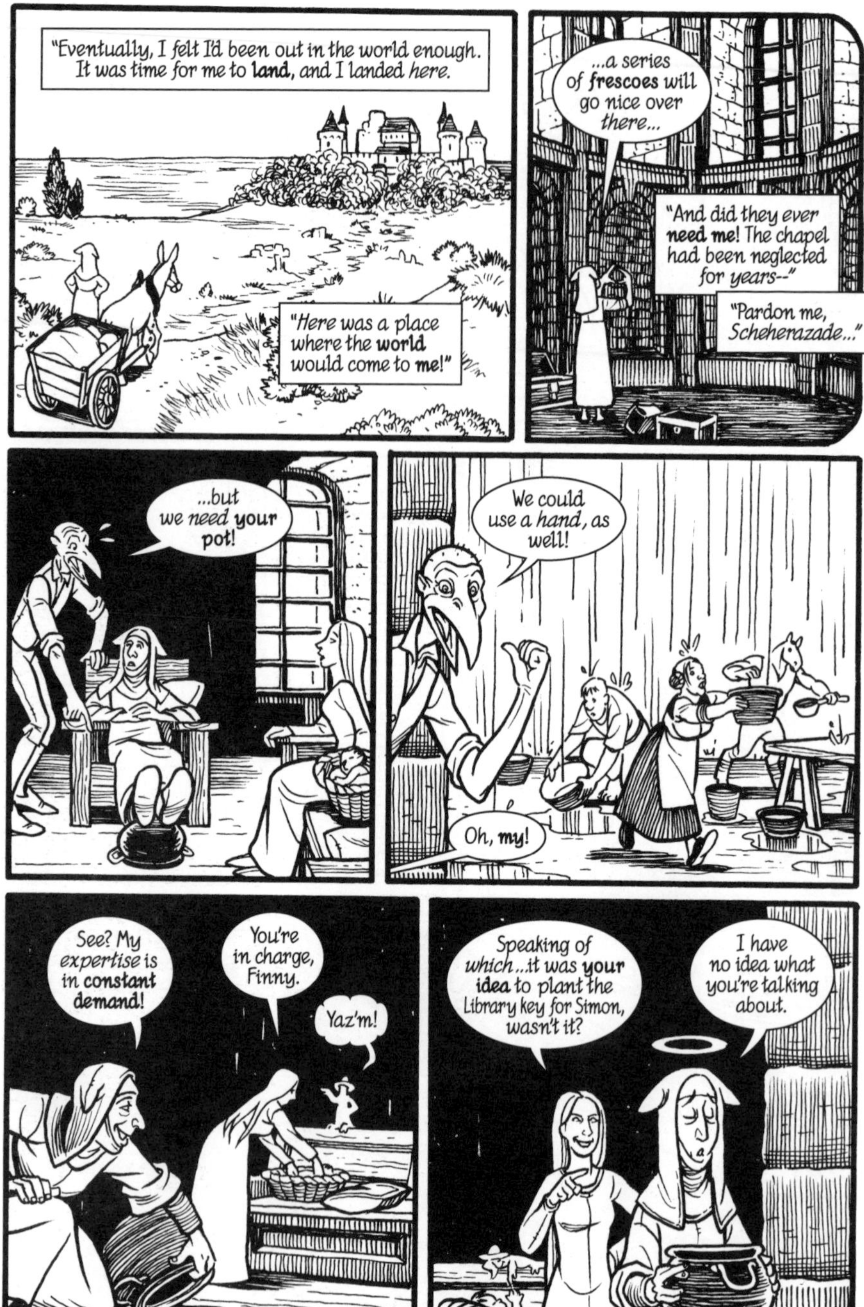
"Eventually, I felt I'd been out in the world enough. It was time for me to land, and I landed here.
"Here was a place where the world would come to me!"
...a series of frescoes will go nice over there...
"And did they ever need me! The chapel had been neglected for years--"
"Pardon me, Scheherazade..."
...but we need your pot!
We could use a hand, as well!
Oh, my!
See? My expertise is in constant demand!
You're in charge, Finny.
Yaz'm!
Speaking of which...it was your idea to plant the Library key for Simon, wasn't it?
I have no idea what you're talking about.

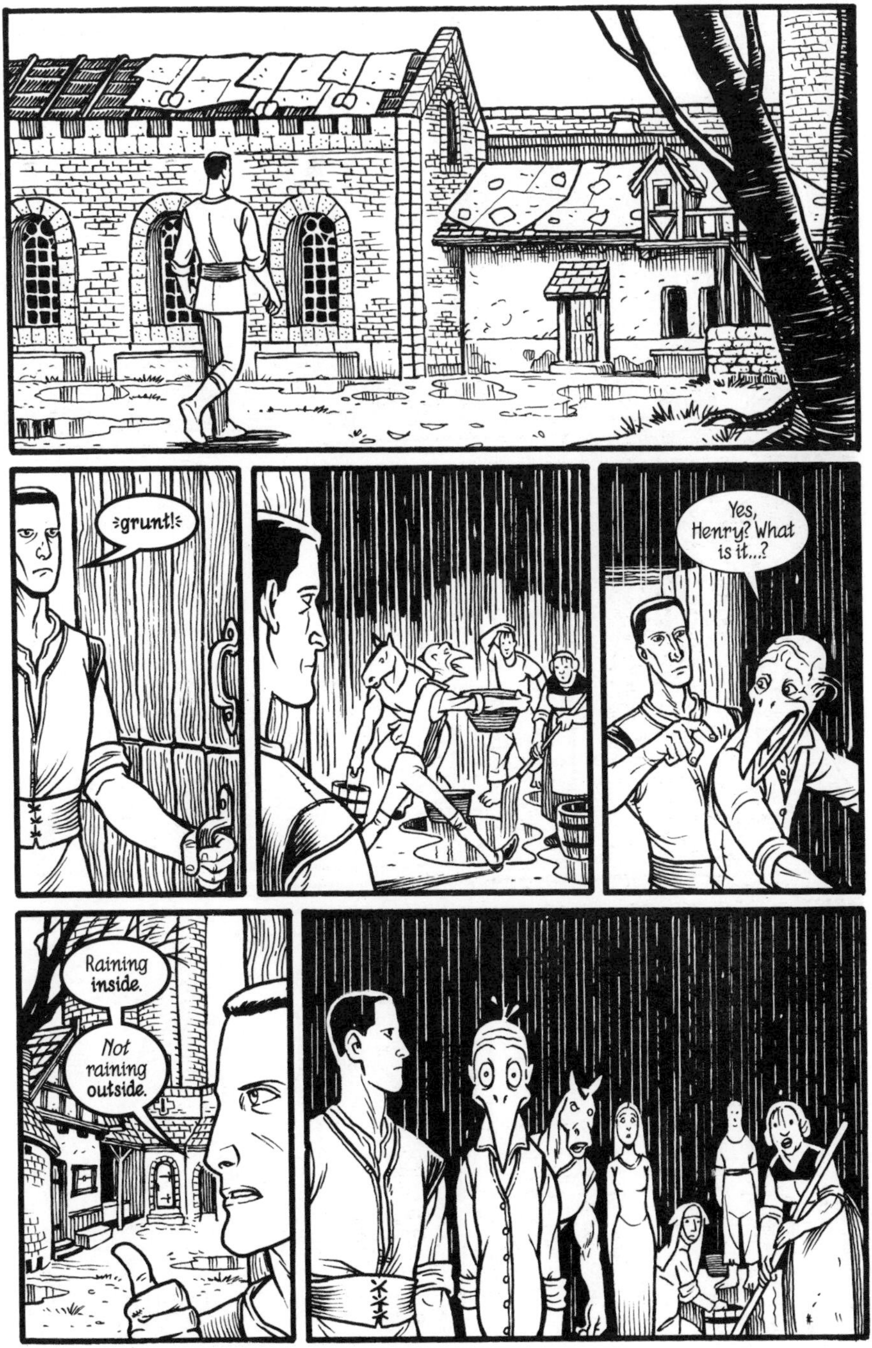
grunt!
Yes, Henry? What is it...?
Raining inside.
Not raining outside.

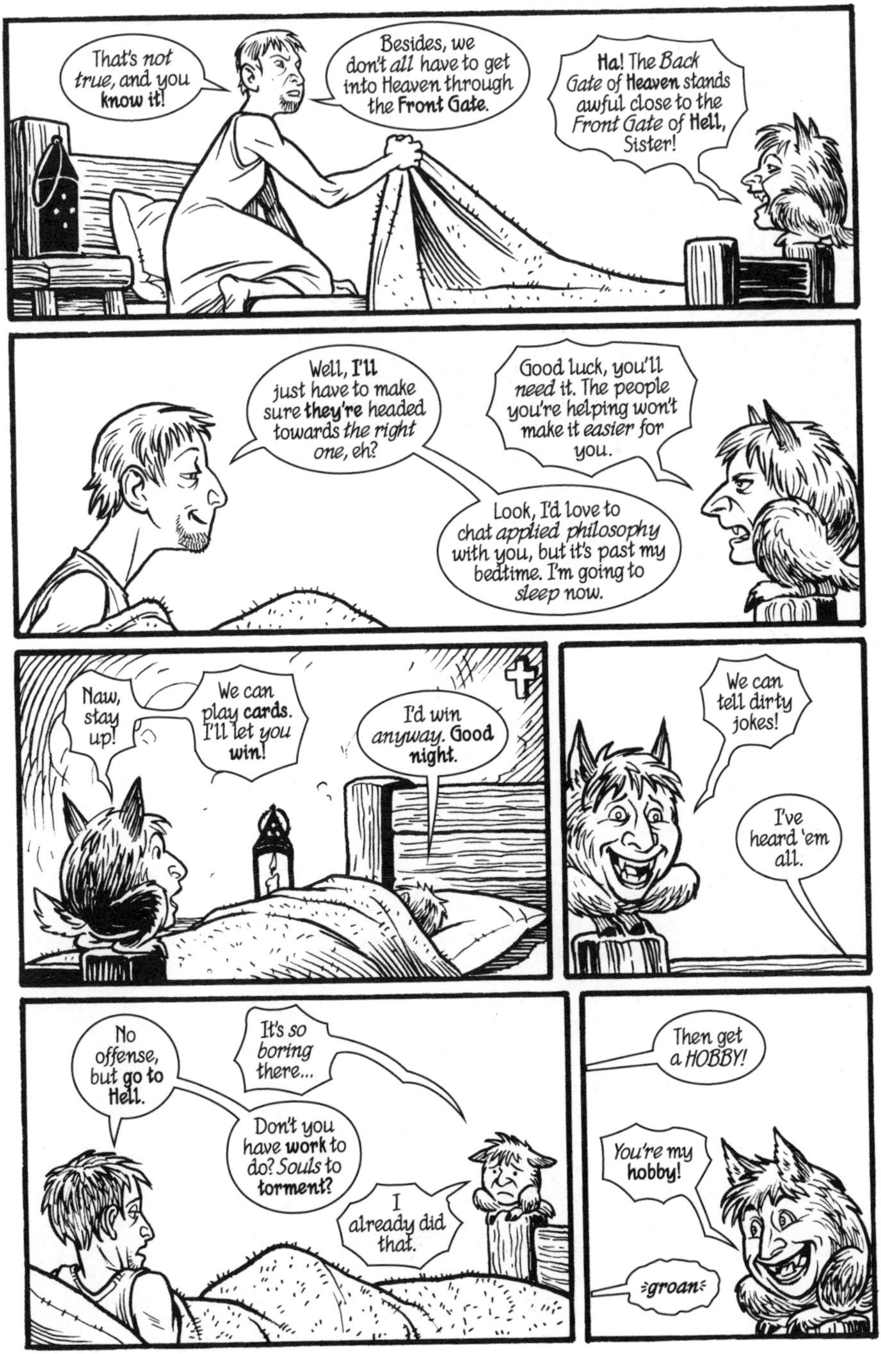
That's *not true*, and you **know it**!
Besides, we don't *all* have to get into Heaven through the **Front Gate**.
Ha! The *Back Gate* of **Heaven** stands awful close to the *Front Gate* of **Hell**, Sister!
Well, **I'll** just have to make sure **they're** headed towards *the right one*, eh?
Good luck, you'll *need* it. The people you're helping won't make it *easier* for you.
Look, I'd love to chat *applied philosophy* with you, but it's past my bedtime. I'm going to *sleep* now.
Naw, stay up!
We can play **cards**. I'll let *you* **win**!
I'd win *anyway*. **Good night**.
We can tell dirty jokes!
I've heard 'em all.
No offense, but **go to Hell**.
It's *so* boring there...
Don't you have **work** to do? *Souls* to **torment**?
I already did that.
Then get a *HOBBY*!
You're my **hobby**!
groan

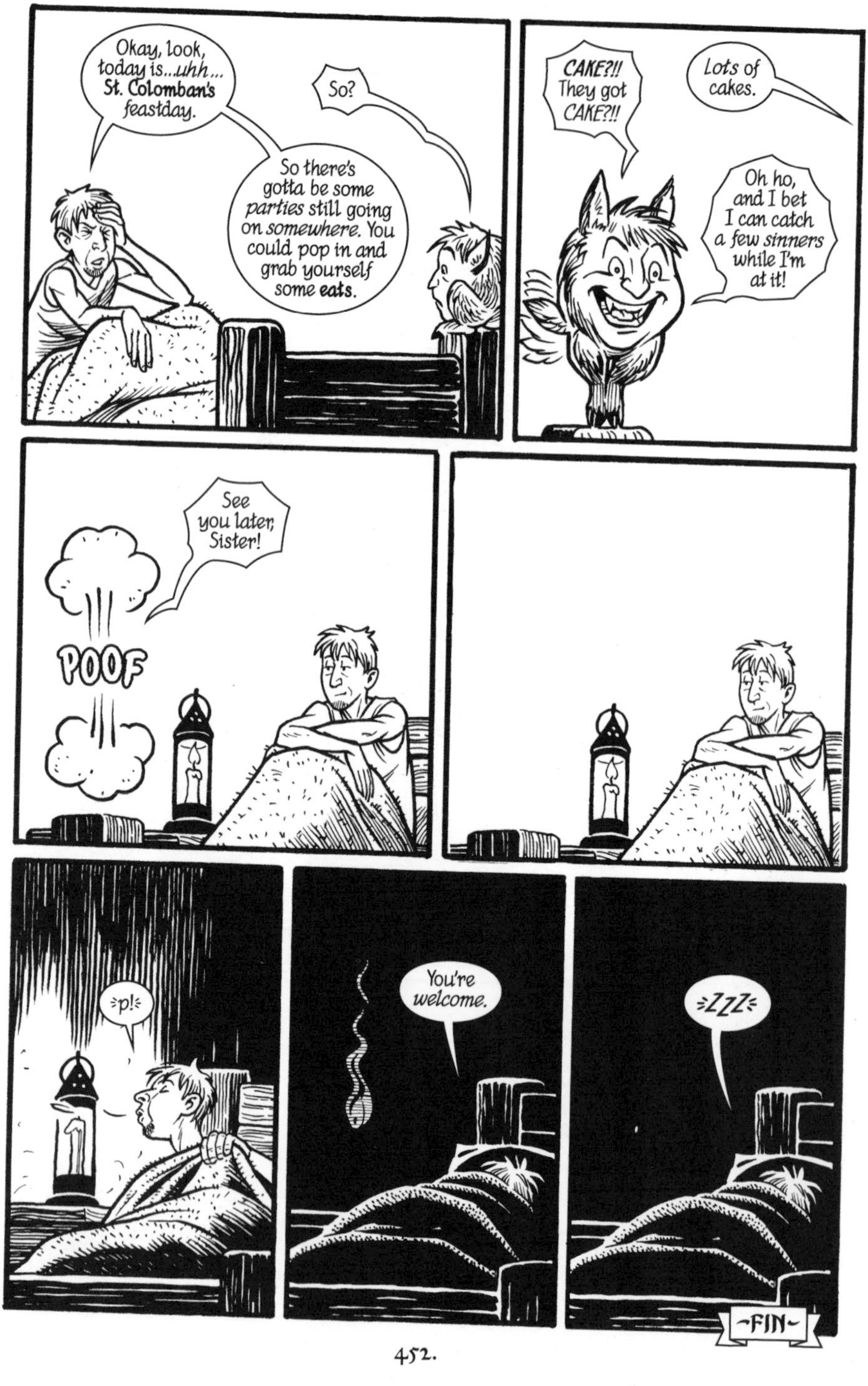
Okay, look, today is...uhh... St. Colomban's feastday.
So?
So there's gotta be some parties still going on somewhere. You could pop in and grab yourself some eats.
CAKE?!! They got CAKE?!!
Lots of cakes.
Oh ho, and I bet I can catch a few sinners while I'm at it!
See you later, Sister!
POOF
p!
You're welcome.
ZZZ
FIN

Epilogue.

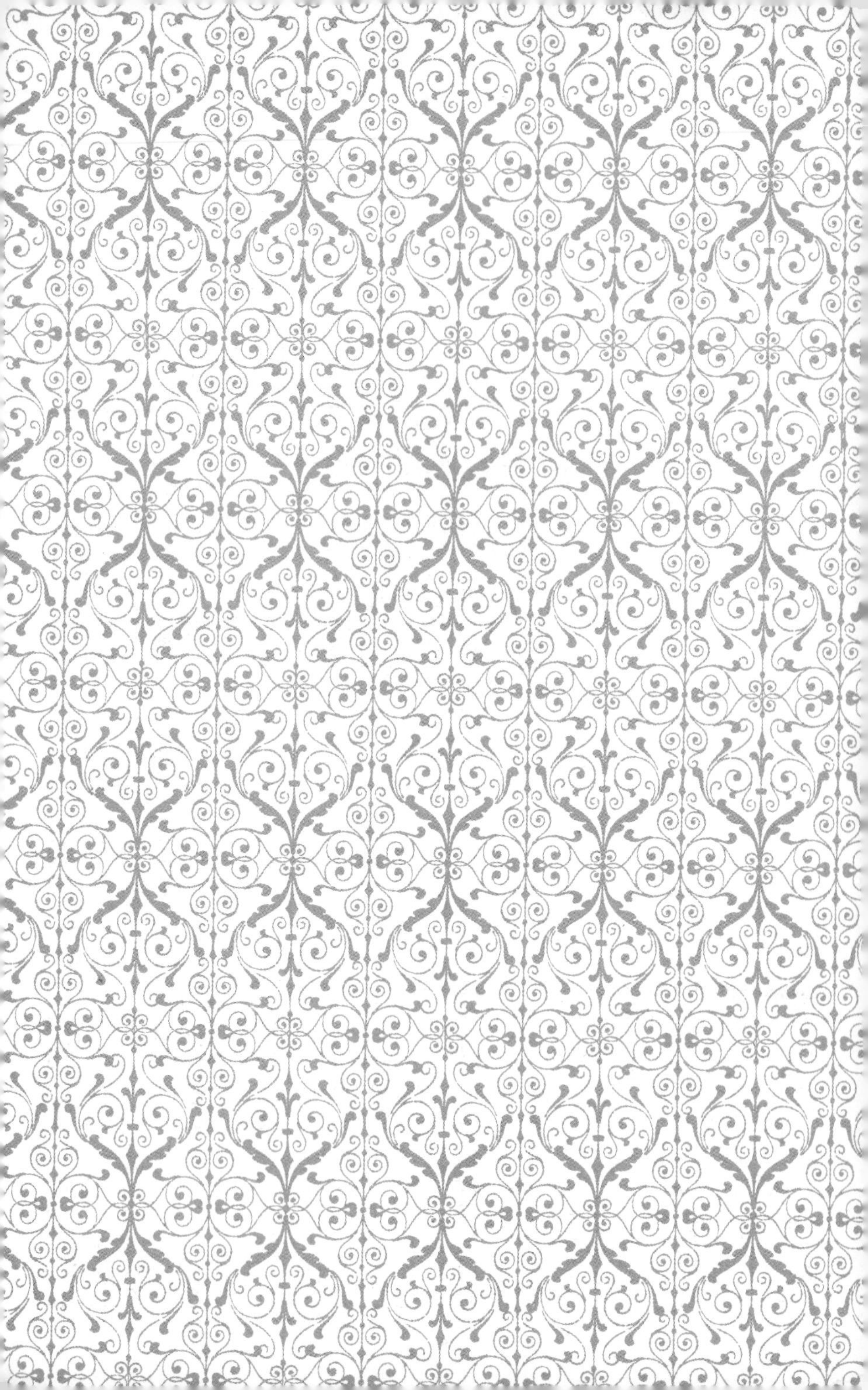

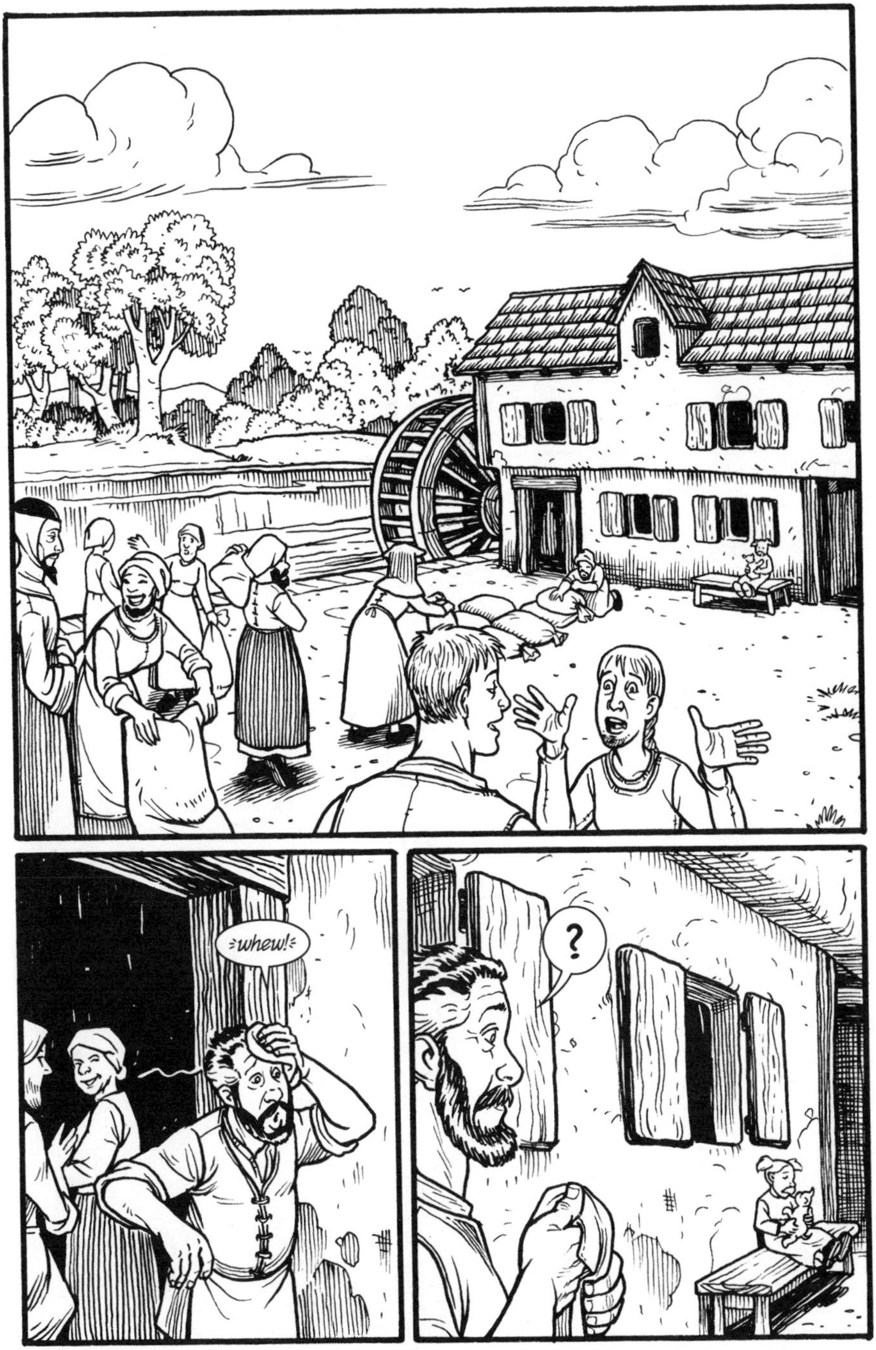
whew!
?

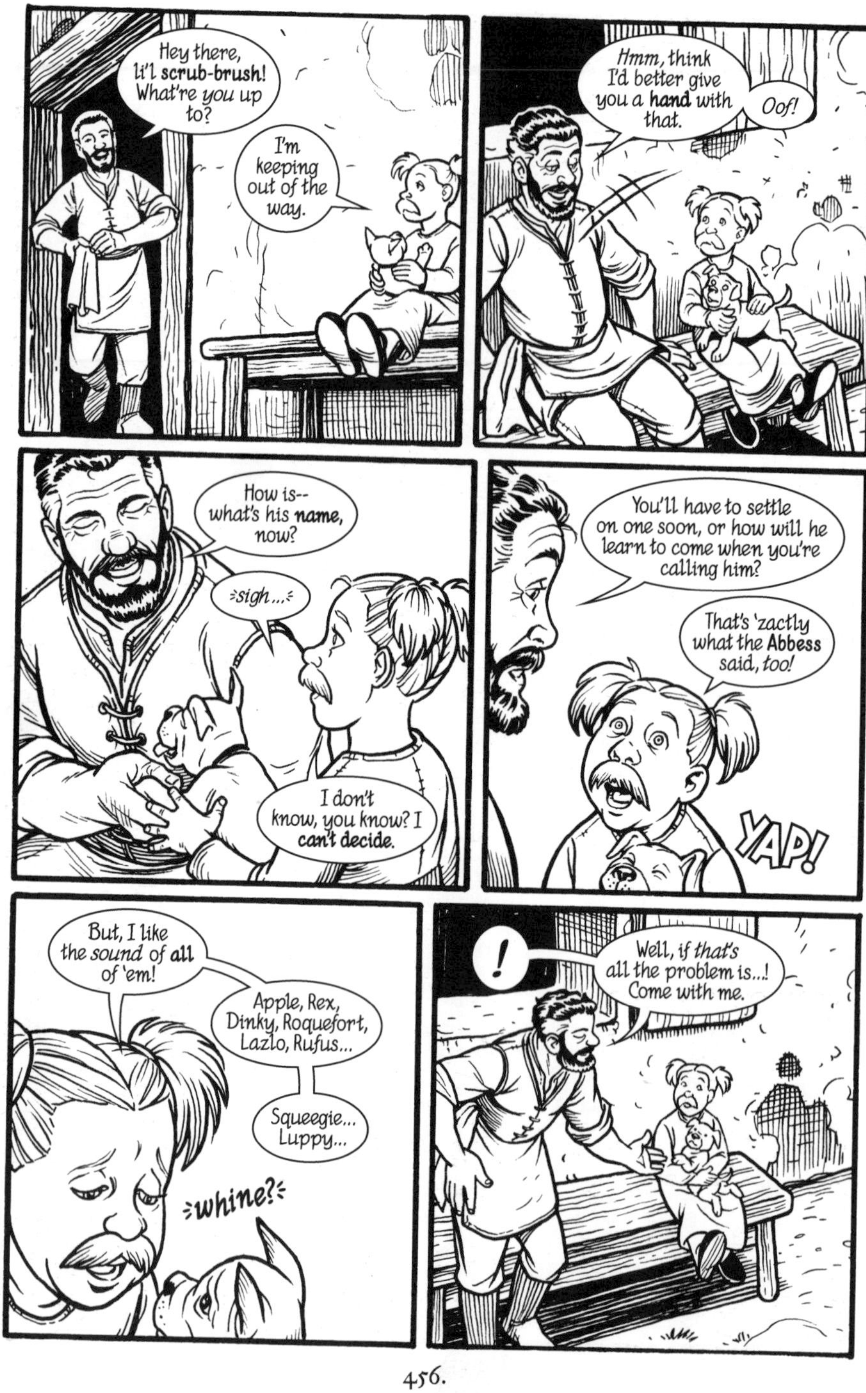
Hey there, li'l scrub-brush! What're you up to?
I'm keeping out of the way.
Hmm, think I'd better give you a hand with that.
Oof!
How is-- what's his name, now?
sigh...
I don't know, you know? I can't decide.
You'll have to settle on one soon, or how will he learn to come when you're calling him?
That's 'zactly what the Abbess said, too!
YAP!
But, I like the sound of all of 'em!
Apple, Rex, Dinky, Roquefort, Lazlo, Rufus...
Squeegie... Luppy...
whine?
!
Well, if that's all the problem is...! Come with me.